Microsoft®

Windows NT® Technical Support

Microsoft® Press

PUBLISHED BY
Microsoft Press
A Division of Microsoft Corporation
One Microsoft Way
Redmond, Washington 98052-6399

Library of Congress Cataloging-in-Publication Data
Microsoft Windows NT Technical Support Training Kit, Deluxe Multimedia Edition / Microsoft Corporation.
p. cm.
Includes index.
ISBN 1-57231-373-0
ISBN 1-57231-833-3 (Deluxe Multimedia Edition)
1. Microsoft Windows NT. 2. Operating systems (Computers)
I. Microsoft Corporation.
QA76.76.063M52435 1997 97-830
005.74--DC21 CIP

Printed and bound in the United States of America.

1 2 3 4 5 6 7 8 9 WCWC 3 2 1 0 9 8

Distributed to the book trade in Canada by Macmillan of Canada, a division of Canada Publishing Corporation.

A CIP catalogue record for this book is available from the British Library.

Microsoft Press books are available through booksellers and distributors worldwide. For further information about international editions, contact your local Microsoft Corporation office. Or contact Microsoft Press International directly at fax (425) 936-7329. Visit our Web site at mspress.microsoft.com.

Project Leads: Sandra Alto, Rick Wallace
Instructional Designers: Sandra Alto, Suzanne E. Sax, Ph.D. (S&T Onsite)
Subject Matter Experts: Beth Nelson, Rick Wallace
Technical Contributors: Paul Adare (FYI TechKnowlogy Services), Keith Cotton, Andrew Mason, Ken Rosen (Ken & Ryan Worldwide)
Software Developer: Wendy Wahl (Madrona Software)
Web Page Development: Karen Berge
Web Page Graphics Design: Ben Chamberlain (Duck Design), Becky Johnson
Graphic Artist: Julie Stone

Acquisitions Editor: Eric Stroo
Project Editor: Saul Candib

Editor: Shari G. Smith (R & S Consulting)
Editing Contributor: Laurie Pritchard
Indexer: Lori Walker (Star Canyon Consulting)
Production Support: Irene Barnett (Barnett Communications)
Manufacturing Support: Bo Galford
Video Producers: Susan Greenberg, Beverly Hare (Media Solutions)
Video Development: Digital Post & Graphics
Video Compression & Processing: "E.J." John Erickson, Brian Snyder (Talent Services)
Product Managers: Dean Murray, Robert Stewart, Elaine Stovall

Part No. 097-0002004

Contents

FOREWORD

Microsoft Windows NT Technical Support

For the past eight years a determined Microsoft team has endeavored to raise the Microsoft Windows operating system to a new level of reliability and function. The team's original goal was to deliver an operating system with reliability characteristics of a minicomputer or mainframe combined with the ease of use and responsiveness of a personal computer. Such a system would be suitable for a broad class of uses ranging from the most demanding business desktop scenarios to usage as a system for one's home.

Every release of Microsoft Windows NT® is a single step toward our goal. With Windows NT 4.0, the right mix of performance, networking support, and usability combined with reliability have yielded the most flexible version of Windows NT thus far. Corporate MIS folks have come to love the reliability and security. End users like the Windows 95 style graphical user interface and soon forget the last time they needed to restart their computer because of a software failure. All of this is good news, but we're not done yet. We're hard at work making the end user experience much more simple. on that. "Plug and Play" and Power Management support are in the works too. Expect them in Windows NT 5.0. Integration with the Internet at a fundamental level is in the works too. As we move the system forward with new features and functions we still remain completely focused on reliability and quality. These will never be sacrificed for any reason.

I've been working on system software for the past thirteen years. The software certainly evolves, but many concepts remain the same. An operating system boots up, manages the hardware resources, and provides an environment in which application programs run. Windows NT is no different in that regard, but there are many detailed concepts to learn and explore. To get the most out of an operating system, you need to know everything about it. A system always seems to work best in the hands of an expert. It takes both knowledge and experience to attain expertise. By taking this course, you are taking the first step to attain the knowledge you need. Your next step is to start up Windows NT system and use it every day. Don't worry about being too rough with it. You won't hurt it!

Frank Artale
Director of Windows NT Program Management

January 18, 1997

About This Book

Welcome to *Microsoft® Windows NT® Technical Support*. This book provides the knowledge, concepts, and skills necessary to install, configure, customize, and troubleshoot Windows NT in a single domain Microsoft Windows NT-based network. In addition, you learn how to integrate Windows NT and Novell NetWare networks. This book also provides you with the prerequisite knowledge and skills required for course 689 *Supporting Microsoft Windows NT Server 4.0—Enterprise Technologies*, and helps to prepare you to meet the certification requirements to become a Microsoft Windows NT Certified Professional.

Note For more information on becoming a Microsoft Certified Professional, please see the section "The Microsoft Certified Professional Program" later in this chapter.

The "About This Book" section provides important setup instructions that describe the hardware and software requirements, as well as the networking configuration, for the two computers that are necessary to complete the hands-on procedures. Read through "About This Book" thoroughly before you start the lessons.

Each chapter in this book is divided into lessons. Most lessons integrate the technical information with hands-on procedures that enable you to practice key concepts and skills. A summary is provided at the end of each chapter. In addition, some chapters contain references to additional information or related topics.

Intended Audience

This book is intended for those who support or administer Microsoft Windows NT Server 4.0 and Windows NT Workstation 4.0, plan to take course 689 *Supporting Microsoft Windows NT Server 4.0—Enterprise Technologies,* or who are on the Microsoft Certified Systems Engineer Windows NT 4.0 track.

Prerequisites

- Working knowledge of an operating system, such as Microsoft Windows® version 3.*x*, Windows 95, Windows NT, Windows for Workgroups, Microsoft MS-DOS®, or UNIX.
- Knowledge of basic computer hardware components, including memory, hard disks, CPUs, communication and printer ports, display adapters, and pointing devices. These concepts and skills are covered in course 683, *Networking Essentials—Self-Paced Training Kit.*
- Working knowledge of major networking components, including clients, servers, local area networks (LANs), network adapter cards, drivers, protocols, services, and network operating systems. These concepts and skills are covered in course 683, *Networking Essentials—Self-Paced Training Kit.*
- Proficiency using the Windows 95 or Windows NT version 4.0 interface, including the ability to use Windows NT Explorer to locate, create, and manipulate folders and files.
- Working knowledge of common Windows NT administrative tasks, including creating user and group accounts, assigning permissions, sharing folders, and auditing. These concepts and skills are covered in the instructor-led course 803, *Administering Microsoft Windows NT 4.0* and in course 753, *Microsoft Windows NT 4.0 Network Administration—Self-Paced Training Kit.*
- Working knowledge of network and end-user support.

Finding the Best Starting Point for You

This book has been designed so that you tailor the content and course flow to meet your training needs. If you decide to complete the chapters out of order, keep in mind that Chapters 3 through 18 require that you first complete the procedures in Chapter 2, "Installing Windows NT." The following table provides suggested learning paths for specific training needs.

If you	Follow this learning path
Are preparing to take the Microsoft Certified Professional examinations: Implementing and Supporting Microsoft Windows NT Server 4.0, exam 70–67 or Implementing and Supporting Microsoft Windows NT Workstation 4.0, exam 70–73.	Read "Getting Started" and complete the procedures in "Setup Instructions" (both located later in "About This Book"). Next, complete all of the procedures in the book. Read and review the information contained in Books Online.
Need to install and configure a small network.	Read "Getting Started" and complete the procedures in "Setup Instructions" (both located later in "About This Book"). Read and complete the procedures in Chapters 2, 3, 5, 6, and 9–11.
Need to install and configure multiple departments, groups, or computers.	Read "Getting Started" and complete the procedures in "Setup Instructions" (both located later in "About This Book"). Read and complete the procedures in Chapters 2–11, and 13.
Need to install and configure TCP/IP.	Read "Getting Started" and complete the procedures in "Setup Instructions" (both located later in "About This Book"). Read and complete the procedures in Chapter 2 and Chapters 9–11.
Need to know the definition of a Windows NT term.	Refer to the glossary included in this book, or to Windows NT Help Glossary.
Need information on a specific topic related to Windows NT.	Refer to the table of contents or index in this book, or refer to Windows NT Help.

Conventions Used in This Book

Before you start any of the lessons, it is important that you understand the terms and notational conventions used in this book.

Features of This Book

- Each chapter opens with an "About This Chapter" section, which provides an overview of the chapter content.
- Where appropriate, each chapter opens with a "Before You Begin" section, which describes the other chapters and procedures that must be completed before continuing.
- Whenever possible, lessons contain practices that give you an opportunity to use the skills being presented and explore each component of Windows NT as it is described.
- The "Review" sections at the end of each chapter allow you to test what you have learned in the lessons included in that chapter.
- The "For more information" table at the end of some chapters lists additional resource locations for information on the concepts and skills covered in the chapter.
- The "Answer Key" section at the end of each chapter contains all of the questions and corresponding answers for that chapter. Each question is referenced by page number.
- The glossary presents a set of definitions of most of the technical terms that appear in this book.

Procedural Conventions

- Hands-on procedures are preceded by a *Practice* heading. A triangular bullet (▸) indicates the beginning of a procedure, and the steps of the procedure are given in numbered lists (1, 2, and so on).

  For example:

  ### Practice

  In these procedures, you explore the HKEY_LOCAL_MACHINE subtree to familiarize yourself with the registry hierarchy.

  ▸ **To explore HKEY_LOCAL MACHINE**

- The word *select* is used for highlighting directories, file names, text boxes, menu bars, and options, and for selecting options in a dialog box.
- The word *click* is used for carrying out a command from a menu or dialog box.

Notational Conventions

- Dialog box names, options, menu names, and menu commands appear in **bold** type.
- Characters or commands that you type appear in **bold lowercase** type.
- Variable information in syntax statements is *italicized*, for example: *cd_rom_drive*:\I386. *Italic* is also used to identify new terms, book titles, and for emphasis in the text.
- Names of files, folders, or directories appear in Title Caps, except when you are to type them directly. Unless otherwise indicated, you can use lowercase letters when you type a folder name or file name in a dialog box or at the command prompt.
- Full capitals are also used for acronyms.
- File name extensions appear in all lowercase.
- Code samples, examples of screen text, or entries that you might type at the command prompt or in initialization files appear in monospace type. For example:

```
I/O Error accessing boot sector file
multi(0)disk(0)rdisk(0)partition(1):\bootsect.dos
```

- Optional items in syntax statements are enclosed in square brackets [ ]. For example, [*filename*] in command syntax indicates that you can choose to type a file name with the command. Type only the information within the brackets, not the brackets themselves.
- Required items in syntax statements are enclosed in braces { }. Type only the information within the braces, not the braces themselves.

Keyboard Conventions

- Names of keys that you press appear in SMALL CAPITALS; for example, TAB and SHIFT.
- A plus sign (+) between two key names means that you must press those keys at the same time. For example, "Press ALT+TAB" means that you hold down ALT while you press TAB.
- A comma (,) between two or more key names means that you must press each of the keys consecutively, not together. For example, "Press ALT, F, X" means that you press and release each key in sequence. "Press ALT+S, R" means that you first press ALT and S together, and then release them and press R.
- You can choose menu commands with the keyboard. Press the ALT key to activate the menu bar, and then sequentially press the keys that correspond to the highlighted or underlined letter of the menu name and the command name. For some commands, you can also press a key combination listed in the menu.

- You can select or clear check boxes or options in dialog boxes with the keyboard. Press the ALT key, and then press the key that corresponds to the underlined letter of the option name. Or you can press TAB until the option is highlighted, and then press SPACEBAR to select or clear the check box or option.
- You can cancel the display of a dialog box by pressing the ESC key.

Icons

The following table describes the icons that are used throughout this book.

Icon	Description
	Identifies content that applies only to computers running Windows NT Server.
	Indicates a hands-on practice.
	Indicates instructions for starting a video clip.
	Identifies content useful when planning.
	Indicates a best practice.
	Identifies content that is useful in identifying and troubleshooting problems.
	Indicates questions that you should answer.

Notes

Notes appear throughout the lessons.

- Notes marked **Tip** contain explanations of possible results or alternative methods.
- Notes marked **Important** are items you should check before completing an action.
- Notes marked **Note** contain supplementary or needed information.
- Notes marked **Caution** contain warnings about possible loss of data.

Chapter and Appendix Overview

This self-paced training kit contains a video, text, hands-on procedures, simulations, and review questions to teach you how to install, configure, and support Windows NT Server and Windows NT Workstation.

The self-paced training book is divided into the following chapters and appendixes:

- Chapter 1, "Overview of Windows NT," provides you with an overview and comparison of the features of Microsoft Windows NT Server 4.0 and Windows NT Workstation 4.0. This chapter also provides you with a review of the components of a Windows NT domain, the administrative differences between a domain and a workgroup, and directory services.
- Chapter 2, "Installing Windows NT," provides you with the hardware requirements and information needed to install Windows NT Server and Windows NT Workstation. The hands-on procedures give you the opportunity to install Windows NT Server from compact disc and configure the computer as a primary domain controller (PDC). You also install Windows NT Workstation from compact disc and then add the computer to the domain. Finally, you create a distribution server for the Windows NT Server source files and use the distribution server to perform an unattended, over-the-network server installation and then configure the computer as a backup domain controller (BDC).
- Chapter 3, "Configuring the Windows NT Environment," provides you with an overview of the registry architecture and introduces you to the tools, Control Panel and Registry Editor, that are used to edit the registry. The hands-on procedures give you an opportunity to use Registry Editor to explore the registry and then use Control Panel to configure the Windows NT environment.
- Chapter 4, "Managing System Policies," introduces you to system policy, a feature of Windows NT Server that enables you to control the user-definable settings in Windows NT user profiles, as well as system configuration settings. The hands-on procedures give you an opportunity to use System Policy Editor to change desktop settings and restrict what users can do from their desktop.
- Chapter 5, "Managing File Systems," provides you with a comparison of the file systems—FAT (file allocation table) and NTFS (Windows NT File System)—and explains issues involved in running them in the Windows NT environment, such as the management of long file names, and file compression. The hands-on procedures give you an opportunity to convert a FAT partition to an NTFS partition, and to create and rename files on a FAT partition and note the effect of these changes on their long file names and aliases. You also use Windows NT Explorer to compress files and folders on an NTFS partition, and then see the effects on compressed files when they are copied or moved into a folder that is not compressed.

- Chapter 6, "Managing Partitions," introduces the types of partitions supported by Windows NT, including primary and extended partitions, volume sets, and stripe sets. The hands-on procedures give you an opportunity to customize Disk Administrator, to create, format, and label the volumes, change the drive letter of a partition, and then extend a partition. Then, you use the Volume Set Simulation to create, format, extend, and delete a volume set.
- Chapter 7, "Managing Fault Tolerance," defines fault tolerance and explains how Windows NT Server provides fault tolerance using two RAID levels: Raid 1–mirror sets, and Raid 5–stripe sets with parity. It also explains the importance of creating a fault tolerance boot disk for use in case of physical disk failure. The hands-on procedures give you the opportunity to use the fault tolerance simulation to implement mirror sets, and stripe sets with parity, and to create a boot disk for the Intel platform that can be used in the event that your computer's boot partition is not accessible.
- Chapter 8, "Supporting Applications," introduces you to the Windows NT operating system architecture. The Windows NT memory model is covered, as well as how Windows NT manages memory and runs applications written for the Windows NT operating system and other operating systems. The hands-on procedures give you the opportunity to manage applications using the Windows NT Task Manager. You determine the effects of a halted Microsoft Win32®-based application on the system, and use Task Manager to end the application that has stopped responding. You observe the effects of a General Protection Fault (GPF) error and the effects of a halted application, and run a Win16-based application in its own memory space.
- Chapter 9, "The Windows NT Networking Environment," describes the components of the Windows NT networking architecture, and how these components communicate with each other and enable a computer running Windows NT to communicate over a network.
- Chapter 10, "Configuring Windows NT Protocols," introduces the Windows network protocols: NWLink IPX/SPX Compatible Transport, NetBEUI, and Transmission Control Protocol/Internet Protocol (TCP/IP). It also describes how network bindings are used to optimize network performance. The hands-on procedures give you an opportunity to install and configure each of these protocols.
- Chapter 11, "Windows NT Networking Services," introduces you to the following services provided by Microsoft Windows NT TCP/IP: Dynamic Host Configuration Protocol (DHCP), Windows Internet Name Service (WINS), and Domain Name Server (DNS). Also covered in this chapter is the Windows NT Computer Browser service which is used by Windows NT to identify and list available network resources. The hands-on procedures give you an opportunity to install and configure DHCP, WINS, and DNS. You create and activate a DHCP scope, use the **ping** and **arp** utilities to help test and troubleshoot DHCP, configure the DHCP server to assign WINS server addresses, and create and configure a DNS Server service primary zone.

- Chapter 12, "Implementing Remote Access Service," introduces you to Microsoft Windows NT Server Remote Access Service (RAS) and the client version of RAS, called Dial-Up Networking. The hands-on procedures give you an opportunity to install RAS and Dial-Up Networking, and include a simulation in which you configure and use Dial-Up Networking.
- Chapter 13, "Internetworking and Intranetworking," introduces you to the Windows NT services used to support publishing and accessing services on the Internet and intranets. These include the Internet Information Server (IIS), Peer Web Services (PWS), and Microsoft Internet Explorer (IE). The hands-on procedures give you an opportunity to install and configure IIS. You examine the Windows NT Server environment before and after installing Microsoft Internet Information Server to determine changes made by IIS. You publish a document on your Web server, and access that document from a client computer running Windows NT Workstation 4.0. Finally, you configure DNS to resolve IP addresses for IIS.
- Chapter 14, "Interoperating with Novell NetWare," explains the Windows NT features and services that enable computers running Windows NT to coexist and interoperate with Novell NetWare servers. Some of these services are included in Windows NT, while others are available as separate products, commonly called add-ons. This chapter describes these NetWare connectivity tools and explains how they can be used to integrate Windows NT and NetWare environments. The hands-on procedures give you the opportunity to install Client Service for NetWare (CSNW). You run a simulation in which you configure CSNW and use it to connect to a NetWare server. You also install and configure Gateway Services for NetWare (GSNW).
- Chapter 15, "Implementing Network Clients," explains the two Windows NT Server client licensing options, Per Server and Per Seat, and introduces you to the tools used to manage client licenses on your network. This chapter describes the client software provided with Windows NT Server 4.0, and the client software that must be installed on a computer so that it can access a computer running Windows NT Server. This chapter also describes Services for Macintosh, which gives you the ability to manage a Windows NT network environment that includes AppleTalk computers. The hands-on procedures give you the opportunity to install the Windows NT Server administrative tools on a client computer, and to install Services for Macintosh.
- Chapter 16, "Implementing File Synchronization and Directory Replication," explains the Microsoft Windows NT Briefcase and the Directory Replicator service used to minimize the administration involved in updating files over a network. The hands-on procedures give you an opportunity to use and configure the Briefcase and the Directory Replicator service.

- Chapter 17, "The Windows NT Boot Process," describes the steps that occur when you start a computer running Windows NT as the operating system and introduces troubleshooting resources that you can use to help you resolve problems when Windows NT will not start. The hands-on procedures give you the opportunity to create a boot disk, and rename system files and reboot to observe error messages. You also disable the keyboard driver and use the Last Known Good configuration to successfully reboot your computer. Finally, you use the **rdisk** utility to update your Emergency Repair Disk and perform an Emergency Repair to inspect your boot sector.
- Chapter 18, "Windows NT Troubleshooting Tools," describes the troubleshooting tools that are available in Windows NT. In addition to learning about these resources, you learn how to use them to diagnose and resolve problems that can occur in administering a Windows NT system or network. The hands-on procedures give you the opportunity to use Event Viewer to view events in the system, security, and application event logs, control the size of the log files, filter events, and search for specific events to locate existing and potential problems. You also use Windows NT Diagnostics (Winmsd) to view configuration information for your local computer and for a remote computer, save a report for the remote computer, and then view the report. You use Performance Monitor to create a chart, and to create and view a log of processor activity. Finally, you install the Network Monitor Tools and Agent, and use them to capture and display network traffic.
- Appendix A, "Comparing Microsoft Windows NT Workstation and Windows 95," provides a comparison of Windows NT Workstation and Windows 95 features and provides criteria to help you choose which operating system will satisfy your organization's requirements.
- Appendix B, "Changes to Kernel Mode, User Mode, and GDI in Microsoft Windows NT 4.0," provides a description of changes to the kernel mode, user mode, and GDI in Windows NT 4.0 and explains how these changes improve the operating system's performance.
- Appendix C, "Implementing DNS Using Microsoft Windows NT 4.0," provides a history of Domain Name Server and explains how to implement DNS in a Windows NT 4.0 network.
- Appendix D, "Using the Point-to-Point Tunneling Protocol," provides detailed information on the function, implementation, and configuration of PPTP in a Windows NT network.
- Appendix E, "The Distributed Component Model," describes how DCOM enhances networking technology over the Internet.

- Appendix F, "Microsoft Services for NetWare," describes each of the Microsoft tools for integrating Windows NT and NetWare networks.
- Appendix G, "Printing from Microsoft Windows NT," examines the Windows NT printing process and describes the components that make it possible.
- Glossary, contains the definitions of most of the technical terms used in this book.

Note The appendixes are located on the *Microsoft Windows NT Technical Support Training Course Materials* compact disc in the Docfiles folder. These files are Microsoft Word for Windows documents and can be viewed and printed with any text editor that can read the RTF file format, such as WordPad.

Cross-References to Windows NT Documentation

You will find references to Windows NT documentation and online Help throughout this book. These references point you to more information about specific tasks.

- Microsoft Windows NT Server *Concepts and Planning* explains how to implement and optimize Windows NT Server. It is designed for new and experienced administrators of small networks and advanced users of operating systems. The online version of Windows NT Server *Concepts and Planning* is included in Books Online on the *Windows NT Server* compact disc.
- The *Microsoft Windows NT Server 4.0 Resource Kit* provides detailed information on the Windows NT Server operating system, and includes utilities and tools that help you to implement and manage Windows NT Server in larger networks.
- The *Microsoft Windows NT Workstation 4.0 Resource Kit* provides detailed information on the Windows NT Workstation operating system, plus topics that are new for version 4.0.
- Help provides references and how-to information for all Windows NT tasks.

Getting Started

This self-paced training contains hands-on procedures to help you learn about Windows NT Server and Windows NT Workstation.

To complete the lessons, you must have two computers. The first computer must be capable of running Microsoft Windows NT Server 4.0. The second computer must be capable of running both Microsoft Windows NT Server 4.0 and Windows NT Workstation 4.0. Both computers must have the following minimum configuration:

- Personal computer with a 486/33 or higher Intel-based processor
- 16 MB of RAM (32 MB recommended)
- A minimum of 450 MB of available hard disk space (on the first computer)
- A minimum of 375 MB of available hard disk space (on the second computer)
- SVGA display adapter and monitor capable of 256 colors
- Microsoft Mouse or compatible pointing device
- Network adapter card and related cables
- One 3.5-inch high-density disk drive
- CD-ROM drive
- Sound card and speakers (optional)
- Null modem cable for testing RAS (optional—for those who do not have the cable, a simulation for RAS is included with the course)
- Serial port for testing RAS practice (optional)

Software Requirements

- *Microsoft Windows NT Server 4.0.* A special 120-day limited use version of Windows NT Server 4.0 is included with this book to enable you to complete the course.
- *Microsoft Windows NT Workstation 4.0.* A special 120-day limited use version of Windows NT Workstation 4.0 is included with this book to enable you to complete the course.

Note Both computers must have an existing Microsoft operating system such as MS-DOS, Windows 3.*x*, Windows 95, or Windows NT 3.*x*. One computer must be able to run multimedia applications so that you can view the video included with the course.

Setup Instructions

1. Set up both computers according to the manufacturer's instructions.
2. The computers need to be networked together, either cabled together using a hub so that the two computers can communicate, or as part of a larger network.
3. Computer1 requires 450 MB of free disk space on drive C.
4. Computer2 requires 200 MB of free disk space on drive C, 125 MB of free disk space on drive D, and 50 MB of unpartitioned disk space in an extended partition.

Caution If your computers are part of a larger network, you *must* verify with your network administrator that the following computer names, domain name, and IP address information do not conflict with network operations. If they do conflict, ask your network administrator to provide alternative values and use those values throughout all of the practices in this book.

Variable	Values used in this course
Computer name for Computer1	Server1
Computer names for Computer2	Server2 and Workstation1
IP address range	131. 107. 2. 200 — 131. 107. 2. 211
Subnet mask	255. 255. 0. 0

Network Configuration Used in This Book

This section provides a description of how your two computers will be configured after completing Chapter 2, "Installing Windows NT," and provides illustrations that show the roles of each computer.

Role of Computer1

Computer1 will act as a server. On Computer1, you install Windows NT Server from the compact disc labeled *Windows NT Server version 4.0 Evaluation Edition 120-day Limit on Use* that is included with this book.

Computer1 will be configured as a primary domain controller (PDC), and will be assigned the computer account name, Server1, and the domain name, Domain1. This computer will act as a domain controller, a file and print server, and an application server in Domain1.

Role of Computer2

Computer2 will act primarily as a workstation for most of the procedures in this course. However, to give you an opportunity to perform an over-the-network installation of Windows NT Server and to perform directory replication, you will also configure Computer2 as a server.

Configuring Computer2 As a Workstation

To configure Computer2 as a workstation, you install Windows NT Workstation from the compact disc labeled *Windows NT Workstation version 4.0 Evaluation Edition 120-day Limit on Use* that is included with this book. This computer is added to Domain1 and is assigned the computer account name Workstation1.

Network Configuration of Server1 and Workstation1

The following illustration shows the roles of Computer1 and Computer2 after installing Windows NT Server on Computer1 and Windows NT Workstation on Computer2.

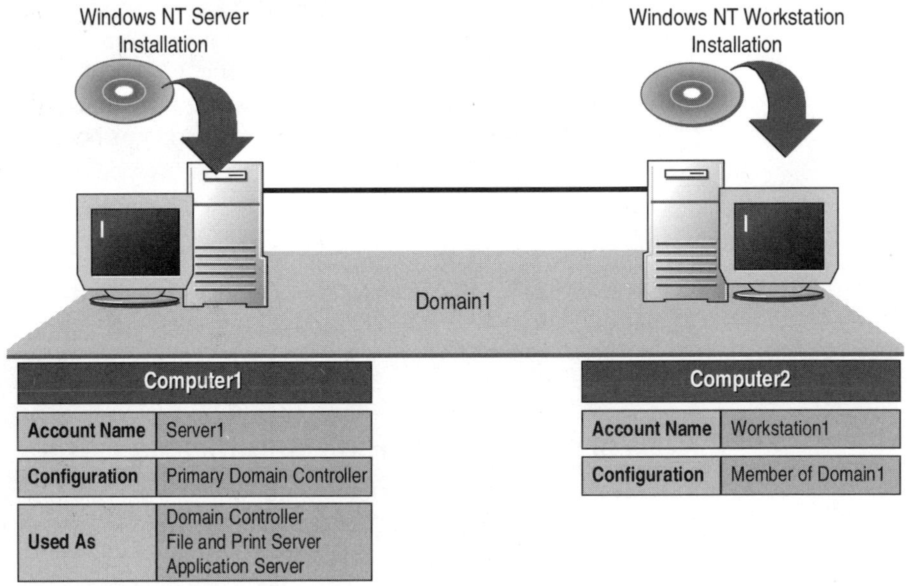

Configuring Computer2 As a Server

To configure Computer2 as a server, you install Windows NT Server. This installation is done during a practice in Chapter 2, "Installing Windows NT." In this practice, Computer2 is configured as a Backup Domain Controller in Domain1 and the computer is assigned the computer account name Server2.

Network Configuration of Server1 and Server2

The following illustration shows the roles of Computer1 and Computer2 after installing Windows NT Server on Computer1 and Computer2.

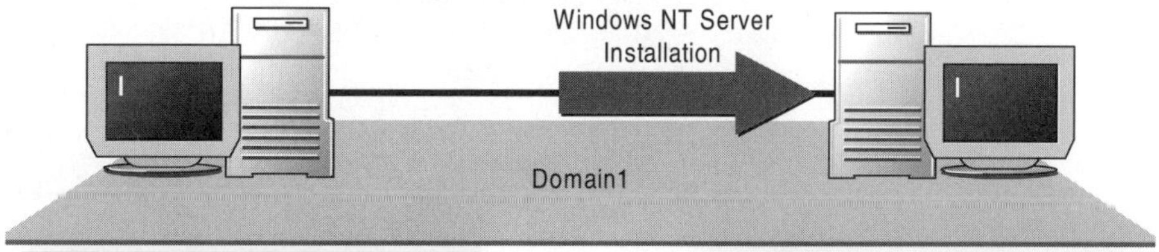

Computer1	
Account Name	Server1
Configuration	Primary Domain Controller
Used As	Domain Controller File and Print Server Application Server

Computer2	
Account Name	Server2
Configuration	Backup Domain Controller

Description of Course Materials Compact Disc

This book includes a compact disc labeled *Microsoft Windows NT Technical Support Training CD-ROM Course Materials.* This compact disc contains the files, simulations, and course Web page that you need in order to complete the procedures in this book. You will install the components on the course materials compact disc onto Server1 and Workstation1 in Chapter 2 "Installing Windows NT."

The following list describes the files that are copied to your computers and the changes that are made to the interface once you have run the course materials Setup program.

1. The lab files used in the procedures are copied to C:\Lab Files.
2. The files required to use the simulations, video, and course Web page are copied to C:\Technical Support Training.

3. The Setup program creates a **Technical Support Training** menu as shown in the following illustration.

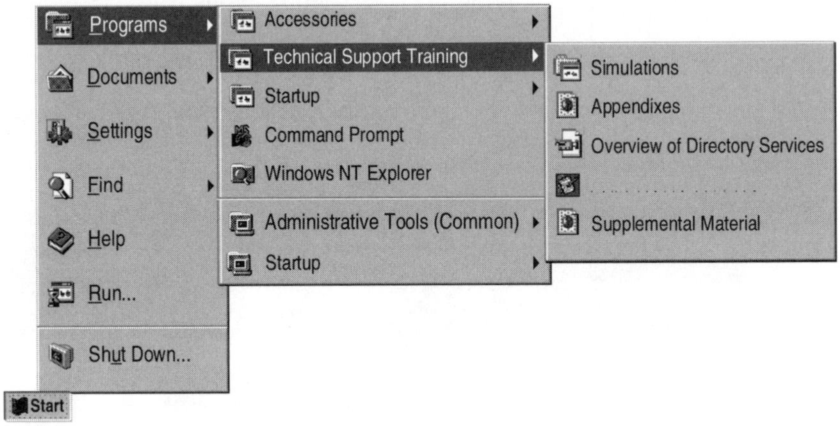

The following list describes the shortcuts on the **Technical Support Training** menu.

- *Simulations.* Pointing to this menu displays the simulations used in this course.
  - *Fault tolerance simulation.* Provides practice using Disk Administrator to create a stripe set with parity, and to create a mirror set.
  - *Novell NetWare simulation.* Provides practice configuring CSNW and then using CSNW to connect to a NetWare server.
  - *RAS simulation.* Provides practice configuring and then using Dial-Up Networking to connect to a RAS server.
  - *Volume set simulation.* Provides practice creating, formatting, extending, and deleting a volume set.
  - *Windows NT Server simulation.* Provides practice installing Windows NT Server as a primary domain controller.
  - *Windows NT Workstation simulation.* Provides practice installing Windows NT Workstation; during this simulation you can choose to install the computer as a member of a workgroup or a domain.
- *Appendixes.* Clicking this option starts the course Web page, and displays a list of the appendixes used in this course. This provides an easy way to view this information online. If you want to print out the appendixes, you can find them on the *Microsoft Windows NT Technical Support Training Course Materials* compact disc in the Docfiles folder. These files are Microsoft Word for Windows documents and can be viewed and printed with any text editor that can read the RTF file format, such as WordPad.

- *Overview of Directory Services.* Clicking this option starts the 7-minute instructional video. The video describes the components in a Windows NT network and the role of user accounts in Windows NT Directory Services. This video can be viewed on either a 32-bit operating system, such as Windows 95 or Windows NT, or on a 16-bit operating system such as Windows 3.1. For more information on running the video, please see the instructions in Chapter 1, "Overview of Windows NT."
- *Self-Assessment Exam.* Clicking this option starts the Microsoft Self-Assessment Program which contains the self-assessment examination for course 803, *Administering Microsoft Windows NT 4.0.* This examination can be used to refresh your knowledge of Windows NT administrative tasks and to identify areas that you may want to study further. If you are interested in learning more about Windows NT administration, you should consider completing the instructor-led course 803, *Administering Microsoft Windows NT 4.0* or course 753, the *Microsoft Windows NT Network Administration* self-paced training kit.
- *Supplemental Material.* Clicking this option starts the course Web page and displays the home page. This Web page provides information on the Microsoft Certified Trainer program, course materials, and links to key Web sites.

Removing Self-Paced Training Files

If you want to remove all files and shortcuts that were created when you installed the self-paced training files, you use the Add/Remove Programs program in Control Panel.

► **To remove the self-paced training files**

1. Click the **Start** button, point to **Settings**, and then click **Control Panel**.

   The Control Panel window appears.

2. Double-click the Add/Remove Programs icon.

   The **Add/Remove Programs Properties** dialog box appears.

3. On the **Install/Uninstall** tab, click **Microsoft Windows NT 4.0 Technical Support Training**, and then click **Add/Remove**.

   The **Microsoft Windows NT 4.0 Technical Support Training Setup** dialog box appears.

4. Click **Remove All**.

   A message appears asking if you want to remove Windows NT 4.0 Technical Support Training.

5. Click **Yes**.

   The **Microsoft Windows NT Technical Support Training** menu is removed from **Programs**, and all related files are removed from your hard disk, including the Lab Files folder (which does not appear on the **Technical Support Training** menu).

6. When a message appears stating that the process has successfully completed, click **OK**.
7. Click **OK** to close the **Add/Remove Programs Properties** dialog box.
8. Close Control Panel.

The Microsoft Certified Professional Program

The Microsoft Certified Professional (MCP) program provides the best method to prove your command of current Microsoft products and technologies. Anyone who must prove his or her technical expertise with Microsoft products should consider completing this program, including systems engineers, product developers, support technicians, system and network administrators, consultants, and trainers.

The Four Certifications

The following table describes the four certifications, based on specific areas of technical expertise.

Certification	Description
Microsoft Certified Product Specialist (MCPS)	MCPSs demonstrate in-depth knowledge of at least one Microsoft operating system. Candidates may pass additional Microsoft certification exams to further qualify their skills with Microsoft BackOffice™ products, development tools, or desktop applications.
Microsoft Certified Systems Engineer (MCSE)	MCSEs are qualified to effectively plan, implement, maintain, and support information systems in a wide range of computing environments with Windows NT Server and the Microsoft BackOffice integrated family of server products.
Microsoft Certified Solution Developer (MCSD)	MCSDs are qualified to design and develop custom business solutions with Microsoft development tools, technologies, and platforms, including Microsoft Office and Microsoft BackOffice.
Microsoft Certified Trainer (MCT)	MCTs are instructionally and technically qualified to deliver Microsoft Official Curriculum through Microsoft Authorized Technical Education Centers.

Certification Requirements

The certification requirements differ for each certification and are specific to the products and job functions addressed by the certification. To become a Microsoft Certified Professional, you must pass rigorous certification exams that provide a valid and reliable measure of technical proficiency and expertise.

The following table describes exam requirements.

Certification	Exam requirements
Microsoft Certified Product Specialist (MCPS)	Pass one operating system exam. In addition, individuals seeking to validate their expertise in a program must pass the appropriate elective exam.
Microsoft Certified Systems Engineer (MCSE)	Pass four operating system exams and two elective exams.
Microsoft Certified Solution Developer (MCSD)	Pass two core technology exams and two elective exams.
Microsoft Certified Trainer (MCT)	Required to meet instructional and technical requirements specific to each Microsoft Official Curriculum course they are certified to deliver.[1]

For More Information See the Certification section of the Web page provided on the compact disc or the Microsoft Training and Certification Web site at http://www.microsoft.com/train_cert/

MCSE Track

This course supports the MCSE Windows NT 4.0 track. To complete this track, it is recommended that you do the following.

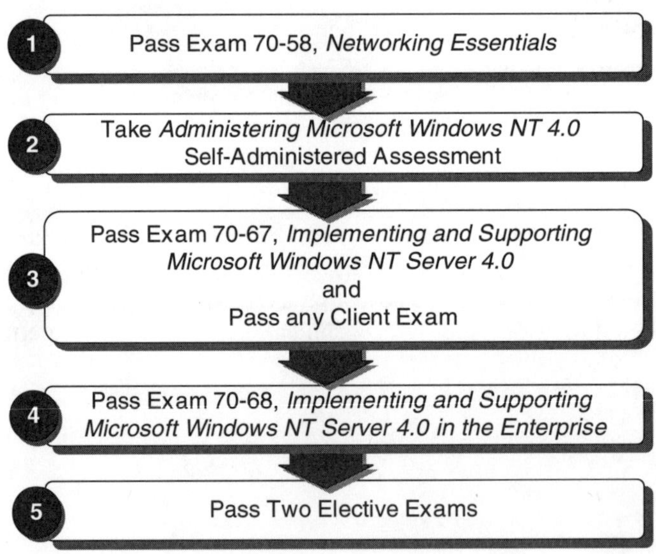

---

[1] *Inside the United States and Canada call (800) 636-7544 for more information on becoming a Microsoft Certified Trainer. Outside the United States and Canada, contact your local Microsoft subsidiary.*

The following table outlines the recommended path to certification.

Step	Pass this exam	Preparation
1	70–58, *Networking Essentials*	Course 683, *Networking Essentials—Self-Paced Training Kit*
2	*Administering Microsoft Windows NT 4.0 self-administered assessment*	Course 803, *Administering Microsoft Windows NT 4.0* –or– *Microsoft Windows NT Network Administration Self-Paced Training*
3	70–67, *Implementing and Supporting Microsoft Windows NT Server 4.0* and any client exam, such as exam 70–73, *Implementing and Supporting Microsoft Windows NT Workstation 4.0*[2] and exam 70–63, *Implementing and Supporting Microsoft Windows 95*	Course 803, *Administering Microsoft Windows NT 4.0* Course 687, *Supporting Windows NT Core Technologies* –or– *Microsoft Windows NT Technical Support Self-Paced Training* Course 564, *Microsoft Windows 95 Training—Instructor-led training*
4	70–68, *Implementing and Supporting Microsoft Windows NT Server 4.0 in the Enterprise*	Course 689, *Supporting Windows NT Server 4.0 Enterprise Technologies*

Important Microsoft Official Curriculum (MOC) helps you to prepare for Microsoft Certified Professional (MCP) exams. However, no one-to-one correlation exists between MOC courses and MCP exams.

[2]For a complete list of client and elective exams, see the Microsoft Training and Certification Web site at http://www.microsoft.com/train_cert/

CHAPTER 1

Overview of Windows NT

About This Chapter

This chapter provides an overview and comparison of the features of Microsoft Windows NT Server version 4.0 and Windows NT Workstation version 4.0. You are introduced to several of the key features of Windows NT Server and Workstation, and you will view a video that provides a review of Windows NT Directory Services.

Before You Begin

To complete the lessons in this chapter, you must have a computer running Microsoft Windows 95 or Windows NT version 3.5 or later, with a CD-ROM drive, an audio board, and headphones or speakers. These operating systems enable you to view the "Overview of Windows NT Directory Services" video contained on the *Course Materials* compact disc.

Lesson 1: Introduction to Windows NT

Windows NT is a multipurpose operating system that can act as both a client and a server in a network environment. Windows NT refers to two different products—Windows NT Server and Windows NT Workstation.

This lesson provides an overview of Windows NT Server and Windows NT Workstation, and the key features of both.

After this lesson, you will be able to:

- Explain the key features in Windows NT Server and Windows NT Workstation.
- Describe the features common to Windows NT Server and Windows NT Workstation, and the differences between the two operating systems.

Estimated lesson time: 10 minutes

What Is Windows NT Server?

Microsoft Windows NT Server 4.0 is:

- A powerful, multipurpose server operating system designed for organizations that must implement mission-critical business systems.
- Optimized to be a file, print, and application server that can handle tasks for organizations ranging from small workgroups to enterprise networks.
- Designed to integrate current and future technologies and to provide competitive advantages through better information access.
- The required operating system for the other Microsoft BackOffice server components, including: Microsoft SQL Server™, Microsoft Systems Management Server, Microsoft SNA Server, Microsoft Proxy Server, and Microsoft Exchange Server.

The following illustration shows some of the key features of the Windows NT Server 4.0 operating system.

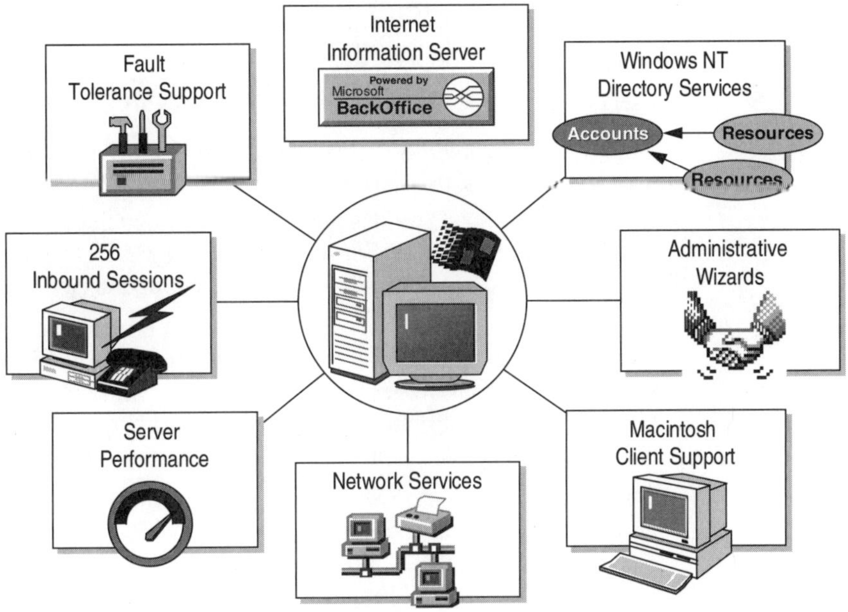

- *The Windows 95 user interface.* Provides a consistent look across desktops and the server, resulting in less training time and a faster rollout of the new network operating system.
- *Internet Information Server (IIS).* The integration of IIS with Windows NT Server 4.0 means that Web server installation and management is simply another part of the operating system. In addition, with IIS 2.0 or later, you can remotely administer your Web site from any computer with a Web browser and provide a fast and secure platform for offering HTTP, FTP, and Gopher services.

  Using Microsoft FrontPage™, a Web authoring and management tool included with Windows NT Server 4.0, you can create Web pages, audit and check the page links, and manage professional-quality Web sites.

- *Windows NT Directory Services.* A directory database that provides a single network logon and a single point of administration.
- *Administrative wizards.* Wizards group the common server management tools, such as User Manager for Domains and Server Manager, in a single place, and walk you through the steps required to add users, create and manage groups of users, manage file and folder access for network clients, and so on.
- *Macintosh client support.* Provides file and print sharing services for Macintosh clients.
- *Network services.* Provides network services, including Microsoft DNS (Domain Name System) Server, Microsoft DHCP (Dynamic Host Configuration Protocol) Server, and Windows Internet Name Service (WINS).
- *Server performance.* Windows NT Server 4.0 is tuned for file, print, and application server performance. The retail version of Windows NT Server supports up to four processors in a symmetric multiprocessing environment. Original equipment manufacturer (OEM) implementations of Windows NT Server support up to 32 processors in a symmetric multiprocessing environment.
- *256 inbound sessions.* Salespeople, home-based employees, traveling workers, and other mobile users connect to Windows NT Server 4.0 using Remote Access Service (RAS), a feature that allows remote users to dial in to their corporate network. Windows NT Server provides support for 256 inbound RAS sessions.
- *Fault tolerance.* Supports software-based *Redundant Array of Inexpensive Disks* (RAID) technology for data protection.

What Is Windows NT Workstation?

Microsoft Windows NT Workstation 4.0 is a powerful desktop operating system for business computing. Optimized for use as a high performance, secure network client and corporate desktop operating system, Windows NT Workstation maximizes the performance of desktop applications running on the local computer. Windows NT Workstation is also designed to improve end-user productivity.

Windows NT Workstation can be used alone as a desktop operating system, networked in a peer-to-peer workgroup environment, or used as a workstation in both a Windows NT Server domain and a Novell NetWare network environment. Windows NT Workstation can be used to access resources on all of the Microsoft BackOffice family of products.

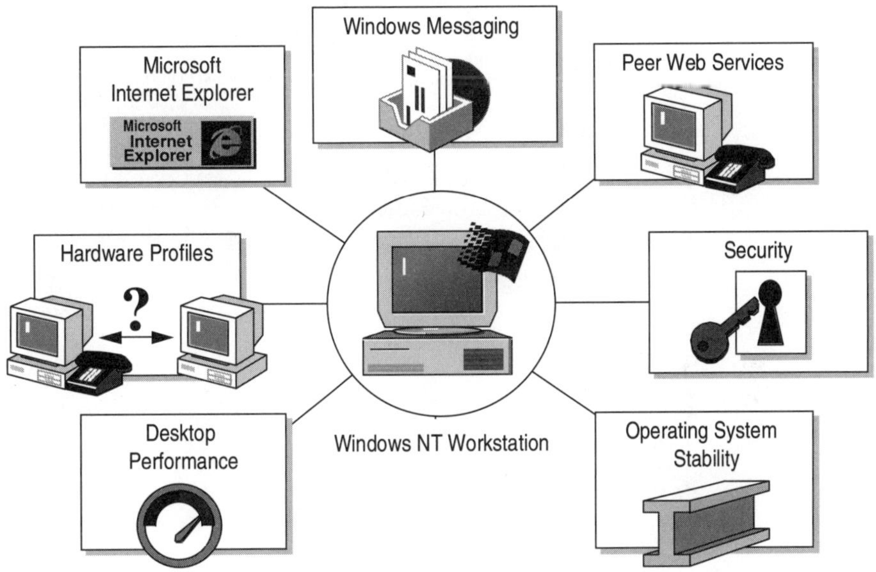

In addition, Windows NT Workstation includes the following features:

- *The Windows 95 user interface.* Provides a consistent look across desktops and the server, resulting in less training time and a faster rollout of the new network operating system.
- *Desktop performance.* Supports preemptive multitasking for all applications. Windows NT Workstation supports multiple processors for true multitasking performance.
- *Hardware profiles.* Creates and maintains a list of hardware configurations to meet specific computer needs.
- *Microsoft Internet Explorer.* Provides a fast and simple-to-use browser for exploring the Internet and the World Wide Web (WWW).
- *Windows messaging.* Receives and stores electronic mail (e-mail), including files and objects created in other applications.

- *Peer Web services.* Provides a personal Web server, optimized to run on Windows NT Workstation 4.0.
- *Security.* Provides local security for files, folders, printers, and other resources. Users must be authenticated by either the local workstation or a domain controller in order to access any resources on the computer or network.
- *Operating system stability.* Supports each application in its own memory address space. Malfunctioning applications will not affect other applications or the operating system.

Windows NT Server vs. Windows NT Workstation

Windows NT Server and Windows NT Workstation have many similar features. For example, both are 32-bit operating systems that provide a fast, multitasking environment. Each operating system also has unique features. This section covers the similarities and differences between Windows NT Server and Windows NT Workstation.

Similarities

The following table describes the common features of both operating systems, and their benefits.

Feature	Benefit
Multiple platforms	Supports Intel or compatible 80486-, Pentium-, and Pentium Pro-based computers, as well as RISC (reduced instruction set computers)-based computers, such as MIPS R4400 and R5000, DEC Alpha AXP, and PowerPC Reference Platform (PReP)-based PowerPC-based systems.
Multitasking and multi-threaded operations	Different applications can run at the same time. Background applications can continue while a user works in the foreground. Multiple threads in an application can operate simultaneously.
Support for MS-DOS-based, Win16-based, Win32-based, OS/2-based, and POSIX-compliant-based applications	Most applications run under Windows NT. Users can work on applications written for other operating systems without having to learn different operating system environments.
Built-in networking	Designed for networking. All utilities are included with the ability to add networking drivers and protocol stacks to meet connectivity requirements. Both systems include a built-in Web browser.

(*continued*)

Feature	Benefit
File systems	Windows NT includes file allocation table (FAT), Windows NT File System (NTFS), and CD-ROM File System (CDFS).
Reliability	Windows NT supports applications in separate memory address spaces. When applications are running in separate memory address spaces, malfunctioning applications will not affect other applications. Furthermore, the Windows NT architecture protects the operating system from applications that attempt to consume too much of the CPU's processing time or to use the operating system's memory address space.

Differences

The primary differences between Windows NT Server and Windows NT Workstation are:

- Windows NT Server contains enhanced features that make it a powerful network server operating system for server-based applications, such as SQL Server, Systems Management Server, SNA Server, and Microsoft Exchange Server. Whereas Windows NT Workstation is designed and tuned as a multitasking desktop operating system.
- The number of concurrent sessions that each operating system can allow. The number of incoming concurrent sessions for Windows NT Server is limited by the number of client licenses, while Windows NT Workstation has a limit of ten incoming concurrent sessions.

Note For a comparison of Windows NT Workstation and Windows 95, see Appendix A, "Comparing Microsoft Windows NT Workstation and Windows 95." You can view this appendix after completing the procedures in Chapter 2, "Installing Windows NT."

Lesson 2: Overview of Windows NT Directory Services

Windows NT Directory Services, one of the services provided by Windows NT Server, allows for centralized administration of the network. Windows NT Directory Services enables each user who has been assigned a unique user name and password to access resources throughout the network. It provides administrators with the ability to view and manage users and network resources from any computer on the network. This lesson provides an instructional video on Windows NT Directory Services, which focuses on a Windows NT environment and the role user accounts play in it.

After this lesson, you will be able to:

- Describe the Microsoft Windows NT Directory Services and the role user accounts play in them.
- Describe the function of the primary domain controller (PDC), backup domain controllers (BDCs), and member servers.
- Explain the function of a trust relationship among domains.

Estimated lesson time: 15 minutes

The video describes the components in a Windows NT network, and defines key terminology used throughout this book. You can view the complete video script on the course Web page, after you have completed the procedures in Chapter 2, "Installing Windows NT."

Practice

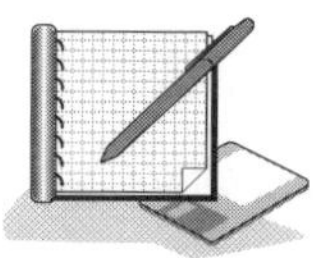

In these procedures, you install the necessary Codec files to run the video, and then you start the video.

Note To view the video, you require a computer running Windows 95 or Windows NT 3.5 or later with a CD-ROM drive.

▸ **To install the Codec files**

1. Insert the *Course Materials* compact disc compact disc in your CD-ROM drive.
2. Using My Computer, Windows NT Explorer, File Manager, or a command prompt, switch to your CD-ROM drive.
3. Change to the Videos\Codec folder.
4. From the Codec folder, run Install.exe.

5. In the **Indeo Video Interactive Install** dialog box, click **Windows 95 or NT**, and then click **OK**.
6. In the **Welcome** dialog box, click **Next**.
7. In the **Software License Agreement** dialog box, click **Yes**.
8. In the **Select Components** dialog box, click the appropriate operating system, and then click **Next**.
9. When prompted to read the Readme file, click **Yes** to read the file or **No** to continue with setup.

   The Codec files are copied to your computer.

▸ **To start the video**

- From the *Course Materials* compact disc, change to the Videos folder, and then double-click **Dirserv.avi**.

Video Review

1. Name three benefits of Windows NT Directory Services.

2. Name the three Windows NT Server types.

3. How many primary domain controllers can there be in each domain? How many backup domain controllers?

4. Name the logical link that combines domains into one administrative unit.

Lesson 3: Workgroups and Domains

A computer running Windows NT operates in either a workgroup or a domain. This lesson covers the administrative differences between workgroups and domains.

After this lesson, you will be able to:

- List the advantages and disadvantages of the workgroup model.
- List the additional advantages and disadvantages of the domain model.

Estimated lesson time: 10 minutes

What Is a Workgroup?

A workgroup is a logical grouping of typically no more than 10 computers. As part of a workgroup, each computer running Windows NT has its own directory database. One of the main advantages of a workgroup is that it allows its users to share resources. Resources and user accounts are managed at each computer in the workgroup.

The Workgroup Model

In the workgroup model, each computer functions as both a server and a client, and maintains its own accounts, administration, and security policies. The following illustration shows the Windows NT workgroup model.

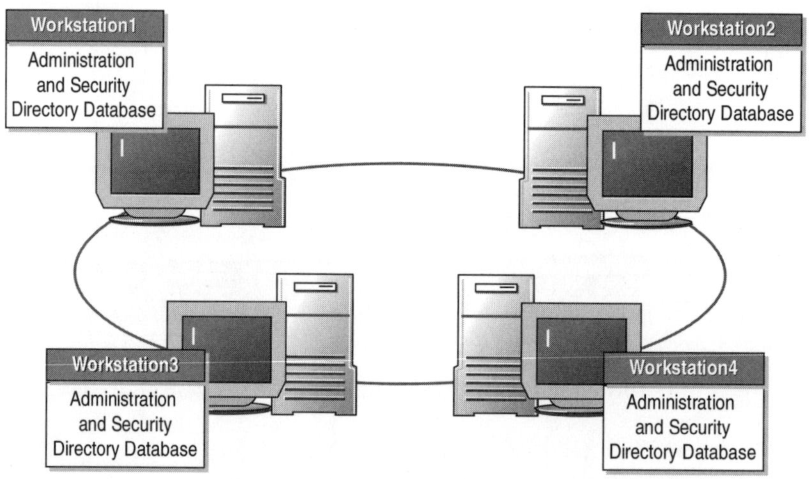

Both Windows NT Workstations and Windows NT Server stand-alone servers can be members of a Windows NT workgroup.

The workgroup model provides the following advantages and disadvantages.

Advantages	Disadvantages
Does not require a Windows NT Server domain controller.	No centralized account management.
Simple design and implementation.	Not recommended for networks that have more than 10 computers.
Convenient for a limited number of computers in close proximity.	

What Is a Domain?

A domain is a collection of computers and users that share a common directory services database. The directory services database allows for central administration of domain account privileges and security and network resources. It is stored on a domain controller.

The Domain Model

While both members of a workgroup and members of a domain can share resources, the domain provides a centralized approach to sharing network resources. The following illustration shows the Windows NT domain model. This example includes one primary domain controller (PDC), two backup domain controllers (BDCs), one computer running Windows NT Server (NTS), and two computers running Windows NT Workstation (NTW).

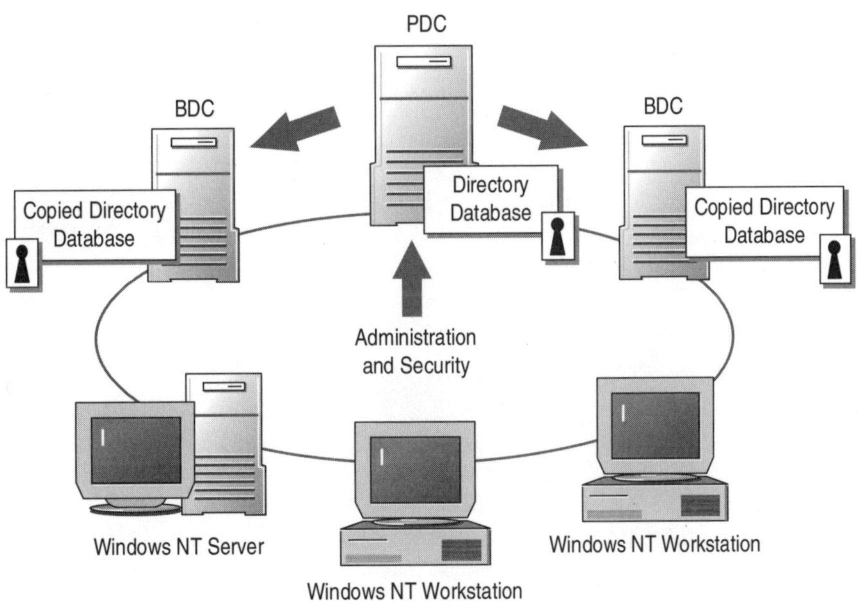

In a domain, computers running Windows NT Workstation and computers running Windows NT Server perform the following tasks:

- Obtain user account validation from the directory database.
- Allow resource access to users defined in the directory database.
- Function as part of a centrally administered group.

Summary

The following information summarizes the key points in this chapter:

- Windows NT refers to two different products—Windows NT Server and Windows NT Workstation.
- Windows NT Server 4.0 is a multipurpose server operating system, optimized to be a file, print, and applications server. Its client/server platform is designed to integrate current and future technologies.
- Windows NT Workstation 4.0 is a desktop operating system that can be used on a stand-alone computer, on a networked computer in a peer-to-peer workgroup environment, or on a networked computer in a Windows NT Server domain or Novell NetWare environment.
- Windows NT Directory Services, one of the services provided by Windows NT Server, allows for centralized administration of the network. The Windows NT Directory Services enables each user who has been assigned a unique user name and password to access resources throughout the network. It provides administrators with the ability to view and manage users and network resources from any computer on the network.
- A workgroup is a logical grouping of typically no more than 10 computers that can share resources. As part of a workgroup, each computer running Windows NT has its own directory database; resources and user accounts are managed at each computer.
- A domain is an administrative unit of Windows NT Directory Services. A domain contains a computer running Windows NT Server configured as a primary domain controller (PDC). The PDC maintains a directory database that stores all of the account and security information for the domain.

Review

1. What is Windows NT Directory Services?

2. Explain the difference between a domain and a workgroup.

3. Which Windows NT operating system provides file and print services for Macintosh clients?

Answer Key

Video Review

Page 9

1. Name three benefits of Windows NT Directory Services.

   Single user logon, universal access to resources, and centralized administration.

2. Name the three Windows NT Server types.

   Primary domain controller, backup domain controller, and member server.

3. How many primary domain controllers can there be in each domain? How many backup domain controllers?

   Each domain must have one and only one primary domain controller. Each domain can have zero or more backup domain controllers; however, at least one is recommended.

4. Name the logical link that combines domains into one administrative unit.

   A trust relationship, or trust.

Review Answers

Page 14

1. What is Windows NT Directory Services?

   Windows NT Directory Services, one of the services provided by Windows NT Server, allows for centralized administration of the network. Windows NT Directory Services enables each user who has been assigned a unique user name and password to access resources throughout the network. It provides administrators with the ability to view and manage users and network resources from any computer on the network.

2. Explain the difference between a domain and a workgroup.

   In a domain, all domain controllers maintain a common directory database, so each user who has been assigned a unique user name and password can log on from any computer that is in the domain. In a workgroup, each computer maintains its own directory database, so a separate user account for each user must exist in each computer's directory database.

3. Which Windows NT operating system provides file and print services for Macintosh clients?

   Windows NT Server.

CHAPTER 2

Installing Windows NT

About This Chapter

This chapter describes the Microsoft Windows NT installation process. You learn what information is required to install Windows NT and how to install it from compact disc or over a network.

Before You Begin

To complete the lessons in this chapter, you must have:

- Two computers that meet the hardware and software requirements as specified in the Getting Started section of "About This Book."
- Nine blank, 1.44 MB high-density disks.

Lesson 1: Preparing for Installation

Before installing Windows NT, you need to determine the computer's configuration, such as the computer's hardware components, the existing partition scheme, existing file systems, and current operating systems. If you are installing Windows NT Server on a computer that will join a domain, you also need to determine the computer's role in that domain. This lesson explains the information that you need to determine before installing Windows NT.

After this lesson, you will be able to:

- Use the NT Hardware Qualifier (NTHQ) program.
- Identify the minimum hardware requirements for installing Windows NT on Intel or RISC-based computers.
- Describe the information required to install Windows NT.

Estimated lesson time: 45 minutes

Hardware Requirements

Before installing Windows NT, you should check to ensure that the computer's hardware is on the Windows NT 4.0 Hardware Compatibility List (HCL). Microsoft supports *only* the devices listed on the HCL. If a device is not on the HCL, contact the device manufacturer to determine if there is a Windows NT driver for the device. The HCL is included on the Windows NT Server and Windows NT Workstation compact disc in a Help file named Hcl.hlp. The most recent version of the HCL is located on the Internet at the following Web site:

http://www.microsoft.com/ntserver/showcase/hwcompatibility.asp

If this Web site is unavailable, please go to the Microsoft home page (http://www.microsoft.com) and search for "compatibility."

Determine the Computer's Hardware

Windows NT provides the NT Hardware Qualifier (NTHQ) to determine the hardware on an Intel *x*86-based computer. NTHQ detects the computer's hardware and can help you avoid installation and start-up problems. You run NTHQ in the following practice. The following illustration shows an example of how NTHQ displays hardware information about a computer.

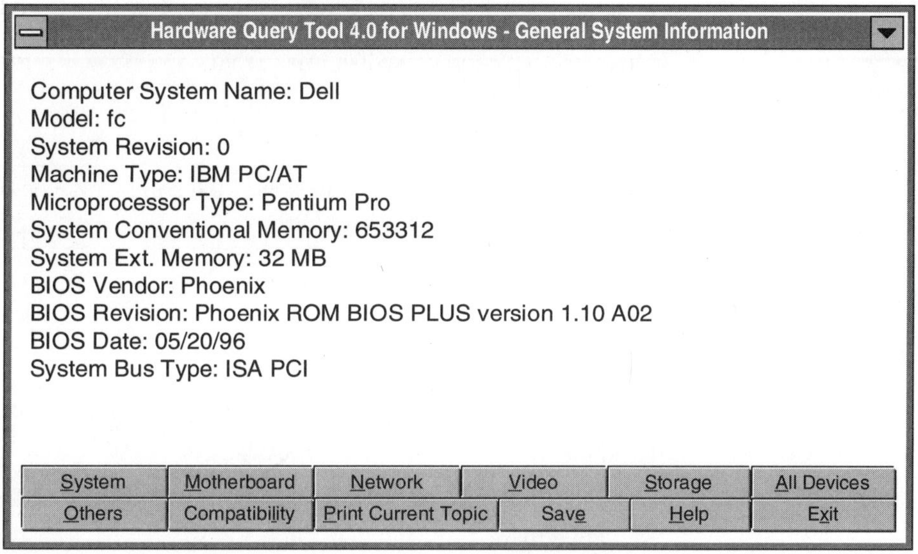

Practice

In these procedures, you create an NTHQ disk and then run NTHQ to determine the hardware components on your system. If any of the hardware components are not on the HCL, your installation of Windows NT Server may not be successful.

Note This procedure requires that you have an operating system installed on a computer that provides the ability to access the CD-ROM drive. This could be the computer that you use to install Windows NT, or a different computer.

▶ To create an NTHQ disk

1. Start the computer and insert the *Microsoft Windows NT Server 4.0* compact disc in the CD-ROM drive.
2. Insert a disk in drive A.

   You can use either a formatted or unformatted disk, because a disk image overwrites any information currently on the disk.
3. Start *cd-rom_drive*:**\Support\Hqtools\Makedisk.bat**

   Makedisk.bat copies the disk image to the floppy disk, creating the NTHQ disk.

▶ To run NTHQ

Note Complete this procedure on each of the computers you use to install Windows NT Server or Workstation.

---

1. Insert the NTHQ disk in drive A, and remove any compact discs from the CD-ROM drive.
2. Shut down and then restart the computer.

   The **Hardware Query Tool 4.0 for Windows** dialog box appears.
3. Read the dialog box, and then click **Yes**.

   The **Detection Method-comprehensive or safe** dialog box appears.
4. Read the dialog box, and then click **Yes**.

   NTHQ runs using comprehensive detection.
5. Explore the NTHQ results for your computer. Use the following table to enter the values for the listed hardware components. You need to click the buttons at the bottom of the display to obtain some of this information.

Hardware component	Value
Computer System Name:	____________
Model:	____________
System Revision:	____________
Microprocessor Type:	____________
BIOS Vendor:	____________
BIOS Date:	____________
System Bus Type:	____________
Network Device:	____________
Network Device IRQ:	____________
Hard Disk Controller Device:	____________
Video Display Device:	____________

6. Verify that your entries in the table are on the HCL.

   The HCL can be found by double-clicking the Hcl.hlp file located in the Support folder of your *Microsoft Windows NT Server 4.0* compact disc.
7. Exit the Hardware Query tool, and then remove the NTHQ disk from drive A.

Minimum Hardware Requirements

The following table describes the minimum hardware requirements for installing Windows NT 4.0.

Hardware component	Minimum hardware requirement
CPU	One of the following microprocessors: 32-bit Intel *x*86-based (80486/33 or higher) processor or compatible. Intel Pentium- or Pentium Pro-based processor. MIPS R4400- or R5000-based processor. Digital Alpha AXP-based processor. PReP-compliant PowerPC-based processor.
Memory	Intel *x*86-based computers: 16 megabytes (MB) of random access memory (RAM) for Windows NT Server and 12 MB of RAM for Windows NT Workstation. RISC-based computers: 16 MB of RAM for Windows NT Server and Windows NT Workstation.
Free hard disk space	Intel *x*86-based computers: approximately 125 MB for a typical installation of Windows NT Server and 110 MB for Windows NT Workstation. RISC-based computers: approximately 160 MB for Windows NT Server and 110 MB for Windows NT Workstation. The amount of free disk space required is also dependent upon the sector size in use on the system partition. For example, to install Windows NT Server on a partition using 16 KB clusters the computer would require about 120 MB of free disk space. By comparison, installing Windows NT Server on a partition using 32 KB clusters requires that the computer have about 200 MB of free disk space. A larger cluster size wastes space, because the entire cluster is not used to store data. For this reason, the unused portion of the cluster is wasted.

(*continued*)

Hardware component	Minimum hardware requirement
Display	Video display adapter with VGA resolution or higher.
Mouse	Microsoft Mouse or other pointing device.
Other drives	Intel *x*86-based computers require a high-density 3.5-inch floppy disk drive and a CD-ROM drive, unless the computer supports the El Torito specification. The El Torito specification does not require the computer to have a floppy disk drive because you can start the computer with a bootable compact disc. For computers without a CD-ROM drive, install Windows NT over a network.
	RISC-based computers require a CD-ROM drive.
Optional hardware components	Network adapter card and appropriate network cabling.

PowerPC Special Requirements

The version of Windows NT compiled to run on the PowerPC platform is designed to run only on systems that conform to the PReP (PowerPC Reference Platform) specification, created by IBM.

Disk Partitioning During Setup

With Windows NT Setup, you can partition the computer's hard disk during installation. A *partition* is a portion of a physical disk that functions as though it were physically a separate unit. Partitions are assigned their own drive letters, and allow the separation of the operating system and user data into logical units. For example, you could store the operating system on one partition and data on another partition. This would save time when backing up and restoring data.

If only one partition exists, then Windows NT stores all of its files on that partition.

System and Boot Partitions

If there is more than one partition, Windows NT copies the hardware-specific files to the *active* partition (ordinarily drive C), also known as the *system* partition. Setup then prompts you to select a folder in which to install the Windows NT operating system files. This folder can be on the system partition or another partition. The partition that contains the operating system files and its supporting files is called the *boot* partition. If both the hardware-specific files and the operating system and its supporting files are installed on one partition, then that partition would be both the system and boot partition.

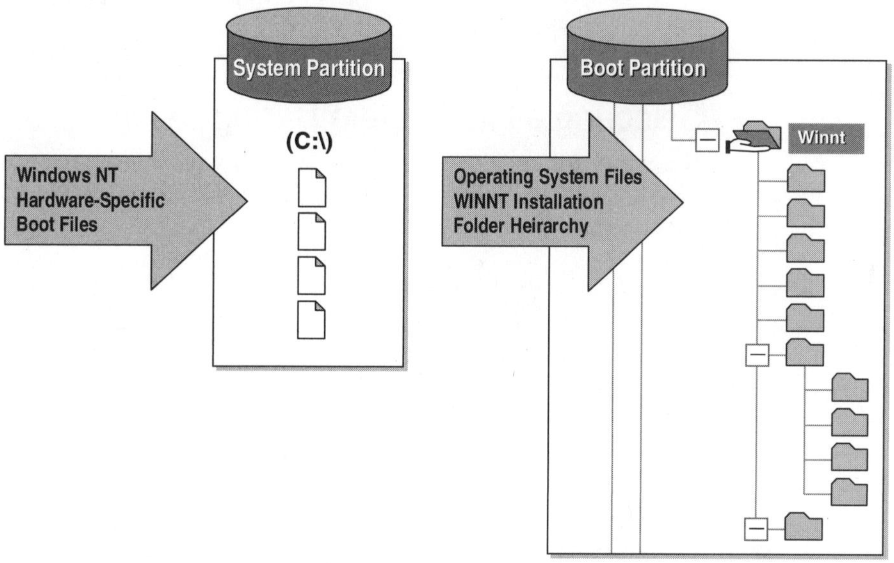

Note If you are familiar with the MS-DOS or Windows 95 operating systems, the Windows NT use of the system and boot partitions may seem confusing. This is because in MS-DOS and Windows 95 the active partition is called the boot drive or partition, whereas in Windows NT, the active partition is called the system partition.

On a RISC-based computer, you use a firmware configuration program to designate the system partition.

Unknown Partition Types

If you are installing Windows NT on a hard disk that already contains *stripe sets, volume sets*, or any areas allocated for *fault tolerance (disk mirroring* and *disk striping with parity)*, they appear on the Setup screen as partitions of an unknown type. If you plan to partition or reformat an unknown partition, but you want to save the data it contains, back up the data before you start Setup, and then restore it after you have completed the Windows NT installation.

Note For more information about stripe sets and volume sets, see Chapter 6, "Managing Partitions." For more information about fault tolerance, see Chapter 7, "Managing Fault Tolerance."

Selecting a File System During Setup

Before installing Windows NT, determine which of the two supported file systems, Windows NT File System (NTFS) or file allocation table (FAT) that you will use for each partition you create.

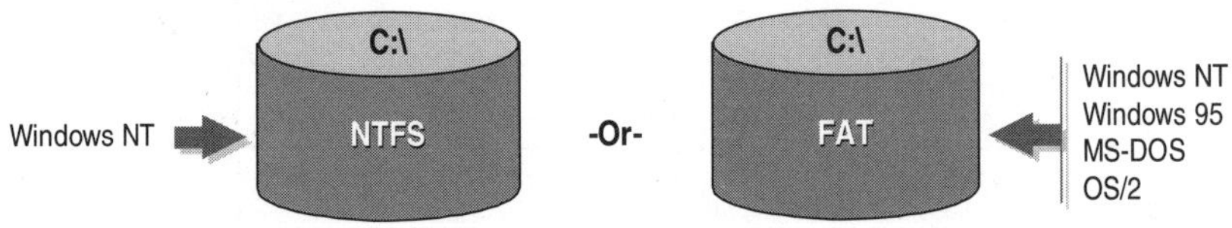

NTFS

NTFS can *only* be accessed by Windows NT and for this reason it provides greater security than the FAT file system. This is because you cannot start the computer with another operating system, such as Windows 95, and access data on an NTFS partition.

Choose NTFS when:

- Windows NT is the only operating system in use.
- Using Services for Macintosh for file sharing.
- File-level security is required.
- Permissions must be preserved while migrating directories and files from a Novell NetWare server.
- Windows NT file compression is required.
- Local security is required.

FAT

The FAT file system can be accessed by Windows NT, Windows 95, MS-DOS, and OS/2 operating systems.

Choose FAT when:

- You require multiple-boot capability between Windows NT and other operating systems, such as Windows 95 or MS-DOS. For this configuration, drive C must be formatted with the FAT file system.
- Installing Windows NT on RISC-based computers. The system partition on a RISC-based computer *must* be formatted with FAT for the firmware to detect the partition as a bootable partition. This partition must be at least 2 MB in size and have enough free hard disk space to store two required Windows NT files: Hal.dll and Osloader.exe.

Common Support Issues

When creating a partition during installation, the partition is always formatted as FAT. Even if you choose to format the partition as NTFS, the initial format is FAT. At the end of the installation, the system restarts and the partition is converted to NTFS.

A problem occurs if you want to create an NTFS partition larger than 4 gigabytes (GB) during installation. Because FAT has a maximum partition size of 4 GB, a partition larger than 4 GB cannot be created during installation.

Solutions

Use one of the following solutions to solve this problem:

- Choose to create a partition of 4 GB or less, then complete the installation. After you finish installing Windows NT, log on as Administrator and start Disk Administrator. You can then use Disk Administrator to extend the NTFS partition. Extending an NTFS partition allows you to add unused disk space to the partition.
- On a different computer that is already running Windows NT, format a partition greater than 4 GB. Remove the drive from that computer and then install it in the computer on which you want to install Windows NT. This computer now has a 4 GB partition where you can install Windows NT.

If you are upgrading from a previous version of Windows NT and want to create an NTFS partition larger than 4 GB, use Disk Administrator to create the partition prior to starting the upgrade.

Note For more information about file systems, see Chapter 5, "Managing File Systems."

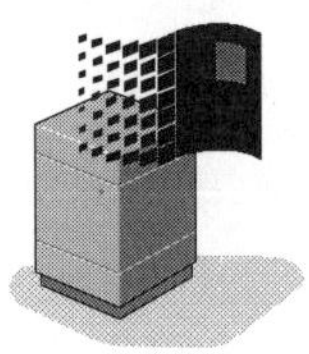

Choosing a Server Role During Setup

Prior to installing Windows NT Server, it is important to plan the configuration of your network and the type of servers you need. When you install Windows NT Server you can choose to configure the computer to be one of the following types of servers:

- Primary domain controller (PDC)
- Backup domain controller (BDC)
- Stand-alone (or member server)

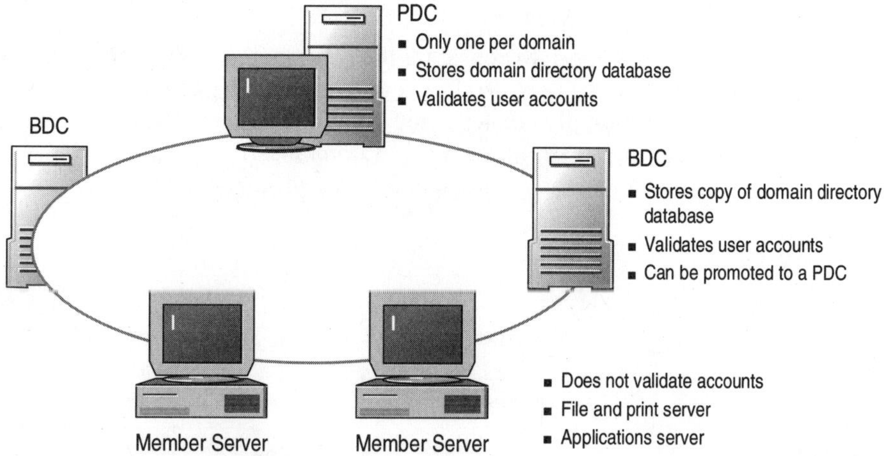

Primary Domain Controller (PDC)

Each domain requires and can contain *only one* PDC. The PDC contains the directory database for the domain. The PDC also authenticates logon requests.

Once the computer is configured as a PDC it must be online before any other computer can join the domain.

Note Any domain controller can authenticate logon requests from the following clients: MS-DOS clients with *enhanced redirector* installed, Windows NT, Windows 95, Windows for Workgroups, and Microsoft LAN Manager.

Creating a Domain

If you choose to configure the computer as a PDC, the Windows NT Server Setup program prompts you for a unique domain name; entering the domain name automatically creates a new domain. When a domain is created, a domain *security identifier* (SID) is created. A domain SID is a unique numeric value that identifies a domain and is included in all user, group, and computer accounts that are created on the domain.

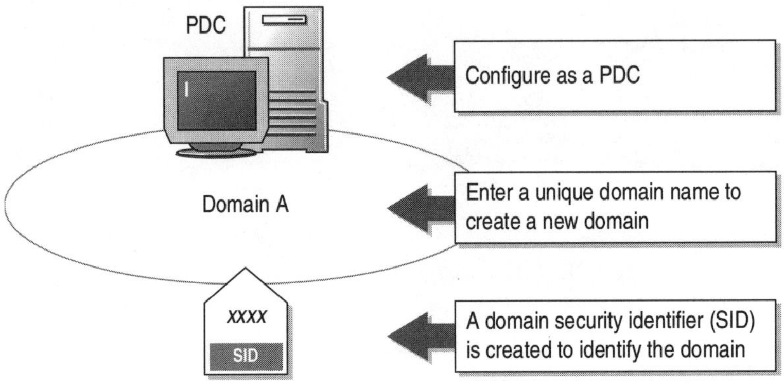

Changing the Domain Name After Installation

You can change the domain name after Windows NT Server is installed, without reinstalling Windows NT Server. This is because the domain SID (rather than the domain name) identifies the domain. The new domain name is associated with the existing SID. However, if you change the domain name you also have to change the domain name for all workstations and servers in the domain. Also, any trust relationships with other domains would have to be re-established.

Computer and domain names are changed using the Network program in Control Panel. Clicking the **Change** button on the **Identification** tab allows you to change the computer name, the domain name, or both.

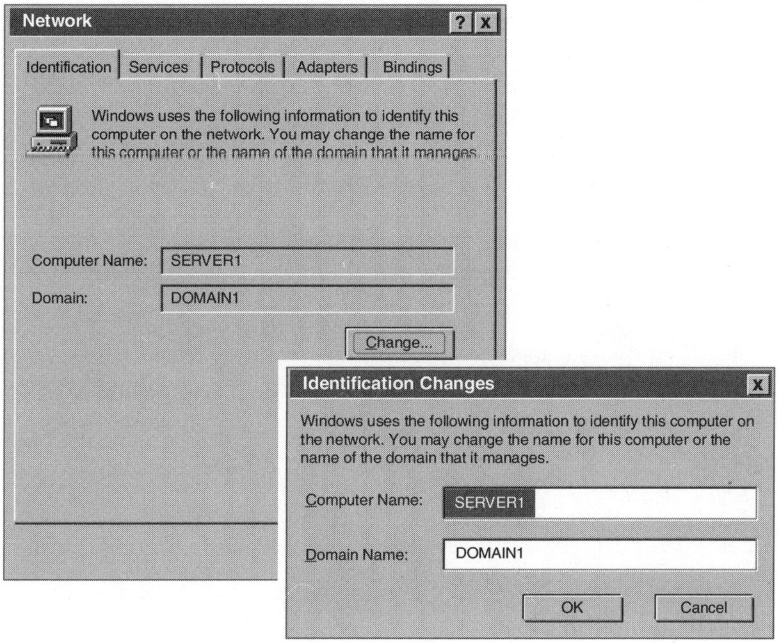

Backup Domain Controller (BDC)

A BDC can also authenticate logon requests; for this reason there are often several BDCs in a domain. If you choose to configure the computer as a BDC, during setup you must supply the name of the domain that the BDC is joining.

Because BDCs can also validate user accounts, the copy of the domain's directory services database, which is stored on the BDC, must be current with the directory services database which is stored on the PDC. To ensure the BDCs remain current, the PDC sends out timed notices that signal the BDCs to request directory changes from the PDC. When the BDC requests changes, it informs the PDC of the last change to the directory database that it received. In this manner, all of the domain controllers remain current.

Furthermore, if the PDC fails, one of the domain BDCs can be promoted to a PDC. The only user account data that would be lost are recent changes that have not yet been replicated to the BDCs.

Moving a Backup Domain Controller to Another Domain

You cannot move a BDC to another domain unless you reinstall Windows NT Server on the BDC. This is because the domain SID cannot be changed without reinstalling Windows NT Server. The best way to avoid reinstallation is to plan your Windows NT network so that PDCs and BDCs remain in the domains in which they were created.

Stand-Alone or Member Server

A stand-alone server may be a member of either a workgroup or a domain. A stand-alone server that is part of a domain is also known as *member* server.

Unlike domain controllers, stand-alone servers do not validate domain user logon requests. For this reason, stand-alone servers provide file, print, and application services more efficiently than domain controllers.

Stand-alone servers and computers running Windows NT Workstation cannot be reconfigured as a BDC or a PDC without reinstalling Windows NT Server.

Moving a Member Server to Another Domain

Unlike a BDC, you can move a member server or a computer running Windows NT Workstation to another domain without reinstalling Windows NT. This is because member servers and computers running Windows NT Workstation maintain their own directory services database. The following illustration shows how the **Identification Changes** dialog box appears when you click the **Change** button on the **Identification** tab. Notice that you can choose to make the computer a member of a workgroup or a domain.

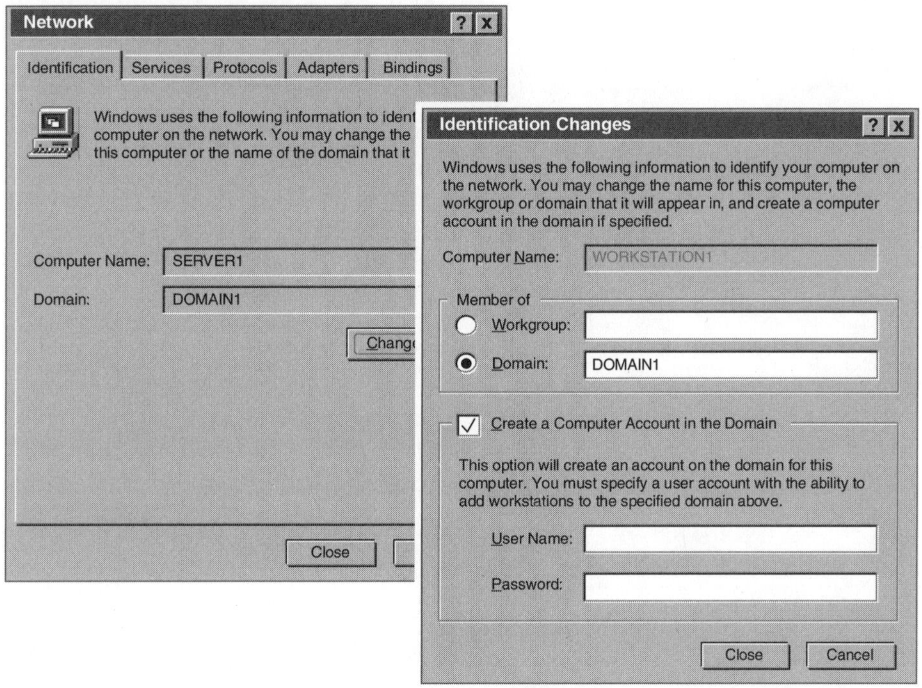

Joining a Domain or Workgroup During Installation

For a BDC, member server, or computer running Windows NT Workstation to participate in a domain, a computer account for that computer must be created and then that computer can join the domain.

For a BDC to join a domain, you must create a computer account on the PDC either prior to or during the installation of the BDC, and supply a computer name and domain name during installation. Stand-alone servers or computers running Windows NT Workstation can join a domain during installation, using the same process as for the BDC. However, stand-alone servers or computers running Windows NT Workstation can also join a domain after installation.

Joining a Workgroup

If the stand-alone server or computer running Windows NT Workstation is joining a workgroup, you supply the name of the workgroup, instead of the name of the domain, during installation. A workgroup does not require a computer account because workgroups do not provide centralized administration of the computer and user accounts in the workgroup.

Choosing a Licensing Mode During Setup

During the installation of Windows NT Server you must choose a licensing mode.

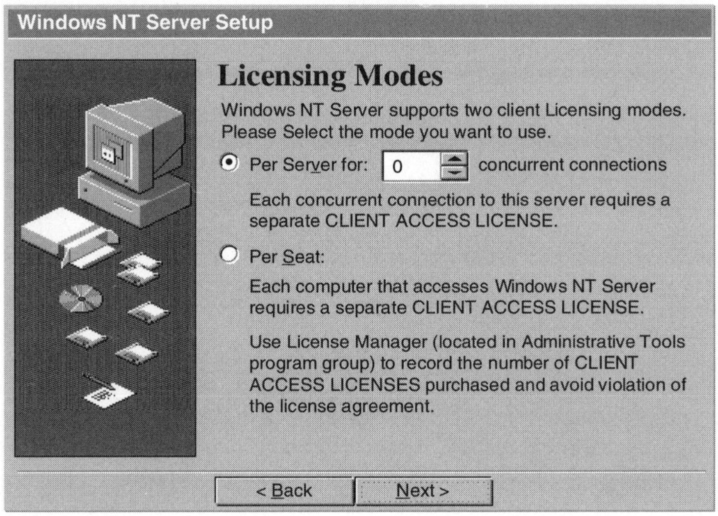

A client access license (CAL) is required in order for a client computer to access resources on a computer running Windows NT Server. A CAL is separate from the desktop operating system software that a client uses to connect to a server. For example, purchasing Microsoft Windows 95, Windows NT Workstation, or any other desktop operating system that connects to a computer running Windows NT Server does not constitute a legal license to connect to a server.

During the installation of Windows NT, you must choose one of the following licensing modes:

- *Per Server licensing mode.* Each CAL is assigned to a specific server and allows one connection to *only* that server for the following basic network services.
    - *File services.* Using and managing files or disk storage.
    - *Printing services.* Using and managing printers.
    - *Macintosh connectivity.* File sharing and printing services.
    - *File and Print Services for NetWare connectivity.* File and printing services for NetWare clients.
    - *Remote access services.* Accessing the server from a remote location through a communication link.

  A connection in Per Server licensing mode is defined as a session between a client and the server. If a client has multiple drive and printer mappings to a single server, the connection would still be considered a single connection for licensing purposes.

- *Per Seat licensing mode.* Requires a separate CAL for each *client* that will access the server for basic network services (file, print, and remote access services). Once a client computer is licensed, it may access any computer running Windows NT Server installed on the network at no additional charge. This means that an unlimited number of computers can have access to a single server, provided each computer is licensed with the appropriate CAL.

  The Per Seat licensing mode is often the most economical one for networks in which clients ordinarily connect to more than one server. For example, in a stock brokerage company users might need persistent connections to an e-mail server, a server running stock quotes, and a server that provides access to the World Wide Web (WWW).

Note If you are not sure which licensing mode to choose, select the Per Server option. After Windows NT Server is installed, you can use the Licensing program in Control Panel for a one-time conversion from the Per Server license to a Per Seat license at no cost. It is not necessary to notify Microsoft to make this change. For more information about client access licenses, see Chapter 15, "Implementing Network Clients."

Lesson 2: Installing Windows NT

This lesson covers the Windows NT installation process and the differences between the installation options when installing Windows NT Workstation or Windows NT Server.

After this lesson, you will be able to:

- Start the setup process on any platform supported by Windows NT.
- Distinguish between the setup types for Windows NT.
- Describe the Windows NT installation process.
- Install Windows NT Server.

Estimated lesson time: 90 minutes

Starting a Windows NT Installation

How you start the Windows NT installation depends on the computer's hardware platform. The Windows NT compact disc includes a version of Windows NT for the Intel *x*86 and RISC (MIPS, Alpha, and PPC) hardware platforms.

Intel *x*86-based Computers

To install Windows NT on an Intel *x*86-based computer, use the three Setup disks and the Windows NT compact disc. The computer must start from the Windows NT Setup Boot Disk (also referred to as Setup Disk #1) and proceed through the other two disks before it can access the Windows NT compact disc. The three Setup disks contain a minimal version of Windows NT, under which the initial Windows NT Setup process runs.

Note If your computer supports the El Torito specification, you do not have to use the disks because you can start the computer with the bootable compact disc.

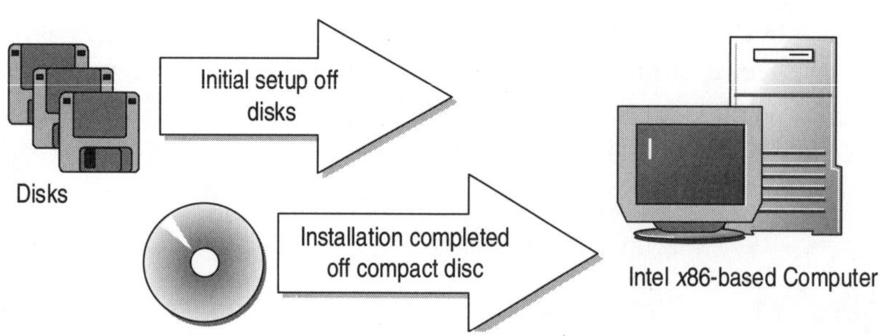

RISC-based Computers

For RISC-based computers, Windows NT Setup must be invoked directly from the compact disc using the Setupldr program. Depending on the version of the computer's firmware, this may be as simple as clicking **Install Windows NT from CD-ROM** on the firmware's supplementary menu. If the computer does not have this option, click **Run a Program** (or an equivalent command) on the firmware menu and then enter the path to Setupldr. Setupldr loads and initializes Windows NT Setup from the compact disc.

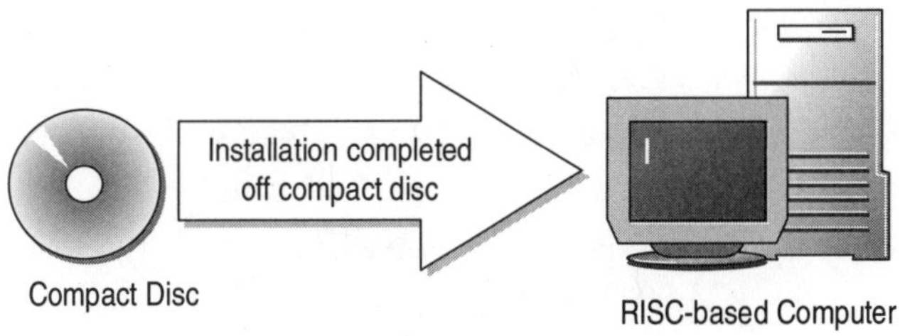

Windows NT Setup Types

Windows NT Workstation provides four setup types: typical, portable, compact, and custom. You can choose one of these types during setup to specify whether or not to include certain components on your computer. Windows NT Server provides only the custom setup type.

The following table describes each setup type.

Setup type	Description
Typical	Designed for most situations, and automatically installs the following components: ▪ Accessibility features. ▪ All Windows NT accessories, except for desktop wallpaper and mouse pointers. ▪ All communications programs. ▪ All multimedia components except Sound Schemes. Windows messaging and games are *not* installed.

(continued)

Setup type	Description
Portable	Designed for notebook and other portable computers and *automatically* installs the following components that are useful for mobile computing: ▪ Accessibility features. ▪ All Windows NT accessories except for Desktop Wallpaper and Mouse Pointers. ▪ All communications programs. ▪ All multimedia components supported by the hardware. Dial-Up Networking is also installed by default. Windows messaging and games are not installed.
Compact	Designed to conserve hard disk space, and automatically installs only components required by Windows NT.
Custom	Designed to let you choose which components to install. This setup type is useful when the you require a configuration that is not provided by one of the other setup types.

Components

The following list describes each installation component.

- *Accessibility options.* Includes choices for changing the keyboard, sound, display, and mouse behavior for users with visual, hearing, or mobility impairments.
- *Accessories.* Includes Calculator, Character Map, Dial-Up Networking, Multimedia applications, Notepad, Telnet, WordPad, and others.
- *Communications programs.* Includes accessories to help you connect to other computers and online services.
- *Games.* Includes FreeCell, Minesweeper, Pinball, and Solitaire.
- *Multimedia.* CD Player, Media Player, Sound Recorder, and Volume Control.
- *Windows messaging.* Includes e-mail and messaging utilities.

The Windows NT Installation Process

Installing Windows NT is a step-by-step process that is easy to follow, especially when you are prepared to enter the appropriate information to complete the installation. The following information provides step-by-step information about the different parts of the Windows NT installation process.

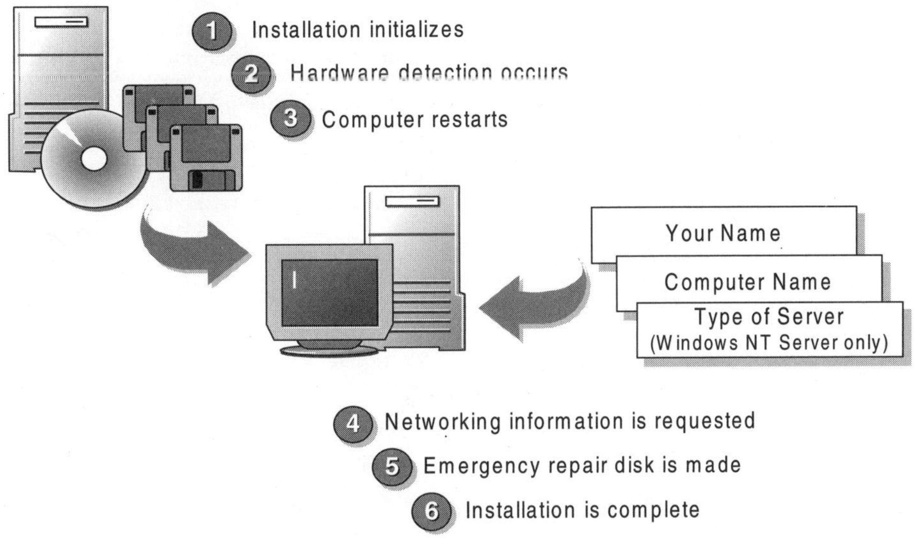

Initializing Installation

After you start the installation, if you are doing an over-the-network installation, the setup initialization begins by copying necessary Windows NT files from the source to the hard disk, and then you are prompted to restart the computer.

Whether you are doing an over-the-network installation or a local installation, Windows NT Setup prompts you for the following information:

1. Whether to upgrade a previous version of Windows NT to Windows NT 4.0 (if there is a version of Windows NT already installed on the computer).
2. Confirmation of the detected hardware—it is normal for a computer's video adapter to be detected as VGA at this point. This ensures that the minimum hardware requirement for the video display is available. Near the end of the installation process you can configure a more advanced video adapter.
3. A partition on which to install Windows NT.
4. A file system on which to install Windows NT—by default, the existing file system for the selected partition is retained, but Setup also provides the option to convert FAT partitions to NTFS.
5. A folder to install the Windows NT files—the default folder is \Winnt. After choosing the folder, Setup begins copying the appropriate files to that folder.

Gathering Information

This part of setup begins by displaying the Windows NT Setup wizard. The following table describes the information required by the Setup wizard when installing Windows NT Workstation or Windows NT Server.

Information required by the Windows NT Setup wizard	Windows NT Workstation	Windows NT Server
Setup type (Typical, Portable, Compact, or Custom)	Choose one of the setup types.	This option does not appear on this operating system.
The name and organization of licensee	Enter the name and organization.	Enter the name and organization.
Registration	Enter the 10 digit CD Key found on the yellow sticker on the back of your compact disc case.	Enter the 10 digit CD Key found on the yellow sticker on the back of your compact disc case.
Choose a licensing mode	This option does not appear on this operating system.	Choose either the **Per Server** or **Per Seat** option.
Computer name	Enter a name unique from all other computers, workgroups, and domain names on the network. The name can be 15 characters or less.	Enter a name unique from all other computers, workgroups, and domain names on the network. The name can be 15 characters or less.
Type of server	This option does not appear on this operating system.	Choose the type of server: **PDC**, **BDC**, or **Stand-alone server**.
Password	Enter and confirm a password for the Administrator account.	Enter and confirm a password for the Administrator account.
Floating Point Divide Problem (only on certain computers)	Choose either **Do not enable** *or* **Enable** the floating-point workaround.	Choose either **Do not enable** *or* **Enable** the floating-point workaround.
Emergency Repair Disk	Choose to create an Emergency Repair Disk. This disk can repair missing or corrupt Windows NT files and restore the registry, including the directory database, security information, disk configuration, and other system information.	Choose to create an Emergency Repair Disk. This disk can repair missing or corrupt Windows NT files and restore the registry, including the directory database, security information, disk configuration, and other system information.
Components	Choose the appropriate components to install.	Choose the appropriate components to install.

Installing Windows NT Networking

The Setup wizard continues by prompting you for the appropriate networking information, such as the type of network adapter card in the computer and the protocols used on the network. If the computer is not part of a network, you can skip this part of setup. The following table describes the networking information required to continue installing either Windows NT Workstation or Windows NT Server.

Networking information	Windows NT Workstation	Windows NT Server
How the computer should participate on the network	Choose one of the following: **Do not connect this computer to a network at this time**, *or* **This computer will participate on a network**. If you choose **This computer will participate on a network**, you can then choose the appropriate networking option(s): **Wired to the network**, or **Remote access to the network**.	Choose the appropriate networking option(s): **Wired to the network**, **Remote access to the network**.
Install Microsoft Internet Information Server (IIS)	This option does not appear on this operating system.	Click **Install Microsoft Internet Information Server** if you want to install this service. You are prompted to configure the appropriate protocols.
Search for installed network adapter cards	Click **Start Search** to have Setup determine the network adapter cards in your computer. If the network adapter card is not automatically detected, click **Select from list** to choose the correct adapter.	Click **Start Search** to have Setup determine the network adapter cards in your computer. If the network adapter card is not automatically detected, click **Select from list** to choose the correct adapter.

(*continued*)

Networking information	Windows NT Workstation	Windows NT Server
Select the appropriate network protocols	Choose the network protocols you want to use on your network: TCP/IP, NWLink IPX/SPX Compatible Transport, NetBEUI Protocol. TCP/IP is the default. If you choose TCP/IP as a protocol, you are prompted as to whether you want to use DHCP. If there is a DHCP server on your network, TCP/IP can be configured to dynamically provide an Internet Protocol (IP) address.	Choose the network protocols you want to use on your network: TCP/IP, NWLink IPX/SPX Compatible Transport, NetBEUI Protocol. TCP/IP and NWLink are the defaults. If you choose TCP/IP as a protocol, you are prompted as to whether you want to use DHCP. If there is a DHCP server on your network, TCP/IP can be configured to dynamically provide an IP address.
Network services	By default, the Computer Browser, NetBIOS Interface, RPC Configuration, Server, and Workstation services are installed. You can click **Select from list** to add other services.	By default, the Computer Browser, NetBIOS Interface, RPC Configuration, Server, and Workstation services are installed. You can click **Select from list** to add other services.
Network Adapter setup	The available options are determined by the network adapter card such as IRQ, I/O Port Address, I/O Channel Ready, and Transceiver type.	The available options are determined by the network adapter card such as IRQ, I/O Port Address, I/O Channel Ready, and Transceiver type.
Configure network bindings	Choose to disable or arrange the order in which the computer finds information on the network.	Choose to disable or arrange the order in which the computer finds information on the network.
Configure the Workgroup or Domain name	Enter a workgroup or domain name. A computer account must exist for the computer to join the domain. If the account does not exist, click **Create computer account in domain** and create the computer account. You must supply a user account, such as the domain Administrator account, and corresponding password, with the ability to add workstations to the specified domain.	Enter a workgroup or domain name. If the computer is a backup domain controller or a member server, a computer account must exist for the computer to join the domain. If the account does not exist, click **Create computer account in domain** and create the computer account. You must supply a user account, such as the domain Administrator account, and corresponding password, with the ability to add workstations to the specified domain.

Finishing Setup

The Setup wizard completes the setup by prompting you for the following information:

1. If you chose to install IIS, you are prompted to specify which IIS options to install.
2. Time zone, date, and time.
3. Video adapter and configuration.

   Your monitor may not support all resolution configurations supported by the video card. If Setup does not recognize the video card, you can install a driver manually after setup using the Display program in Control Panel.

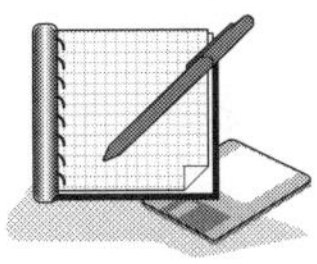

Practice

In these procedures, you install Windows NT Server from the compact disc onto drive C of Computer1. You name the computer Server1, and configure it as a primary domain controller in Domain1. Then you assign Server1 the *IP address* 131.107.2.200 and *subnet mask* 255.255.0.0.

Before you begin the installation, you create the three Setup boot disks needed for the Windows NT Server installation.

To complete these procedures, you need four blank disks. You also need access to a computer that has an operating system and a CD-ROM drive accessible through that operating system.

Important If your computer is part of a larger network, verify with your network administrator that the computer name, domain name, and IP address information do not conflict with network operations. If they do conflict, ask your network administrator to provide alternate values, and use those values for all of the procedures in this book.

► **To create Windows NT Server Setup disks**

In this procedure, you create the three Setup disks needed to complete a Windows NT Server compact disc installation.

Note This procedure requires that you have an operating system installed on a computer that provides the ability to access the CD-ROM drive.

---

1. Insert the *Microsoft Windows NT Server 4.0* compact disc in the CD-ROM drive.
2. Start a command prompt.

   If you are using a computer running Windows 95 or Windows NT, click the **Start** button, point to **Programs**, and then click **Command Prompt**.

3. If you are using a computer running MS-DOS, Windows 3.1, Windows for Workgroups, or Windows 95, at the command prompt, type:

   cd-rom_drive_letter:**\I386\winnt /ox**

   substituting the appropriate letter for your CD-ROM drive.

   If you are using a computer running Windows NT, at the command prompt, type:

   cd-rom_drive_letter:**\I386\winnt32 /ox**

   substituting the appropriate letter for your CD-ROM drive.

Note For example, if your CD-ROM drive letter is **e**, type **e:\I386\winnt /ox**

---

4. Press ENTER.

   The **Windows NT 4.00 Upgrade/Installation** dialog box appears, prompting for the location of the Windows NT Server files.
5. In the path or location box, type *cd-rom_drive_letter*:**\I386** and then press ENTER or click **Continue**.
6. When prompted, label a blank disk as Windows NT Server Setup Disk #3, insert the disk in drive A, and then press ENTER or click **OK**.
7. When prompted, label a blank disk as Windows NT Server Setup Disk #2, insert the disk in drive A, and then press ENTER or click **OK**.
8. When prompted, label a blank disk as Windows NT Server Setup Boot Disk, insert the disk in drive A, and then press ENTER or click **OK**.

   When Winnt or Winnt32 has finished creating the disks, the application quits.
9. Remove the disk from drive A and the compact disc from the CD-ROM drive.

► **To start the Windows NT Server installation**

In these procedures, you install Windows NT Server.

Note Complete these procedures on Computer1.

---

1. Insert the Windows NT Server Setup Boot Disk (also referred to as Setup Disk #1) in drive A, and then start your computer.

   You receive the message that Setup is inspecting your computer hardware. Setup then loads files.
2. When prompted, insert the Windows NT Server Setup Disk #2 in drive A, and then press ENTER.

   Setup continues to load files. The **Welcome to Setup** screen appears.

3. Read the **Welcome to Setup** screen, and then press ENTER to continue.
4. Press ENTER to have Windows NT Setup automatically detect mass storage devices.
5. When prompted, insert the Windows NT Server Setup Disk #3 in drive A, and then press ENTER.

   Setup continues to load files, and then displays the recognized mass storage devices.
6. When prompted, press ENTER to confirm the detected devices.
7. When prompted, insert the Windows NT Server CD-ROM in the CD-ROM drive, and then press ENTER.

   The Windows NT Licensing Agreement appears.
8. Use the PAGE DOWN key to scroll through and read the Licensing Agreement.
9. Press F8 to accept the terms of the agreement.

   Setup looks for versions of Windows installed on your computer that can be upgraded.
10. If prompted, press N to cancel the upgrade of any existing version of Windows NT, and instead install a fresh copy of Windows NT.
11. Review the detected hardware and software components, and if you need to make changes, follow the directions on your screen. Press ENTER to confirm the hardware and software components.
12. Select partition C, and then press ENTER to install Windows NT Server on drive C.
13. If there is information on your computer that you need to keep, click **Leave the current file system intact (no changes)**, and then press ENTER.

    If you want to reformat your partition to ensure a clean install, click **Format FAT**, and then press ENTER. You are prompted to press F to begin the format.
14. Press ENTER to confirm the default installation directory of Winnt.
15. Press ENTER to have Setup examine your hard disk.

    Setup copies files to the hard disk. This process may take a few minutes.
16. When prompted, remove the disk from drive A. Also remove the *Windows NT Server CD-ROM* from the CD-ROM drive, and then press ENTER to restart your computer.

▸ **To complete the gathering information part of setup**

1. When prompted, insert the *Windows NT Server CD-ROM* in the CD-ROM drive, and then click **OK**.

   Note If you click **OK** before the CD-ROM drive has had time to read the compact disc, you are prompted to insert the *Windows NT Server CD-ROM*. Click **OK** to continue with setup.

   Setup continues to copy files, and then the Windows NT Server Setup wizard appears.

2. Click **Next**.

   Windows NT Setup creates the folder hierarchy for your installation.

3. Type your name and organization, and then click **Next**.
4. In the **CD-Key** box, type **040** followed by **0048126** and then click **Next**.
5. Click **Per Server**, enter **10** concurrent connections, and then click **Next**.
6. In the **Name** box, type **Server1** and then click **Next**.
7. Click **Primary Domain Controller**, and then click **Next**.
8. In the **Password** and **Confirm Password** boxes, type **password** for the Administrator account password, and then click **Next**.
9. If you see a message indicating that your computer exhibits a floating-point divide problem, click **Do not enable the floating-point workaround**, and then click **Next**.
10. Click **Yes, create an emergency repair disk (recommended)**, and then click **Next**.
11. Click **Next** to accept the default components.

▸ **To install Windows NT Networking**

1. Click **Next** to begin installing Windows NT Networking.
2. Click **Next** to confirm that your computer is wired to the network.
3. Clear the **Install Microsoft Internet Information Server** check box, and then click **Next** to skip installation of Internet Information Server.
4. Click **Start Search** to have Windows NT Server Setup detect your network adapter card.
5. If there is only one network adapter card in your computer, or if you are sure that the network adapter card you want to use has been detected, click **Next** to confirm the detected network adapter card.

   If the wrong network adapter card is detected, you must manually select your network adapter card. For example, if you have two network adapter cards in your computer and your cable is plugged into one card, but the other one is detected, you must click **Select from list**. Then select the appropriate network adapter card and click **OK**.
6. Clear the **NWLink IPX/SPX Compatible Transport** check box, verify that **TCP/IP** is the only protocol selected, and then click **Next**.
7. Click **Next** to confirm the selected network services.
8. Click **Next** to install the selected network components.
9. If prompted, enter the appropriate configuration settings for your network adapter card, and then click **Continue**.
10. Click **No** so that your computer will not use DHCP.

    Windows NT Server Setup installs and configures the networking components. The **Microsoft TCP/IP Properties** dialog box appears on the **IP Address** tab.
11. Click **Specify an IP address**.
12. In the **IP Address** box, type **131.107.2.200**
13. Click **OK** to accept the default **Subnet Mask** of 255.255.0.0 and a blank **Default Gateway**.
14. Click **Next** to accept the default bindings.
15. Click **Next** to start the network.
16. In the **Domain** box, type **Domain1** and then click **Next** to create the domain.

▸ **To complete Windows NT Server setup**

1. In the **Windows NT Server Setup** dialog box, click **Finish**.
2. When prompted, in the **Time Zone** list, click the correct time zone for your location, confirm that the **Date** and **Time** options are correct, and then click **Close**.
3. Click **OK** to confirm the detected video adapter.
4. Click **Test** to test the settings for your video adapter, and then click **OK**.
5. If you did not see the test bitmap, adjust your settings and test them again. If you did see the test bitmap, click **Yes**, and then click **OK**.
6. Click **OK** to confirm the video settings.

   Windows NT Server Setup copies additional files to the hard disk, and saves the configuration to the emergency repair folder.
7. When prompted, label a blank disk as Emergency Repair Disk, insert it in drive A, and then click **OK**.

   Windows NT formats the disk and then copies the emergency repair information.
8. When prompted, remove the disk from drive A and the compact disc from the CD-ROM drive, and then click **Restart Computer**.

   The computer restarts.
9. When the operating system selection list appears, select the default Windows NT Server version 4.0, and then press ENTER.

Installing the Course Materials on Server1

Now that you have installed Windows NT Server, you need to install the course materials to continue with the course. The course materials include lab files, and the course Web page which contains supplemental material, such as appendixes and links to important Microsoft Web sites.

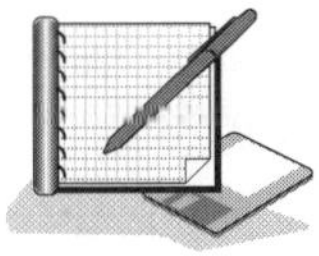

Practice

▸ **To install the course materials on Server1**

1. Insert the *Course Materials* compact disc in the CD-ROM drive of Server1.
2. Log on as Administrator.

Note Throughout this course the password for the administrator is *password.*

---

3. From the *Course Materials* compact disc, run Setup.exe.

   The **Microsoft Windows NT 4.0 Technical Support** dialog box appears.
4. Click **Continue**.
5. In the **Name** box, type your name.
6. In the **Organization** box, type the name of your organization or leave this box empty, and then click **OK**.
7. Click **OK** to confirm that the Name and Organization information was entered correctly.
8. Click the **Setup** button.

   The required course files are copied to and installed on the hard disk.
9. Click **OK**.

▸ **To install Microsoft Internet Explorer 3.0**

1. In the *Course Materials* compact disc, open the IE_Setup folder, and then run Msie30.exe.

   A **Microsoft Internet Explorer 3.0** dialog box appears prompting if you want to install Microsoft Internet Explorer 3.0.

2. Click **Yes** to install Microsoft Internet Explorer 3.0.

   A **Microsoft Internet Explorer Setup** dialog box appears indicating that files are being copied to a temporary folder on your hard disk.

3. Read the End-User License Agreement for Microsoft Internet Explorer, and then click **I Agree** to accept the terms of the agreement and continue the installation.

   A **Microsoft Internet Explorer Setup** dialog box appears indicating that files are being copied and Microsoft Internet Explorer is being set up on your computer.

4. When prompted to restart your computer, click **Yes**.

Lesson 3: Adding a Computer Account to a Domain

Before a computer running Windows NT can join a domain, a computer account must be created or added to the domain directory database. In this lesson, you configure Computer2 by adding a computer account to Domain1, installing Windows NT Workstation on Computer2, and then configure Workstation1 to join Domain1.

After this lesson, you will be able to:

- Identify who can add computer accounts to a domain.
- Create a computer account.
- Install Windows NT Workstation.
- Join a domain.

Estimated lesson time: 90 minutes

Only users who have the user right *add workstations to a domain* can create a computer account. Members of the Administrators, Domain Admins, or Account Operators groups have this user right, by default. You can use the following methods to create a computer account:

- Create the account during installation.
- Use the **Add to Domain** option in Server Manager—you can add the computer account prior to installation and then delegate the task of actually installing Windows NT by providing the computer account name to the person who completes the installation. This is common in organizations where end-users or help desk technicians install Windows NT but are not granted Administrator privileges.

  Once the computer account is added to the domain, the computer must join the domain. This can be done during the Windows NT installation or after installation by using the Network program in Control Panel (on the local computer).

- On the local computer, use the Network program in Control Panel. When you click the **Change** button on the **Identification** tab, the options to change the computer name, join a workgroup or domain, and create a computer account in the domain are displayed. If the computer is configured as a PDC, you can only use this program to rename the computer or domain.

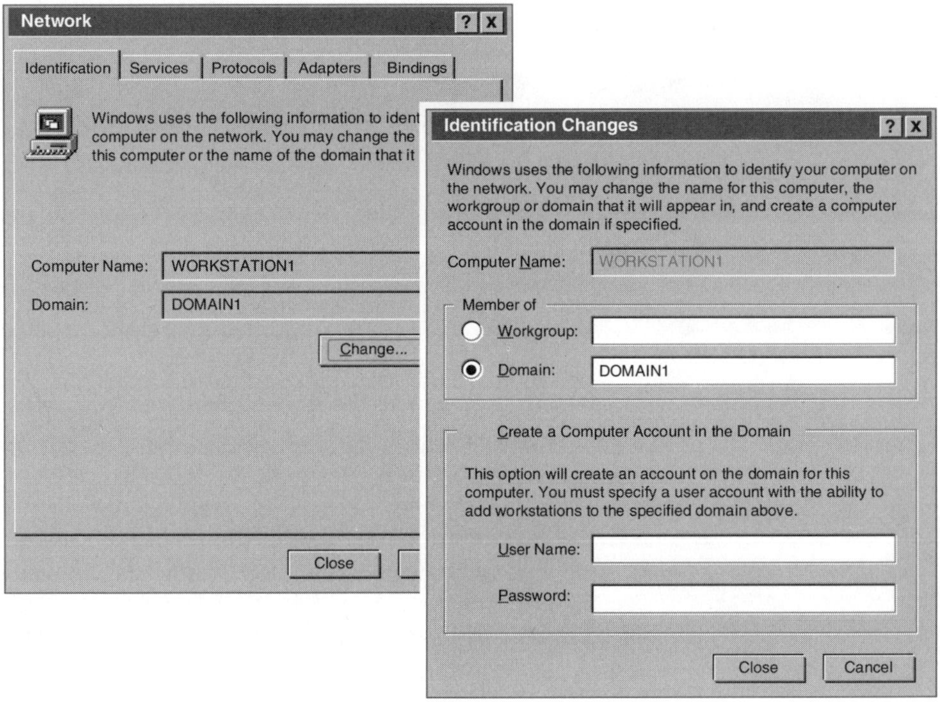

Practice

In this procedure, you use Server Manager to create a computer account named *Workstation1*.

▶ **To add a computer account to a domain**

Note Complete this procedure on Server1.

---

1. Log on as Administrator.
2. Click the **Start** button, point to **Programs**, point to **Administrative Tools (Common)**, and then click **Server Manager**.
3. On the **Computer** menu, click **Add to Domain**.
4. In the **Add Computer to Domain** dialog box, click **Windows NT Workstation or Server**.
5. In the **Computer Name** box, type **Workstation1** and then click **Add**.

   A computer account for Workstation1 is added to the domain directory database.
6. Click **Close**.

   The computer Workstation1 appears in the Server Manager window.
7. Close Server Manager.

Practice

In these procedures, you install Windows NT Workstation from compact disc on drive C of Computer2. You name the computer Workstation1, and it will join Domain1. You have already created a computer account for Workstation1 in Domain1. Assign the computer the IP address 131.107.2.201 and subnet mask 255.255.0.0. To complete these procedures, you need four blank disks.

Important If your computer is part of a larger network, verify with your network administrator that the computer name, domain name, and IP address information do not conflict with network operations. If they conflict, ask your network administrator to provide alternative values, and use those values throughout all of the procedures in this book.

▸ To create Windows NT Workstation Setup disks

In this procedure, you create the three Setup disks needed to complete a Windows NT Workstation compact disc installation.

Note Complete this procedure on Server1.

---

1. Log on as Administrator.
2. Insert the *Microsoft Windows NT Workstation 4.0* compact disc in the CD-ROM drive, and then close the Microsoft CD-ROM window.
3. Click the **Start** button, and then click **Run**.
4. In the **Open** box, type *cd-rom_drive_letter*:**\I386\winnt32 /ox** substituting the appropriate letter for your CD-ROM drive, and then press ENTER or click **OK**.

   The **Windows NT 4.00 Upgrade/Installation** dialog box appears, indicating the location of the Windows NT Workstation files.
5. Click **Continue**.
6. When prompted, label a blank disk as Windows NT Workstation Setup Disk #3, insert the disk in drive A, and then press ENTER or click **OK**.
7. When prompted, label a blank disk as Windows NT Workstation Setup Disk #2, insert the disk in drive A, and then press ENTER or click **OK**.
8. When prompted, label a blank disk as Windows NT Workstation Setup Boot Disk, insert the disk in drive A, and then press ENTER or click **OK**.

   When Winnt32 has finished creating the disks, the application quits.
9. Remove the disk from drive A and the compact disc from the CD-ROM drive.

▸ To install Windows NT Workstation

In this procedure, you install Windows NT Workstation on drive C of Computer2. You name the computer Workstation1, and it will initially be a member of the default workgroup, Workgroup.

Note Complete this procedure on the Computer2.

---

1. Insert the Windows NT Workstation Setup Boot Disk in drive A, and then start your computer.
2. When prompted, insert the Windows NT Workstation Setup Disk #2 and Disk #3 in drive A, and then press ENTER.
3. When prompted, insert the Windows NT Workstation CD-ROM in the CD-ROM drive, and then press ENTER.

4. Install Windows NT Workstation using the information in the following table.

When this information is requested	Use
MS-DOS-based portion of Setup	
If prompted, upgrade or new fresh copy	**N** to install a fresh copy
Partition to install on	**C:**
File system	Leave the current file system intact (no changes)
Location where files are to be installed	\WINNT
Phase 1: Gathering Information	
Setup Options	Typical
Name and Organization	Your name and organization
Computer Name	Workstation1
Administrator Account password	password
Emergency Repair Disk	Yes, create
Windows NT Components	Install the most common components
Phase 2: Installing Windows NT Networking	
How this computer will participate on a network	Wired to the network
Network Adapters	The correct network adapter card for your computer
Network Adapter Properties	The correct network adapter card settings for your computer
Network Protocols	TCP/IP Protocol
Do you wish to use DHCP?	No
IP Address	131.107.2.201
Subnet mask	255.255.0.0
Make this computer a member of workgroup or domain	Workgroup
Workgroup name	Workgroup
Phase 3: Finishing Setup	
Date, time, and time zone	The correct values for your location
Display	The correct display for your computer

5. When the installation has completed, restart your computer.

Installing the Course Materials on Workstation1

Now that you have installed Windows NT Workstation, you also need to install the course materials to continue with the course. The course materials include lab files, and the course Web page which contains supplemental material, such as appendixes and links to important Microsoft Web sites.

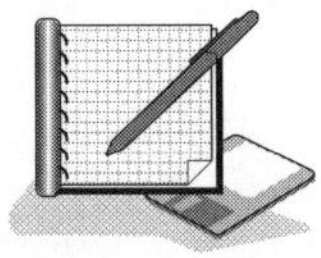

Practice

In these procedures, you install the course materials and Microsoft Internet Explorer 3.0 on Workstation1.

Note Complete this procedure on Workstation1.

► **To install the course materials on Workstation1**

1. Insert the *Course Materials* compact disc in the CD-ROM drive of Workstation1.
2. Log on as Administrator.
3. From the *Course Materials* compact disc, run Setup.exe.

   The **Microsoft Windows NT 4.0 Technical Support** dialog box appears.
4. Click **Continue**.
5. In the **Name** box, type your name.
6. In the **Organization** box, type the name of your organization or leave this box empty, and then click **OK**.
7. Click **OK** to confirm that the Name and Organization information was entered correctly.
8. Click the **Setup** button.

   The required course files are copied to and installed on the hard disk.
9. Click **OK**.

► **To install Microsoft Internet Explorer 3.0**

1. In the *Course Materials* compact disc, open the IE_Setup folder, and then run Msie30.exe.

   A **Microsoft Internet Explorer 3.0** dialog box appears prompting if you want to install Microsoft Internet Explorer 3.0.
2. Click **Yes** to install Microsoft Internet Explorer 3.0.

   A **Microsoft Internet Explorer Setup** dialog box appears indicating that files are being copied to a temporary folder on your hard disk.

3. Read the End-User License Agreement for Microsoft Internet Explorer, and then click **I Agree** to accept the terms of the agreement and continue the installation.

   A **Microsoft Internet Explorer Setup** dialog box appears indicating that files are being copied and Microsoft Internet Explorer is being set up on your computer.

4. When prompted to restart your computer, click **Yes**.

Joining a Domain

Once the computer account is created or added to the domain, use the Network program in Control Panel to join the computer to the domain.

Note If you want a computer to join to a domain, and the computer currently has a session with the PDC of that domain, the process fails and you receive a message indicating that you already have a connection. Therefore, you must disconnect all sessions that the computer has with the PDC before attempting to have it join the domain.

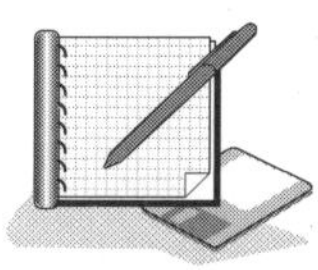

Practice

In this procedure, you have Workstation1 join Domain1.

► **To join a domain**

Note Complete this procedure on Workstation1.

---

1. Log on as Administrator.
2. Double-click the Network icon in Control Panel.
3. Click the **Identification** tab to display the current computer name and the domain or workgroup name to which the computer belongs.
4. Click the **Change** button.

   The **Identification Changes** dialog box appears.

5. In the **Member of** box, click **Domain**, and then type **Domain1** for the name of the domain to join.

Note Because you have already created a computer account in Domain1, you can just click **OK**.

If you had not previously created the computer account, you would have to click **Create Computer Account in the Domain**, supply a user account that has been granted the **Add Workstations to Domain** user right (Administrators and Server Operators have this right by default) and the appropriate password, and then click **OK**.

---

6. Click **OK**.
7. Click **OK** to acknowledge the **Welcome to the Domain1 domain** dialog box.
8. Click **Close**.
9. Click **Yes** to restart your computer.

Note If the computer has had Windows NT reinstalled on it, or for some other reason needs to rejoin the domain, then the computer name must be deleted and recreated at the domain controller. If this is not done, an error message refers the administrator to check the computer account on the domain.

Lesson 4: Logging On to a Computer or Domain

To access resources on a computer running Windows NT or on a domain, you must log on and be validated by the appropriate directory database. To log on you must provide a user name and password that is unique to the directory database for the computer or the domain. For example, when you log on to a domain, you are validated by the domain directory database and given permission to access resources on the domain. By contrast, when you log on locally to a computer running Windows NT, you are validated by the directory database on that computer and are given access to resources on that computer. The mandatory logon process is a security feature of Windows NT, and cannot be disabled.

After this lesson, you will be able to:

- Describe the resources that are available when you log on to a computer, domain, or workgroup.

Estimated lesson time: 20 minutes

Logging On to a Computer or Domain

The following information describes the logon procedures and the resources available to you when you start Windows NT on a computer that is a domain member.

- *Workstation or member server.* When you log on at a workstation or a member server that is a member of a domain, you can choose to log on to the local computer or to the domain. This is done by clicking either the computer name or the domain name from the **Domain** box in the **Logon Information** dialog box.

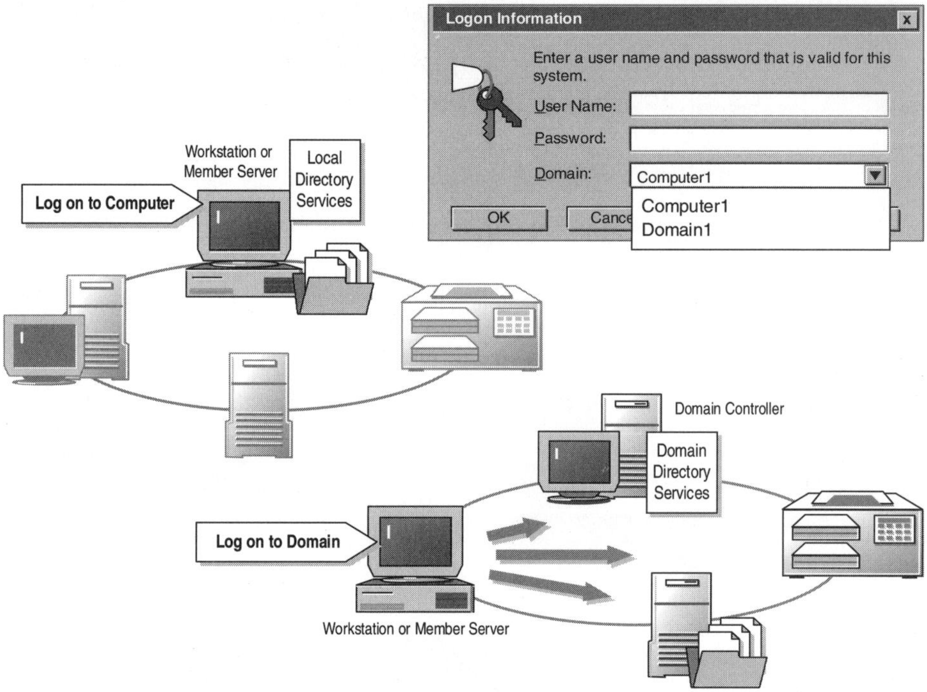

If you specify the computer name in the **Domain** box, then you are specifying the local directory services database stored on that computer. You can still view resources in the domain while logged on to the local computer. For example, you would be able to view the shared folders on another computer in the domain. However, you cannot access the contents of the shared folders unless you connect to a resource on the domain, and specify a valid domain user account and password.

You would use the following steps to map a network drive:

1. Start Windows NT Explorer.
2. On the **Tools** menu, click **Map Network Drive**.
3. In the **Path** box, enter a universal naming convention (UNC) path for the domain resource. For example, *server_name\shared_folder_name.*
4. In the **Connect as** box, enter the domain name and user account name using the following format *domain_name\domain_user_account_name*.
5. You are prompted to enter the appropriate password.

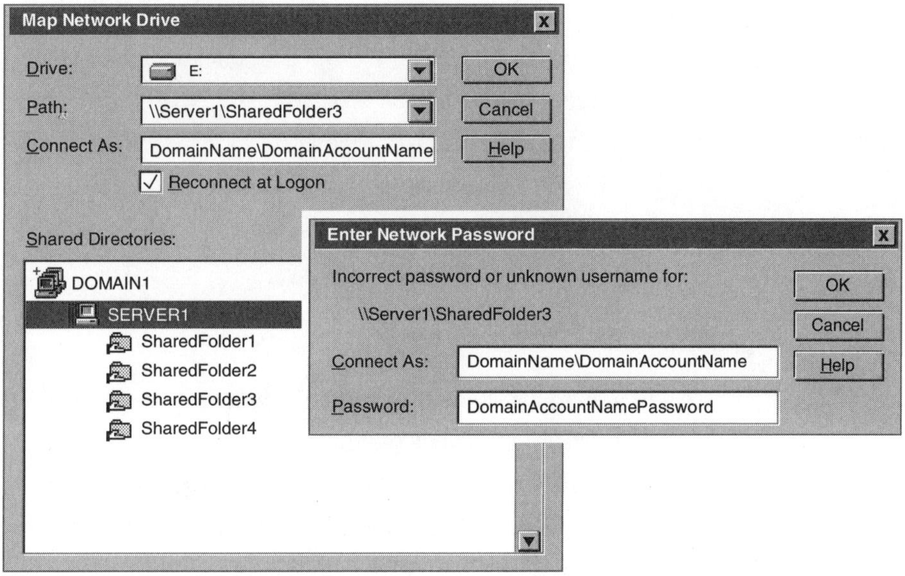

Logging On at a Domain Controller

When you log on at a domain controller, you cannot choose to log on to the local computer, you can only log on to the domain. If the appropriate trust relationships exist with other domains, you can choose to log on to another domain instead. This is because the local directory services database on domain controllers is also the domain directory services database.

When you specify the domain name in the **Domain** box, you are specifying the domain directory services database stored on the domain controllers. This means that you have access to domain resources.

Practice

In this procedure, you log on to Domain1.

▸ To log on to a domain

In this procedure, you examine the contents of the **Domain** box in the **Logon Information** dialog box of a domain controller, and then log on to the domain.

Note Complete this procedure on Server1.

---

1. If you are logged on at Server1, then log off.

   To log off, press CTRL+ALT+DELETE, click **Logoff**, and then click **OK**.

   The **Begin Logon** dialog box appears.
2. Press CTRL+ALT+DELETE to log on.

   The **Logon Information** dialog box appears.
3. In the **Domain** box, click the list box.

   What appears in the list?

   ____
4. Log on to the domain as Administrator.
5. Press CTRL+ALT+DELETE.

   The **Windows NT Security** dialog box appears.

   Why does the **Logon Information** dialog box show that you are logged on as DOMAIN1\Administrator?

   ____

Practice

In this procedure, you log on to the computer named Workstation1.

▸ To log on to a computer

In this procedure, you examine the contents of the **Domain** box in the **Logon Information** dialog box of a computer running Windows NT Workstation that is a member of a domain, and you then log on to the computer.

Note Complete this procedure on Workstation1.

---

1. If you are logged on at Workstation1, then log off.

   The **Begin Logon** dialog box appears.
2. Press CTRL+ALT+DELETE to log on.

   The **Logon Information** dialog box appears.
3. In the **Domain** box, click the list box.

   What appears in the list?

   ____

   ____
4. In the **Domain** box, click **WORKSTATION1**.
5. Log on to Workstation1 as Administrator.
6. After you have logged on and the Windows NT interface appears, press CTRL+ALT+DELETE.

   The **Windows NT Security** dialog box appears.

   Why does the **Logon Information** dialog box show that you are logged on as WORKSTATION1\Administrator?

   ____

   ____

Logging On to a Computer Running Windows NT in a Workgroup

To log on to a computer running Windows NT in a workgroup, you enter the user name and password in the **Logon Information** dialog box. Unlike logging on to a computer that is a member of a domain, you cannot choose other workgroups to log on to. The user name and password that you enter is validated against the local directory services database on that computer. If you need to access resources on another computer in the workgroup, you would have to have a user account in the directory database on that computer.

If you want to join a different workgroup, you would use the Network program in Control Panel. You would click the **Change** button and, in the **Identification Changes** dialog box, you would type in the name of the workgroup you want to join.

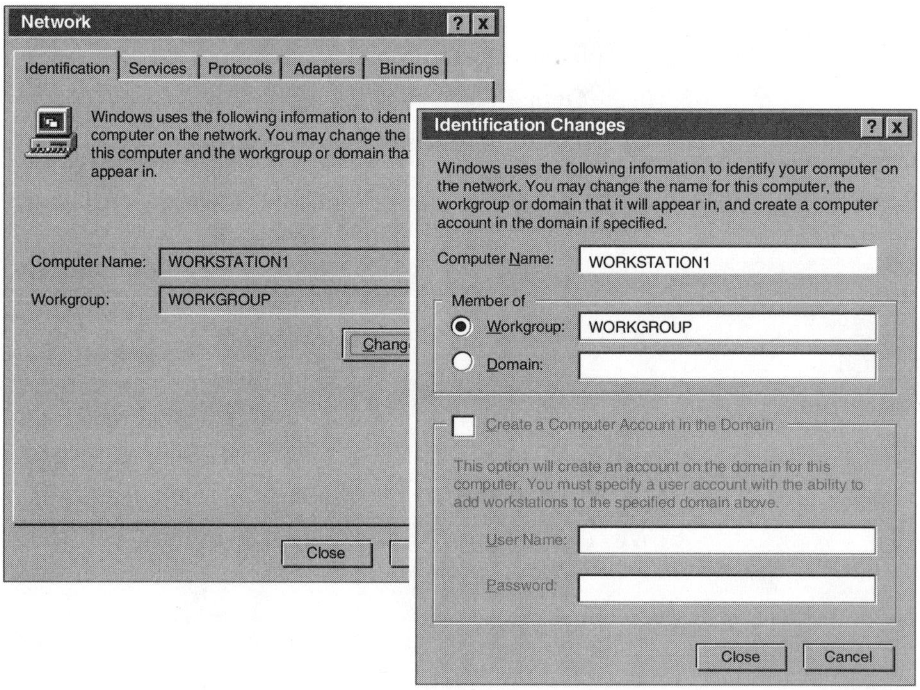

Practice

In this procedure, you log on to the domain named Domain1.

▸ **To log on to a domain from a workstation computer**

In this procedure, you examine the contents of the **Domain** box in the **Logon Information** dialog box of a workstation that is a member of a domain, and you then log on to the domain.

Note Complete this procedure on Workstation1.

---

1. If you are logged on at Workstation1, then log off.

   The **Begin Logon** dialog box appears.

2. Press CTRL+ALT+DELETE to log on.

   The **Logon Information** dialog box appears.

3. In the **Domain** box, click **DOMAIN1**.
4. Log on as Administrator.
5. After you have logged on and the Windows NT interface appears, press CTRL+ALT+DELETE.

   The **Windows NT Security** dialog box appears.

   Why does the **Logon Information** dialog box show that you are logged on as DOMAIN1\Administrator?

   ____

   ____

Lesson 5: Installing Windows NT Server from a Network Share

If you want to install Windows NT on multiple computers, you can streamline the installation by copying the Windows NT files to a network server. You would then log on to each of the computers, connect to the share containing the Windows NT files, and then run Setup from the server. This installation method, utilizing a network share containing the Windows NT source files, is known as a *server-based installation.* This lesson covers the procedures to perform a server-based installation.

After this lesson, you will be able to:

- Create a *distribution server* that has a network share containing the Windows NT installation files.
- Create an Unattend.txt file to prepare for an unattended installation.
- Install Windows NT on an Intel *x*86-based computer in an unattended installation using a distribution server.
- Explain why Windows NT cannot upgrade a Windows 95 installation.
- Explain how to upgrade from Windows 3.*x* to Windows NT.
- Describe how to remove Windows NT.

Estimated lesson time: 100 minutes

Performing a Server-based Installation

To perform a server-based installation, you need to create a *distribution server.* Create a distribution server by copying the Windows NT source files from the Windows NT compact disc to a shared folder that you created on the distribution server. You determine which source files to copy based on the type of computer on which you install Windows NT. Once you know the required platform(s), copy the appropriate I386, Mips, Ppc, or Alpha folder(s) containing the source files.

Note On RISC-based computers, you can use this server-based installation method only to upgrade or reinstall the operating system when Windows NT is already installed.

To copy the files, use the Windows NT Explorer or the **xcopy** command. If you use the **xcopy** command, include the **/s** switch to make sure that subfolders are copied. Furthermore, if your computer requires any drivers that are located in the Drvlib folder, you need to copy the Drvlib folder to the shared folder on your distribution server.

Note If you are using Windows NT Explorer to copy the files, you must change the Windows NT Explorer default settings in order to allow files with extensions such as .dll, .sys, and .vxd to be displayed. Files that are not displayed are not copied. To change the default settings, click **View**, click **Options**, and then in the **Hidden Files** box, click **Show all files**.

Windows NT provides two Setup programs, named Winnt.exe and Winnt32.exe, that are used for server-based installations.

- *Winnt.exe.* This file is used to install Windows NT on a client computer running Windows 95 or MS-DOS.
- *Winnt32.exe.* This file is used to install or upgrade Windows NT on a computer already running Windows NT. For example, if you are upgrading from Windows NT 3.51 to Windows NT 4.0, then you would install Windows NT 4.0 in the same folder where Windows NT 3.51 was installed, thus preserving your desktop and configuration settings.

  If you want to retain your current version of Windows NT, you should install Windows NT 4.0 in a separate folder. For example, if you are a support engineer that needs to dual boot between Windows NT Workstation and Windows NT Server, or a previous version of Windows NT, you would install Windows NT 4.0 in a separate folder.

Once the files are copied to a network server and the folder is shared, you can connect to the network share from the client computer where you want to install Windows NT, and then run Winnt.exe or Winnt32.exe. The network share method streamlines installation. You can start concurrent installations on several computers by connecting to the server from each client computer and running the Winnt.exe or Winnt32.exe program.

The following illustration shows a distribution server being used to install Windows NT Server on two computers: one to be configured as a PDC and the other as a member server. The distribution server is also being used to install Windows NT Workstation on a third computer. The distribution server would have to have both the Windows NT Server and Windows NT Workstation source files on it.

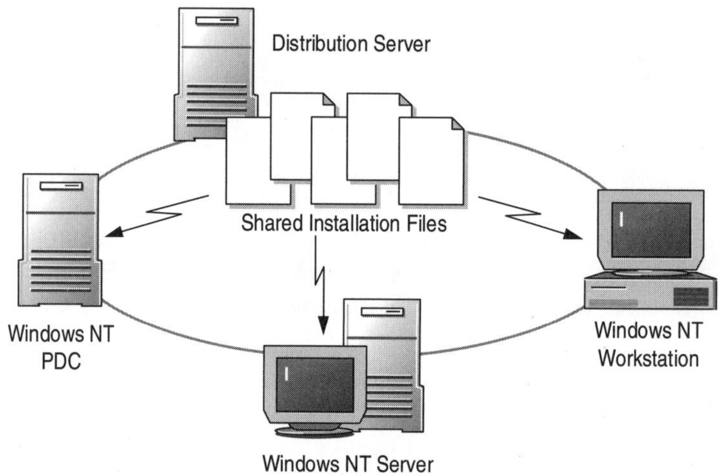

Note If you do not have enough hard disk space on a network server to copy all of the appropriate Windows NT installation files, then you could share the I386, Mips, Ppc, or Alpha folder on the Windows NT Server compact disc. To share a folder, connect from the client computers to the shared folder on the compact disc and then run Setup. However, this method is much slower than installing Windows NT from the server's hard disk.

Practice

In this procedure, you create a distribution server for the Windows NT Server source files. You copy the I386 folder on the Windows NT Server compact disc to a folder on Server1, and then share the folder. You use this distribution server later in this chapter to perform an over-the-network installation.

▸ **To create a distribution server for the Windows NT Server files**

Note Complete this procedure on Server1. This procedure typically requires approximately 105 MB of free disk space on a disk partition. If you do not have sufficient free disk space, you can share the compact disc directly.

---

1. Start Server1 and log on as Administrator.
2. Insert the *Microsoft Windows NT Server 4.0* compact disc in the CD-ROM drive.
3. Create a folder on your hard disk named Nts_source.
4. Use Windows NT Explorer to drag and drop the I386 folder from your *Microsoft Windows NT Server 4.0* compact disc to the Nts_source folder.
5. Use Windows NT Explorer to share the Nts_source folder, assigning the share name of Nts_source, and assigning Read permissions for the group Everyone.
6. Remove the *Microsoft Windows NT Server 4.0* compact disc from the CD-ROM drive.

Installing from a Network Server to a Client Computer Running Windows 95 or MS-DOS

The Windows NT Winnt.exe Setup program is used to install Windows NT from a network server to a client computer running Windows 95 or MS-DOS.

To start the server-based installation, you use the following steps:

1. From the computer where you want to install Window NT, connect to the shared folder containing the Windows NT distribution files.
2. Run Winnt.exe.

Winnt.exe performs the following steps:

1. Winnt.exe creates three Setup boot disks. (These are copies of the disks used for the compact disc installation described earlier in this chapter.) This step requires three blank formatted disks.
2. Winnt.exe creates a Win_nt.~ls temporary folder on the client computer, and then copies Windows NT files from the network shared installation files to this folder.
3. Winnt.exe prompts you to insert the first Setup boot disk in drive A, and then to restart the computer.

Customizing a Server-based Installation

The following table describes switches that can be used with Winnt.exe to control how Setup runs.

Switch	Description
/x	Prevents Setup from creating Setup boot disks. Use this when you have already created Setup boot disks.
/ox	Specifies that Setup only create boot disks for installing from the compact disc. This option can be used to replace the disks that are included with the Windows NT product, if they have been lost or damaged.
/b	Causes the boot files to be loaded on the computer's hard disk rather than on floppy disks, so that floppy disks do not need to be loaded or removed by the user. The **/b** switch requires an extra 4–5 MB of hard disk space on the computer where Windows NT is being installed. This setup option creates a Ldr file and a Win_nt.~bt temporary folder on the hard disk of the client computer.
/u:answer_file	Specifies the location of an answer file that provides answers for an unattended installation that the user would otherwise be prompted for during the setup process.
/udf:id [,UDF_file]	Specifies the identifier that is to be used by the Setup program to apply sections of the Uniqueness Database File (UDF) file in place of the same section in the answer file. A UDF can be used during an unattended installation to identify settings such as the video adapter or computer name that are unique to a specific computer. If no UDF is specified, the Setup program prompts the user to insert a disk that contains a file named $UNIQUE$.UDF. If a UDF is specified, Setup looks for the identifier in that file.

(*continued*)

Switch	Description
/s	Specifies the location of the Windows NT source files. This switch can be used in conjunction with the **/u** switch to bypass the normal prompt for the source file location. This switch also allows you to specify multiple source file locations to significantly speed up installation.
/f	Prevents Winnt.exe from verifying files as they are copied. You can use this switch to accelerate installation.
/i:*inffil*	Specifies the file name (no path) of the setup information file. The default is Dosnet.inf. You can modify this file to customize how Setup runs.
/t:*tempdrive*	Forces Setup to place temporary files on the specified drive. If not specified, Setup uses the partition on the computer where Windows NT is being installed that has the most free hard disk space.
/l	Creates a log file named $Winnt.log on the computer where Windows NT is being installed. This file lists any errors encountered when Winnt.exe copies files to the temporary folder.

Installing from a Network Server to a Computer Running Windows NT

The Windows NT distribution files include the Setup program Winnt32.exe for installing Windows NT on computers that are already running Windows NT. It is used to upgrade from earlier version of Windows NT or to install Windows NT in a different folder on the same computer. Winnt32.exe uses all of the switches listed in the preceding table for Winnt.exe, with the exception of the **/f** and **/l** switches.

Performing an Unattended Installation

In an unattended setup, the Setup program runs over a network, using the Winnt.exe or Winnt32.exe programs with the **/u** switch. The **/u** switch is used to specify an *answer file*. The answer file is a script that you create to automate the installation.

Creating Answer Files

You can create different answer files for various computer configurations in an organization. Answer files can be further customized with UDFs. For example, you can create one answer file for each geographic location, or for each corporate division. To customize individual user and computer names you would create a UDF with a section for each computer that specifies the user name and computer name. The user can then run the customized installation by specifying the appropriate answer and UDF file when they run Winnt.exe or Winnt32.exe.

Unattended answer files can be created either by using the Setup Manager utility provided on the Windows NT Server compact disc in the Support\Deptools*platform* folder, or by modifying the sample Unattend.txt file found on the Windows NT Server compact disc in the respective platform folders. An unattended answer file can be given any legal file name.

The unattended answer file is comprised of several sections containing information that is to be used during the installation.

Note For more information on using unattended answer files and installations, see the *Microsoft Windows NT Workstation Resource Kit.*

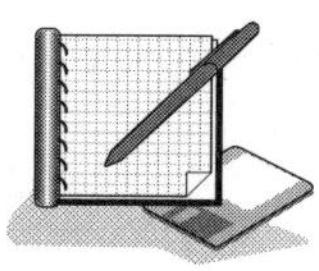

Practice

In this procedure, you create an Unattend.txt file using Setup Manager, and then modify the file to include additional information. This Unattend.txt file is used later in this lesson to perform an unattended, over-the-network installation.

▸ **To create an Unattend.txt file**

Note Complete this procedure on Server1. This procedure assumes you have created and shared the Nts_source folder on Server1.

---

1. Run the **Support\Deptools\I386\Setupmgr** program from the *Microsoft Windows NT Server 4.0* compact disc.

   The **Windows NT Setup Manager** dialog box appears.

2. Click **General Setup**.

3. Use the tabs to complete the information in the following table.

On this tab	In this box	Do this action
User Information	User Name	Type your name
	Organization	Type your organization
	Computer Name	Type **Server2**
	Product ID	Type **040-0048126**
Computer Role	Select the role of the computer	Click **Backup domain controller**
	Enter the domain name	Type **Domain1**
Install Directory	Directory	Click **Specify installation directory now**
		Type **Server2**
Display Settings	Automatically use the above settings	Select the check box
Time Zone	Select the time zone for the user's location	Click the time zone for the user location
License Mode	Per Server	Click this option
	users permitted	Type **10**

4. Click **OK**.
5. In the **Windows NT Setup Manager** dialog box, click **Networking Setup**.
6. Use the tabs in the **Networking Options** dialog box to complete the information in the following table.

Note If Setup did *not* correctly detect and install your network adapter card during the Windows NT Workstation installation performed in Lesson 3, then click **Manual Network Installation** and go to step 7.

On this tab	In this box	Do this action
General		Click **Unattended Network Installation**
	Unattended Network Installation	Click **Automatically detect and install first adapter**
Protocols	List of Protocols	Click **Add**; in the drop-down list box, choose **TCP/IP**, and then click **OK**

(*continued*)

On this tab	In this box	Do this action
		Click **Parameters**
	Do not use DHCP	Select the check box
	IP Address	Type **131.107.2.211**
	Subnet	Type **255.255.0.0** and then click **OK**
Internet	Do not install Internet Server	Select the check box

7. Click **OK**.
8. In the **Windows NT Setup Manager** dialog box, click **Advanced Setup**.
9. Use the tabs to complete the information in the following table.

On this tab	In this box	Do this action
General	Reboot	Select the **After Text Mode** and **After GUI Mode** check boxes
	Skip Welcome wizard page	Select the check box
	Skip Administrative Password wizard page	Select the check box
File System	File System	Click **Use current file system**

10. Click **OK**.
11. Click **Save**.

    The **Save as an Answer File** dialog box appears.
12. In the **Save in** box, double-click the **Nts_source** shared folder.
13. In the **File name** box, type **Unattend**
14. In the **Save as type** box, click **Text Files (*.txt)**.
15. Click **Save**, and then click **Exit** to quit Windows NT Setup Manager.
16. In Windows NT Explorer, double-click the **Nts_source\Unattend.txt** file.

    The file is opened in Notepad.

17. Edit the **Nts_source\Unattend.txt** file using the information in the following table.

In this section	Add this line	To bypass this prompt
[unattended]	OEMSkipEula=yes	Licensing agreement
[network]	CreateComputerAccount= Administrator, password	Credentials and password used to create the computer account

18. Save the file and close **Notepad**.

Customizing the Installation with Uniqueness Database Files

When implementing a complete, unattended installation of Windows NT to numerous computers, some of the information that must be supplied through answer files, such as the computer name, must be unique to each computer. With Windows NT, use a single answer file for the information that applies to all users, and use one or more Uniqueness Database Files (UDFs) to supply information that is specific to a single computer or a small group of computers.

UDFs are used to provide replacements for sections of the answer file, or supply additional sections. The replacement sections are specified in a text file similar to the answer file. This file is indexed by means of strings called *uniqueness IDs*.

The UDF is used to specify a set of sections that should be merged into the answer file at the start of Setup. Setup then uses the merged file to perform the customized unattended installation.

The first section of the UDF is the [UniqueIds] section. This section lists all uniqueness IDs that are supported by this database. Following the [UniqueIds] section are the sections referenced in [UniqueIds]. For example:

```
[UniqueIds]
katedresen = UserData, Unattended
aaronco = UserData, Unattended
elang = UserData, KeyboardDrivers, PointDeviceDrivers

[UserData]
FullName = "Kate Dresen"
...
[Unattended]
NtUpgrade = no
...
```

Following the [UniqueIds] section are the sections referenced in [UniqueIds].

Specifying a UDF During Installation

To specify a uniqueness ID during setup, the user must run the **Winnt** or **Winnt32** command with the following parameter:

Winnt /U:answer_filename /UDF:ID[,database_filename]

Where *ID* is the uniqueness ID to use while installing Windows NT on this computer, and where *database_filename* is the file name, including the full path, of the UDF.

Practice

In this procedure, you install Windows NT Server on drive D of Computer2 by performing an unattended installation. To accomplish this, you connect from Workstation1 to the distribution share \\Server1\Nts_source and run Setup using the Unattend.txt file created earlier in this lesson. This installation configures Computer2 as a BDC in Domain1, and names the computer Server2.

► **To perform an unattended setup**

Note Complete this procedure on Workstation1. You must have at least 125 MB of disk space available on drive D.

---

1. Log on to the domain as Administrator.
2. Use Windows NT Explorer to map network drive S to **\\Server1\Nts_source**. Clear the **Reconnect at Logon** check box.
3. Click the **Start** button, and then click **Run**.
4. In the **Open** box, type **S:\I386\winnt32 /u:S:\unattend.txt /t:D** and then click **OK**.

   The installation starts, and you can watch the progress on the computer's screen.

5. If you configured Unattend.txt for manual network installation, when prompted, configure the network components using the information in the following table.

Note Use the information in the following table *only* if you clicked **Manual Network Installation** in the Unattend.txt file.

When this information is requested	Do this action
How this computer will participate on a network	Check only the **Wired to the network** box
Microsoft Internet Information Server	Clear this check box
Network Adapters	Click **Select from list**, and then select the correct network adapter card for your computer
Network Protocols	Select only the **TCP/IP** protocol
Network Adapter Properties	Select the correct settings for your network adapter card
Do you wish to use DHCP?	Click **No**
IP Address	**131.107.2.211**
Subnet Mask	**255.255.0.0**
Domain	**Domain1**
Administrator Name	**Administrator**
Administrator Password	**password**

When installation is complete, your computer automatically restarts.

6. Start Server2 and log on as Administrator.

Upgrading from Windows 95 to Windows NT 4.0

Because Windows NT and Windows 95 do not use the same *registry* settings or hardware device support, Windows NT cannot upgrade a Windows 95 installation. Instead, you would install Windows NT 4.0 to a separate folder. After Windows NT is installed, you need to start your computer under Windows NT and reinstall all of your applications. Your applications can be installed in the same folders that were used when they were installed under Windows 95. Reinstalling your applications under Windows NT updates the Windows NT registry. After the applications are installed, you can delete the folder where Windows 95 was installed.

Note If you intend to dual boot between Windows 95 and Windows NT, for example, if you are evaluating or supporting both operating systems, then do not delete the Windows 95 folder.

Upgrading from Windows NT 3.*x* to Windows NT 4.0

If you are installing Windows NT 4.0 on a computer running Windows NT 3.*x*, Windows NT 4.0 Setup prompts you to upgrade your version of Windows NT. If you decide to upgrade rather than complete a new installation, the following settings are preserved:

- User and group accounts
- Network settings and configuration
- The desktop environment
- Preferences set for administrative tools

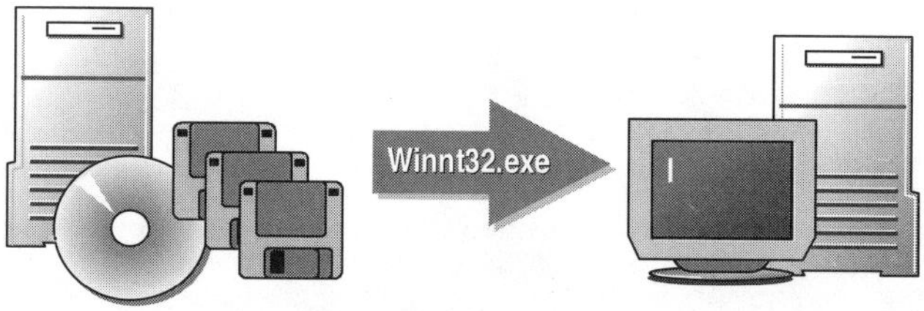

Upgrading preserves the following Windows NT 3.*x* data:
- User and group accounts
- Network settings and configuration
- Desktop environment
- Administrative tools preferences

To upgrade Windows NT 3.*x* to Windows NT 4.0, click **Yes** in response to the upgrade question during the setup process, and then follow the upgrade instructions.

Removing Windows NT

You can use one of the following methods to remove Windows NT.

- Remove the partition Windows NT is installed on. This also removes any other information on this partition.
- Remove only Windows NT. This method can only be used on a FAT partition.

Removing a Partition

Use the following procedure to remove a partition.

Caution These steps are provided for your information. If you remove Windows NT, you cannot complete the course without reinstalling Windows NT.

---

1. Start the computer from the Setup boot disk.
2. When prompted to create or choose a partition, click the partition where the Windows NT files are located, and then press D to delete the partition.
3. When prompted, press F3 to exit Setup.

   The partition is removed from the computer at this time.

The following list contains alternative methods for removing partitions:

- Use the OS/2 1.*x* installation disk A to delete all partitions on the first physical disk.
- Use an MS-DOS 5.0 (or later) boot floppy disk and run **fdisk**.

  Note **fdisk** will not remove an NTFS logical drive in an extended MS-DOS partition.

Removing Windows NT from a FAT Partition

If you want to remove Windows NT from a FAT partition on drive C, but you want to leave Windows 95 or MS-DOS on the FAT partition, then use the following procedure.

Caution These steps are provided for your information. If you remove Windows NT, you cannot complete the course without reinstalling Windows NT.

---

1. Start the computer from a Windows 95 or MS-DOS system disk that contains the Sys.com file.
2. From drive A, type **sys c:**

   This transfers the Windows 95 or MS-DOS system files to the boot track on drive C.
3. After the system files are successfully transferred, restart the system from the hard disk.
4. To free space on the hard disk, delete the following:
   - C:\Pagefile.sys
   - C:\Boot.ini (marked as hidden, system, and read-only)
   - C:\Nt*.* (marked as hidden, system, and read-only)
   - C:\Bootsect.dos (marked as hidden, system, and read-only)
   - *systemroot* folder
   - Program files\Windows NT

Lesson 6: Viewing the Windows NT Documentation

User documentation for Windows NT Workstation and Windows NT Server are included on their corresponding compact discs.

After this lesson, you will be able to:

- Describe the user documentation available on the Windows NT Workstation and Windows NT Server compact discs.
- Install Books Online.

Estimated lesson time: 10 minutes

The Windows NT Workstation compact disc includes support documentation that covers the installation and new features of Windows NT Workstation. The documents are stored in the Support\Books folder. They are Microsoft Word for Windows documents, and can be viewed with applications that can read Word for Windows document files, such as WordPad.

To view the contents of the online documentation, double-click Wfront.doc. The number of each chapter listed in Wfront.doc corresponds to the number in the document name listed in the Support\Books folder. Double-click the document name to view a particular document.

The Windows NT Server compact disc also includes support documentation. The documents are stored in the Support\Books folder. Included in this folder are two books that you might find useful, *Concepts and Planning* (Book_cp.hlp) and *Networking Supplement* (Book_net.hlp). You can view these support files by using the Help viewer, Books Online, which is installed during the Windows NT Server installation.

Note The first time Books Online is run, you are prompted to enter the path to the documentation files. By default, the files are stored on the compact disc. You can copy the files to the local computer or to a network file server and then set the path when you start Books Online. If you move the files to another location after you have set the path, Books Online prompts you to reset the path the next time Books Online is started.

Practice

In this procedure, you start Books Online and review the Windows NT registry topic.

► **To use Books Online**

Note Complete this procedure on Server1.

---

1. Log on as Administrator.
2. Use Windows NT Explorer to create a Support folder in the Nts_source folder on your computer.
3. Use Windows NT Explorer to drag and drop the Support\Books folder from the *Microsoft Windows NT Server 4.0* compact disc to the Nts_source\Support folder on your computer.
4. Remove the *Microsoft Windows NT Server 4.0* compact disc from the CD-ROM drive.
5. Click the **Start** button, point to **Programs**, and then click **Books Online**.
6. In the **Location of Books Online Files** box, type:

   drive_letter:**\nts_source\support\books**

   substituting the correct drive letter for your computer, and then click **OK**.

   The **Help Topics: Windows NT Server 4.0 Books Online** dialog box appears.
7. Open and explore the books available in Books Online.
8. Exit Books Online.

Note Books Online is only available on Windows NT Server.

Summary

The following information summarizes the key points in this chapter:

- Before installing Windows NT on a computer you should determine:
  - That the computer's hardware is listed on the most recent version of the Windows NT Hardware Compatibility List. You can use the Windows NT Hardware Qualifier program to determine the computer's hardware.
  - How the hard disk(s) should be partitioned.
  - Which file system(s), FAT or NTFS, to use.
  - When installing Windows NT Server, whether the computer should be configured as a PDC, BDC, or stand-alone server.
- A domain can contain only one PDC. When you configure a computer as a PDC, you are creating a domain. If the computer is to be configured as a PDC, you must also choose either the Per Server or Per Seat licensing mode.
- Before a computer running Windows NT can join a domain, a computer account must be created or added to the domain directory database. Only users with the right to *add workstations to a domain*, can create computer accounts.
- If a workstation is a member of a domain, a user with the appropriate user rights can choose to log on to either the computer or the domain. If the user logs on to the workstation, the user has access to the resources on that computer. If the user logs on to the domain, the user has access to domain resources.
- When Windows NT must be installed on many computers, copy the Windows NT files to a shared network location. Then connect to the network share from the client computer and run Setup. This installation method is known as a server-based installation.
- By creating answer files and Uniqueness Database Files (UDFs), you can both automate and customize Windows NT installations.
- Windows NT cannot upgrade a Windows 95 installation.
- Windows NT can be removed by removing the partition it was installed on, or Windows NT can be removed from a FAT partition.
- The Windows NT Server compact disc and the Windows NT Workstation compact disc contain supporting documentation.

Review

1. You want to install Windows NT Server on an Alpha-based computer. You want to protect your files and folders with local security, and you will be supporting Macintosh clients. How should you partition your disk or disks?

2. You are installing Windows NT Workstation, and want to include Microsoft Exchange in the installation. What type of installation must you choose?

3. You have been told to automate the setup of Windows NT Workstation 4.0 on multiple machines in your department. You have 40 machines in five different configurations. How can you do this in the easiest possible way?

4. You are trying to install Windows NT Server as a BDC, but Setup reports that a primary domain controller cannot be found. What should you check?

5. Your computer runs only Windows NT Server 3.51. The hard disk is formatted entirely with NTFS. You want to upgrade the operating system to version 4.0 while minimizing the amount of downtime necessary to perform the upgrade. What is the quickest and least disruptive way to upgrade the server?

6. A user sent you an e-mail message asking a question that you cannot answer. How can you get the answer in electronic form, so that you can paste it into your reply?

7. You have been testing Windows NT Workstation on a computer, and now want to return to running Windows 95 only. You delete all of the Windows NT operating system files, including the hidden files in the system partition. But when you start the computer, you receive a messages stating "BOOT: Couldn't find NTLDR. Please insert another disk." The Windows 95 boot process does not proceed. What is causing this behavior?

Answer Key

Procedure Answers

Page 60

▸ **To log on to a domain**

3. In the **Domain** box, pull down the list box.

   What appears in the list?

   Domain1, which is the domain name of this domain controller.

5. Press CTRL+ALT+DELETE.

   The **Windows NT Security** dialog box appears.

   Why does the **Logon Information** dialog box show that you are logged on as DOMAIN1\Administrator?

   Because the domain's directory services database, stored on the domain controller, validated the logon.

Page 61

▸ **To log on to a computer**

3. In the **Domain** box, pull down the list box.

   What appears in the list?

   Domain1, which is the domain that this computer has joined, and Workstation1, which is the computer name for this computer.

6. After you have logged on and the **Windows NT** interface appears, press CTRL+ALT+DELETE.

   The **Windows NT Security** dialog box appears.

   Why does the **Logon Information** dialog box show that you are logged on as WORKSTATION1\Administrator?

   Because the workstation's directory services database, stored on the workstation, validated the logon.

Page 63

▸ **To log on to a domain from a workstation computer**

5. After you have logged on and the Windows NT interface appears, press CTRL+ALT+DELETE.

   The **Windows NT Security** dialog box appears.

   Why does the **Logon Information** dialog box show that you are logged on as DOMAIN1\Administrator?

   Because the domain's directory services database, stored on the PDC, validated the logon.

Review Answers

Page 82

1. You want to install Windows NT Server on an Alpha-based computer. You want to protect your files and folders with local security, and you will be supporting Macintosh clients. How should you partition your disk or disks?

   A very small FAT system partition (Alphas require FAT system partitions), with the rest of the disk or disks formatted as NTFS.

2. You are installing Windows NT Workstation, and want to include Microsoft Exchange in the installation. What type of installation must you choose?

   Custom.

3. You have been told to automate the setup of Windows NT Workstation 4.0 on multiple machines in your department. You have 40 machines in five different configurations. How can you do this in the easiest possible way?

   Create an answer file for the generic settings and five UDFs to handle the five configurations for the specific sections. Use the answer file with the appropriate UDF to automate the installations.

4. You are trying to install Windows NT Server as a BDC, but Setup reports that a primary domain controller cannot be found. What should you check?

   Check the spelling of the domain name, make sure the PDC is up and running, make sure the BDC is using the same protocol as the PDC, and make sure that the network adapter card settings for the BDC are correct.

5. Your computer runs only Windows NT Server 3.51. The hard disk is formatted entirely with NTFS. You want to upgrade the operating system to version 4.0 while minimizing the amount of downtime necessary to perform the upgrade. What is the quickest and least disruptive way to upgrade the server?

   By using the Winnt32.exe utility, because it copies all of the files from the compact disc or network to the hard disk while the server is still running. Using the Setup disks and compact disc requires the server to be inoperative for a longer period of time.

6. A user sent you an e-mail message asking a question that you cannot answer. How can you get the answer in electronic form, so that you can paste it into your reply?

   Look up the topic in Books Online, highlight the text, and then copy and paste it into your reply.

7. You have been testing Windows NT Workstation on a computer, and now want to return to running Windows 95 only. You delete all of the Windows NT operating system files, including the hidden files in the system partition. But when you start the computer, you receive a messages stating "BOOT: Couldn't find NTLDR. Please insert another disk." The Windows 95 boot process does not proceed. What is causing this behavior?

   The Windows 95 boot sector must be restored with the Win95 sys command.

CHAPTER 3

Configuring the Windows NT Environment

About This Chapter

One of the most significant challenges for system administrators and technical support engineers is managing and supporting the hardware, operating systems, and applications on personal computers and network servers. Microsoft Windows NT contains a *registry* to help simplify this task by providing a secure, unified database that stores configuration data for the local computer. In this chapter, you learn about the registry architecture and some of the tools provided by Windows NT, such as Control Panel and Registry Editor, which are used to edit the registry on both local and remote computers.

Before You Begin

To complete the lessons in this chapter, you must have:

- Two computers that meet the hardware and software requirements as specified in the Getting Started section of "About This Book."
- Completed all practices in Chapter 2, "Installing Windows NT."

Lesson 1: The Windows NT Registry

This lesson describes the Windows NT registry and how Windows NT uses it to store and access all hardware and software configuration settings.

After this lesson, you will be able to:

- Describe the purpose of the Windows NT registry.
- Describe how Windows NT components use the registry.
- Identify the structural components of the registry hierarchy.

Estimated lesson time: 30 minutes

What Is the Registry?

The *registry* is a unified database where Windows NT stores all hardware and software configuration information for the local computer. The registry controls the Windows NT operating system by providing the appropriate initialization information to start applications and load components such as device drivers and network protocols.

The following list describes the type of information contained in the registry:

- The hardware installed on the computer, including the central processor, bus type, pointing device or mouse, and keyboard.
- Installed device drivers.
- Installed applications.
- Installed network protocols.
- Network adapter card settings. For example, the Interrupt Number, the Memory Base Address, the I/O Port Base Address, I/O Channel Ready, and Transceiver type.
- User account information. For example, the user's group membership, rights, and permissions are stored in the registry.

Viewing the Registry

To view the registry, Windows NT provides Registry Editor. Registry Editor can be used to make direct changes to the registry. However, Windows NT provides applications such as Control Panel, User Manager, and *System Policy Editor* that change the registry based on configuration information you supply. These applications provide an easy-to-use interface to help you to correctly configure your system. As you review this lesson, run Registry Editor so that you can view the contents of the registry on your local computer.

Caution You must be *very* careful when changing values using Registry Editor. Registry Editor does *not* recognize errors in syntax or other semantics, and therefore you are *not* warned if you have made an incorrect entry. If an incorrect entry is made, the operating system may be rendered unusable.

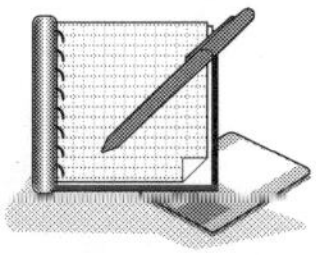

Practice

In these procedures, you create a shortcut for Registry Editor and then start Registry Editor to view the registry on Server1. The following illustration shows how the Registry Editor icon appears on the desktop.

Note Complete this procedure on Server1.

► **To create a shortcut for Registry Editor**

1. Right-click the desktop.
2. Click **New**, and then click **Shortcut**.
3. In the **Command line** box, type **regedt32.exe**
4. Click **Next**, and then click **Finish**.

   A shortcut icon for Regedt32.exe appears on your desktop.

► **To view the registry**

1. Start Registry Editor by double-clicking the shortcut icon.

   Registry Editor appears.
2. On the **Options** menu, click **Read Only Mode**.

   There should be a check mark by **Read Only Mode** indicating that it is selected. This prevents you from making any unintentional changes to the registry.

   When Registry Editor is opened, it displays five windows. Each window displays a *subtree*; each subtree is used to access different areas of the registry.
3. List the names of the five subtrees displayed by Registry Editor.

   ____

   ____
4. Minimize Registry Editor.

How Windows NT Components Use the Registry

Windows NT stores and checks all configuration information in only one location—the registry. The following illustration shows some of the various Windows NT components that use the registry.

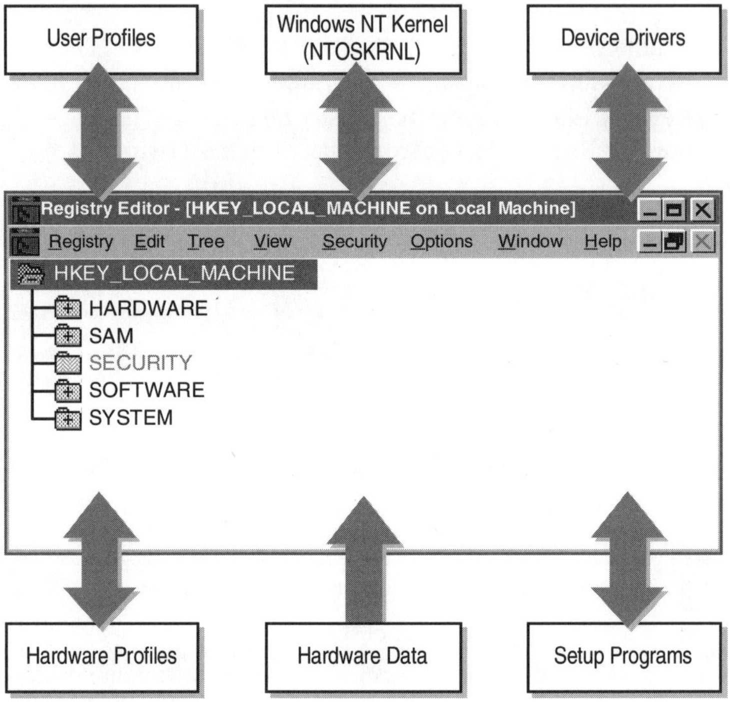

The following table specifies how applications and the Windows NT operating system components use the registry to store and retrieve information.

Component	Description
Hardware profiles	A list of the hardware devices and services to be enabled or disabled when you start Windows NT can be stored in the registry by creating a hardware profile. For example, if you are using a portable computer, you may want to enable particular devices and services, depending on whether your computer is docked or undocked. When you start your computer, you can choose the appropriate hardware profile and when Windows NT starts, it uses that profile.
User profiles	Configuration information is stored on a user-by-user basis in the registry. This information includes all of the per-user settings of the Windows NT environment, such as the desktop arrangement, personal program groups and the program items in those groups, screen saver settings, network connections, printer connections, mouse settings, window size and position, and more.
Windows NT kernel	During startup, the Windows NT kernel (Ntoskrnl.exe) reads information from the registry to determine which device drivers to load and the order that they should be loaded. The kernel also passes back information on itself, such as its version number.
Device drivers	Device drivers pass data to the registry, and also receive load and configuration parameters from the registry. A device driver tells the registry what system resources it is using, such as hardware interrupts or direct memory access (DMA) channels. Device drivers can also report discovered configuration data.
Setup programs	A Setup program can add new configuration data to the registry. It can also query the registry to determine if a component has already been installed, and whether to install a more recent version of the component.
Hardware data	Each time Windows NT is started, hardware and configuration data are collected and the registry is updated. On *x*86-based computers, this hardware detection is done through a program named Ntdetect.com. On RISC-based computers this information is extracted from the computer's firmware and then stored in the registry.

The Registry Structure

The registry is structured as a set of five databases called subtrees that contain per-computer and per-user databases. Access to information in the registry occurs through these subtrees.

The per-computer databases include information about hardware and software installed on the specific computer. The per-user databases include the information in *user profiles*, such as desktop settings, individual preferences for certain software, and personal printer and network settings.

The following table identifies and defines the five registry subtrees.

Subtree	Description
HKEY_LOCAL_MACHINE	Contains all configuration data about the local computer. This data is used by applications, device drivers, and the Windows NT operating system to set computer configuration. Part of the data is used to start Windows NT. Data in this subtree determines which device drivers and services to load during startup. The data in this subtree is constant, regardless of the user.
HKEY_USERS	Contains two subkeys: ▪ DEFAULT—Contains the system default settings (system default profile) used when the CTRL+ALT+DEL logon screen is displayed ▪ The security identifier (SID) of the user currently logged on the computer.
HKEY_CURRENT_USER	Contains data about the user currently logged on interactively. A copy is stored for each user account that has ever been logged on to the computer in the *systemroot*\Profiles*user_name* folder in a file named Ntuser.dat. This subkey points to the same data that can be accessed under HKEY_USERS*SID_of_the_currently_logged_on_user*. This subtree takes precedence over HKEY_LOCAL_MACHINE for duplicated data.
HKEY_CLASSES_ROOT	Contains information about file associations and data associated with COM objects, and points to the CLASSES subkey under HKEY_LOCAL_MACHINE\SOFTWARE.
HKEY_CURRENT_CONFIG	Contains data about the active hardware profile. This data is extracted from the SOFTWARE and SYSTEM keys of HKEY_LOCAL_MACHINE.

The Registry Hierarchy

The registry is organized in a hierarchical structure similar to the hierarchical structure of folders and files on a disk. The following illustration labels each component of the hierarchy.

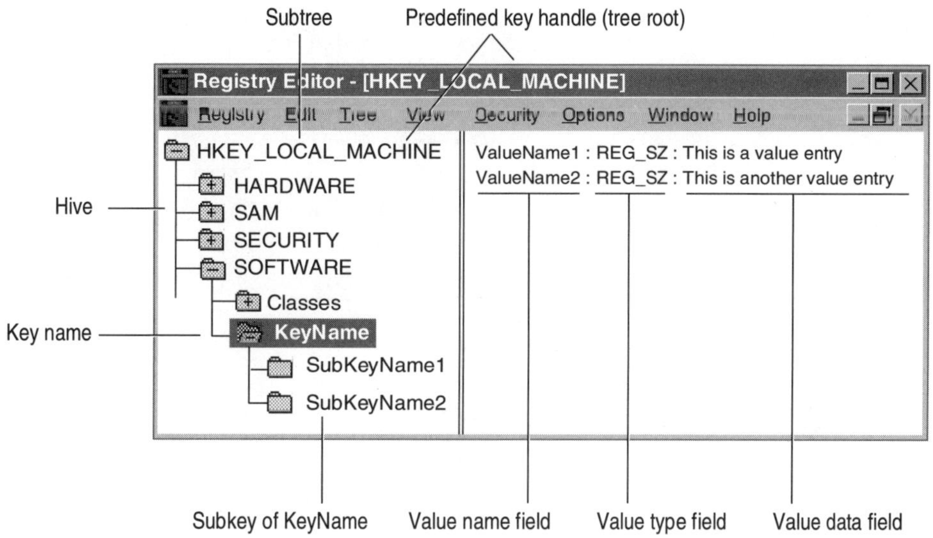

This section of the lesson describes the hierarchical organization of the registry and defines the overall structure of the *subtrees, hives,* and *value entries*. The following table identifies and describes each of the hierarchical components of the registry.

Hierarchical component	Description
Subtree	A subtree (or subtree key) is analogous to the root folder of a disk. The registry contains the following five predefined subtrees: HKEY_LOCAL_MACHINE HKEY_USERS HKEY_CURRENT_USER HKEY_CLASSES_ROOT HKEY_CURRENT_CONFIG

(continued)

Hierarchical component	Description
Hive	A hive is a discrete body of keys, subkeys, and values. Each hive has a corresponding registry file and .log file. By default, most hives, such as Default, SAM, Security, and System, and the corresponding hive files are located in *systemroot*\System32\Config folder. The .log file is used to record changes to the registry and to ensure the integrity of the registry.
Keys and subkeys	Keys and subkeys are analogous to folders and subfolders. Each hive can contain keys and subkeys, just as a folder can have subfolders.
Values	Values are analogous to files because they come at the end of the hierarchy. Keys and subkeys can contain one or more values. A value entry has three parts—the name, data type, and value itself (or configuration parameter).
Value Data Types	REG_DWORD. Only one value is allowed, and it must be a string of 1–8 hexadecimal digits. **REG_SZ**. Only one value is allowed, and it is interpreted as the string to be stored. **REG_EXPAND_SZ**. This is similar to **REG_SZ**, except that the text can contain a replaceable variable. For example, in the string %Systemroot%\Ntvdm.exe, %Systemroot% would be replaced with the path to the Windows NT System32 folder. **REG_BINARY**. Only one value is allowed, and it is a string of hexadecimal digits, each pair of which is interpreted as a byte value. **REG_MULTI_SZ**. Multiple values are allowed; each value is a string and is interpreted as a component of the **MULTI_SZ**. Entries are separated by a null character.

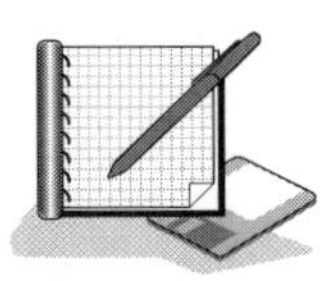

Practice

In this procedure, you explore the HKEY_LOCAL_MACHINE subtree to familiarize yourself with the registry hierarchy.

Note Complete this procedure on Server1.

▸ To explore the HKEY_LOCAL_MACHINE

1. Maximize Registry Editor.
2. On the **View** menu, verify that **Tree and Data** is selected.
3. Click the HKEY_LOCAL_MACHINE window, and maximize the window.

   Notice that the HKEY_LOCAL_MACHINE subtree has five subkeys—HARDWARE, SAM, SECURITY, SOFTWARE, and SYSTEM.

4. Double-click **HARDWARE** to expand the HARDWARE key.
5. Double-click **DESCRIPTION** to expand the DESCRIPTION key, and then double-click the **System** key.

   Notice the value names, value types, and value listed in the right window.

   For example: **Identifier : REG_SZ : AT/AT COMPATIBLE**

   Identifier is the value name; **REG_SZ** is the value type; and **AT/AT COMPATIBLE** is the value.
6. Explore a few of the other subkeys to see the information they contain.
7. When you are done exploring, close Registry Editor.

Subkeys of HKEY_LOCAL_MACHINE

The HKEY_LOCAL_MACHINE subtree has five subkeys: HARDWARE, SAM, SECURITY, SOFTWARE, and SYSTEM. The SECURITY, SAM, SOFTWARE, and SYSTEM subkeys are all considered *hives* because they have corresponding files located in the *systemroot*\System32\Config folder.

The subkeys in HKEY_LOCAL_MACHINE are described in the following table.

Subkey	Description
HARDWARE	The HARDWARE subkey is volatile. It is constructed from information gathered each time the computer is started. This key contains information that an application can query to determine the type and state of physical devices attached to the local computer. The HARDWARE subkey does not map to a file on the hard disk because the parameter values are volatile, meaning that they are not saved, but built each time the computer is started. The information under HKEY_LOCAL_MACHINE\HARDWARE can be used to determine the following information: ▪ The appropriate driver to install for a piece of hardware. This is done by starting Windows NT and then seeing what hardware device was detected. ▪ Whether a device driver is failing to load because the hardware is no longer being detected. It is possible that there has been a hardware failure or conflict with a new piece of hardware that was installed.

(***continued***)

Subkey	Description
SAM	The SAM (Security Accounts Manager) database hive contains the directory database for the computer. If the computer is a domain controller, the SAM database hive contains the master directory database. The SAM hive maps to the SAM and Sam.log files in the *systemroot*\System32\Config folder. This hive is a pointer to the same data that can be accessed under HKEY_LOCAL_MACHINE\SECURITY\SAM. Data in the SAM or SECURITY keys *cannot* be viewed unless the permissions on the keys are changed. *By default, this data cannot be viewed.* Be careful if you make changes to the permissions on these keys, or you may render your operating system unusable.
SECURITY	The SECURITY database hive contains all of the security information for the local computer. By default, none of the keys contained in SECURITY can be modified by an application. The SECURITY hive maps to the Security and Security.log files in the *systemroot*\System32\Config folder.
SOFTWARE	The SOFTWARE database hive contains information about the software on the local computer that is independent of per-user configuration information. Examples include the manufacturer and version number of software. This hive maps to the Software and Software.log files in the *systemroot*\System32\Config folder and also contains file associations and OLE information.
SYSTEM	The SYSTEM hive contains information about the devices and services on the system. When device drivers or services are installed or configured, they add or modify information under this hive. The SYSTEM hive maps to the System and System.log files in the *systemroot*\System32\Config folder. A backup of the data in the SYSTEM hive is kept in the System.alt file.

Lesson 2: Modifying Settings Using Control Panel

Lesson 1 presented a foundation for understanding where and how Windows NT system changes take place. Many of the settings contained in the registry are configured using the programs in Control Panel.

Users can manage their own environments through programs in Control Panel. For example, each user that can log on to a computer running Windows NT can use the Display program to select a screen saver. These types of settings are called per-user settings, and they are stored in the registry in the Control Panel key under HKEY_CURRENT_USER.

Other Control Panel programs are used to configure computer settings, such as using the Network program to add or configure network adapter cards. These computer settings are stored in the registry in the HKEY_LOCAL_MACHINE subtree, and are in effect regardless of the user that has logged on to the computer. Only administrators can configure these types of system settings.

This lesson identifies the Control Panel programs that are used to modify per-user and computer settings.

After this lesson, you will be able to:

- Identify user and computer programs in Control Panel.
- Configure a user's local profile.
- Configure serial (COM) ports.
- Configure the display.
- Configure SCSI adapters and tape devices.
- Configure an uninterruptible power supply (UPS).
- Configure PC Card devices.

Estimated lesson time: 90 minutes

System Configuration Overview

The following illustration shows the default Windows NT Server Control Panel programs.

Note The same default Control Panel programs are installed with Windows NT Workstation, with the exception of the Licensing program; a Client Access License is not required to access Windows NT Workstation.

As you review this lesson, review the Control Panel programs that are covered in this lesson.

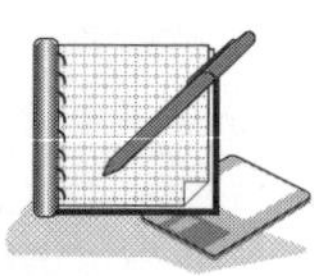

Practice

In this procedure, you start Control Panel.

Note Complete this procedure on Server1.

▸ **To start Control Panel**

1. Log on as Administrator.
2. Click the **Start** button, point to **Settings**, and then click **Control Panel**.

Modifying Per-User Settings

Several Control Panel programs control configuration settings on a per-user basis. The following table describes each Control Panel program that effects user settings.

Program	Description
Accessibility Options	Configures the keyboard, sound, display, and mouse behavior for users with visual, hearing, or mobility impairments.
Console	Configures the display, features, and functionality of the MS-DOS console.
Display	Changes the look of a user's computer desktop, including the wallpaper and screen saver.
Keyboard	Specifies the keyboard repeat rate and delay.
Mouse	Changes mouse settings such as tracking speed, double-click sensitivity, and determining the active mouse button.
Regional Settings	Specifies regional or international settings such as country and language.
Sounds	Assigns sounds to system events.

Changes made through the previous Control Panel programs are saved to the logged-on user's *local profile*. Each user can thus configure the desktop according to individual preferences. Each time a user logs on, the user environment is configured according to the last saved settings in their user profile.

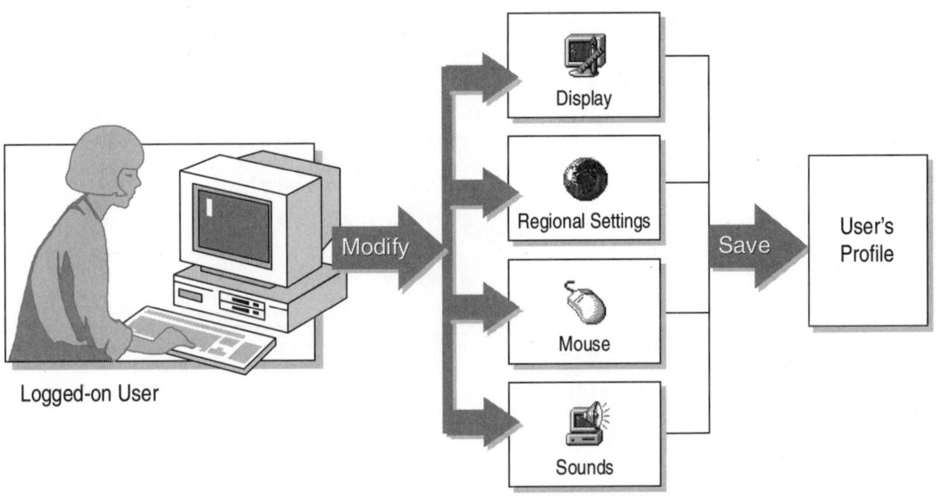

Managing User Profiles

When a user logs on for the first time from a client computer running Windows NT, the system checks to see if a user profile exists for that user. If there is not an existing user profile, the system makes a copy of the default user profile which becomes the user profile for that user. The user profile defines such things as the appearance of a user's desktop environment, and the user's network and printer connections. The user profile ensures that multiple users sharing the same computer can maintain separate desktop environments. When the user logs off, any changes that have been made to the user profile are saved.

Note For more information on configuring user profiles, see Microsoft Windows NT Server *Concepts and Planning*.

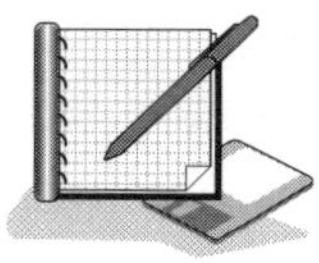

Practice

In these procedures, you log on to Server1 and create a new user, User1, in Domain1. You grant the Everyone group the right to log on locally at Server1. You then log on as User1 and change your Display background. When you log back on as User1, you verify that the changes are retained.

Note Complete these procedures on Server1.

▸ To create a new user

In this procedure, you create a new user on Domain1. This user is used to test user profiles later in this practice.

1. Click the **Start** button, point to **Programs**, point to **Administrative Tools (Common)**, and then click **User Manager for Domains**.
2. On the **User** menu, click **New User**.
3. Use the following information to complete the fields in the **New User** dialog box.

In this box	Do this action
Username	Type **user1**
Password	Type **password**
Confirm Password	Type **password**
User Must Change Password at Next Logon	Clear this check box

4. Click **Add**.
5. Click **Close**.

► To allow the Everyone group to log on locally

In this procedure, you allow the Everyone group to log on locally.

1. In the **User Manager for Domains** dialog box, on the **Policies** menu, click **User Rights**.
2. In the **Right** drop-down list box, click **Log on Locally**.
3. Click **Add**.
4. In the **Names** box, click **Everyone**, and then click **Add**.

   The group Everyone now appears on the **Add Names** box.
5. Click **OK**.

   The group Everyone now appears on the **Grant To** box.
6. Click **OK**, and then close **User Manager for Domains**.

► To change a user's profile

In this procedure, you log on as User1, change your desktop configuration, and then log off. You log back on to verify that your changes were retained.

1. Log off, and then log on as User1.
2. Start Registry Editor (Regedt32.exe), and then on the **Options** menu, select **Read Only Mode**.
3. Expand the HKEY_CURRENT_USER\Control Panel\Desktop key.

   What is the value of the **Pattern** field?

   ____
4. Close Registry Editor.
5. Click the **Start** button, point to **Settings**, and then click **Control Panel**.
6. Double-click **Display**.
7. In the **Pattern** box, select a pattern that is not your current pattern, and then click **OK**.

   Notice that the pattern of your display is the one you just selected.
8. Log off, and then log on as User1.

   Notice that the pattern of your display was saved.

9. Start Registry Editor, and then expand the HKEY_CURRENT_USER\Control Panel\Desktop key.

   What is the value of the **Pattern** field?

   ____

10. Close Registry Editor.
11. Log off, and then log on as Administrator.

Modifying Computer Settings

Other Control Panel programs allow you to control per-computer configurations. These configuration settings are used regardless of which user is logged on to the computer running Windows NT.

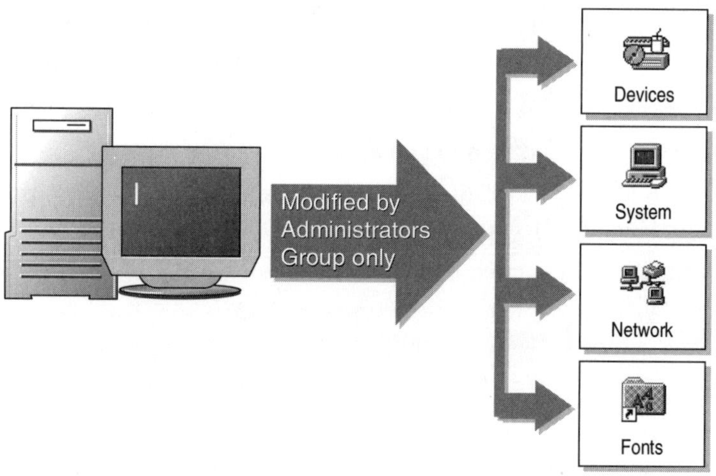

You must be a member of the Administrators group to modify most hardware configuration options. If you are not an administrator, a message appears stating that you do not have administrative permission to change settings or that access is denied. The following table describes the Control Panel programs that are used to configure the hardware on the computer.

Control Panel programs	Description
Date/Time	Changes the date, time, and time zone of your computer's clock. The Time Zone feature allows a correct international time zone to be selected for each computer. Each user thus views time stamps for his or her own time zone. For example, a file saved in New York (US Eastern time) at 6:00 PM shows a 3:00 PM time to a user in Seattle (US Pacific time).
Devices	Starts and stops device drivers, and configures the startup type for each device driver.
Display	Installs and configures the display drivers.
Fonts	Adds and removes fonts, and sets TrueType options.
Internet	Configures settings for Microsoft Internet Explorer.
Multimedia	Installs and removes multimedia device drivers.
Network	Installs and removes network adapter cards, protocols, and software, and configures network bindings.
Ports	Specifies the communications settings for the serial (COM) port(s).
Printers	Installs and removes printers, and sets printer options.
SCSI Adapters	Displays installed SCSI adapters and drivers, adds and removes SCSI adapter drivers.
Server	Displays who is connected to the computer's shared resources. Also controls replication and files that are open.
Services	Configures, starts, pauses, and stops services such as the Computer Browser and Net Logon services. A service can continue to be active even after you log off the computer.
System	Controls the computer's startup settings, such as virtual memory, environment variables, tasking, hardware profiles, and the Boot Loader Operating System Selection menu on Intel *x*86-based computers. This menu shows the operating systems installed on a computer and lets you choose which operating system to load for a session.
Tape Devices	Displays installed tape backup devices and drivers.
UPS	Installs and configures an uninterruptible power supply (UPS).

Configuring COM Ports

The Ports program in Control Panel is used to specify the communication settings for a selected serial (COM) port. Only administrators can configure the I/O port address and the IRQ options in the **Advanced Settings on COM*x*** dialog box.

The following table describes the purpose of each option in the **Ports** dialog box.

Option	Description
Settings	Configures port settings, such as baud rate and flow control.
Add	Adds COM ports, up to port 256.
Delete	Deletes the selected port.

The **Ports** dialog box lists only COM ports that are *not in use* by the computer. For example, if a serial mouse is attached to COM1, that port does not appear in the Ports program in Control Panel. The following illustration shows the screens used to configure COM ports. In this specific example, the **Ports** dialog box shows that COM2 is not in use.

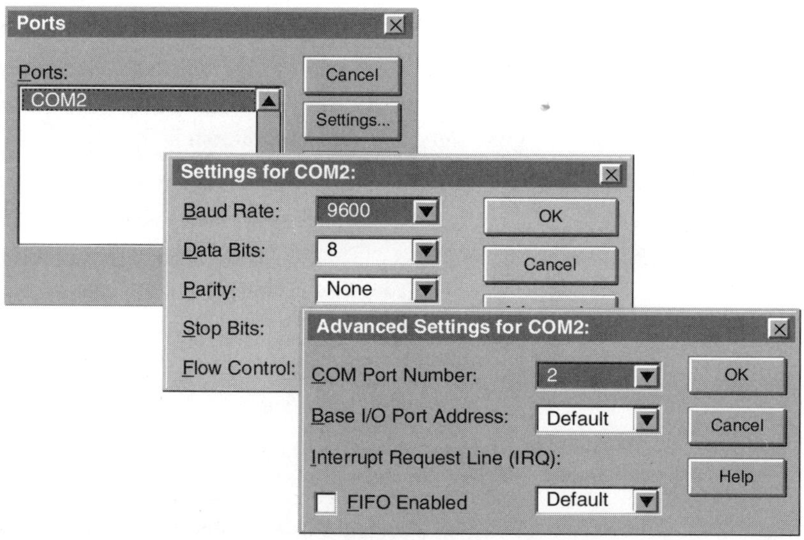

If all COM ports were listed, then none of the COM ports would be in use. Because COM1 is not listed, you know it is in use. If you want to determine which device is using COM1, locate the SerialController key. You can find it by using Registry Editor to view the following key:

HKEY_LOCAL_MACHINE\HARDWARE\Description\System

Below this key, depending on the hardware devices in your computer, you would then look at either the MultifunctionAdapter or EisaAdapter, and then continue to look through their subkeys (0, 1, or 2, depending on your computer) until you find the SerialController key.

Under the SerialController key are subkeys for each port, with 0 for COM1, 1 for COM2, and so on. If you want to determine what is attached to COM1, look at the value 0. For example, if there were a mouse attached to COM1, there would be a PointerPeripheral subkey.

Configuring the Display

The Display program in Control Panel is used to configure user settings such as the background display, screen saver, and the number of colors. It can also be used to configure computer settings, such as video resolution, font sizes, and refresh frequency.

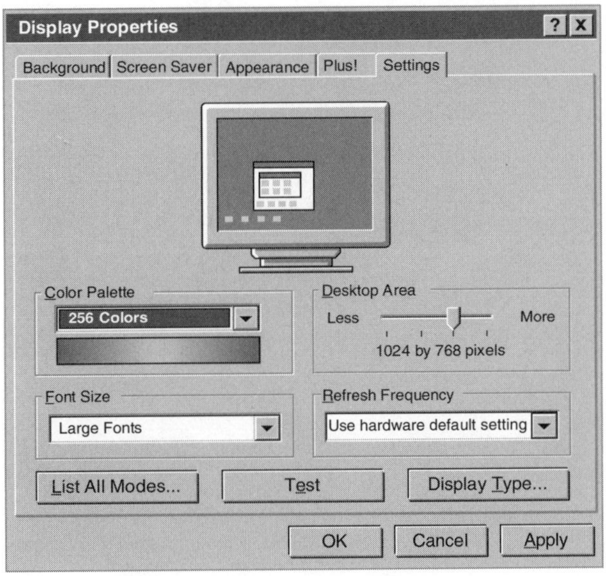

Display Options

The following table describes the options in the **Settings** tab in the **Display Properties** dialog box. Any changes made to these settings affect all users of this computer.

Option	Use to
Color Palette	List color options for the display adapter.
Desktop Area	Configure the screen area used by the display. The larger the desktop area, the smaller the objects will appear on the screen.
Font Size	Change the font size to small or large.
Refresh Frequency	Configure the frequency of the screen refresh rate for high-resolution drivers only. The higher the refresh rate, the less flicker there is on the screen. Do not select a refresh rate that is not supported by the monitor at the selected resolution. If you are unsure what refresh rates your monitor supports, select the lowest refresh rate option.
List All Modes button	Configure color, desktop, and refresh frequency all at once.
Test button	Test screen choices. The Test option works only when old and new drivers do not conflict. For example, if the VGA driver is installed, the SVGA driver cannot be tested because it conflicts with the VGA video driver.
Display Type button	Display information about the display device driver and allows installation of a new driver. Only users with the user right "Load and unload device drivers" can change and test video device drivers. By default, only the Administrators group has this user right.

Configuring SCSI Adapters and Tape Devices

The SCSI Adapters and Tape Devices Control Panel programs are used to install and start the appropriate drivers for each of these devices.

Both utilities have these two tabs:

- Devices
- Drivers

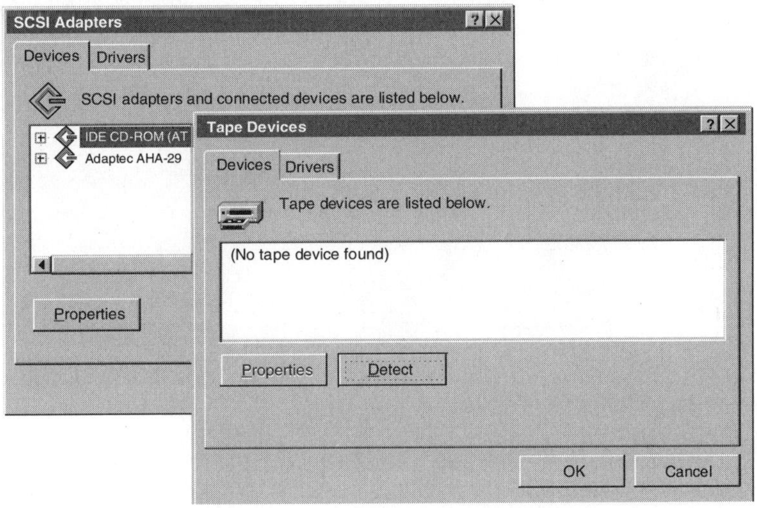

When adding SCSI adapter drivers, the computer must be restarted for the SCSI adapter driver to start.

Windows NT automatically detects tape devices when the **Detect** button on the **Devices** tab in the **Tape Devices** dialog box is clicked. To find tape device information such as SCSI ID number, firmware information, and SCSI host adapter, click the **Properties** button on the **Devices** tab in the **Tape Devices** dialog box. The computer does not need to be restarted for the tape device driver to start.

Configuring a UPS

An *uninterruptible power supply* (UPS) provides uninterrupted power if the main power source fails. The UPS is usually rated to provide power for a specific time period. Power for the UPS comes from batteries that are continuously charged while the main power source is available.

UPS settings are controlled through the UPS program in Control Panel. The following illustration shows the **UPS** dialog box.

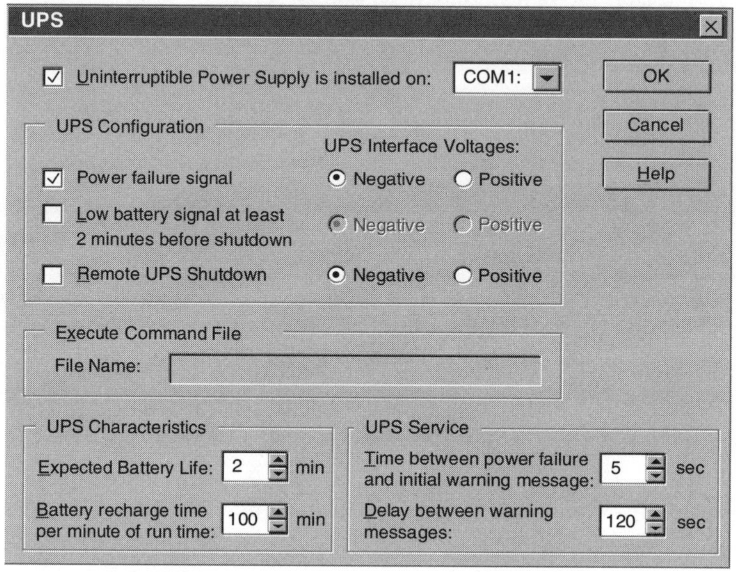

UPS Operation

During a power failure, the UPS service for Windows NT communicates with the UPS to keep the system running until one of the following events occurs:

- Power is restored.
- The system is shut down, either by the administrator or the UPS service.
- The UPS signals that its batteries are low.

The UPS service immediately pauses the Server service during a power failure, so that users do not establish new connections with a failing computer. The UPS service then notifies users of the impending shutdown and advises them to terminate their sessions with the failing server. When signaled to shut down, the UPS service performs a safe system shutdown. If power is restored before the shutdown starts, a message tells users that power is restored and normal operations have resumed.

Note The UPS communicates with the service through a standard RS-232 serial port. However, the cable used between the UPS and the serial port does not use standard pinouts; a special UPS cable is required for the UPS to be able to communicate with the computer. Check the HCL for supported UPSs and their cable part numbers.

Important Be sure to test the UPS service after it has been configured, particularly on Intel *x*86-based computers. During startup, Ntdetect.com sends a detection signal to the serial ports to detect the attached hardware. Some UPS units switch off in response to this signal. If testing the newly configured UPS shows that it shuts off in this way, add the **/NoSerialMice** switch in the Boot.ini file to prevent the detection signal from being sent to the serial port. For more information, see Chapter 3, "Disk Management Basics," in the *Resource Guide* of the *Microsoft Windows NT Server Resource Kit.*

The following table describes the options available in the **UPS** dialog box.

Select this check box	If	Corresponds to
Power failure signal	The UPS device can send a message when the power supply fails.	Clear to send (CTS) cable signal for the UPS serial port connection.
Low battery signal at least 2 minutes before shutdown	The UPS device can send a warning when battery power is low.	Data carrier detect (DCD) cable signal for the UPS serial port connection.
Remote UPS Shutdown	The UPS device can accept a signal from the UPS service to shut down.	Data terminal ready (DTR) cable signal for the UPS serial port connection.

Note For the previous options, the UPS Interface Voltages can be set to either Negative or Positive. The default is Negative. Refer to the UPS manufacturer's instructions for the correct settings.

Select this check box	To	Use these parameters
Execute Command File	Execute a command file immediately before shutdown.	The command file can be any file with a .cmd, .bat, .com, or .exe extension, and has 30 seconds to complete its task.

Use this option	To adjust	Use these parameters
Expected Battery Life	The time, in minutes, that the system can run on battery power.	Range: 2–720 minutes. Default: 2 minutes.

Caution Be sure to enter the number of minutes in the **Expected Battery Life** box when **Power failure signal** is selected but **Low battery signal** is not. Also enter an appropriate number of minutes in the **Battery recharge time per minute of run time** box.

(continued)

Use this option	To adjust	Use these parameters
Battery recharge time per minute of run time	The amount of time to recharge the battery, typed as the number of minutes of recharge time per minute of battery run time.	Range: 1–250 minutes. Default: 100 minutes.
Time between power failure and initial warning message	The time between a power failure and the first message sent to notify users of the failure.	Range: 0–120 seconds. Default: 5 seconds.
Delay between warning messages	The interval between power failure messages sent to users notifying them that the system may shut down.	Range: 5–300 seconds. Default: 120 seconds.

Configuring PC Card Devices

The PC Card (PCMCIA) program in Control Panel is used to configure PC card devices. The program shows which PC card devices are installed, in which sockets they are installed, how they are configured, and which resources the PC Card controller is using.

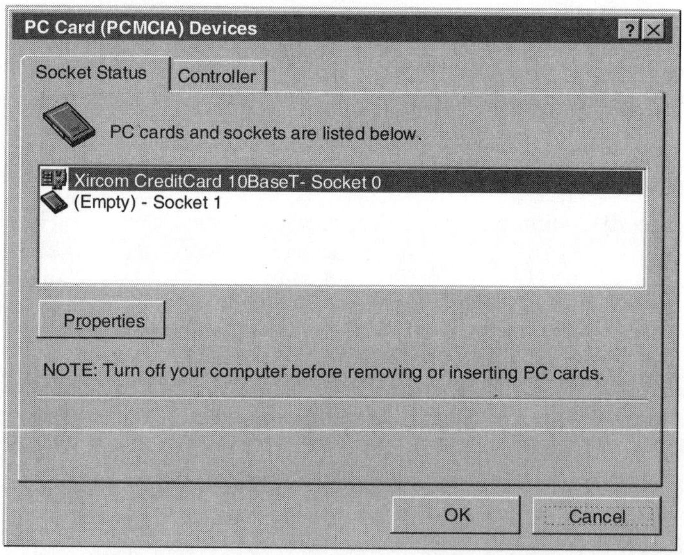

Note Turn the computer off before adding or removing a PC card. When the system restarts, Windows NT recognizes the change in hardware. For many PC card devices, PC Card in Control Panel suggests the correct device driver.

Lesson 3: Modifying System Settings Using Control Panel

This lesson introduces some of the Control Panel programs that are used to configure the operating system and other software on a computer running Windows NT.

After this lesson, you will be able to:

- Use System in Control Panel to change startup and shutdown settings.
- Use System in Control Panel to configure a hardware profile.
- Use System in Control Panel to configure virtual memory.
- Use System in Control Panel to set environment variables.
- Use Add/Remove Programs in Control Panel to customize a Windows NT installation.

Estimated lesson time: 90 minutes

Changing Startup and Shutdown Settings

You can change startup and shutdown settings for a computer running Windows NT by using the System program in Control Panel. These options are configured on the **Startup/Shutdown** tab as shown in the following illustration. There are two groups of information on the tab: **System Startup** and **Recovery**.

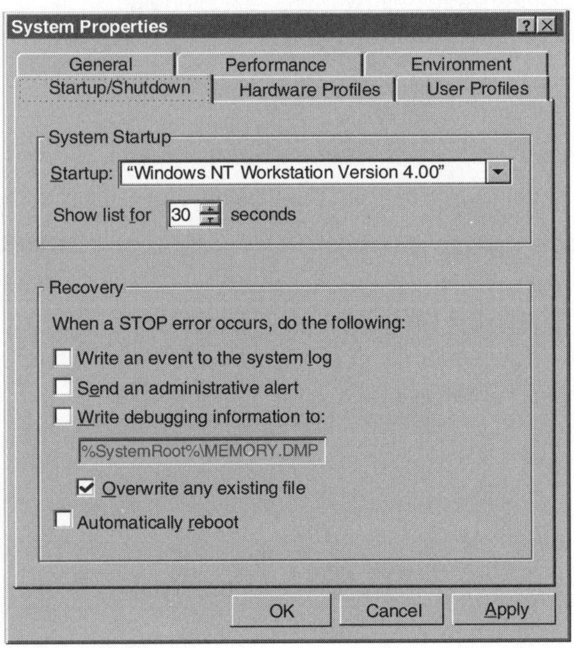

System Startup

If a computer has several operating systems installed, they are displayed when the computer is turned on so that the user can determine which operating system to run. You can configure the order in which the operating systems are displayed, and the number of seconds to pause on this display so that a user can choose which operating system to use. You can specify the default operating system in the **Startup** box and set the number of seconds to wait before the default operating system starts automatically in the **Show list for** box. If the user does not make a selection, then the default operating system initializes when the time set in the **Show list for** box expires.

Note The default setting in the **Startup** box is the last operating system installed. The default setting in the **Show list for** box is 30 seconds. If you do not want users to be able to choose which operating system to run, set the time in the **Show list for** box to 0 seconds.

Recovery

Under **Recovery** there are options to configure Windows NT for specified tasks if a STOP error (Fatal System error) occurs. When a STOP error occurs, Windows NT stops all processes and requires that the computer is restarted. The **Recovery** section includes these options:

- Write an event to the system log.
- Send an administrative alert to the users and computers specified in the **Alerts** dialog box of the Server program in Control Panel.
- Write debugging information to a specified file name. Use of this option requires the following:
  - The paging file must be on the boot partition.
  - The paging file must be at least as big as physical RAM.
  - You must have the necessary disk space for the specified file.

  If you want to overwrite an existing file select the **Overwrite any existing file** check box.
- Automatically reboot. Do this *only* when the **Write debugging information to** check box has been selected.

Note As a best practice, you should *always* select the **Write debugging information to** check box and enter a path and file for this information. The information in this file provides important information that can help Microsoft Technical Support solve reported problems.

Practice

In this procedure, you set the boot delay by changing the number of seconds of delay before the default operating system is loaded.

Note Complete this procedure on Server1.

► **To set the boot delay**

1. Shut down and restart Windows NT Server to observe the number of seconds before Windows NT Server automatically loads.
2. Log on as Administrator.
3. Double-click the System icon in Control Panel.
4. Click the **Startup/Shutdown** tab.
5. In the **Show list for** box, set the number of seconds to **10**, and then click **OK**.
6. Shut down and then restart Windows NT Server to see the results of your boot delay setting.

Practice

In this procedure, you set your default operating system as Windows NT Workstation on the computer that dual-boots as Workstation1 and Server2.

Note Complete this procedure on Server2.

► **To change the default operating system**

1. Log on as Administrator.
2. Double-click the System icon in Control Panel.
3. Click the **Startup/Shutdown** tab.
4. In the **Startup** box, click **Windows NT Workstation Version 4.0**, and then click **OK**.
5. Shut down and then restart your computer to see the results.
6. Start your computer as Workstation1.

Configuring Hardware Profiles

A hardware profile stores the configuration for a set of devices and services. Windows NT can store different hardware profiles to meet a user's needs. For example, a portable computer may use different hardware configurations than a desktop computer, depending on whether the portable computer is docked or undocked. A portable computer user could create a hardware profile for each state (docked and undocked), and choose the appropriate profile when starting the operating system. Hardware profiles are created by starting the System program in Control Panel and clicking the **Hardware Profiles** tab as shown in the following illustration.

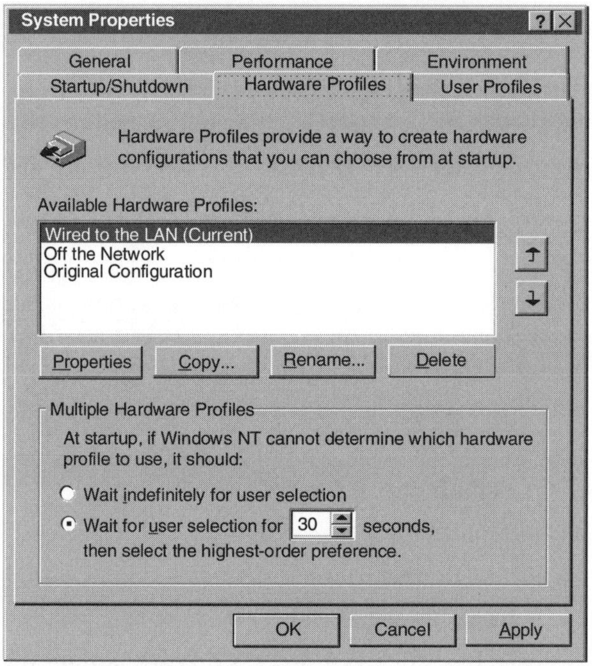

Creating and Modifying Hardware Profiles

You create a hardware profile by copying and then modifying the default hardware profile that is created when Windows NT is installed. The default hardware profile appears as **Original Configuration (Current)** in the **Available Hardware Profiles** list. Once you create a hardware profile, it is added to the **Available Hardware Profiles** list. To configure a specific device or service for a hardware profile, use the Devices and Services programs in Control Panel. Each of these programs contains a **Hardware Profiles** button that allows you to assign the configuration to a specific hardware profile.

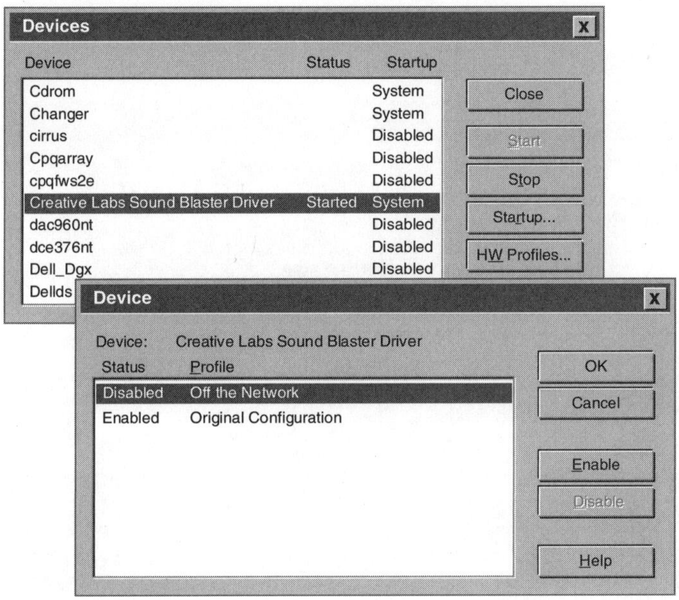

Note As a best practice, make a copy of the default hardware profile and use the copy as your hardware profile. That way, if you make a change or revision to the copy that prevents the system from starting, then you can always start the system with the original default hardware profile. For example, when you modify hardware profiles, be careful not to disable one of the boot devices. If a required boot device is disabled, Windows NT may not start.

Configuring for Multiple Hardware Profiles

When your computer is configured with multiple hardware profiles, you can specify which profile is the default, and how long to wait before automatically starting the default profile.

The first profile in the list is the default profile. To change the order of the profiles, you can use the arrow buttons on the **Hardware Profiles** tab to move the profiles up or down in the list.

To configure the computer to pause for a number of seconds before loading the first hardware profile, click **Wait for user selection for** and enter a number of seconds. The default profile can be configured to start automatically by setting the number of seconds in the **Wait for user selection for** option to 0.

Loading a Hardware Profile

The order in which hardware profiles appear in the **Available Hardware Profiles** list also determines how the profiles appear at startup and which one is loaded. If more than one profile is in the **Available Hardware Profiles** list, Windows NT prompts you to choose a hardware profile during startup. The following illustration shows a computer with two hardware profiles and how those profiles appear when Windows NT is started.

```
  Hardware Profile/Configuration Recovery Menu

This menu allows you to select a hardware profile
to be used when Windows NT is started.

If your system is not starting correctly, then you may switch to a previous
system configuration, which may overcome startup problems.
IMPORTANT: System configuration changes made since the last successful
startup will be discarded.
  Original Configuration
  Off the Network

Use the up and down arrow keys to move the highlight
to the selection you want. Then press ENTER.
To switch to the Last Known Good configuration, press 'L'.
To Exit this menu and restart your computer, press F3.

Seconds until highlighted choice will be started automatically: 30
```

To load a hardware profile, you can select the profile when this screen appears. If you do not select a profile, then the first one in the list is loaded.

Configuring a Network-Disabled Profile

For computers that are not always attached to the network, you can configure a hardware profile to disable all networking devices and services. A user could then choose this profile when using a computer when it is not attached to the network. To configure a network-disabled profile, use the System program to copy an existing profile. In the **Properties** dialog box for the copied profile, click the **Network** tab and then click **Network-disabled hardware profile**.

For example, you can create a network-disabled hardware profile for your laptop computer. When not connected to the network, having a network-disabled hardware profile for the laptop can decrease your startup time and prevent startup error messages such as "One or more services failed to start." This error message occurs when starting a computer running Windows NT that is configured to start networking devices and services, but is not attached to a network.

Practice

In these procedures, you create a network-disabled hardware profile for Workstation1. You then test the profile, verifying that the networking functions have been disabled. Finally, you delete the network-disabled hardware profile.

Note Complete this procedure on Workstation1. Server1 must be online.

▸ To create a network-disabled hardware profile

In this procedure, you use the System program to create a network-disabled hardware profile for Workstation1.

1. Log on to Domain1 as Administrator.
2. Double-click the System icon in Control Panel.
3. Click the **Hardware Profiles** tab.
4. Click **Rename**.

   The **Rename Profile** dialog box appears.
5. In the **To** box, type **On the Network** and then click **OK**.
6. Click **Copy**.

   The **Copy Profile** dialog box appears.
7. In the **To** box, type **Off the Network** and then click **OK**.
8. In the **Available Hardware Profiles** box, click **Off the Network**, and then click **Properties**.
9. Click the **Network** tab.
10. Select the **Network-disabled hardware profile** check box, and then click **OK**.
11. Under **Multiple Hardware Profiles**, in the **Wait for user selection for** box, change the value to 10 seconds.
12. Click **OK**.

▸ To choose a hardware profile at system startup

In this procedure, you test your Off the Network hardware profile.

1. Shut down and then restart Workstation1.
2. On the **Hardware Profile/Configuration Recovery** menu, select **Off the Network**, and then press ENTER.
3. Log on to Domain1 as Administrator.

   What message appears?

   ___

   ___

   ___

   ___

   Why does this message appear?

   ___

   ___

   ___

   ___

4. Click **OK**.
5. Shut down and then restart Workstation1, using the On the Network profile.

▸ To delete a hardware profile

In this procedure, you delete the Off the Network hardware profile that you created.

1. Log on to Domain1 as Administrator.
2. Double-click the System icon in Control Panel.
3. Click the **Hardware Profiles** tab.
4. Under **Available Hardware Profiles**, click **Off the Network**, and then click **Delete**.
5. Click **Yes** to confirm that you want to delete the profile.
6. Click **OK** to close System.

Common Support Issue

When trying to determine why a user cannot connect to the network, remember to first check the hardware profile a user has loaded to make sure that it is *not* configured as a network-disabled profile. The reason you should check the profile is because the Services program in Control Panel and the **net start** command at a command prompt show all network services as started, even when a network-disabled profile is loaded.

Configuring Virtual Memory

Windows NT uses a process called *demand paging* to swap data between RAM and one or more paging files located on one or more hard drives. When Windows NT is installed, Setup creates a virtual-memory paging file, Pagefile.sys, on the partition with the most free disk space.

Paging File Size

The following list specifies the default size of the paging file for Windows NT.

- *Windows NT Server.* The default paging file size is the amount of physical RAM or, if you have less than 22 MB of RAM, the default paging file size is 22 MB or the amount of available disk space, whichever is smaller.
- *Windows NT Workstation.* The paging file size is equal to the total amount of RAM plus 12 MB, or the amount of available disk space, whichever is smaller. The minimum size is 2 MB. A typical paging file is 24 MB or larger.

Often, the size of the paging file can stay at the default value assigned during installation. In some circumstances, such as a large number of applications running simultaneously, a larger paging file or multiple paging files may be advantageous.

Configuring the Paging File

The paging file is configured by clicking the **Change** button on the **Performance** tab of the System program in Control Panel. The **Virtual Memory** dialog box appears, from which virtual memory parameters can be edited. The following illustration shows the **Virtual Memory** dialog box.

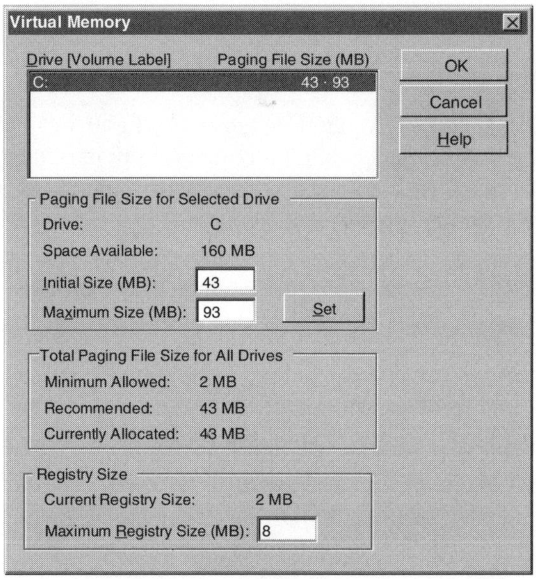

The **Virtual Memory** dialog box shows the drives on which the paging files reside, and has fields for adjusting the following parameters:

- Paging file size for the selected drive.
- Maximum registry size.

To move the paging file to another partition, or to create a paging file on each hard disk, use the **Virtual Memory** dialog box.

After a paging file is created, it does not shrink below its initial size. Unused space in the paging file is always available to the internal Windows NT Virtual Memory Manager. If the initial paging file is sized significantly below the recommended size, then when you log on, Windows NT displays a Limited Virtual Memory message. You are then prompted to use the System program in Control Panel to create a paging file or increase the initial paging file size. Only an administrator can log on and use the System program to correct this problem.

As needed, a paging file grows from its initial size to the maximum size configured. Once the maximum paging file size is reached, system performance may degrade if additional applications, requiring more virtual memory, are started or continue to run.

When a computer running Windows NT is restarted, all paging files are resized to the initial size specified.

Enhancing Performance

Several options are available to you to increase system performance. For example, if a system has multiple hard disks, consider creating a paging file for each disk. If the hard disk controller can read from and write to multiple hard disks simultaneously, the distribution of information across multiple paging files can significantly improve performance.

You may also be able to improve system performance by moving the paging file off the drive that contains the Windows NT *systemroot* folder. Placing the paging file on a drive that does not contain the boot partition avoids competition between various reading and writing requests. If the paging file is placed on the boot partition to facilitate the recovery feature, you can increase performance by creating multiple paging files that reside on other drives. Because the Virtual Memory Manager alternates write operations between paging files, the paging file on the boot partition is accessed less frequently.

Another way to increase system responsiveness is to set the initial size of the paging file to the optimal size required by the system. This eliminates the time required to enlarge the file.

Note When applying new settings, be sure to click the **Set** button before clicking **OK**.

Remember that changes made to virtual memory are not dynamic. They take effect only after the system restarts.

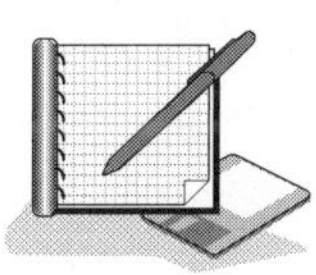

Practice

In this procedure, you use the System program to change the size of the Windows NT paging file on Server1.

Note Complete this procedure on Server1.

► **To change the paging file size**

1. Log on as Administrator.
2. Double-click the System icon in Control Panel.
3. In the **System Properties** dialog box, click the **Performance** tab.

4. Click the **Change** button.

   The **Virtual Memory** dialog box appears.
5. In the **Drive** box, click the drive that currently contains your paging file.
6. In the **Initial Size (MB)** box, increase the value by 10, and then click **Set**.

   If you do not click **Set**, the change does not occur.
7. Click **OK**, and then click **Close**.

   The **System Settings Change** dialog box appears.
8. Click **Yes** to shut down and then restart Windows NT Server.
9. After Windows NT Server restarts, log on as Administrator and confirm the new settings using the System program in Control Panel.

Setting Environment Variables

Environment variables are strings containing information such as a drive, path, or file name. Environment variables provide information that Windows NT requires to control the behavior of various applications. For example, the TEMP environment variable specifies the location where applications place temporary files.

In the **System Properties** dialog box in the System program in Control Panel, the **Environment** tab (as shown in the following illustration) allows administrators to change two types of environment variables:

- System environment variables
- User environment variables for *logged_on_user_name*

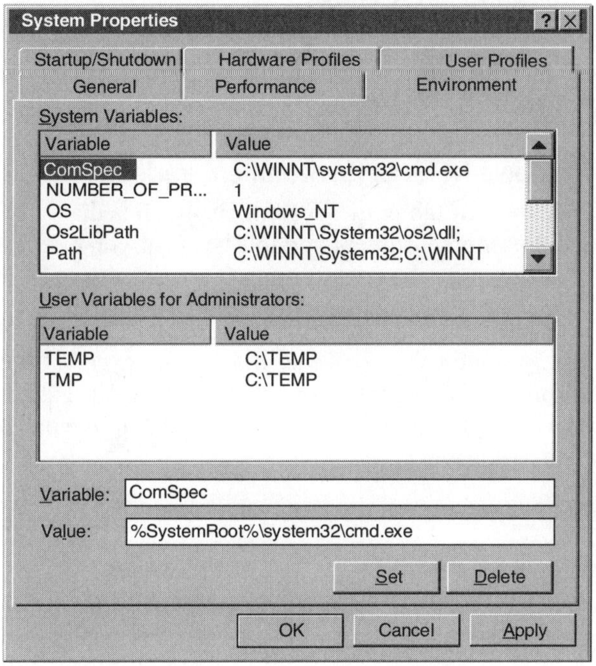

System Environment Variables

Administrators can change or add environment variables that apply to the system, and thus to all users of the system. These are called system environment variables. During installation, Windows NT Setup configures the default system variables, such as the path to the Windows NT files.

User Environment Variables

The user environment variables are different for each user of a particular computer. The variables include any that are set by the user, as well as any variables defined by applications, such as the path to the location of the application files.

How Windows NT Sets Environment Variables

The **Environment** tab in the **System Properties** dialog box displays all of the system and user environment variables currently in effect. Any user can add, modify, or remove a user environment variable, but only an administrator can add, modify, or remove a system environment variable.

By default, Windows NT searches the C:\Autoexec.bat file, if one exists, and sets any environment statements. For example, the PATH statement in the C:\Autoexec.bat file is automatically appended to the default system path every time any user logs on.

Windows NT sets environment variables in this order:

1. Autoexec.bat variables
2. System environment variables
3. User environment variables

For example, if the line "SET TMP=C:\" is placed in Autoexec.bat and a User variable "TMP=X:\TEMP" is set, the User variable setting overrides the prior setting. Therefore, the TMP environment variable is equal to X:\TEMP.

A registry entry can be set to prevent Windows NT from searching the C:\Autoexec.bat file. To enable this feature, an administrator can use Registry Editor to edit the following registry parameter and make the value ParseAutoexec: **REG_SZ = 0**.

\HKEY_CURRENT_USER\Software\Microsoft\
Windows NT\CurrentVersion\Winlogon\ParseAutoexec **REG_SZ = 0**

Optionally, System Policy Editor can be used to edit this registry parameter. Under the Local User hierarchy, choose **Windows NT System** and clear the **Parse Autoexec.bat** check box to prevent parsing of Autoexec.bat.

Note System Policy Editor is covered in Chapter 4, "Managing System Policies."

Adding and Removing Windows NT Components

An administrator can add or remove any of the Windows NT components that are not required by the system through Add/Remove Programs in Control Panel. The **Add/Remove Programs Properties** dialog box contains the following tabs:

- **Windows NT Setup**
- **Install/Uninstall**

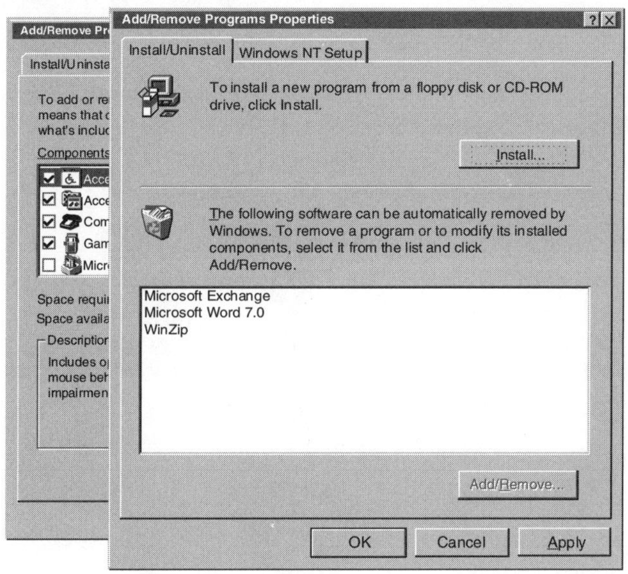

Windows NT Setup

Use the **Windows NT Setup** tab to add or remove Windows NT components. The **Windows NT Setup** tab displays the same list of optional components that is presented during installation. Adding more components or removing existing ones requires the original Windows NT 4.0 compact disc or shared installation files to be available. Restarting the computer may be required following the addition or removal of components, depending on the software that was added or removed.

Install/Uninstall

Use the **Install/Uninstall** tab to install new applications or to uninstall existing applications. Any application that uses Setup.exe or Install.exe to install itself can be both installed and uninstalled.

Clicking the **Install** button on the **Install/Uninstall** tab prompts Windows NT to scan first the floppy disk drives and then the CD-ROM drive for Setup.exe or Install.exe. Windows NT runs the first instance of a program named SETUP or INSTALL that it finds.

Applications that use the Install/Uninstall application programming interface (API) appear on the list of installed programs above the **Add/Remove** button. Clicking the **Add/Remove** button runs the original Setup program for the selected application. Additional components of that application, or the application itself, can then be added or removed, following the application's Setup program.

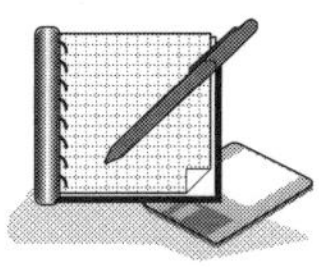

Practice

In this procedure, you use the Add/Remove Programs program to install the Windows NT games and wallpaper.

Note Complete this procedure on both Server1 and Workstation1.

► **To add additional Windows NT components**

1. Log on as Administrator.
2. Double-click the Add/Remove Programs icon in Control Panel.
3. Click the **Windows NT Setup** tab.
4. Select the **Games** check box.
5. Select the **Accessories** check box, and then click **Details**.
6. In the **Components** list, click **Desktop Wallpaper**, and then click **OK**.

7. Click **OK**.

   The **Insert Disk** dialog box appears.

8. Click **OK**.

   The **Files Needed** dialog box appears.

9. In the **Copy files from** box:

   On Server1, type **\\Server1\nts_source\I386** and then click **OK**.

   On Workstation1, insert the *Microsoft Windows NT Workstation 4.0* compact disc, type *cd-rom drive letter*:**\I386** and then click **OK**.

   The files are installed.

10. Check the contents of your Accessories folder to confirm that the games have been installed.

11. Using the Display program in Control Panel, click the **Background** tab to confirm that the wallpapers have been installed.

Lesson 4: Modifying System Settings Using Registry Editor

Windows NT Registry Editor is the most powerful tool available for editing the registry. It is the only Windows NT program that can be used to edit all of the local keys in the registry. It also allows an administrator to edit the HKEY_LOCAL_MACHINE and HKEY_USERS keys on a remote computer running Windows NT. This enables administrators to provide either local or remote support of Windows NT.

After this lesson, you will be able to:

- Use Registry Editor to view information in the registry.
- Use various commands of Registry Editor to explore the registry.

Estimated lesson time: 45 minutes

Guidelines for Using Registry Editor

The Windows NT Registry Editor allows administrators to manually edit the registry and it enables troubleshooting by displaying the contents of the registry. Registry Editor (Regedt32.exe) is installed in the *systemroot*\System32 folder during the Windows NT setup but is not added to any of the folders on the **Start** menu.

Appropriate Use of Registry Editor

The primary purpose of Registry Editor is to help with troubleshooting and problem resolution. For example, sections of the registry can be saved to disk and transported to another computer for analysis or system documentation purposes, or the registry can be viewed over the network.

Note For more information on editing the registry, see the *Microsoft Windows NT Server Resource Kit.*

By default, administrators have Full control over the registry. Users have Full control over their HKEY_CURRENT_USER subtree, and have Read access to other parts of the registry. An administrator can change the registry permissions through the **Security** menu in Registry Editor.

Though Registry Editor is a dedicated administrative tool, in most cases it is not the appropriate tool for modifying the system configuration. Most configuration changes can be made through Control Panel or System Policy Editor, as described later in this book. However, some configuration settings can only be set directly through Registry Editor.

Caution Incorrect use of Registry Editor can cause serious problems that may require reinstallation of Windows NT. Microsoft cannot guarantee that problems due to incorrect use of Registry Editor can be solved without reinstallation. When using Registry Editor to view data, click **Read Only Mode** on the **Options** menu to prevent accidental edits to the registry.

Useful Registry Editor Commands

Some of the most useful Registry Editor commands are on the **View** and **Registry** menus of the **Registry Editor** dialog box. The following table describes these commands.

Command	Description
View Menu:	
Find Key	Searches only for keys, not values. Use this command to search the registry for a specific key. Key names appear on the left of the Registry Editor window. The search begins at the currently selected key and parses all descendant keys for the specified key name. The search is local to the subtree in which the search begins; for example, a search for keys under HKEY_LOCAL_MACHINE does not include keys under HKEY_CURRENT_USER.
Registry Menu:	
Save Key	Saves part of the registry in binary format. It saves the currently selected key and all subkeys. This binary file can then be used with the Restore command to reload a set of values after testing a modification.
Restore	Loads the data in the selected file under the currently selected key. If the selected key was saved in the data file, Registry Editor overwrites the key with the values in the file.
Save Subtree As	Saves the selected key and all subkeys in a text file. The text file can then be searched in a text editor for a specific value or key that was added or modified. If an administrator is unsure as to which value may have been modified, this command can be used to determine which keys had values modified and when those modifications were made.

(*continued*)

Command	Description
Select Computer	Accesses the registry of a remote computer. By default, Windows NT Server allows remote access to only the Administrators group; Windows NT Workstation allows remote access by any valid user account. The remote access permissions for either platform can be modified by setting permissions on this registry key: HKEY_LOCAL_MACHINE\SYSTEM\CurrentControlSet\Control\SecuredPipeServers\winreg By default, this key exists on Windows NT Server. The key does *not* exist on Windows NT Workstation, but you can add it through Registry Editor.

Windows 95 Registry Editor

Windows NT Setup also installs the Windows 95 Registry Editor (Regedit.exe). Because Regedit.exe does not have a security menu, or a read-only mode, and because it does not support all of the data types that Regedit32.exe supports, it is not the recommended Registry Editor for Windows NT. However, Regedit.exe does contain a more powerful search engine that allows you to find keys, values, and data in the registry. Regedt32.exe allows you to search only for keys.

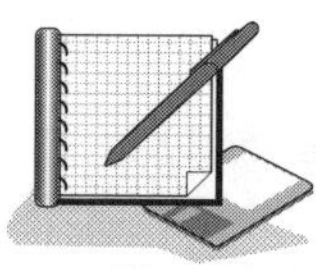

Practice

In these procedures, you use Registry Editor to locate and view information in the registry.

Note Complete these procedures on Server1.

▸ **To locate information in the registry**

In this procedure, you use Registry Editor to view information in the registry.

1. Verify that you are logged on as Administrator.
2. Start Registry Editor (Regedt32.exe).
3. On the **Options** menu, verify that **Read Only Mode** is selected.
4. On the **View** menu, verify that **Tree and Data** is selected.
5. Minimize all windows except HKEY_LOCAL_MACHINE on Local Machine.

6. Expand the HARDWARE\DESCRIPTION\System subkey. Locate the system subkeys, and value and string for each item in the Hardware configuration column in the second table, using the subkeys under the System key. The first table provides an example of system subkeys, values and strings.

Hardware configuration	System subkeys	Value and string
Processor type (example)	CentralProcessor\0	Identifier:80486
Bus type (example)	MultifunctionAdapter\0	Identifier:ISA
Pointer controller type (example)	MultifunctionAdapter\0\ PointerController\0\ PointerPeripheral\0\	Identifier:MICROSOFT PS2 MOUSE
Pointer controller type (EISA example)	EisaAdapter\0\ PointerController\0\ PointerPeripheral\0\	Identifier:MICROSOFT PS2 MOUSE
Processor type	____________	____________
Bus type	____________	____________
Pointer controller type	____________	____________

7. Expand the SOFTWARE\Microsoft\Windows NT\CurrentVersion subkey and locate the value and string for each item listed under Software configuration in the following table.

Software configuration	Value and string
Current Build Number	____________
Current Version	____________
Registered Organization	____________
Registered Owner	____________

▸ To use the Find Key command

In this procedure, you use Regedt32.exe to find a specified key in the registry.

1. Select the HKEY_LOCAL_MACHINE subkey located at the top of the path. This ensures that the entire subtree is searched.
2. On the **View** menu, click **Find Key**.
3. In the **Find what** box, type **serial** and then click **Find Next**.

   Note the locations in the registry that are found.
4. Click **Find Next** until a **Warning** dialog box appears stating "Registry Editor cannot find the desired key."
5. Click **OK** to close the dialog box.
6. In the **Find** dialog box, click **Cancel** to end the search.

▸ **To view a configuration change in the registry**

In this procedure, you make a change using Control Panel and verify that the configuration information was written to the registry.

1. Double-click the System icon in Control Panel.
2. In the **System Properties** dialog box, click the **Environment** tab.
3. In the **System Variables** box, click any variable.

   The focus is now set on the **System Variables** box.
4. In the **Variable** box, type **TEST**
5. In the Value box, type **yes** and then click Set.
6. Click **OK**.
7. Switch to Registry Editor.

   Does the TEST variable appear in HKEY_LOCAL_MACHINE\SYSTEM\CurrentControlSet\Control\Session Manager\Environment?

   ____

8. Close Control Panel.

▸ **To search a subtree for a specific value using Regedt32.exe and Notepad**

In this procedure, you use Regedt32.exe and Notepad to search for a registry value's data.

1. Switch to Registry Editor.
2. Click **HKEY_LOCAL_MACHINE\SOFTWARE**.
3. On the **Registry** menu, click **Save Subtree As**.
4. Save the file with the name Software.txt.
5. Close Registry Editor.
6. Open the Software.txt file that you just created.

   Notepad displays the file.
7. On the **Search** menu, click **Find**.
8. In the **Find what** field, type **CurrentBuildNumber** and then click **Find Next**.
9. Click **Cancel** to close the **Find** dialog box.
10. Scroll down (if necessary) to see the data for **CurrentBuildNumber**. What is the current build?

    ____

11. Close Notepad.

▸ To search the registry for a specific value using Regedit.exe

The Windows 95 Registry Editor, Regedit.exe, provides an alternate way of viewing data directly in the registry. In this procedure, you use Regedit.exe to search for a registry value's data.

1. Click the **Start** button, and then click **Run**.
2. In the **Open** box, type **regedit.exe** and then click **OK**.
3. On the **Edit** menu, click **Find**.
4. In the **Find what** box, type **CurrentBuildNumber** and then click **Find Next**.

   What is the current build?

   ____

5. Close Regedit.exe.

Summary

The following information summarizes the key points in this chapter:

- The Windows NT registry is a unified database where Windows NT stores all system configuration information for the local computer.
- Windows NT provides tools such as Control Panel, System Policy Editor, and other administrative tools that are used to configure the hardware, software, and operating system settings.
- The Windows NT Registry Editor is a tool that provides access to the entire registry, and should be used to view the registry to identify whether the proper system settings are being loaded. You should be very careful when using Registry Editor to edit the registry. Registry Editor does not check for mistakes made in syntax or semantics, so you are not warned if you have improperly entered a value into the registry.

For more information on	See
The registry	*Microsoft Windows NT Workstation Resource Kit* The *Resource Guide* of the *Microsoft Windows NT Server Resource Kit* –or– "Using Registry Editor" in Microsoft Windows NT Server *Concepts and Planning*

Review

1. Based on what you know of the registry, in which subtrees (HKEY_LOCAL_MACHINE or HKEY_CURRENT_USER) do you think the following configuration parameters reside?
   - TCP/IP:

     ____

   - Video:

     ____

   - Hardware profiles:

     ____

   - Mouse pointer acceleration:

     ____

2. You use a portable computer both at home and in a docking station on the network at your office. When you start Windows NT at home, you get the following message: "One or more services failed to start. See Event Viewer for details." This message does not appear when you start Windows NT while your computer is docked at work. What is causing this message, and what can you do to stop it?

   ____

   ____

   ____

3. You configured your computer to dual-boot between Windows NT Workstation and Windows NT Server. You almost always use Windows NT Workstation rather than Windows NT Server. However, because you installed Windows NT Server after Windows NT Workstation, your computer always starts into Windows NT Server by default. How can you configure Windows NT Workstation to start by default?

4. When you attempt to access the registry of a computer running Windows NT Server remotely using Registry Editor, you get an "Access Denied" message. What is the likely cause of the message?

Answer Key

Procedure Answers

Page 89

▶ **To view the registry**

3. List the names of the five subtrees displayed by Registry Editor.

   HKEY_LOCAL_MACHINE, HKEY_CLASSES_ROOT, HKEY_CURRENT_USER, HKEY_CURRENT_CONFIG, HKEY_USERS

Page 101

▶ **To change a user's profile**

3. Expand the HKEY_CURRENT_USER\Control Panel\Desktop key.

   What is the value of the **Pattern** field?

   (None)

9. Start Registry Editor, and then expand the HKEY_CURRENT_USER\Control Panel\Desktop key.

   What is the value of the **Pattern** field?

   It is a numeric value for the new pattern.

Page 118

▶ **To choose a hardware profile at system startup**

3. Log on to Domain1 as Administrator.

   What message appears?

   A domain controller for your domain could not be contacted. You have been logged on using cached account information.
   Changes made to your profile since you last logged on may not be available.

   Why does this message appear?

   This messages appears because network-related services and drivers are not running. This prevents dependent services and drivers from starting, and it also prevents the workstation from communicating with a domain controller during logon.

Page 131

▸ **To locate information in the registry**

6. Expand the HARDWARE\DESCRIPTION\System subkey and locate the information requested in the second table, using the subkeys under the System key.

Hardware configuration	System subkeys	Value and string
Processor type	________	________
Bus type	________	________
Pointer controller type	________	________

Answers will vary.

7. Expand the SOFTWARE\Microsoft\Windows NT\CurrentVersion subkey and locate the information in the following table.

Software configuration	Value and string
Current Build Number	1381
Current Version	4.0
Registered Organization	________
Registered Owner	________

Answers will vary.

Page 132

▸ **To view a configuration change in the registry**

7. Switch to Registry Editor.

   Does the TEST variable appear in HKEY_LOCAL_MACHINE\SYSTEM\CurrentControlSet\Control\Session Manager\Environment?

   Yes, if the system environment variable was entered correctly.

Page 132

▸ **To search a subtree for a specific value using Regedt32.exe and Notepad**

10. Scroll down (if necessary) to see the data for **CurrentBuildNumber**. What is the current build?

    1381.

Page 133

▸ **To search the registry for a specific value using Regedit.exe**

4. In the **Find what** box, type **CurrentBuildNumber** and then click **Find Next**.

   What is the current build?

   1381.

Review Answers

Page 135

1. Based on what you know of the registry, in which subtrees (HKEY_LOCAL_MACHINE or HKEY_CURRENT_USER) do you think the following configuration parameters reside?
   - TCP/IP: **HKEY_LOCAL_MACHINE**
   - Video: **HKEY_LOCAL_MACHINE**
   - Hardware profiles: **HKEY_LOCAL_MACHINE**
   - Mouse pointer acceleration: **HKEY_CURRENT_USER**
2. You use a portable computer both at home and in a docking station on the network at your office. When you start Windows NT at home, you get the following message: "One or more services failed to start. See Event Viewer for details." This message does not appear when you start Windows NT while your computer is docked at work. What is causing this message, and what can you do to stop it?

   The network services are not loading because the network adapter card is in the docking station. Create separate hardware profiles to solve the problem.

3. You configured your computer to dual-boot between Windows NT Workstation and Windows NT Server. You almost always use Windows NT Workstation rather than Windows NT Server. However, because you installed Windows NT Server after Windows NT Workstation, your computer always starts into Windows NT Server by default. How can you configure Windows NT Workstation to start by default?

   Change the startup option on the Startup/Shutdown tab of Control Panel System so that Windows NT Workstation is selected.

4. When you attempt to access the registry of a computer running Windows NT Server remotely using Registry Editor, you get an "Access Denied" message. What is the likely cause of the message?

   You are using an account that is not recognized as an administrator's account on the remote computer. Computers running Windows NT Server restrict registry remote access to members of the Administrators group.

CHAPTER 4

Managing System Policies

About This Chapter

System policies enable you to control the user-definable settings in Windows NT and Windows 95 user profiles, as well as system configuration settings. You can use *System Policy Editor* to change desktop settings and restrict what users can do from their desktops. In this chapter, you learn how to implement a system policy in a domain.

Before You Begin

To complete the lessons in this chapter, you must have:

- Two computers that meet the hardware and software requirements as specified in the Getting Started section of "About This Book."
- Completed all practices in Chapter 2, "Installing Windows NT."
- Completed the practices in Chapter 3, "Configuring the Windows NT Environment," in which you used Add/Remove Programs in Control Panel to install the Windows NT games and wallpaper, and in which you used User Manager for Domains to create User1.

Lesson 1: The Purpose of System Policies

A system policy provides administrators with increased control and manageability of desktop computers running Windows NT or Windows 95 across a domain. This lesson provides an overview of the settings you can control with a policy.

After this lesson, you will be able to:

- Define the function of system policies.
- Identify which Windows NT operating system includes System Policy Editor.
- Identify who can implement system policy.
- Start System Policy Editor.
- Describe what settings are configured in a computer policy.
- Describe what settings are configured in a user policy.

Estimated lesson time: 25 minutes

What Is a System Policy?

A system policy is a set of rules that controls what a user sees on their desktop and what they can do with their computer. When a system policy is used in a domain, it can establish a uniform set of rules, or policy, for all users and computers running Windows NT or Windows 95. System policies can also be configured to provide custom desktop and computer configurations for specific users, groups, and computers.

A system policy gives you the ability to:

- Restrict options in Control Panel, such as hiding the Screen Saver tab in the Display program, which would prevent users from changing or configuring their screen savers.
- Customize parts of the desktop, such as specifying the corporate standard wallpaper on all computers.
- Control network logon and access, such as creating a logon banner to display a message when a user logs on.

Note A system policy is created with an administrative tool, System Policy Editor (Poledit.exe). System Policy Editor is only included with Windows NT Server 4.0 and appears on the **Administrative Tools (Common)** menu. Only administrators can create and change system policies.

As you review this lesson, review the options in System Policy Editor that are covered in this chapter.

Practice

In this procedure, you create a shortcut for System Policy Editor and then start System Policy Editor.

Note Complete this procedure on Server1.

▶ **To create a shortcut for and start System Policy Editor**

1. Log on to as Administrator.
2. Create a shortcut for Poledit.exe.

   The following illustration shows how the shortcut icon appears on your desktop.

3. Start System Policy Editor from the shortcut for Poledit.exe.

   System Policy Editor appears. Notice that the System Policy Editor window is empty. This is because a policy file must first be created or opened before it can appear in the System Policy Editor window.
4. On the **File** menu, click **New Policy**.
5. What two icons appear in the System Policy Editor window?

   ____

Computer Policy and User Policy

When you create a new policy, System Policy Editor displays two icons, Default Computer and Default User. These icons display the individual policy options that give you the ability to configure a computer policy for all computers in the domain that are running Windows NT or Windows 95 and a user policy for all users that log on to one of these computers.

- *Default Computer.* Computer policy options are used to configure logon and network settings. These options apply to all computers in the domain and effect all users that log on to those computers. When you need to customize a specific computer policy for a specific computer, you can add the computer using the **Edit** menu in System Policy Editor.

- *Default User.* User policy options are used to configure the user's desktop. You can set these options to effect all users that log on to the domain. When you need to customize a specific user policy that is different from the default, you can add users or groups using the **Edit** menu in System Policy Editor.

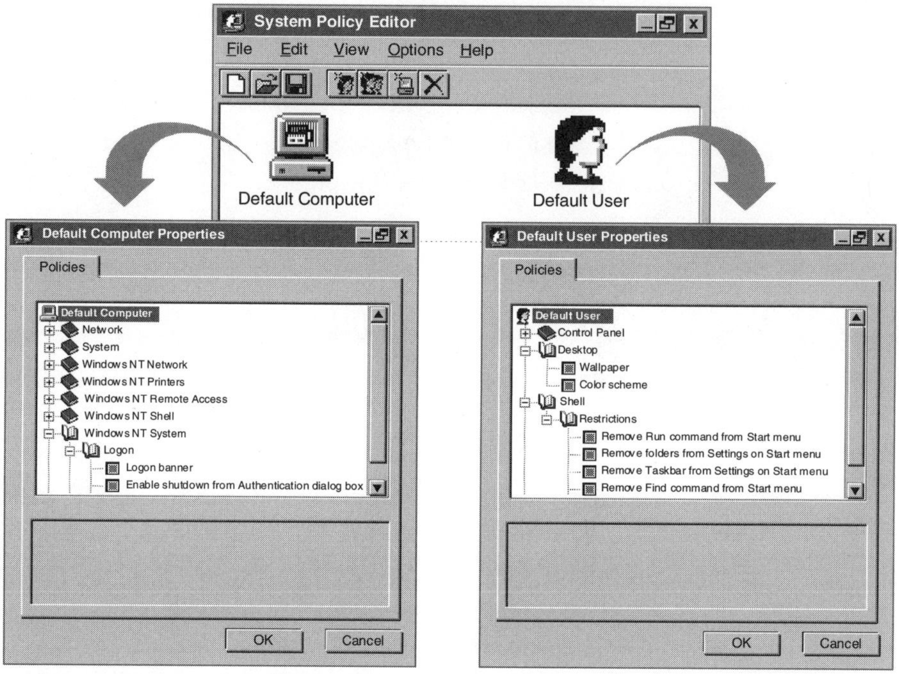

Practice

In this procedure, you explore the policy options in Default User and Default Computer.

Note Complete this procedure on Server1.

▸ To explore Default User and Default Computer

1. In System Policy Editor, double-click **Default User**.
2. Expand **Shell** by clicking the plus sign (+) beside **Shell**, and then expand **Restrictions**.
3. Explore the various Default User options.

   The Default User options are explained later in this chapter.
4. Click **Cancel** to close the **Default User Properties** dialog box.
5. Double-click **Default Computer**.

6. Expand **Windows NT System**, and then expand **Logon**.
7. Explore the various Default Computer options.

   These Default Computer options are explained later in this chapter.
8. Click **Cancel** to close the **Default Computer Properties** dialog box.
9. Close System Policy Editor and do *not* save any changes.

Lesson 2: Implementing a System Policy

In this lesson, you learn how a system policy is implemented in a domain. This includes what happens when a user logs on, and the priority order in which policies are implemented. You also learn how to implement a local policy when you want a computer to use a policy other than the domain policy.

After this lesson, you will be able to:

- Describe the process to implement a system policy in a domain.
- Describe how a user policy is implemented when a user logs on to the domain.
- Describe how a computer policy is implemented when a user logs on to a domain.
- Describe how to implement a local policy.

Estimated lesson time: 20 minutes

Implementing a System Policy in a Domain

The following steps provide an overview of how a system policy is implemented in a domain.

1. Use System Policy Editor to create a new policy file. Set the appropriate policy options in Default Computer and Default User.
2. If you need to set specific policy options for a user, group, or specific computer account, use the **Edit** menu to add the account and then set the policy options.

   The following illustration shows a domain system policy that also includes separate policies for a specific computer (Computer1), user (User1), and group (Account Operators).

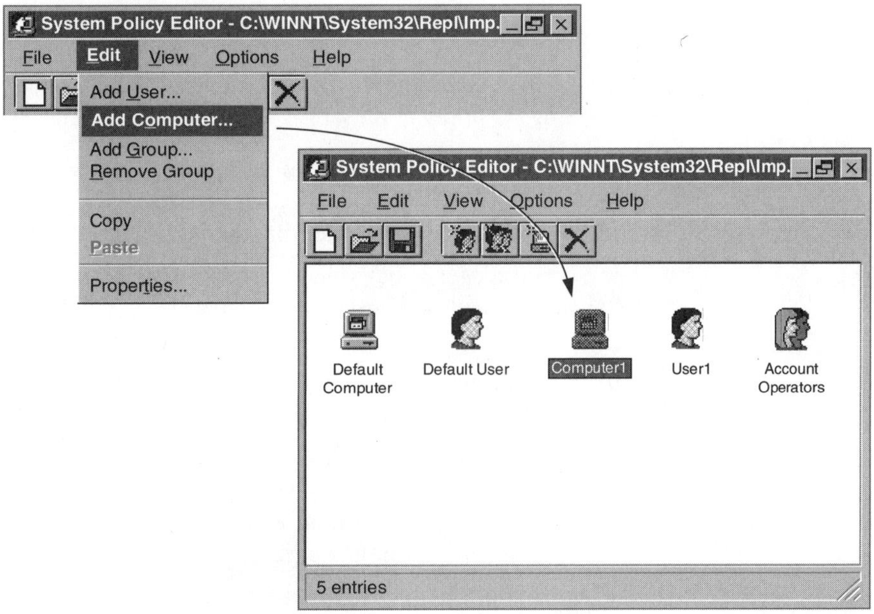

3. By default, Windows NT searches for the Ntconfig.pol policy file stored on the PDC in the Netlogon share. Therefore, name the policy file Ntconfig.pol on the PDC in the following folder:

   systemroot\System32\Repl\Import\Scripts

   On domain controllers, the Windows NT installation automatically shares this folder with the share name Netlogon.

4. Enable *replication* on all domain controllers so that the Ntconfig.pol file is replicated to the same folder on all backup domain controllers.

Note For more information on replication see Chapter 16, "Implementing File Synchronization and Directory Replication."

How a User Policy Is Implemented When a User Logs On

The following list describes the process used by Windows NT to determine which *user* settings to apply to a user logging on to a domain:

- When a users logs on to the domain from a computer running Windows NT, the user's user profile is loaded. Next, Windows NT searches for the Ntconfig.pol file on the domain controller that authenticated the user logon request.
- If a specific user policy exists for that user, those policy settings are merged into the current user portion of the registry (HKEY_CURRENT_USER).
- Even if user policy is not defined for a specific user, the system policy may include a group policy that has been defined for a *group* of which the user is a member. If a user is a member of more than one group, the group with the highest priority defines the policy settings for the user. The group's policy settings are then merged into HKEY_CURRENT_USER.

  A group's priority is configured in System Policy Editor by clicking **Group Priority** on the **Options** menu.
- If system policy is not defined for the user or for the user's group(s), the *Default User policy* settings are merged into HKEY_CURRENT_USER.

Note Policies are applied only at the time a user logs on. If a user is logged on when a system policy change is implemented, the user must log off and log back on for the policy change to take effect.

The following illustration diagrams how user and computer policies are implemented when a user logs on.

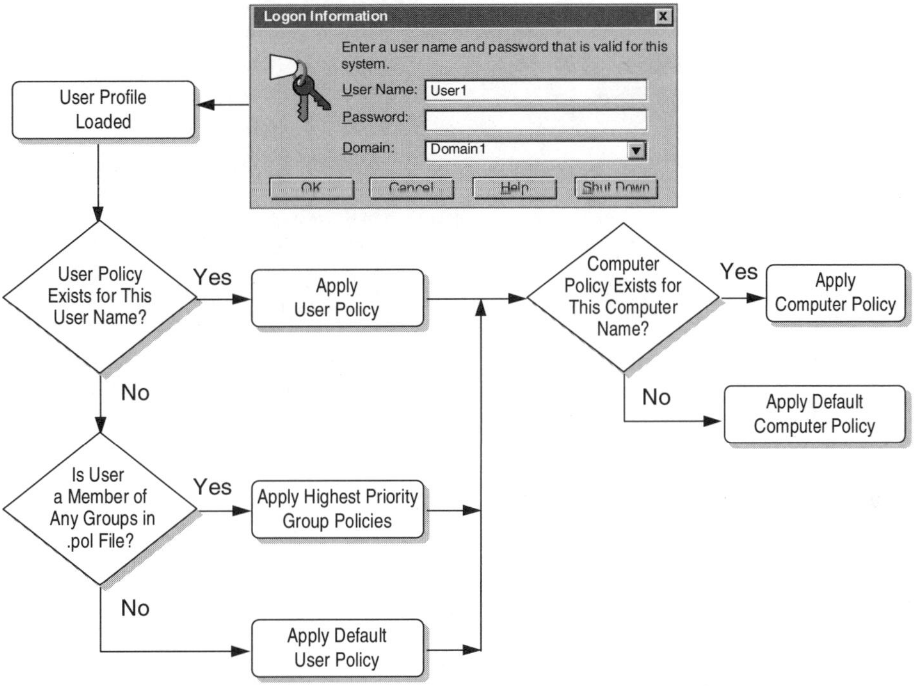

How a Computer Policy Is Implemented When a User Logs On

If a specific computer policy is defined for the computer at which the user is logging on, those policy settings are merged into the local computer portion of the registry (HKEY_LOCAL_MACHINE). Otherwise, the *Default Computer policy* settings are merged into HKEY_LOCAL_MACHINE.

Note To apply system policies in a network that uses both Windows 95 and Windows NT Workstation, System Policy Editor must be run once from each platform. When you use System Policy Editor on a computer running Windows 95, you save the policy settings to a file named Config.pol. This file is similar to the Ntconfig.pol file, but has a different file format and reflects differences in the registries of the two operating systems. Save the Config.pol file to the Netlogon share on the PDC. For more information on using system policy for computers running Windows 95, see the *Microsoft Windows 95 Resource Kit*.

Implementing a Local Policy

You are not restricted to using only one system policy in a domain. However, by default a computer running Windows NT automatically downloads the information in the Ntconfig.pol file from the domain controller that authenticated the user logon request. Therefore, if you want to use a system policy from a computer that is not a domain controller, you would change the **Remote update** setting from *automatic* in the computer policy portion of the system policy to *manual,* and specify the computer and path to the system policy file.

You would use the following steps to set up a manual update path on a computer running Windows NT Workstation. This is done by using System Policy Editor on a computer running Windows NT Server to create a system policy file on the computer running Windows NT Workstation.

Note The following steps are informational and should *not* be performed at this time.

---

1. Start System Policy Editor on a computer running Windows NT Server.
2. On the **File** menu, click **New Policy**.
3. Double-click **Default Computer**, and then expand **Network**.
4. Expand **System policies update**.
5. Select **Remote update** (there should be a check in the check box).

   Notice at the bottom of the screen that the **Settings for Remote update** dialog box appears.
6. In the **Update mode** box, click the down arrow, and then click **Manual (use specific path)**.
7. In the **Path for manual update** box, enter *path\unique_file_name*.pol. For example, **C:\Ws1.pol**
8. Click **OK**.
9. Click **File** and, then click **Save**.
10. In the **Save in** box, click the down arrow.
11. Click **Network Neighborhood**, and then double-click the name of the computer for which you want to change the remote update setting.

    The name of the computer running Windows NT Workstation now appears in the **Save in** box, so that you can save the policy file on it.
12. In the **File name** box, type the file name that you specified in the system policy file. In our example, it was Ws1.pol.

    By default, Ws1.pol is saved in the root directory of the drive containing *systemroot*. Therefore, you must make sure that the path and file name of the policy file match the one you entered in the **Path for manual update** box.

Lesson 3: Using System Policy Editor to Manage a System Policy

Now that you have learned how a system policy is implemented in a domain, you learn how to create and manage a system policy using System Policy Editor.

After this lesson, you will be able to:

- Describe the two Registry Editor modes: registry mode and policy mode.
- Describe the computer and user policy options.
- Configure a computer policy within a system policy.
- Describe the function of the system policy templates.

Estimated lesson time: 60 minutes

System Policy Editor is available in the Administrative Tools (Common) folder on computers running Windows NT Server 4.0. System Policy Editor is used to:

- Modify default settings for the computer and user policy for the domain.
- Create custom settings that apply to individual users, groups of users, or individual computers.
- Specify the manner and location from which to download policy for some or all users.

Note Educate users about the system policy implemented in the domain or on a computer. If a user is familiar with the default Windows NT interface, they may interpret policy restrictions or customizations as a problem with the operating system. For example, if the policy hides the **Run** command on the **Start** menu, a user may report that the operating system is not working properly, because the user cannot find the **Run** command.

System Policy Editor Modes

System Policy Editor has two modes, registry mode and policy mode. When System Policy Editor starts, it is not in any specific mode.

Registry Mode

In registry mode, you can edit portions of the registry of the local computer or a remote computer. This is a *direct* edit of the local registry and changes are reflected almost immediately. To simplify administration, avoid using this mode and instead make changes to the domain system policy. When the registry is opened (by clicking **Open Registry** or **Connect** on the **File** menu), System Policy Editor is placed in registry mode. The title bar displays **Local Registry**.

Changing Registry Settings on a Local or Remote Computer

When System Policy Editor is used in registry mode, changes are made by selecting or clearing specific registry options in **Local Computer** or **Local User**.

Using registry mode exposes certain keys in HKEY_CURRENT_USER and HKEY_LOCAL_MACHINE. Changes made to the Local Computer or Local User policy are updated in these registry keys when the settings are saved and the registry is closed. The user does not need to log off or restart the computer to see the changes.

To make changes to the Windows NT registry settings on a remote computer, click **Connect** on the System Policy Editor **File** menu. This feature allows remote adjustment to computer registries.

Note To simplify administration, avoid using registry mode to change individual computer registry settings. A uniform system policy for the domain is easier to maintain. If a specific user or computer incompatibility problem occurs, instead of making *direct changes* to registry settings, create a separate policy entry for that user or computer within the domain system policy (Ntconfig.pol).

Policy Mode

Policy mode is the mode you use to create and modify a system policy for a domain. The policy mode is used to create or modify system policy files (.pol). However, changes to the registry on the computers receiving the policy are not implemented for users or computers until the following procedures are completed:

1. The policy file is saved as Ntconfig.pol in the Netlogon share on the PDC.
2. Ntconfig.pol is replicated to the BDCs in the domain.
3. Users log on to the domain.

When you create a policy file by clicking **New Policy** on the **File** menu, System Policy Editor is placed in policy mode. The title bar displays **Untitled**. When you modify an existing system policy by clicking **Open Policy** on the **File** menu and typing in the existing policy file name, System Policy Editor is also placed in policy mode.

Check Box Selection Levels

The check boxes for individual policies can appear dimmed, selected, or cleared as shown in the following illustration.

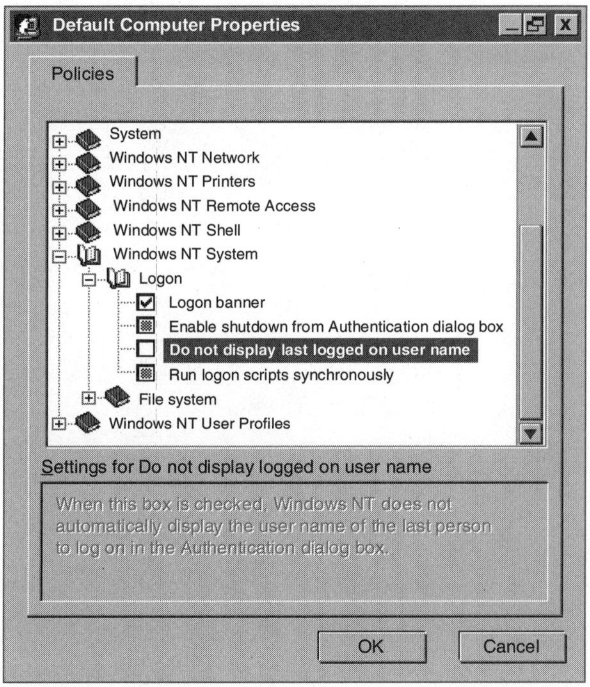

- *Dimmed.* The registry key for the policy is not modified. This is the default setting.
- *Selected.* The policy is implemented.
- *Cleared.* The policy is not implemented.

When the policy file is created, only the selected and cleared policy settings are saved to the policy file (.pol). You would leave a check box dimmed to increase logon speed. This is because dimmed options are not saved to the policy file and are not loaded across the network.

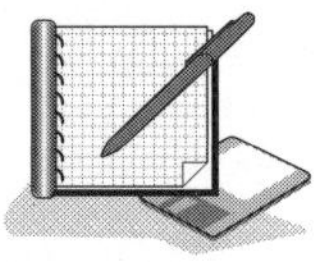

Practice

In these procedures, you use System Policy Editor on Server1 to examine the various options available for creating and modifying system policy.

Note Complete these procedure on Server1.

▸ **To explore the File menu options in System Policy Editor**

1. Start **System Policy Editor**.
2. Click **File**.

   The following table describes the options on the **File** menu.

File option	Allows you to
New Policy	Create a new system policy.
Open Policy	View and modify an existing system policy.
Open Registry	View and modify the information stored in the local registry.
Save	Save any changes you have made to system policy.
Save As	Allows you to create a new system policy based on the one you are currently editing. Any change made since the last save are only saved in the new system policy.
Close	Close the open system policy file.
Connect	To make changes to the Windows NT registry settings on a remote computer.
Exit	Close or exit System Policy Editor.

▸ **To create a new system policy**

- On the **File** menu, click **New Policy**.

  System Policy Editor displays two icons, Default Computer and Default User.

▸ To explore system policy for default computer

1. Double-click **Default Computer**.

   The **Default Computer Properties** dialog box appears.

2. Explore the Default Computer settings.

   The following table describes the system policy settings available for Default Computer.

Computer system policy option	Use the option
Network	To perform system policy updates. Remote Update options include a choice of two modes: an automatic default path (which updates from Ntconfig.pol on a domain controller), or a manually entered path to update system policy from a computer other than a domain controller. There are also options to enable display of error messages if the policy file cannot be found, and to enable *load balancing* for computers running Windows 95.
System	To configure the Simple Network Management Protocol (SNMP) entry and specify the contents of the **Run** entry that is used to specify which applications should run at startup.
Windows NT Network	To enable creation of hidden shares for each drive letter upon system startup.
Windows NT Printers	To disable the print spooler browser, to change the priority of print job assignments, or set the print spooler to beep every 10 seconds if there is an error condition for a print job on a remote print server.
Windows NT Remote Access	To use a remote access server, set a maximum number for unsuccessful authentication retries, and a maximum time limit for authentication. There is also an option for the time interval between call-back attempts and a time limit for automatic disconnection from the server.
Windows NT Shell	To create custom shared folders for all users at the computer.
Windows NT System	To modify **Logon** options: Altering the logon banner, changing the default user name and password, enabling shutdown from the **Authentication** dialog box, and disabling display of the last logged-on user name. To modify **File system** options for enabling or disabling 8.3 file names, for using extended characters for 8.3 file names, and for updating the last access time attribute of a file.

(continued)

Computer system policy option	Use the option
Windows NT User Profiles	To define a slow connection to a logon server and allow the computer to automatically detect a slow connection when a user attempts to log on. Use these settings in conjunction with the options on the **User Profile** tab of the System program in Control Panel to optimize performance when logging on through a slow connection.
FTP System (appears if FTP server service is enabled)	To configure the File Transfer Protocol (FTP) server service.

3. After you have finished exploring the Default Computer options, click **Cancel**. Do not change the default settings at this time.

▸ To explore system policy for the default user

1. Double-click **Default User**.

   The **Default User Properties** dialog box appears.

2. Explore the Default User options.

   The following table describes the system policy options in **Default User**.

User system policy option	Use the option
Control Panel	To restrict the user activity in the Display program in Control Panel or to deny any access to the Display program.
Desktop	To specify the background wallpaper and color scheme for the desktop.
Shell	To customize desktop folders and restrict what appears on the desktop, and restrict the use of the **Run**, **Find**, and **Shut Down** commands. You can create custom folders by entering paths to program items, desktop icons, startup items, Network Neighborhood items, and **Start** menu items that you want to come from a location other than user profile folders. You can provide locations for custom desktop icons, applications you want in the Startup folder, or even replace the entire **Start** menu.

(continued)

User system policy option	Use the option
System	To disable Windows NT Registry Editor (Regedt32.exe) and Windows 95 Registry Editor (Regedit.exe) so that users cannot edit the registry files. You can also enter a list of Windows-based applications users can use. Any application *not* in the list is unavailable to the user.
Windows NT Shell	To customize the desktop by specifying a path to a custom Programs folder, desktop icons, Startup folder, Network Neighborhood and **Start** menu, and to hide the **Start** menu subfolders. Also used to remove common program groups from the **Start** menu.
Windows NT System	To merge the environmental variables from the **Parse** Autoexec.bat file with the user's environment variables.

3. After you have finished exploring the Default User options, click **Cancel**.

   Do not change the default settings at this time.
4. Close System Policy Editor.

Customizing System Policy for Users, Groups, and Computers

The default settings established by system policy can affect the entire domain. If you have users, groups, or computers that require settings that are different from the default settings, you can add these accounts to the domain system policy and configure them as needed.

Users, groups, or computers with settings that are different from the default system policy settings receive separate entries in the Ntconfig.pol file. For example, if User1 requires settings different from the default system policy settings, you would need to use System Policy Editor to add a user profile for User1 to the Ntconfig.pol file. The same would be true of a group or computer requiring settings that were different from the default settings.

When a user or group member who has special policy settings in Ntconfig.pol logs on, the system finds Ntconfig.pol and also the special settings that apply specifically to the user or group member. Similarly, if a computer is added and special settings are entered using System Policy Editor, anyone logging on to that computer receives those computer settings.

To add special policies for a user, a group, or a computer, you would use the following steps:

1. Log on as Administrator and start System Policy Editor.
2. On the **Edit** menu, click the appropriate selection:
   - Click **Add User** to create an entry for a specific user.
   - Click **Add Group** to create an entry for a specific group.
   - Click **Add Computer** to create an entry for a specific computer.
3. Enter the appropriate user, group, or computer name.
4. Click **OK**.
5. You would then open the icon for the user, group, or computer and modify the settings for that account.

Example: Configuring a System Policy to Secure Computers

System Policy Editor provides two computer policy options that enable you to configure the **Logon Information** dialog box to secure a computer using the following methods:

- *Prevent the display of the last logged on user.* By default, each time a user presses CTRL+ALT+DELETE, the **Logon Information** dialog box displays the user name of the last person to log on to the system. To prevent the display of the last user that logged on, configure the **Windows NT System\Logon\Do not display last logged on user name** option in the appropriate computer policy.

- *Display a warning to users against unauthorized system use.* This is done by configuring the **Windows NT System\Logon\Logon Banner** option in the appropriate computer policy. You can set this option in the Default Computer policy for all computers in the domain, or in a specific computer name.

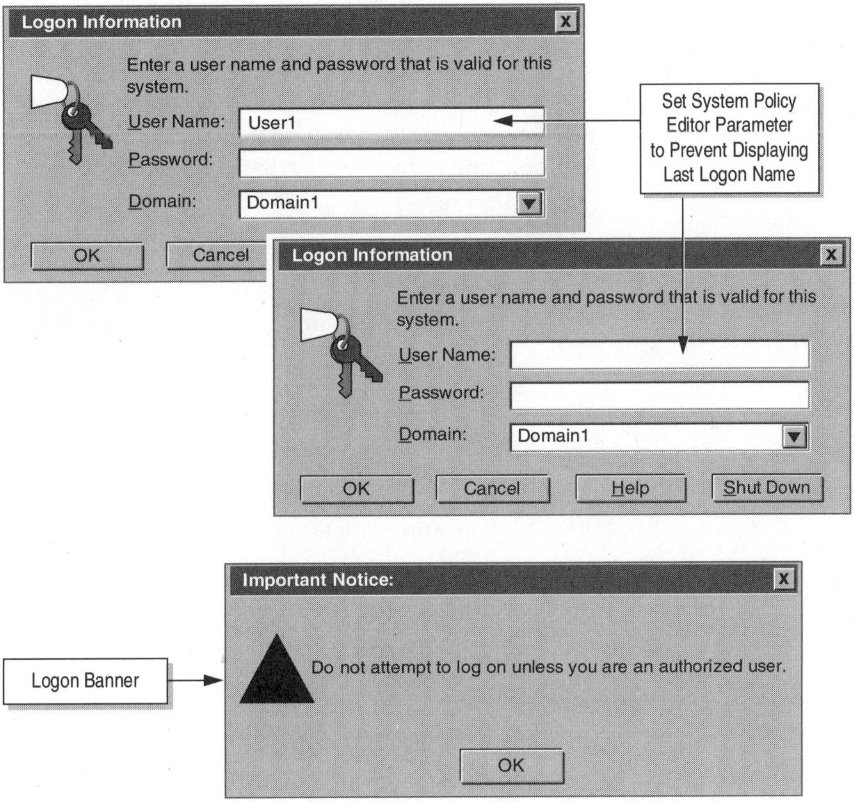

Note You can set these two policy options for all computers in the domain by modifying the Default Computer policy, or for a specific computer by modifying its settings.

Practice

In these procedures, you use System Policy Editor to create a domain system policy containing a computer policy for Workstation1. You then configure the computer policy to display a logon banner that appears whenever a user logs on to Workstation1, and to prevent the display of the last logged on user name.

Note Complete these procedures on Server1 logged on as Administrator.

► **To create a domain system policy for Workstation1 that displays a logon banner**

1. Start System Policy Editor.
2. On the **File** menu, click **New Policy**.
3. On the **Edit** menu, click **Add Computer**.
4. In the **Add Computer** dialog box, type **Workstation1** and then click **OK**.
5. Double-click the Workstation1 icon.

   The **Workstation1 Properties** dialog box appears.
6. Expand **Windows NT System**.
7. Expand **Logon**.
8. Click the **Logon Banner** option.

   Notice at the bottom of the screen that a **Settings for Logon banner** dialog box appears. If this box appears dimmed, you have not yet selected this option (there is not a check mark in the check box).
9. In the **Caption** box, type **Attention:**
10. In the **Text** box, type **Unauthorized use of Workstation1 is prohibited.**
11. Click **OK**.

Note System Policy Editor stores this information in two values (LegalNoticeCaption and LegalNoticeText) in the registry under:

HKEY_LOCAL_MACHINE\SOFTWARE\Microsoft\Windows NT\CurrentVersion\Winlogon

▸ **To disable the display of the last logged on user name on Workstation1**

1. Double-click the Workstation1 computer profile icon.
2. Expand **Windows NT System**, and then expand **Logon**.
3. Click the **Do not display last logged on user name** check box.
4. Click **OK**.

▸ **To save the new system policy file in Netlogon**

1. On the **File** menu, click **Save**.
2. Save the file in the C:\Winnt\System32\Repl\Import\Scripts folder, and name it Ntconfig.

   System Policy Editor automatically appends the .pol extension.
3. Close System Policy Editor.

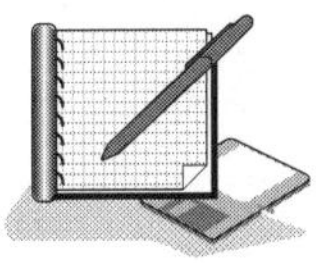

Practice

In this procedure, you test the domain system policy and the computer policy for Workstation1.

▸ **To test the new system policy**

Note Complete this procedure on Workstation1. Server1 must be running.

---

1. If you are currently logged on at Workstation1, log off.
2. Press CTRL+ALT+DELETE.
3. Are the policy settings in effect? Why or why not?

   ____

   ____

   ____

   ____

4. Log on to Domain1 as Administrator, and then log off.

5. Press CTRL+ALT+DELETE to log on.
6. Are the policy settings in effect? Why or why not?

____

____

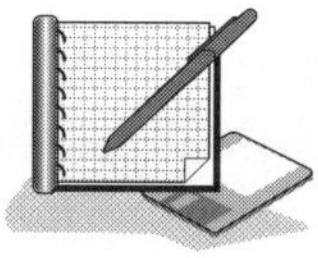

Practice

In these procedures, you use System Policy Editor to add a user policy to the domain system policy, and then you test the user policy for User1.

► **To add a user to the Ntconfig.pol system policy**

Note Complete this procedure on Server1 logged on as Administrator.

---

1. Open System Policy Editor.
2. On the **File** menu, click **Open Policy**.
3. In the **File Name** box, type the following:

   c:\winnt\system32\repl\import\scripts\ntconfig.pol
4. Click **Open**.
5. On the **Edit** menu, click **Add User**.
6. In the **Add User** dialog box, type **User1** and then click **OK**.
7. Double-click the User1 icon.

   The **User1 Properties** dialog box appears.
8. Expand **Desktop**.
9. Select the **Wallpaper** check box.

   The **Settings for Wallpaper** dialog box appears at the bottom of the screen.
10. In the **Wallpaper Name** box, type **C:\Winnt\Blue Monday**

    Note If you did not complete the practice in Chapter 3, "Configuring the Windows NT Environment," in which you used Add/Remove Programs in Control Panel to install the Windows NT games and wallpaper, the Blue Monday wallpaper is not available.

    ---
11. Select the **Tile Wallpaper** check box.
12. On the **Policies** tab, select the **Color Scheme** check box.

    The **Settings for Color Scheme** dialog box appears at the bottom of the screen.

13. In the **Scheme name** box, click **Rose 256**, and then click **OK**.
14. Close System Policy Editor, and then save changes to Ntconfig.pol.

▸ **To test the user profile portion of system policy**

Note Complete this procedure on Workstation1.

---

1. If you are currently logged on at Workstation1, log off.
2. Log on to Domain1 as User1.
3. Are the policy settings in effect? Why or why not?

____

____

____

Restricting the User Environment

System Policy Editor provides policy options that enable you to restrict the user's environment. Use the following steps to enable these options.

Caution The following steps are provided for your information and should *not* be done as part of the course. If you make changes to any of these settings, you may not be able to complete the remainder of the course.

---

1. Start System Policy Editor.
2. On the **File** menu, click **Open Policy**.
3. Open *systemroot*\System32\Repl\Import\Scripts\Ntconfig.pol.
4. Open **Default User**.
5. Expand **Shell**.
6. Expand **Restrictions**.

   The following table explains some of the Restriction policy options.

Individual policy option	Description
Remove Run command from Start menu	The **Run** command no longer appears as an option on the **Start** menu.
Hide Network Neighborhood	The Network Neighborhood no longer appears on the desktop.
Hide all items on desktop	All items are missing from the desktop.
Disable the Shut Down command	The **Shut Down** command no longer appears as an option on the **Start** menu.

Supporting Windows 95 System Policy

You have learned that system policies allow you to override local registry values for user or computer settings. When a user logs on, system policy settings overwrite the current settings in the user's registry to enable administrators to control individual desktop and registry settings.

For computers running Windows 95, the following rules also apply:

- System policies can only be stored on the domain controllers.
- Group policies, if used, must be enabled on each computer running Windows 95. You can enable group policies when you install Windows 95, using a custom setup script, or use Add/Remove Programs in Control Panel after Windows 95 is installed.
- Windows 95 policy must be saved in a file named Config.pol (*not* Ntconfig.pol), and stored in the Netlogon share of the primary domain controller (PDC).

Note Remember that system policy files created on computers running Windows NT cannot be used on computers running Windows 95, and vice versa. Therefore, when modifying system policy for a computer running Windows 95, you run System Policy Editor on a computer running Windows 95 and you save the policy settings to a file named *Config.pol* in the Netlogon share on the PDC. For more information on using system policy for computers running Windows 95, see the *Microsoft Windows 95 Resource Kit*.

Load Balancing

Ordinarily, computers running Windows 95 get policy settings from the PDC only. Load balancing allows computers running Windows 95 to take policies from multiple domain controllers. Therefore, enabling load balancing can prevent network slowdown when many Windows 95 clients try to access the same policy file.

To enable load balancing, use the Windows 95 System Policy Editor to open Config.pol, then double-click the Default Computer icon, open **Network\Update\Remote Update Policy**, and then check **Load-balanced**.

System Policy Templates

The policies that appear in System Policy Editor are provided by template files. Windows NT requires both the Winnt.adm and the Common.adm system policy templates.

Note Because policy files are basically registry entries, it is possible to add options to System Policy Editor by editing the existing templates or creating and adding in new template files. For more information on the system policy templates, see Microsoft Windows NT Server *Concepts and Planning*, or see "Adding policy templates" in System Policy Editor Help.

System Policy Issues

Verify the following items when troubleshooting problems with system policies:

- The individual policy option is set properly in the policy (.pol) file.
- The policy file is located in the correct network location, and the network location is accessible from the computer running Windows NT or Windows 95.
- The user name, group name, and computer name are correct, and groups contain the appropriate members.

The following table describes common policy issues and their resolutions.

Issue	Resolutions
Downloading system policies is very slow.	Although there is no limit to the number of individual users, groups, or computers that can be added to a policy file, delays may occur if too many users log on at the same time. Enable load balancing on the computers running Windows 95 to better balance network resources. On computers running Windows NT, in **Remote update**, click **Manual**, and use computers other than the domain controllers to store the system policy files.
User policies are downloaded for a user when logged on to a computer running Windows 95, but are not downloaded when the user logs on to a computer running Windows NT.	Although computers running Windows NT and computers running Windows 95 support system policy files created with System Policy Editor, the policy files are not named the same and are not interoperable. If a user uses a computer running Windows 95 and a computer running Windows NT, you must create a user policy in both system policy files (Config.pol and Ntconfig.pol).

(*continued*)

Issue	Resolutions
User policies are downloaded for a user when logged on to a computer running Windows NT, but are not downloaded when the user logs on to a computer running Windows 95.	Same as above.
User policies restrict access to Control Panel options, but the icons still appear in Control Panel.	System policies can restrict access to Control Panel options, but they cannot remove the icons. In order to remove the icons from Control Panel, modify the [don't load] section of Control.ini.
The wallpaper assigned in the system policy file does not appear on all client computers.	Some system policy settings require components to be installed locally on the computer where the policy is applied. In this example, the wallpaper bitmap is not present in the path specified by the policy file.
Group policies are not processed by all client computers running Windows 95.	Group Policy must be installed on a computer running Windows 95 not only to create group policies, but to process them. Unlike Windows NT, group policies are not installed by default with System Policy Editor. Add group policy support through the Add/Remove Programs option of Control Panel.

Summary

The following information summarizes the key points in this chapter:

- Prior to implementing a system policy, plan the types of restrictions and customizations that will be implemented by the policy. Identify any specific policies for users, groups, and computers. Notify users and groups before the policy is implemented to avoid possible confusion once the policy is implemented.
- A system policy is made up of computer policy, user policy, group policy, or any combination of these policies.
- By default, to implement a domain system policy on computers running Windows NT, the policy settings must be stored in a file named Ntconfig.pol in the Netlogon share of the PDC.
- By default, to implement a domain system policy on computers running Windows 95, use the Windows 95 System Policy Editor to create system policy on that operating system. These system policy settings must be saved to a file named Config.pol in the Netlogon share of the PDC.
- Both Ntconfig.pol and Config.pol must be stored on the PDC in the following folder: *systemroot*\System32\Repl\Import\Scripts. By default this folder is shared as Netlogon.
- Replication must be enabled for all domain controllers to receive copies of the Ntconfig.pol and Config.pol files. Remember that load balancing must be enabled on computers running Windows 95 in order for them to access Config.pol on BDCs.
- You can specify customized settings for individual users, groups, and computers to meet the needs of your organization.
- System Policy Editor can be used to directly edit portions of the registry.

Review

1. Describe the purpose of system policy.

2. Who can implement system policy?

3. Name two major functions of System Policy Editor.

4. Name two policies that you might create to secure a computer.

5. If a user logs on to a domain that has system policy, but system policy has not been defined for that user, what happens next?

6. Your network has 165 computers running Windows 95, and 200 computers running Windows NT Workstation. The Windows 95 users are complaining that the network is really slow when everyone is trying to log on in the morning. What can cause this problem and how do you resolve it?

Answer Key

Procedure Answers

Page 143

▶ **To create a shortcut for and start System Policy Editor**

5. What two icons appear in the System Policy Editor window?

   Default Computer and Default User.

Page 161

▶ **To test the new system policy**

3. Are the policy settings in effect? Why or why not?

   No, because system policies are not downloaded until a user logs on. When you complete the logon process, your computer policy is downloaded, and the next time you attempt to log on to the computer the policy settings are in effect.

6. Are the policy settings in effect? Why or why not?

   Yes, because the system policy was downloaded when you logged on in step 4.

Page 163

▶ **To test the user profile portion of system policy**

3. Are the policy settings in effect? Why or why not?

   Yes, because User1 now has the Blue Monday wallpaper and the color scheme is Rose256. System policy overwrites the local user profile on Workstation1.

Review Answers

Page 168

1. Describe the purpose of system policy.

   To establish a uniform set of rules to maintain computer and user environments across a domain.

2. Who can implement system policy?

   An administrator.

3. Name two major functions of System Policy Editor.

   Modify default settings for the computer and user policy for the domain.

   Create custom settings that apply to individual users, groups of users, or individual computers.

   Specify the location from which to download system policy.

4. Name two policies that you might create to secure a computer.

   Create a logon banner that is seen by anyone logging on to the computer.

   Disable the display of the last user's logon name.

5. If a user logs on to a domain that has system policy, but system policy has not been defined for that user, what happens next?

   Windows NT checks to see whether system policy exists for a group that the user is in, and if it does exist, the group settings are merged into HKEY_CURRENT_USER. If a group does not exist, then the default user policy settings are merged into HKEY_CURRENT_USER.

6. Your network has 165 computers running Windows 95, and 200 computers running Windows NT Workstation. The Windows 95 users are complaining that the network is really slow when everyone is trying to log on in the morning. What can cause this problem and how do you resolve it?

   A potential slowdown on the network can occur because by default the computers running Windows 95 always search for their policies on the PDC. If load balancing is selected, after the initial logon the Windows 95 client takes its policy from whichever logon server authenticates a user.

CHAPTER 5

Managing File Systems

About This Chapter

This chapter covers the Microsoft Windows NT file systems—FAT (file allocation table), also used by other operating systems, such as Microsoft MS-DOS; and NTFS (Windows NT File System), used only on computers running Windows NT—and explains the issues involved in running them in the Windows NT environment. In addition, management of long file names (LFNs) is discussed, including how long file names are converted to 8.3 entries and the concerns when using long file names on a FAT partition. Finally, methods of file compression are explained, along with the effects that copying and moving files have on the compression attributes of the files.

Before You Begin

To complete the lessons in this chapter, you must have:

- Two computers that meet the hardware and software requirements as specified in the Getting Started section of "About This Book."
- Completed all practices in Chapter 2, "Installing Windows NT."

Lesson 1: File Systems Supported by Windows NT

Windows NT supports different file systems on the same computer running Windows NT. You can format multiple partitions with different file systems on the same computer running Windows NT. The file system(s) you choose depend on the operating system(s) and the security needs of your organization. This lesson describes the file systems supported by Windows NT and identifies their major distinguishing features.

After this lesson, you will be able to:

- Describe the features of the FAT file system.
- Describe the features of the NTFS file system.
- Identify important considerations in NTFS implementation.
- Compare the advantages and disadvantages of FAT and NTFS.
- Convert FAT partitions to NTFS.

Estimated lesson time: 25 minutes

The following table shows the file systems in Windows NT and the operating systems that support them.

File system	Supporting operating systems
File allocation table (FAT)	Windows NT, Microsoft Windows 95, MS-DOS, and IBM OS/2
Windows NT File System (NTFS)	Windows NT
CD-ROM File System (CDFS)	Windows NT and Windows 95

Note CDFS is used to read from CD-ROM drives. Because CDFS is a read-only, special-purpose file system, it is not described in this course.

FAT File System

The file allocation table (FAT) file system is an enhanced version of the file system that has been used for years with computers running MS-DOS. FAT is required for computers running Windows 95 and MS-DOS. Therefore, if you want to dual-boot a computer running Windows NT with another operating system, such as Windows 95 or MS-DOS, the system partition must be formatted with the FAT file system.

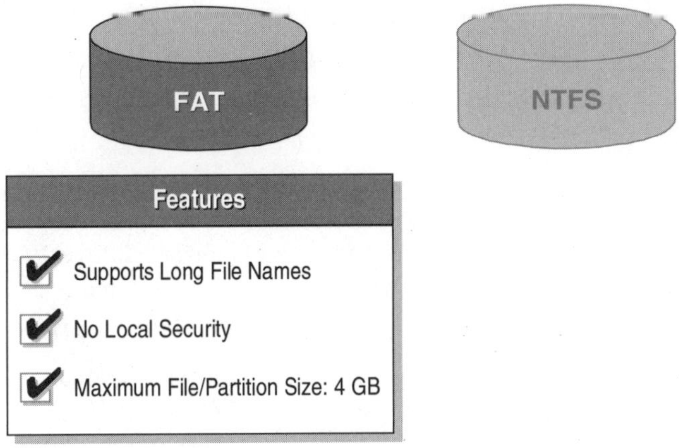

Note Windows NT cannot read FAT32 file systems, which are available on some OEM versions of Windows 95.

Some important considerations when using the FAT file system are naming conventions, security concerns, and file and partition size.

FAT Naming Conventions

Under Windows NT, the FAT file system is enhanced to support long file names (LFNs). The following criteria apply to file names on a Windows NT partition that has been formatted with the FAT file system:

- The file name, including the full path location, can be up to 255 characters.
- The name must start with either a letter or a number, and can contain any characters except the following:

  / \ : | * = ? " ; [ ] , ^
- The name can contain multiple spaces.
- The name can contain multiple periods, with the characters after the last period treated as the extension.
- Names preserve case, but are not case-sensitive.

FAT Security

A FAT partition cannot be protected by *local* file or folder security features of Windows NT. The only security available on FAT partitions is provided through Windows NT directory-level sharing mechanisms.

FAT File and Partition Size

FAT is the preferred file system for partitions less than 200 MB in size. The maximum file and partition size for FAT is 4 GB.

Other FAT File System Considerations

The following considerations are important when implementing a FAT file system for Windows NT:

- You cannot undelete a file because undelete utilities access the hardware directly, which is not allowed under Windows NT. However, if the deleted file is on a FAT partition, and the system is restarted under MS-DOS, it may be possible to undelete the file if it has not been written over.
- FAT has minimal file-system overhead (less than 1 MB per partition).
- Performance declines with large numbers of files because FAT uses a linked list for the folder structure. If the amount of data in a file grows, the file becomes fragmented on the hard disk, and the process of retrieving the file from the disk becomes slower.
- FAT is the required file system for the system partition on ARC-compliant computers, which are RISC-based computers supported by Windows NT.

NTFS File System

The Windows NT File System (NTFS) is the preferred file system under Windows NT for a number of reasons, primarily security. NTFS can only be used on computers running Windows NT.

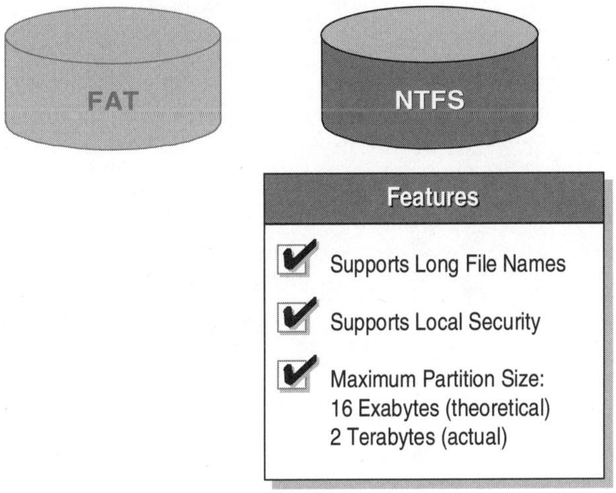

NTFS Naming Conventions

The following rules apply to NTFS file names:

- File and folder names can be up to 255 characters, including extensions.
- In general, names are not case-sensitive but are case-preserving. There is an exception: within a POSIX application, NTFS allows the coexistence of two identically named files that differ only in case. POSIX (Portable Operating System Interface) is a standard developed by the Institute of Electrical and Electronics Engineers, Inc. (IEEE).
- Names can contain any characters, including spaces, except the following: / \ : | * ? " < >

NTFS Security

NTFS should be used when security is required for servers and personal computers. NTFS supports discretionary access control and ownership privileges important to ensure the integrity of data. While folders shared by a computer running Windows NT can have assigned permissions regardless of the file system used, NTFS files and folders can have assigned permissions whether or not they are shared. NTFS is the only file system on Windows NT that allows permissions to be assigned to individual files and folders.

NTFS File and Partition Size

NTFS supports larger file and partition sizes than the FAT file system, theoretically up to 16 exabytes for both files and partitions.

- The maximum file size is between 4 GB and 64 GB, depending on the computer's hardware. The functional maximum partition size for NTFS on typical hardware is 2 terabytes due to industry-standard limitations on the maximum number and size of disk sectors.
- The recommended minimum partition size for an NTFS partition is 50 MB, because of the overhead involved in using NTFS.

Additional Features

NTFS has the following additional features that make it a powerful and flexible file system:

- *Support for file compression.* File compression reduces text-oriented application or data file size by about 50 percent and reduces executable file size by about 40 percent.
- *Transaction-based recoverability.* NTFS has high reliability. It is a recoverable file system that uses transaction logging to log all folder and file updates automatically. This is used by Windows NT to repeat or undo operations that failed due to system failure or power loss.
- *Support for cluster remapping.* If an error occurs because of a bad sector on the hard disk, NTFS allocates a new cluster to replace the cluster with the bad sector. NTFS then stores the address of the cluster containing the bad sector so that the bad sector is not reused. This is transparent to any applications performing disk I/O.
- *Support for Macintosh files.* You can install Services for Macintosh on computers running Windows NT Server. This allows Macintosh computers to store their files on the computer running Services for Macintosh.
- *Support for POSIX requirements.* NTFS is the Windows NT POSIX.1-compliant supported file system and supports the following POSIX.1 requirements:
  - *Case-sensitive naming.* Under POSIX, file names are case-sensitive, so that README.TXT, Readme.txt, and readme.txt are different files.
  - *Additional time stamp.* This supplies the time the file was last accessed.
  - *Hard links.* A hard link occurs when two different file names, which can be located in different folders, point to the same data.

Note You can run POSIX applications from any Windows NT file system. However, if the application requires access to file system resources, then NTFS is required.

- *Support for file and folder security.*
- *Provides a separate Recycle Bin for each user.*
- *Reduces file fragmentation.* Reduces file fragmentation by attempting to write files contiguously on the partition. A file can become fragmented as it grows in size, depending on the disk's space usage.

For more information on Windows NT file systems, see *Inside the Windows NT File System,* by Helen Custer.

Converting to NTFS

Windows NT includes an executable file, Convert.exe, that converts an existing FAT hard disk partition to NTFS. Note that conversion is a one-way process; there is no way to convert an NTFS partition to FAT.

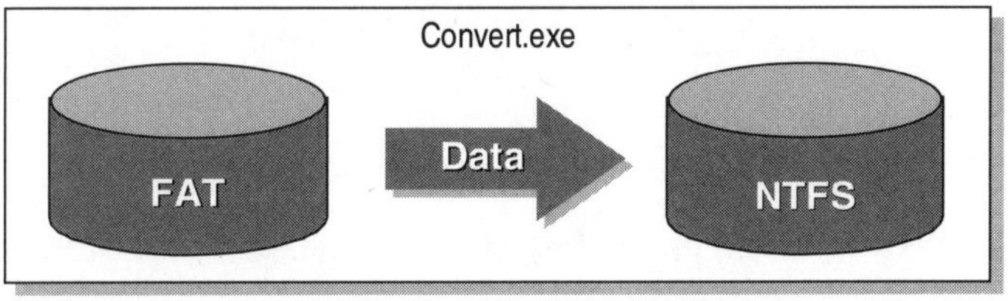

Converting a partition from FAT to NTFS preserves all data on the partition, unlike formatting the partition, which destroys all data.

The **convert** command uses the following command prompt syntax:

convert *drive*: **/fs:ntfs**

where *drive* is the letter of the logical drive to be converted to NTFS.

If a process, including Windows NT itself, is currently accessing the drive, an error message appears. The error message provides an option to schedule the drive for conversion when the system restarts.

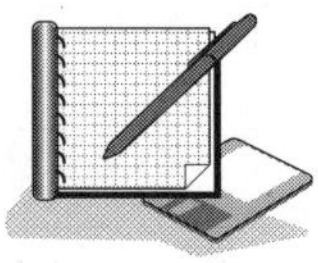

Practice

In this procedure, you convert your Server2 boot partition (drive D) from FAT to NTFS. You then observe what happens when you attempt to convert a partition on which there are open files.

▸ To convert a FAT partition to NTFS

Note Complete this practice on Server2.

---

1. Start Server2 and log on as Administrator.
2. Click the **Start** button, point to **Programs**, and then click **Command Prompt**.
3. Type **convert d: /fs:ntfs** and then press ENTER.

   A message appears stating the **convert** command cannot gain exclusive access to drive D and cannot convert it now.

   Why does this message occur?

   ____

4. Type **y** and then press ENTER to schedule the conversion to take place the next time the system restarts.
5. Shut down and then restart the computer as Server2.

   The conversion process occurs.

   Note The system restarts itself a second time. Make sure you start your computer as Server2.

   ---

6. After Server2 has restarted, log on as Administrator.
7. Right-click **My Computer**, and then click **Explore**.

   Windows NT Explorer starts.

8. Right-click **drive D**, and then click **Properties**.

   What file system is on drive D?

   ____

9. Click **Cancel**.
10. Close Windows NT Explorer.

Changing File Systems

File systems can be changed on any partition after running Setup. Windows NT provides Convert.exe to convert a FAT partition to NTFS with no loss of data. You cannot convert an NTFS partition to FAT. If you want to change a partition from NTFS to FAT, you must do the following:

1. Back up all files.
2. Reformat the partition (this action deletes all of the files), specifying the file system, using either the **format** command or Disk Administrator.
3. Restore the files from the backup.

Lesson 2: Working with File Names

Long file name (LFN) support on Windows NT frees users from the limitations of the 8.3 file naming convention used by MS-DOS. This lesson examines how Windows NT handles long file names on FAT and NTFS file systems. This lesson also describes treatment of case-sensitive file names on partitions.

After this lesson, you will be able to:

- Explain the process for converting long file names to 8.3 entries.
- Identify concerns when using long file names on a FAT partition.

Estimated lesson time: 40 minutes

Autogenerated 8.3 File Names

The previous lesson explained that Windows NT supports long file names (LFNs) for both the FAT and NTFS file systems. To allow Windows 3.*x*- and MS-DOS-based applications to recognize and load LFN files, Windows NT automatically generates an 8.3 alias for each long file name.

Generating 8.3 File Names

Converting file names from the LFN to 8.3 format follows this process:

1. All file name characters that are not allowed under MS-DOS are removed, such as spaces.
2. The conversion takes the first six characters of the long file name and uses a *~number* suffix to keep the name unique. For example:
   - My Term Paper A.doc becomes MYTERM~1.DOC.
   - If additional files have the same first six characters, and the same characters after the period, the successive iterations would be: MYTERM~2.DOC, MYTERM~3.DOC, and MYTERM~4.DOC.
3. After the fourth file with the same first 6 characters, and the exact same 3 characters after the last period in the LFN, the naming convention changes. The fifth iteration keeps the first 2 characters of the LFN, but the next 4 characters are generated by a hashing algorithm. The random characters improve seek performance by distinguishing otherwise similar file names. For example:
   - My Term Paper E.doc becomes MY0F58~1.DOC.
   - Only when the hashing of the middle 4 characters (0F58) fails to produce a unique name is the ~1 incremented to ~2, and so on. This method is used on both FAT and NTFS partitions to create aliases for long file names.

The following illustration shows the long file name-to-8.3 alias generation.

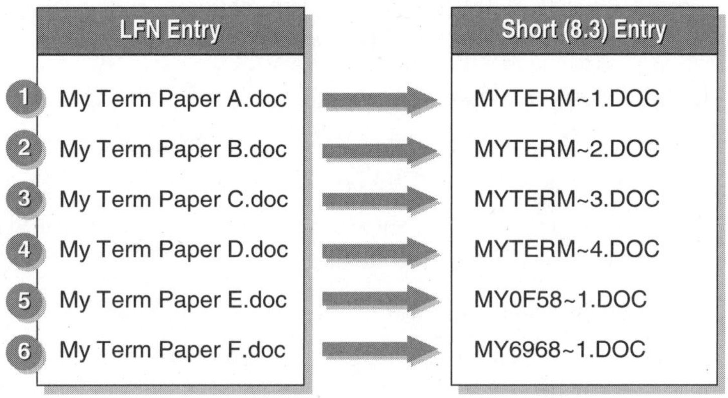

Long File Name Considerations

There are several important considerations when using long file names:

- When using long file names on files that are read by MS-DOS-based applications, consider creating files with unique combinations of the first six characters.
- Windows NT does not generate an alias for files created by a POSIX-based application. MS-DOS- and 16-bit Windows-based applications are not able to access a file created by a POSIX-based application if its file name exceeds the MS-DOS 8.3 file naming convention.
- When using long file names from the command prompt, if there are any spaces in the path, the path must be in quotes. For example, if Microsoft Word for Windows is installed in the folder D:\Word for Windows, all references to the folder path and files from the command prompt should be in quotation marks. To start Word from a command prompt, you would type the following: "D:\Word for Windows\winword.exe"

  If quotation marks are not placed around the path, an invalid path error message appears. The exception is the **chdir** (or **cd**) command, which does not require quotation marks.

Caution Some 16-bit applications save data to a temporary file, delete the original file, and then rename the temporary file to the original file name. In some cases this deletes the long file name and, when the file is on an NTFS partition, any permissions that were associated with the original file.

Long File Names on FAT Partitions

On a FAT partition, Windows NT automatically creates a short file name, or alias, for each long file name (LFN). The LFNs are retained in secondary folder entries.

Alias Folder Entries

For every LFN on a Windows NT FAT partition, an autogenerated short file name provides an alias for the long file names. Aliases are stored as MS-DOS-compatible FAT folder entries.

There are two ways to view an alias:

- Through Command Prompt
  1. Click the **Start** button, point to **Programs**, and then click **Command Prompt**.
  2. Type **dir /x**

     Both the LFN and the alias are listed for each file.
- Through Windows NT Explorer
  1. Start Windows NT Explorer, and then select the file.
  2. On the **File** menu, click **Properties**.

     The alias appears as the 8.3 character MS-DOS name of the file.

Secondary Folder Entries

On FAT partitions, an LFN creates one folder entry for its alias and a hidden secondary folder entry for every 13 characters of the LFN. For example, the file name, *This is a Long Name.txt*, is 23 characters, and has three folder entries: one folder entry for the alias and two secondary folder entries for the LFN.

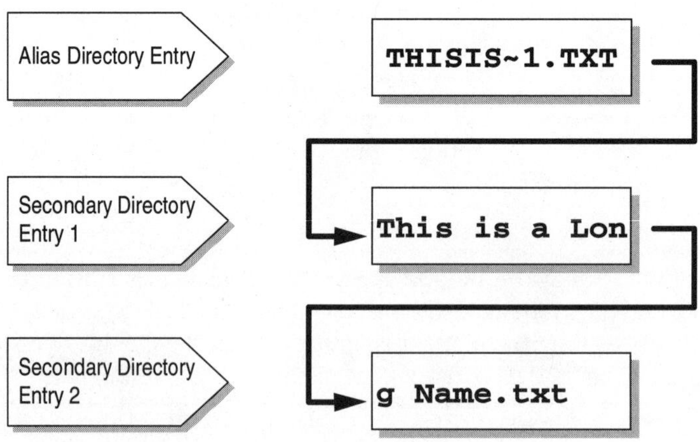

Caution The FAT root folder has a hard-coded limit of 512 entries. If many LFN files are stored in the root folder, the user could run out of entries in the root folder. As a result, the user would be unable to create any more LFN files, 8.3 files, or folders in the root folder.

Note When a system is started under MS-DOS, some third-party disk utilities that directly manipulate FAT can destroy LFN entries, or even the file itself. Users should be careful when using these utilities. They give errors indicating that there is something wrong with FAT. It is more likely that the LFN entries are causing the error message, rather than FAT.

LFN entries are not harmed by either the MS-DOS version 6.*x* tools, SCANDISK, DEFRAG, and CHKDSK, or the disk utilities designed for Windows 95.

Windows NT can be configured to prevent the use of LFNs on FAT partitions by changing the following registry value to 1:

HKEY_LOCAL_MACHINE\SYSTEM\CurrentControlSet\Control\FileSystem\Win31FileSystem.

Mixed-Case File Names

Windows NT preserves case-sensitive file names. Therefore, on a FAT partition, a mixed-cased file name generates an uppercase alias, even if the original file name meets the other 8.3 naming convention requirements. For example, MyFile.Txt generates an alias of MYFILE.TXT on a FAT partition. However, this same file on an NTFS partition does not generate an alias.

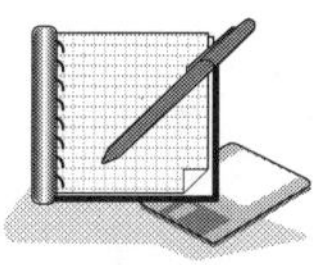

Practice

In this procedure, you create and rename files on a FAT partition (drive C) and note the effect of these changes on their long file names and aliases. When creating the files, type the names exactly as the procedure specifies; remember that Windows NT preserves the uppercase and lowercase formatting of file names.

Note Complete this procedure on Server2.

▸ **To create long file names**

1. Log on as Administrator.
2. Right-click **My Computer**, and then click **Explore**.

   Windows NT Explorer starts.
3. On the **View** menu, click **Options**.

4. On the **View** tab, verify that **Hide file extensions for known file types** is selected, and then click **OK**.
5. Click the icon for drive C.
6. On the **File** menu, point to **New**, and then click **Folder** to create a new folder. Name the folder LFN Lab Exercise.
7. Inside the LFN Lab Exercise folder, create the following text documents using Windows NT Explorer:

   Long filename.lab.exercise

   Long filename.exercise.lab

   Longfilename.exercise.lab

   Exercise.long filename.lab

   Lab.long filename.exercise

   Test.Txt
8. At a command prompt, change to the root folder of drive C (C:\). Use the **dir /x** command to list the root folder.

   How does the LFN Lab Exercise folder that you just created appear in the folder list?

   ____

9. Type **cd LFN Lab Exercise** and then press ENTER to change to the folder you created.
10. Type **dir /x** to list the folder. Record the 8.3 file names below.

8.3 file names	Long file names
____________________	Long filename.lab.exercise.txt
____________________	Long filename.exercise.lab.txt
____________________	Longfilename.exercise.lab.txt
____________________	Exercise.long filename.lab.txt
____________________	Lab.long filename.exercise.txt
____________________	Test.Txt.txt

   Why does Test.Txt have two extensions when listed from the command prompt?

   ____

11. Rename LONGFI~1.TXT to LFN.LAB by typing **ren LONGFI~1.TXT LFN.LAB** and then pressing ENTER.

12. List the folder and note the file name and alias.

    What happened to the file name and alias of the file you renamed?

    ____

13. Type **ren "Long filename.exercise.lab.txt" LONG.TXT** and then press ENTER.

    Be sure to use quotation marks around the long file name because the **ren** command does not recognize blank spaces.

14. List the folder contents.

    What happened to the file name and alias of the file you renamed?

    ____

15. Type **ren LONG.TXT Long.Txt** and then press ENTER.

16. List the folder contents.

    What happened to the file name and alias of the file you renamed?

    ____

    Why does Long.Txt have an alias while LONG.TXT does not?

    ____

17. Minimize the command prompt.

Lesson 3: Managing NTFS Compression

This lesson discusses file compression on NTFS partitions and issues that can result when you compress and decompress files and folders.

After this lesson, you will be able to:

- Compress and decompress files and folders using Windows NT Explorer or the **compact** command.
- Describe the effects that copying and moving files has on the compression attributes of the files.

Estimated lesson time: 30 minutes

Compressing and Decompressing Files and Folders

The NTFS file system supports automatic compression and decompression of files and folders. Compression can be performed on individual files, folders, and even entire drives.

Note By default Windows NT files and folders are decompressed. To compress them you must select the compression attribute.

Although both Windows NT Server and Windows NT Workstation support file compression, performance degradation can occur on systems that experience heavy write traffic, such as some types of dedicated servers.

Note For performance reasons, compression is not supported on NTFS partitions with cluster sizes greater than 4 KB.

Compression Attribute

On an NTFS partition, each file and folder has an attribute for compression. The compression attribute of a file is different from that of a folder in the following ways:

- If the compression attribute is set for a file, it indicates that the file is compressed.
- If the compression attribute is set for a folder, it indicates that any files created in the folder are automatically compressed.

In Windows NT Explorer, files and folders that have a compressed attribute can be configured to display in blue text. To do this, on the **View** menu, click **Options**, click the **View** tab, and then click the **Display compressed files and folders with alternate color** check box.

Note Blue is the only color option that Windows NT Explorer provides to designate compressed files and folders; therefore, using a blue background is not recommended.

Methods for Compressing and Decompressing

Windows NT includes the following two methods to compress and decompress files and folders:

- Windows NT Explorer
- Compact.exe

Note Neither Windows NT Explorer nor Compact.exe will compress an open file.

Windows NT Explorer

When you use Windows NT Explorer to examine the attributes of a folder on an NTFS partition, the **General** tab in the **Properties** dialog box includes a **Compress** check box.

Note The **Properties** dialog box of a *file* on an NTFS partition includes a **Compressed** check box.

The following illustration shows the properties of a folder named Reports.

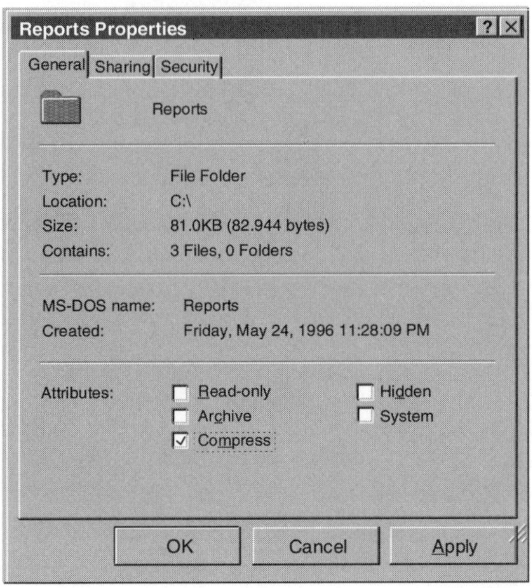

When you compress or decompress a folder, Windows NT Explorer prompts you to indicate whether to compress or decompress existing subfolders in the selected folder. Each existing subfolder in compressed or decompressed folders retains its compression state unless you change it.

Compact.exe

You can also compress files and folders by using Compact.exe from the command prompt. Compact.exe supports the following options.

Option	Action performed
/c	Compresses the specified files. Folders are marked so that files added after the initial compression are compressed.
/u	Decompresses the specified files. Folders are marked so that files added after the decompression are not compressed.
/s	Performs the specified operation on files in the given folder and all subfolders. The default folder is the current folder.
/a	Displays files with the hidden or system attributes. These files are omitted by default.
/i	Continues performing the specified operation even after errors have occurred. By default, Compact.exe stops when an error is encountered.
/f	Forces the compress operation on all specified files, even those that are already compressed. This switch is useful if a large file is being compressed and power is lost. When a file is compressed, it is initially marked as compressed before the compression actually occurs. If the power is lost during compression, the file may not be fully compressed. This switch can be used to complete the compression process on the file.
/q	Reports only the summary information.

If Compact.exe is used without any options, it displays the compression state of the current folder and any files within the current folder.

Note Any user that has Read and Write permissions can use Windows NT Explorer or Compact.exe to compress and decompress files and folders on an NTFS partition.

Compressing the Windows NT Installation

If Windows NT is installed on an NTFS partition, it is possible to compress the entire *systemroot* folder and all subfolders. However, it is not possible to compress the Windows NT Boot Loader (NTLDR) if you are booting from an NTFS partition on an Intel *x*86-based computer.

Paging files cannot be compressed while in use. A closed paging file from another Windows NT installation can be compressed, but when that installation restarts, the paging file is immediately decompressed.

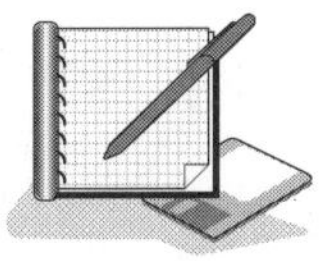

Practice

In these procedures, you use Windows NT Explorer to compress files and folders on an NTFS partition.

Note Complete these procedures on Server2, where drive D is formatted as an NTFS partition.

► **To prepare for this practice**

1. Start Windows NT Explorer.
2. Create a new folder in the root of drive D named Student.
3. Copy the C:\Lab Files\Ntfs\Student folder and all of its subfolders and files to D:\Student.

► **To compress a folder**

1. Right-click drive D, and then click **Properties**.

   The **Properties** dialog box appears.

   What is the total capacity of drive D?

   ____

   What is the free space for drive D?

   ____

2. Select the **Compress D:** check box, and then click **Apply**.

   An **Explorer** dialog box appears that contains the following messages: "Compress all files in D:\." "This action compresses all files but does not compress subfolders."

3. Select the **Also compress subfolders** check box, and then click **OK**.

   A Windows NT Explorer dialog box appears with a message that Windows NT Explorer cannot change the compress attributes for D:\Pagefile.sys.

4. Click **Ignore All** to continue.

   How much free space is available on drive D after compression?

   ____

5. Click **OK**.

▸ **To confirm that files have been compressed**

1. On the **View** menu in Windows NT Explorer, click **Options**.
2. On the **View** tab, select the **Display compressed files and folders with alternate color** check box.
3. Click **OK**.

   The compressed files and folders are displayed in blue.

▸ **To decompress a folder**

1. In Windows NT Explorer, expand the icon for drive D.
2. Expand the Student folder.
3. In the Student folder, right-click the Archives folder.
4. Click **Properties**.
5. Clear the **Compress** check box, and then click **OK**.

   An **Explorer** dialog box appears that contains the following messages: "Uncompress all files in D:\Student\Archives." "This action uncompresses all files but does not uncompress subfolders."

   This dialog box contains a check box option to decompress subfolders.
6. Select the **Also uncompress subfolders** check box, and then click **OK**.

   The Archives folder name should now be displayed in black. If not, press F5 to refresh the display.

Copying and Moving Compressed Files

When files are copied or moved on NTFS partitions, their compression attributes can change.

Copying

When a file is copied from one folder to another, the compression attribute of the file changes to that of the target folder. In the same way that permissions are inherited on a copied file, the file inherits the compression setting of the target folder.

Note When copying a file to a compressed folder, the file is first copied, and then compressed. For this reason, if the partition on which the compressed folder resides does not have enough space for the file in its decompressed state, the copy fails, even though there is enough space for the compressed file.

Moving

When a file is moved from one folder to another on the same NTFS partition, the file retains its compression attribute, regardless of whether or not the target folder is compressed. Again, as was true for permissions, the file retains its compression setting when a file is moved.

When a file is moved between two NTFS partitions, just as with permissions, the file inherits the compression attribute from the target folder. This occurs because a move between partitions is actually a copy-and-delete operation.

Note When a compressed file is moved to a folder that is not compressed, the folder does not appear in blue in Windows NT Explorer. The only time a folder appears in blue is when the folder has the compression attribute set.

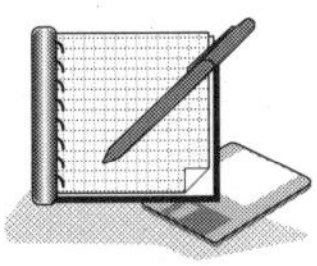

Practice

In these procedures, you see the effects that copying and moving files have on compressed files.

Note Complete these procedures on Server2, where drive D is a compressed NTFS partition containing the Student folder.

▸ **To copy a compressed file to a decompressed folder**

1. Examine the properties for Dna.txt in D:\Student\Reports\Statistics.

   Is Dna.txt compressed or decompressed?

   ____

2. Copy Dna.txt to the Archives folder on drive D.

   Make sure you copy (hold down the CTRL key) and do not move the file.

3. Examine the properties for Dna.txt in the Archives folder.

   Is Dna.txt compressed or decompressed?

   ___

   Why?

   ___

4. Close Windows NT Explorer.

▸ **To move a compressed file to a decompressed folder**

1. Examine the properties of Labor.txt in the D:\Student\Reports\Tech folder.

   Is Labor.txt compressed or decompressed?

   ___

2. Move Labor.txt to the Archives folder.
3. Examine the properties of Labor.txt in the Archives folder.

   Is Labor.txt compressed or decompressed?

   ___

   Why?

   ___

Summary

The following information summarizes the key points in this chapter:

- Windows NT 4.0 supports both the file allocation table (FAT) and Windows NT File System (NTFS).
- The following table compares the basic characteristics of FAT and NTFS.

	FAT	NTFS
File name and folder length	255 characters	255 characters
File size	4 GB (2^{32} bytes)	4 GB–64 GB actual, based on current hardware; 16 exabytes (2^{64} bytes) theoretical based on Windows NT software
Partition size	4 GB (2^{32} bytes)	2 terabytes actual, based on current hardware; 16 exabytes (2^{64} bytes) theoretical based on Windows NT software
Attributes	Read Only, Archive, System, Hidden	Further extended and extensible
Accessible through	Windows NT, Windows 95, MS-DOS, and OS/2	Windows NT
Built-in security	No	Yes
Supports file compression	No	Yes

- The following table shows advantages and disadvantages of FAT and NTFS.

	Advantages	Disadvantages
FAT	Low system overhead. Suitable for drives or partitions up to 400 MB.	No file or directory permissions. Using FAT with drives or partitions larger than 400 MB can decrease performance.
NTFS	Suitable for volumes of 400 MB or larger. More robust than FAT. Supports local security.	Not efficient for volumes smaller than 400 MB, because of disk space overhead of an NTFS partition. Disk space overhead ranges from 1–5 MB or more, depending on the size of the partition.

- Windows NT supports long file names (LFNs) for both the FAT and NTFS file systems. Windows NT automatically generates an 8.3 alias for each LFN.
- The NTFS file system supports automatic compression and decompression of files and folders. Compression can be performed on individual files, folders, and even entire drives.

For more information on	See
Windows NT file systems	*Inside the Windows NT File System,* by Helen Custer.

Review

1. If you must support long file names on all partitions, need the ability to dual-boot between MS-DOS and Windows NT Workstation, and want to provide file compression for Windows NT, which file system or systems should you choose?
   a. FAT and NTFS
   b. FAT on all partitions
   c. NTFS on all partitions

   ____

2. You get a telephone call from a user, saying that he got a message that something is wrong with the FAT file system. As you ask the user questions, you learn that an error was generated when a third-party disk utility was in use. What do you think caused the problem?

   ____

   ____

   ____

3. You get a telephone call from a user who wants to know why she is unable to create a file in the root folder. She is using LFNs, the root folder is on a FAT partition, and she has 278 entries in the folder. What do you suspect is the problem?

   ____

   ____

   ____

4. You install Windows NT Workstation on a computer that previously ran Windows 95. One of your FAT partitions is not accessible under Windows NT Workstation. Why not? How can you make this partition accessible under Windows NT?

5. You create a folder named Archives on an NTFS partition and compress it. You use this folder to store files that are eventually backed up to tape, but when you move files into this folder, some get compressed and some do not. Why is the compression status not consistent?

Answer Key

Procedure Answers

Page 180

► **To convert a FAT partition to NTFS**

3. Type **convert d: /fs:ntfs** and then press ENTER.

   A message appears stating the **convert** command cannot gain exclusive access to drive D and cannot convert it now.

   Why does this message occur?

   Drive D is the boot partition and is currently in use by the operating system.

8. Right-click **drive D**, and then click **Properties**.

   What file system is on drive D?

   NTFS.

Page 185

► **To create long file names**

8. At a command prompt, change to the root folder of drive C (C:\). Use the **dir /x** command to list the root folder.

   How does the LFN Lab Exercise folder that you just created appear in the folder list?

   The command dir /x shows both the alias and the long file name: LFNLAB~1 and LFN Lab Exercise.

10. Type **dir /x** to list the folder. Record the 8.3 file names below.

8.3 file names	Long file names
LONGFI~1.TXT	Long filename.lab.exercise.txt
LONGFI~2.TXT	Long filename.exercise.lab.txt
LONGFI~3.TXT	Longfilename.exercise.lab.txt
EXERCI~1.TXT	Exercise.long filename.lab.txt
LABLON~1.TXT	Lab.long filename.exercise.txt
TESTTX~1.TXT	Test.Txt.txt

   Why does Test.Txt have two extensions when listed from the command prompt?

   By default, Windows NT Explorer hides extensions. When you created a new text document, a .txt extension was appended to the file name that you provided (Test.Txt). The new file name is Test.Txt.txt.

12. List the folder and note the file name and alias.

    What happened to the file name and alias of the file you renamed?

    The file name was changed to LFN.LAB and the alias was deleted because it was no longer necessary.

14. List the folder contents.

    What happened to the file name and alias of the file you renamed?

    The file was renamed to LONG.TXT and the alias was deleted.

16. List the folder contents.

    What happened to the file name and alias of the file you renamed?

    The file was renamed to Long.Txt with an alias of LONG.TXT.

    Why does Long.Txt have an alias while LONG.TXT does not?

    Aliases are only created when a file name exceeds the FAT 8.3 limitation, or when a mixed-case file name is created.

Page 191

▸ **To compress a folder**

1. Right-click drive D, and then click **Properties**.

   The **Properties** dialog box appears.

   What is the total disk space for drive D?

   Answers will vary.

   What is the total free disk space for drive D?

   Answers will vary.

4. Click **Ignore All** to continue.

   How much free disk space is available on drive D after compression?

   Answers will vary.

Page 193

▸ **To copy a compressed file to a decompressed folder**

1. Examine the properties for Dna.txt in D:\Student\Reports\Statistics.

   Is Dna.txt compressed or decompressed?

   Compressed.

3. Examine the properties for Dna.txt in the Archives folder.

   Is Dna.txt compressed or decompressed?

   Decompressed.

   Why?

   A copied file inherits the compression attribute of the target folder.

Page 194

▸ **To move a compressed file to a decompressed folder**

1. Examine the properties of Labor.txt in the D:\Student\Reports\Tech folder.

   Is Labor.txt compressed or decompressed?

   Compressed.

3. Examine the properties of Labor.txt in the Archives folder.

   Is Labor.txt compressed or decompressed?

   Compressed.

   Why?

   When a file is moved to a new folder on the same partition, its compression attribute does not change.

Review Answers

Page 197

1. If you must support long file names on all partitions, need the ability to dual-boot between MS-DOS and Windows NT Workstation, and want to provide file compression for Windows NT, which file system or systems should you choose?

   a. FAT and NTFS

   b. FAT on all partitions

   c. NTFS on all partitions

   Answer a., because FAT is required for MS-DOS, and NTFS is required for file compression.

2. You get a telephone call from a user, saying that he got a message that something is wrong with the FAT file system. As you ask the user questions, you learn that an error was generated when a third-party disk utility was in use. What do you think caused the problem?

   When a system is started under MS-DOS, some third-party disk utilities that directly manipulate FAT and long file name entries are probably causing the error. Check to see whether the user is using LFNs and whether they have been warned that the disk utility could destroy the LFNs and leave only the 8.3 aliases, and possibly destroy the file itself. Determine the reason for running the utility and suggest an alternative such as SCANDISK, DEFRAG, or CHKDSK in Windows 95 or MS-DOS 6.*x*; these utilities do not harm LFN entries.

3. You get a telephone call from a user who wants to know why she is unable to create a file in the root folder. She is using LFNs, the root folder is on a FAT partition, and she has 278 entries in the folder. What do you suspect is the problem?

   The FAT root directory has a hard-coded limit of 512 entries. On FAT partitions, an LFN takes one directory entry for each 13 characters, plus another directory entry for its alias. For example, if a file name is 15 characters long, it has two directory entries for the LFN and another for the alias. A 36-character LFN takes three directory entries for the LFN plus another for its alias, for a total of four directory entries. If a large number of the 278 entries in the root directory are LFNs, the user could have run out of entries in the root directory and could be unable to create any more files in the root directory.

4. You install Windows NT Workstation on a computer that previously ran Windows 95. One of your FAT partitions is not accessible under Windows NT Workstation. Why not? How can you make this partition accessible under Windows NT?

   The partition is probably FAT32, which is supported by some versions of Windows 95, but not by Windows NT. You must back up any files on the partition that you want to keep. You can then reformat the partition so that Windows NT can access it. Finally, you would need to restore the files you backed up.

5. You create a folder named Archives on an NTFS partition and compress it. You use this folder to store files that are eventually backed up to tape, but when you move files into this folder, some get compressed and some do not. Why is the compression status not consistent?

   The files are probably being moved from multiple partitions. Moving files within the same partition does not change the compression attribute, so decompressed files stay decompressed even when they are moved into a compressed folder. Moving a file from one partition to another actually creates a new instance of the file and deletes the original. New files inherit the compression attribute from their parent folder.

CHAPTER 6

Managing Partitions

About This Chapter

In this chapter, you learn about the types of partitions supported by Windows NT, including primary and extended partitions, volume sets, and stripe sets. You also learn about and use Disk Administrator—a Windows NT tool used to create, manage, and delete partitions. Finally, you will learn maintenance and troubleshooting solutions for partition management problems.

Before You Begin

To complete the lessons in this chapter, you must have:

- Two computers that meet the hardware and software requirements as specified in the Getting Started section of "About This Book."
- Completed all practices in Chapter 2, "Installing Windows NT."
- At least 50 MB of free space in an extended partition on Workstation1.

Lesson 1: Partitioning a Disk

Before a hard disk can be formatted with a file system, the disk must first be partitioned. Partitioning a disk involves specifying which portion and how much of the hard disk can be formatted with a file system. You can divide a hard disk into a maximum of four partitions. When a partition is created, Windows NT assigns it a drive letter.

Partitioning of disk space serves a number of purposes for computers running Windows NT. You can have the dual-boot capability discussed in Chapter 5, "Managing File Systems," and can manage your disk space to maximize the efficiency and performance of your system.

Windows NT supports several types of partitions. These include primary and extended partitions, volume sets, and stripe sets. This lesson describes the partition options in Windows NT.

After this lesson, you will be able to:

- Explain the differences between primary and extended partitions.
- Explain the benefits and disadvantages of a volume set.
- Explain the benefits and disadvantages of a stripe set.
- Describe hardware-related issues that affect Windows NT when adding additional hard disks.

Estimated lesson time: 30 minutes

Primary and Extended Partitions

Partitions are created in hard disk *free space*. Free space is the unused (or unpartitioned) portion of a hard disk. Free space can be divided into two types of partitions: primary or extended. Multiple primary partitions and one extended partition can coexist on the same disk. There can be up to four partitions on a hard disk.

Primary Partitions

A primary partition is a portion of a disk that can be marked as active and used by the system to start the computer. There can be up to four primary partitions per disk (or up to three, if there is an extended partition). A primary partition cannot be divided into smaller partitions.

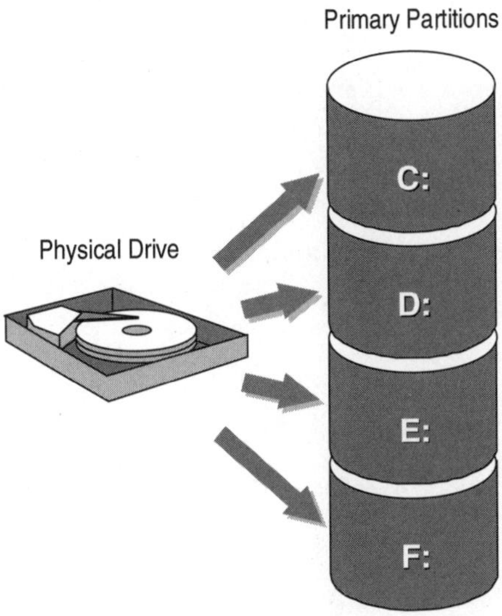

All partitions used by the Microsoft Windows 95 or Microsoft MS-DOS operating system must be formatted with the FAT file system.

On RISC-based computers, the primary partition created by the manufacturer's configuration program must be FAT, and at least 2 MB in size.

Some operating systems, such as MS-DOS version 5.0, can recognize only one primary partition per disk, even if other primary partitions are formatted with a file system that the operating system can use.

Extended Partitions

An extended partition is a method for avoiding the four-partition limit, and for configuring a hard disk into more than four logical volumes. Similar to a primary partition, an extended partition is created from free space on a hard disk.

You can have one extended partition on a hard disk. An extended partition is effectively a logical disk. Unlike a primary partition, you do not format the extended partition, nor is it assigned a drive letter. Instead, you can create one or more logical drives within the extended partition, and each logical drive is assigned a drive letter. You format each logical drive with a particular file system; this allows additional drive letters for organizing applications, data files, e-mail, multiple file systems, and so on. The following illustration shows how disk space can be divided into primary and extended partitions.

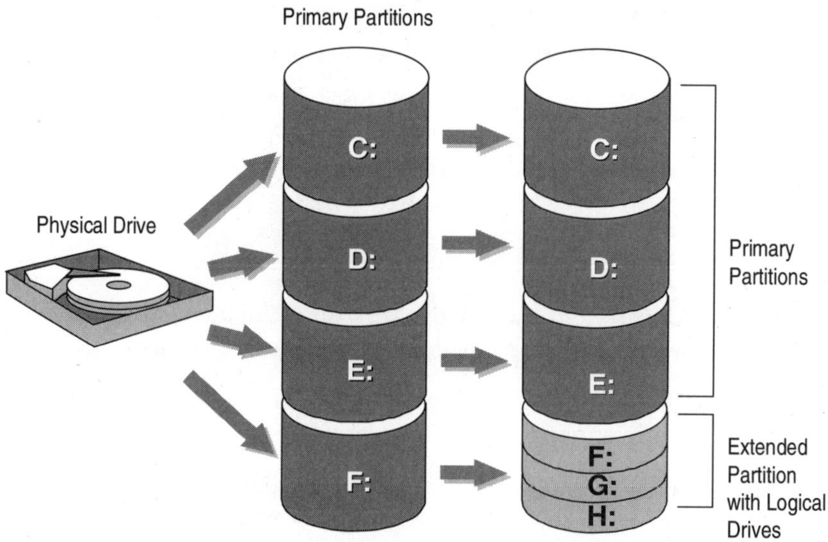

Theoretically, you could allocate disk space according to the preceding illustration, in which one primary partition was replaced by an extended partition divided into logical drives. However, the following illustration represents a more typical distribution of your hard disk space when using both primary and extended partitions. Typically the C partition would contain the system and boot files, and the remaining disk space would be an extended partition with space distributed among one or more logical drives to complement your working environment.

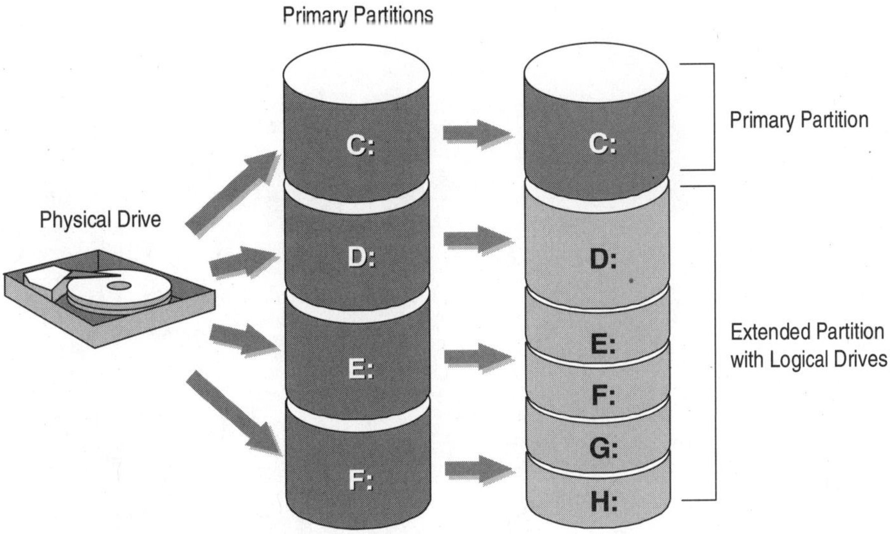

System and Boot Partitions

The Windows NT system partition must be a primary partition. The Windows NT boot partition can be either a primary partition or a logical drive in an extended partition.

What Is a Volume Set?

A volume set is a partition formed by collecting 2 to 32 areas of unformatted free space on one or more hard disks. Each area is referred to as a member of the volume set. The members form one large logical volume set, which is treated as a single partition. Though this does not improve performance, volume sets do increase the disk space available for a single logical drive and free up drive letters for other purposes. For example, in the following illustration, 100 MB of free space from Disk 0 is combined with 50 MB of free space from Disk 1 to create a 150 MB partition called a volume set.

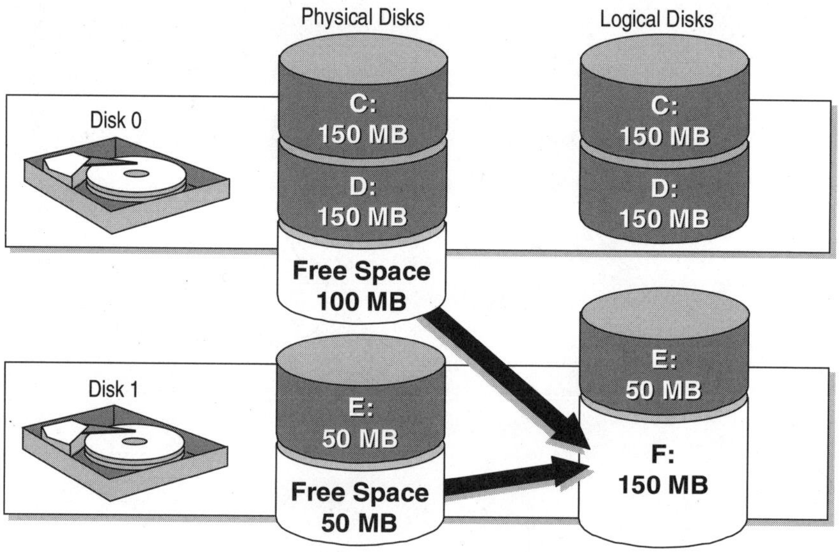

A volume set can combine areas from different types of hard disks, including small computer system interface (SCSI), enhanced small device interface (ESDI), and integrated device electronics (IDE). When creating a volume set, the free space can be an unallocated area within an extended partition, or an unpartitioned area elsewhere on the disk.

Create a volume set when you have disk space from two or more unused areas that can be combined into a single large partition, or when an application requires a larger amount of disk space than you have on any single hard disk.

Guidelines for Managing Volume Sets

Keep the following points in mind when implementing volume sets:

- You cannot reclaim portions of disk space used in a volume set for other purposes without losing the entire volume set and all of the data stored on it.
- The Windows NT boot and system partitions cannot reside in a volume set.
- If a computer running Windows NT is configured to allow booting of another operating system that does not support volume sets, such as Windows 95 or MS-DOS, that operating system cannot access information in a volume set.
- Volume sets do not provide any *fault tolerance* (the ability of a computer or operating system to respond to a catastrophic event, such as a power outage or hardware failure, so that no data is lost and work in progress is not corrupted) because there is no data redundancy. In fact, volume sets spanning multiple hard disks are more susceptible to failure because a failure on any of the hard disks will destroy the full volume set.
- In a volume set, data is written to one member of the set at a time until no space remains on that member. Data is then written to the next member in the volume set, and so on.

Note For more information about fault tolerance, see Chapter 7, "Managing Fault Tolerance."

What Is a Stripe Set?

Stripe sets are similar to volume sets in that they also combine areas of unformatted free space into one large logical drive.

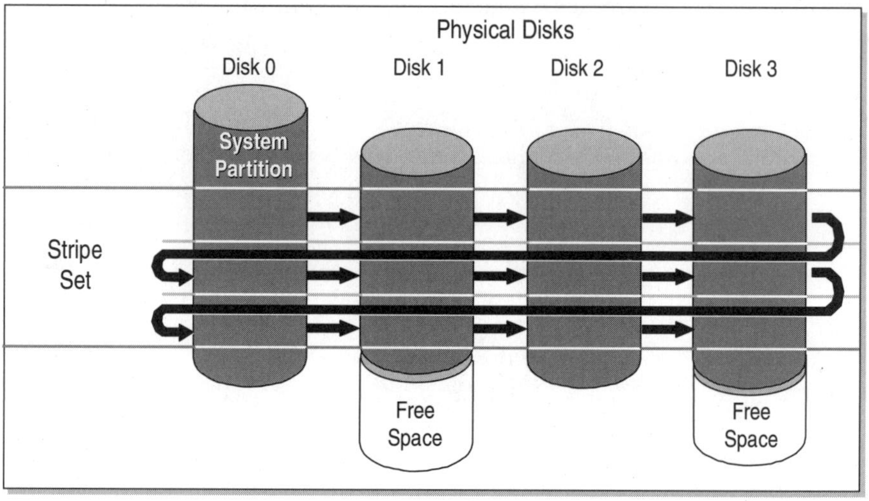

Unlike a volume set, which can be implemented with a single hard disk, a stripe set requires at least two hard disks. Stripe sets, like volume sets, can include disk space from as many as 32 hard disks and can combine areas on different types of hard disks, such as SCSI, ESDI, and IDE. The amount of space used on each disk will be equal to the smallest unpartitioned space that you selected on the disks.

In a stripe set, data is written evenly across all of the physical disks, one row at a time. The Windows NT implementation of stripe sets writes these in 64 KB units.

All of the hard disks belonging to the stripe set perform the same functions as a single hard disk. This allows concurrent I/O commands to be issued and processed on all hard disks simultaneously. In this way, stripe sets can increase the speed of system I/O.

Guidelines for Managing Stripe Sets

Stripe sets are similar to volume sets in the following ways:

- You cannot reclaim portions of disk space used in a stripe set for other purposes without losing the entire stripe set and all of the data stored on it.
- The Windows NT boot and system partitions cannot reside in a stripe set.
- If a computer running Windows NT is configured to allow booting of another operating system that does not support stripe sets, such as Windows 95 or MS-DOS, that operating system cannot access information in a stripe set.
- Stripe sets inherently do not provide any fault tolerance because there is no data redundancy. In fact, a stripe set is more susceptible to failure because it spans two or more hard disks, and a failure on any of the hard disks will destroy the full stripe set.

Note Windows NT Server includes a mechanism, adding *parity* to stripe sets, that can enable stripe sets to provide fault tolerance. For more information about fault tolerance, see Chapter 7, "Managing Fault Tolerance."

Comparing a Stripe Set to a Volume Set

The following table compares the features of stripe sets and volume sets.

Condition	Stripe set	Volume set
Can it be created on one hard disk?	No	Yes
Can it contain the system or boot partition?	No	No
What is the maximum number of areas that can be combined?	32	32
Must the areas combined be of approximately the same size?	Yes	No
Can it combine areas on different types of hard disks such as SCSI, ESDI, and IDE?	Yes	Yes
Is the area on one hard disk filled before starting to fill the next hard disk?	No	Yes
Can it improve I/O performance?	Yes	No

Note A volume set can appear to slightly improve performance on reads if the controller has the ability to do concurrent reads. The small read performance gains that can occur when using a volume set is actually a function of the hardware, and not the volume set.

Other Disk Management Considerations

In addition to creating, formatting, and deleting partitions, other disk management tasks may have to be performed on a computer running Windows NT. These include adding hard disks and configuring a disk for removable media.

Adding Hard Disks

The number of hard disks that can be added to a computer depends on the following variables:

- The physical configuration of the computer, such as the number of slots or bays available.
- The number of devices that can be connected to a disk controller or SCSI bus controller.
- The number of controllers in the computer.

When a new hard disk is added to the computer, the Disk Administrator program updates the registry when the computer is shut down and restarted. There is no need to indicate to Windows NT that a new hard disk has been added. As long as the drivers are installed for the disk controller, Windows NT automatically detects the hard disk and allows it to be partitioned and used. To partition and format the hard disk, run Disk Administrator.

Removable Media

Removable media can have only one partition, and it must be a primary partition. Removable media cannot be part of a volume set or stripe set, and cannot contain a system or boot partition. Windows NT supports formatting removable media as either FAT or NTFS. However, if the removable disk is formatted as NTFS, the computer must be shut down and restarted to change disks.

Lesson 2: Managing Partitions Using Disk Administrator

You have learned about the different types of file systems and the partitions supported by Windows NT. This lesson describes *Disk Administrator*, the Windows NT tool that is used to manage hard disks. You use Disk Administrator to create, format, and delete partitions, volume sets, and stripe sets.

After this lesson, you will be able to:

- Create, format, and delete partitions.
- Describe the purpose of an active partition.
- Create, format, extend, and delete volume sets.
- Create, format, and delete stripe sets.
- Describe drive letter assignments.
- Commit changes from within Disk Administrator.
- Secure the system partition on a RISC-based computer.

Estimated lesson time: 60 minutes

What Is Disk Administrator?

Disk Administrator is an administrative tool for managing hard disks. Disk Administrator can be thought of as a graphical Windows NT version of the MS-DOS **fdisk** utility.

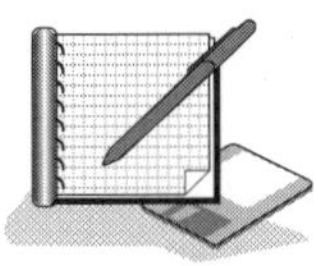

Practice

In this procedure, you start the Disk Administrator program.

- Customize the Disk Administrator legend.
- Set the Disk Administrator window to display disk areas as "equal" regions, rather than as proportional.

► **To start Disk Administrator**

Note Complete this procedure on Workstation1.

1. Shut down Server2, and then restart the computer as Workstation1.
2. Log on as Administrator.
3. Click the **Start** button, point to **Programs**, and then point to **Administrative Tools (Common)**.

4. On the **Administrative Tools (Common)** menu, click **Disk Administrator**.

   If this is the first time Disk Administrator has run, you will see one of the following messages:

   ```
   Disk Administrator has determined that this is the first time Disk
   Administrator has been run, or that one or more disks have been added
   to your computer since Disk Administrator was last run....
   ```

   –or–

   ```
   No signature found on Disk 0. Writing a signature is a safe operation
   and will not affect your ability to access this from other operating
   systems, such as DOS....
   ```

5. If you get the first message, click **OK**. If you get the second message, click **Yes**.

   Disk Administrator starts.

Clicking **Yes** creates a 32-bit signature that identifies the disk. The signature is written in the Master Boot Record of the disk. Even if a disk is moved to a different controller, or its identification is changed, Disk Administrator and the Windows NT fault tolerance driver (Ftdisk.sys) recognize it.

Disk Administrator displays the computer's disk resources through a status bar and legend. This legend can be customized by colors and patterns to display disk regions and disk usage.

Note The following illustration shows Disk Administrator on Windows NT Server. The **Fault Tolerance** menu is included only on Windows NT Server Disk Administrator. Fault tolerance can only be administered on computers running Windows NT Server.

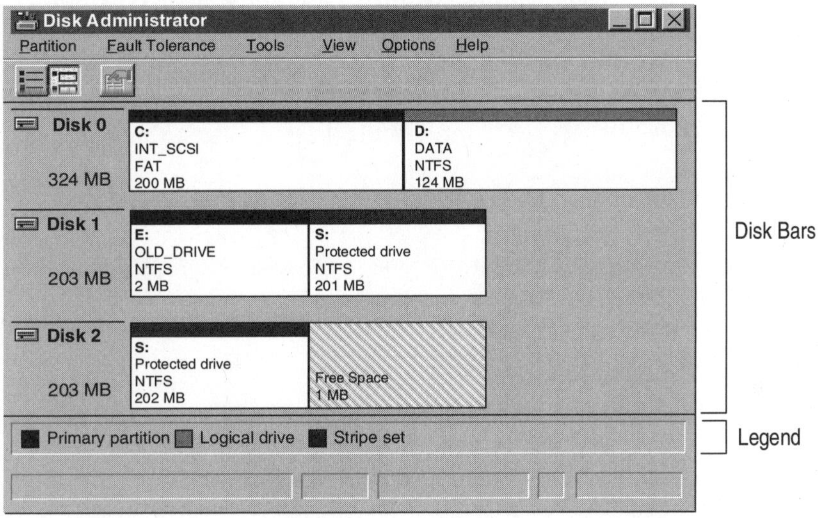

Practice

In these procedures, you start Disk Administrator, customize the Disk Administrator legend and set the Disk Administrator window to display disk areas as "equal" regions.

Note Complete these procedures on Workstation1.

▸ To customize the Disk Administrator legend

In this procedure, you set the color indicator of the primary partition to white.

1. Verify that Disk Administrator is displayed on your screen.
2. On the **Options** menu, click **Colors and Patterns**.
3. Click the down arrow in the **Color and pattern for:** box.

   List the options for which you can customize the color and pattern.

   ____

   ____

4. In the **Color and pattern for:** box, click **Primary Partition**.
5. In the **Colors** box, click the white box, and then click **OK**.

   The Disk Administrator window appears. Notice that the color indicator of the primary partition C: is now white.

▸ **To use Disk Administrator to set up the display window**

In this procedure, you set the window to display the areas representing the disk space in equal rather than proportional regions.

What file systems are currently used on drives C and D?

According to the information in the Disk Administrator window, how much free disk space does your computer have?

---

1. On the **Options** menu, click **Region Display**.
2. In the **Which disk** box, click **All disks**.
3. Click **Size all regions equally**, and then click **OK**.

   The Disk Administrator window appears. Notice that the size of block representing all partitions is the same, regardless of the actual size of the partition.

Creating and Formatting Partitions

To create and format partitions, use the Disk Administrator **Partition** and **Options** menus. You specify the location and when prompted, specify the size of the partition. When a partition is created, Windows NT assigns the next available drive letter.

After the hard disk is partitioned, the partitions must be formatted with a file system. A partition can be formatted in one of two ways:

- Use the **format** command in a command prompt with the following syntax:

  format d: /fs:FAT|NTFS
- Use the **Format** option on the **Tools** menu in Disk Administrator.

Both options allow formatting of a partition as either FAT or NTFS and assigning a volume label.

Practice

In these procedures, you use Disk Administrator to do the following:

- Create a new partition.
- Format a partition and label a volume.
- Change the drive letter of the newly-created volume.
- Save the changes.

Note Complete these procedures on Workstation1.

▸ To create a new partition

1. Click an area of free space to select it.

   The area should now have a dark outline around it, indicating that it is selected.
2. On the **Partition** menu, click **Create**.
3. In the **Create logical drive of size** box, type **25** and then click **OK**.

   The partition is created using the next available drive letter.
4. On the **Partition** menu, click **Commit Changes Now**.

   A **Confirm** dialog box appears asking if you want to save the changes.
5. Click **Yes**.

   A **Disk Administrator** dialog box appears stating that disks were updated successfully.
6. Click **OK**.

▸ To format a partition and label a volume

In this procedure, you format and label the partition that you just created.

1. Click the new unformatted partition, and then on the **Tools** menu, click **Format**.

   The **Format** dialog box appears.
2. In the **File System** box, click **NTFS**.
3. In the **Volume Label** box, type **ntfs-vol**
4. Select the **Quick Format** check box, and then click **Start**.

   A **Format** dialog box appears, warning that formatting will erase all data on this disk.

5. Click **OK**.

   A **Format Complete** dialog box appears.

6. Click **OK**.
7. Click **Close** to close the **Format** dialog box.

   Notice that Disk Administrator now displays the label, the type of file system, and the size of the newly formatted partition.

▸ **To change the drive letter**

In these procedures, you change the drive letter of the 25 MB partition you created.

1. Click the ntfs-vol partition.
2. On the **Tools** menu, click **Assign Drive Letter**.
3. In the **Assign drive letter** box, click **I:**, and then click **OK**.

   A **Confirm** dialog box appears, stating that the new drive letter assignment will happen immediately.

4. Click **Yes**.
5. On the **Partition** menu, click **Exit**.

Deleting Partitions

Use the Disk Administrator **Delete** command, located on the **Partition** menu, to delete partitions. Partitions can be deleted at any time, except under the following conditions:

- The system and boot partitions cannot be deleted from within Windows NT. You can remove the system and boot partitions by either of the following methods:
  - Booting with another operating system such as MS-DOS and then deleting the partitions.
  - Booting from the Windows NT Setup Disk 1, as if doing an installation. You are then prompted to insert Setup Disks 2 and 3, and are asked where to install Windows NT. You can also create and delete partitions from this screen. Select the system partition and then press **d**. Follow the prompts on the screen to finish deleting the partitions.
- A partition containing an open file cannot be deleted. This includes the partition that contains Pagefile.sys, the Windows NT paging file.

Marking Partitions As Active

The active partition contains the system files.

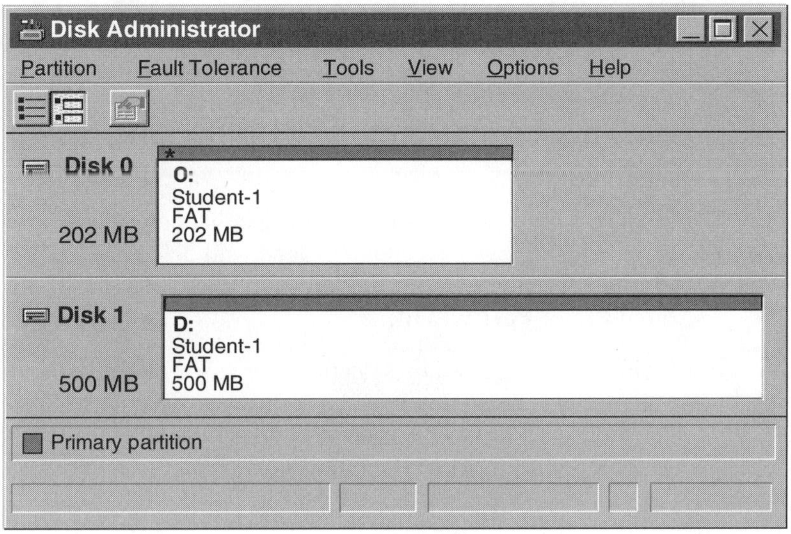

In order for an operating system to start, the partition containing the startup file must be marked as active. On Intel *x*86-based computers, the active partition is a primary partition containing the system boot files. The active partition is on the disk that the computer accesses when starting up. Use the Disk Administrator **Partition** menu to mark a partition as active. Disk Administrator displays the active partition with an asterisk in its color bar. Only one partition should be marked as active at a time.

Note The default color for primary partitions can make it difficult to see the asterisk. You may want to use the **Colors and Patterns** option on the **Options** menu of Disk Administrator to change the color of the primary partitions, as you did in an earlier procedure.

If you want to use an operating system, for example UNIX or OS/2, that is located on a partition other than the partition currently marked active, you must mark the system partition of the other operating system as active. Then shut down and restart the computer.

When a system partition is marked active, the active designation of any other partition is removed.

Note On RISC-based computers, partitions are not marked active. Instead, they are configured by a hardware configuration program supplied by the manufacturer.

Creating, Formatting, Extending, and Deleting Volume Sets

You have learned that a volume set is a collection of free space combined to create a single logical drive. To create, extend, and delete a volume set you use the **Create Volume Set**, **Extend Volume Set**, and **Delete** commands on the Disk Administrator **Partition** menu.

A volume set is created by selecting free space on the computer's hard disks. After a volume set is created, it must be formatted. Volume sets can be formatted with either FAT or NTFS. This is done by using the Disk Administrator **Format** command, which is located on the **Tools** menu.

Volume sets are also created when an NTFS partition is extended. You can also extend an existing NTFS volume set. In these circumstances, the extended partition is automatically formatted with NTFS when the computer is restarted.

Deleting a volume set deletes all information on all parts of the volume set, and returns free space.

Extending a Volume Set

You add space to an existing volume set by extending it. You can only extend a volume set that is formatted with NTFS.

For example, in the following illustration, a 150 MB NTFS volume set is extended by adding 100 MB of free space to create one 250 MB volume set.

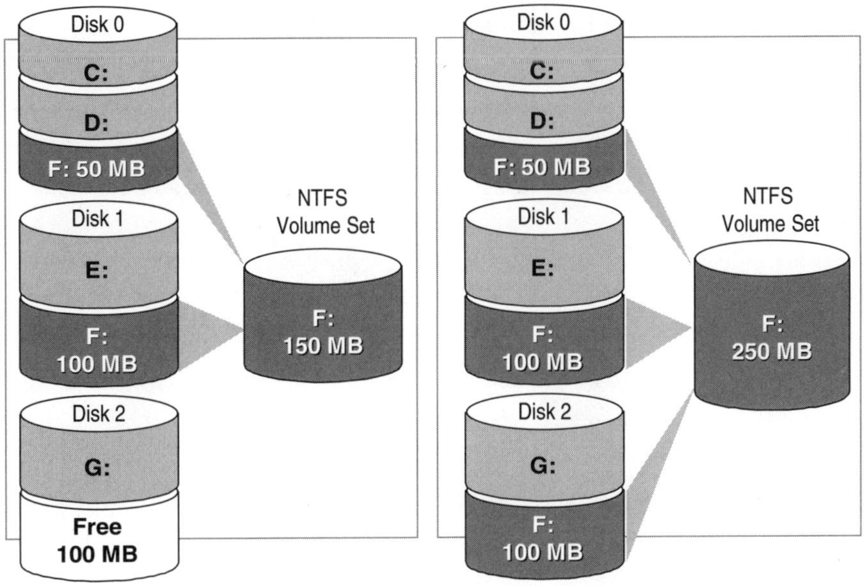

An existing volume set is extended by selecting the volume set and one or more areas of free space, and then clicking **Extend Volume Set** on the **Partition** menu in Disk Administrator.

Note There is no way to extend a FAT volume set. If you have a FAT volume set you want to extend, you must first convert the volume to NTFS. Then you can extend it.

It is necessary to shut down and restart the computer when a volume set is created or extended. Shutting down and restarting the computer after a volume set is extended automatically formats the new area or areas when the computer starts.

Important After a volume set is extended and the configuration is saved, space cannot be reclaimed without deleting the entire volume set.

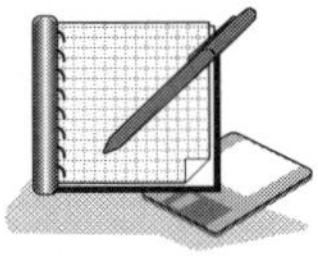

Practice

In these procedures, you use the Volume Set Simulation to create, format, extend and delete a volume set.

Note Complete these procedures on Server1.

▶ To start the simulation

1. Log on as Administrator.
2. Click the **Start** button, point to **Programs**, point to **Technical Support Training**, point to **Simulations**, and then click **Volume Set Simulation**.

   The simulations starts, and Disk Administrator appears.

▶ To create a volume set

1. Click an area of free space on Disk 0.

   The area should now have a dark outline around it, indicating that it is selected.
2. Hold down the CTRL key, and then click an area of free space on Disk 1.

   Both areas should now appear selected.
3. On the **Partition** menu, click **Create Volume Set**.

   The **Create Volume Set** dialog box appears. Notice in **Create Volume Set of Total Size** that the default is the actual total of the two areas of free space you selected.
4. Click **OK** to create a volume set of the maximum size possible on Disk 0 and Disk 1.

   The new volume set is created. Notice that the next available drive letter, G, has been assigned and the color bar has changed. The new volume set is unformatted.
5. On the **Partition** menu, click **Commit Changes Now**.

   A **Confirm** message box appears, stating that changes have been made to your disk configuration.
6. Click **Yes** to save the changes.

   A **Confirm** message box appears, stating that the changes requested will require you to restart your computer.
7. Click **Yes** to continue with the changes.

   A **Disk Administrator** message box appears, stating that the disks were updated successfully.

8. Click **OK**.

   A **Disk Administrator** message box appears, stating that changes have been made which require you to restart your computer.

9. Click **OK** to initiate system shutdown.

   A **Volume Set Simulation** message box appears, stating that the simulation will proceed as if a shutdown occurs and you have logged on as Administrator.

10. Click **OK**.

    A message box appears prompting you to please wait while the system writes unsaved data to the disk.

    The simulation continues with Disk Administrator open.

► **To format a volume set**

1. In Disk Administrator, click the unformatted volume set, drive G, and then on the **Tools** menu, click **Format**.
2. In the **File System** box, select **NTFS**, and then click **Start**.
3. Click **OK** to continue to format the volume set.

   A **Formatting** message box appears indicating the format is complete.

4. Click **OK**.
5. Click **Close**.

   The volume set now appears in Disk Administrator as an NTFS volume set.

► **To extend a volume set**

1. In Disk Administrator, click drive G, and then while you hold down the CTRL key, click an area of free space on Disk 2. Both areas should be selected.
2. On the **Partition** menu, click **Extend Volume Set**.

   The **Extend Volume Set** dialog box appears. Notice in **Create Volume Set of Total Size** that the default is the maximum total size of the areas you selected.

3. Click **OK** to extend the volume set.

   You have extended an existing NTFS volume. Notice that drive G appears in all three region displays for this volume set.

4. On the **Partition** menu, click **Exit**, and then click **Yes** to save your changes.

   A **Disk Administrator** dialog box appears, indicating your disks were updated successfully.

5. Click **OK**.

   A **Disk Administrator** dialog box appears indicating that the requested changes require you to restart your computer.

6. Click **OK** to restart your computer.

   A **Volume Set Simulation** dialog box appears, stating that the simulation will proceed as if a shutdown occurs and you have logged on as Administrator.
7. Click **OK**.

   A dialog box appears prompting you to please wait while the system writes unsaved data to the disk.

   The simulation continues with Disk Administrator open.

▸ **To delete a volume set**

1. In Disk Administrator, click drive G. All areas of drive G should now be selected.
2. On the **Partition** menu, click **Delete**.

   A **Confirm** dialog box appears indicating that all data in the volume set will be lost.
3. Click **Yes** to delete the selected volume.
4. On the **Partition** menu, click **Exit**, and then click **Yes** to save your changes.

   A **Disk Administrator** dialog box appears indicating that the disks were updated successfully.
5. Click **OK**.

   Disk Administrator closes, and the Volume Set Simulation ends.

Creating, Formatting, and Deleting Stripe Sets

Procedures for creating and deleting stripe sets are similar to procedures for creating and deleting volume sets.

You have learned the structure and use of stripe sets, and that a stripe set is similar to a volume set. Areas of free space are combined to form a single logical drive. However, while a volume set can consist of space on one or more hard disks (up to a maximum of 32), a stripe set requires space on two or more (up to 32) hard disks. Use the **Disk Administrator** menu commands to create, format, and delete stripe sets. Unlike a volume set, a stripe set cannot be extended.

The partitions combined to create a stripe set must be approximately the same size. If they are not, Disk Administrator makes each partition of the stripe set approximately the same size.

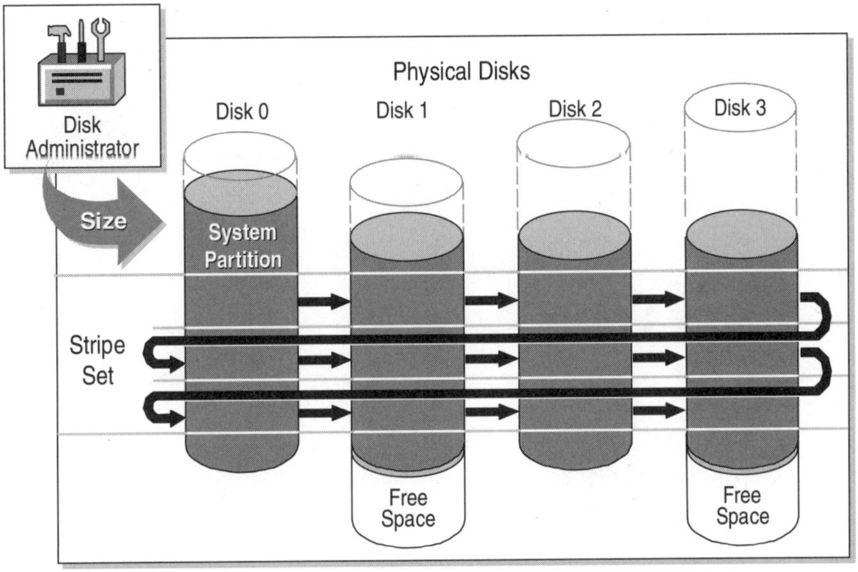

It is necessary to shut down and restart the computer when a stripe set is created.

Caution Deleting a stripe set deletes all of the information stored in the stripe set.

Committing Changes

If you have made changes to partitions using Disk Administrator, on exit, a dialog box appears requiring confirmation before changes are committed, or saved.

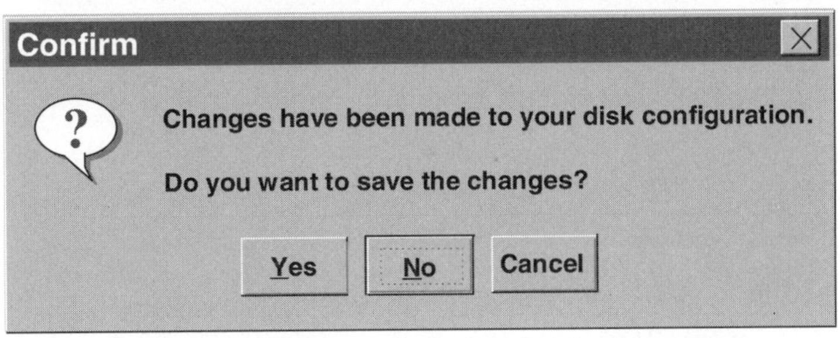

Changes can also be confirmed by using the **Commit Changes Now** command on the **Partition** menu. Changes do not take effect until they have been confirmed.

Primary and extended partitions can be removed, reconfigured, and formatted without restarting the computer. However, it *is* necessary to shut down and restart the computer when a volume set is created or extended, or when a stripe set is created.

Partition Renumbering

Windows NT assigns partition numbers to all primary partitions before assigning partition numbers to any logical drives within an extended partition. The following illustration shows how logical partitions are sequentially numbered after the primary partition.

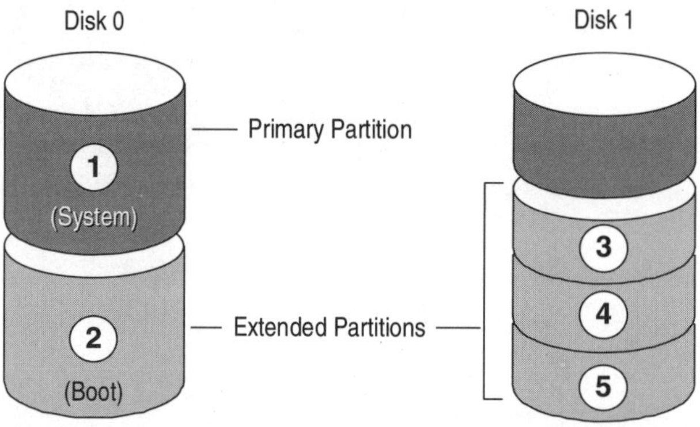

If you create another primary partition, regardless of the hard disk that it is created on, the new primary partition receives a number lower than any logical drive on an extended partition. Then the logical partitions are renumbered. The following illustration shows an example of partition renumbering. A primary partition was created on Disk 1, and was assigned the number 2. The logical partitions were reassigned numbers (3, 4, 5, 6) following the number of the newly-created primary partition (2).

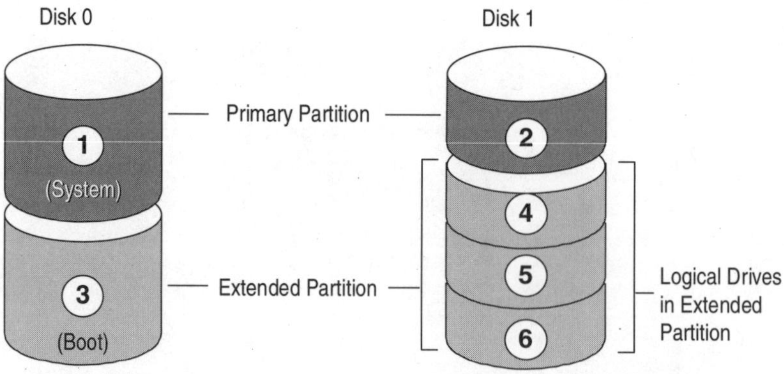

Support Issue

Windows NT uses a file named Boot.ini to find the boot partition. If the boot partition resides on an extended partition that was subsequently renumbered (as shown in the preceding illustration), then the Boot.ini file *must* be manually updated so that it points to the boot partition; otherwise, Windows NT will not start.

If you use Disk Administrator to create additional partitions on computers that are sold with small hidden partitions containing diagnostic utilities, the partition table is rewritten to include the hidden partition as partition 1. In this situation a message appears that prompts you to edit the Boot.ini file. Again, Windows NT will not start unless the Boot.ini file is correctly updated.

Note For more information about editing the Boot.ini file, see Chapter 7, "Managing Fault Tolerance."

Automatic Assignment of Drive Letters by Windows NT

Until Disk Administrator is run for the first time, Windows NT dynamically assigns drive letters using the following procedure:

1. Starting with Disk 0, the first primary partition on each disk is assigned a consecutive drive letter, beginning with the active system partition as drive C. In the following illustration, the primary partition on Disk 0 is assigned C, Disk 1 has no primary partition, Disk 2 is assigned D, and Disk 3 is assigned E.
2. Then, starting with Disk 0, logical drives on each disk are assigned the next consecutive letter(s). In the following illustration, Disk 1 has three logical drives, which are assigned F, G, and H.

3. The remaining primary partitions on each disk with unassigned partitions are each assigned a letter. In the following illustration, Disk 0 has a second primary partition which is assigned the letter I.

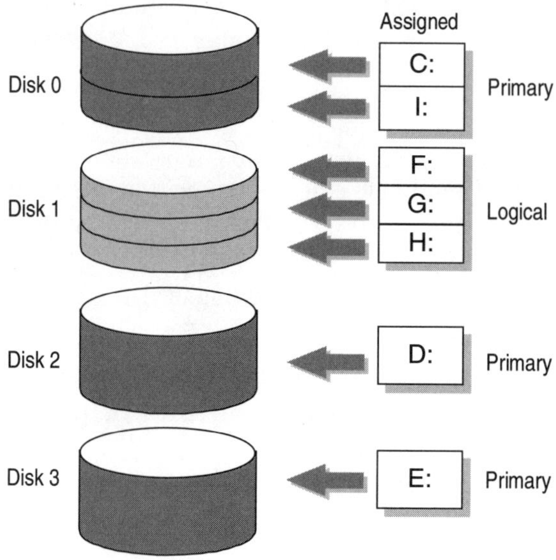

After Disk Administrator is run for the first time, it assigns static drive letters to partitions.

Reassigning Drive Letters Through Disk Administrator

Drive letters can be reassigned though the **Drive Letter** command on the Disk Administrator **Tools** menu. A partition can be statically assigned any letter that is not already in use by a local device, such as a CD-ROM drive, or in use by a network connection. Be careful not to change the drive letter of the system partition because many programs make reference to the C drive.

Assigning CD-ROM Drive Letters Through Disk Administrator

A drive letter for a CD-ROM drive can be assigned using the **CD-ROM Drive Letter** command on the **Tools** menu in Disk Administrator.

Note All drive letter modifications made with Disk Administrator can be done without restarting the computer, if the selected partition does not contain Windows NT system files.

Securing the System Partition

You learned about selecting a file system for the system partition in Chapter 2, "Installing Windows NT." Although only NTFS provides local security, FAT may be required for the system partition. For example, RISC-based computers require system partitions to be formatted with FAT, regardless of the operating system. This is because these computers will only start from a FAT file system.

Securing a FAT System Partition on a RISC-based Computer

Because FAT partitions cannot be protected with local security, the system partitions on a RISC-based computer are vulnerable unless the system partition is secured through Disk Administrator or with a third-party utility.

Note The **Secure System Partition** command is only present on RISC-based computers.

On RISC-based computers, when the **Secure System Partition** command is used in Disk Administrator, only members of the Administrators group on that computer are able to access the system partition. All other users receive an access denied message. Security is not applied until the computer is restarted.

Lesson 3: General Maintenance and Troubleshooting

This lesson covers problems that you may encounter with partition management, such as failure to recognize a hard disk or partition, or file corruption, and some potential solutions to these problems. In addition, it introduces a method to restore your current disk configuration.

After this lesson, you will be able to:

- State the solutions for the following maintenance and troubleshooting issues:
  - Recovering disk configuration information
  - Failure to recognize hard disks or partitions
  - Corrupted files or directories
  - Problems with MS-DOS-based disk utilities
  - Problems with 1 GB IDE hard disks

Estimated lesson time: 15 minutes

Recovering Disk Configuration Information

Disk configuration information is initially stored on the Emergency Repair Disk and in the *systemroot*\Repair folder at system installation. After making changes such as assigning drive letters, creating volume sets or stripes sets, and creating new partitions, Disk Administrator provides an option for saving and later restoring this configuration information in the *systemroot* folder. It also prompts you to update your Emergency Repair Disk. You must update the Emergency Repair Disk, or the information will not match the actual hard disk configuration on your computer, if an emergency repair is required.

Restoring saved disk configuration information is useful in the following situations:

- The computer was recently recovered with the Emergency Repair process and the registry was reset to its initial state. At this point, the current disk configuration will be as it was when the system was originally installed.
- A new version of Windows NT is being installed.

The Rdisk.exe utility, in the *systemroot*\System32 folder, can also be used to restore the configuration to its previous state in the last update operation.

Note Use the Rdisk.exe utility to update the Emergency Repair Disk. For more information on Rdisk.exe see Chapter 17, "The Windows NT Boot Process."

File System Problems and Solutions

Further file system problems fall into two categories: failure to recognize the hard disk or partition, and corrupted files. The following table offers solutions to some of these file system problems.

Problem	Solution
Failure to recognize hard disks or partitions.	Check to make sure there are no hardware incompatibility or hard disk problems. If Windows NT does not recognize the disk, then there is probably an incompatibility problem. If Windows NT recognizes the disk but cannot access the partition, then the problem is in either the partition table or the boot sector. Detected hardware appears in the registry under HKEY_LOCAL_MACHINE\HARDWARE.
File system corruption.	In the case of damaged directories, files with scrambled names, and minor corruption, remove the offending folder or file. More serious problems may require use of a file system repair utility. In general, if a logical drive appears corrupted and a backup exists, then reformat the drive and restore the files.
Corrupted or lost files when running MS-DOS-based utilities on dual-boot FAT partitions.	When a computer is booted under MS-DOS, some third-party disk utilities that directly manipulate FAT can destroy long file name (LFN) entries, or even the file itself. Users should be careful when using these utilities; the utilities give errors indicating that there is something wrong with FAT. It is more likely that the LFN entries are causing the error message, rather than FAT. LFN entries will not be harmed by either the MS-DOS 6.*x* tools, SCANDISK, DEFRAG, and CHKDSK, or the disk utilities designed for Windows 95. Windows NT can be configured to prevent the use of LFNs on FAT partitions by changing the following registry value to 1: HKEY_LOCAL_MACHINE\SYSTEM\CurrentControlSet\Control\FileSystem\Win31FileSystem.

(*continued*)

Problem	Solution
Problems with 1-GB IDE disks. These disks follow the EIDE standard.	Windows NT generally cannot gain access to all of the space on the disk because the disks do not translate in a way that Windows NT recognizes. This is due to a BIOS limit of 1024 cylinders, not an operating system limit. To overcome this limit, either the computer's BIOS must be able to circumvent the limit (by sector translation or by using relative cluster addressing, as SCSI hard disks do), or Windows NT must be able to communicate directly with the controller. Windows NT can currently communicate only with WD 1003-compatible controllers. Windows NT includes support for the OnTrack Systems Disk Manager partitioning utility in the hard disk device driver, Atdisk.sys. Disk Manager provides support for large (greater than 540 MB) IDE hard disks under MS-DOS. Disk Manager works by embedding BIOS extension code into Track 0 (zero) of the hard disk. Disk Manager makes sure that the MBR (Master Boot Record) invokes code that loads the BIOS extensions before anything else, such as NTLDR. The BIOS extensions, combined with the Disk Manager partition type, are used to transparently support large hard disks.

Summary

The following information summarizes the key points in this chapter:

- Windows NT supports primary and extended partitions.
- A physical disk can have as many as four partitions, or as few as one. If there are four partitions, up to four can be primary, but only one can be extended.
- Windows NT also supports volume sets and stripe sets.
- A volume set is a partition formed by collecting areas of free space to form one large logical volume. This both increases the disk space available for a single logical drive and frees up drive letters for other purposes.
- Stripe sets are similar to volume sets in that they also combine areas of unformatted free space into one large logical drive. However, a stripe set requires at least two hard disks.
- Stripe sets, like volume sets, can include disk space from as many as 32 hard disks and can combine areas on different types of hard disks, such as SCSI, ESDI, and IDE.
- In a stripe set, data is written evenly across all of the physical disks, one row at a time. The amount of space used on each disk will be equal to the smallest unpartitioned space that you selected on the disks.
- The hard disks belonging to a stripe set perform the same functions as a single hard disk, allowing concurrent I/O commands to be issued and processed on all hard disks simultaneously, thereby increasing the speed of computer I/O.
- Disk Administrator is the graphical tool provided by Windows NT that is used to create, manage, and delete partitions, volume sets, and stripe sets.
- Problems may arise relating to partitions, such as failure to recognize a hard disk or partition, or file corruption. These problems can usually be resolved by following general maintenance and troubleshooting procedures.
- The Emergency Repair Disk can be used to restore your current disk configuration when emergency repair is required.

Review

1. Name at least two reasons for using volume sets.

2. Name at least two differences between volume sets and stripe sets.

3. If you want to start an operating system that is on your computer, but is not on the active partition, what would you do?

4. If you access Disk Administrator and the **Fault Tolerance** menu is missing, what would you conclude?

5. You have created and formatted a volume set using Disk Administrator, but you are not able to write to the partition. What must you do?

   ____

6. If you are installing a new version of Windows NT, and would like to restore your present computer configuration, what should you do?

   ____

   ____

   ____

7. Where would you find information regarding detected hardware?

   ____

   ____

8. What is the likely cause of a lost file when running an MS-DOS-based utility on dual-boot FAT partitions?

   ____

   ____

Answer Key

Procedure Answers

Page 215

▶ **To customize the Disk Administrator legend**

3. Click the down arrow in the **Color and pattern for:** box.

   List the options for which you can customize the color and pattern.

   Primary partition, Logical drive, Stripe Set, Stripe Set with parity, Mirror set, and Volume set.

Page 216

▶ **To use Disk Administrator to set up the display window**

What file systems are currently used on drives C and D?

Drive C is FAT, and drive D is NTFS.

According to the information in the Disk Administrator window, how much free disk space does your computer have?

Answers will vary.

Review Answers

Page 234

1. Name at least two reasons for using volume sets.

   To enable using an application that requires more disk space than you have on any single drive.

   To arrange disk space more efficiently, such as combining several partitions into one.

   To free up drive letters for other functions.

2. Name at least two differences between volume sets and stripe sets.

   Volume sets can reside on a single hard disk; stripe sets require two or more hard disks.

   A volume set can consist of areas of varying sizes; a stripe set requires that the areas included in the partition be of approximately the same size.

   In a volume set, data is written to one member of the set at a time until no space remains; in a stripe set, data is written evenly across all of the physical disks, one row at a time.

   Volume sets can be extended; stripe sets cannot.

3. If you want to start an operating system that is on your computer, but is not on the active partition, what would you do?

   Use Disk Administrator to mark the partition containing the operating system as active.

4. If you access Disk Administrator and the **Fault Tolerance** menu is missing, what would you conclude?

   Your computer is running Windows NT Workstation, rather than Windows NT Server.

5. You have created and formatted a volume set using Disk Administrator, but you are not able to write to the partition. What must you do?

   You must shut down and restart the computer.

6. If you are installing a new version of Windows NT, and would like to restore your present computer configuration, what should you do?

   Use Disk Administrator to save your current computer configuration. Then install the new version of Windows NT and restore the current configuration.

7. Where would you find information regarding detected hardware?

   In the registry under HKEY_LOCAL_MACHINE\HARDWARE

8. What is the likely cause of a lost file when running an MS-DOS-based utility on dual-boot FAT partitions?

   The changes to FAT for long file names may not be supported by the utility.

CHAPTER 7

Managing Fault Tolerance

About This Chapter

Fault tolerance is the ability of a computer or operating system to respond to a catastrophic event, such as a power outage or a hardware failure, so that no data is lost, and that work in progress is not corrupted.

Microsoft Windows NT Server provides fault tolerance through a system called Redundant Array of Inexpensive Disks (RAID). Data protected by fault tolerance can be recovered and restored. This chapter covers the two RAID levels that are supported by Windows NT Server: *mirror sets* and *stripe sets with parity*. Furthermore, you will practice configuring these two methods of fault tolerance.

Before You Begin

To complete the lessons in this chapter, you must have:

- Two computers that meet the hardware and software requirements as specified in the Getting Started section of "About This Book."
- Completed all practices in Chapter 2, "Installing Windows NT" and Chapter 6, "Managing Partitions."
- One blank, 1.44 MB high-density disk.

Lesson 1: Fault Tolerance

This lesson discusses the various forms of fault tolerance including hardware and software solutions provided by Redundant Arrays of Inexpensive Disks (RAID).

After this lesson, you will be able to:

- Identify supported RAID levels and features.
- Describe the mirror sets function of RAID 1.
- Describe the disk striping function of RAID 5.
- Compare the features of RAID 1 with the features of RAID 5.
- Implement RAID 1 and RAID 5.

Estimated lesson time: 25 minutes

Fault tolerance is the ability of a system to continue functioning when part of the system fails. Fault tolerance is designed to combat problems with disk failures, power outages, or corrupted operating systems, which can include boot files, the operating system itself, or system files. Fully fault-tolerant systems include redundant disk controllers, power supplies, and uninterruptible power supplies (UPSs), which safeguard against local power failure.

Caution Although the data is available and current in a fault-tolerant system, you still need to make backups to protect the information on your hard disks from erroneous deletions, fire, theft, or other disasters. Always remember that fault-tolerant systems should never be used as a replacement for the regular backup of servers and local hard disks. A carefully planned backup strategy is the best insurance for recovering lost or damaged data.

RAID Systems

Windows NT Server provides a software implementation of a fault tolerance technology known as RAID. RAID technology is standardized and categorized in levels. Each level offers various mixes of performance, reliability, and cost. Windows NT Server supports RAID levels 1 and 5 to provide fault tolerance.

How does RAID operate to protect your system? RAID provides fault tolerance by implementing *data redundancy*. With data redundancy, data is written to more than one disk in a manner that allows recovery of the data in the event of a single hard disk failure. This lesson describes the types of RAID that can be implemented by Windows NT Server, and the implications of using each type.

Hardware and Software Implementations of RAID

RAID fault tolerance can be implemented as either a hardware solution or a software solution. The following are points to consider when deciding whether to implement fault tolerance in hardware or software:

- Fault-tolerant software is available only on Windows NT Server. Windows NT Workstation does not provide fault tolerance.
- Software fault tolerance is less expensive than a hardware fault tolerance solution.
- System performance is usually faster with hardware fault tolerance.
- A hardware fault tolerance solution may lock you into a single hardware vendor.
- In a hardware fault tolerance implementation, some hardware vendors allow replacement of a failed drive without shutting down the system.

Regardless of whether you implement fault tolerance by using hardware or software, implementing fault tolerance does not reduce the need for regular backups.

Furthermore, following a failure, there is no fault tolerance until the fault is repaired. If a second fault occurs before the data lost from the first fault is regenerated, you cannot recover the data without restoring it from a backup.

Hardware Implementations of RAID

In a hardware solution, the disk controller interface handles the creation and regeneration of redundant information. Some hardware vendors implement RAID data protection directly into their hardware, as with disk array controller cards. Because these methods are vendor-specific and bypass the fault tolerance software drivers of the operating system, they usually offer performance improvements over software implementations of RAID.

Note For information about hardware implementation of RAID, consult vendor product documentation.

Software Implementations of RAID

Windows NT Server supports two software implementations of RAID: RAID 1, mirror sets, and RAID 5, stripe sets with parity.

RAID 1: Mirror Sets

Mirror sets (RAID 1) use the Windows NT fault tolerance driver (Ftdisk.sys) to simultaneously write the same data to two physical drives. Through duplication, or mirroring, RAID 1 helps to ensure the survival of data in case of failure.

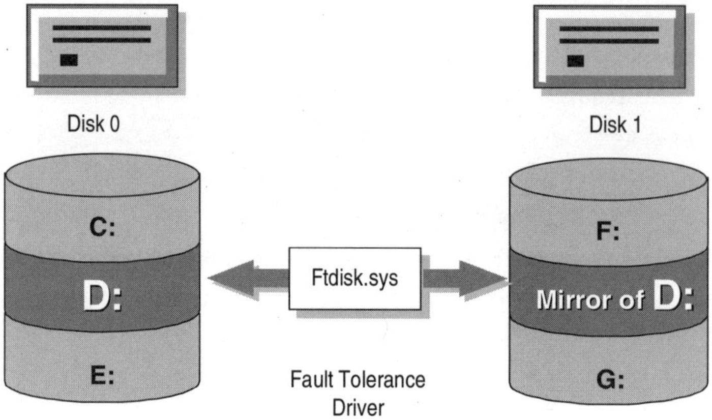

With mirror sets the data on a partition is duplicated on another physical disk. In the preceding illustration, data written to drive D on Disk 0 is duplicated on Disk 1. Any partition, including the boot or system partitions, can be mirrored. This strategy protects a single disk against failure. Windows NT Server configures fault tolerance at the level of the logical drive letter, not the physical disk level. For example, if your computer has one physical disk containing drives C and D, and a second physical disk with sufficient unpartitioned disk space, you can choose to mirror drive C, or drive D, or both.

In terms of cost per megabyte, mirror sets is more expensive than other forms of fault tolerance because disk space use is only 50 percent. However, for peer-to-peer and small server-based LANs, mirror sets usually have a lower initial cost because it requires only two disks.

Mirror sets can provide enhanced read performance because the fault tolerance driver can read from both members of the mirror set at the same time. There can be a slight decrease in write performance when writing to a mirror set because the fault tolerance driver must write to both members simultaneously. When one member of a mirror set fails, read performance returns to normal because the fault tolerance driver works with only the single partition.

Note If either the boot partition or the system partition is part of a mirror set, you should create a fault tolerance boot disk and test it in order to ensure a smooth and rapid data recovery. See the following lesson for the steps to create a fault tolerance boot disk.

Disk Duplexing

A member of a mirror set is one of the physical disk partitions that make up the set. If both physical disks that comprise a mirror set are controlled by the same disk controller, and the disk controller fails, both members of the mirror set are inaccessible. However, a second controller can be installed in the computer so that each disk in the mirror set has its own controller. In this way, the mirror set is protected against both controller failure and disk failure. This arrangement is called *disk duplexing*. Duplexing also reduces bus traffic and potentially improves read performance.

Note Disk duplexing is a hardware enhancement to a Windows NT Server mirror set. No additional software configuration is necessary.

RAID 5: Stripe Sets with Parity

The following illustrations shows stripe sets with parity.

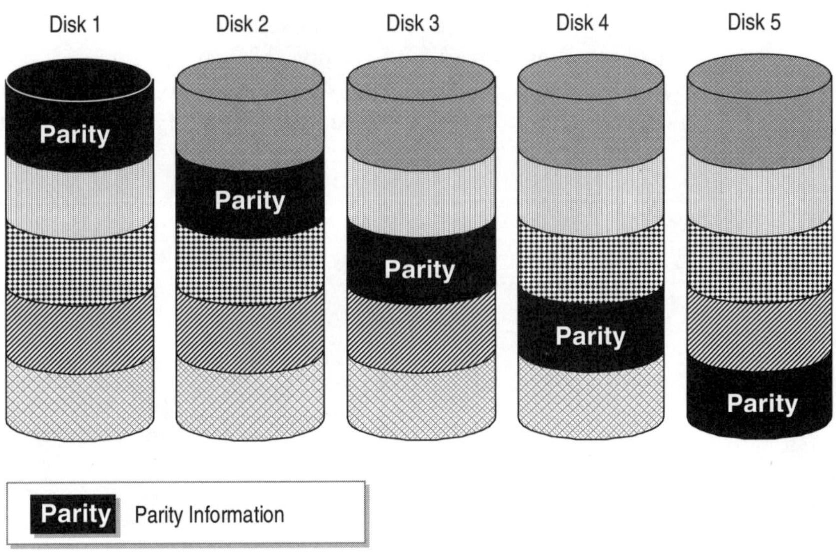

Stripe sets were discussed in Chapter 6, "Managing Partitions." Data written in stripe sets can be protected by the fault tolerance mechanism, stripe sets with parity (RAID 5), which is supported by Windows NT Server.

Parity is a mathematical method of verifying data integrity. Fault tolerance is achieved by adding a parity-information stripe to each disk partition in the volume. In a stripe set with parity, 3 to 32 disks are supported. The parity stripe block is used to reconstruct data for a failed physical disk. If a single disk fails, data is not lost because the Windows NT Server fault tolerance driver has spread the information across the remaining disks. The data can be completely reconstructed. For example, if Disk 3 fails and must be replaced, data for the new disk can be regenerated using the data and parity information in each stripe on the remaining four disks.

All normal write operations on a stripe set with parity are substantially slower than writing to stripe sets without parity due to the parity calculation.

However, stripe sets with parity can offer better read performance than mirror sets, especially with multiple controllers, because data is distributed among multiple drives. However, if a disk fails, the read performance on a stripe set with parity slows because data is being reconstructed using parity information.

Stripe sets with parity can offer a cost advantage over mirror sets because disk utilization is optimized. For example, if there are four disks in a stripe set with parity, the disk space overhead is 25 percent, compared to 50 percent disk space overhead with mirror sets. Stripe sets with parity is currently the most popular approach to fault tolerance.

Note Neither the boot partition nor the system partition can be part of the Windows NT implementation of a stripe set with parity.

RAID 1 vs. RAID 5

The previous section describes RAID 1 (mirror sets) and RAID 5 (stripe sets with parity). The major differences between mirror sets and striping with parity are hardware requirements, performance, and cost. The following illustration shows the major features of the two methods of fault tolerance.

Mirror Sets	Stripe Sets with Parity
■ Supports FAT and NTFS	■ Supports FAT and NTFS
■ Can mirror system or boot partition	■ Cannot stripe system or boot partition
■ Requires two hard disks	■ Requires minimum of three hard disks
■ Has higher cost per megabyte (50 percent utilization)	■ Has lower cost per megabyte
■ Has good read and write performance	■ Has moderate write performance ■ Has excellent read performance
■ Uses less system memory	■ Requires more system memory
	■ Supports up to 32 hard disks

Implementing RAID 1 and RAID 5

Mirror sets and stripe sets with parity can coexist on the same computer. Because a stripe set with parity cannot include the system or boot partition, consider mirroring the system and boot partitions, and protecting the remaining data in stripe sets with parity. For example, as shown in the following illustration, the system and boot partition are located on drive C, which is part of a mirror set. The remaining data on drive D is part of a stripe set with parity.

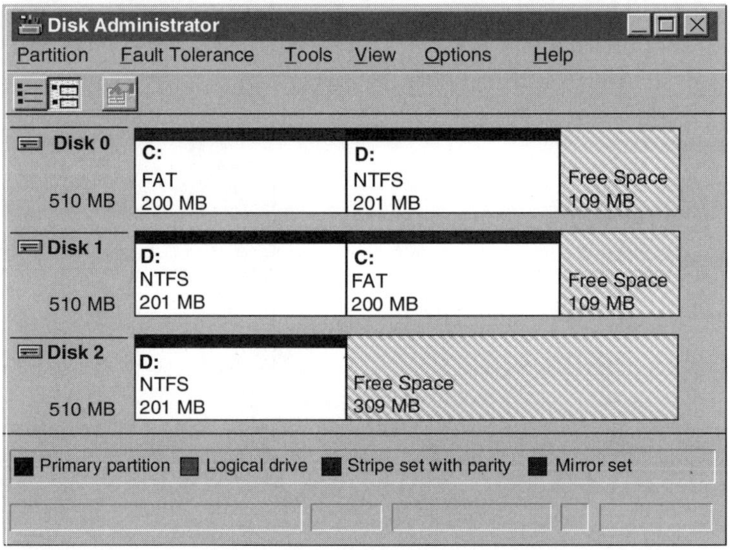

Note that the Windows NT Server Disk Administrator has an additional menu named **Fault Tolerance**, from which both mirror sets and stripe sets with parity are managed.

Considerations When Creating and Deleting a Stripe Set with Parity

The free spaces that are combined to create a stripe set with parity must be the same size. If they are not, Disk Administrator makes each partition of the set approximately the same size and leaves the unused portions of the partitions as usable free space.

Note It is necessary to shut down and then restart the computer after a stripe set with parity is created.

Caution Deleting a mirror set or stripe set with parity deletes all of the information stored in that volume.

Practice

In this procedure, you use the fault tolerance simulation to implement stripe sets with parity, and mirror sets.

Note Complete these procedures on Server1.

▶ **To configure stripe sets with parity**

1. Log on as Administrator.
2. Click the **Start** button, point to **Programs**, point to **Technical Support Training**, point to **Simulations**, and then click **Implementing Fault Tolerance Simulation**.

   The simulation starts, and Disk Administrator appears.
3. Click an area of free space on Disk 0 to be used for creating a stripe set with parity.
4. Hold down the CTRL key and click an area of free space on Disk 1 and an area of free space on Disk 2.
5. On the **Fault Tolerance** menu, click **Create Stripe Set with Parity**.

   The Create Stripe Set with Parity dialog box appears. The default size is three times the size of the smallest area of selected free space.
6. In the **Create stripe set of total size** box, type **300** and then click **OK**.

   The partitions now have the same drive letter (G) and are highlighted in green. This indicates that they are part of a stripe set with parity.

▶ **To configure mirror sets**

1. Click drive D to begin creating a mirror set.
2. Hold down the CTRL key and click an area of free space on Disk 1.

   The area must be equal to or greater than the partition selected in the preceding step.
3. On the **Fault Tolerance** menu, click **Establish Mirror**.

   The partitions should now have the same drive letter (D) and be highlighted in purple. This indicates that they are part of a mirror set.

▶ **To exit and save changes**

- On the **Partition** menu, click **Exit** to end the simulation.

  If this had not been a simulation, Disk Administrator would have prompted you to save your changes.

Lesson 2: Recovering from Hard Disk Failure

Fault tolerance duplicates system and user data in case of disk failure. The previous lesson described the implementation of mirror sets and stripe sets with parity. This lesson describes procedures to recover data that was saved by mirror sets and stripe sets with parity.

When a member of a mirror set or a stripe set with parity fails (as may occur in a power loss or hardware failure), the fault tolerance driver directs all I/O to the remaining members of the fault-tolerant volume. This ensures continuous service. If you have used Server Manager to configure the computer to send administrative alerts, and the Alerter service is running, then an alert message is sent to notify the specified accounts that this failure has occurred.

If the failed disk is part of a mirror set that contains the boot partition, and if the failed disk is the primary physical drive, then a fault tolerance boot disk will be required to restart the system.

After this lesson, you will be able to:

- Describe the procedure for recovering from the failure of a member of a stripe set with parity.
- Describe the procedure for recovering from the failure of a member of a mirror set.
- Create a fault tolerance boot disk.
- Describe how Advanced RISC Computing (ARC) paths identify partitions.

Estimated lesson time: 40 minutes

Regenerating a Stripe Set with Parity

If a member of a stripe set with parity fails, the computer continues to operate and to gain access to all data. However, as data is requested, the Windows NT Server fault tolerance driver uses the parity bits to regenerate the missing data in RAM. When this happens, system performance slows down.

To regenerate the data and return the computer to its previous performance level, use Disk Administrator to select an area of free space to replace the failed member and then click the **Regenerate** command on the **Fault Tolerance** menu. If you do not have sufficient free space, replace the failed drive and then regenerate your data.

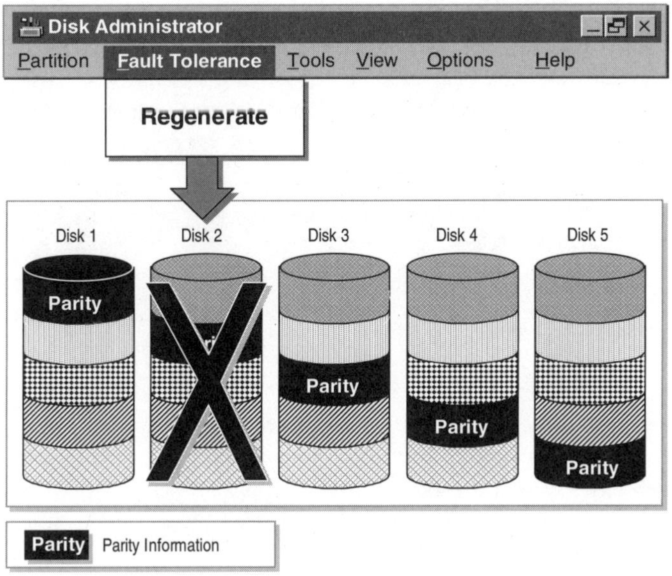

The fault tolerance driver reads the parity information from the stripes on the other member disks. It then recreates the data of the missing member and writes the data to the new member.

Recovering from Mirror Set Failure

Because of the data duplication involved in mirror sets, the system continues to function when a member of the mirror set fails. In order to replace the failed member, an administrator must first "break" the mirror set.

In order to break a mirror set, do the following:

1. From Disk Administrator, use the **Break Mirror** command on the **Fault Tolerance** menu to break the mirror set. Break the mirror set relationship to isolate the remaining *working* partition as a separate volume. Regardless of which disk contains the fault, when the mirror set is broken, Disk Administrator assigns the mirrored volume the next available drive letter.

In the following illustration, drive D on Disk 0 is mirrored on Disk 1. Drive D on Disk 1 is the secondary member of the mirror set. When the mirror set is broken, drive D on Disk 1 is assigned the next available drive letter, H.

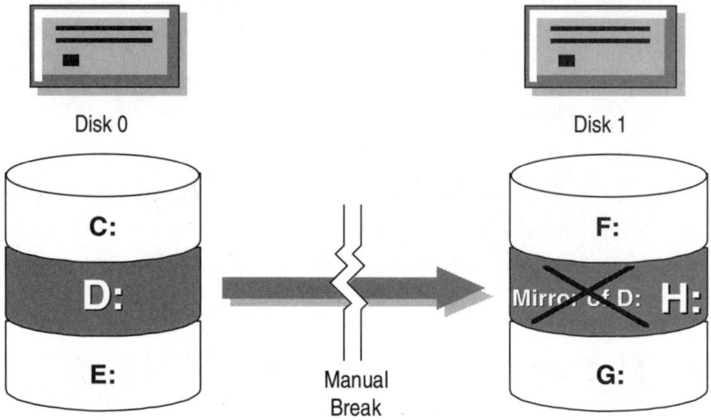

2. If the failed drive is the primary member of the mirror set, it may be necessary to assign the drive letter that was previously assigned to the complete mirror set to the working member of the mirror set. For example, if the disk has any shared resources, or if a shortcut points to a location on a particular drive letter, you would need to reassign the drive letter to maintain your computer's functionality.

   In the preceding illustration, assume that the failure occurred on Disk 0. The working member (now drive H) needs to retain the drive letter D assignment. Using Disk Administrator, first unassign drive D on Disk 0, and then reassign drive letter D to drive H.

3. Delete the *failed* partition.

   Note You can use Event Viewer to look at the System log to determine which partition failed.

4. Using free space on another disk, create a new mirror set relationship.

   For the procedure to establish a mirror set, see "Establishing a Mirror Set" in Windows NT Server Help. When the computer is restarted, the data from the good partition is copied to the new member of the mirror set.

Note Replacing a failed member is not the only reason that you would break a mirror set. You would also break the mirror set if you wanted to reclaim the disk space for other purposes.

Creating a Fault Tolerance Boot Disk

When making a mirror set for the boot partition or system partition of a computer running Windows NT Server, it is important to create a fault tolerance boot disk for use in case of physical disk failure.

Remember that in a software implementation of RAID, the system and boot partitions cannot be members of a stripe set with parity; only mirror sets can provide fault tolerance for the system and boot partitions.

The following illustration outlines the steps involved in creating a fault tolerance boot disk.

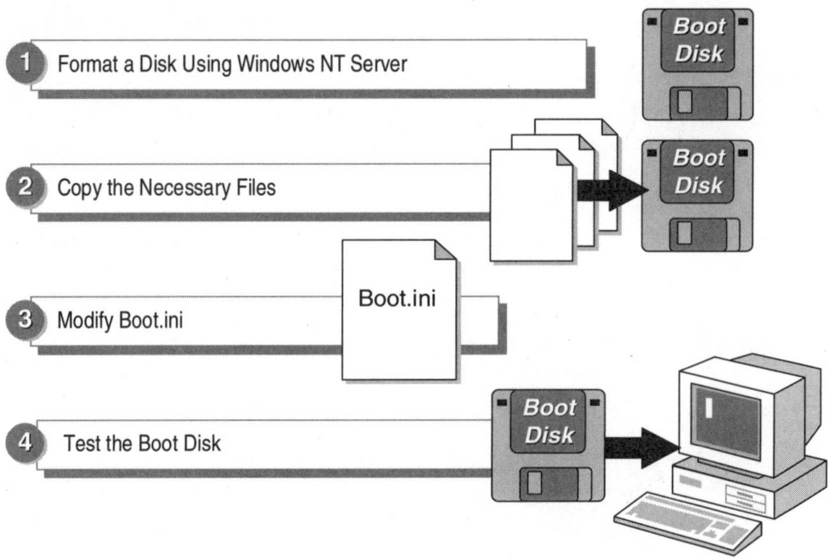

The following explanation describes the steps used to create a fault tolerance boot disk in detail:

1. Format a floppy disk on a computer running Windows NT Server. This writes information to the boot track of the disk so that it looks for the appropriate loader file when the system is started.

   Note A fault tolerance boot disk must be formatted on a computer running Windows NT Server.

2. Copy the following files from the primary partition of the computer running Windows NT Server to the boot disk. Several of the files are ordinarily hidden in the root folder. Use Windows NT Explorer to display hidden files.

*x*86-based computers	RISC-based computers
Ntldr	Osloader.exe
Ntdetect.com	Hal.dll
Ntbootdd.sys (for SCSI disks not using SCSI BIOS)*	*.pal (contains PAL code—software subroutines that provide an operating system with direct control of the processor)
Boot.ini	

   *The Ntbootdd.sys file appears only on SCSI systems in which the SCSI BIOS is not used.

3. On Intel *x*86-based computers, edit Boot.ini to change your operating system entry to point to the mirrored copy of the boot partition.

   On RISC-based computers, modify the firmware variables shown in the following table.

Variable	Value
OSLOADER	multi(0)disk(0)fdisk(0)\Osloader.exe
SYSTEMPARTITION	multi(0)disk(0)fdisk(0)
OSLOADPARTITION	path to the secondary mirrored partition
OSLOADFILENAME	path to the Windows NT Server root directory

4. Test the boot disk to ensure that it works and boots using data from the mirrored copy of the boot partition; do this by shutting down Windows NT Server, inserting the fault tolerance boot disk, and then restarting the computer.

Whenever partition path information has been changed, it is important to update the Boot.ini file on the fault tolerance boot disk.

Note For more information on creating fault tolerance boot disks, see Chapter 7, "Protecting Data," in Microsoft Windows NT Server *Concepts and Planning*.

Practice

In these procedures, you create a boot disk for the Intel platform that can be used in the event that your computer's boot partition is not accessible. Then, you test the boot disk by starting the computer using the Windows NT boot disk.

Note Complete these procedures on Server1.

▸ **To create a Windows NT boot disk**

1. Format a floppy disk using the Windows NT Explorer, or go to a command prompt and use the **Format.exe** command.
2. Copy the following files from the root of drive C to the root of drive A.

   Ntldr

   Ntdetect.com

   Boot.ini

   Bootsect.dos (only if it exists)

   Ntbootdd.sys (only if it exists)
3. Do not remove the disk from the drive.

▸ **To test the Windows NT boot disk**

1. Shut down and then restart your computer using the Windows NT boot disk you just created.

   Did Windows NT start successfully?

2. Remove the floppy from the disk drive.

Understanding ARC Paths

Creating a fault tolerance boot disk for recovery of a mirrored boot or system partition requires editing the Advanced RISC Computing (ARC) names in the Boot.ini file. You need to change the ARC path so that it points to the secondary or mirrored partition rather than the primary or boot or system partition. You are familiar with identifying the paths of *x*86-based computers by supplying a drive letter, such as C:\ or D:\. The ARC paths in the Boot.ini file use a different naming convention, which is explained in this section.

When you install Windows NT, a Boot.ini file is generated. The Boot.ini file contains the ARC paths used to point to location(s) of the operating system(s) files. The following represents an ARC path in the boot.ini file:

multi(0)disk(0)rdisk(1)partition(2)

The following table describes the ARC naming conventions used by Windows NT to generate the ARC paths:

Convention	Description
multi/scsi	Identifies the hardware adapter/disk controller as either multi or SCSI. SCSI indicates a SCSI controller on which SCSI BIOS is not enabled. All other adapters or disk controllers are represented by multi. These include SCSI disk controllers with the BIOS enabled so that the SCSI disk is accessed by the SCSI BIOS. For Windows NT Server, this could be a disk supported by the Atdisk, Abiosdsk, or Cpqarray drivers. Remember, use multi in all cases except when Ntbootdd.sys is on your system. The Ntbootdd.sys file appears only on SCSI systems in which the SCSI BIOS is not used.
(x)	Ordinal number of the hardware adapter. For example, if there are two SCSI adapters in the system, the first to load and initialize is assigned the ordinal number 0 and the next adapter is assigned the ordinal number 1.
disk(*y*)	SCSI bus number. For settings of multi, this value is always 0.
rdisk(*z*)	Ordinal number of the disk (ignored for SCSI controllers).
partition(*a*)	Ordinal number of the partition.

RISC-based computers use the SCSI naming convention. In both multi and SCSI conventions, multi/scsi, disk, and rdisk numbers are assigned starting with (0), while partition numbers are assigned starting with (1). All non-extended partitions are assigned numbers first, followed by all logical drives in extended partitions.

Note SCSI and multi ARC naming conventions are similar except that the SCSI notation varies the disk( ) parameter for successive disks on one controller, while the multi format varies the rdisk( ) parameter.

The following illustration shows a computer running Windows NT Server that has three hard disks divided into five partitions. It also shows the ARC path for the boot partition that is located on drive G.

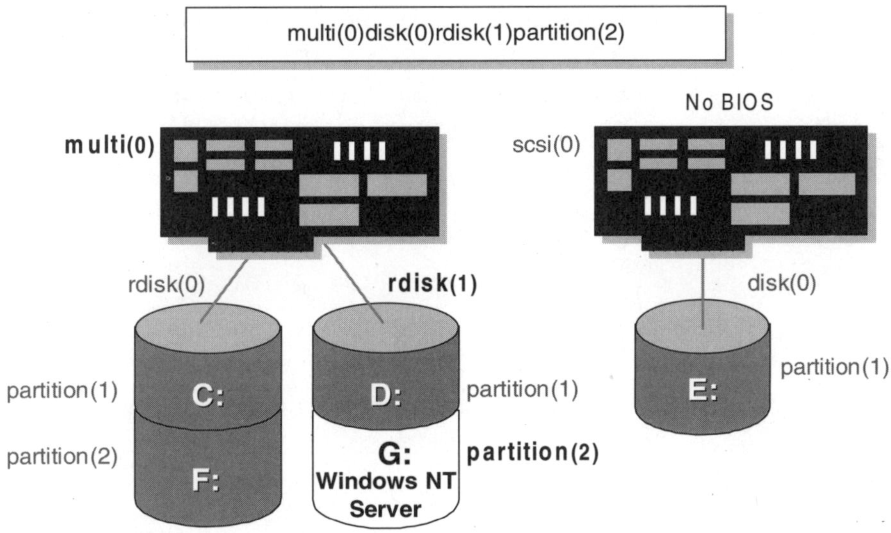

What would the ARC path be if the system files were located on drive C?

___

What would the ARC path be if the system files were located on drive E?

___

Summary

The following information summarizes the key points in this chapter:

- Fault tolerance is the ability of a system to protect against loss of data when part of the system fails. Both hardware and software fault tolerance solutions are available. While hardware solutions can provide enhanced performance over software solutions, they can also be more costly.
- Windows NT Server supports two software fault tolerance methods, mirror sets and stripe sets with parity. The factors that influence whether to use either one or both methods include cost, performance, and reliability.
- When you implement fault tolerance, keep the following considerations in mind:
  - Fault tolerance is *not* a substitute for regular backups.
  - Following a failure, fault tolerance has not been achieved until the fault is repaired and the data is restored.
  - Create a fault tolerance boot disk to restore the system in the case of a physical disk failure of a mirror set containing the boot or system partition.

For more information on	See
RAID, RAID terminology, and disk arrays	*The RAIDbook, a Source Book for Disk Array Technology*
Stripe sets, mirror sets, and stripe sets with parity on Windows NT Server	Chapter 7, "Protecting Data," in Microsoft Windows NT Server *Concepts and Planning*
Configuring, and recovering from failures of, mirror sets and stripe sets with parity	"Preparing for and Performing Recovery" in the *Resource Guide* of the *Microsoft Windows NT Server Resource Kit*
Creating fault tolerance boot disks	Chapter 7, "Protecting Data," in Microsoft Windows NT Server *Concepts and Planning*

Review

1. Your computer running Windows NT Server has the following disk configuration:
   - Disk 0: drive C (300 MB, system/boot partition), drive D: (700 MB, data), and 500 MB of free space.
   - Disk 1: 750 MB free space.
   - Disk 2: 1 GB free space.

   You want to install additional Microsoft BackOffice components on this computer. How can you protect your computer's data and optimize its performance using Windows NT fault tolerance?

2. The disk containing the system/boot partition for your computer running Windows NT Server failed. The system/boot partition was part of a mirror set, but your computer only tries to boot from the original system/boot partition. How can you successfully boot Windows NT Server from the mirrored system/boot partition?

Answer Key

Procedure Answers

Page 253

▸ **To test the Windows NT boot disk**

1. Shut down and then restart your computer using the Windows NT boot disk you just created.

   Did Windows NT start successfully?

   Yes. The boot disk was created properly.

   No. Verify that you formatted the floppy disk using Windows NT, and then compare the files on your boot disk with those listed in the preceding procedure.

Page 255

Understanding ARC Paths

What would the ARC path be if the system files were located on drive C?

multi(0)disk(0)rdisk(0)partition(1)

What would the ARC path be if the system files were located on drive E?

scsi(0)disk(0)rdisk(0)partition(1)

Review Answers

Page 257

1. Your computer running Windows NT Server has the following disk configuration:

   - Disk 0: drive C (300 MB, system/boot partition), drive D: (700 MB, data), and 500 MB of free space.
   - Disk 1: 750 MB free space.
   - Disk 2: 1 GB free space.

   You want to install additional Microsoft BackOffice components on this computer. How can you protect your computer's data and optimize its performance using Windows NT fault tolerance?

   Mirror drive C on Disk 2, and create a 1.5 GB stripe set with parity spanning all three disks.

2. The disk containing the system/boot partition for your computer running Windows NT Server failed. The system/boot partition was part of a mirror set, but your computer only tries to boot from the original system/boot partition. How can you successfully boot Windows NT Server from the mirrored system/boot partition?

   With a fault-tolerance boot disk. You must edit the Boot.ini file to point to the mirrored boot partition.

CHAPTER 8

Supporting Applications

About This Chapter

Microsoft Windows NT is designed to run applications written for existing operating systems such as Microsoft MS-DOS, OS/2, POSIX, and Microsoft Windows 3.*x*. It achieves this through *environment subsystems*, which emulate different operating system environments. This chapter describes each of the Windows NT environment subsystems and their configurations. The chapter also addresses general application management.

Before You Begin

To complete the lessons in this chapter, you must have:

- Two computers that meet the hardware and software requirements as specified in the Getting Started section of "About This Book."
- Completed all practices in Chapter 2, "Installing Windows NT."

Lesson 1: Windows NT Architecture Overview

A working knowledge of Windows NT begins with an understanding of the system architecture. This lesson introduces key aspects of the Windows NT architecture that affect the operating system functionality and performance.

After this lesson, you will be able to:

- Define the two processor modes used by Windows NT: user mode and kernel mode.
- Describe the function of the components that make up the Windows NT architecture.
- Describe the Windows NT memory model.

Estimated lesson time: 20 minutes

User Mode vs. Kernel Mode

Windows NT uses two modes, *user mode* and *kernel mode*, to maintain operating efficiency and integrity. The following illustration shows the components of the Windows NT architecture, separated into user mode components and kernel mode components.

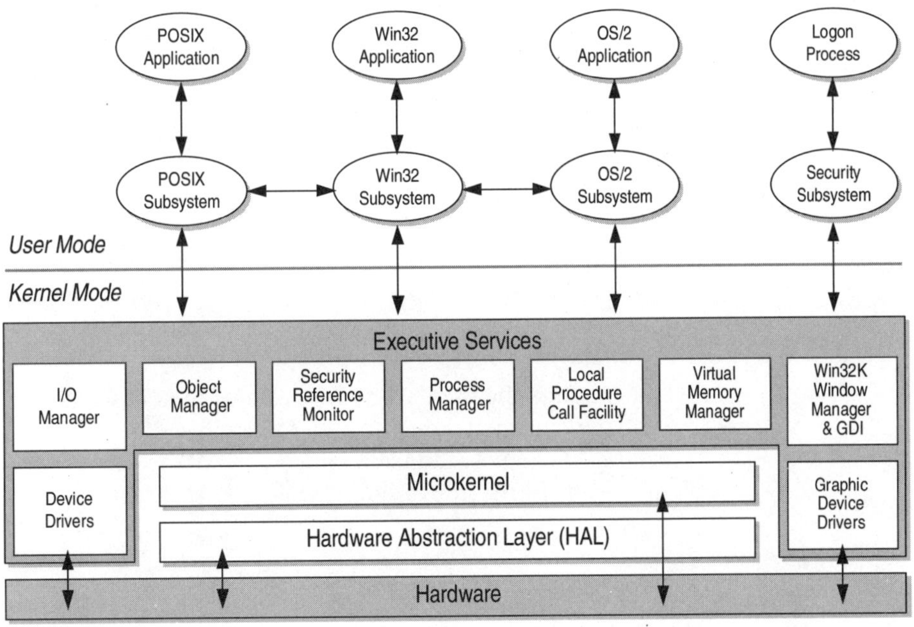

User Mode

User mode is a less privileged processor mode than kernel mode, and has no direct access to hardware. Code running in user mode acts directly only in its own address space. It uses well-defined operating system application program interfaces (APIs) to request system services. Applications, and the subsystems that support them, run in user mode. When an application is started, a Windows NT *process* is created. A process is implemented as an *object*. An object consists of an executable program, a set of virtual memory addresses, and one or more threads.

User mode processes:

- Have no direct access to hardware. To protect against malfunctioning applications or unauthorized user access, user mode processes cannot directly access hardware. Hardware access requests must be granted by a kernel mode component.
- Are limited to an assigned address space. Windows NT helps protect the operating system by limiting the areas of memory that a user mode process can access. This limitation is accomplished by assigning only certain addresses to the user mode process.
- Can be paged out of physical memory into virtual RAM on a hard disk. *Virtual memory,* also known as virtual RAM, allows hard disk space to be used as if it were additional memory. In this manner, the user mode processes have access to more memory than is actually available to them. The details of virtual memory are covered later in this lesson.
- Process at a lower priority than kernel mode components. User mode processes are lower in priority—and therefore typically have less access to the CPU cycles—than processes that run in kernel mode. This ensures that the operating system does not slow down or have to wait while an application finishes processing.

The user mode environment subsystems shown in the preceding illustration are covered in the next lesson.

Kernel Mode

Kernel mode is the privileged mode of operation in which the code has direct access to all hardware and all memory, including the address spaces of all user mode processes. The following list outlines some of the capabilities of the kernel mode components. Kernel mode components:

- Can access hardware directly.
- Can access all of the memory on the computer.
- Are not moved to the virtual memory page file on the hard disk.
- Process at a higher priority than user mode processes.

The kernel mode in Windows NT is comprised of the Windows NT Executive, which includes the Executive Services, the microkernel, and the hardware abstraction layer (HAL).

Windows NT Executive

Windows NT Executive is the generic name for a number of subsystems and components of the operating system that run in kernel mode.

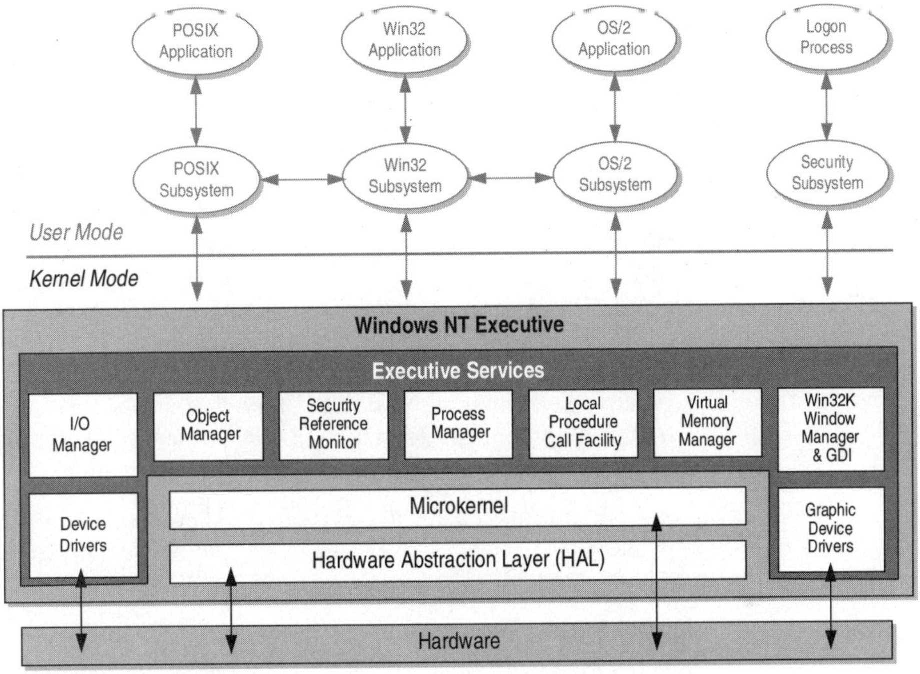

Windows NT Executive provides support for user applications and environment subsystems. Within the Windows NT Executive, basic functions of the operating system are integrated through three layered components; the Executive Services, the microkernel, and the HAL.

Executive Services Components

The Windows NT Executive Services are central to all major operating system functions; therefore, it is important to protect them from user mode applications and subsystems. This is accomplished by having the Executive Services run in kernel mode.

The following table describes the function of each component of Executive Services.

Executive Service	Function
Managers	Various modules that manage I/O, objects, security, processes, interprocess communications (IPC), virtual memory, and window and graphics management.
Device drivers	Software components that control hardware access.

Note If you are familiar with the previous releases of Windows NT, you may notice a change in the components listed as Executive Services. In Windows NT version 3.51 or earlier, the Window Manager and graphics device interface (GDI) were located in the Win32 subsystem. In Windows NT 4.0, this functionality is provided by the Win32K Window Manager and GDI of the Windows NT Executive Services. The Win32K Window Manager and GDI are responsible for handling all graphical user interface (GUI)-related I/O requests, maintaining the display, and providing a common GUI for all applications.

For more information about user mode and kernel mode in Windows NT, see Appendix B "Changes to Kernel Mode, User Mode, and GDI in Windows NT 4.0."

Microkernel

The microkernel provides the most basic operating system services, such as thread scheduling, first-level interrupt handling, and deferred procedure calls. The microkernel resides between the Executive Services and HAL layers.

Hardware Abstraction Layer

The HAL is a kernel-mode library of hardware-manipulating routines provided by Microsoft or by the hardware manufacturer. This software layer hides the characteristics of the platform behind standard entry points so that all platforms and architectures look alike to the operating system. It enables the same operating system to run on different platforms with different processors. For example, it allows Windows NT to run on single or multiprocessor computers and enables higher-level device drivers, such as graphics display drivers, to format data for different kind of monitors.

The Windows NT Memory Model

The memory architecture for Windows NT is a demand-paged, virtual memory system. It is based on a flat, linear 32-bit address space, which allows each process in Windows NT to have access to up to 4 GB of memory.

Virtual Memory Architecture

With *virtual memory*, all applications seem to have a full range of memory addresses available. Windows NT does this by giving each application a private memory range called a *virtual memory space* and by mapping that virtual memory to physical memory.

Windows NT maps physical and virtual memory addresses in 4 KB blocks called *pages*. Each virtual memory space has room for 4 GB of addresses. This address space is made up of 1,048,576 (1 MB) 4 KB pages.

Because few systems contain enough RAM to provide 4 GB for each application, the operating system allocates the available physical RAM pages between the virtual memory spaces. While the application operates as though it is in RAM, in reality, the pages are often in virtual memory. Pages in virtual memory can have one of the following three characteristics:

- Most of the pages are actually empty, because the application is not using them.
- Pages that are being used are redirected by a pointer, invisible to the application, to physical RAM.
- Some pages that have not been used recently contain another pointer, also invisible to the application, to a 4 KB section of the *paging file* on the hard disk.

Note For information on how to configure virtual memory, see Chapter 3, "Configuring the Windows NT Environment."

Virtual Memory Process

The virtual memory process makes use of the paging file(s) on the hard disk (Pagefile.sys). With virtual memory in Windows NT, some of the application code and other information is kept in RAM while other information can be temporarily paged into virtual memory. When the paged information is required again, Windows NT reads it back into RAM, paging other information to virtual memory if necessary.

The process of managing which pages are stored in RAM, and which are stored in the paging file, is called *demand paging*. The Windows NT demand paging procedure is shown in the following illustration.

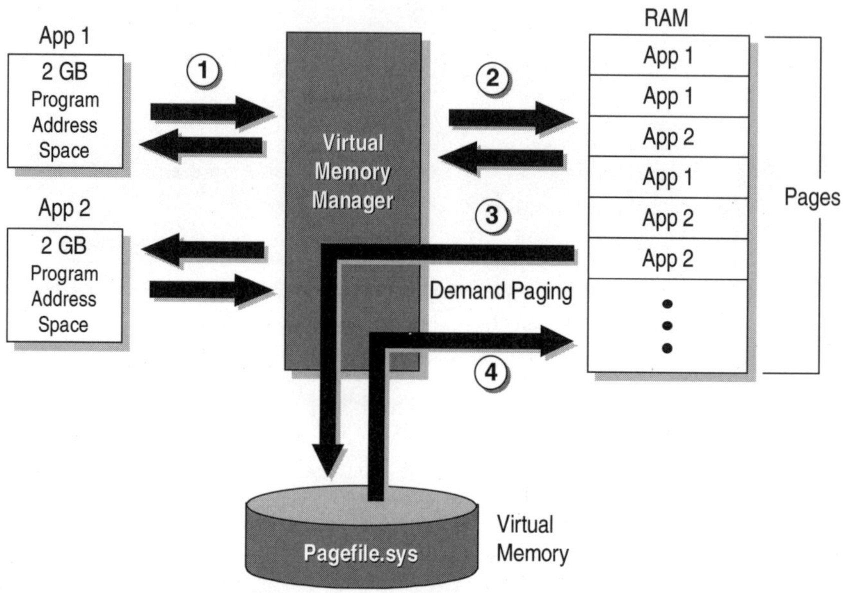

The following steps describe this procedure:

1. An application attempts to store data in memory.
2. The Virtual Memory Manager intercepts the request, determines how many pages are needed to fill the request, and maps unused physical memory to any empty address spaces in the application's virtual memory space, as needed. The Virtual Memory Manager hides the organization of physical memory from the application. When an application calls for a memory location, it maps to a non-conflicting memory address.
3. If there is not enough unused physical memory available, the Virtual Memory Manager uses demand paging to find pages of RAM that have not been used recently. It then copies these pages to the paging file (Pagefile.sys) on the hard disk. The newly freed RAM is remapped to fill the application's request.
4. When data stored in the paging file is needed, the pages are copied back into RAM. The new RAM location is mapped back to the same virtual address required by the application.

Virtual Memory Advantages

The linear addressing scheme used by the Virtual Memory Manager helps make Windows NT portable because it is compatible with the memory addressing of processors such as the MIPS R4000, IBM RS/6000, and DEC Alpha AXP.

Windows NT makes memory use efficient, and consistent. As a result, it allows programmers to write large and concise applications. It also allows users to run more applications at one time than a system's physical memory would otherwise allow.

Note For more information about Windows NT architecture, see Chapter 5, "Windows NT 4.0 Workstation Architecture," in the *Microsoft Windows NT Workstation Resource Kit.*

Lesson 2: Subsystems Overview

Windows NT supports applications by using environment subsystems. An environment subsystem provides API services to applications written for a specific environment or operating system. This lesson describes the subsystem architecture that allows these applications to run, and specifically describes the function of the Win32 subsystem.

After this lesson, you will be able to:

- Explain the purpose and function of the environment subsystems.
- Describe the Windows NT subsystem architecture.

Estimated lesson time: 5 minutes

The following illustration shows the relationships that exist between the environment and Win32 subsystems and Executive Services.

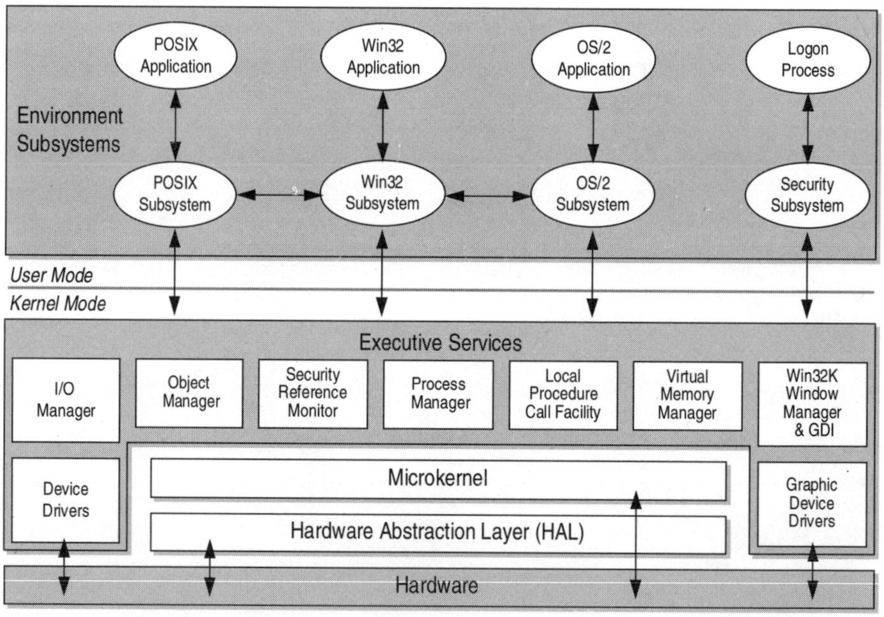

Environment Subsystems

An environment subsystem in Windows NT is an intermediary between an application designed for a specific operating environment, and the Executive Services. The environment subsystem translates environment-specific instructions from an application into instructions that the Executive Services can carry out. There are two Windows NT environment subsystems that support applications designed for other operating environments: the POSIX subsystem and the OS/2 subsystem. These subsystems receive all function requests from the applications that they support. A subsystem either carries out the request itself or passes it to the Windows NT Executive Services.

The Win32 Subsystem

The Win32 subsystem is sometimes referred to as the client/server subsystem, the CSR subsystem, or CSRSS. It supports Win32-, MS-DOS-, and Windows 3.*x*-based applications and the environment subsystems. The Win32 subsystem also supports console applications—applications not written for the Microsoft Windows GUI—application shutdown, and error handling functions.

Note The security subsystem supports the logon process. It does not support other applications.

Subsystems Interactions with Executive Services

The Windows NT Executive Services perform basic operating system functions for all subsystems. The Executive Services reside in kernel mode. This provides stability for the operating system, because no application can directly access the Executive Services. In this way, a malfunctioning user-mode component (such as an application) cannot unintentionally stop a kernel mode component.

All GUI-related I/O requests are channeled to the Win32K Window Manager and GDI component of Executive Services which is responsible for maintaining the display. This provides a common GUI for all applications.

The subsystems build on the Executive Services to produce environments that meet the specific needs of their client applications. In this way, common operating system functions are implemented once in the Executive Services, rather than duplicated in each subsystem. This reduces the effort required to develop new subsystems and makes them easier to maintain.

Lesson 3: Windows NT Task Manager

Task Manager is a Windows NT utility that provides information about the current processes running in Windows NT. In this lesson, you learn the functions of Task Manager and how to use Task Manager to manage applications and processes.

After this lesson, you will be able to:

- Describe the function and capabilities of Task Manager.
- Use Task Manager to view running applications and processes.
- Use Task Manager to prioritize applications.
- Use Task Manager to end a process.
- User Task Manager to view system performance.

Estimated lesson time: 20 minutes

You use Task Manager to monitor and prioritize applications and processes, and to view system performance data.

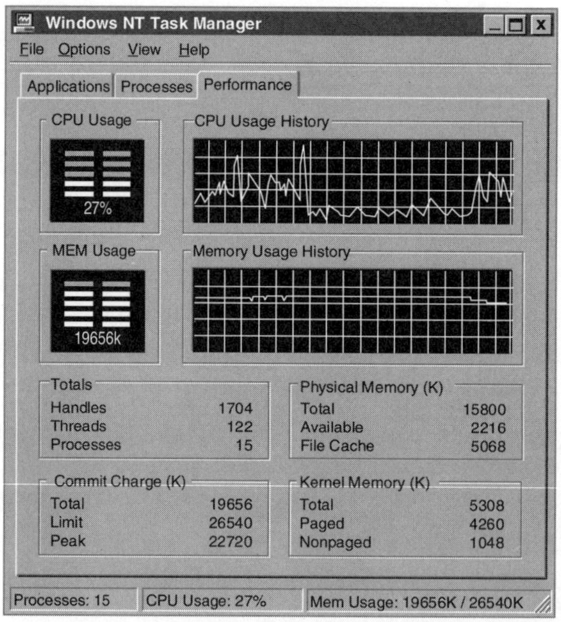

Task Manager Capabilities

Task Manager includes the following capabilities:

- Displays running applications and processes, including 16-bit processes.
- Displays the most commonly used performance measures for processes, including processor time, physical memory usage, virtual memory size, page faults, base priority, and thread count.
- Displays line graphs and instantaneous values of CPU and memory use for the computer.
- Sets processor affinity for an application on a multiprocessor computer, changes the base priority of a process, and activates a debugger if you have one.

Task Manager Tabs

There are three tabs in the **Windows NT Task Manager** dialog box: Applications, Processes, and Performance. The **Applications** tab shows the status of the programs or tasks that are currently running on your computer. From this window you can end, switch to, or start a program. The **Processes** tab shows information about the processes that are currently running on your computer. The **Performance** tab is used to monitor your computer's system performance.

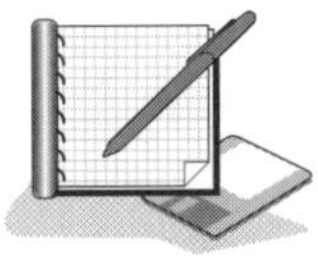

Practice

In these procedures, you use Task Manager to view the applications running on your desktop and the processes executing in the background.

Note Complete these procedures on Workstation1.

▶ **To access Task Manager**

- Start Task Manager using one of these methods:
  - Press CTRL+SHIFT+ESC.
  - Right-click the Windows NT taskbar, and then click **Task Manager**.
  - Press CTRL+ALT+DELETE, and then click **Task Manager**.

► **To start applications**

1. Click the **Start** button, point to **Programs**, point to **Accessories**, and then click **Calculator**.
2. Click the **Start** button, point to **Programs**, point to **Accessories**, and then click **Paint**.
3. Click the **Start** button, point to **Programs**, point to **Accessories**, and then click **WordPad**.
4. Minimize Calculator, Paint, and WordPad.

► **To view running applications using Task Manager**

1. Switch to Task Manager.
2. Click the **Applications** tab.

   You see a list of the running applications. Notice that there are buttons that allow you to end an application, switch to an application window, or to start a new application.
3. Click **Document - WordPad**, and then click **End Task**.

   WordPad is no longer listed in the task list.

► **To view the processes options**

1. In Task Manager, click the **Processes** tab.

   You see a list of running processes and measures of their performance. The Task Manager process table includes every process that runs in its own address space, including all applications and system services.
2. On the **View** menu, click **Select Columns**.

   A **Select Columns** dialog box appears, displaying a list of options that allows you to obtain additional information about a process.
3. Select the **Base Priority** check box, and then click **OK**.
4. On the **Options** menu, select **Show 16-bit tasks**.

   This option allows you to include 16-bit applications in the process table.
5. Use Task Manager to close **Calculator** and **Paint**.

Practice

In these procedures, you use Task Manager to change the base priority of an active process and to end a process.

Note Complete these procedures on Workstation1.

► To view the priority of a running application

1. From C:\Lab Files\Apps, start **Counter**.
2. Start a second instance of Counter.
3. Arrange Task Manager and the two Counters windows so that you can view them all on the screen.
4. In Task Manager, click the **Processes** tab.
5. If necessary, resize the Task Manager window until you can see the **Base Priority** column.

   What is the priority of each Counter?

► To change the priority of a running application

1. On the **Processes** tab, right-click either instance of Counter.exe.
2. Point to **Set Priority**, and then click **Low**.

   A **Task Manager Warning** dialog box appears.
3. Click **Yes** to change the priority of Counter.exe.

   The low-priority instance of Counter.exe runs significantly slower than the normal-priority instance.
4. On the **Processes** tab, right-click the instance of Counter.exe that is running at low priority.
5. Point to **Set Priority**, and then click **High**.

   A **Task Manager Warning** dialog box appears.
6. Click **Yes** to change the priority of Counter.exe.

   The high-priority instance of Counter.exe runs significantly faster than the normal-priority instance.

▸ **To end a process using Task Manager**

1. On the **Processes** tab, right-click the instance of Counter.exe that is running at high priority.
2. Click **End Process**.

   A **Task Manager Warning** dialog box appears.
3. Click **Yes** to terminate this instance of Counter.exe.
4. Use Task Manager to end the instance of Counter.exe that is running at normal priority.

Assigning a Process to a Processor

On multiprocessor computers, processor affinity assigns the threads of a process to run on the various processors. The Windows NT microkernel distributes processing over all processors, based on priority. Often, the threads of a single process run on more than one processor. Windows NT uses an algorithm called *soft affinity* to distribute processor load. This means that when possible, Windows NT reassigns threads to the same processor on which they previously ran, but Windows NT does not block the threads to wait for that processor if it is in use.

You can limit the execution of an application to one or more processors. This is known as *hard affinity*. To select processors for a process, right-click the process name on the Task Manager **Processes** tab, click **Set Affinity**, and then click one or more processors from the list. The **Set Affinity** option is visible only on multiprocessor computers. Although it is possible to reserve a processor for a specific thread, this usually results in a decrease in overall performance because all other threads can only use the remaining processors.

Monitoring System Performance

When Task Manager is running, a CPU usage gauge that shows system performance appears on the taskbar in the status area at the end opposite the **Start** button. When the cursor is paused over this icon, the ToolTip displays the percentage of CPU usage.

The status bar at the bottom of the **Performance** tab also displays performance data. It shows the total number of processes, CPU usage, and memory use of the system.

Practice

In this procedure, you use the Task Manager **Performance** tab to monitor your computer's performance.

Note Complete this procedure on Workstation1.

► To view the performance

1. In Task Manager, click the **Performance** tab.

   Notice the dynamic overview of system performance, including a graph and numeric display of processor and memory usage.

2. Double-click the **CPU Usage History** box.

   The **CPU Usage History** box is expanded.

3. Double-click the **CPU Usage History** box.

   The **Performance** tab appears.

4. Close Task Manager.

Note For additional information on the Task Manager, see the *Microsoft Windows NT Workstation Resource Kit.*

Lesson 4: Supporting Win32-based Applications

The Win32 subsystem maintains the display and manages user input for all applications. This lesson describes the APIs used by Win32-based applications and describes the Microsoft DirectX™ set of APIs supported by Windows NT.

After this lesson, you will be able to:

- Describe how Windows NT supports Win32-based applications.
- Describe Windows NT support for OLE/ActiveX™ and OpenGL (Graphics Language) APIs.
- Describe the DirectX APIs supported by Windows NT.

Estimated lesson time: 10 minutes

Win32-based Applications

Win32-based applications benefit from the inherent reliability of Windows NT and can take full advantage of the following features of Windows NT:

- Multithreading, to enhance system performance
- OLE/ActiveX and OpenGL support
- DirectX set of APIs in Windows NT

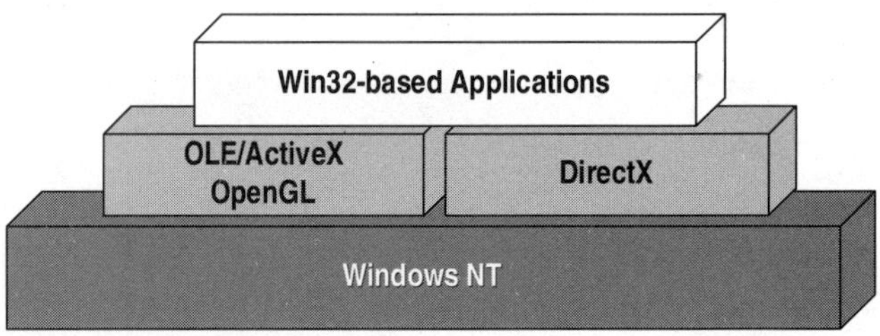

Multithreaded Applications

Win32-based applications can simultaneously execute multiple threads, or execution units of a process. For example, a Win32-based Setup program can be broken into three threads:

- One that decompresses files.
- One that copies files.
- One that modifies the system configuration files.

The threads are completely independent of each other as shown in the following illustration. They run at the same time, thereby increasing system performance.

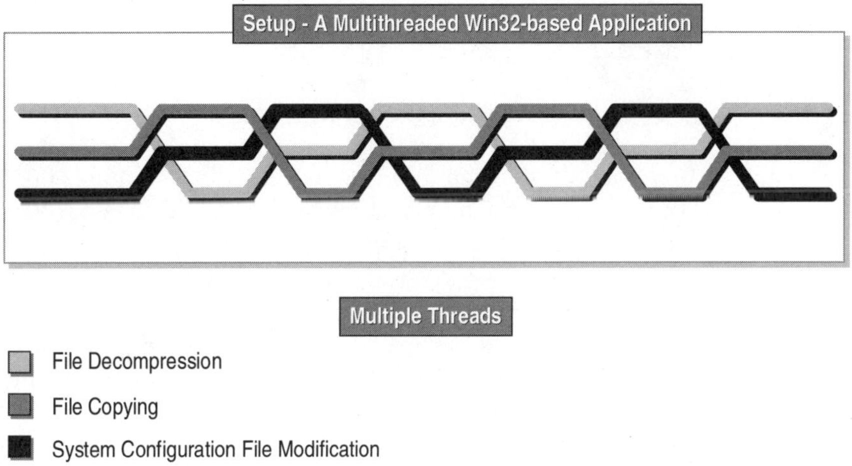

Reliability

Each Win32-based application runs in its own 2 GB address space. For this reason, a Win32-based application cannot corrupt the memory of another Win32-based application. In other words, if one Win32-based application fails, it does not affect other Win32-based applications.

OLE/ActiveX, OpenGL, and DirectX

Windows NT supports OLE/ActiveX and OpenGL APIs and DirectX, a high-performance media interface. This section describes each of these interfaces.

OLE/ActiveX Support

OLE/ActiveX is a method for transferring and sharing information between applications. Windows NT includes both 16-bit and 32-bit versions of OLE, and fully supports interoperability between Win16 and Win32 OLE applications.

While Microsoft ActiveX and OLE are both based on the Component Object Model (COM), they provide substantially different services to developers. COM provides the low-level object-binding mechanism that enables objects to communicate with each other. OLE uses COM to provide high-level application services such as linking and embedding to enable users to create compound documents. ActiveX, on the other hand, provides a substantially pared down infrastructure to enable controls to be embedded in Web sites and respond interactively to events. While OLE is optimized for end-user usability and integration of desktop applications, ActiveX is optimized for size and speed. ActiveX also adds a number of important innovations for the Internet, including a substantial reduction in size (50 to 75 percent) of the controls, and support for incremental rendering and asynchronous connections.

OpenGL

OpenGL (Graphics Language) is an industry-standard software interface for producing two- and three-dimensional graphics. OpenGL allows applications to create high-quality color graphics independent of windowing systems, operating systems, and hardware.

Several 3-D screen savers are included with Windows NT and are examples of OpenGL utilities. Use the Display program in Control Panel to select these 3-D screen savers.

Note The OpenGL screen savers included with Windows NT use more CPU time than a non-OpenGL screen saver. Therefore, it is not recommended to use an OpenGL screen saver on a busy file, print, or application server, as it may affect performance.

DirectX

DirectX is a low-level API designed specifically for high-performance applications such as games. DirectX is designed to provide high-speed, real-time response to the user interface.

The following table describes the three DirectX components included in Windows NT 4.0.

DirectX component	Description
Microsoft DirectDraw™	DirectDraw for Windows NT 4.0 supports a 32-bit API for accelerated drawing. Unlike DirectDraw for Windows 95, DirectDraw for Windows NT does not communicate directly with the display driver or with any hardware. All DirectDraw calls are mediated by the GDI. DirectDraw achieves high performance by providing a thin layer above the video hardware, enabling device-independent access to graphics accelerator hardware.
Microsoft DirectPlay™	DirectPlay simplifies communication between computers, allowing DirectX programs to run over a network or by means of a modem.
Microsoft DirectSound™	DirectSound provides device-independent access to audio accelerator hardware. It provides features such as real-time mixing of audio streams and control over effects such as volume and panning during playback. DirectSound API calls communicate directly with the I/O Manager.

Note For additional information on supporting Win32 applications, or for additional information on DirectX, see the *Microsoft Windows NT Workstation Resource Kit*.

Lesson 5: Supporting MS-DOS-based and Win16-based Applications

Windows NT supports MS-DOS-based applications in an *NT Virtual DOS Machine (NTVDM)*. An NTVDM can also support Win16-based applications in an emulated Win16 on Win32 (WOW) environment. This lesson describes the components and configuration of NTVDMs and the WOW environment.

After this lesson, you will be able to:

- Describe the components of an NT Virtual DOS Machine (NTVDM).
- Configure an NTVDM to run MS-DOS-based applications.
- Describe the components of the Win16 on Win32 (WOW) environment.
- Identify the advantages and disadvantages of running Win16-based applications in multiple NTVDMs.
- Configure a Win16-based application to start in its own memory space in a separate NTVDM.

Estimated lesson time: 60 minutes

MS-DOS-based applications run in a special Win32-based application called an NT Virtual DOS Machine (NTVDM). The NTVDM provides a simulated MS-DOS environment for MS-DOS-based applications.

The NT Virtual DOS Machine (NTVDM)

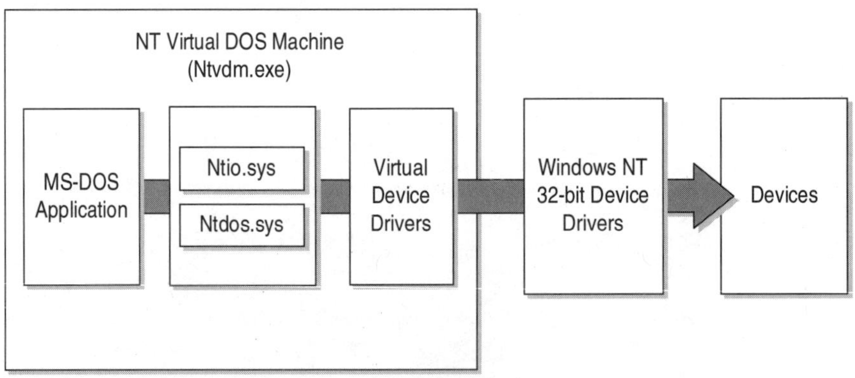

NTVDM Operation and Components

Each MS-DOS-based application has its own NTVDM, and each NTVDM has a single thread. Each NTVDM is independently supported in its own address space, so that if one NTVDM fails, all other NTVDMs remain unaffected. The function of each of the key components of the NTVDM is described in the following table.

Component	Function
Ntvdm.exe	Runs in kernel mode. This program provides the MS-DOS emulation and manages the NTVDM.
Ntio.sys	Equivalent of the MS-DOS Io.sys.
Ntdos.sys	Equivalent of Msdos.sys.

Note On RISC-based computers, the NTVDM also includes an Instruction Execution Unit that emulates an Intel 80486 processor.

MS-DOS Virtual Device Drivers

Many MS-DOS-based applications attempt to access hardware directly. However, you have learned that applications that run in user mode do not have direct access to hardware. The NTVDM uses *virtual device drivers* (VDDs) to allow MS-DOS-based applications to access the system hardware. The VDDs intercept the application's hardware calls and interact with the Windows NT 32-bit device driver. This process of communicating with the hardware is transparent to the application.

Windows NT supplies VDDs for the mouse, keyboard, printer, and COM port. The VDDs are loaded into every NTVDM based on values stored in the registry. Information about the VDDs is found in the following registry path:

HKEY_LOCAL_MACHINE\System\CurrentControlSet\Control\
VirtualDeviceDrivers

Configuring the MS-DOS NTVDM

An NT Virtual DOS Machine (NTVDM) can be customized for a specific MS-DOS-based application by changing settings in the application's program information file (PIF). To create, modify, and save PIFs, right-click the application file name in Windows NT Explorer; if you click **OK** after changing any of the settings in the **Properties** dialog box, you create a PIF (a shortcut) for the application.

The settings available in Windows NT PIFs are similar to Windows 3.*x* PIFs with the addition of two settings: the Autoexec Filename setting and the Config Filename setting. In MS-DOS there was only one Autoexec.bat file and one Config.sys file, while in Windows NT you can have multiple Autoexec files and Config files. These additional settings allow you to specify the Autoexec and Config files to use with a specific application.

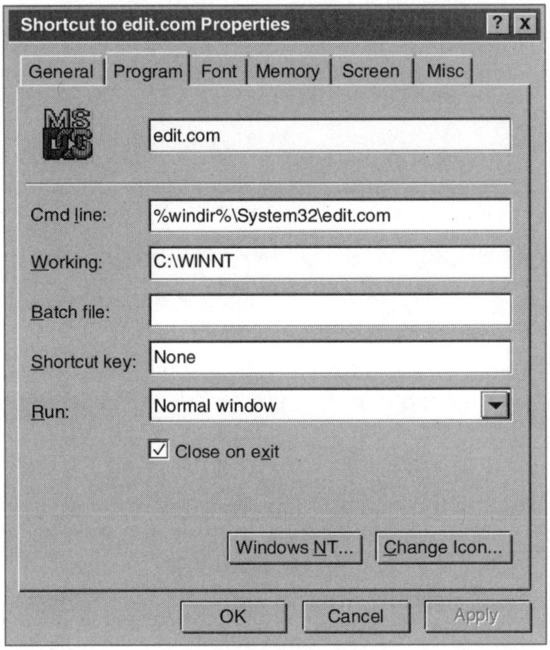

Although most MS-DOS-based commands work under Windows NT, any MS-DOS drivers or executable files that attempt to directly access a device for which there is no VDD will fail. Windows NT protects the system from such access.

Autoexec and Config Windows NT File Names

When an MS-DOS-based application starts, a new NTVDM automatically starts, and its Autoexec and Config files are run. These are the Windows NT equivalents of the MS-DOS files, Autoexec.bat and Config.sys. The default files are Autoexec.nt and Config.nt, and are located in *systemroot*\System32.

To specify different Autoexec and Config files to be used with a specific MS-DOS-based application, click the **Windows NT...** button (as shown in the preceding illustration) on the **Program** tab of the PIF for the application. The dialog box shown in the following illustration appears.

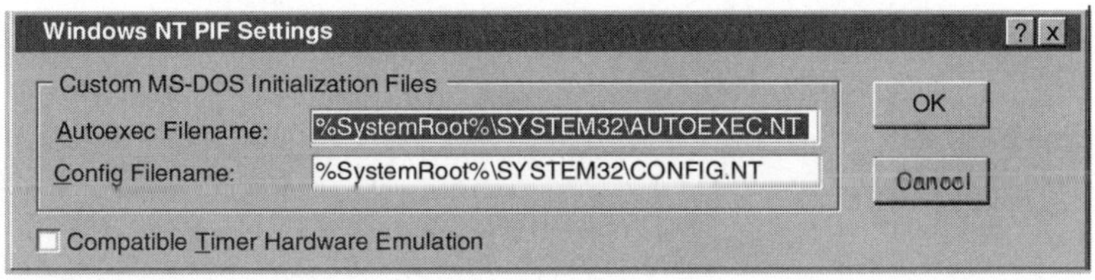

You must edit the PIF associated with an application to specify different Config and Autoexec files for each application. PIFs can be created for MS-DOS-based applications by modifying the default properties for the applications. A change to a setting in either Autoexec.nt or Config.nt takes effect as soon as the changes are saved and the application restarts.

Windows NT supports the same commands in the Autoexec file that are supported by MS-DOS 5.0. If a command that is not supported by Windows NT is used in the Config file, it is ignored.

Note Remember that there is nothing new added to MS-DOS after version 5.0 that Windows NT does not already have built in. For more information about supported commands, see *What's New and Different from MS-DOS* in Windows NT Help.

WOW and Win16-based Applications

Win16 on Win32 (WOW) is a 32-bit user-mode program in Windows NT that allows Win16-based applications to run in a Win32 environment. Because Windows 3.*x* is itself an MS-DOS-based program, Win16 applications require an NT Virtual DOS Machine (NTVDM). WOW components operate in the context of this NTVDM.

WOW Components

The WOW environment consists of several components, as described in the following table.

Component	Description
Wowexec.exe	Provides the Windows 3.1 emulation for the NTVDM.
Wow32.dll	Provides the DLL portion of the Windows 3.1 emulation layer.
Win16 application	The 16-bit application running in the WOW.
Krnl386.exe	A modified version of the Windows 3.1 386 kernel for Intel *x*86-based computers, which translates many operations to Win32 services.
User.exe	A modified version of the Windows 3.1 User.exe, which translates API calls to Win32 services.
Gdi.exe	A modified version of the Windows 3.1 Gdi.exe, which translates API calls to Win32 services.

Note 16-bit Windows 3.*x* VDDs are *not* supported under WOW. Win16-based applications that rely on these drivers may not function correctly under Windows NT.

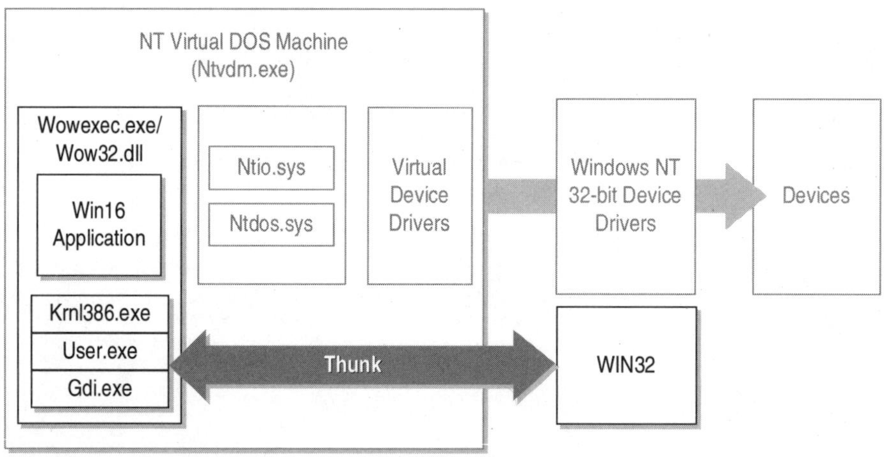

WOW Operation

WOW translates, or *thunks*, 16-bit calls to 32-bit calls. Thunking is the process of translating 16-bit calls into 32-bit calls and vice versa. When an application calls a Windows 3.*x* function, WOW intercepts the call and passes control to the equivalent Win32 function. As a result, Windows 3.*x*-based applications use Win32 functions.

If the Win32 function needs to return anything to the calling application, it must be translated from 32 bits to 16 bits. Although these translations incur some overhead, the loss may be offset by the speed gained by carrying out 32-bit instructions.

WOW provides the nonpreemptive multitasking environment for which Win16-based applications were designed.

By default, a single NTVDM starts when the first Win16-based application is initialized, and all Win16-based applications run in that NTVDM.

WOW Limitations

The WOW environment has these limitations:

- If one Win16-based application fails, it can adversely affect all other Win16-based applications running in the NTVDM. For example, if a Win16-based application does not release the processor, the other Win16-based applications cannot get access to it, because WOW provides nonpreemptive multiprocessing within that environment. Other Windows NT–based applications can still access the processor, but in order for the other Win16-based applications running in that NTVDM to gain access to the processor, the failed Win16-based application must be closed.
- There is no shared memory between the applications running in WOW and other applications running under Windows NT. Win16-based applications cannot call 32-bit DLLs, and Windows NT–based applications cannot call Win16 DLLs.

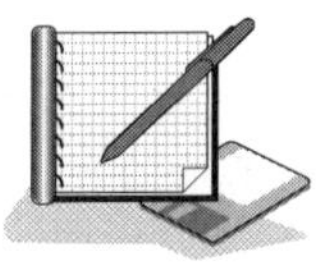

Practice

In these procedures, you start a few applications, and then use Task Manager to view the active processes and applications on the system. You then determine the effects of a halted Win32 application on the system and end the application that has stopped responding.

Note Complete these procedures on Workstation1.

► **To view running applications and system processes**

1. Open the C:\Lab Files\Apps folder.
2. In the Apps folder, start BadApp32, Spind16, and Spind32. Do not close the Apps folder.
3. Click the SpinDIB:32 window, and then click **Open**.
4. Click **Billg.bmp**, and then click **Open**.
5. Click the SpinDIB:16 window, and then click **Open**.

6. Click **Billg.bmp**, and then click **Open**.
7. Arrange your desktop so that you can see the Apps folder, Spind16, Spind32, and BadApp32 (the title bar shows BadApp) at the same time.
8. To verify that the SpinDIB:32 and SpinDIB:16 applications are running, click **Spin!** on each application.
9. Start Task Manager.

   According to the **Applications** tab, what tasks are currently running?

   ____

   ____

   ____

10. Click the **Processes** tab.

    According to Task Manager, what processes are currently running?

    ____

    ____

    ____

    Why does Spind16.exe appear indented under Ntvdm.exe?

    ____

11. On the **Options** menu in Task Manager, select **Always on Top**, so that the check box is *not* selected.

▸ **To view the effects of a Win32 application that has stopped responding**

1. On the BadApp32 **Action** menu, click **Hang**.

   In the BadApp32 window, the fuse burns down, and then the bomb explodes. At this point the application halts.
2. Move the mouse pointer over BadApp32. What is the status of BadApp32?

   ____

3. Are SpinDIB:32 and SpinDIB:16 still active? (Can you spin Bill?)

   ____

▸ **To terminate an application that has stopped responding**

1. Switch to Task Manager, and then click the **Applications** tab.
2. Click **BadApp**, and then click **End Task**.

   The **BadApp** dialog box appears, indicating that the application cannot respond to the End Task request.
3. In the **BadApp** dialog box, click **End Task** to clear the dialog box and end BadApp32.

   SpinDIB:32 and SpinDIB:16 should still be running.

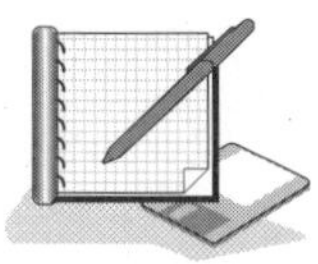

Practice

In these procedures, you observe the effects of a General Protection Fault (GPF) error and the effects of a halted application. You also run a Win16-based application in its own memory space.

Note Complete these procedures on Workstation1.

▸ **To observe the effects of a 16-bit application General Protection Fault**

1. In the Apps folder, open Badapp16.
2. In the Bad App window, click the bomb.

   When the fuse burns down, the bomb explodes. At this point an error message occurs.
3. Do *not* click **Close** or **Ignore**.
4. Click **SpinDIB:32**.

   Is the application active? Why or why not?

   ____
5. Click **SpinDIB:16**.

   Is the application active? Why or why not?

   ____
6. In the **BADAPP** dialog box containing the error message, click **Close**.

   An **Application Error** dialog box appears.
7. Click **Close**.
8. Click **SpinDIB:16**.

   Is the application active? Why or why not?

   ____

▸ **To observe the effects of a Win16 application that halts**

1. With SpinDIB:32 and SpinDIB:16 still active, open Badapp16.
2. On the **Action** menu, click **Hang**.

   When the fuse burns down, the bomb explodes. At this point the application halts.
3. Move the mouse pointer over SpinDIB:16.

   What is the status of SpinDIB:16?

   ____
4. Move the mouse pointer over SpinDIB:32.

   What is the status of SpinDIB:32?

   ____
5. Use Task Manager to end the Bad App application.
6. Switch to SpinDIB:16 to verify that it is still active.
7. Close SpinDIB:16 and SpinDIB:32.

Multiple NTVDMs

Win16-based applications can be configured to run in their own memory spaces, on an application-by-application basis, thereby creating multiple NT Virtual DOS Machines (NTVDMs).

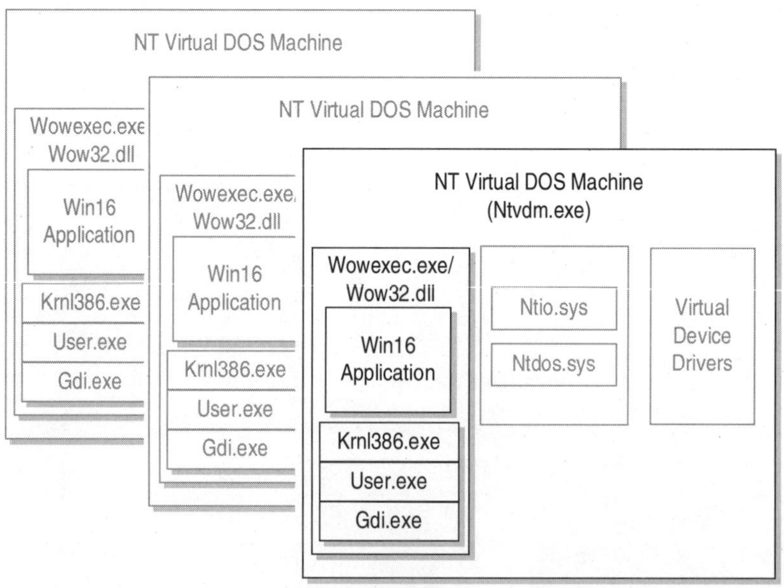

When a Win16-based application is configured to run in its own memory space, a new NTVDM is created when the application starts. Inside the new NTVDM, a new WOW application environment starts. Each Win16-based application configured to run in its own memory space creates another WOW application environment within another NTVDM.

Advantages of Multiple NTVDMs

There are several advantages to running Win16-based applications in separate NTVDMs:

- *Reliability.* A single faulty Win16-based application does not affect any other Win16-based applications.
- *Interoperability.* If Win16-based applications follow the OLE and dynamic data exchange (DDE) specifications, they can interoperate with other applications in separate memory spaces.
- *Preemptive multitasking.* If several Win16-based applications are running in a shared memory space, one busy application prevents the others from being used. Running each Win16-based application in its own memory space, however, keeps all of the applications usable, even when one is busy.
- *Multiprocessing.* Multitasking and true multiprocessing of Win16-based applications is enabled on multiprocessor computers. If all of the Win16-based applications are running in a shared memory space, only one Win16-based application is ever running at one time. Therefore, even on a multiprocessor system, only one Win16-based application can run, and the Win16-based applications do not take advantage of any additional processors on the system. However, if each Win16-based application is configured to run in a separate memory space, it can run simultaneously if the system has enough available processors.

Disadvantages of Multiple NTVDMs

There are potential disadvantages to running Win16-based applications in separate NTVDMs:

- *Additional memory usage.* Starting multiple Win16-based applications in their own memory spaces introduces additional overhead into the system. Each Win16-based application that is started in its own memory space starts another NTVDM and WOW application environment. This overhead can potentially be approximately 2 MB of page file space and approximately 1 MB of RAM per separate memory space used. Depending on the amount of RAM in the computer, this overhead could affect system performance.
- *Lack of interoperability.* If Win16-based applications do not follow the OLE and DDE standards, or if they rely on shared memory to exchange data, these Win16-based applications do *not* function correctly in separate memory spaces. To function properly, such applications must be run in the default (shared) NTVDM and WOW application environment.

Note Once started, the default (shared) NTVDM and WOW application environment remains open, even if all Win16-based applications that were running in it are closed. You can use Task Manager to close the shared NTVDM and WOW application environment.

However, when a Win16-based application is started in a separate memory space, an additional NTVDM and WOW application environment is started. When you close this Win16-based application, its NTVDM and WOW application environment is also closed. The default NTVDM is not affected.

Starting a Win16-based Application in Its Own NTVDM

A Win16-based application can be started in its own NTVDM in the following ways:

- From a command prompt

  Type **start /separate [path] application_executable**

- From the **Start** menu

  Click **Run**, and in the **Open** box, type **[path] application_executable** and then click the **Run in Separate Memory Space** check box.

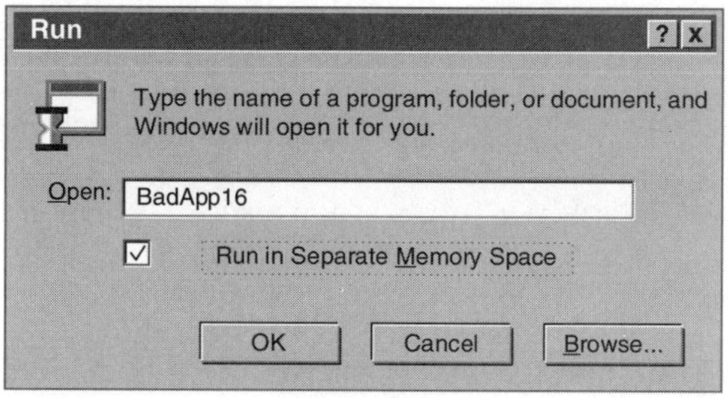

Note If the **Run in Separate Memory Space** check box appears dimmed, the application is not a 16-bit Windows application, or the system cannot find the application.

- From a shortcut

  Create a shortcut, and on the **Properties Shortcut** tab, click the **Run in Separate Memory Space** check box.

- By file association

  On the Windows NT Explorer **View** menu, click **Options**, click the **File Types** tab, and then click the Win16-based application to be edited.

  Click **Edit**, and then double-click **Open**.

  Edit the open line to include the **/separate** switch using the following syntax:

  cmd /c start **/separate** <path><application_executable> %1

Note File association can also be done from the command prompt by using the **ftype** and **assoc** commands.

Practice

In these procedures, you run Win16-based applications in separate NTVDMs.

Note Complete these procedures on Workstation1.

▸ To start a Win16-based application in a separate NTVDM for a single instance from a command prompt

1. Start a command prompt.
2. Type the following:

   start /separate C:\ "Lab Files"\Apps\Spind16

   and then press ENTER.

▸ To start a Win16-based application in a separate NTVDM for a single instance from the Start menu

1. On the **Start** menu, click **Run**.
2. In the **Run** dialog box, type **"C:\Lab Files\Apps\BadApp16"** and then select the **Run in Separate Memory Space** check box.
3. Click **OK**.

   You should now see SpinDIB:16 and BadApp running.
4. Use Task Manager to verify they are running in separate NTVDMs.
5. Close SpinDIB:16 and BadApp.

Note Each Win16-based application runs either in the default shared NTVDM or in its own NTVDM. Only one NTVDM can allow shared Win16-based applications.

If you want to configure a Win16-based application to always start in a separate NTVDM, create a shortcut for the application. Right-click the shortcut and then click **Properties**. In the **Properties** dialog box, click the **Shortcut** tab. On the **Shortcut** tab, click the **Run in Separate Memory Space** check box. Each time you start the application using the shortcut you created, it is automatically started in a separate NTVDM.

Practice

In this procedure, you create and configure a shortcut to start Spind16, a Win16-based application, in a separate NTVDM.

Note Complete this procedure on Workstation1.

▸ **To create and configure a shortcut to start Spind16 in a separate NTVDM**

1. In the Apps folder, right-click **Spind16**, and then click **Create Shortcut**.

   A new Shortcut to Spind16 appears in the Apps folder.
2. Rename the shortcut file name from **Shortcut to Spind16** to **SpinDIB16 (separate WOW)**.
3. Right-click **SpinDIB16 (separate WOW)**.
4. Click **Properties**.
5. Click the **Shortcut** tab.
6. Select the **Run in Separate Memory Space** check box.
7. Click **OK** to close the **SpinDIB16 (separate Wow) Properties** dialog box.
8. Start **SpinDIB16 (separate WOW)**.

   Notice that it takes somewhat longer to start SpinDIB16 this time. This is because a new NTVDM and WOW must be loaded.

You saw earlier in this lesson that when all Win16-based applications are running in a single NTVDM, if one Win16-based application stops responding, it causes the rest of the Win16-based applications to stop responding as well. You now determine what happens when a Win16-based application running in a separate NTVDM stops responding.

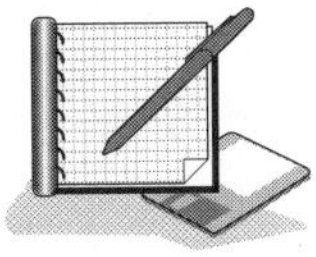

Practice

In this procedure, you determine the effect of a non-responding Win16-based application that is running in a separate NTVDM on other Win16-based applications running in the default (shared) NTVDM.

Note Complete this procedure on Workstation1.

- **To determine the effect a non-responding Win16-based application, running in a separate NTVDM, has on other Win16-based applications**

1. With the instance of SpinDIB:16 you started from the SpinDIB16 (separate WOW) shortcut still active, start **Badapp16**.
2. Arrange your desktop so that you can see SpinDIB:16 and Bad App at the same time.
3. On the Badapp16 **Action** menu, click **Hang**.
4. When Bad App stops responding, switch to SpinDIB:16.

   Is SpinDIB:16 still active? Why?

   ____

5. Use Task Manager to end the Bad App application.
6. Close **SpinDIB:16** and **Task Manager**, and if the **Apps** window is open, close it.

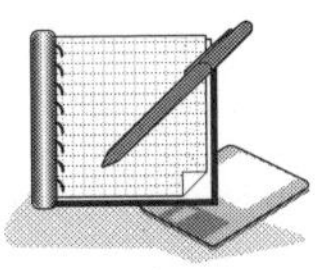

Practice

In these procedures, you rename key subsystem files and observe the resulting effects on running MS-DOS-based, Win16-based, and Win32-based applications.

Note Complete these procedures on Workstation1.

- **To observe effects on MS-DOS-based, Win16-based, and Win32-based applications when Ntvdm.exe is missing**

1. In the C:\Winnt\System32 folder, rename Ntvdm.exe to Ntvdm.old.
2. Shut down and then restart Workstation1.
3. Log on as Administrator, and then start a command prompt.
4. From C:\Lab Files\Apps, try to run Edit.com, and record the resulting behavior in the following table.

5. From C:\Lab Files\Apps, try to run Spind16.exe, and record the resulting behavior in the following table.
6. From C:\Lab Files\Apps, try to run Spind32.exe, and record the resulting behavior in the following table.

Application	Record the results here
Edit.com	_____ _____ _____ _____
Spind16.exe	_____ _____ _____ _____
Spind32.exe	_____ _____

7. In the C:\Winnt\System32 folder, rename **Ntvdm.old** to **Ntvdm.exe**.

▸ **To observe effects on MS-DOS-based, Win16-based, and Win32-based applications when Wowexec.exe is missing**

1. In the C:\Winnt\System32 folder, rename Wowexec.exe to Wowexec.old.
2. Shut down and then restart Workstation1.
3. Log on as Administrator, and then start a command prompt.
4. From the C:\Lab Files\Apps folder, try to run Edit.com, and record the resulting behavior in the following table.
5. From C:\Lab Files\Apps folder, try to run Spind16.exe, and record the resulting behavior in the following table.

6. From the C:\Winnt\System32 folder, try to run Spind32.exe, and record the resulting behavior in the following table.

Application	Record the results here
Edit.com	
Spind16.exe	
Spind32.exe	

7. In the C:\Winnt\System32 folder, rename **Wowexec.old** to **Wowexec.exe**.

▸ **To observe effects on MS-DOS-based, Win16-based, and Win32-based applications when Krnl386.exe is missing**

1. In the C:\Winnt\System32 folder, rename Krnl386.exe to Krnl386.old.
2. Shut down and then restart Workstation1.
3. Log on as Administrator, and then start a command prompt.
4. From the C:\Lab Files\Apps folder, try to run Edit.com, and record the resulting behavior in the following table.
5. From C:\Lab Files\Apps folder, try to run Spind16.exe, and record the resulting behavior in the following table.

6. From the C:\Winnt\System32 folder, try to run Spind32.exe, and record the resulting behavior in the following table.

Application	Record the results here
Edit.com	
Spind16.exe	
Spind32.exe	

In which situations did Edit.com fail? Why?

In which situations did Spind16.exe fail? Why?

In which situations did Spind32.exe fail? Why?

7. In the C:\Winnt\System32 folder, rename Krnl386.old to Krnl386.exe.
8. Shut down and then restart Workstation1.

Lesson 6: Supporting Applications on Different Hardware Platforms

Because Windows NT can run on multiple platforms, there are compatibility issues that should be considered. This lesson discusses the compatibility issues you need to understand in deciding which applications to select for a specific platform.

After this lesson, you will be able to:

- List platform capabilities and limitations.
- Choose the appropriate version of an application for a given platform.

Estimated lesson time: 10 minutes

The following illustration summarizes the different hardware platforms that Windows NT runs on, and the compatibility issues that are involved.

Hardware Platform	Win32 Applications	Windows 3.*x* and MS-DOS Applications	POSIX Applications	OS/2 1.*x* Applications
Intel *x*86	Source-compatible	Binary-compatible	Source-compatible	Binary-compatible
RISC - Alpha MIPS PowerPC	Source-compatible	Binary-compatible	Source-compatible	Binary-compatible (Bound Applications Only)

Source Compatibility

A source-compatible application must be recompiled for each hardware platform. For example, the Win32 version of Microsoft Word for Windows runs only on the hardware platform for which it was compiled. Although many Win32-based applications are available for all hardware platforms supported by Windows NT, many other Win32-based applications are specific to the Intel *x*86-based platform.

Binary Compatibility

A binary-compatible application can run on any hardware platform supported by Windows NT, with no recompilation necessary.

Windows 3.*x*–based and MS-DOS-based Applications

Many users migrating to Windows NT use applications written for MS-DOS and Windows 3.*x*. All of these applications contain Intel *x*86 instructions. One of the goals of Windows NT is to make these existing applications binary-compatible on all computers running Windows NT, including those that do not have built-in support for Intel *x*86 instructions.

To support this goal, versions of Windows NT developed for non-Intel *x*86 computers contain code that emulates Intel 80486 instructions. When an MS-DOS- or Windows 3.*x*–based application runs on RISC-based computers, each instruction the application carries out is emulated by one or more instructions in the processor's native machine language. Emulating these instructions takes time and slows the application's execution. However, the decrease in performance is small, because a RISC-based computer is several times faster than an Intel 80486. Windows 3.*x*–based and MS-DOS-based applications are binary-compatible across all computers running Windows NT.

OS/2 Applications

The Windows NT OS/2 subsystem supports OS/2 1.*x* character-based applications on Intel-based computers. OS/2 applications are binary-compatible across all Intel *x*86-based computers.

Because there is no OS/2 subsystem on RISC-based computers running Windows NT, the only OS/2 applications capable of running on these computers are *bound* applications. Bound applications are applications designed to run under either OS/2 or MS-DOS using a single executable file. OS/2 bound applications can run on RISC-based computers running Windows NT because they run in MS-DOS mode in a NTVDM.

To run the 16-bit OS/2 1.*x* Presentation Manager application on Windows NT, an add-on subsystem is required. The Windows NT Add-on Subsystem for Presentation Manager is designed to aid in the migration from OS/2 to Windows NT. It is not included with any version of Windows NT, and must be purchased separately. The Windows NT Add-on Subsystem for Presentation Manager is a replacement OS/2 subsystem, and is supported only on Intel *x*86-based computers.

Win32-based and POSIX-based Applications

POSIX is a standard for versions of UNIX and UNIX-like operating systems. POSIX allows software developers to create applications that meet the U.S. Federal Information Processing Standard 151. POSIX.1 is a library of functions implemented as system calls. Windows NT File System (NTFS) is the only POSIX.1-compliant file system.

Win32 and POSIX are portable APIs. Applications written to these APIs are source-compatible across all Windows NT platforms.

Interoperability

One of the strengths of Windows NT is its support for sharing data between applications. All Windows NT–based applications can share data using the Windows NT Clipboard. Windows 3.*x*-based and Win32-based applications can share data using OLE and DDE. This level of interoperability is possible because all of the subsystems rely on the Win32 subsystem and Win32K Executive Service for user interactions.

Lesson 7: Distributed Component Object Model

Distributed computing users seek a common application infrastructure for building applications made up of multiple components spread across multiple platforms. This lesson explains how the distributed Component Object Model (DCOM) functions and how it can be configured to improve the networking capabilities of a computer running Windows NT.

After this lesson, you will be able to:

- Explain the function and purpose of DCOM.
- Configure DCOM.

Estimated lesson time: 15 minutes

DCOM Overview

DCOM uses remote procedure calls (RPCs) and Windows NT security features, such as permissions, to enable applications to communicate across networks. In addition, DCOM provides a programming model for software developers that can be used to create distributed applications.

One example of an application requiring DCOM would be a stock quote service. Using DCOM on a computer running Windows NT Server, stock quotes are distributed to clients on the network. A second DCOM conversation takes that data and compares it to trading rules from an object on a third computer. For example, you can create a rule specifying when to buy a specific stock. If the price for that stock falls below a predetermined level, a notification to buy would be sent out. The result of the data and rule, "Buy stock," creates a trading advisory that is displayed on a fourth computer. DCOM provides the infrastructure that connects the distributed objects so that clients receive needed information.

DCOM uses the same tools and technologies as COM. Remember that COM is the basis of OLE. COM is the standard by which software components can make use of, or be used by, one another, integrating features among diverse applications. Distributed COM is network OLE—that is, COM with a longer wire. It is a fast transport for distributed applications built with COM.

Note Existing COM (OLE) applications can use DCOM. They require only minor modification to a system's configuration, but none to the application code itself. The programming model is identical to ActiveX technologies, so integration is seamless. However, you should test existing OLE applications before deploying them with DCOM.

DCOM includes the features described in the following table.

Feature	This feature provides Windows NT with the ability to
Distribution	Run applications across a network, including the Internet.
Remote Activation	Start an application by calling a component.
Security	Support launch, access, and context security. Administrators use Windows NT security to set permissions for DCOM applications, and vary them for local and remote execution.
DCOM Configuration Tool	Configure 32-bit applications to communicate over a network and set the applications' properties.

DCOM and Remote Procedure Calls

Remote procedure calls (RPCs) provide the basis of communication and interoperability between the various DCOM services. RPCs allow an application to carry out procedures on a remote computer. In a DCOM application, a program uses the network as a means of carrying out individual components on other hosts at remote locations.

For example, a client application carries out a call to a *stub code* that takes the place of a procedure located on the client computer. The stub code uses both communication and data conversion facilities from an RPC library to carry out the requested routine within a process on a remote server.

Note Stub code is a piece of programming code designed to emulate a local routine that actually resides on a remote computer.

DCOM uses an RPC to enable existing applications to interact across multiple computers in a network. The following illustration shows the flow of a client application call to a server object.

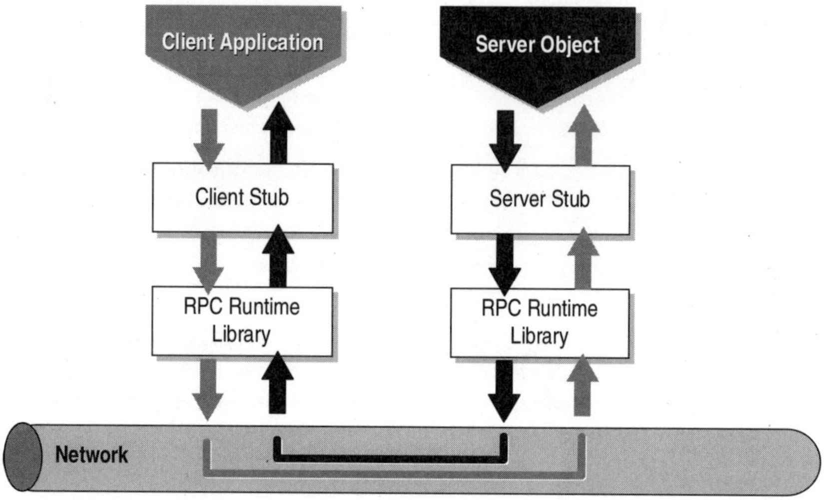

1. A client application initiates an RPC.
2. The RPC client stub packages the call, and the RPC run-time library transmits the package to the server.
3. The server's RPC runtime library receives the package and forwards it to its RPC server stub, which converts the package into the RPC.
4. The RPC is carried out.
5. The RPC server stub packages the procedure results, and the RPC runtime library transmits the package to the client running the application.
6. The client RPC runtime library receives the package and forwards it to the client stub, which unpackages it into the data for the client application.

Configuring DCOM

DCOM is installed during Windows NT setup. Use the **Distributed COM Configuration Properties** dialog box to enable DCOM and to set DCOM properties, such as security and the location for an application. Access this tool through a command prompt by typing **dcomcnfg**. Dcomcnfg.exe is located in the *systemroot*\System32 folder.

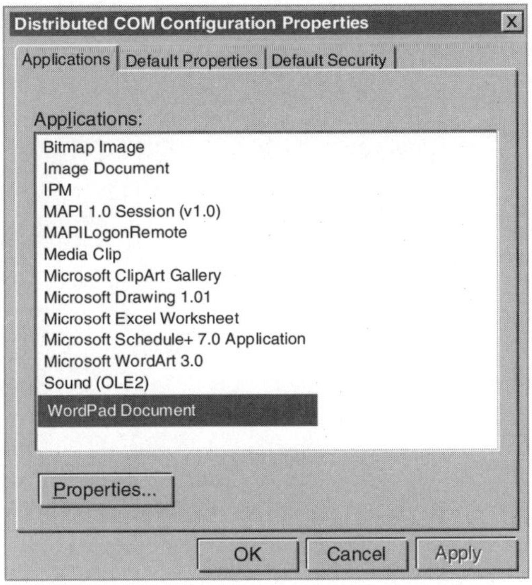

DCOM Configuration Options

The following table lists the DCOM configuration options available through the **Distributed COM Configuration Properties** dialog box.

Tab	Use this tab to
Applications	View current applications and set properties for each application. To view and configure the properties for an application, select the application, and then click the **Properties** button. The following tabs appear: **General** tab. Describes the properties of the DCOM application: the application name, the type of application (including whether the application is on the local computer or on another computer in the network), and the path. **Location** tab. Is used to designate the computer on which the application will run. Using this tab, an administrator can set applications to run on the computer where the data is located, on the local computer, or on another network computer. **Security** tab. Is used to set the following permissions: *access* permissions which allow or deny users or groups access to the application, *launch* permissions which allow or deny users or groups to start the application, and *configuration* permissions which allow users or groups to view or change the application configuration information stored in the registry. **Identity** tab. Contains user account options that allow the administrator to specify whose permissions should be used to run the object. The choices include *interactive user*, *launching user*, or *this user*. The option, *this user*, allows you to specify a specific user or service account.
Default Properties	Enable DCOM on the local computer and set default communication properties, such as Default Authentication and Default Impersonation Level. The Default Authentication properties sets packet-level security on communication between applications. The Default Impersonation Level specifies the level of permissions a client application grants to a server application to perform processing tasks on its behalf.
Default Security	Set default security permissions for Access, Launch, and Configuration.

Note The computers running the client application and the server application must both be configured for DCOM. On the computer running as a client, you must specify the location of the server application that is accessed or started. For the computer running the server application, you must specify the user account that has permission to access or start the application, and the user account that is used to run the application.

For additional information on DCOM, see Appendix E, "The Distributed Component Object Model," included with this book, or Chapter 1, "Windows NT Networking Architecture," in the *Networking Guide* of the *Microsoft Windows NT Server Resource Kit.*

Lesson 8: Managing Applications

In this chapter, you learned about and used Task Manager to manage running applications. This lesson introduces the tools, Command Prompt and the Console and System programs in Control Panel, which are used to start programs and can also be used to manage applications running under Windows NT.

After this lesson, you will be able to:

- Use the Console program in Control Panel to configure the Command Prompt.
- Prioritize applications running under Windows NT.
- Use the System program in Control Panel to change the relative responsiveness of the foreground application.

Estimated lesson time: 20 minutes

Using the Command Prompt

The Windows NT Command Prompt (Cmd.exe) in the Programs folder on the **Start** menu starts a 32-bit character mode interface to Windows NT and all of its subsystems. Starting the Command Prompt does *not* start an NT Virtual DOS Machine (NTVDM). An NTVDM only starts when an MS-DOS-based application is launched.

From the Command Prompt, a user can do the following tasks:

- Start applications, including Windows NT (32-bit), Windows 3.*x* (16-bit), MS-DOS, OS/2 1.*x* character-based, or POSIX applications.
- Start any batch file with the extension .bat or .cmd.
- Issue any Windows NT command.
- Administrate or use network resources.
- Cut and paste information between applications, including applications running in different subsystems.
- Mix commands from the different subsystems (for example, pipe between an MS-DOS and a POSIX application).

Configuring the Command Prompt

Use the **Console** program in **Control Panel** to configure the default settings for any instance of the Command Prompt that the logged-on user runs.

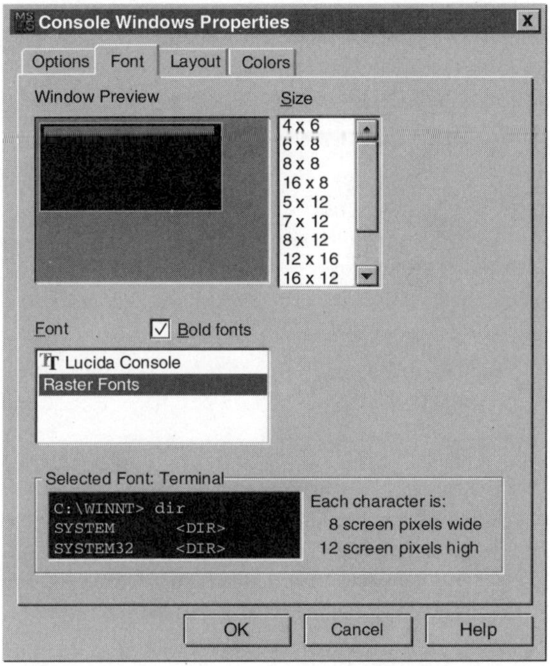

These settings are stored on a user-by-user basis in the registry in the following location:

\HKEY_CURRENT_USER\Console

Each user can configure default settings for the Command Prompt.

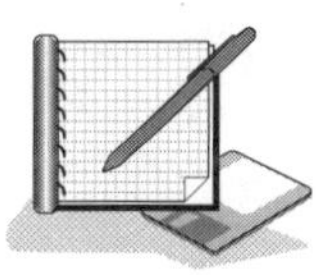

Practice

In this procedure, you configure the default settings for the Command Prompt, and then test your configuration.

Note Complete this procedure on Workstation1.

► **To configure the default settings for the Command Prompt**

1. Log on as Administrator.
2. Click the **Start** button, point to **Settings**, and then click **Control Panel**.
3. In Control Panel, start the Console program.

4. Explore the options on each of the tabs.
5. Make one or more changes to default command prompt settings. For example, change the screen background color and screen text color.
6. Click **OK** to apply the change(s); the Console program closes.
7. Start a Command Prompt to test your changes.
8. Close the Command Prompt.

Configuring Individual Command Prompts

In order to configure a Command Prompt that is currently running, click the **MSDOS** icon in the upper-left corner of the Cmd.exe window. Click **Properties** and use the "Command Prompt" **Properties** dialog box to configure a Command Prompt in one of following ways:

- Apply properties to the current window only.

  This applies the settings only to the current Command Prompt window; if another Command Prompt is started, it will have the default settings.

- Modify the shortcut which started this window.

  If you started Command Prompt by means of a shortcut, you can modify the configuration settings for the shortcut. Any Command Prompt started by this shortcut uses these settings. If you start another Command Prompt by clicking the **Start** button, pointing to **Programs**, and clicking **Command Prompt** or by running Cmd.exe, the Command Prompt that starts uses the default configuration set up through the Console program.

Prioritizing Applications

Windows NT prioritizes applications and distributes processing time among them.

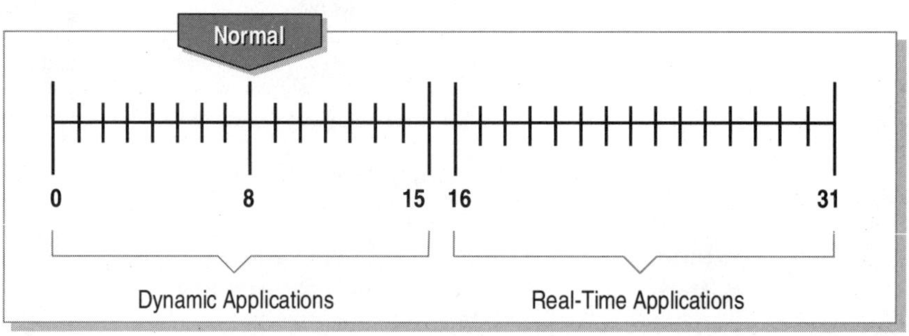

- Normal Priority = 8
- Dynamic Applications Use Priority Levels 0–15
- Real-Time Applications Use Priority Levels 16–31

Priority Levels

Priority levels range from 0 to 31. The base priority is normal (8). Critical system applications use higher priorities; others can use lower levels.

Priority	Used by
0–15	Dynamic applications: User applications and most operating system functions that are not crucial to the performance of the system and can be written to the page file.
16–31	Real time applications, such as the kernel, that cannot be written to the page file.

Starting Applications at a Specified Priority

In a preemptive, multitasking operating system such as Windows NT, the microkernel schedules threads for the processor in order of their priority and interrupts running threads if a higher priority thread is ready to run. You may want to increase the priority of a process, or decrease the priority of competing processes to improve the response.

If you want to start an application and change its base priority, use the **start** command and one of these options:

/realtime (sets base priority to 24)

/high (sets base priority to 13)

/normal (sets base priority to 8)

/low (sets base priority to 4)

For example, to start Notepad.exe at low priority, type the following at the Command Prompt:

start /low notepad

Important Changing the base priority class of a process to Real-Time can destabilize your system. A busy, Real-Time process can prevent other processes and system services from running.

To change the base priority class of a process, click the process name on the Task Manager **Processes** tab, click the highlighted name with the right mouse button, click **Set Priority**, and then click a new priority class from the **Set Priority** menu.

Note Using the **start** command to run an application at high priority may slow performance because other applications get less I/O time. This is why only users with Administrator privileges can use the **/realtime** option.

Changing Foreground Application Responsiveness

Windows NT changes the priorities of applications automatically. To improve system performance, you can manually change the relative priority of foreground and background applications. In **Control Panel**, double-click **System**. On the **Performance** tab in the **System Properties** dialog box, use your mouse or the arrow keys to select one of the three **Application Performance** settings to adjust foreground application responsiveness.

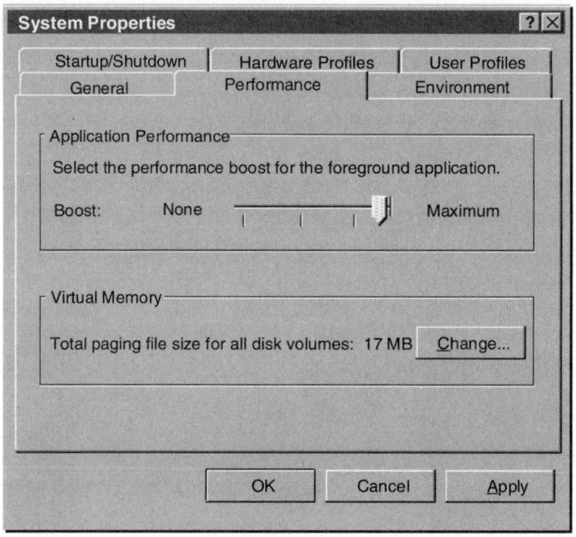

If the **Application Performance** box **Boost** setting is set to **None**, the foreground application priority is not changed. All foreground and background applications retain base priority levels. Use this setting when all applications are equally important to the current task. For example, running an administrative utility on an application server should not slow performance on clients connected to the server.

If the **Application Performance** box **Boost** setting is set to the middle setting, the foreground application's priority increases by one level. Background applications maintain base priority levels. Use this selection for non-critical situations—for example, when a game needs to receive faster response time than a file that is being spell-checked.

If the **Application Performance** box **Boost** setting is set to **Maximum**, the foreground application's priority increases by two levels. Background applications maintain their base priority levels. Use this setting to run an important application that must receive as much CPU time as possible, but still allow background applications to have minimal access to system resources. For example, a mission-critical data file should receive the most CPU time to process mathematical computations, while a file spools on the printer at the same time.

Summary

The following information summarizes the key points in this chapter:

- Windows NT architecture uses a layered approach where applications and the subsystems that support them operate in user mode. The system components, including Executive Services, microkernel, and HAL, operate in kernel mode, which is protected and has a higher priority than user mode. This architecture serves to increase system stability and reliability.
- Windows NT includes enhanced memory management. Virtual RAM allows hard disk space to be used as if it were additional memory. In this manner, the user mode processes have access to more memory than is actually available on the system.
- Through environmental subsystems, Windows NT can support applications written for other operating systems, such as MS-DOS, POSIX, and OS/2. Common operating system functions are implemented once in the Executive Services, rather than duplicated in each subsystem. This consolidation of operating system functions in the Executive Services reduces the effort required to develop new subsystems and makes them easier to maintain.
- In Windows NT 4.0, the Win32K Window Manager and GDI are incorporated into the Windows NT Executive Services. The Win32K Window Manager and GDI are responsible for handling all GUI-related I/O requests, maintaining the display, and providing a common GUI for all applications. Having Window Manager and GDI run in kernel mode enhances system performance.
- There are system compatibility issues involved with supporting applications from a variety of operating systems. For example, some applications attempt to directly access hardware, which is not allowed under the security system of Windows NT.
- Windows NT also includes several system management tools, including Task Manager, Control Panel, and the Command Prompt, which enable you to optimize your system's performance, and prioritize your applications in terms of their access to system resources.

Review

1. You are running several Win32-based applications on a computer running Windows NT Workstation. One of your Win32-based applications encounters an error and stops responding. What impact does this have on the rest of the operating system, and how can you terminate the unresponsive application?

2. You are running two Win16-based applications on a computer running Windows NT Server. Your computer has two processors, but Task Manager shows that only one is being heavily utilized, while the other is relatively idle. How can you improve your system's performance so that both processors are carrying out application code?

3. You download a Win32-based application from the Internet, but it does not run on your PowerPC-based Windows NT Workstation computer. Why?

4. Your company uses a suite of multitier client/server applications. What Microsoft Windows NT service would you configure to let these applications run in a fully distributed, multiple-computer environment? What default parameters must be changed?

5. You have a graphics-intensive program that takes a long time to render when operating in the background. You need to be able to check e-mail and work in other applications, but you do not want to slow the rendering process. How can you optimize your system's performance?

Answer Key

Procedure Answers

Page 273

▸ **To view the priority of a running application**

5. If necessary, resize the Task Manager window until you can see the **Base Priority** column.

   What is the priority of each Counter?

   Normal.

Page 285

▸ **To view running applications and system processes**

9. Start Task Manager.

   According to the **Applications** tab, what tasks are currently running?

   Answers will vary, but should include BadApp, SpinDIB:16, SpinDIB:32, and Exploring–Apps (if you opened Apps through Windows NT Explorer) or Apps (if you did not use Windows NT Explorer).

10. Click the **Processes** tab.

    According to Task Manager, what processes are currently running?

    Answers will vary, but should include Ntvdm.exe, Badapp32.exe, Spind32.exe, Taskmgr.exe, Services.exe, Explorer.exe, Csrss.exe (client/server subsystem services which is the Win32 subsystem), and others.

    Why does Spind16.exe appear indented under Ntvdm.exe?

    Spind16 is a 16-bit application that runs within an NT Virtual DOS Machine (NTVDM), created and maintained by Ntvdm.exe.

Page 286

▸ **To view the effects of a Win32 application that has stopped responding**

2. Move the mouse pointer over BadApp32. What is the status of BadApp32?

   An hourglass appears, meaning that the application has halted.

3. Are SpinDIB:32 and SpinDIB:16 still active? (Can you spin Bill?)

   Yes, both applications should still be active.

Page 287

▸ **To observe the effects of a 16-bit application General Protection Fault**

4. Click **SpinDIB:32**.

   Is the application active? Why or why not?

   Yes. SpinDIB:32 is a 32-bit Windows-based application and has its own memory space.

5. Click **SpinDIB:16**.

   Is the application active? Why or why not?

   No. SpinDIB:16 is a 16-bit Windows-based application and uses the same memory space as Badapp16.

8. Click **SpinDIB:16**.

   Is the application active? Why or why not?

   Yes, Badapp16 is closed.

Page 288

▸ **To observe the effects of a Win16 application that halts**

3. Move the mouse pointer over SpinDIB:16.

   What is the status of SpinDIB:16?

   An hourglass appears, meaning that the application has halted.

4. Move the mouse pointer over SpinDIB:32.

   What is the status of SpinDIB:32?

   SpinDIB:32 is still active.

Page 293

▸ **To determine the effect a non-responding Win16-based application, running in a separate NTVDM, has on other Win16-based applications**

4. When Bad App stops responding, switch to SpinDIB:16.

   Is SpinDIB:16 still active? Why?

   Yes, because it is running in its own memory space.

Page 293

▸ To observe effects on MS-DOS-based, Win16-based, and Win32-based applications when Ntvdm.exe is missing

4. From C:\Lab Files\Apps, try to run Edit.com, and record the resulting behavior in the following table.
5. From C:\Lab Files\Apps, try to run Spind16.exe, and record the resulting behavior in the following table.
6. From C:\Lab Files\Apps, try to run Spind32.exe, and record the resulting behavior in the following table.

Application	Record the results here
Edit.com	It fails to run because Windows NT cannot find the file C:\Lab Files\Apps\Edit.com. MS-DOS-based applications require Ntvdm.exe to run.
Spind16.exe	It fails to run because Windows cannot find C:\Lab Files\Apps\Spind16.exe. Win16-based applications require Ntvdm.exe to run.
Spind32.exe	It runs as expected because Win32-based applications are not dependent on Ntvdm.exe to run.

Page 294

▸ To observe effects on MS-DOS-based, Win16-based, and Win32-based applications when Wowexec.exe is missing

4. From the C:\Lab Files\Apps folder, try to run Edit.com, and record the resulting behavior in the following table.
5. From C:\Lab Files\Apps folder, try to run Spind16.exe, and record the resulting behavior in the following table.
6. From the C:\Winnt\System32 folder, try to run Spind32.exe, and record the resulting behavior in the following table.

Application	Record the results here
Edit.com	It runs as expected. MS-DOS-based applications are not dependent on Wowexec.exe to run.
Spind16.exe	It fails to run (no error message). Win16-based applications require Wowexec.exe to run.
Spind32.exe	It runs as expected. Win32-based applications are not dependent on Wowexec.exe to run.

Page 295

▸ **To observe effects on MS-DOS-based, Win16-based, and Win32-based applications when Krnl386.exe is missing**

4. From the C:\Lab Files\Apps folder, try to run Edit.com, and record the resulting behavior in the following table.
5. From C:\Lab Files\Apps folder, try to run Spind16.exe, and record the resulting behavior in the following table.
6. From the C:\Winnt\System32 folder, try to run Spind32.exe, and record the resulting behavior in the following table.

Application	Record the results here
Edit.com	It runs as expected. MS-DOS-based applications are not dependent on Krnl386.exe to run.
Spind16.exe	It fails to run (no error message). Win16-based applications are dependent on Krnl386.exe to run.
Spind32.exe	It runs as expected. Win32-based applications are not dependent on Krnl386.exe to run.

In which situations did Edit.com fail? Why?

When Ntvdm.exe was missing. MS-DOS-based applications require Ntvdm.exe to emulate the MS-DOS environment.

In which situations did Spind16.exe fail? Why?

When Ntvdm.exe was missing. Win16-based applications require Ntvdm.exe to emulate the MS-DOS environment, which is required for the WOW component.

When Wowexec.exe was missing. Win16-based applications require Wowexec.exe to emulate the Windows environment.

When Krnl386.exe was missing. Win16-based applications require Krnl386.exe to translate many operations to Win32 services.

In which situations did Spind32.exe fail? Why?

Spind32.exe did not fail because it is a Win32-based application and does not require any of these files to operate.

Review Answers

Page 312

1. You are running several Win32-based applications on a computer running Windows NT Workstation. One of your Win32-based applications encounters an error and stops responding. What impact does this have on the rest of the operating system, and how can you terminate the unresponsive application?

   All other applications, as well as the rest of the operating system, continue to process normally, because each Win32-based application maintains its own threads, separate from all other processes. Use Task Manager to end the unresponsive application.

2. You are running two Win16-based applications on a computer running Windows NT Server. Your computer has two processors, but Task Manager shows that only one is being heavily utilized, while the other is relatively idle. How can you improve your system's performance so that both processors are carrying out application code?

   The Win16-based applications are most likely running in the same NTVDM. Because the Win16-based applications alternate use of a common thread, the microkernel can only schedule this thread on one processor. To optimize performance, start each Win16-based application in its own NTVDM.

3. You download a Win32-based application from the Internet, but it does not run on your PowerPC-based Windows NT Workstation computer. Why?

   The application is probably specific to the Intel platform. Win32-based applications are source-compatible across Windows NT platforms; they must be compiled for a specific platform in order to function on that platform.

4. Your company uses a suite of multitier client/server applications. What Microsoft Windows NT service would you configure to let these applications run in a fully distributed, multiple-computer environment? What default parameters must be changed?

   DCOM. The service must first be enabled, and permissions need to be set so that the appropriate users have permissions to access, change, or delete components as needed.

5. You have a graphics-intensive program that takes a long time to render when operating in the background. You need to be able to check e-mail and work in other applications, but you do not want to slow the rendering process. How can you optimize your system's performance?

   Use the System program in Control Panel to set your dynamic priorities so that the foreground application's threads receive a one-level priority boost rather than a two-level priority boost. The actual setting is the middle setting on the Application Performance slider bar.

CHAPTER 9

The Windows NT Networking Environment

About This Chapter

Knowledge of the networking components that make up the Microsoft Windows NT networking architecture enhances your ability to support Windows NT. This chapter defines the components of Windows NT networking architecture and describes how these components communicate with each other to enable a computer running Windows NT to communicate over a network.

Lesson 1: Windows NT Network Architecture

The Windows NT operating systems are designed for client/server computing. Client/server computing generally means connecting a single-user, general-purpose workstation (client) to multi-user, general-purpose servers, with the processing load shared between both. The client requests services, and the server responds by providing the services. Windows NT also provides file and print sharing capabilities as well as the ability to use file and print resources on the network. All of these networking capabilities are built into the Windows NT operating system. Because of this integrated network support, a single computer running Windows NT can simultaneously interoperate with the following network environments:

- Microsoft networks, including Windows NT, Microsoft Windows 95, Microsoft Windows for Workgroups, and Microsoft LAN Manager.
- Transmission Control Protocol/Internet Protocol (TCP/IP) networks, including UNIX hosts.
- Remote access systems.
- AppleTalk-based networks (made possible through the Windows NT Server Services for the Macintosh).
- Novell NetWare 3.*x* and 4.*x* networks.

These networking capabilities differentiate Windows NT from other operating systems, such as Microsoft MS-DOS and Microsoft Windows, which install network capabilities separately from the core operating system.

After this lesson, you will be able to:

- Describe the network components that make up the Windows NT network architecture.
- Describe the network transport protocols included with Windows NT.

Estimated lesson time: 30 minutes

Network Component Overview

I/O Manager, a component of Executive Services, contains most of the Windows NT networking components. The components contained within I/O Manager are organized into the following architectural layers:

- *Network adapter card drivers* that are compatible with the network device interface specification (NDIS 4.0). These drivers link computers running Windows NT to the network through corresponding network adapter cards and protocols.
- *Protocols* that enable the reliable flow of data between computers on a network.
- *File system drivers* that enable applications to access local and remote system resources.

The following illustration shows the networking components in I/O Manager.

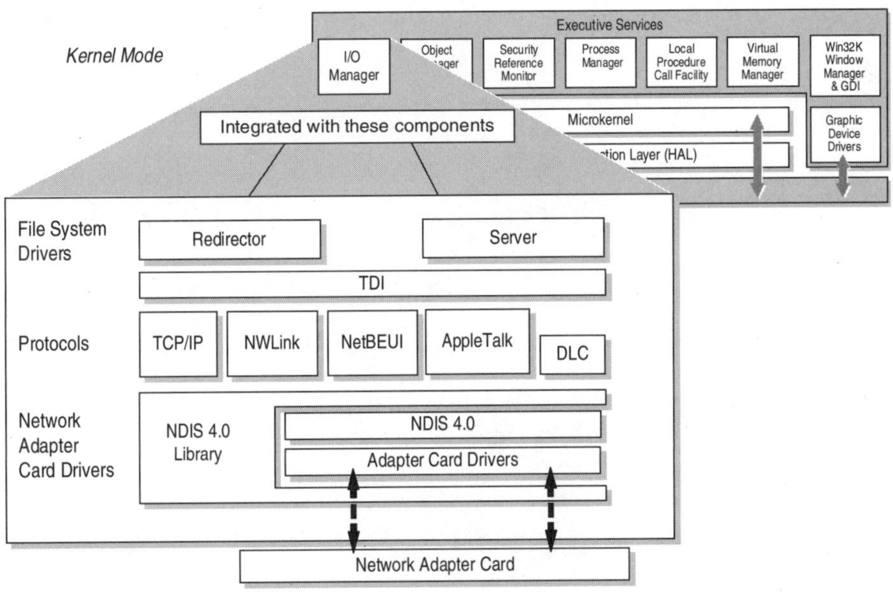

Each component communicates through programming interfaces called *boundaries*. A boundary is the unified interface between the functional layers in the Windows NT network architecture model. Creating boundaries as breakpoints in the network layers helps open the networking components of the operating system to outside development by making it easier for vendors to develop network drivers and services. These boundary layers modularize the Windows NT network architecture and provide a platform for developers to build distributed applications. For example, vendors developing transport protocols need to program only between the boundary layers instead of programming for the entire Open Systems Interconnection (OSI) model.

There are two boundary layers in the Windows NT networking architecture model: transport driver interface (TDI) and network device interface specification (NDIS) 4.0, which are described later in this chapter.

NDIS-Compatible Network Adapter Card Drivers

NDIS-compatible network adapter card drivers coordinate communications between network adapter cards and the computer's hardware, firmware, and software. Network adapter cards are the physical interface between the computer and the network cable.

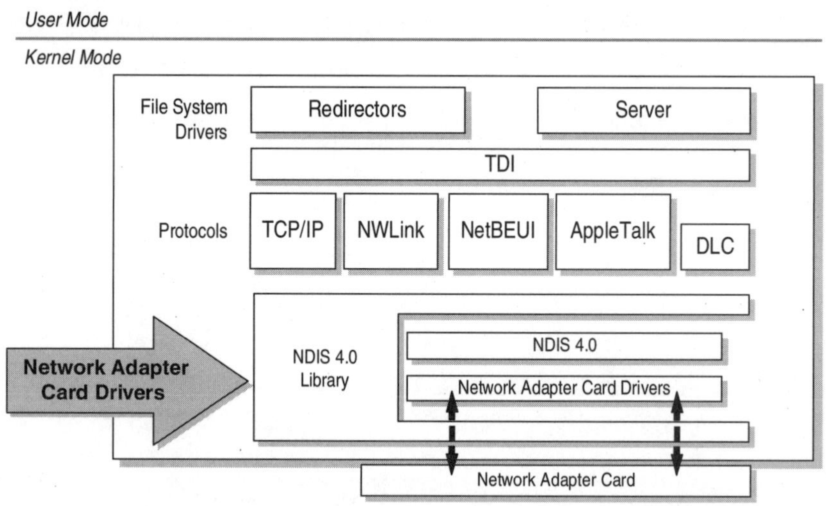

Each network adapter card can have one or more corresponding drivers. These drivers must be compatible with NDIS 4.0 to operate with computers running Windows NT 4.0. With NDIS 4.0, one or more protocols can be bound, independently, to one or more network adapter card drivers.

Because network adapter cards and their corresponding drivers are independent of the protocols, changing protocols does not require a reconfiguration of network adapter cards.

Network Device Interface Specification 4.0

The network device interface specification (NDIS) 4.0 defines the software interface used by protocols to communicate with network adapter card drivers. Any NDIS 4.0–compatible protocol can communicate with any NDIS 4.0–compatible network adapter card driver. Therefore, a protocol does not need to include blocks of code written for specific network adapter card drivers.

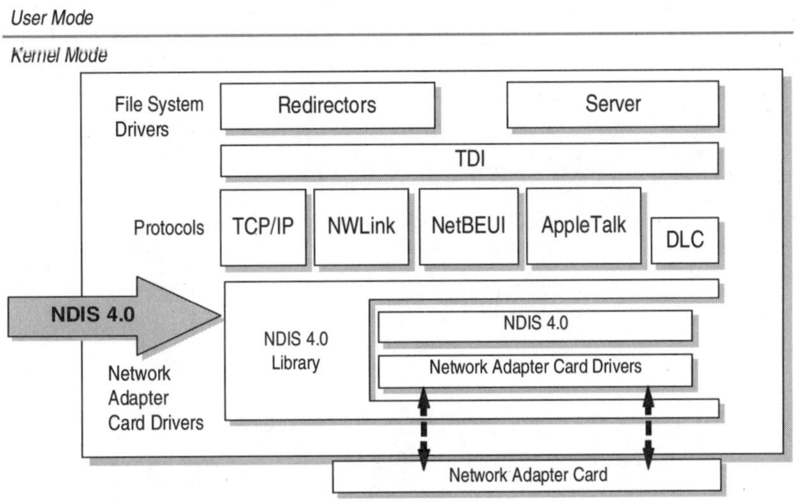

The initial communication channel between the protocol and the network adapter card driver is established through a process called *binding*.

Note For more information on binding, see Chapter 10, "Configuring Windows NT Protocols."

In Windows NT, NDIS 4.0 is implemented in a module called Ndis.sys which is referred to as the NDIS 4.0 library or *wrapper.* The NDIS 4.0 library is code surrounding all of the NDIS device drivers. The library provides a uniform interface between protocol drivers and NDIS device drivers, and contains supporting routines that make it easier to develop an NDIS driver.

In Windows NT, NDIS 4.0 allows:

- Communication links between network adapter cards and associated drivers.
- Protocols and network adapter card drivers to remain independent of each other.
- An unlimited number of network adapter cards.
- An unlimited number of protocols to be bound to a single network adapter card.

Protocols

Protocols govern communication between two or more host computers. Some protocols are commonly referred to as transport protocols. For example, TCP/IP, NWLink, NetBEUI, and AppleTalk are transport protocols. In the Windows NT network architecture, protocols are located above the NDIS 4.0 interface, as shown in the following illustration. Protocols communicate with network adapter cards through NDIS 4.0–compatible network adapter card drivers. Windows NT supports multiple protocols, bound simultaneously to one or more adapters.

In the following illustration, *data link control* (DLC) is also listed as a protocol. However, the DLC protocol is not a transport protocol. DLC is used primarily for accessing printers connected directly to the network and for accessing systems network architecture (SNA) mainframes.

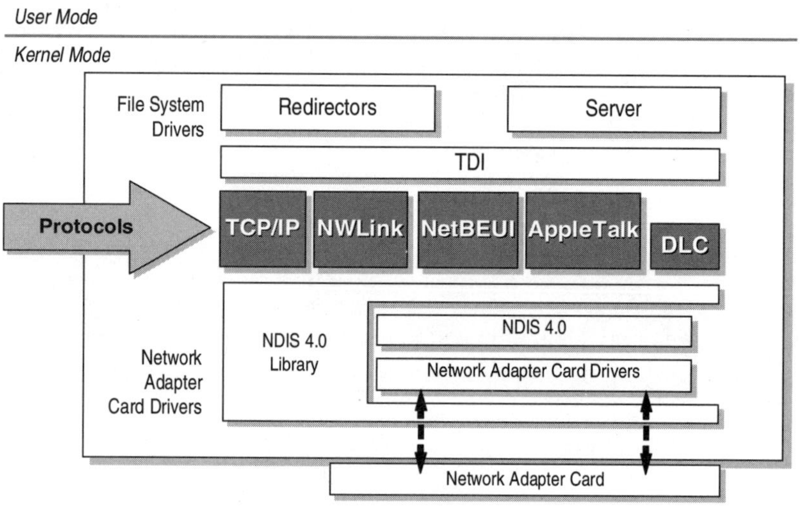

The following protocols are included with Windows NT Server and Windows NT Workstation:

- *Transmission Control Protocol/Internet Protocol (TCP/IP).* A routable networking protocol that supports wide area networks (WANs). TCP/IP is the protocol used on the Internet.
- *NWLink IPX/SPX compatible transport.* An NDIS 4.0–compatible version of the Internetwork Packet Exchange/Sequenced Packet Exchange (IPX/SPX) protocol. NWLink allows users to communicate with MS-DOS, OS/2, Windows, or other computers running Windows NT through remote procedure calls (RPCs), Windows Sockets, or Novell NetBIOS IPX/SPX.

- *NetBEUI.* A very fast and efficient non-routable protocol that relies heavily on broadcasts, and is commonly used in smaller networks. NetBEUI provides compatibility with existing LAN Manager, LAN Server, Windows 95, and Windows for Workgroups installations.
- *AppleTalk.* Used with Services for Macintosh on a computer running Windows NT Server to host connections from Apple Macintosh clients.
- *Data link control (DLC).* Traditionally used as an interface with SNA mainframes and printers that are directly connected to the network. It cannot be used, however, to establish file and print connections to another computer.

Note For more information on protocols, see Chapter 10, "Configuring Windows NT Protocols," or see *Networking Supplement* in Books Online.

Transport Driver Interface

The Transport Driver Interface (TDI) is a boundary layer that provides a common programming interface for file system drivers, such as the Workstation service (Redirector) or Server service (Server), to communicate with the transport protocols. The TDI allows the Redirector and Server to remain independent of the protocols. The Redirector and Service services are covered later in this chapter.

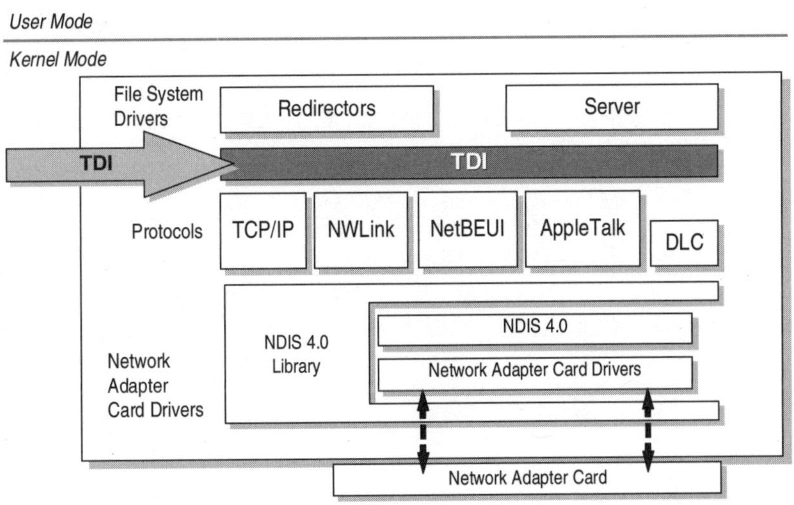

Because the TDI allows networking components to be independent of each other, protocols can be added, removed, or changed without reconfiguring the entire network subsystem.

Note For more information on installing and configuring protocols, see Chapter 10, "Configuring Windows NT Protocols."

File System Drivers

File system drivers are used to access files. Any time you request a file, whether it is a request to perform a read or write operation, a file system driver is involved. For example, if you request a file on an NTFS partition, the Ntfs.sys file system driver is involved in servicing your request. Several major networking components are implemented as file system drivers, such as the Workstation (Redirector) and Server services.

The I/O Manager controls file system drivers. I/O Manager can store files locally on a hard disk, using a file system driver such as Ntfs.sys, or on a remote networked computer using the Redirector file system driver. In the Windows NT network architecture, file system drivers are located above the TDI and allow user-mode applications to access system resources, such as a read call from an I/O operation to an NTFS partition, or a read call to a remote resource that uses the Workstation (Redirector) service.

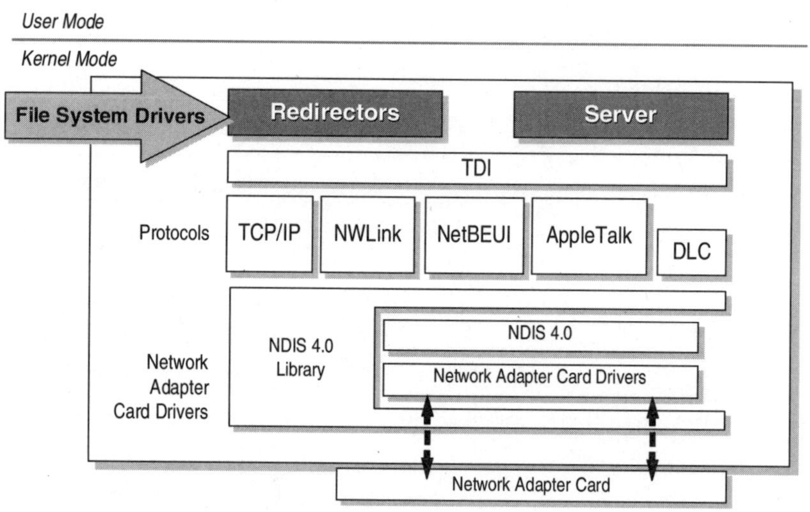

Redirector

The I/O Manager determines if an I/O request is for a local disk or for a network resource. If the I/O request is for a network resource, the Redirector accepts the I/O requests and sends or redirects the request to the appropriate network resource. The Windows NT Redirector (RDR) is a component that resides above the TDI and communicates with the transport protocols by means of the TDI interface. The Redirector allows connection to Windows for Workgroups, LAN Manager, LAN Server, and other Microsoft network-based servers.

The Redirector is implemented as a Windows NT file system driver. Implementing a redirector as a file system driver provides the following benefits:

- Applications can call the Windows NT I/O API to access files on both local and remote computers. From the I/O Manager perspective, there is no difference between accessing files stored locally on a hard disk and using the Redirector to access files stored remotely on a computer on the network.
- The Redirector can run in kernel mode and directly call other drivers and other kernel-mode components, such as Cache Manager, thereby improving the performance of the Redirector.
- The Redirector can be dynamically loaded and unloaded, like any other file system driver.
- The Redirector can easily coexist with other vendor's redirectors that have been installed on your computer.

Server

Windows NT includes a second component, the Server service (Server). Like the Redirector, the Server resides above the TDI, is implemented as a file system driver, and directly interacts with various other file system drivers to satisfy I/O requests, such as reading or writing to a file.

The Server service supplies the connections requested by client-side redirectors and provides them with access to the resources they request.

When the Server service receives a request from a remote computer asking to read a file that resides on the server's local hard drive, the following steps occur:

- The low-level network drivers receive the request and pass it to the Server service.
- The Server service passes a read-file request to the appropriate local file system driver.
- The local file system driver calls lower-level, disk device drivers to access the file.
- The data is passed back to the local file system driver.
- The local file system driver passes the data back to the Server service.
- The Server service passes the data to the lower-level network drivers for transmission back to the client computer.

Lesson 2: Distributed Processing

As more and more enterprises adopt the client/server paradigm for their networks, standards-based distributed processing becomes a key factor in the success of that effort. A computer running Windows NT can divide applications into components: a front-end component that runs on a client, and a back-end component that runs on a server. This distribution allows an application to take better advantage of hardware resources, such as multiple processors or large amounts of RAM, that are distributed on the network. Computers running Window NT use interprocess communication (IPC) mechanisms to create client/server connections that support distributed processing.

After this lesson, you will be able to:

- Explain the function of distributed processing.
- Describe the IPC mechanisms that enable client/server connections.

Estimated lesson time: 10 minutes

Distributed Application Overview

In a typical distributed application, a computing task is divided into processes: front-end processes that require minimal resources and run on a client, and back-end processes that require large amounts of data, number calculations, shared processing rules, or specialized hardware that run on a server. The server shares its processing power, carrying out tasks on behalf of clients.

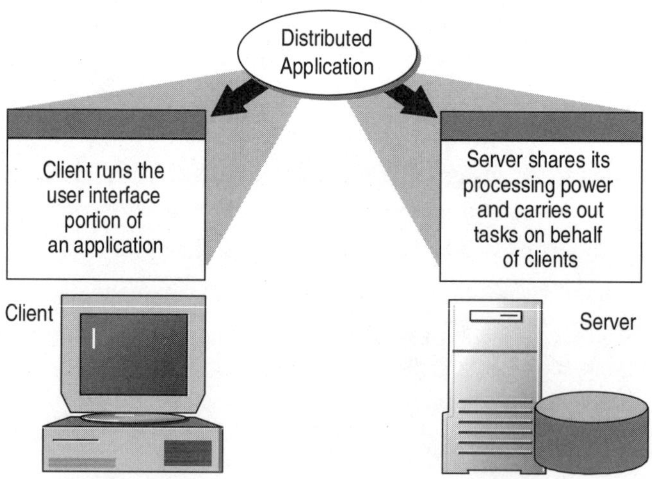

Note Computers running Windows NT can perform the role of either the client or the server for distributed application support. The client and server components can be parts of a common application, such as a Microsoft Exchange Server, or can be parts of different applications, such as Microsoft Access communicating with Microsoft SQL Server.

IPC Mechanisms

In distributed processing, a network connection that allows data to flow in both directions must exist between the client and server portions of a distributed application. The following table describes the Windows NT IPC mechanisms that are used to achieve these connections.

IPC mechanism	This IPC mechanism is used to
Named pipes	Build a bidirectional communication channel between a client and a server. Named pipes provide guaranteed messaging services for distributed applications. Once a pipe is open, both client and server can read data from, and write data to, the pipe. The WinLogon process is an example of an application that uses named pipes.
Mailslots	Build a unidirectional communication channel between a client and server. Mailslots provide second-class, non-guaranteed messaging services for distributed applications. They can be used to identify other computers or services on a network, such as the Browser service.
Windows Sockets (WinSock)	Enable a distributed application to access transport protocols, such as TCP/IP and IPX. WinSock can be used to build a bidirectional, guaranteed communication channel between a client and a server.
Remote procedure calls (RPCs)	Allow a distributed application to call procedures available on various computers in a network.
Network dynamic data exchange (NetDDE)	Share information between applications. NetDDE uses NetBIOS APIs to communicate with the underlying network components. Chat is an example of a NetDDE-based utility.
Distributed Component Object Model (DCOM)	Distribute processes, using RPCs, across multiple computers so that the client and server components of an application can be placed in optimal locations on the network. DCOM is a Microsoft ActiveX technology, and its design enables it to work with both Java™ applets and ActiveX components through use of the Component Object Model (COM).

Lesson 3: Accessing File and Print Resources

Windows NT includes networking components that are necessary to share network resources from a server, and to gain access to network resources from a Windows NT client.

After this lesson, you will be able to:

- Describe the file and print sharing components supported by Windows NT.
- Describe how a computer running Windows NT can access file and print resources on a network.

Estimated lesson time: 10 minutes

File and Print Sharing Components

A computer running Windows NT typically has at least one redirector and a server component that are used for accessing and sharing file and print resources on a network. Along with these components, there are additional components called the multiple universal naming convention provider (MUP) and the Multiple Provider Router (MPR) that are needed to access file and print resources on a network. The following table describes the purpose of each of these components.

Component	Purpose
Workstation service (RDR)	Identify the appropriate service that can provide the resources requested by an application. The redirector does this by accepting I/O requests for remote files, named pipes, or mailslots and redirecting the I/O request to a network service on another computer. The redirector enables a client to gain access to network resources, including the ability to log on to a domain, connect to shared folders and printers, and use distributed applications.
Server service (SRV)	Share and secure resources, such as directories and printers. The Server service accepts incoming I/O requests, such as a request to read or write to a file, and routes the requested resources back to the clients.

(continued)

Component	Purpose
Multiple universal naming convention provider (MUP)	Connect to a remote computer that accepts the universal naming convention (UNC). The UNC is a naming convention for describing network servers. An example of a UNC name is *server_name**share_name**subfolder**file_name*. The MUP frees applications from having to maintain UNC provider listings. This allows a client computer with multiple redirectors installed to browse and access network resources without having to provide a unique syntax to each network redirector.
Multiple Provider Router (MPR)	Support multiple redirectors, including Windows NT, NetWare, and Banyan VINES. For each redirector that is installed, there is also a corresponding *Provider*.dll. The MPR is responsible for routing network requests to the appropriate provider and redirector. For example, if a computer running Windows NT has multiple redirectors installed, Multiple Provider Router is used to direct browser requests to the appropriate redirector for the network that is chosen.

File and Print Sharing Process

When a process on a computer running Windows NT attempts to open a file that resides on a remote computer, the Workstation (Redirector) and Server services complete the following steps to fulfill the I/O request:

1. A client initiates an I/O request through a network command that tells the I/O Manager to open a file.
2. The I/O Manager recognizes the remote file request. With the assistance of the MUP or the MPR, it passes the request to the Redirector.
3. The Redirector (RDR) passes the request to lower-level network drivers, which transmit it to the remote server for processing.
4. The Server service (SRV) receives a request from a remote computer asking it to read a file that resides on the server's local hard disk.
5. The Server service (SRV) passes the request to the I/O Manager.
6. The I/O Manager passes the read request to the local file system driver.
7. The local file system driver calls lower-level disk device drivers to access the file. Once the file is located, it is returned to the client that requested it through the same path.

The following illustration diagrams this process.

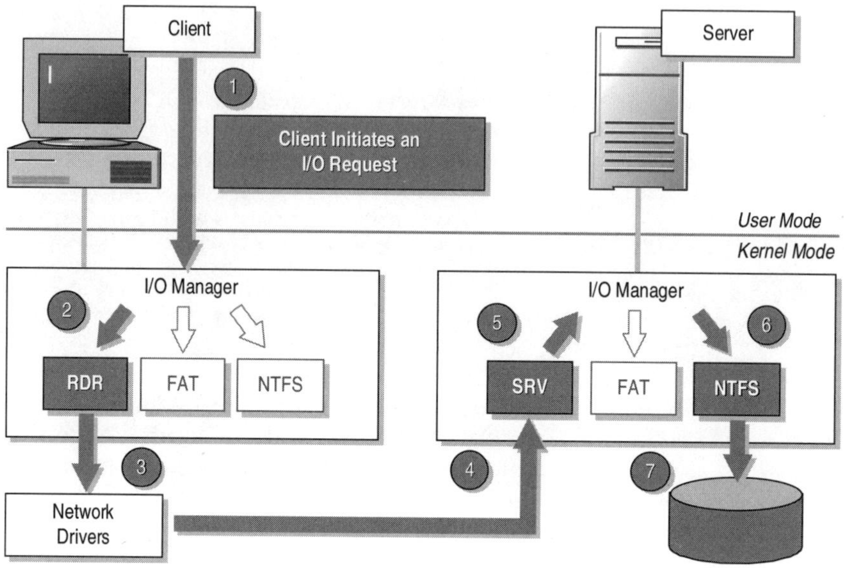

Summary

The following information summarizes the key points in this chapter:

- Networking capabilities are fully integrated into the Windows NT operating system. By providing both client and server capabilities, a computer running Windows NT can be either a client or a server in a distributed application environment. Windows NT also provides file and print sharing capabilities.
- I/O Manager, a component of the Executive Services, contains most of the Windows NT networking components. These components include network adapter cards and their drivers, network protocols, and file system drivers.
- NDIS 4.0 defines the software interface used by protocols to communicate with network adapter card drivers. Any NDIS 4.0–compatible protocol can communicate with any NDIS 4.0–compatible network adapter card driver.
- Computers running Windows NT use IPC mechanisms to create client/server connections that support distributed processing. These include named pipes, mailslots, Windows Sockets, remote procedure calls (RPCs), network dynamic data exchange (NetDDE), and distributed Component Object Model (DCOM).

For more information	See
Windows NT network architecture	Chapter 1 in the *Networking Guide* of the *Microsoft Windows NT Server Resource Kit*

Review

1. Your network includes NetWare-based servers and UNIX-based computers. You must install both the NWLink IPX/SPX compatible transport and TCP/IP protocols on your computer running Windows NT Server so that it can support all of the computers on the network. What is the minimum number of network adapter cards required for the computer running as a Windows NT server to support both protocols?

2. You are able to connect from your computer running Windows NT Workstation to shared folders on any other computer running Windows NT. However, no other computers can connect to the shared folders on your computer. In addition, although you are logged on as an Administrator, your shared folders do not appear with the shared symbol in Windows NT Explorer. What is the likely cause of the problem?

Answer Key

Review Answers

Page 334

1. Your network includes NetWare-based servers and UNIX-based computers. You must install both the NWLink IPX/SPX compatible transport and TCP/IP protocols on your computer running Windows NT Server so that it can support all of the computers on the network. What is the minimum number of network adapter cards required for the computer running as a Windows NT server to support both protocols?

   One. NDIS 4.0 enables multiple transport protocols to be bound to a single network adapter card.

2. You are able to connect from your computer running Windows NT Workstation to shared folders on any other computer running Windows NT. However, no other computers can connect to the shared folders on your computer. In addition, although you are logged on as an Administrator, your shared folders do not appear with the shared symbol in Windows NT Explorer. What is the likely cause of the problem?

   The Server service is probably disabled. Without the Server service, your computer cannot share resources.

CHAPTER 10

Configuring Windows NT Protocols

About This Chapter

Microsoft Windows NT includes the following network protocols: NWLink IPX/SPX Compatible Transport, NetBIOS extended user interface (NetBEUI), and TCP/IP. These protocols can be added, removed, or configured using the Network program in Control Panel. In addition, the Network program in Control Panel can be used to optimize network performance by configuring network bindings. This chapter covers the installation and configuration of Windows NT networking protocols.

Before You Begin

To complete the lessons in this chapter, you must have

- Two computers that meet the hardware and software requirements as specified in the Getting Started section of "About This Book."
- Completed all practices in Chapter 2, "Installing Windows NT."

Lesson 1: Using the Network Program in Control Panel

The Network program in Control Panel is used to install and configure Windows NT networking components such as protocols and network adaptercard drivers, and to configure bindings. It is also used to change a computer name, specify a workgroup or domain, and establish a domain account for the computer. This lesson describes how to use the Network program to install and configure network adapter card drivers and protocols.

After this lesson, you will be able to:

- Install and configure network adapter card drivers.
- Install and configure protocols.

Estimated lesson time: 10 minutes

Installing and Configuring Network Adapter Card Drivers

Network adapter card drivers are typically installed during Setup, when hardware is changed, or when drivers need to be updated. Use the **Adapters** tab in the **Network** dialog box in Control Panel to configure network adapter card drivers. The following illustration shows the **Adapters** tab in the **Network** dialog box.

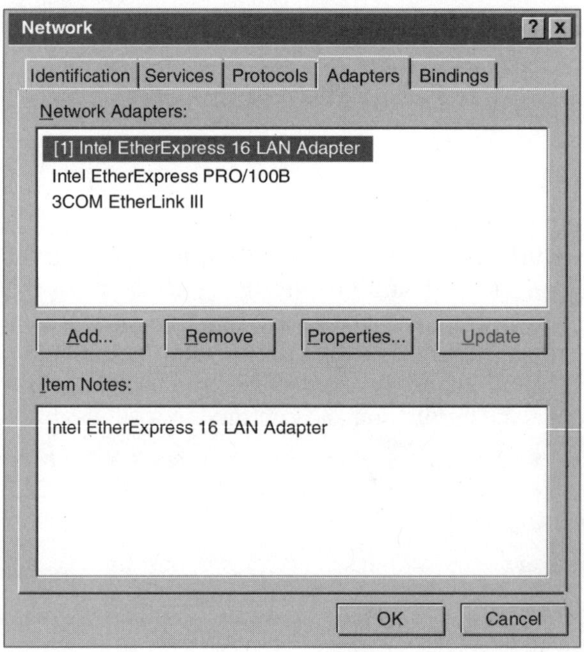

The following table describes the options on the **Adapters** tab.

Option	Use this option to
Add	Add a network adapter card driver to a computer.
Remove	Remove the selected network adapter card driver from the system configuration. Removing the driver does not delete the file from the hard drive. Therefore, you can add the driver again, if necessary.
Properties	View and change the settings for the selected driver. Click the **Properties** button and the **Setup** dialog box appears for the selected network adapter card driver. Use the **Setup** dialog box to configure the appropriate settings, such as the IRQ level, I/O port address, I/O channel, and the transceiver type for a selected network adapter card.
Update	Update the driver information for a selected network adapter card. When you click this button, you are prompted to provide a path to the upgrade driver files.

Installing and Configuring Protocols

Protocols, such as NWLink IPX/SPX Compatible Transport, NetBEUI, and TCP/IP provide a mechanism for computers to connect with each other and exchange information over a network. Protocols communicate with network adapter cards by means of NDIS 4.0–compatible network adapter card drivers. In addition, Windows NT supports multiple protocols, bound to one or more adapters, simultaneously.

Use the **Protocols** tab in the **Network** dialog box in Control Panel to install and configure protocols. The following illustration shows the **Protocols** tab in the **Network** dialog box.

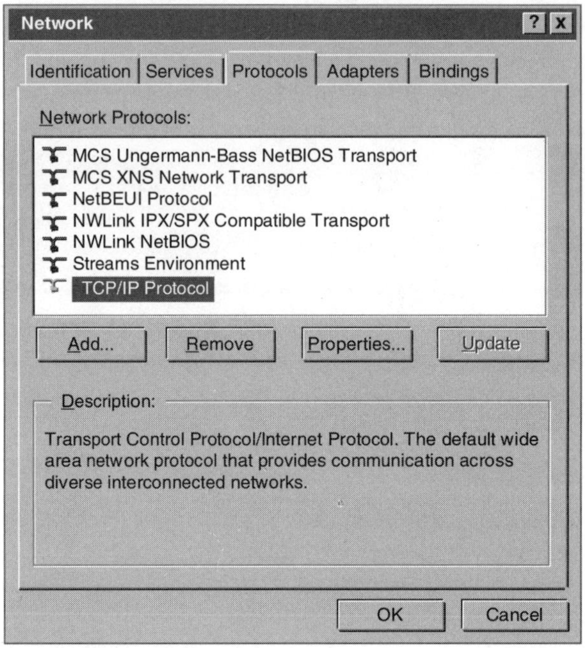

The following table defines the functions of each option in the **Protocols** tab.

Option	Function
Add	Add a protocol to the system configuration.
Remove	Remove the selected protocol from the system configuration. Removing the protocol does not delete the protocol files from the hard disk. Although the protocol can be added again by using the files that are currently on the hard disk, the recommended method is to use the original source, such as a network share or the Microsoft Windows NT operating system compact disc.
Properties	View and configure settings for the selected protocol.
Update	Update the selected protocol. When you click the **Update** button, you are prompted for the path to the upgrade files.

Lesson 2: NWLink

NWLink IPX/SPX Compatible Transport protocol is the Microsoft 32-bit NDIS 4.0–compliant version of Novell's Internetwork Packet Exchange/Sequenced Packet Exchange (IPX/SPX) protocol. This lesson describes NWLink's function and configuration in a Windows NT environment.

After this lesson, you will be able to:

- Describe the purpose of the NWLink IPX/SPX Compatible Transport.
- Install and configure NWLink IPX/SPX Compatible Transport.

Estimated lesson time: 20 minutes

NWLink Overview

NWLink is most commonly used in network environments where Microsoft clients need to access client/server applications running on Novell NetWare servers, or NetWare clients need to access client/server applications running on computers running Windows NT. NWLink allows computers running Windows NT to communicate with other network devices that are using IPX/SPX, such as HP JetDirect printers. NWLink can also be used in small network environments that only use Windows NT and Microsoft clients.

NWLink supports the following networking APIs that provide IPC services:

- Windows Sockets (WinSock) support existing NetWare applications written to comply with the NetWare IPX/SPX Sockets interface. WinSock is commonly used for communicating with NetWare Loadable Modules (NLMs). Customers implementing client/server solutions using NLMs can port them to Windows NT Server and still retain compatibility with their clients.
- NetBIOS over IPX, implemented as NWLink NetBIOS, supports communication between a NetWare workstation running NetBIOS and a Windows NT–based computer running NWLink NetBIOS.

Note For more information on configuring computers running Windows NT so that they can access file and print resources on a NetWare server, and on configuring NetWare clients so that they can access file and print resources stored on the computer running Windows NT, see Chapter 14, "Interoperating with Novell NetWare."

Configuring NWLink

The frame type and network number are options that must be configured when installing and configuring NWLink IPX/SPX Compatible Transport.

Frame Types

A frame type defines the way in which the network adapter card formats data to be sent over a network. For computers running Windows NT and NetWare servers to communicate, you need to configure NWLink on the computer running Windows NT with the same frame type as the one used by NetWare servers. Setting an incorrect frame type prevents computers running Windows NT from communicating with NetWare servers.

The following table lists the topologies and frame types supported by NWLink.

Topology	Supported frame type
Ethernet	Ethernet II, 802.3, 802.2, and Sub Network Access Protocol (SNAP), which defaults to 802.2
Token Ring	802.5 and SNAP
FDDI (fiber distributed data interface)	802.2 and SNAP

Note On Ethernet networks, the standard frame type for NetWare 2.2 and NetWare 3.11 is 802.3. Starting with NetWare 3.12, the default frame type was changed to 802.2.

For further information about Ethernet, Token Ring, and FDDI topologies, see *Networking Essentials,* by Microsoft Press®.

Automatically Detected Frame Types

When NWLink is installed on a computer running Windows NT, the frame type is automatically detected. This allows Windows NT to determine the IPX frame type being used on the network and sets the NWLink frame type accordingly. If multiple frame types are detected in addition to the 802.2 frame type, NWLink defaults to the 802.2 frame type.

It is possible for a connection to be established between two computers that are using different frame types on the network, when one of those computers is a NetWare computer acting as a *router*. A router is a device that is used to connect networks of different types, such as those using different architectures and protocols. The NetWare computer could route the network traffic between the two frame types. However, this is not efficient and, depending on the number of computers using the two frame types, this routing could potentially result in a bottleneck. If a connection is successfully established through NWLink but is very slow, verify that the two systems are using the same frame type.

Configuring Frame Types

Frame types are configured through the Network program in Control Panel. Use the **NWLink IPX/SPX Properties** dialog box to designate a frame type for each network adapter card on a computer. Windows NT can be set to automatically detect a frame type for the network. If frame type detection is set to manual, you would need to specify the frame type. A computer running Windows NT can be configured to use multiple frame types simultaneously. The following illustration shows the **General** tab in the **NWLink IPX/SPX Properties** dialog box on a computer running Windows NT Server.

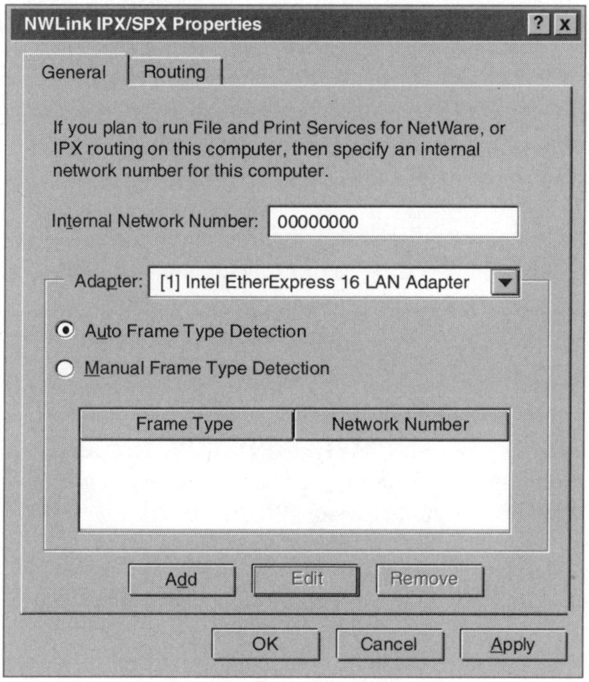

Network Number and Internal Network Number

The NWLink IPX/SPX protocol included with Windows NT uses two types of network numbers, the Network Number and the Internal Network Number, each of which serves a distinctly different function. The Network Number identifies the network segment that you need to access; the Internal Network Number identifies your computer on the network.

Network Number

Windows NT uses an IPX network number for routing purposes. This number is sometimes referred to as the *external network number*, and must be unique for each network segment. If you do not know the appropriate network numbers to use, you must obtain them from the NetWare administrator. You then assign a network number to each configured frame type and adapter combination on your computer.

Internal Network Number

Windows NT also uses an internal network number to uniquely identify the computer on the network for internal routing. This internal network number, also known as a *virtual network number*, is represented by an eight-digit hexadecimal number. By default, the internal network number is (00000000).

Windows NT does not automatically detect the internal network number. In each of the following situations, you need to manually assign a unique non-zero internal network number:

- You have File and Print Services for NetWare (FPNW) installed, and you choose multiple frame types on a single adapter.
- You have bound NWLink to multiple adapters in your computer.
- Your computer is acting as a Windows NT server for an application that uses the NetWare Service Advertising Protocol (SAP), such as SQL or SNA.

Routing Information Protocol

Use the **Routing** tab in the **NWLink IPX/SPX Properties** dialog box to enable or disable the Routing Information Protocol (RIP). Using RIP routing over IPX, a Windows NT Server can act as an IPX router.

RIP allows a router to exchange information with neighboring routers. A RIP router is a computer or other piece of hardware that broadcasts routing information, such as network addresses. As a router becomes aware of any change in the internetwork layout—for example, a downed router—it broadcasts the information to neighboring routers.

Practice

In these procedures, you create a shortcut for the Network program. You install the Microsoft NWLink IPX/SPX Compatible Transport protocol on both Server1 and Workstation1, and test the NWLink IPX/SPX Compatible Transport protocol installation.

Note Complete these procedures on both Server1 and Workstation1.

▸ To create a shortcut to the Network program in Control Panel

1. Log on to the domain as Administrator.
2. In Control Panel, drag the Network icon to your desktop.

   A dialog box appears, asking if you want to create a shortcut.
3. Click **Yes**.

   A shortcut icon for the Network program appears.

▸ To install NWLink

1. Double-click the Shortcut to Network icon.

   The **Network** dialog box appears.
2. Click the **Protocols** tab, and then click **Add**.

   The **Select Network Protocol** dialog box appears.
3. Click **NWLink IPX/SPX Compatible Transport**, and then click **OK**.

   The **Windows NT Setup** dialog box appears.
4. Type the path to your Microsoft Windows NT Setup files in the text box:
   - On Workstation1, insert the *Windows NT Workstation* compact disc, type *cd-rom_drive*:**\I386** and then click **Continue**.
   - On Server1, type **\\Server1\Nts_source\I386** and then click **Continue**.

   All of the files that you need are copied to your computer.

   What are the two new protocols displayed on the **Protocols** tab in the **Network** property sheet?

   ____

   ____
5. Click **TCP/IP Protocol**, and then click **Remove**.

   A **Warning** dialog box appears.

6. Click **Yes**, and then click **Close**.

   Notice that the installation process continues and binds your network adapter card to NWLink IPX/SPX protocol. The **Network Setting Change** dialog box appears when the installation process is completed. It asks if you want to restart your computer now.
7. Click **Yes** to restart your computer.

► **To test your installation of the Microsoft NWLink IPX/SPX Compatible Transport protocol**

Note Complete this procedure on Workstation1.

---

1. Log on to the domain as Administrator.
2. Click the **Start** button, and then click **Run**.
3. Type **\\Server1** and then click **OK**.

   Can you connect to Server1? If a window appears displaying Server1 in the title bar and showing the shares available on Server1, you successfully connected to Server1.

   ____

4. Close the Server1 window.

Lesson 3: NetBEUI

NetBIOS extended user interface (NetBEUI) is a protocol developed for small departmental local area networks (LANs) of 20 to 200 computers. NetBEUI is not suitable for wide-area networks because it cannot be routed.

After this lesson, you will be able to:

- Identify the purpose and function of NetBEUI.
- Identify compatible operating systems for NetBEUI.
- Install NetBEUI.

Estimated lesson time: 10 minutes

NetBEUI provides compatibility with existing LANs that use the NetBEUI protocol and provides interoperability with older network systems, such as Microsoft LAN Manager and Microsoft Windows for Workgroups, version 3.11.

NetBEUI provides computers running Windows NT with the following capabilities:

- Connection-oriented and connectionless communication between computers.
- Self-configuration and self-tuning.
- Error protection.
- Small memory overhead.

Windows NT–based computers running NetBEUI must be connected using bridges instead of routers. A bridge is a device that joins two LANs.

NetBEUI is a non-routable, broadcast-based protocol. Because NetBEUI relies on broadcasts for many of its functions, such as name registration and discovery, its use causes more broadcast traffic than other protocols.

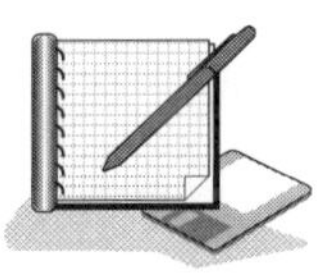

Practice

In these procedures, you install Microsoft NetBEUI and verify that the installation was successful.

► **To install Microsoft NetBEUI**

Note Complete this procedure on both Server1 and Workstation1.

---

1. Log on to the domain as Administrator.
2. Double-click the Shortcut to Network icon.
3. In the **Network** dialog box, click the **Protocols** tab.

4. Click **Add**.
5. Click **NetBEUI Protocol**, and then click **OK**.

   A **Windows NT Setup** dialog box appears and prompts you for the path of the files to be copied.
6. Type the path to your Microsoft Windows NT Setup files in the text box:
   - On Workstation1, insert the *Windows NT Workstation* compact disc, type *cd-rom_drive*:**\I386** and then click **Continue**.
   - On Server1, type **\\Server1\Nts_source\I386** and then click **Continue**.

   Once the NetBEUI Protocol is installed, the **Protocols** tab in the **Network** dialog box reappears.
7. Click **NWLink IPX/SPX Compatible Transport**, and then click **Remove**.

   A **Warning** dialog box appears.
8. Click **Yes**, and then click **Close**.

   The binding process starts and finishes and the **Network Settings Change** dialog box appears.
9. When prompted, click **Yes** to restart the computer.

▸ **To verify that your installation was successful**

Note Complete this procedure on Workstation1. Both Workstation1 and Server1 must be restarted after you install NetBEUI on them.

---

1. Log on to the domain as Administrator.
2. Click the **Start** button, and then click **Run**.
3. Type **\\Server1** and then click **OK**.

   Can you connect to Server1?

   ____

4. Close the Server1 window.

Lesson 4: Microsoft TCP/IP

TCP/IP is a networking protocol that provides communication across interconnected networks made up of computers with diverse hardware architectures and various operating systems. Microsoft TCP/IP on Windows NT enables enterprise networking and connectivity on your computer running Windows NT. This lesson provides an overview of the function, installation, and configuration of Microsoft TCP/IP.

After this lesson, you will be able to:

- Explain the purpose and function of Microsoft TCP/IP.
- Identify the components included in the Microsoft TCP/IP protocol suite.
- Configure TCP/IP manually, when given an IP address, the subnet mask, and the default gateway.
- Identify the TCP/IP utilities included with Windows NT.
- Test the TCP/IP configuration and validate connections to other computers.

Estimated lesson time: 45 minutes

TCP/IP is a flexible suite of protocols designed for wide area networks (WANs) and adaptable to a wide range of network hardware. TCP/IP can be used to communicate with Windows NT systems, with devices that use other Microsoft networking products, and with non-Microsoft systems, such as UNIX systems.

Microsoft TCP/IP Overview

Microsoft TCP/IP is a routable, enterprise networking protocol. Adding it to a Windows NT system configuration provides the following capabilities:

- A standard, routable, enterprise networking protocol for Windows NT.
- An architecture that facilitates connectivity in heterogeneous environments.
- Access to the Internet and its resources.

Microsoft TCP/IP Protocol Suite

TCP/IP is a suite of protocols designed for internetworks. The Microsoft TCP/IP core protocols provide a set of standards for how computers running Windows NT communicate in a network environment. The following illustration provides an overview of the Microsoft TCP/IP protocol suite.

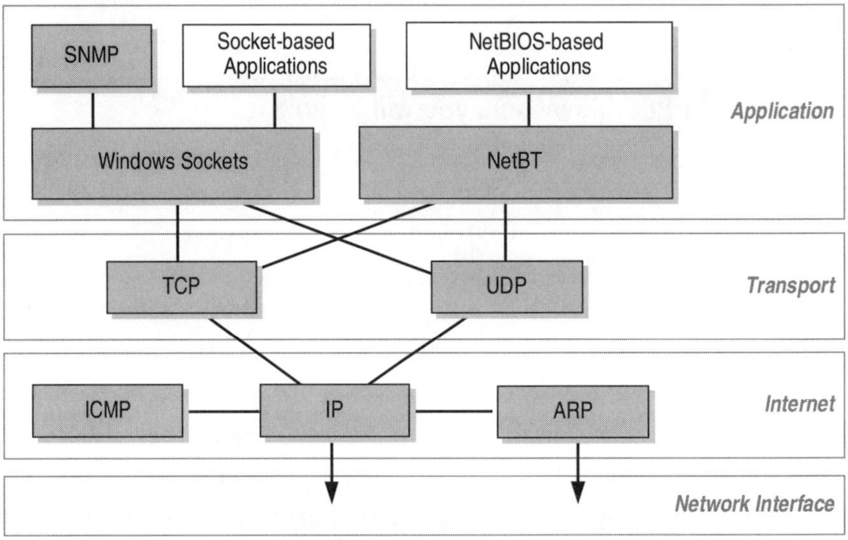

The following table describes the protocols included with Microsoft TCP/IP.

Protocol	This protocol provides
Simple Network Management Protocol (SNMP)	Management Information Base (MIBs) monitoring data contained in SNMP.
Windows Sockets (WinSock)	Standard interface between socket-based applications and TCP/IP protocols.
NetBIOS over TCP/IP (NetBT)	NetBIOS services, including name, datagram, and session services. It also provides a standard interface between NetBIOS-based applications and TCP/IP protocols.
Transmission Control Protocol (TCP)	Connection-oriented, guaranteed packet delivery services.
User Datagram Protocol (UDP)	Connectionless packet delivery services that are not guaranteed.

(continued)

Protocol	This protocol provides
Internet Control Message Protocol (ICMP)	Special communication between hosts. Reports messages and errors regarding packet delivery.
Internet Protocol (IP)	Address and routing functions.
Address Resolution Protocol (ARP)	IP address mapping to the media access control sublayer address. An IP address is required for each computer that runs TCP/IP. An IP address is a logical 32-bit address used to identify a TCP/IP host. The media access control sublayer communicates directly with the network adapter card and is responsible for delivering error-free data between two computers on a network.

Configuring TCP/IP Manually

If you are not using Dynamic Host Configuration Protocol (DHCP) to automatically assign the IP addresses, you have to configure TCP/IP manually. To configure TCP/IP manually after it has been installed, you use the **Protocols** tab in the Network program in Control Panel.

The following illustration shows the **Microsoft TCP/IP Properties** dialog box with the **Specify an IP address** option selected.

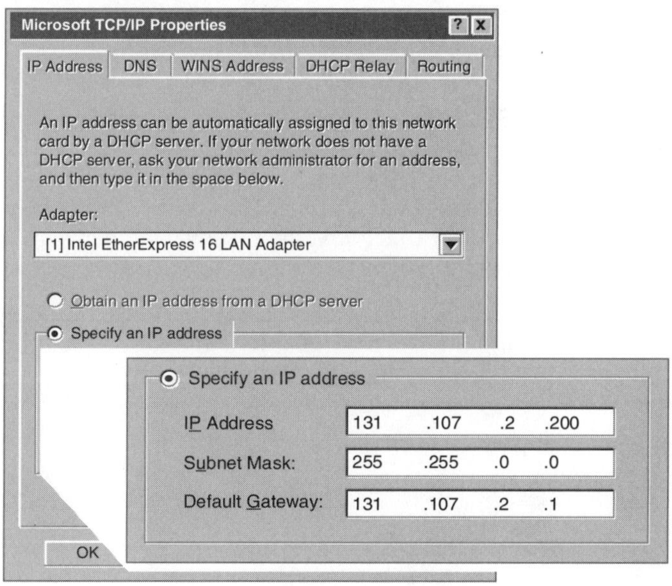

When configuring TCP/IP manually, you can:

- Assign an IP address.
- Assign a subnet mask.
- Add a default gateway.

These parameters are required for each network adapter card in the computer that uses TCP/IP. The following table describes these parameters.

Parameter	Description
IP address	An IP address is a logical 32-bit address that is used to identify a TCP/IP host. Each IP address has two parts: the network ID and the host ID. The network ID identifies all hosts that are on the same physical network. The host ID identifies a host on the network. Each computer running TCP/IP requires a unique IP address, such as 131.107.2.200. In this example, 131.107 is the network ID, and 2.200 is the host ID.
Subnet mask	A subnet is a network in a multiple network environment that uses IP addresses derived from a single network ID. Using subnets, an organization can divide a single large network into multiple physical networks and connect them with routers. A subnet mask is used to block out a portion of the IP address so that TCP/IP can distinguish the network ID from the host ID. When TCP/IP hosts try to communicate, the subnet mask is used to determine whether the destination host is located on a local or a remote network. A sample subnet mask is 255.255.0.0. In order for computers to communicate on a network, they must have the same subnet mask.
Default gateway	For communication with a host on another network, an IP address should be configured for the default gateway. TCP/IP sends packets that are destined for remote networks to the default gateway, if no other route is configured on the local host to the destination network. If a default gateway is not configured, communication may be limited to the local network (subnet). A sample default gateway is 131.107.2.1.

Important Be careful when assigning IP addresses; IP communications can fail when multiple devices use the same IP address.

Practice

In these procedures, you remove NetBEUI, install TCP/IP, and then verify your installation.

▸ To remove NetBEUI, and install and manually configure TCP/IP

Note Complete this procedure on both Server1 and Workstation1.

---

1. Log on to the domain as Administrator.
2. Double-click the Shortcut to Network icon.

   The **Network** dialog box appears.
3. Click the **Protocols** tab.
4. Click **NetBEUI Protocol**, and then click **Remove**.

   A **Warning** dialog box appears.
5. Click **Yes**.
6. Click **Add**.

   The **Select Network Protocol** dialog box appears.
7. Click **TCP/IP Protocol**, and then click **OK**.

   The **TCP/IP Setup** dialog box appears. You will not be using DHCP at this time.
8. Click **No**.
9. Type the path to your Microsoft Windows NT Setup files in the text box:
   - On Workstation1, insert the *Windows NT Workstation* compact disc, type *cd-rom_drive*:**\I386** and then click **Continue**.
   - On Server1 type **\\Server1\Nts_source\I386** and then click **Continue**.

   All of the files that you need are copied to your computer.
10. Click **Close**.

    The **Microsoft TCP/IP Properties** dialog box appears, with the **IP Address** tab in the foreground.

11. Click **Specify an IP address**, and then complete the configuration settings as indicated in the following table.

In this box	Use
IP Address	131.107.2.200 on Server1
	131.107.2.201 on Workstation1
Subnet Mask	255.255.0.0
Default Gateway	Leave this blank

12. Click **OK**.
13. Click **Yes** to restart your computer.

► **To verify that your installation was successful**

Note Complete this procedure on Workstation1. Both Workstation1 and Server1 must have restarted after you installed NetBEUI on them.

---

1. Log on to the domain as Administrator.
2. Click the **Start** button, and the click **Run**.
3. Type **\\Server1** and then click **OK**.

   Can you connect to Server1?

   ____

4. Close the Server1 window.

Configuring TCP/IP Automatically

Windows NT provides a service called the Dynamic Host Configuration Protocol (DHCP) server service. When a DHCP server is configured on a network, clients that support DHCP, such as Windows NT Server and Windows NT Workstation, can request the TCP/IP configuration parameters (IP address, subnet mask, and a default gateway) from the DHCP server.

When a DHCP server is available, TCP/IP can be configured automatically by selecting the **Obtain an IP address from a DHCP server** option on the **IP Address** tab in the **Microsoft TCP/IP Properties** dialog box.

The following illustration shows the **Microsoft TCP/IP Properties** dialog box, with **Obtain an IP address from a DHCP server** selected.

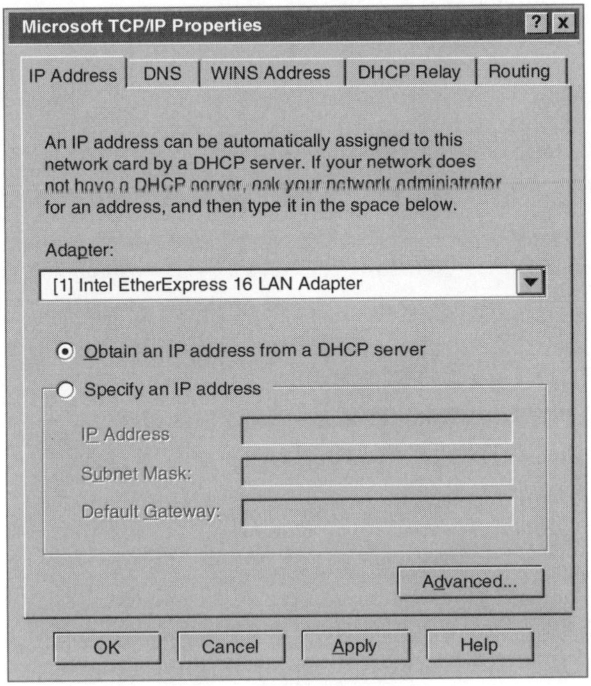

When **Obtain an IP address from a DHCP server** is selected, the DHCP client contacts a DHCP server for its configuration information. After receiving this request, the DHCP server assigns an IP address, subnet mask, and default gateway to the DHCP client.

Note The Windows NT Server's DHCP Server service is discussed in more detail in Chapter 11, "Windows NT Networking Services."

Using TCP/IP Utilities

The following table describes the Windows NT utilities that work with TCP/IP protocols to provide networking capabilities.

Utility	Function
Packet Internet Groper (PING)	Verifies configurations and tests connections.
File Transfer Protocol (FTP)	Provides bidirectional file transfers between a computer running Windows NT and any TCP/IP host running FTP.
Trivial File Transfer Protocol (TFTP)	Provides bidirectional file transfers between a computer running Windows NT and a TCP/IP host running TFTP.
Telnet	Provides terminal emulation to a TCP/IP host running Telnet.
Remote Copy Protocol (RCP)	Copies files between a computer running Windows NT and a UNIX host.
Remote Shell (RSH)	Runs commands on a UNIX host.
Remote Execution (REXEC)	Runs a process on a remote computer.
Finger	Retrieves system information from a remote computer that supports TCP/IP and the finger service.
Microsoft Internet Explorer (IE)	Locates resources on the Internet.
ARP	Displays a cache of locally resolved IP addresses to physical addresses.
ipconfig	Displays the current TCP/IP configuration.
nbtstat	Displays protocol statistics and connections using NetBIOS over TCP/IP.
netstat	Displays TCP/IP protocol statistics and connections.
Route	Displays or modifies the local routing table.
Hostname	Returns the local computer's host name for authentication by the RCP, RSH, and REXEC utilities.
Tracert	Checks the route to a remote system.

Testing TCP/IP with Ipconfig and Ping

After TCP/IP is configured and the computer is restarted, it is a good idea to test the configuration and connections to other TCP/IP hosts and networks. This is accomplished through the Command Prompt using the ipconfig and ping utilities.

The Ipconfig Utility

The ipconfig utility is used to verify the TCP/IP configuration parameters on a host. This is useful in determining whether the configuration is initialized or if a duplicate IP address has been configured. The ipconfig command syntax is: **ipconfig /all**.

If a configuration has initialized, the IP address, subnet mask, and, if it is assigned, default gateway appear. If a duplicate IP address has been configured, it appears as configured; however, the subnet mask appears as 0.0.0.0. In addition, if DHCP is being used, and the computer is unable to obtain an IP address, the IP address appears as 0.0.0.0.

The Ping Utility

After the TCP/IP configuration is verified with the ipconfig utility, use the Packet Internet Groper (PING) utility to test connectivity. Ping is a diagnostic tool used to test TCP/IP configurations and diagnose connection failures. Ping determines whether a particular TCP/IP host is available and functional. The ping command syntax is: **ping *IP_address***.

The following steps outline procedures for verifying a computer's configuration and for testing router connections using ping.

1. Ping the loopback address (127.0.0.1) to verify that TCP/IP is installed and loaded correctly.
2. Ping the IP address of your computer to verify that it was added correctly and to check for possible duplicate IP addresses.
3. Ping the IP address of the default gateway to verify that default gateway is up and running, and that you can communicate with the local network.
4. Ping the IP address of a remote host to verify that you can communicate through a router.

Tip If you start with step 4 and can ping successfully, then steps 1 through 3 are successful by default. If the ping is not successful, ping another remote host.

If ping is successful, it responds, by default, with the following message four times: **Reply from** *IP_address*.

Practice

In these procedures, you use ping to verify IP connectivity, and use ipconfig to display the TCP/IP configuration.

Note Complete these procedures on both Server1 and Workstation1.

▸ To test that the TCP/IP and configuration is correct

1. Log on to the domain as Administrator.
2. Start a command prompt.
3. To test that IP is working and bound to your adapter, type **ping 127.0.0.1** and then press ENTER.

   Four "Reply from 127.0.0.1" messages should appear indicating that the internal loop-back test was successful.
4. Type **ping 131.107.2.200** and then press ENTER.

   Four "Reply from 131.107.2.200" messages should appear.

   Note If you are on Workstation1, you are testing the connectivity to Server1 by pinging the Server1 IP address.

   If you are on Server1, you are testing to verify that the IP address was added correctly and to check for possible duplicate IP addresses.

   ---
5. Type **ping 131.107.2.201** and then press ENTER.

   Four "Reply from 131.107.2.201" messages should appear.

   Note If you are on Server1, you are testing the connectivity to Workstation1 by pinging the Workstation1 IP address.

   If you are on Workstation1, you are testing to verify that the IP address was added correctly and to check for possible duplicate IP addresses.

   ---
6. Type **ping 131.107.2.222** and then press ENTER.

   Four "Request timed out." messages should appear. This is an invalid IP address; if it is a valid address on your network repeat step 6 using an invalid address.

▸ **To use ipconfig to verify the TCP/IP configuration**

1. Type **ipconfig /all** and then press ENTER.
2. Fill in the following tables.

Windows NT IP configuration	Server1	Workstation1
Host name	____________	____________

Adapter	Server1	Workstation1
Description	____________	____________
Physical address	____________	____________
DHCP enabled	____________	____________
IP address	____________	____________
Subnet mask	____________	____________
Default gateway	____________	____________

Lesson 5: Network Bindings

Network *bindings* are links that enable communication between network adapter card drivers, protocols, and services. This lesson describes the function of bindings in a network and the process of configuring them.

After this lesson, you will be able to:

- Define the function of bindings in a network.
- Configure bindings for a network that uses NetBEUI, NWLink, and TCP/IP.

Estimated lesson time: 15 minutes

As you have learned, the Windows NT network architecture consists of a series of interdependent layers. The bottom layer of the network architecture ends at the network adapter card, which places the information on the cable, allowing information to flow between computers.

Binding is the process of linking network components on different levels to enable communication between those components. You can bind a network component to one or more network components above or below it. The services each component provides can be shared by all other components bound to it. For example, the installed protocols are bound to the Workstation service as well as the Server service.

In the following illustration all three protocols are bound to the Workstation service, but only the routable protocols, NWLink and TCP/IP, are bound to the Server service. You can also select which protocols to bind to the network adapter cards. Network adapter card (0) is bound to all three protocols, while network adapter card (1) is only bound to the routable protocols. Administrators have full control over which components are bound together.

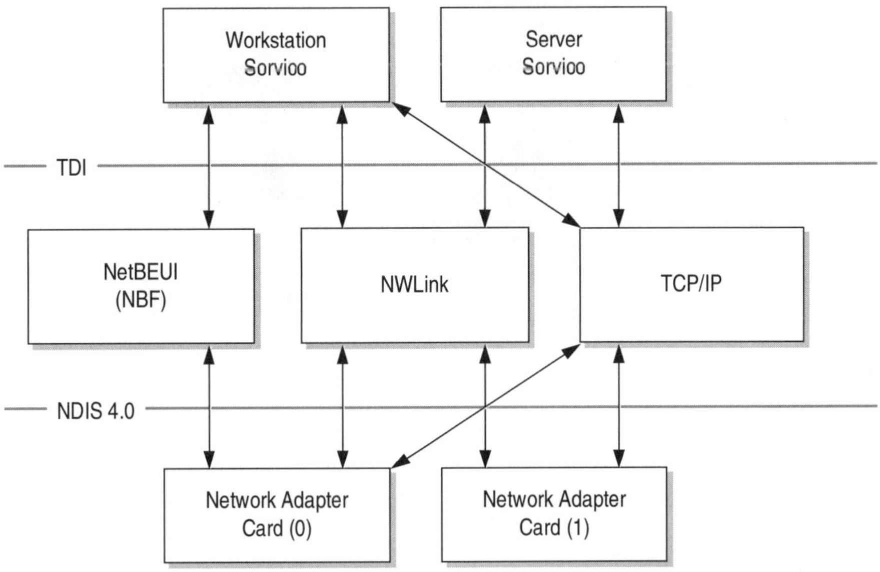

When adding network software, Windows NT automatically binds all dependent network components. NDIS 4.0 provides the capability to bind multiple protocols to multiple network adapter card drivers.

Configuring Network Bindings

To configure network bindings, click the **Bindings** tab in the **Network** dialog box in Control Panel. The **Bindings** tab shows the bindings of the installed network components, from the upper-layer services and protocols to the lowest layer of network adapter card drivers. Bindings can be enabled and disabled, based on your use of the network components installed on your system. The following illustration shows the **Bindings** tab in the **Network** dialog box.

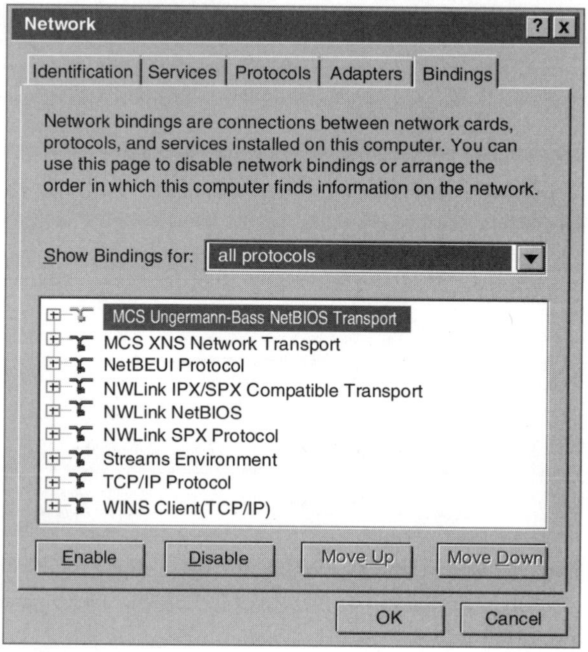

Bindings can also be ordered to optimize the network. For example, if a computer running Windows NT Workstation has NetBEUI, NWLink IPX/SPX, and TCP/IP installed on it, and the majority of servers that it is connected to are running only TCP/IP, the Workstation bindings should be examined. In looking at the Workstation bindings, verify that the Workstation binding to TCP/IP is listed *before* the Workstation binding to NetBEUI, as shown in the following illustration. In this way, when a user attempts to connect to a server, the Workstation service first tries using TCP/IP to establish connection.

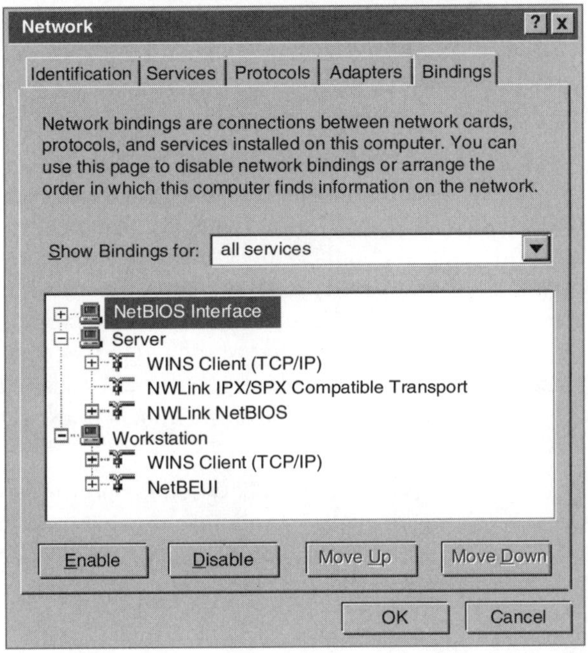

The following table describes the options available on the **Bindings** tab.

Option	Use this option to
Show Bindings for	View bindings for installed services, protocols, and adapters installed on the computer.
Enable	Enable the selected binding path. It also enables all connections in the hierarchy beneath the selected component.
Disable	Disable the selected binding path. It also disables all connections in the hierarchy beneath the selected component.
Move Up or **Move Down**	Move the selected binding up, or down, in the binding list, for computers using more than one network protocol or adapter.

Summary

The following information summarizes the key points in this chapter:

- Windows NT network protocols, network adapter card drivers, and bindings are added, removed, and configured using the Network program in Control Panel.
- NWLink is the Microsoft implementation of the IPX/SPX protocol. NWLink allows NetWare clients to access client/server applications on computers running Windows NT, and allows Microsoft clients to access client/server applications on a NetWare server.
- NetBEUI is a protocol used to support small LANs. It is not suitable for wide area networks because it cannot be routed. NetBEUI is mostly used for older, existing LANs because it is compatible with the NetBEUI protocol driver shipped with older Microsoft networking products.
- Microsoft TCP/IP enables networking and connectivity on computers running Windows NT. To configure TCP/IP manually you must supply an appropriate value for the IP address and the subnet mask. For communication with a remote network, you must also specify a default gateway. The default gateway is where the IP sends packets that are destined for remote networks. If you do not specify a default gateway, communications are limited to the local network. TCP/IP configuration values can also be configured automatically by using a DHCP server. Use the Ping utility to test network connections after TCP/IP is configured.
- Network bindings provide the links between the protocols, network adapter card drivers, and services and enable communication between these components. Windows NT automatically binds all dependent network components. However, bindings can be enabled, disabled, and ordered to optimize network communication.

For more information on	See
DHCP	Chapter 11, "Windows NT Networking Services."
File and Print Services	Chapter 14, "Interoperating with Novell NetWare."

Review

1. Your computer running Windows NT Server can communicate with some, but not all, of the NetWare servers on your network. Some of the NetWare servers are running frame type 802.2 and some are running 802.3. What is the likely cause of the problem?

2. Your computer running Windows NT Workstation was configured manually for TCP/IP. You can connect to any host on your own subnet, but you cannot connect or even **ping** any host on a remote subnet. What is the likely cause of the problem, and how would you fix it?

3. Your computer running Windows NT Server runs TCP/IP as its primary protocol. The server also has NWLink installed, for the sole purpose of hosting connections from NetWare clients. How would you optimize the bindings for this server?

Answer Key

Practice Answers

Page 345

▶ **To install NWLink**

4. Type the path to your Microsoft Windows NT Setup files in the text box:

   On Workstation1, insert the *Windows NT Workstation* compact disc, type *cd-rom_drive*:**\I386** and then click **Continue**.

   On Server1, type **\\Server1\Nts_source\I386** and then click **Continue**.

   All of the files that you need are copied to your computer.

   What are the two new protocols displayed on the **Protocols** tab in the **Network** property sheet?

   The two new protocols displayed are NWLink IPX/SPX Compatible Transport and NWLink NetBIOS.

Page 346

▶ **To test your installation of the Microsoft NWLink IPX/SPX Compatible Transport protocol**

3. Type **\\Server1** and then click **OK**.

   Can you connect to Server1? If a window appears displaying Server1 in the title bar and showing the shares available on Server1, you successfully connected to Server1.

   Yes, if your NWLink IPX/SPX Compatible Transport installation is working.

Page 348

▶ **To verify that your installation was successful**

3. Type **\\Server1** and then click **OK**.

   Can you connect to Server1?

   Yes, if both computers are running NetBEUI.

Page 354

▶ **To verify that your installation was successful**

3. Type **\\Server1** and then click **OK**.

   Can you connect to Server1?

   Yes, if TCP/IP is configured correctly on both computers.

Page 359

▸ **To use ipconfig to verify the TCP/IP configuration**

2. Fill in the following tables.

Windows NT IP configuration	Server1	Workstation1
Host name	server1	workstation1

Adapter	Server1	Workstation1
Description	____________	____________
Physical address	____________	____________
DHCP enabled	No	No
IP address	131.107.2.200	131.107.2.201
Subnet mask	255.255.0.0	255.255.0.0
Default gateway	Blank	Blank

Review Answers

Page 365

1. Your computer running Windows NT Server can communicate with some, but not all, of the NetWare servers on your network. Some of the NetWare servers are running frame type 802.2 and some are running 802.3. What is the likely cause of the problem?

   Although the NWLink implementation in Windows NT can automatically detect a frame type for IPX/SPX compatible protocols, it can only automatically detect one frame type. This network uses two frame types, so both frame types (802.2 and 802.3) will need to be configured manually.

2. Your computer running Windows NT Workstation was configured manually for TCP/IP. You can connect to any host on your own subnet, but you cannot connect or even **ping** any host on a remote subnet. What is the likely cause of the problem, and how would you fix it?

   The default gateway is probably missing or incorrect. It can be added or changed in the Microsoft TCP/IP Properties dialog box accessed through the Network program in Control Panel. Other possibilities: the default gateway is offline, or the subnet mask is incorrect.

3. Your computer running Windows NT Server runs TCP/IP as its primary protocol. The server also has NWLink installed, for the sole purpose of hosting connections from NetWare clients. How would you optimize the bindings for this server?

   For the Server service, order the bindings so that TCP/IP is first, and NWLink is second. Disable the binding between the Workstation service and NWLink, because the server will never need to establish connections or authenticate users over NWLink.

CHAPTER 11

Windows NT Networking Services

About This Chapter

In this chapter, you learn how to install and configure the following services provided by Microsoft Windows NT for Transmission Control Protocol/Internet Protocol (TCP/IP): Dynamic Host Configuration Protocol (DHCP), Windows Internet Name Service (WINS), and Domain Name System (DNS).

You also learn about the Computer Browser service, which is used by Windows NT to identify and list the available network resources.

Before You Begin

To complete this chapter, you must have:

- Two computers that meet the hardware and software requirements as specified in the Getting Started section in "About This Book."
- Completed all practices in Chapter 2, "Installing Windows NT."
- Read Chapter 9, "The Windows NT Networking Environment."
- Read and complete all practices in Chapter 10, "Configuring Windows NT Protocols."

Lesson 1: Installing Network Services

Windows NT network services provide a computer running Windows NT with access to the network and its resources. In this lesson, you learn how to install network services.

After this lesson, you will be able to:

- Describe the procedures to add and remove networking services from a computer running Windows NT.
- Identify the options available for installing network services.

Estimated lesson time: 5 minutes

You install network services by using the **Services** tab in the Network program in Control Panel. The following illustration shows the **Services** tab in the **Network** dialog box in Control Panel and the dialog box that appears when you click the **Add** button on the **Services** tab.

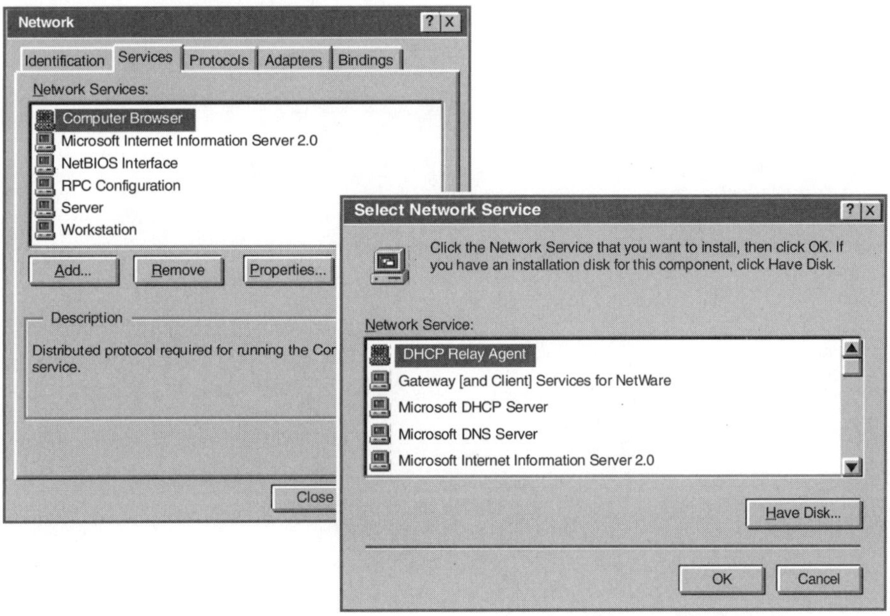

Use the **Services** tab to perform the functions listed in the following table.

Option	Use this option to
Add	Add a service to a computer.
Remove	Remove a selected service.
Properties	View or configure settings for a selected network service.
Update	Update the settings for a service. The system prompts the user for the path of the upgrade files.

Lesson 2: Dynamic Host Configuration Protocol Overview

In order to manually assign and maintain IP address information on a network, you must do the following:

- Maintain a list of the IP addresses assigned to your company.
- Configure or make sure that you correctly configure TCP/IP on each computer on the network and assign a valid IP address to that computer.
- Maintain a list of any unassigned IP addresses.

In this lesson, you learn how the Dynamic Host Configuration Protocol (DHCP) helps reduce administration by *automatically* assigning IP addresses.

After this lesson, you will be able to:

- Explain the function of DHCP.
- List the requirements for using DHCP.
- Explain how DHCP assigns an IP address.
- Install DHCP Server service.
- Create and configure a DHCP scope.
- Configure TCP/IP on a client to obtain an IP address from a DHCP server.

Estimated lesson time: 60 minutes

What Is DHCP?

The Dynamic Host Configuration Protocol (DHCP) is a protocol that centralizes and manages the allocation of TCP/IP configuration information by automatically assigning IP addresses to computers that have been configured to use DHCP. Implementing DHCP eliminates some of the configuration problems and administration associated with manually configuring TCP/IP. In this lesson, you learn how a DHCP server assigns an IP address, and how to install and configure the DHCP Server service.

You use DHCP to define global and subnet TCP/IP parameters for an internetwork. TCP/IP configuration parameters that can be dynamically assigned by a DHCP server include:

- IP addresses for each network adapter card in a computer.
- Subnet masks that identify the portion of an IP address that is the physical segment (subnet) network identifier.
- Default gateway (router) that connects the subnet to other network segments.
- Additional configuration parameters that can be optionally assigned to DHCP clients, such as a domain name.

Each time a DHCP client starts, it requests this TCP/IP configuration information from a DHCP server. When a DHCP server receives a request, it selects an IP address from a pool of addresses defined in its database and offers it to the DHCP client. If the client accepts the offer, the IP address is leased to the client for a specified period of time.

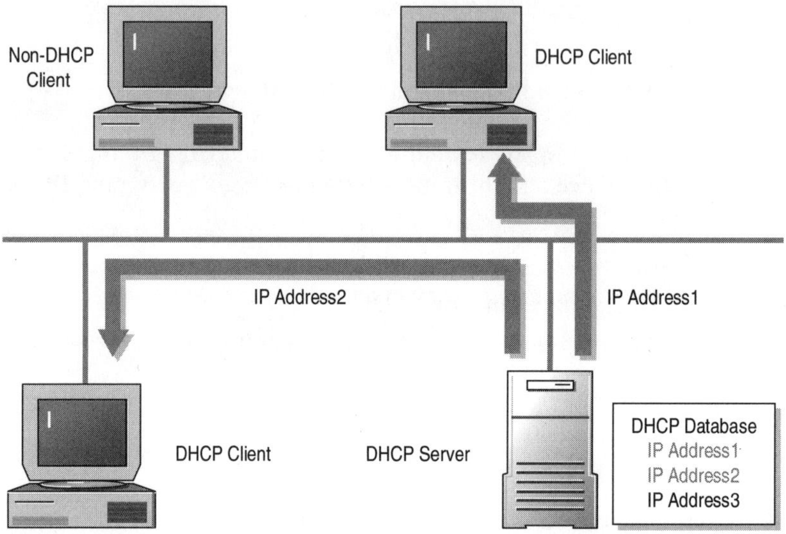

Important If no IP address is available to lease to a client, the client cannot initialize TCP/IP.

Manual vs. Automatic IP Address Configurations

To understand why DHCP is beneficial in configuring IP addresses on client computers, it is useful to contrast the manual method of configuring TCP/IP with the automatic method using DHCP.

Manually Configuring IP Addresses

The impact on administration and the potential problems associated with manually entering and configuring IP addresses include the following:

- The administrator of a client computer can enter a random IP address instead of obtaining a valid, unassigned IP address from the network administrator. Entering an address that is currently in use or that is invalid can lead to network problems that can be difficult to trace to the source of the problem.
- Entering an incorrect subnet mask or default gateway can cause communication problems. For example, if the default gateway is entered incorrectly, you may not be able to communicate beyond your local network.
- There is administrative overhead on internetworks where computers are frequently moved from one subnet to another. For example, the IP address and default gateway address must be changed to enable the computer to communicate from its new location.

Using DHCP to Configure IP Addresses

Using DHCP to automatically configure IP addresses ensures that:

- The client computer always receives a valid IP address.
- The configuration information is correct, thereby eliminating many difficult-to-trace network problems.

How DHCP Works

DHCP uses a four-phase process to configure a DHCP client. The following illustration shows the DHCP process.

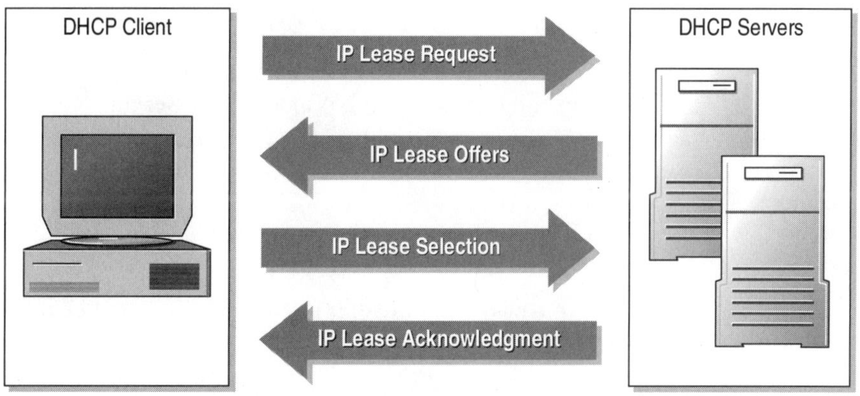

The following table describes the phases of the DHCP process.

Phase	Description
IP lease request	The client initializes a limited version of TCP/IP and broadcasts a request for the location of a DHCP server and IP addresses.
IP lease offers	All DHCP servers that have valid IP addresses available send an offer to the client.
IP lease selection	The client selects the IP address from the first offer it receives and broadcasts a message requesting to lease the IP address in the offer.
IP lease acknowledgment	The DHCP server that made the offer responds to the message, and all other DHCP servers withdraw their offers. The IP addressing information is assigned to the client and an acknowledgment is sent to the client. The client finishes initializing and binding the TCP/IP protocol. Once the automatic configuration process is complete, the client can use all TCP/IP services and utilities for normal network communications and connectivity to other IP hosts.

Note If a client has multiple network adapter cards, the DHCP process occurs separately over each network adapter card. A unique IP address is assigned to each adapter in the computer.

DHCP Requirements

To implement DHCP, the following requirements must be met for the DHCP Server service and the DHCP client.

DHCP Server

- The DHCP Server service must be installed and properly configured on a computer running Microsoft Windows NT Server.

  Note The DHCP server does not have to be a domain controller.

- A DHCP server must be configured with a static IP address, subnet mask, and optionally, a default gateway.
- If your IP routers do not support RFC 1542, then a DHCP server is required on each subnet.
- A DHCP scope must be created on the DHCP server. A DHCP scope consists of a range, or pool, of IP addresses that the DHCP server can assign, or lease, to DHCP clients: for example, 131.107.3.51 through 131.107.3.200.

DHCP Client

- A DHCP client must be running one of the following supported operating systems:
  - Windows NT Server 3.5 or later (but not running the DHCP Server service)
  - Microsoft Windows NT Workstation
  - Microsoft Windows 95
  - Microsoft Windows for Workgroups 3.11
  - Microsoft Network Client 3.0 for MS-DOS
  - Microsoft LAN Manager 2.2c
- The TCP/IP protocol must be configured to obtain an IP address from a DHCP server.

Installing and Configuring DHCP

To install the DHCP Server service on your Windows NT Server, use the Network program in Control Panel. On the **Services** tab, click **Add**, and then click **Microsoft DHCP Server**. You need to restart your computer for the service to start.

After installing the DHCP Server service, Windows NT–based DHCP configuration is performed through DHCP Manager. DHCP Manager is located in the Administrative Tools (Common) group on computers running Windows NT Server that have the DHCP Server service installed.

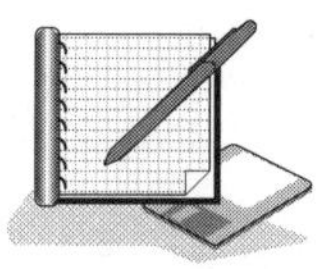

Practice

In this procedure, you install the DHCP Server service.

► **To install the DHCP Server service**

Note Complete this procedure on Server1.

---

1. Log on as Administrator.
2. In Control Panel, double-click the Network icon.

   The **Network** dialog box appears.
3. Click the **Services** tab.
4. Click **Add**.

   The **Select Network Service** dialog box appears.
5. Click **Microsoft DHCP Server**, and then click **OK**.

6. When prompted for the location of the Windows NT distribution files, type **\\Server1\Nts_source\I386** and then click **Continue**.

   The appropriate files are copied to your computer and a dialog box appears stating that if any adapters are using DHCP to obtain an IP address, they are now required to use a static IP address.

7. Click **OK**, and then click **Close**.
8. Click **Yes** to restart the computer.

Configuring a DHCP Scope

Once the DHCP Server service has been installed and started, then you need to create a scope. A scope consists of a range of IP addresses, such as 131.107.3.51 through 131.107.3.200, which the DHCP server can assign or lease to DHCP clients. Every DHCP server requires at least one scope with a pool of IP addresses available for leasing to clients.

To create a DHCP scope, use DHCP Manager. On the **Scope** menu in DHCP Manager, click **Create**. The following illustration shows the **Create Scope** dialog box.

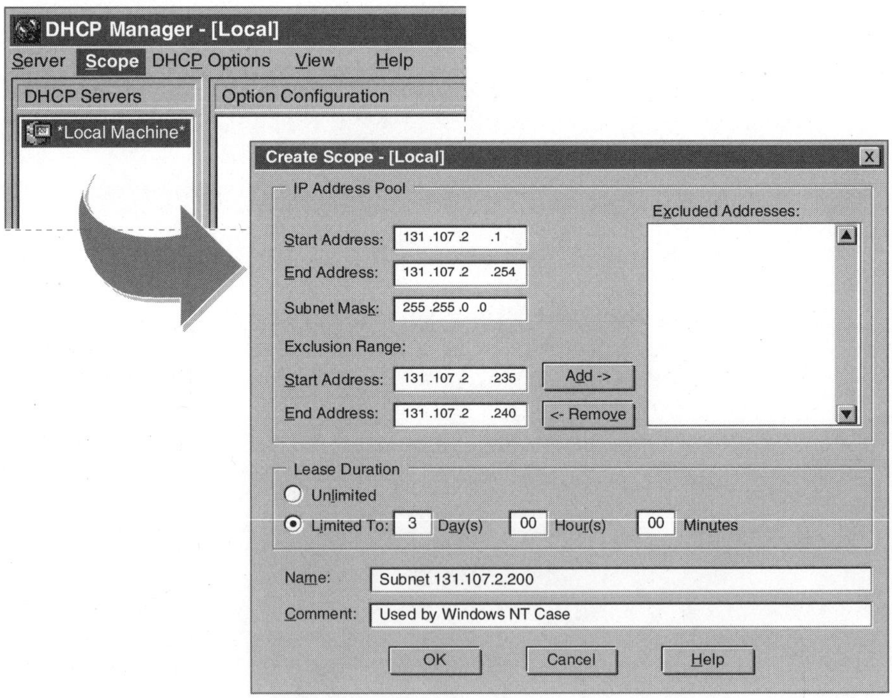

The options listed in the following table can be configured from the **Create Scope** dialog box.

Option	This option configures
IP Address Pool Start Address	First IP address that can be assigned to a DHCP client. This is a required field.
IP Address Pool End Address	Last IP address that can be assigned to a DHCP client. This is a required field.
Subnet Mask	Subnet mask to be assigned to all DHCP clients in this scope. This is a required field.
Exclusion Range Start Address	Starting IP address to be excluded from the IP address pool of addresses. The addresses in this exclusion are not assigned to DHCP clients. This is important if there are static IP addresses configured on non-DCHP clients. This is not a required field.
Exclusion Range End Address	Ending IP address to be excluded from the IP address pool of addresses. The addresses in this exclusion are not assigned to DHCP clients. This is important if there are static IP addresses configured on non-DCHP clients. This is not a required field.
Unlimited	DHCP leases assigned to clients that never expire.
Limited To	Number of days, hours, and minutes that a DHCP client lease is available before it must be renewed.
Name	A name to be assigned to the DHCP scope. The name is displayed after the IP address in the DHCP Manager. This is a required field.
Comment	Optional comments for the scope.

A scope must be activated before the DHCP server can provide a DHCP client with a valid IP address defined by the scope. You can activate the scope when you create it, or at a later time.

Practice

In this procedure, you create a DHCP scope that consists of a pool of IP addresses and an assigned lease time of 1 day.

▸ To create a DHCP scope

Note Complete this procedure on Server1.

---

1. Log on as Administrator.
2. In Control Panel, double-click the Services icon.

   What are the names of the two DHCP-related services?

   ____

   What are the status and startup values of these two services?

   ____

3. Close **Services**.
4. Click the **Start** button, point to **Programs**, point to **Administrative Tools (Common)**, and then click **DHCP Manager**.

   The DHCP Manager window appears.
5. Click **Scope**.

   Notice that no options on the menu are available because you have not yet specified the computer on which the scope will be created.
6. In the **DHCP Servers** pane, double-click ***Local Machine***

   Now that you have selected this computer, notice that (Local) now appears on the title bar for DHCP Manager.
7. On the **Scope** menu, click **Create**.

   The **Create Scope** dialog box appears.
8. Configure the scope using the following information.

In this box	Type this
IP Address Pool Start Address	**131.107.2.201**
IP Address Pool End Address	**131.107.2.209**
Subnet Mask	**255.255.0.0**
Lease Duration Limited To (Days)	**1**

9. When you are finished, click **OK**.

   A **DHCP Manager** dialog box appears, indicating that the scope was successfully created, and now needs to be activated.

10. Click **No**. You will activate the scope later in this lesson.

    A dialog box appears stating that no more data is available.

11. Click **OK**.

    The DHCP Manager window appears with the new scope added. Notice the gray light bulb next to the IP address, indicating an inactive scope.

Configuring Client Reservations

You can reserve a specific IP address for a specific client computer. You would do this if the client must use a specific IP address, typically one that was previously assigned using another method of TCP/IP configuration. To create a client reservation, click **Add Reservations** on the **Scope** menu in DHCP Manager. Once you have created a client reservation, you can then configure additional options for the specific client.

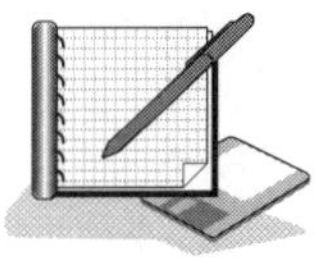

Practice

In this procedure, you use the Ping and Arp utilities to determine the physical address of the network adapter card of the computer running Windows NT Workstation. You then create a reservation for the workstation.

► **To add a client reservation**

Note Complete this procedure on Server1.

---

1. Start a command prompt, type **ping 131.107.2.201** and then press ENTER.
2. Type **arp -a** and then press ENTER to obtain the physical address of Workstation1's network adapter card. Document the address here for reference.

    ____

3. Switch to DHCP Manager and ensure your scope is selected.
4. On the **Scope** menu, click **Add Reservations**.

    The **Add Reserved Clients** dialog box appears.

5. In the **IP Address** box, type **131.107.2.201**
6. In the **Unique Identifier** box, type the physical address (without the hyphens) of Workstation1's network adapter card.
7. In the **Client Name** box, type **Workstation1** and then click **Add**.
8. Click **Close** to return to DHCP Manager.

Other DHCP Options

Many other networking options can be made available to DHCP clients. These options can be configured globally or for a specific scope or client reservation using the DHCP Manager. The following illustration shows the **DHCP Options: Global** dialog box of DHCP Manager.

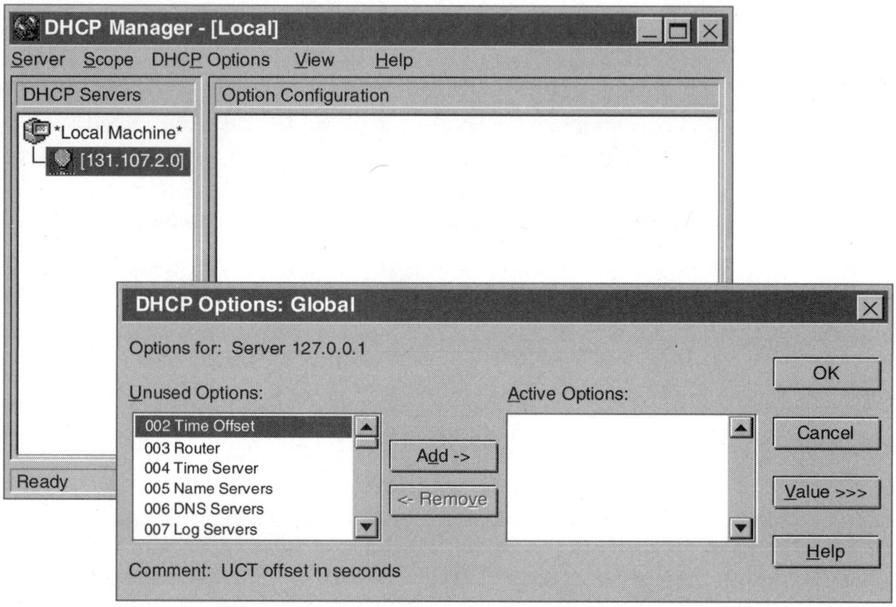

Some common options are listed in the following table.

Option	This option configures a
003 Router	Default gateway.
006 DNS Servers	List of IP addresses for name servers for the client.
044 WINS/NBNS Servers	List of IP addresses for NetBIOS name servers.

Global Options

Global options apply to all DHCP scopes defined on the selected DHCP server and all DHCP clients that lease an address from any of these scopes. Global options are used when all clients on all subnets require the same configuration information. For example, all clients can be configured to use the same WINS server. Global options are always used, unless the Scope or Client options are configured. To configure global options, click **Global** on the **DHCP_Options** menu in DHCP Manager.

Scope Options

Scope options apply to only the specified scope and clients that lease an address from that scope. For example, if there is a different scope for each subnet, you must specify the appropriate default gateway address for each subnet. Scope options override Global options. Therefore, the default gateway specified in the Scope options will be used in place of any specified in the Global options. To configure Scope options, click **Scope** on the **DHCP_Options** menu in DHCP Manager.

Client Options

Client options apply to a specific client that has a reserved DHCP address lease. Client options override Scope or Global options. To configure Client options, first create a client reservation. Then, click **Active Leases** on the **Scope** menu in DHCP Manager. Click the client, click **Properties**, and then click the **Options** button in the **Client Properties** dialog box.

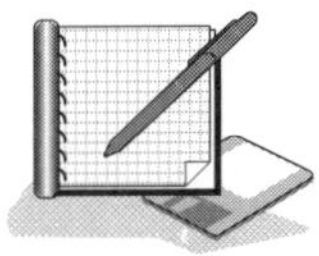

Practice

In these procedures, you activate the DHCP scope option 003 Router. This option automatically assigns a default gateway address for use by the DHCP clients. You then activate the scope.

Note Complete these procedures on Server1.

▸ **To configure a DHCP Scope option**

1. From the **DHCP Options** menu, click **Scope**.

   The **DHCP Options: Scope** dialog box appears.

2. Under **Unused Options**, click **003 Router**, and then click **Add**.

   The **003 Router** option appears in the **Active Options** box.

3. Click **Value**.

   The **DHCP Options: Scope** dialog box expands to add the **IP Address** box.

4. Click **Edit Array**.

   The **IP Address Array Editor** dialog box appears.

5. In the **New IP Address** box, type **131.107.2.200** (your Server1 IP address) and then click **Add**.

   The new IP address appears under **IP Addresses**.

6. Click **OK** to return to the **DHCP Options: Scope** dialog box.

7. In the **DHCP Options: Scope** dialog box, click **OK** to close, and then click **OK** to acknowledge no more data is available.

▸ **To activate the DHCP scope**

1. On the **Scope** menu, click **Activate**.

   Notice the yellow light bulb next to the IP address, indicating an active scope.
2. Close DHCP Manager.

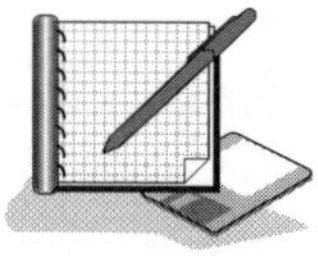

Practice

In these procedures, you configure Workstation1 as a DHCP client, and then test your DHCP server's configuration.

Note Complete these procedures on Workstation1.

▸ **To configure a DHCP client**

1. Log on to the domain as Administrator.
2. In Control Panel, double-click the Network icon.
3. Click the **Protocols** tab.
4. Click **TCP/IP Protocol**, and then click **Properties**.
5. Click **Obtain an IP address from a DHCP server**.

   A **Microsoft TCP/IP Properties** dialog box appears, asking if you want to enable DHCP.
6. Click **Yes**.
7. Click **OK** to close the **Microsoft TCP/IP Properties** dialog box.
8. Click **OK** to close **Network**.

▸ **To test the DHCP configuration**

1. Start a command prompt, type **ipconfig /all** and then press ENTER to view the new TCP/IP configuration.

   What IP address was assigned to the computer running Windows NT Workstation by the DHCP server?

   ____

   What is the DHCP server address?

   ____

What is the address of the default gateway?

____

When does the lease expire?

____

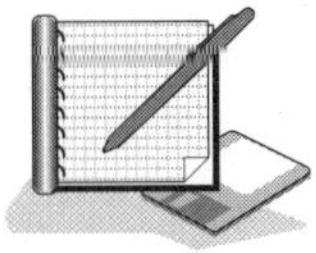

Practice

In these procedures, you explore DHCP and troubleshoot various DHCP configuration errors.

Note These procedures contain procedures for both computers. Make sure that you complete the correct procedure on the correct computer.

▸ To view DHCP assigned addresses

In this procedure, you view the DHCP server listing of leased addresses.

Note Complete this procedure on Server1.

---

1. Start DHCP Manager, and double-click ***Local Machine***
2. Click the local scope.
3. On the **Scope** menu, click **Active Leases**.

   The **Active Leases** dialog box appears, displaying the list of IP addresses that have been leased to clients.
4. Click **Cancel** to return to the **DHCP Manager** window.
5. Close DHCP Manager.

▸ To renew a DHCP lease

In this procedure, you release and then renew the lease assigned to Workstation1.

Note Complete this procedure on Workstation1.

---

1. Start a command prompt, type **ipconfig /all** and then press ENTER to view the lease information.

   When does the lease expire?

   ____

2. Type **ipconfig /release** and then press ENTER.

   What message did you receive?

   ____

3. Type **ipconfig /all** and then press ENTER to view the IP configuration.

   What is your IP address?

   ____

4. Type **ipconfig /renew** and then press ENTER to renew the lease.

   The Windows NT IP configuration information for the assigned address is displayed.

5. Type **ipconfig /all** and then press ENTER to view the lease information again.

   When does the lease expire?

   ____

Practice

In these procedures, you stop the DHCP Server service and then determine what effect this has when a DHCP client attempts to renew a lease.

▸ To stop the DHCP Server service

In this procedure, you stop the Microsoft DHCP Server service to prevent IP address lease assignments and renewals.

Note Complete this procedure on Server1.

---

1. From Control Panel, start Services.
2. Click **Microsoft DHCP Server**, and then click **Stop**.
3. Click **Yes** when prompted.

   The Microsoft DHCP server stops.

▸ To attempt lease renewal when the DHCP server is unavailable

In this procedure, you use the **ipconfig** utility to attempt to renew the lease assigned to Workstation1 while the DHCP server is unavailable.

Note Complete this procedure on Workstation1.

---

1. Start a command prompt, type **ipconfig /renew** and then press ENTER.

   Could you successfully renew the lease?

   ____

2. Type **ping 131.107.2.200** and then press ENTER to verify that TCP/IP can still communicate with Server1.

   Ping should respond with four success messages.

   Even though you were unable to renew your IP address lease, it is still a valid lease. The IP address you leased remains active until the lease expires or until you use the **ipconfig /release** command to return the address to the IP address pool. Therefore, TCP/IP communications are still possible using the IP address that you had obtained earlier from the DHCP server.

▸ To release a DHCP address

In this procedure, you use the **ipconfig** utility to release the IP address lease assigned to Workstation1.

Note Complete this procedure on Workstation1.

---

1. Start a command prompt, type **ipconfig /release** and then press ENTER.

   The Windows IP configuration information appears.

   What message did you receive?

   ____

2. Type **ping 131.107.2.200** and then press ENTER to test TCP/IP communications with Server1.

   Ping should respond with four *Destination host unreachable* messages.

3. Shut down and restart Workstation1.
4. Log on to the domain as Administrator.

   A **Logon Message** dialog box appears, stating that a domain controller could not be found.

   Why does this message appear?

   ____

5. Start a command prompt, type **ipconfig /all** to view the IP configuration.

   What is the IP address? Why?

   ____

▸ To start the DHCP Server service

In this procedure, you start the Microsoft DHCP Server service to allow IP address lease assignments and renewals.

Note Complete this procedure on Server1.

- Use either the **Services** program in Control Panel, or Server Manager to start the Microsoft DHCP Server service.

▸ To renew a DHCP lease

In this procedure, you use the **ipconfig** utility to renew the lease assigned to the computer running Windows NT Workstation.

Note Complete this procedure on Workstation1.

---

1. Start a command prompt, type **ipconfig /renew** and then press ENTER.
2. Type **ipconfig /all** and then press ENTER.

   When does the lease expire?

   ____

Lesson 3: Windows Internet Name Service

Computers use IP addresses to identify each other, but computer users usually find it easier to work with computer names. A mechanism must be available on a TCP/IP network to resolve computer names, which are NetBIOS names, to IP addresses. To ensure that both computer name and IP address are unique, the computer running Windows NT using TCP/IP registers its name and IP address on the network during system startup. In this lesson, you learn about NetBIOS name resolution and how Windows NT computers can use the Windows Internet Name Service (WINS) in TCP/IP internetworks to ensure accurate name resolution between Windows NT computers names (NetBIOS names) and IP addresses.

After this lesson, you will be able to:

- Define NetBIOS name.
- Explain the function of WINS.
- Define WINS server and client requirements.
- Install and configure the WINS Server service.
- Configure a WINS client.

Estimated lesson time: 45 minutes

Name Resolution

People typically assign meaningful, easy-to-remember names to their computers. For example, in this book you named the computer running Windows NT Server Server1. Using easy-to-remember names simplifies connecting to resources through the **net use** command or Windows NT Explorer. The Windows NT computer name, assigned during setup, is a NetBIOS name.

TCP/IP devices use IP addresses rather than the computer name to locate a computer on the internetwork. Thus, TCP/IP internetworks require a name resolution method that can match and convert computer names to IP addresses and IP addresses to computer names.

What Is a NetBIOS Name?

A NetBIOS name is used for NetBIOS processes to communicate with each other. In Windows NT, NetBIOS names are created (registered) when services initialize, such as the Server and Workstation services, or when a NetBIOS application starts.

A computer's NetBIOS name:

- Is the computer name, such as Server1, assigned during installation.
- Is stored as an entry in the registry, and can be changed through the Network program in Control Panel.
- Is always specified in Windows NT commands, such as **net use** and **net view**.
- Can be determined by typing **nbtstat -n** at a command prompt.
- Can be 15 characters in length. A 16th character can be added to the name to designate the service or application that registered the name. This extra character is added by the service or application.

What Is NetBIOS Name Resolution?

In order to communicate successfully on a TCP/IP-based network, hosts need to identify each other's media access control address. The media access control address is the physical address assigned to the network adapter card, for example the burned-in address. The physical address is sometimes referred to as the hardware address. The process of converting a computer name to a media access control address is also known as name resolution. Name resolution in a TCP/IP network is really a two-step process. Starting with a computer name, the first step is to resolve the computer name to an IP address. Once the IP address has been determined, the hardware address can be resolved.

Note This lesson only covers name resolution between NetBIOS names and IP addresses.

Microsoft TCP/IP can use any of the methods in the following table to resolve computer names to IP addresses.

Method of resolution	Description
NetBIOS name cache	The local cache containing the locally registered computer names and the computer names that the local computer recently resolved to IP addresses.
NetBIOS Name Server (NBNS), such as the Windows Internet Name Service (WINS)	A server implemented under RFC 1001/1002 to provide name resolution of NetBIOS computer names. The Microsoft implementation of this is WINS.

(continued)

Method of resolution	Description
Local broadcast	A broadcast on the local network for the IP address of the destination NetBIOS name.
LMHOSTS file	A local text file that maps IP addresses to the NetBIOS computer names of Windows networking computers on remote networks.
HOSTS file	A local text file in the same format as the 4.3 Berkeley Software Distribution (BSD) UNIX/etc/hosts file. This file maps host names to IP addresses. This file is typically used to resolve host names for TCP/IP utilities.
Domain Name Server (DNS)	A server configured with the DNS daemon that maintains a database of IP address/computer name (host name) mappings. A DNS is common to UNIX environments.

Note This chapter covers the installation and configuration of the WINS and DNS name resolution methods, because they are installed and configured as Windows NT Server services. For more information on name resolution methods, see the *Networking Guide* of the *Microsoft Windows NT Server Resource Kit.*

NetBIOS Over TCP/IP Name Resolution Modes

Windows NT provides support for all of the NetBIOS over TCP/IP name resolution modes defined in the Request for Comments (RFCs) 1001 and 1002. The RFC is a series of documents that contain the standards for TCP/IP. Each mode resolves NetBIOS names differently.

Mode	Description
b-node (broadcast)	Uses broadcasts (UDP datagrams) for name registration and resolution. b-node has two major problems: 1. In a large internetwork, broadcasts can increase the network load, and 2. Routers typically do not forward broadcasts, so only computers on the local network can respond.
p-node (peer-peer)	Uses a NetBIOS Name Server (NBNS), such as WINS to resolve NetBIOS names. p-node does not use broadcasts; instead, it queries the Name Server directly. Because broadcasts are not used, computers can span routers. The most significant problems with p-node are that all computers must be configured with the IP address of the NBNS, and if the NBNS is down, computers will not be able to communicate even on the local network.

(continued)

Mode	Description
m-node (mixed)	A combination of b-node and p-node. By default, an m-node functions as a b-node. If it is unable to resolve a name by broadcast, it uses the NBNS of p-node.
h-node (hybrid)	A combination of p-node and b-node. By default, an h-node functions as a p-node. If it is unable to resolve a name through the NetBIOS Name Server, it uses a b-node broadcast to resolve the name.
Microsoft enhanced b-node	An enhanced b-node for resolving NetBIOS computer names of remote hosts. Enhanced b-node utilizes the LMHOSTS file, which is a static file that maps a remote computer's NetBIOS name to its IP address. Entries in the LMHOSTS file that marked with #PRE are cached when TCP/IP initializes. Before a b-node broadcast is sent, the cache is checked for the NetBIOS name/IP address mapping. If the mapping is not found in cache, a b-node broadcast is initiated. If the broadcast is not successful, the LMHOSTS file is parsed in an attempt to resolve the name.

What Is WINS?

WINS is a NetBIOS Name Service that is designed to provide a flexible solution to the problem of locating NetBIOS resources in routed TCP/IP-based networks. It is a dynamic database for registering and resolving NetBIOS name-to-IP address mappings in a network.

How WINS Works

Before two NetBIOS-based hosts can communicate, the destination NetBIOS name must be resolved to its IP address. This is necessary because TCP/IP requires an IP address to communicate; TCP/IP cannot establish communication using a NetBIOS computer name.

The procedure for registering and resolving NetBIOS names using WINS is as follows:

1. In a WINS environment, each time a WINS client starts, it registers its NetBIOS name/IP address mapping with a designated WINS server. In the following illustration, Student 3 registers its NetBIOS name and IP address with the WINS server.
2. When a WINS client, Student 1, initiates a NetBIOS command to communicate with another host (Student 3), the name query request is sent directly to the WINS server instead of being broadcast on the local network.

3. If the WINS server finds a NetBIOS name/IP address mapping for the destination host, Student 3, in this database, it returns the destination host's IP address to the WINS client, Student 1. Because the WINS database obtains NetBIOS name/IP address mappings dynamically, it is always current. If the WINS server is unavailable, the client switches to b-node and sends the query as a broadcast message on the local subnet.

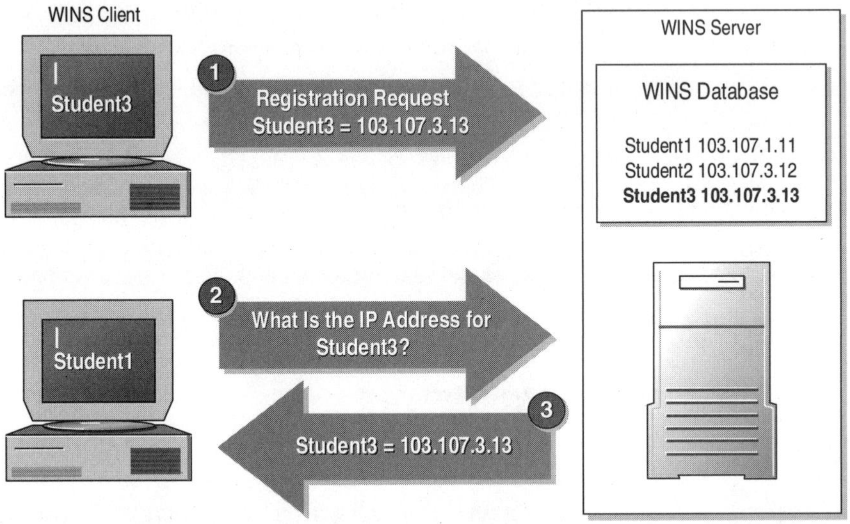

Note For more information on name registration and resolution, see Chapter 3, "Implementation Considerations," in the *Networking Supplement* in Books Online.

WINS Servers

A WINS server handles name registrations and queries. It maintains a database that maps the NetBIOS computer names of WINS clients to their IP addresses. When a WINS client requests an IP address, a WINS server retrieves the IP address from its database and returns it to the client.

WINS Clients

A WINS client registers its computer name and IP address with a WINS server during system startup. It then queries the WINS server for computer name resolution.

Windows-based networking clients, such as WINS-enabled computers running Windows NT, Windows 95, or Windows for Workgroups 3.11, can use WINS directly. Non-WINS computers that use broadcasts can access WINS through proxies. Proxies are WINS-enabled computers that listen to name-query broadcast messages, forward the request to the WINS server, and then respond for names that are not on the local subnet.

WINS Requirements

To implement WINS, both the server and client require configuration.

Server Requirements

A WINS server requires:

- The WINS Server service configured on at least one computer within the TCP/IP internetwork running Windows NT Server. (It does not have to be a domain controller.)
- A static IP address.

Client Requirements

A WINS client requires:

- A computer running any of the following supported operating systems:
  - Windows NT Server 3.5 or later.
  - Windows NT Workstation 3.5 or later.
  - Windows 95.
  - Windows for Workgroups 3.11 running Microsoft TCP/IP-32.
  - Microsoft Network Client 3.0 for MS-DOS with the real-mode TCP/IP driver included on the *Microsoft Windows NT Server* compact disc.
  - LAN Manager 2.2c for MS-DOS (included on the *Microsoft Windows NT Server* compact disc). LAN Manager 2.2c for OS/2 is not supported.
- The IP address of a WINS server.

Installing and Configuring WINS

To install the WINS Server service on a computer running Windows NT Server, use the Network program in Control Panel. On the **Services** tab, click **Add**, and then click **Windows Internet Name Service**. You must shut down and restart your computer for the service to start.

After installing the WINS Server service, all Windows NT-based WINS management and configuration are performed through WINS Manager. WINS Manager is located in the Administrative Tools (Common) group on computers running Windows NT Server that have installed the WINS Server service. WINS Manager (shown in the following illustration) allows you to obtain detailed information about your WINS servers, as well as viewing the mappings database or adding static mappings to the database.

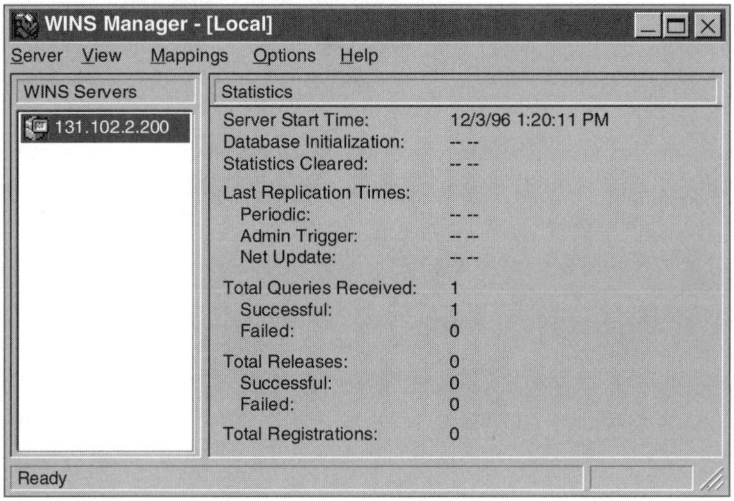

Practice

In this procedure, you install a WINS server on Server1, and you configure Server1 to use itself as its WINS server.

► **To install and configure the WINS Server service**

Note Complete this procedure on Server1.

---

1. Log on as Administrator.
2. In Control Panel, double-click the Network icon.

   The **Network** dialog box appears.
3. Click the **Services** tab, and then click **Add**.

   The **Select Network Service** dialog box appears.

4. Click **Windows Internet Name Service**, and then click **OK**.

   A **Windows NT Setup** dialog box appears asking for the full path to the software.
5. Type **\\Server1\Nts_source\I386** and then click **Continue**.

   The appropriate files are copied to your computer.
6. Click the **Protocols** tab.

   You now configure Server1, which is not a DHCP client, to use its own address for a WINS server.
7. Double-click **TCP/IP Protocol**.

   The **Microsoft TCP/IP Properties** dialog box appears.
8. Click the **WINS Address** tab.
9. In the **Primary WINS Server** box, type **131.107.2.200** (your IP address) and then click **OK**.

   The **Network** dialog box appears.
10. Click **Close**.

    A **Network Settings Change** dialog box appears, indicating that the computer needs to be restarted to initialize the new configuration.
11. Click **Yes** to restart Server1.

Configuring a WINS client

There are two ways to configure a WINS client, either manually or in conjunction with DHCP.

Manually

You can manually configure a WINS client by using the Network program in Control Panel. On the **Protocols** tab, click **TCP/IP**, and then click **Properties**. In the **Microsoft TCP/IP Properties** dialog box, click the **WINS Address** tab. You then provide the address of the primary, and optionally secondary, WINS server.

In Conjunction with DHCP

When you configure your DHCP server to work in conjunction with your WINS server, you save the administrative overhead of individually configuring your DHCP clients to also be WINS clients.

You can use DHCP Manager to add and configure the following DHCP options:

044 WINS/NBNS Servers. Your DHCP server can provide the address of a WINS server to be used for name registration and resolution to the DHCP clients.

046 WINS/NBT Node Type. Must be used to automatically configure the client's node type for use in name resolution.

Note For more information about installing, configuring, and managing WINS servers, see the *Network Guide* of the *Microsoft Windows NT Server Resource Kit.*

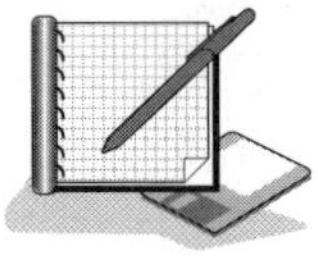

Practice

In this procedure, you configure the DHCP server to supply the appropriate WINS server addressing information and node type to DHCP clients.

Note Complete this procedure on Server1.

► **To configure the DHCP server to assign WINS server addresses**

1. Log on as Administrator.
2. From the Administrative Tools (Common) group, start DHCP Manager.

   The DHCP Manager window appears.
3. Double-click *__Local Machine__*

   The local scope IP address appears.
4. Click the local scope's IP address.

   The local scope options appear under **Option Configuration**.
5. On the **DHCP Options** menu, click **Scope**.

   The **DHCP Options: Scope** dialog box appears.
6. Under **Unused Options**, click **044 WINS/NBNS Servers**, and then click **Add**.

   A **DHCP Manager** message box appears, indicating that for WINS to function properly, you must add the **046 WINS/NBT Node Type** option.
7. Click **OK**.

   The **044 WINS/NBNS Servers** option now appears under **Active Options**.
8. Click **Value**.

   The **DHCP Scope: Options** dialog box expands.
9. Click **Edit Array**.

   The **IP Address Array Editor** dialog box appears.
10. Under **New IP Address**, type **131.107.2.200** (your IP address) and then click **Add**.

    The new IP address appears under **IP Addresses**.
11. To return to the **DHCP Options: Scope** dialog box, click **OK**.
12. Under **Unused Options**, click **046 WINS/NBT Node Type**, and then click **Add**.

    The **046 WINS/NBT Node Type** option now appears under **Active Options**.

13. In the **Byte** box, type **0x8** and then click **OK**.

    The DHCP Manager window appears. Under **Option Configuration**, the following active scope options appear: **003 Router**, **044 WINS/NBNS Servers**, and **046 WINS/NBT Node Type**.

14. Exit DHCP Manager.

Practice

In this procedure, you test the configuration of the DHCP server to automatically assign the WINS server address and NetBIOS node types to DHCP clients. At Workstation1, your DHCP client, you renew your IP address, view the information supplied, and ping a computer using the computer name.

Note Complete this procedure on Workstation1.

▸ **To test the configuration of the DHCP server to assign WINS server addresses**

1. Log on to the domain as Administrator.
2. Start a command prompt, type **ipconfig /renew** and then press ENTER to renew your IP address.
3. Type **ipconfig /all** and then press ENTER to view your IP addressing information.

   What is the address of the primary WINS server?

   ____

   What is the node type?

   ____

4. Type **ping server1** and then press ENTER.

   Why were you successful in pinging a NetBIOS computer name?

   ____

5. Close the command prompt.

Lesson 4: Domain Name System

This lesson explains the function of the Domain Name System (DNS) Server service and how it can be configured to locate resources on an internetwork. In addition, it examines how WINS is integrated with DNS, which allows computers running Windows NT to access information on the Internet using Internet naming conventions.

Note DNS is a complex topic, and this book does not attempt to explain it fully. For more information on DNS, see the *Microsoft Windows NT Server Resource Kit,* or *DNS and BIND,* by Paul Albitz and Cricket Liu, published by O'Reilly and Associates.

After this lesson, you will be able to:

- Describe the purpose of DNS.
- Install and configure the DNS Server service.
- Explain the advantages of integrating WINS and DNS.

Estimated lesson time: 45 minutes

What Is DNS?

The Domain Name System (DNS) is a distributed database providing a hierarchical naming system for identifying hosts on the Internet. DNS was developed to solve the problems that arose when the number of hosts on the Internet grew dramatically in the early 1980s. DNS specifications are defined in RFCs 1034 and 1035. DNS computer names consist of two parts: a host name and a domain name, which combine to form the fully qualified domain name (FQDN). For example, research.widgets.com is a FQDN where *research* is the host name and *widgets.com* is the domain name.

Note The term *domain,* when used in the context of DNS, is not related to the term domain used when discussing Windows NT Directory Services.

An Internet domain is a unique name that identifies an Internet site. In order to register a domain name, you must contact the Internet Network Information Center (InterNIC). Visit the InterNIC home page on the Internet at http://internic.net.

What Is the DNS Server Service?

The DNS Server service is a name resolution service that resolves a FQDN to the IP address that is then used by the internetwork. For example, you can use Microsoft Internet Explorer to open research.widgets.com, and a DNS server can resolve this friendly name to the correct IP address on the Internet.

Comparing WINS and DNS

Although DNS might seem similar to WINS, there are two major differences. The following table summarizes the differences.

DNS	WINS
Resolves Internet names to IP addresses.	Resolves NetBIOS names to IP addresses.
Static database of computer name to IP address mappings. It must be manually updated.	Dynamic database of NetBIOS names and IP addresses. It is dynamically updated.

DNS Benefits

Using DNS on your computer running Windows NT allows you to:

- Access UNIX-based systems using friendly names.
- Connect to Internet systems using Internet naming conventions.
- Maintain a consistent hierarchical naming scheme across your organization.

How DNS Works

DNS uses a client/server model, where DNS servers (name servers) contain information about a portion of the DNS database (zone) and make this information available to clients (resolvers).

DNS name servers perform name resolution by interpreting network information to find a specific IP address. The name resolution process is outlined below:

1. A resolver (or client) passes a query to its local name server.
2. If the local name server does not have the data requested in the query, it queries other name servers on behalf of the resolver.
3. When the local name server has the address requested, it returns the information to the resolver.

The Domain Name Space

The DNS database is a tree structure called the *domain name space*. Each domain (node in the tree structure) is named and can contain subdomains. The domain name identifies the domain's position in the database in relation to its parent domain. A period (.) separates each part of the name for each network node in the DNS domain. For example, in the following illustration, the DNS domain name csu.edu, specifies the csu subdomain whose parent is the edu domain; microsoft.com specifies the microsoft subdomain whose parent is the com domain. The following illustration shows the parent-child relationships of DNS domains.

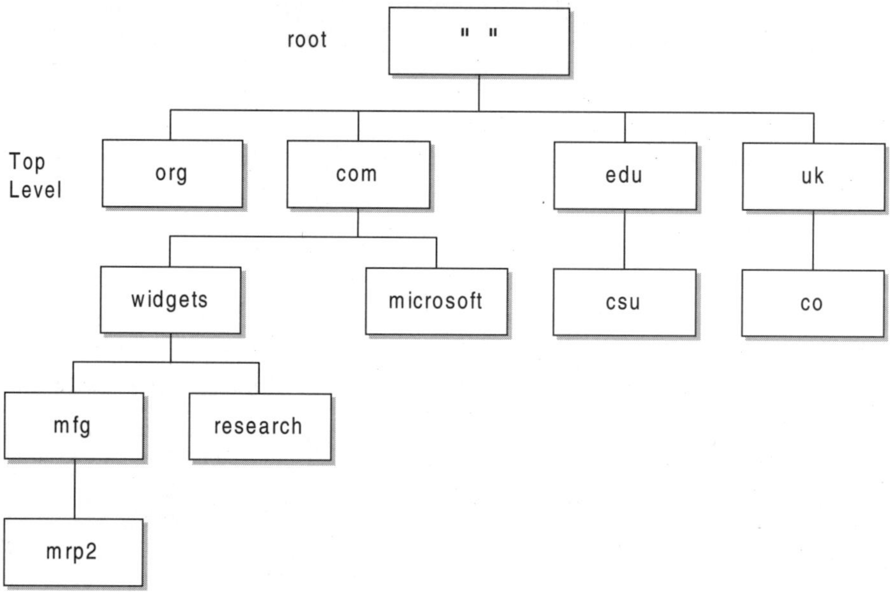

As shown in the preceding illustration, the root node of the DNS database is unnamed (" " which is used to represent null).

The root node is referenced in DNS names with a trailing period (.). For example, in the name: "research.widgets.com." it is the period after com that denotes the DNS root node.

Top-Level Domains

The root and top-level domains of the DNS database are managed by the InterNIC. In most of the world, top-level domain names consist of geographical 2-character country codes such as .uk for the United Kingdom. In the United States many top-level domains are organizational, 3-character names, for example .com for commercial organizations and .edu for educational organizations.

Delegation

Responsibility for managing the DNS name space below the top level is delegated to other organizations by the InterNIC. These organizations further subdivide the name space and delegate responsibility down the hierarchical tree structure. This decentralized administrative model allows DNS to be autonomously managed at the levels that make the most sense for each organization involved.

Zones

The administrative unit for DNS is the zone. A zone is a subtree of the DNS database that is administered as a single separate entity. It can consist of a single domain or a domain with subdomains. The lower-level subdomains of a zone can also be split into separate zone(s). The following illustration shows the relationship between DNS domains and zones.

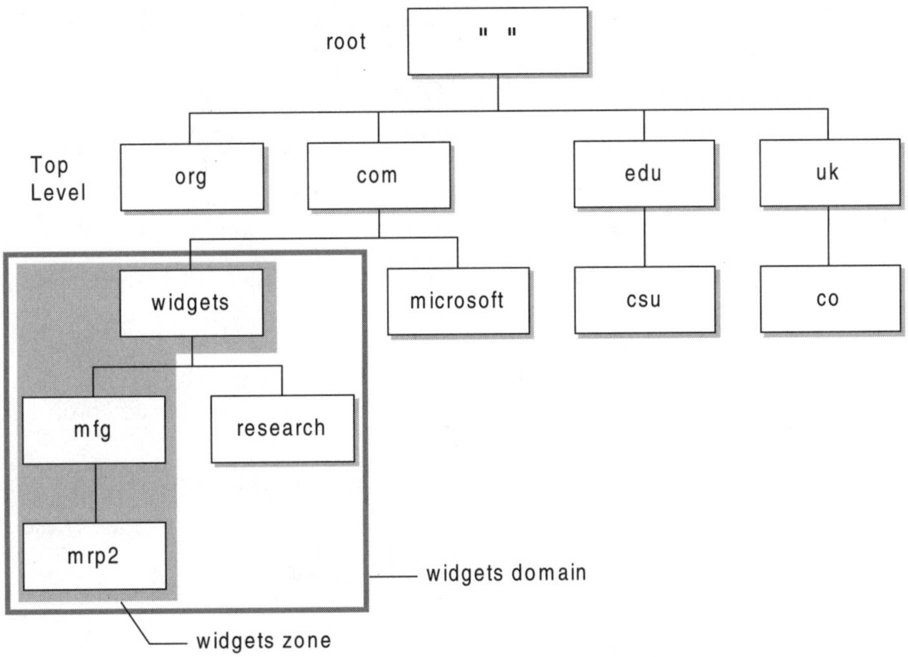

Fully Qualified Domain Names

With the exception of the root, each node in the DNS database has a name (label) of up to 63 characters. Each subdomain must have a unique name within its parent domain. This ensures name uniqueness throughout the DNS name space. DNS domain names are formed by following the path from the bottom of the DNS tree to the root. The node names are concatenated, and a period (.) separates each part. An optional period (.) that signifies the root can appear at the end of the name. Such names are known as fully qualified domain names (FQDN). The following is an example of an FQDN:

mrp2.mfg.widgets.com.

Note For more information about DNS, see Appendix C, "Implementing DNS Using Microsoft Windows NT 4.0."

Installing and Configuring DNS

To install the DNS Server service on a computer running Windows NT Server, use the Network program in Control Panel. On the **Services** tab, click **Add**, and then click **Microsoft DNS Server**. You must restart your computer for the service to start. DNS servers require a static IP address.

All DNS management and configuration is performed through DNS Manager located in the Administrative Tools (Common) group. Its primary function is to configure DNS objects. Each of these objects has a defined set of manageable properties (or attributes). DNS Manager can be used to visually identify any one of these objects, and to view, add, or modify associated properties.

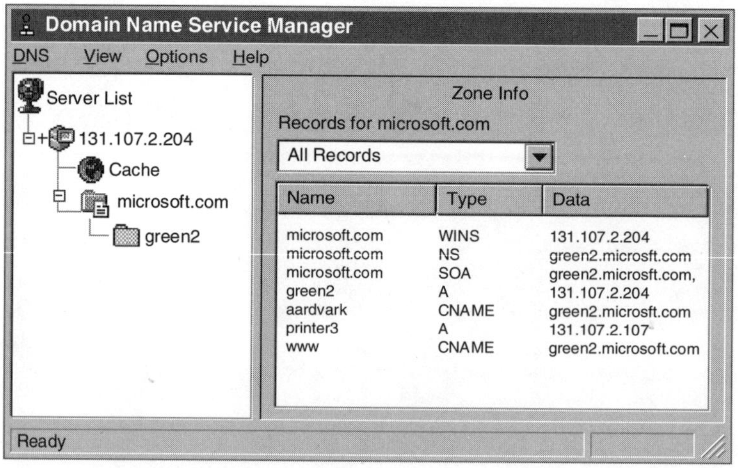

The following table lists the objects that are configured using DNS Manager.

Object	Description
DNS Resource Record (RR)	The RR is the principal object in DNS. It is the component that contains the actual information elements managed by DNS. Three common properties are common to all RR types: owner, class, and TTL (Time to Live).
DNS Domain	A node in the DNS tree. It contains all of the resource records for that domain.
DNS Zone	A subtree of the DNS database that is administered as a single entity. It may contain a single domain, or a domain with subdomains.
DNS Server	Administers at least one DNS zone.
Server List	Contains the DNS servers that can be administered with DNS Manager. New DNS servers can be added as needed.

The Resource Record (RR) property set depends on the RR type. The three properties listed in the following table, however, are common to all RR types.

Property	Function
Owner	Identifies the DNS domain or host to which the RR applies.
Class	Identifies a defined and standardized family of RR types. Almost all RRs in use today are of the 'IN' or Internet class.
TTL (Time to Live)	Indicates how long the information in the RR will remain valid.

Note DNS servers contain a database that Windows NT searches for computer names. Servers are searched in the order they appear in DNS Manager.

Configuring a DNS Client

Windows NT Server, Windows NT Workstation, Windows 95, and Windows for Workgroups 3.11 with Microsoft TCP/IP-32 installed all include DNS-resolver functionality.

There are two ways to configure a Windows NT client to use the DNS server to resolve Internet names, either manually or in conjunction with DHCP.

Manually

You can manually configure a DNS client by using the Network program in Control Panel. On the **Protocols** tab, click **TCP/IP Protocol**, and then click **Properties**. In the **Microsoft TCP/IP Properties** dialog box, click the **DNS** tab. You then provide the domain name for the client, and the IP addresses and search order for all DNS servers that you want to use to resolve host names.

In Conjunction with DHCP

When you configure your DHCP server to work in conjunction with your DNS server, you save the administrative overhead of individually configuring your DHCP clients to also be DNS clients. By using DHCP Manager to add and configure the DHCP option, 006 DNS Servers, your DHCP server can provide the address of a DNS server to be used for Internet name resolution to the DHCP clients.

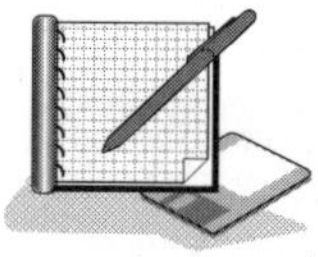

Practice

In these procedures, you install, configure, and test the Microsoft DNS Server service on Server1. Your DNS domain name is corp1.com.

Note Complete these procedures on Server1.

► **To install the Domain Name System Server service**

1. Log on as Administrator.
2. In Control Panel, double-click the Network icon.

   The **Network** dialog box appears.
3. Click the **Services** tab, and then click **Add**.

   The **Select Network Service** dialog box appears.
4. In the **Network Service** list, click **Microsoft DNS Server**, and then click **OK**.

   Windows NT Setup displays a dialog box requesting the full path to the Windows NT distribution files.
5. Type **\\Server1\Nts_source\I386** and then click **Continue**.

   All necessary files, including the sample files, are copied to your hard disk.
6. In the **Network** dialog box, click **Protocols**.
7. On the **Protocols** tab, double-click **TCP/IP Protocol**.

   The **Microsoft TCP/IP Properties** dialog box appears.
8. Click the **DNS** tab.
9. In the **Domain** box, type **corp1.com** and then click **OK**.
10. In the **Network** dialog box, click **Close**.
11. When prompted, click **Yes** to restart Server1.

▸ To configure the DNS Service search order

In this procedure, you configure the DNS search order by entering the IP address of Server1.

Note Complete this procedure on Server1.

---

1. Log on as Administrator.
2. In Control Panel, double-click the Network icon.

   The **Network** dialog box appears.
3. Click the **Protocols** tab, and then double-click **TCP/IP Protocol**.
4. Click the **DNS** tab.
5. In the **DNS Service Search Order** box, click **Add**.
6. In the **DNS Server** box, type **131.107.2.200** which is the IP address for Server1, and then click **Add**.
7. Click **OK**.

   The **Network** dialog box appears.
8. Click **OK** to close the **Network** dialog box.

▸ To configure the DNS Server service primary zone

In this procedure, you create a primary zone within your domain.

Note Complete this procedure on Server1.

---

1. Click the **Start** button, point to **Programs**, point to **Administrative Tools (Common)**, and then click **DNS Manager**.

   The Domain Name Service Manager window appears.
2. On the **DNS** menu, click **New Server**.

   The **Add DNS Server** dialog box appears.
3. In the **DNS Server** box, type **Server1** and then click **OK**.
4. Right-click **Server1**, and then click **New Zone**.

   The **Creating new zone for Server1** dialog box appears.

5. Click **Primary**, and then click **Next**.
6. In the **Zone Name** box, type **corp1.com**
7. Press the TAB key.

   Corp1.com.dns is automatically entered in the **Zone File** box.
8. Click **Next**, and then click **Finish**.

   Notice that the Server List now shows a zone name, corp1.com. In the right pane, notice the Zone Info entries that have been added.

▸ **To add your workstation computer as a New Host in your domain**

In this procedure, you add a host name, Workstation1, for your workstation computer to your domain.

Note Complete these procedure on Server1.

---

1. In the left pane, right-click your zone name, **corp1.com**.
2. On the menu that appears, click **New Host**.

   The **New Host** dialog box appears.
3. In the **Host Name** box, type **Workstation1**
4. In the **Host IP Address** box, type **131.107.2.201** which is your workstation's IP address, and then click **Add Host**.
5. Click **Done**.

▸ **To add an alias for your workstation computer to your zone**

In this procedure, you add an alias, work1, for Workstation1. The only reason you are creating this alias is to test that DNS is correctly installed and configured.

Note Complete these procedure on Server1.

---

1. Right-click your zone name, and then click **New Record**.

   The **New Resource Record** dialog box appears.
2. Under **Record Type**, click **CNAME Record**.
3. In the **Alias Name** box, type **work1**
4. In the **For Host DNS name** box, type **workstation1.corp1.com**
5. Click **OK**.

▶ To add a Name Server record to your domain

In this procedure, you add a Name Server record for Workstation1 to your domain.

Note Complete these procedure on Server1.

---

1. Right-click your zone name, and then click **New Record**.

   The **New Record** dialog box appears.
2. Under **Record Type**, click **NS Record.**

   Notice that the domain is already filled in with your domain name.
3. In the **Name Server DNS Name** box, type **workstation1**
4. Click **OK**.
5. Close DNS Manager.

▶ To resolve an IP address using DNS

In this procedure, you ensure that DNS is correctly installed and configured by resolving the alias work1. The alias name, work1, only exists in the DNS entries, and not in the WINS database. When the alias is resolved, your installation and configuration of DNS is now verified.

Note Complete these procedure on Server1.

---

1. Start a command prompt.
2. Type **ping work1** and then press ENTER.

   What IP address did it return?

   ____

Integrating WINS and DNS

The structure of a DNS zone changes whenever a new host is added or when an existing host is moved to a different subnet. Because DNS is not dynamic, you must manually change the DNS database files if the zone is to reflect the new configuration. This results in increased administrative overhead, especially on zones that change frequently.

The Windows NT DNS Server service can be configured to use WINS for host name resolution. You can install WINS and DNS on the same computer or on different computers running Windows NT Server 4.0.

This integration creates a form of dynamic DNS Server service that takes advantage of the best features of both DNS and WINS. With it, you can direct DNS to query WINS for name resolution of the lower levels of the DNS tree in your zones. This final WINS resolution is transparent to the client, which perceives the DNS name server as handling the entire process.

The following illustration shows how name resolution works when WINS is integrated with DNS. A user at the resolver computer is trying to connect to the widgets.universal.com host.

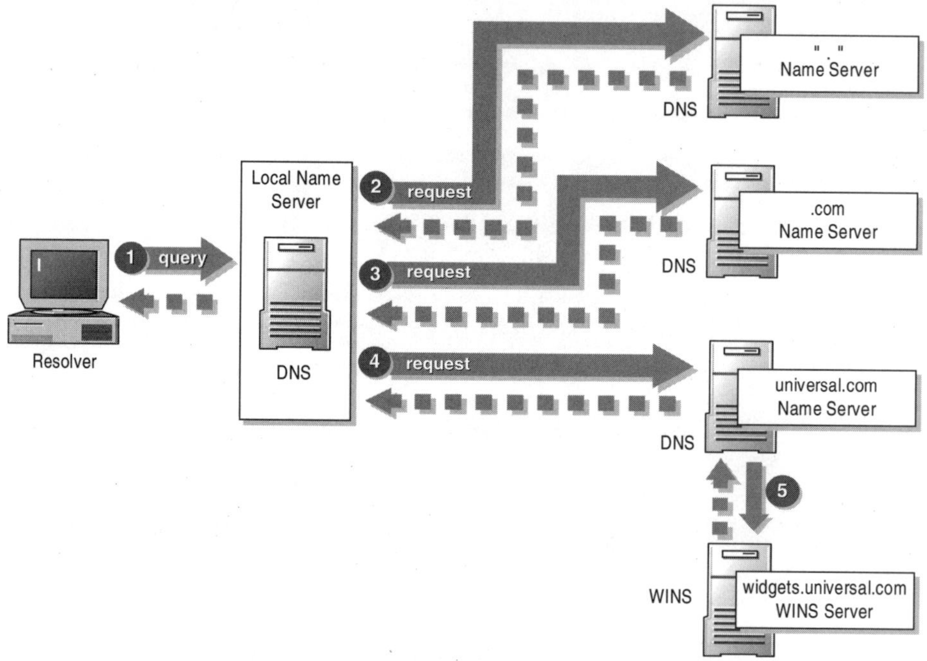

1. A resolver (or client) passes a query to its local name server.
2. The local name server sends an iterative request to one of the DNS root servers requesting resolution of the FQDN. The DNS root server returns a referral to the name servers that are authoritative for the *com* DNS domain.
3. The local name server sends an iterative request to one of the *com* name servers, which responds with a referral to the *universal* name servers.

4. The local name server sends an iterative request to one of the *universal* name servers.
5. The *universal* name servers are running the DNS server on a computer running Windows NT Server. They are configured to use WINS to resolve the leftmost portion (host name) of the FQDN. When the *universal* name server receives the request from the local name server, it passes the *widgets* piece of the DNS name to its local WINS server for resolution. WINS returns the IP address for *widgets* to the *universal* name server, which returns the IP address of the FQDN to the local DNS server, which then sends it back to the client resolver.

To configure DNS to use WINS to resolve the host name of a FQDN, use DNS Manager. Right-click the zone that will consult the WINS database for name resolution, and then click **Properties**. Click the **WINS Lookup** tab, and then select the **Use WINS Resolution** check box and type the WINS server IP address that will be used for resolution.

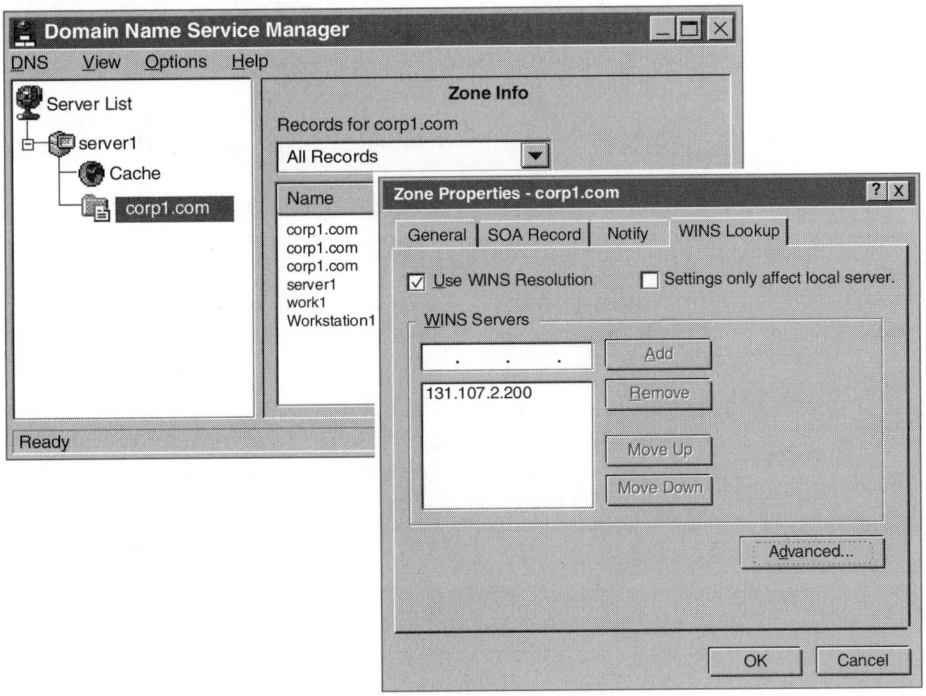

Lesson 5: Computer Browser Service

In this lesson, you learn how browsing for NetBIOS resources occurs in a internetwork.

After this lesson, you will be able to:

- Identify the roles a computer running Windows NT can perform in the browser process.
- Explain how the Windows NT Computer Browser service locates available servers on the network.
- Configure a computer to become a browser.

Estimated lesson time: 15 minutes

To use resources across a network efficiently, users must be able to find out what resources are available. Windows NT uses the Computer Browser service to display a list of currently available network resources.

The Computer Browser service maintains a centralized list of available network resources. This list is distributed to specially assigned computers that perform browsing services, along with their other normal services. Browser computers eliminate the need for all computers to maintain a list of all shared resources on the network. By assigning the browser role to specific computers, the Computer Browser service reduces the amount of network traffic required to build and maintain a list of all shared resources on the network. This also frees the CPU time each computer would have had to use in creating a network resource list.

Note For this lesson, a server is defined as any computer that provides resources to the network. For example, in the context of the Browser service, a computer running Windows NT Workstation is a server if it shares file or print resources with other networked computers.

The Browser Process

The following illustration shows the browser process.

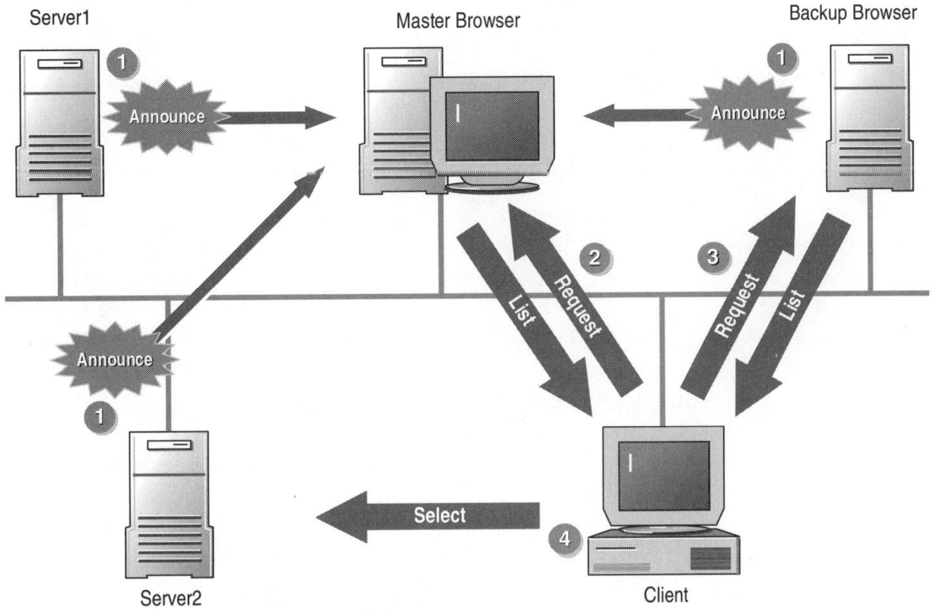

The Windows NT Computer Browser service operates as follows:

1. After startup, all computers that are running a Server service announce their presence to the master browser in their workgroup or domain. This happens regardless of whether or not they have shared resources to advertise.
2. The first time a client computer attempts to locate available network resources, it contacts the master browser of the domain or workgroup for a list of backup browsers.
3. The client then requests the network resource list from a backup browser, which responds to the requesting client with a list of domains and workgroups and the list of servers local to the client's domain or workgroup.
4. The user at the client selects a server, searches for the appropriate resource, and contacts the appropriate server to establish a session to use that resource.

Browser Roles

The responsibility of providing a list of servers to clients is distributed among multiple computers on a network. The browsing roles of these computers are known to the Browser service as potential browser, master browser, backup browser, and browser clients (non-browsers). Computers running Windows NT can perform any of the Browser service roles. These computers collect and maintain a list of available network resources, as defined in the following table.

Browser role	Description
Domain Master Browser	The domain master browser is the computer that collects and maintains the master list of available network servers, as well as the names of other domains and workgroups. It distributes this list to the master browser of each subnet in the Windows NT domain. There is only one domain master browser in a Windows NT domain, and it is the primary domain controller (PDC).
Master Browser	The master browser is the computer that collects and maintains the list of available network servers in its workgroup or subnet. It shares this list with the domain master browser, and receives information on other workgroups, domains, and subnets from the domain master browser, incorporating the information into its list of available resources. It distributes its list, referred to as the browse list, to the backup browsers. There is one master browser for each workgroup or subnet of a domain.
Backup Browsers	A backup browser is a computer that receives a copy of the browse list from the master browser. It then distributes the list to the browser clients upon request.
Potential Browser	A potential browser is not a browser server at all. It is, however, a computer that is capable of becoming a browser (either backup or master) if instructed to do so by a master browser.
Non-Browser	A non-browser is a computer that has been configured so that it will not maintain a browse list. Peer-to-peer networking computers are commonly non-browsers despite their having server services.

Browser Elections

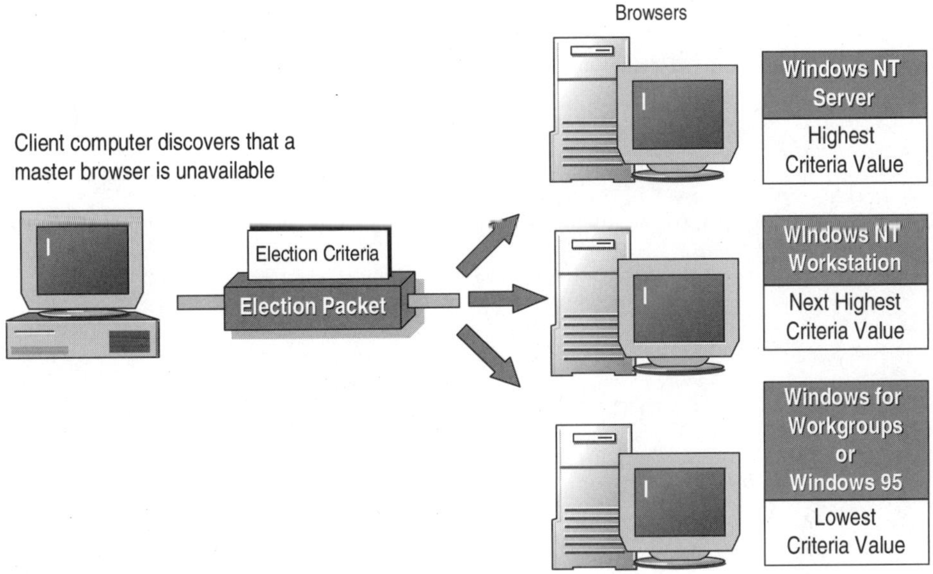

When a client computer cannot locate a master browser, or when a backup browser attempts to update its network resource list and cannot locate the master browser, a new master browser must be selected. This selection process is called a browser election. The election process ensures that *only one* master browser exists per workgroup or segment in a domain.

Election Process

Network computers can initiate an election by broadcasting a special message called an election packet. This election packet contains the requesting computer's criteria value. All browsers process the election packet.

When a browser receives an election packet, it examines the packet and compares the requesting computer's criteria value with its own election criteria. If the receiving browser has a higher election criteria than the issuer of the election packet, the browser issues its own election packet and enters what is referred to as an "election-in-progress" state. This process continues until a master browser is elected, based on the highest ranking criteria value.

Browser Criteria

Browser criteria determine the hierarchical order of the different types of computer systems that are in the workgroup or domain. Each browser computer has certain criteria, depending on the type of system it is. Among other things, the criteria include:

- The operating system:
  - Windows NT Server
  - Windows NT Workstation
  - Microsoft Windows 95
  - Microsoft Windows for Workgroups
- The operating system version, for example, Windows NT 4.0, 3.51, 3.5, or 3.1.
- Its configured role in the browsing environment:
  - Browser
  - Potential browser
  - Non-browser

The criteria ranking is used during an election. An election is used to determine which computer should be the master browser if the current master browser is unavailable.

Configuring Browsers

Computers running Windows NT can be configured to be a browser, to never participate as a browser, or to be a potential browser. Use Registry Editor to configure the following parameter:

\HKEY_LOCAL_MACHINE\SYSTEM\CurrentControlSet\Services
\Browser\Parameters**MaintainServerList**

The following table describes the value entries you can set for **MaintainServerList**.

Value entry	This value entry configures the computer to
No	Never participates as a browser server. Use this value entry to prevent computers that are frequently taken offline, such as mobile or test computers, from becoming a browser server.
Yes	Attempt to become a browser server. Yes is the default value entry for Windows NT Server domain controllers.
Auto	Possibly become a browser server, depending on the number of currently active browsers. This computer, referred to as a potential browser, is notified by the master browser as to whether it should become a backup browser. Auto is the default value for computers running Windows NT Server (non-domain controllers) and Windows NT Workstation.

Note To determine whether a computer running Windows NT will become a browser, when the computer initializes, the Computer Browser service looks in the registry for the value entry that has been configured for the computer.

Note For more information about browsing, see Chapter 3, "Windows NT Browser Service," in the *Networking Guide* of the *Microsoft Windows NT Server Resource Kit.*

Summary

The following information summarizes the key points in this chapter:

- Windows NT provides the following related services for TCP/IP that are added and configured using the **Services** tab in the Network program in Control Panel.
  - *DHCP.* Reduces administration by automatically assigning IP addresses to computers configured to use DHCP.
  - *WINS.* Is a name resolution service. It maintains a dynamic database for registering and resolving NetBIOS name-to-IP address mappings in a network.
  - *Windows NT DNS Server service.* Is a name resolution service. It uses a static database that resolves host names to IP addresses as required by the internetwork.
- The Windows NT DNS Server service is not dynamic, but it can be configured to use WINS for host name resolution, thereby creating a form of dynamic DNS Server service that takes advantage of the best features of both DNS and WINS.
- You can configure your DHCP server to work in conjunction with your WINS server and save the administrative overhead of individually configuring your DHCP clients to also be WINS clients.
- You can configure your DHCP server to work in conjunction with your DNS server and save the administrative overhead of individually configuring your DHCP clients to also be DNS clients.
- The Computer Browser service maintains a centralized list of available network resources. This list is distributed to specially assigned computers that perform browsing services, which reduces the amount of network traffic required to build and maintain a list of all shared resources on the network. It also reduces the CPU time each computer would have had to use in creating a network list, and allows users to locate network resources.

Review

1. How do you install Windows NT network services?

____

____

2. What role does the DHCP Server service play in the Windows NT networking environment?

____

____

3. Explain how the DHCP Server service assigns an IP address.

____

____

____

____

4. Your new computer running Windows NT Workstation cannot view or access any network resources. You have tried pinging other hosts unsuccessfully. Upon examining your TCP/IP configuration, you discover that your IP address is 0.0.0.0, even though it is a DHCP client. What do you suspect is the cause of the problem?

____

____

5. You are experiencing duplicate IP addressing problems. When you troubleshoot the problems, you discover that you accidentally assigned the same IP address to multiple scopes. Why did this create a problem?

____

6. What roles do WINS and DNS services play in the networking environment, and how do they differ?

7. Explain the advantages of integrating WINS and DNS.

8. You have a Windows NT network with TCP/IP as the only protocol available on your network. You have a computer running Windows NT Workstation that is configured to use DNS and WINS. Although you can connect to the computers running Windows NT Server in your domain, you are unable to **ftp** to any UNIX host on your network using the UNIX host's host name. What do you suspect is the cause of the problem?

Answer Key

Procedure Answers

Page 380

▶ **To create a DHCP scope**

2. In Control Panel, double-click the Services icon.

   What are the names of the two DHCP-related services?

   DHCP Client and Microsoft DHCP Server.

   What are the status and startup values of these two services?

   DHCP Client: blank status, and Disabled startup. Microsoft DHCP Server: Started status and Automatic startup.

Page 384

▶ **To test the DHCP configuration**

1. Start a command prompt, type **ipconfig /all** and then press ENTER to view the new TCP/IP configuration.

   What IP address was assigned to the computer running Windows NT Workstation by the DHCP server?

   The reserved client address, 131.107.2.201

   What is the DHCP server address?

   It is 131.107.2.200, the IP address of the Server1 DHCP server.

   What is the address of the default gateway?

   131.107.2.200 (as assigned by DHCP).

   When does the lease expire?

   Approximately 24 hours from the current time.

Page 386

▶ **To renew a DHCP lease**

1. Start a command prompt, type **ipconfig /all** and then press ENTER to view the lease information.

   When does the lease expire?

   Approximately 24 hours from the time you last renewed your lease.

2. Type **ipconfig /release** and then press ENTER.

   What message did you receive?

   IP address 131.107.2.201 successfully released for adapter "*network_adapter_card*".

3. Type **ipconfig /all** and then press ENTER to view the IP configuration.

   What is your IP address?

   0.0.0.0

5. Type **ipconfig /all** and then press ENTER to view the lease information again.

   When does the lease expire?

   Approximately 24 hours from the current time.

Page 387

▸ **To attempt lease renewal when the DHCP server is unavailable**

1. Start a command prompt, type **ipconfig /renew** and then press ENTER.

   Could you successfully renew the lease?

   No. You receive the following error message: "Error: DHCP Server Unavailable: Renewing adapter '*network_adapter_card*'".

Page 388

▸ **To release a DHCP address**

1. Start a command prompt, type **ipconfig /release** and then press ENTER.

   The Windows IP configuration information appears.

   What message did you receive?

   IP address 131.107.2.201 successfully released for adapter "*network_adapter_card*".

4. Log on to the domain as Administrator.

   A **Logon Message** dialog box appears, stating that a domain controller could not be found.

   Why does this message appear?

   Your computer does not have an IP address and therefore cannot communicate with other computers.

5. Start a command prompt, type **ipconfig /all** to view the IP configuration.

   What is the IP address? Why?

   The IP address is 0.0.0.0 because the DHCP server is disabled, so no IP address was assigned.

Page 389

▸ **To renew a DHCP lease**

2. Type **ipconfig /all** and then press ENTER.

   When does the lease expire?

   Approximately 24 hours from the current time.

Page 399

▸ **To test the configuration of the DHCP server to assign WINS server addresses**

3. Type **ipconfig /all** and then press ENTER to view your IP addressing information.

   What is the address of the primary WINS server?

   It is the IP address of the \\SERVER1 DHCP server.

   What is the node type?

   It is hybrid, indicating that it is h-node.

4. Type **ping server1** and then press ENTER.

   Why were you successful in pinging a NetBIOS computer name?

   The WINS server resolved the NetBIOS name to its IP address.

Page 409

▸ **To resolve an IP address using DNS**

2. Type **ping work1** and then press ENTER.

   What IP address did it return?

   Your workstation's address.

Review Answers

Page 419

1. How do you install Windows NT network services?

   From the Network program in Control Panel, click the Services tab, and then click Add. Select the required service and then click OK.

2. What role does the DHCP Server service play in the Windows NT networking environment?

   It automatically assigns IP addresses to computers, eliminating common configuration problems that can occur when manually configuring TCP/IP.

3. Explain how the DHCP Server service assigns an IP address.

   The client sends out a request. Each of the DHCP servers that receives the request selects an address from the pool of addresses defined in its database and offers the address to the client. The client then accepts one of the offers, and the IP address is leased for a specific period of time.

4. Your new computer running Windows NT Workstation cannot view or access any network resources. You have tried pinging other hosts unsuccessfully. Upon examining your TCP/IP configuration, you discover that your IP address is 0.0.0.0, even though it is a DHCP client. What do you suspect is the cause of the problem?

   Either a DHCP server is unavailable or all IP addresses in the scope for your subnet are already being leased.

5. You are experiencing duplicate IP addressing problems. When you troubleshoot the problems, you discover that you accidentally assigned the same IP address to multiple scopes. Why did this create a problem?

   Because the same address is being leased by multiple computers.

6. What roles do WINS and DNS services play in the networking environment, and how do they differ?

   Both WINS and DNS are name resolution services.

   WINS is used to register NetBIOS computer names and resolve them to IP addresses. The WINS database is updated automatically.

   The DNS service is used to resolve fully qualified domain names to IP addresses. DNS computer names consist of two parts, a host name and a domain name, which together form the fully qualified domain name. The DNS database is static.

7. Explain the advantages of integrating WINS and DNS.

   It significantly decreases the administrative burden of updating DNS zone changes. The integration creates a dynamic DNS service that takes advantage of the best features of both DNS and WINS.

8. You have a Windows NT network with TCP/IP as the only protocol available on your network. You have a computer running Windows NT Workstation that is configured to use DNS and WINS. Although you can connect to the computers running Windows NT Server in your domain, you are unable to **ftp** to any UNIX host on your network using the UNIX host's host name. What do you suspect is the cause of the problem?

   The DNS server is either unavailable or does not contain a resource record for the UNIX host. Because DNS is not dynamic, you must manually enter resource records for your hosts. Connections to computers running Windows NT are successful because these connections use WINS, not DNS.

CHAPTER 12

Implementing Remote Access Service

About This Chapter

This chapter introduces you to Microsoft Windows NT *Remote Access Service* (RAS). When RAS is installed on Windows NT Server, clients can connect over telephone lines through the Remote Access Service to a remote network. The RAS server acts as a gateway between the remote client and the network. After a user has made a connection, the telephone lines become transparent to the user, and the user can access all network resources as if sitting at a computer in an office that is directly attached to the network. For example, RAS makes a modem act like a network adapter card, projecting your remote computer onto a local area network (LAN).

In Windows NT version 4.0, RAS on the client side is called *Dial-Up Networking* and has a user interface that is consistent with Microsoft Windows 95. Thus, RAS is installed on Windows NT servers and Dial-Up Networking is installed on clients.

You will learn the basic operation of Windows NT RAS and Dial-Up Networking, as well as how to install and configure the key components that are required to support remote networks.

Before You Begin

To complete the lessons in this chapter, you must have:

- Two computers that meet the hardware and software requirements as specified in the Getting Started section of "About This Book."
- Completed all practices in Chapter 2, "Installing Windows NT."

Lesson 1: RAS and Dial-Up Networking

RAS and Dial-Up Networking enable you to extend your network beyond a single location and meet the diverse business needs of remote and mobile employees.

- RAS enables incoming connections from remote clients that are using Dial-Up Networking or other Point-to-Point Protocol (PPP) or Serial Line Internet Protocol (SLIP) dial-up software.
- Dial-Up Networking provides low-speed connections and is used by clients connecting to a RAS server or Internet service provider (ISP).

After this lesson, you will be able to:

- Describe the purpose of RAS and Dial-Up Networking.
- Explain the WAN support included in RAS.
- Identify the remote access protocols that are included in RAS.
- Explain the function of the NetBIOS gateway and routers.
- Describe the Point-to-Point Tunneling Protocol.
- Explain the security features included with RAS.

Estimated lesson time: 40 minutes

Using Windows NT RAS and Dial-Up Networking, a business can extend its networks over Public Switched Telephone Networks (PSTN), Integrated Services Digital Networks (ISDN), X.25, and the Internet. RAS provides an organization with a standards-based, remote networking system that supports computing for remote clients.

Because RAS supports wide area network (WAN) connections, protocols, and Windows NT security features, remote clients can use the network as if they were directly connected to it.

The following illustration lists some of the principal features of RAS and illustrates the resources that are made available to the Dial-Up Networking client.

- **WAN Connectivity**
- **Remote Access Protocols**
- **Gateways and Routers**
- **Point-to-Point Tunneling Protocol (PPTP)**
- **RAS Security Features**

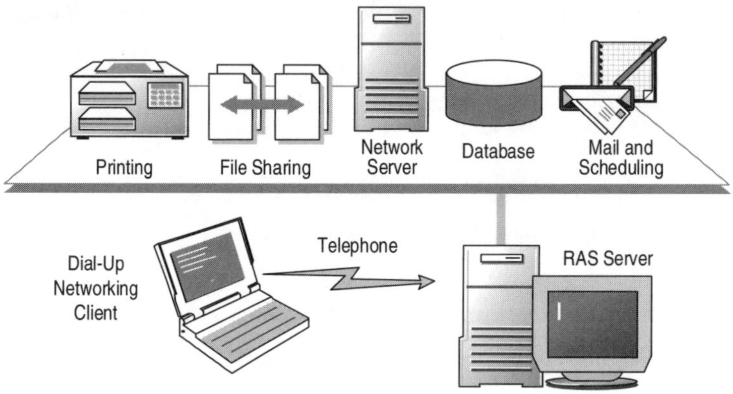

Furthermore, with Dial-Up Networking installed, clients can use the phonebook feature of Dial-Up Networking to record telephone numbers that are needed to connect to remote networks.

WAN Connectivity

Remote clients can connect directly to a RAS server through a Public Switched Telephone Network (PSTN), X.25 network, or Integrated Services Digital Network (ISDN). They may also connect remotely over a TCP/IP (Transmission Control Protocol/Internet Protocol) network, such as the Internet, using the Point-to-Point Tunneling Protocol (PPTP).

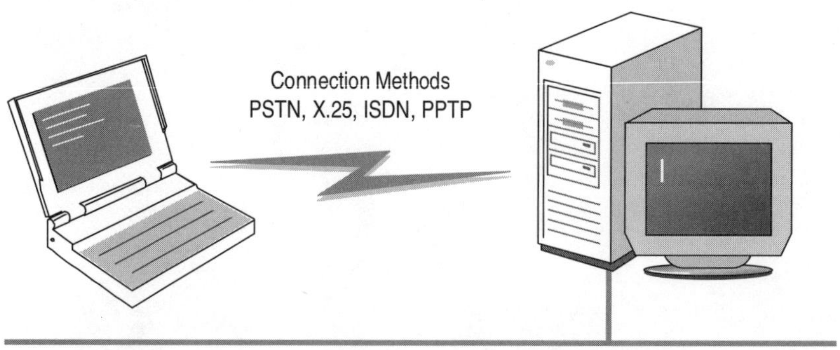

Public Switched Telephone Networks and Modems

Windows NT RAS uses standard modem connections over Public Switched Telephone Networks (PSTNs). A key advantage of PSTN is worldwide availability.

Most modems that comply with industry standards can interoperate with other modems. However, many difficult-to-diagnose problems can result from incompatible modems.

Windows NT can automatically detect modems. This is especially useful for remote clients, when users are not sure which modem is installed (for example, if their computer has an internal modem installed). If there is a problem detecting a modem automatically, it is possible to install a modem manually through the Modems program in Control Panel.

Integrated Services Digital Network

Integrated Services Digital Network (ISDN) is a digital system that offers much faster communication speed than a PSTN, communicating at speeds of 64 kilobits per second (Kbps) or faster. ISDN lines must be installed at both the server and remote site. ISDN requires that an ISDN adapter be installed in both the server and the remote client.

X.25

An X.25 network transmits data with a packet-switching protocol. This protocol relies on data communications equipment (DCEs), an elaborate worldwide network of packet-forwarding nodes that participate in delivering an X.25 packet to its designated address, for example, a modem.

Dial-Up Networking clients can directly access an X.25 network by using an X.25 packet assembler/disassembler (PAD). Dial-Up asynchronous PADs constitute a practical choice for remote access clients because they do not require an X.25 line plugged into the back of the computer. Their only requirement is the telephone number of the PAD service for the carrier.

RAS provides access to the X.25 network in one of two ways, depending on the operating systems involved.

Client/server	Configuration
Client (for Windows 95 or Windows NT operating systems)	Asynchronous packet assemblers/disassemblers (PADs)
Server and client (for Windows NT systems only)	Direct connection to the X.25 network through an X.25 smart card

Note The ISDN adapter and the X.25 adapter are treated as network adapter cards, thereby giving remote computers a direct data feed across a WAN to the LAN.

Packet Assemblers/Disassemblers

The PAD converts serially transmitted data into X.25 packets. When the PAD receives a packet from an X.25 network, it puts the packet out on a serial line making communication possible between the client and the X.25 network.

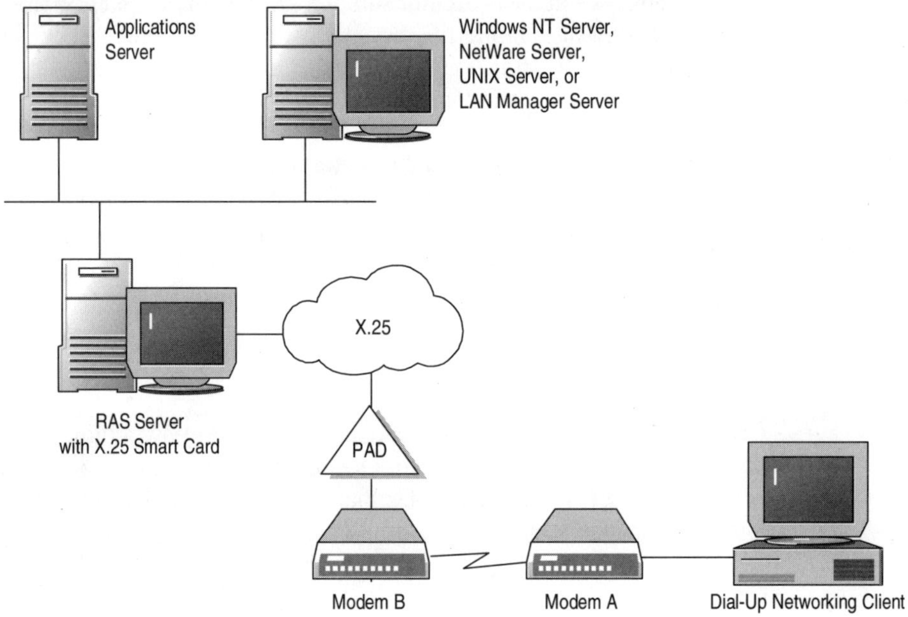

Smart Cards

An X.25 smart card is a hardware card with a PAD embedded in it. The smart card acts like a modem. To the personal computer, a smart card looks like several communication ports attached to PADs.

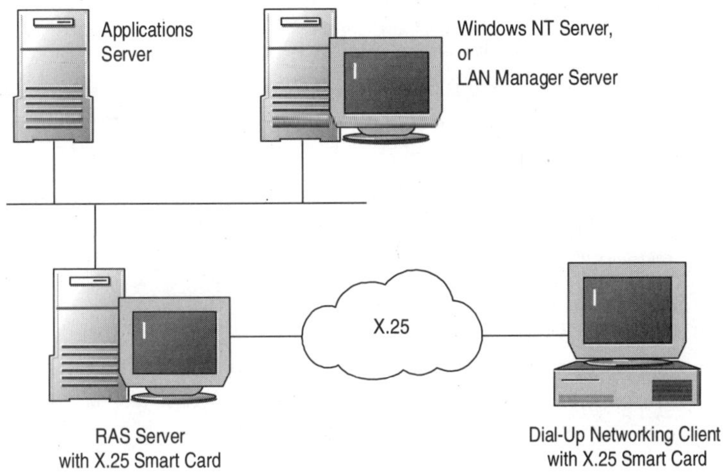

Point-to-Point Tunneling Protocol

Point-to-Point Tunneling Protocol (PPTP) is a technology that supports multiprotocol virtual private networks (VPNs). This support enables you to remotely access your corporate network securely across the Internet. Using PPTP, you establish a connection to the Internet and then establish a connection to the RAS server on the Internet using PPTP.

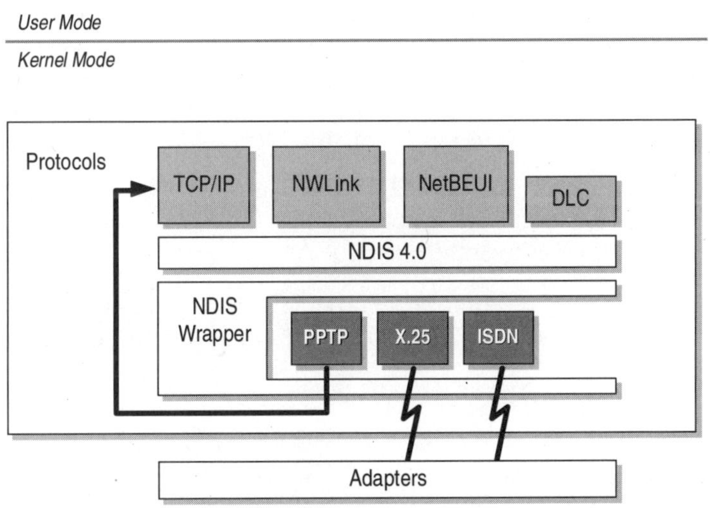

PPTP Advantages

Using PPTP to connect to a remote network offers computers running Windows NT the following advantages:

- *Lower Transmission Costs.* If you have local access through an Internet Service Provider (ISP), access to the remote network will be less expensive than a long-distance telephone call or using an 800 number.
- *Lower Hardware Costs.* If PPTP is used, a RAS server needs only a connection to the Internet. It is not necessary for the RAS server to have multiple modems, ISDN, or X.25 cards.
- *Lower Administrative Overhead.* With PPTP in Windows NT 4.0, you manage and secure your network at the RAS server. You need to manage only the user accounts and RAS dial-in permissions.
- *Security.* PPTP provides security through data encryption. A PPTP connection over the Internet is encrypted and works with the NetBEUI, TCP/IP, and IPX protocols. Data sent by means of a PPTP tunnel consists of encapsulated PPP packets. If Dial-Up Networking is configured to use data encryption, the data sent by means of PPTP is encrypted when sent.

How PPTP Works

PPTP provides a way to route IP, IPX, or NetBEUI PPP packets over a TCP/IP network. Because PPTP allows multiprotocol encapsulation, any of these packets can be sent over the TCP/IP network.

PPTP treats the existing corporate network as a PSTN, ISDN, or X.25 network. This virtual WAN is supported through public carriers, such as the Internet.

Comparing PPTP to Other WAN Protocols

When using PSTN, ISDN, or X.25, a remote access client establishes a PPP connection with a RAS server over a switched network. After the connection is established, PPP packets are sent over the switched connection to the RAS servers to be routed to the destination LAN.

In contrast, when using PPTP instead of a switched connection to send packets over the WAN, a transport protocol such as TCP/IP is used to send the PPP packets to the RAS server over the virtual WAN.

The resulting benefit for the corporation is a savings in transmission costs by using the Internet rather than long distance dial-up connections.

PPTP Access Over the Internet

A Dial-Up Networking client that has a PPTP driver as its WAN driver can connect to a Windows NT 4.0 RAS server using the Internet by either connecting directly to the Internet or calling an ISP.

If a direct connection to the Internet is required, the client must have a PPTP driver, and the RAS server must have a PPTP-enabled adapter.

If an ISP provides the connection, and the ISP's Point of Presence (POP) supports PPTP, then PPTP does not have to be installed on the client. (A POP is a physical site in a geographical area where an ISP has equipment to which users connect to get access to the Internet. This is typically done by dialing in over a modem and telephone line.) The client establishes a connection to the ISP and calls the Windows NT RAS server to establish the PPTP tunnel.

Note For more information about PPTP, see Appendix D, "Using the Point-to-Point Tunneling Protocol."

Protocols

You learned about Windows NT protocols in Chapter 10, "Configuring Windows NT Protocols." This discussion will focus upon the protocols that are specifically relevant to RAS, including which protocols to install, and their implications in implementing RAS.

Protocols supported by RAS can be examined according to their functions: those protocols that transmit data over LANs and those that transmit data over WANs. Windows NT supports LAN protocols such as TCP/IP, IPX/SPX, NWLink, and NetBEUI; and remote access protocols such as PPP, SLIP, and the Microsoft RAS protocol.

The Microsoft RAS protocol is a proprietary remote access protocol supporting the NetBIOS standard. The Microsoft RAS protocol is supported in all previous versions of Microsoft RAS and is used on Windows NT version 3.1, Windows for Workgroups, MS-DOS, and LAN Manager clients. A RAS client dialing in to an older version of Windows (for example, Windows NT version 3.1 or Windows for Workgroups) must use the NetBEUI protocol. The RAS server then acts as a "gateway" for the remote client, providing access to servers that use the NetBEUI, TCP/IP, or IPX protocols.

LAN Protocols

Windows NT RAS supports NetBEUI, TCP/IP, and IPX. Thus, you can integrate Windows NT RAS into existing Microsoft, UNIX, or NetWare networks using the PPP remote access standard. Windows NT RAS clients can also connect to existing SLIP-based remote access servers (primarily UNIX servers).

When you install and configure RAS, any protocols already installed on the computer (such as NetBEUI, TCP/IP, and IPX) are automatically enabled for RAS.

Remote Access Protocols

RAS connections can be established through SLIP or PPP.

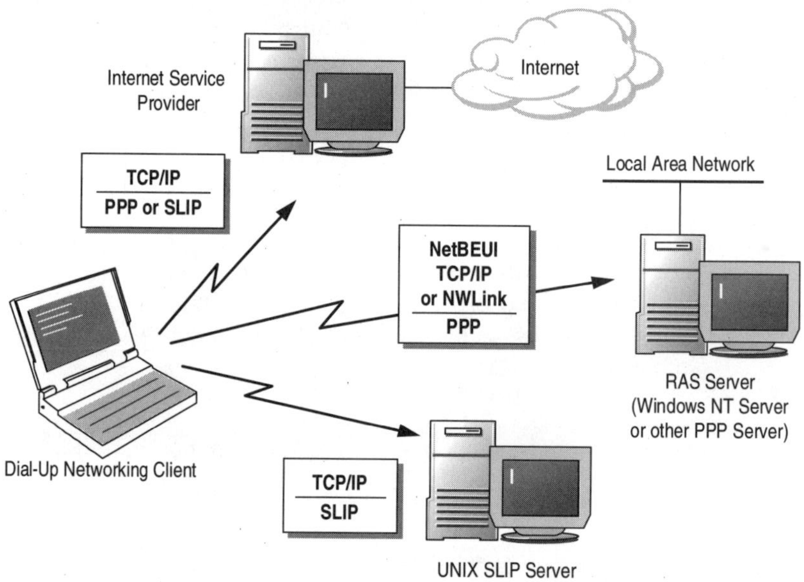

Serial Line Internet Protocol

Serial Line Internet Protocol (SLIP) is an industry standard that addresses TCP/IP connections made over serial lines. SLIP was first developed in 1984 to support TCP/IP networking over low-speed serial interfaces. SLIP is supported by Windows NT Dial-Up Networking and gives Windows NT clients easier access to Internet services.

SLIP has several limitations when compared to the newer Point-to-Point Protocol (PPP). SLIP servers cannot utilize DHCP/WINS. SLIP connections typically rely on text-based logon sessions and usually require a scripting system to automate the logon process. Although SLIP supports TCP/IP, it does not support IPX/SPX or NetBEUI. In addition, unlike PPP, SLIP transmits authentication passwords as clear text, thereby making the system less secure.

Note Windows NT RAS server does not have a SLIP server component, so it cannot be used as a SLIP server.

Point-to-Point Protocol

The Point-to-Point Protocol (PPP) was designed as an enhancement to the original SLIP specification. PPP is a set of industry standard framing and authentication protocols that enable RAS clients and servers to interoperate in a multivendor network. It provides a standard method of sending network data over a point-to-point link. PPP supports several protocols, including AppleTalk, DECnet, Open Systems Interconnection (OSI), NetBEUI, TCP/IP, and IPX. Windows NT supports NetBEUI, TCP/IP, and IPX.

Windows NT Protocol Support Over PPP

PPP support enables computers running Windows NT to dial in to remote networks through any server that complies with the PPP standard. PPP compliance also enables a computer running Windows NT Server to receive calls from, and provide access to, other vendors' remote access software.

The PPP architecture enables clients to load any combination of NetBEUI, TCP/IP, and IPX. Applications written to the Windows Sockets (WinSock), NetBIOS, or IPX interface can be run on a remote computer running Windows NT Workstation.

Supporting TCP/IP makes Windows NT "Internet ready," and allows remote clients to access the Internet through WinSock applications.

RAS clients that have both the IPX interface and Client Service for NetWare (CSNW) installed can access NetWare servers.

RAS clients that do *not* have CSNW installed can still access a NetWare server if Gateway Services for NetWare (GSNW) is installed on a RAS server. The RAS server then functions as a gateway to a NetWare server. In this case, IPX is not required.

RAS Setup automatically binds to NetBEUI, TCP/IP, and IPX if they are already installed on the computer when RAS is installed. After RAS is installed, each protocol can be configured separately for use with RAS.

PPP Multilink Protocol

The PPP Multilink Protocol (MP) provides the means to increase data transmission rates. MP accomplishes this by combining multiple physical links into a logical bundle to increase bandwidth. Based on the Internet Engineering Task Force (IETF) standard RFC 1717, RAS using PPP Multilink Protocol lets you easily combine analog modem paths, ISDN paths, and even mixed analog and digital communications links on both your client and server computers. For example, a client with two 28.8 Kbps modems and two PSTN lines can use MP to establish a single 57.6 Kbps connection to an MP server. This will speed up your access to the Internet or to your intranet, and cut down on the amount of time you have to be remotely connected, thus reducing your costs for remote access.

Both the Dial-Up Networking client and RAS server need to have MP enabled for this protocol to be used.

Remote access protocol standards are defined in RFCs, which are published by the IETF and other working groups. The RFCs supported in this version of Windows NT RAS are listed in the following table.

Request for Comment	Subject
RFC 1662	PPP in HDLC-like Framing
RFC 1552	The PPP Internetwork Packet Exchange Control Protocol (IPXCP)
RFC 1334	PPP Authentication Protocols
RFC 1332	The PPP Internet Protocol Control Protocol (IPCP)
RFC 1661	Link Control Protocol (LCP)
RFC 1717	PPP Multilink Protocol
RFC 1144	Compressing TCP/IP Headers for Low-Speed Serial Links
RFC 1055	A Nonstandard for Transmission of IP Datagrams Over Serial Lines: SLIP

Gateways and Routers

Windows NT RAS can act as a gateway or router in several situations.

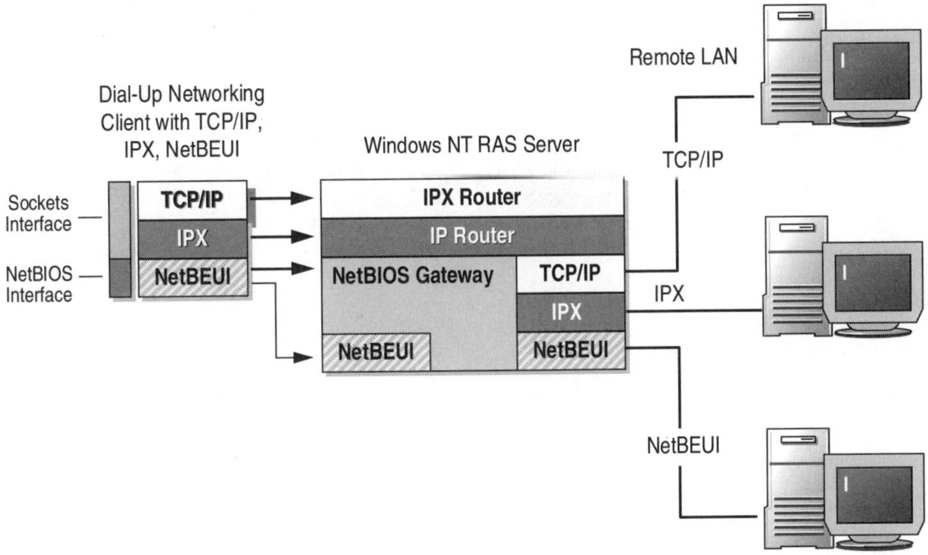

NetBIOS Gateway

Windows NT RAS includes a NetBIOS gateway that enables remote clients to access NetBIOS resources, such as file and print services, on a network. This enables clients running NetBEUI to access remote servers regardless of which protocol is installed on the remote server. The NetBIOS gateway does this by translating the NetBEUI packets into IPX or TCP/IP formats that can be understood by remote servers.

IP and IPX Routers

Windows NT enhances the RAS architecture by adding IP and IPX router capabilities. RAS servers that have IP and IPX routers installed can perform the following functions:

- Act as a router to link LANs and WANs.
- Connect LANs that have different network topologies such as Ethernet and Token Ring.

In addition, a RAS server can be an IPX router and Service Advertising Protocol (SAP) agent for Dial-Up Networking clients. SAP is similar in functionality to the Windows NT Browser service. Once configured, RAS servers enable remote clients to access NetWare file and print services, and to take advantage of Windows Sockets applications.

RAS Security Features

Windows NT RAS implements a number of security measures to validate remote client access to a network.

Integrated Domain Security

Windows NT Server provides for enterprise-wide security using a trusted domain, single-network logon model. This eliminates the need for duplicate user accounts across a multiple-server network. The single-network logon model extends to RAS users. The RAS server uses the same user account database as the computer running Windows NT. This allows easier administration, because clients can log on with the same user accounts that they use at the office. This feature ensures that clients have the same privileges and permissions they ordinarily have while in the office.

To connect to a RAS server, clients must have a valid Windows NT user account as well as the RAS dial-in permission. Clients must first be authenticated by RAS before they can log on to Windows NT.

Encrypted Authentication and Logon Process

By default, all authentication and logon information is encrypted when transmitted over RAS. However, it is possible to allow any authentication method, including clear text. In addition, it is possible to configure RAS and Dial-Up Networking so that all data that passes between a client and server is encrypted.

Auditing

With auditing enabled, RAS generates audit information on all remote connections, including processes such as authentication and logging on.

Intermediary Security Hosts

It is possible to add another level of security to a RAS configuration by connecting a third-party intermediary security host between the RAS client or clients and the RAS server or servers. When an intermediary security host is used, clients must type a password or code to get past the security device before a connection is established with the RAS server.

Callback Security

The RAS server can be configured to provide callbacks as a means of increasing security. When callback security is used, the server receives the call from the client computer, disconnects the connection, and then calls the client back either at a preset telephone number or at a number that was provided during the initial call. This allows another level of security by guaranteeing that the connection to the local network was made from a trusted site, such as a branch office.

PPTP Filtering

When using PPTP, the RAS server must have a direct connection to the Internet and a company's corporate network. This could pose a security risk because the corporate network could be accessed through the RAS server. Use PPTP filtering to help ensure security on a corporate network. When PPTP filtering is enabled, all protocols other than PPTP will be disabled on the selected network adapter card.

Note The following steps are presented for informational purposes only and are not intended to be completed as a practice.

To enable PPTP filtering, you would do the following:

1. Click the **Start** button, point to **Settings**, and click **Control Panel**.
2. Double-click the Network icon in Control Panel.
3. Click the **Protocols** tab.
4. Click **TCP/IP Protocols**, and then click the **Properties** button.
5. Click the **IP Address** tab in the **Microsoft TCP/IP Properties** dialog box.
6. Click the **Advanced** button.
7. Select the **Enable PPTP Filtering** check box in the **Advanced IP Addressing** dialog box.

   PPTP filtering would now be enabled.

Lesson 2: Telephony API

The Windows NT Telephony API (TAPI) provides a standard way for communications applications to control telephony functions for data, fax, and voice calls. TAPI virtualizes the telephone system by acting as a device driver for a telephone network. TAPI manages all signaling between a computer and a telephone network, including such basic functions as establishing, answering, and terminating calls. It can also include supplementary functions such as hold, transfer, conference, and call park, found in Private Branch Exchanges (PBXs), ISDN, and other telephone systems.

After this lesson, you will be able to:

- Describe the function of TAPI.
- Describe the TAPI settings.
- Configure a TAPI location.

Estimated lesson time: 10 minutes

TAPI Settings

TAPI allows you to centrally configure your computer for local dialing parameters. The basic TAPI settings for a system are set up when a TAPI-aware program is run for the first time. Dial-Up Networking is a TAPI-aware application. If a TAPI-aware application has not been run, the TAPI configuration will be automatically installed when you install Dial-Up Networking.

Location Setup

A *location* in Windows NT Dial-Up Networking is a set of information that TAPI uses to analyze telephone numbers in international number format, and to determine the correct sequence of numbers to be dialed. A location does not need to correspond to a particular geographic location, although it usually does. A location could include the special numbers needed to dial out from an office or hotel room. Locations can be named anything that is helpful for remembering them later.

Location information includes:

- Area (or city) code.
- Country code.
- Outside line access codes, for both local and long distance calls.
- Preferred calling card.

Calling Card

TAPI uses calling cards to create the sequence of numbers to be dialed for a particular card. The number is stored in scrambled form and will not be displayed once it is entered. This is a security feature that is used to prevent unauthorized access to the number. Multiple calling cards can be defined.

Drivers

TAPI drivers, also known as TAPI Service Providers (TSPs), are software components that control TAPI hardware (for example, a PBX, voice mail card, telephone system, or other equipment). Usually, TAPI drivers are installed with the TAPI hardware. However, the TAPI driver for modems (Unimodem.tsp) is automatically installed with the operating system.

Note All TAPI Service Providers (TSPs) run in the same memory space, so it is possible for a malfunctioning TSP to affect other TSPs.

Configuring a TAPI Location

You can configure a single TAPI location and use it from any TAPI-aware application.

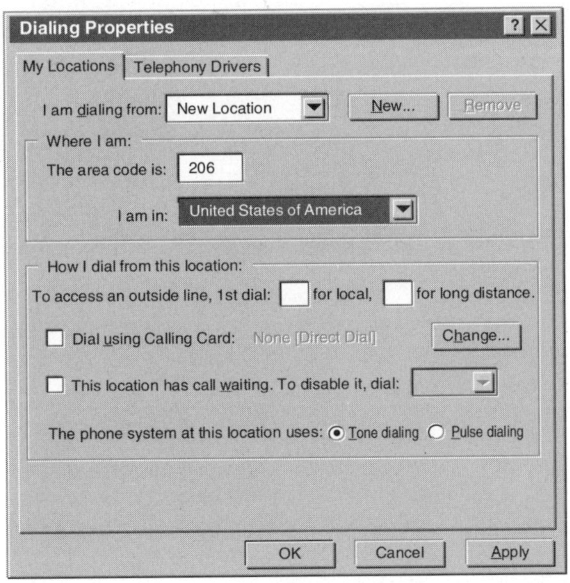

Preparing a computer running Windows NT to use TAPI involves configuring a TAPI location. Configure TAPI locations through the **Dialing Properties** dialog box accessible through the **Telephony** program in Control Panel. This **Dialing Properties** dialog box contains tabs through which various TAPI options can be configured.

The following table lists the configuration options available through the **My Locations** tab in the **Dialing Properties** dialog box.

Option	Use this option to
I am dialing from list and **New** button:	List the locations that are currently set up. To set up an additional location, click **New**.
The area code is	Enter the area code for the TAPI location. If the location is in a country other than the United States, type the city code, without leading 0(s). For example, if the city code is 071, type 71.
I am in	Select the current country name.
To access an outside line	Type the number(s) required to access an outside line for local and long distance calls. In many cases, these two numbers will be the same. If no number is required to access an outside line, leave both spaces blank.
Dial using Calling Card	Specify that the displayed calling card will be used when calling from this location. In the preceding illustration, a calling card has not been specified.
Change button	Change the calling card to be used for this location.
This location has call waiting. To disable it, dial	Specify whether this location uses call waiting. Call waiting should be turned off when dialing from a computer. Contact the local telephone company for information about how to disable call waiting.
The phone system at this location uses	Specify either tone or pulse dialing.

Lesson 3: Installing and Configuring RAS

RAS can be installed either during or after the installation of Windows NT 4.0. If you select "Remote access to the network" during setup, both RAS and Dial-Up Networking will be automatically installed. You can install either one or both services manually after installation. This lesson will cover the installation and configuration of RAS on Server1.

After this lesson, you will be able to:

- Install RAS software.
- Use the automatic modem detection feature of RAS.
- Configure the RAS server to support the various protocols.
- Grant RAS permission to clients.

Estimated lesson time: 50 minutes

Installing RAS

Whether you install RAS during Windows NT installation or later through the Network program in Control Panel, RAS requires the following information for installation:

- The model of modem that will be used.
- The type of communication port to use for the RAS connection.
- Whether this computer will be used to dial in, dial out, or both.
- The protocols to be used.
- Any modem settings such as baud or Kbps rate.
- Security settings including callback.

Note Windows NT 4.0 Server supports 256 simultaneous inbound RAS connections, while Windows NT 4.0 Workstation supports only one.

Configuring a RAS Server

Configuring a RAS server differs from configuring Dial-Up Networking clients. While Dial-Up Networking clients are configured primarily to dial in to remote networks, RAS servers are configured to provide access to network services for these clients. RAS server configuration involves configuring communication ports, network protocols (such as NetBEUI, TCP/IP, and IPX), and encryption settings.

The first step in configuring a RAS server is to specify the hardware that RAS will use, including the type of modem and the port to which the modem will be connected. In the following illustration, the modem is a Hayes Optima 288 V.34 and it is connected to COM1.

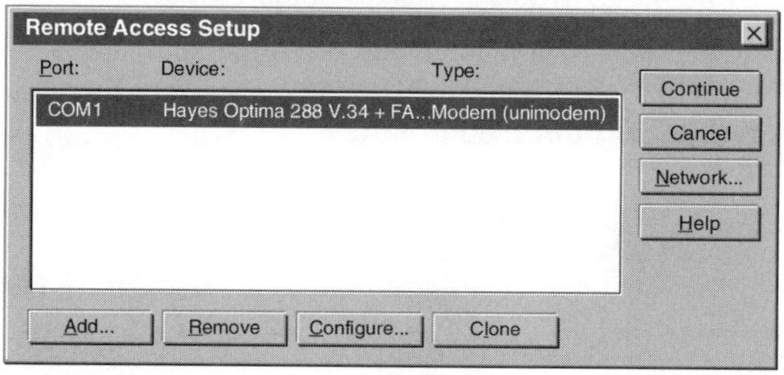

The drivers and ports used by RAS servers are configured through the **Remote Access Setup** dialog box. To access this dialog box, start the Network program in Control Panel. Click the **Services** tab and select the Remote Access Service. Then click the **Properties** button. The **Remote Access Setup** dialog box appears. The following table lists the configuration options available through this dialog box.

Option	Use this option to
Add	Make a port available to RAS and install a modem or X.25 PAD.
Remove	Make a port unavailable to RAS.
Configure	Change the RAS settings for the port, such as the attached device or the intended usage (dialing out only, receiving calls only, or both).
Clone	Copy the same modem setup from one port to another.
Network	Configure network protocol, Multilink, and encryption settings.

RAS Server Port Configuration Options

Click the **Configure** button in the **Remote Access Service** dialog box to configure the RAS server ports. The following illustration shows a possible configuration.

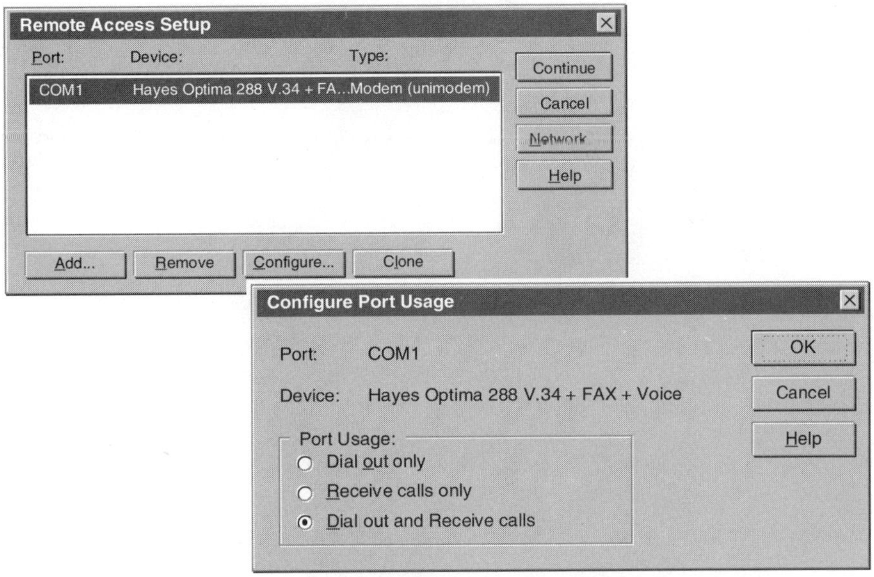

The following table explains the options listed in the **Configure Port Usage** dialog box.

Option	Use this option to enable
Dial out only	Dial-Up Networking clients to use that port to initiate calls.
Receive calls only	RAS servers to receive calls from Dial-Up Networking clients on that port.
Dial out and Receive calls	RAS servers to use that port for either Dial-Up Networking client or server functions.

Port configuration options affect only the specified port. For example, if the server's COM1 port is configured to receive calls and the COM2 port is configured to dial out and receive calls, a remote client could call in on either COM port, but a local user could only use COM2 for outbound RAS calls.

Once you select the appropriate Port Usage option, click **OK** and the **Remote Access Setup** dialog box reappears.

Configuring Protocols on the Server

Click the **Network** button in the **Remote Access Setup** dialog box, and the **Network Configuration** dialog box appears. In the following illustration, one of the dial-out options has been selected and all three protocols are being used.

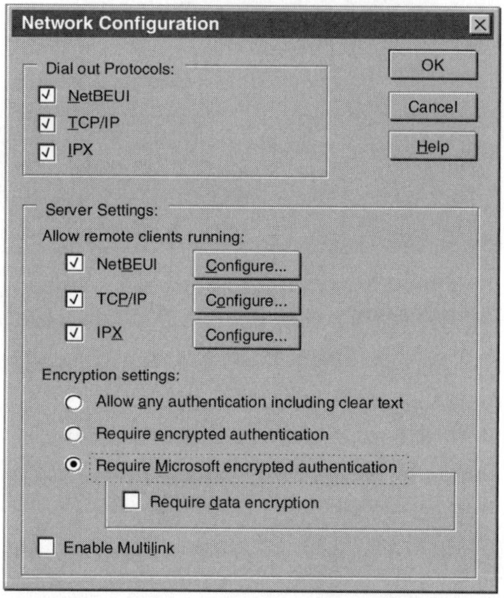

Note In the preceding illustration, the **Enable Multilink** check box is only available on computers running Windows NT Server.

Use the **Network Configuration** dialog box to select and configure the LAN protocols. Network protocol configuration applies to RAS operations on all RAS-enabled ports.

The following table describes the protocol configuration options available through the **Network Configuration** dialog box.

Options	Use this option to
Dial out Protocols	Select the dial-out protocols.
Server Settings	Select and configure the protocols the RAS server can use for servicing remote clients.
Encryption settings	Select an authentication level ranging from clear text for down level clients to Microsoft Encrypted Authentication for Windows NT and Windows 95 clients. If **Require Microsoft encrypted authentication** is selected, **Require data encryption** can also be selected.
Enable Multilink	Enable the Dial-Up Networking PPP Multilink Protocol. To use Multilink, both the client and the server must have Multilink enabled.

Note The next lesson provides an explanation of how Dial-Up Networking clients enable the Multilink Protocol.

Configuring a RAS Server to Use NetBEUI

If the NetBEUI protocol has been installed, the RAS Setup enables NetBEUI and the NetBIOS gateway by default. RAS servers use NetBEUI to provide remote clients with access to small workgroups or department-sized LANs.

To configure a RAS server to use NetBEUI, in the **Network Configuration** dialog box, make sure that NetBEUI is selected and then click **Configure** next to **NetBEUI**. The **RAS Server NetBEUI Configuration** dialog box appears.

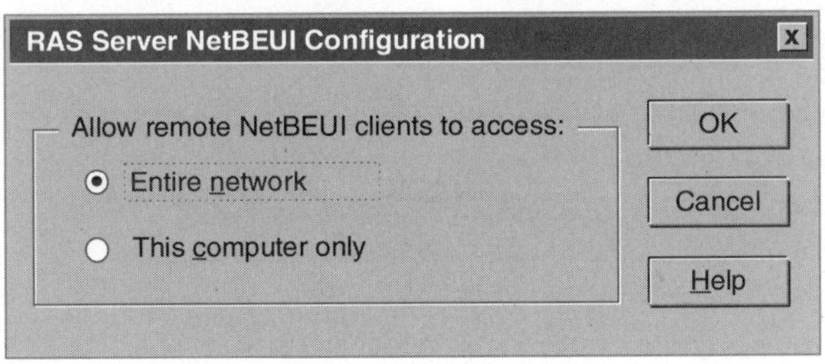

Use the **RAS Server NetBEUI Configuration** dialog box to allow remote NetBEUI clients to access:

- **Entire network**. This option grants remote clients permission to access resources on the network.
- **This computer only**. This option grants remote clients permission to access only the resources on the RAS server.

Configuring a RAS Server to Use TCP/IP

Servers can be configured to support not only Microsoft clients but also PPP clients from other vendors.

Dial-Up Networking clients and servers are assigned to the same WINS and DNS servers. Also, Dial-Up Networking clients in small networks where IP addresses do not change can use a Hosts or Lmhosts file for name resolution.

To configure a RAS server to use TCP/IP, on the **Network Configuration** dialog box, make sure that TCP/IP is selected and then click **Configure** next to **TCP/IP**. The **RAS Server TCP/IP Configuration** dialog box appears.

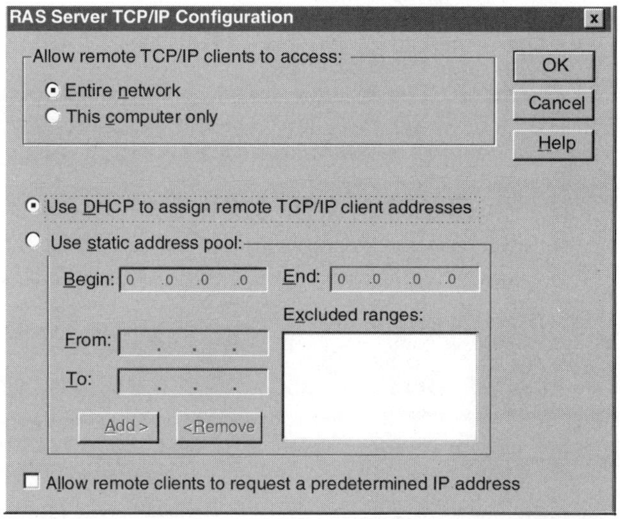

Use the **RAS Server TCP/IP Configuration** dialog box to grant network access permissions and IP addresses to Dial-Up Networking clients. The following table describes the configuration options available through this dialog box.

Option	Use this option to
Allow remote TCP/IP clients to access	Allow Dial-Up Networking clients to access the **Entire network** or the **This computer only** options.
Use DHCP to assign remote TCP/IP client addresses	Use a DHCP server to dynamically assign an IP address to a Dial Up Networking client. Dial-Up Networking clients require an IP address to communicate on TCP/IP networks.
Use static address pool	Configure the IP address range. Designate beginning and ending values for the IP address range. Use the Add and Remove buttons to exclude any IP addresses that are not to be used.
Allow remote clients to request a pre-determined IP address	Enable Dial-Up Networking clients to request a predetermined IP address.

Configuring a RAS Server to Use IPX

Use the **RAS Server IPX Configuration** dialog box to grant remote IPX clients access to the network and to allocate network numbers.

To configure a RAS server to use IPX, on the **Network Configuration** dialog box, make sure that IPX is selected. Click **Configure** next to **IPX**, and the **RAS Server IPX Configuration** dialog box appears.

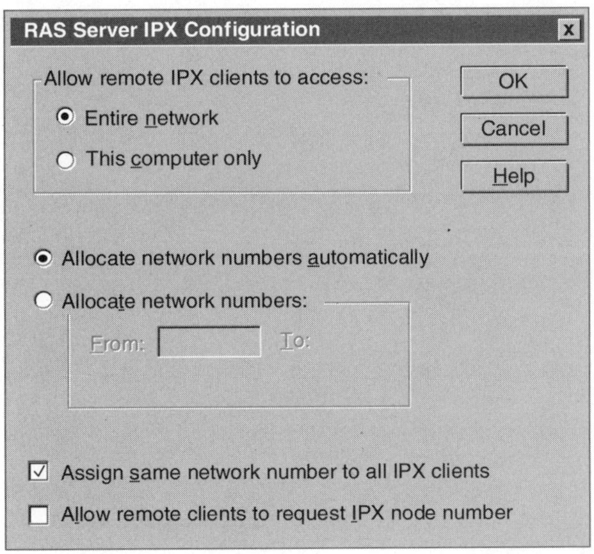

Dial-Up Networking clients can access Novell NetWare server file and print sharing resources through RAS servers that support IPX.

Use the **RAS Server IPX Configuration** dialog box to grant network access permissions and allocate Novell network numbers to Dial-Up Networking clients. The following table outlines the configuration options available through this dialog box.

Option	Use this option to
Allow remote IPX clients to access	Allow Dial-Up Networking clients to access the **Entire network** or **This computer only**.
Allocate network numbers automatically	Assign network numbers automatically to Dial-Up Networking clients. The same network number can be assigned to all IPX clients.
Allocate network numbers	Assign network numbers manually to Dial-Up Networking clients.
Assign same network number to all IPX clients	Assign a single network number to all IPX clients. Only one network number will be added to your routing table for all active Dial-Up Networking clients.
Allow remote clients to request IPX node number	Enable Dial-Up Networking clients to request an IPX node number rather than use the node number assigned by the RAS server.

Practice

In these procedures, you install RAS and configure it to use a serial modem cable.

Note Complete these procedures on Server1, logged on as Administrator.

▸ To prepare to install RAS

1. Log on as Administrator.
2. In Control Panel, double-click the Network icon.
3. Install NetBEUI Protocol and NWLink IPX/SPX Compatible Transport.
4. Shut down and then restart Server1 for your changes to take effect.

▸ To install RAS

1. Log on as Administrator.
2. In Control Panel, double-click the Network icon.
3. Click the **Services** tab, and then click **Add**.
4. In the **Select Network Service** dialog box, click **Remote Access Service**, and then click **OK**.

5. When prompted for the path to the distribution files, type **\\Server1\Nts_source\I386** and then click **Continue**.

   A **Remote Access Setup** dialog box appears, asking if you want RAS Setup to invoke the modem installer.

6. Click **Yes**.

   The Install New Modem wizard appears.

7. Select the **Don't detect my modem, I will select it from a list** check box, and then click **Next**.

   The Install New Modem wizard continues.

8. Under **Manufacturers**, click **(Standard Modem Types)**. Under **Models**, click **Dial-Up Networking Serial Cable between 2 PCs**, and then click **Next**.

   The Install New Modem wizard continues.

9. Click **Selected ports**, click **COM1**, and then click **Next**.

Important If COM1 is already in use on your computer and is therefore not available, you must select an available COM port. All other references to COM1 in these procedures would have to change to the selected COM port.

Note If you have already configured TAPI, you will not be prompted for the options in steps 10–13.

---

10. In the **Location Information** dialog box, select the appropriate country under **What country are you in now?**
11. In the **What area (or city) code are you in now?** box, type your area or city code.
12. If you are in a location where you need to dial a number or numbers to access an outside line, type in the appropriate number(s) in the specified box.
13. Click **Tone dialing** or **Pulse dialing**, depending on your telephone.
14. Click **Next**.
15. Click **Finish**.

    The **Add RAS Device** dialog box appears. You should see **COM1-Dial-Up Networking Serial Cable between 2 PCs** in the **RAS Capable Devices:** box.

16. Click **OK**.

    The **Remote Access Setup** dialog box appears. You have finished installing RAS, and will complete the configuration in the next practice.

▸ To configure RAS

Note Complete this procedure on Server1, logged on as Administrator.

1. Click **Configure** in the **Remote Access Setup** dialog box.

   The **Configure Port Usage** dialog box appears.
2. Click **Dial out and Receive calls**, and then click **OK**.

   The **Remote Access Setup** dialog box appears.
3. Click the **Network** button.

   The **Network Configuration** dialog box appears.
4. In the **Dial out Protocols** box, verify that **NetBEUI**, **TCP/IP**, and **IPX** are selected.
5. Under Server Settings, verify that the **Allow remote clients running** check boxes for **NetBEUI**, **TCP/IP**, and **IPX** are selected.
6. Next to **NetBEUI**, click **Configure**.

   The **RAS Server NetBEUI Configuration** dialog box appears.
7. Click **Entire network**, and then click **OK**.

   The **Network Configuration** dialog box appears.
8. Next to **TCP/IP**, click **Configure**.

   The **RAS Server TCP/IP Configuration** dialog box appears.
9. Under **Allow remote TCP/IP clients to access**, click **Entire network**.
10. Click **Use DHCP to assign remote TCP/IP client addresses**.
11. Click **OK**.

    The **Network Configuration** dialog box appears.
12. Next to **IPX**, click **Configure**.

    The **RAS Server IPX Configuration** dialog box appears.
13. Under **Allow remote IPX clients to access**, click **Entire network**.
14. Click **Allocate network numbers automatically**.
15. Select the **Assign same network number to all IPX clients** check box, and then click **OK**.

    The **Network Configuration** dialog box appears.
16. Click **OK**.

    The **Remote Access Setup** dialog box appears.
17. Click **Continue**.

    An **RIP for NWLink IPX Configuration** dialog box appears asking if you want to enable NetBIOS Broadcast Propagation.

18. Click **No**.

    A **Setup Message** dialog box appears indicating that RAS has been successfully installed.

19. Click **OK**.

    The **Network** dialog box appears.

20. Click **Close**.
21. An **NWLink IPX/SPX** dialog box appears offering you the chance to change the internal network numbers now, click **No**.
22. Click **Yes** to restart the computer.

Granting Remote Access Permissions

After installing RAS on a server, you must grant Remote Access permissions to users before they can to connect through Dial-Up Networking. You use the Remote Access **Admin** utility or User Manager for Domains to grant RAS permission.

Practice

▸ **To assign permission to RAS users**

Note Complete this procedure on Server1.

---

1. Log on as Administrator
2. Click the **Start** button, point to **Programs**, point to **Administrative Tools (Common)**, and then click **Remote Access Admin**.

   This starts the **Remote Access Admin** program on your server.

3. On the **Users** menu, click **Permissions**.

   The **Remote Access Permissions** dialog box appears.

4. Click **Grant All**.

   A **Remote Access Admin** dialog box appears, with the "Grant Remote Access permission to all SERVER1 users?" prompt.

5. Click **Yes**.

   The **Remote Access Permissions** dialog box appears.

6. Click **OK**.
7. Exit the **Remote Access Admin** program.

Lesson 4: Installing and Configuring Dial-Up Networking

Dial-Up Networking enables remote clients to connect to a network from a remote site, such as home or a hotel. It functions by calling the RAS server and establishing a telephone connection with the network. After the connection has been made, a Dial-Up Networking client can work as if connected directly to the network.

There are a number of configuration options that can be set in Dial-Up Networking. You learned about TAPI configuration earlier in this chapter. Other configuration options include configuring phonebook entries, logging on using a dial-in entry, and the AutoDial feature.

After this lesson, you will be able to:

- Install Dial-Up Networking.
- Configure a phonebook entry.
- Log on to a Windows NT domain through Dial-Up Networking.
- Explain the AutoDial feature.

Estimated lesson time: 30 minutes

Installing Dial-Up Networking

You learned earlier that Dial-Up Networking is automatically installed during Windows NT installation if you selected **Remote access to the network** during Setup. It is also automatically installed when you install Remote Access Service if you configure RAS to dial out and receive calls, or dial out only.

You can also manually install Dial-Up Networking by double-clicking the Dial-Up Networking icon in My Computer.

Practice

In these procedures, you install and configure Dial-Up Networking on Workstation1.

Note Complete these procedures on Workstation1, logged on to the domain as Administrator.

► **To prepare to install Dial-Up Networking**

1. Double-click the Shortcut to Network icon.
2. Install **NetBEUI Protocol** and **NWLink IPX/SPX Compatible Transport**.
3. Shut down, and then restart Workstation1 for your changes to take effect.

▸ **To install Dial-Up Networking**

1. Log on to the domain as Administrator.
2. On the desktop, double-click My Computer, and then double-click Dial-Up Networking.
3. Click **Install**.
4. If a **Files Needed** dialog box appears, insert the *Microsoft Windows NT Workstation* compact disc, type *cd-rom_drive*:**\I386** and then click **OK**.
5. When the **Remote Access Setup** dialog box appears, asking if you want RAS Setup to invoke the modem installer, click **Yes**.

   The Install New Modem wizard appears.
6. Select the **Don't detect my modem, I will select it from a list** check box, and then click **Next**.

   The Install New Modem wizard continues.
7. Under **Manufacturers**, click **(Standard Modem Types)**. Under **Models**, click **Dial-Up Networking Serial Cable between 2 PCs**, and then click **Next**.

   The Install New Modem wizard continues.
8. Click **Selected ports**; click **COM1** (if COM1 is already in use, select an available COM port on your computer), and then click **Next**.

   A **Location Information** dialog box appears.

Note Steps 9–12 are not necessary when using a null modem cable to connect two computers, as you are doing in this procedure.

---

9. In the **What country are you in now?** box, select the appropriate country.
10. In the **What area (or city) code are you in now?** box, type your area or city code.
11. In the **If you dial a number to access an outside line, what is it?** box, type the appropriate number(s).
12. Click **Tone dialing** or **Pulse dialing** depending on your telephone, and then click **Next**.
13. Click **Finish**.

    The **Add RAS Device** dialog box appears. You should see **COM1-Dial-Up Networking Serial Cable between 2 PCs** in the **RAS Capable Devices:** box.
14. Click **OK**.

    The **Remote Access Setup** dialog box appears.

▸ **To configure Dial-Up Networking**

1. Click **Configure**.

   The **Configure Port Usage** dialog box appears.

2. Click **Dial out only**, and then click **OK**.

   The **Remote Access Setup** dialog box reappears.

3. Click the **Network** button.

   The **Network Configuration** dialog box appears.

4. In the **Dial out Protocols** box, verify that **NetBEUI**, **TCP/IP**, and **IPX** are selected, and then click **OK**.

5. Click **Continue**.

   A **Dial-Up Networking** dialog box appears asking if you would like to restart your computer.

6. Click **Restart**.

Configuring Phonebook Entries

Dial-Up Networking connects a client to remote networks using a modem, ISDN, or other WAN adapter. A *phonebook* entry stores all of the settings needed to connect to a particular remote network.

The Dial-Up Networking client stores all of its configuration data for a single connection in a phonebook file. Phonebooks can be specific to an individual user or shared among all users on the computer. When a phonebook is shared among all users, it is called a system phonebook. To create or edit phonebook entries, you can access Dial-Up Networking through either My Computer or the **Accessories** menu, which is accessed through clicking the **Start** button, and then pointing to **Programs**.

The first time a new phonebook entry is created, you should use the New Phonebook Entry wizard. After you feel comfortable creating phonebook entries, you can turn off the wizard by selecting the **I know all about phonebook entries and would rather edit the properties directly** check box.

Note If you would like to use the New Phonebook Entry wizard again, access **Dial-Up Networking** and click the **More** button. Click **User Preferences**, and then click the **Appearance** tab. On the **Appearance** tab, select **Use wizard to create new phonebook entries**, and then click **OK**. The next time you create a new phonebook entry, the wizard will automatically start.

To create or configure a phonebook entry, double-click the Dial-Up Networking icon in **My Computer**, and then click **New**. If you have disabled the New Phonebook Entry wizard, when you click **New**, the **New Phonebook Entry** dialog box appears.

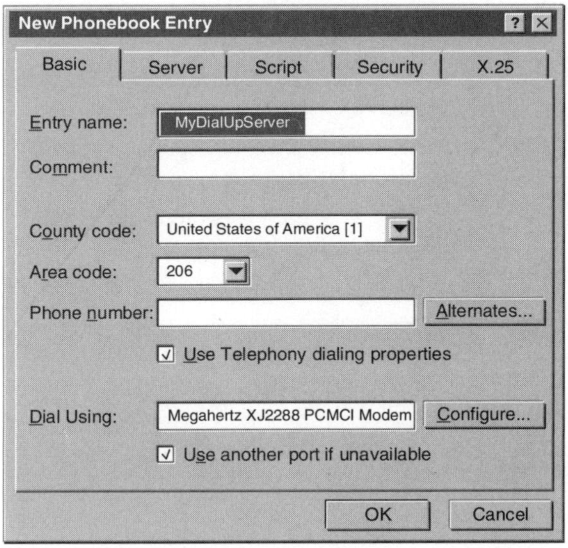

Note In the preceding illustration, if the **Use Telephony dialing properties** option is *not* selected, the **Country code** and **Area code** boxes will not appear.

New Phonebook Entry Configuration

Use the tabs in the **New Phonebook Entry** dialog box to configure the parameters described in the following table.

Tab	Use this tab
Basic	To configure a name for the phonebook entry.
	To enter the telephone number and any alternate telephone numbers, and to use Telephony dialing properties, such as when you are calling long distance or are using a credit card.
	To specify and configure the device used by the phonebook entry. To enable the PPP Multilink Protocol, select **Multiple Lines** in the **Dial Using** box, and then click **Configure**. In order to use the Multilink Protocol, you must have multiple devices installed, such as modems.
Server	To select the Dial-up server, type PPP, SLIP, or an older RAS protocol.
	To select a network protocol, click NetBEUI, TCP/IP, or IPX/SPX Compatible Transport.
Script	To specify a terminal window or script file if manual intervention is required before or after dialing to establish a remote access session.
Security	Select a level of authentication and encryption.
X.25	Select an X.25 network provider and configure connectivity information required by the X.25 network provider.

In addition, the following TCP/IP settings (available on the **Server** tab) may need to be configured, based on the **Dial-up server type** selected. The TCP/IP settings are only available for PPP and SLIP servers.

Option	Description
IP address	Automatically assigned by the dial-up server, or manually configured on clients.
Name server addresses	Assign DNS and WINS server addresses. These can be assigned by a DHCP server or manually configured at the client.
Use IP header compression	Enable header compression for low-speed serial links.
Use default gateway on remote network	Select this check box if the Dial-Up Networking client is using a network adapter card to connect simultaneously to a LAN. When it is checked, packets that cannot be routed on the local network are forwarded to the default gateway on the remote network. In addition, address conflicts between the remote and local networks are resolved in favor of the remote network.

Practice

In this procedure, you create a phonebook entry.

► **To create a phonebook entry**

Note Complete this procedure on Workstation1, logged on as Administrator.

---

1. Log on as Administrator, and then double-click the Dial-Up Networking icon in **My Computer**.

   The **Dial-Up Networking** dialog box appears, stating that the phonebook is empty.

2. Click **OK**.

   The New Phonebook Entry wizard starts.

3. In the **Name the new phonebook entry** box, type **Server1** and then click **Next**.

   A **Server** dialog box appears.

4. Verify that all check boxes are cleared, and then click **Next**.

   A **Phone Number** dialog box appears.

5. Leave the Phone number box blank, and then click **Next**.

   You have just created a phonebook entry for Server1. In this case, the telephone number is blank because this computer is configured for a direct connection to Server1, using the **Dial-Up Networking Serial Cable between 2 PCs** option.

6. Click **Finish** to exit the New Phonebook Entry wizard.

   The **Dial-Up Networking** dialog box appears.

7. Click **New**.

   The **New Phonebook Entry Wizard** dialog box appears.

8. Select the **I know all about phonebook entries and would rather edit the properties directly** check box, and then click **Finish**.

   The **Dial-Up Networking** dialog box appears.

9. Click **New**.

   The **New Phonebook Entry** dialog box appears.

10. Click **Cancel** to close the **New Phonebook Entry** dialog box and to return to the **Dial-Up Networking** dialog box.

Logging on Through Dial-Up Networking

When Dial-Up Networking is installed, Windows NT includes a logon option that enables users to log on to a domain using Dial-Up Networking. When this check box is selected, users have the opportunity to select a Dial-Up Networking phonebook entry that will be used for logging on. Dial-Up Networking will then establish a connection to the RAS server so that a domain controller for the specified domain can validate the client's logon request.

The dial-up settings for establishing a connection for logging on are configured using the **Logon Preferences** dialog box in the Dial-Up Networking client. To access this dialog box, click the **More** button in the **Dial-Up Networking** dialog box, and then select **Logon Preferences** on the **More** menu.

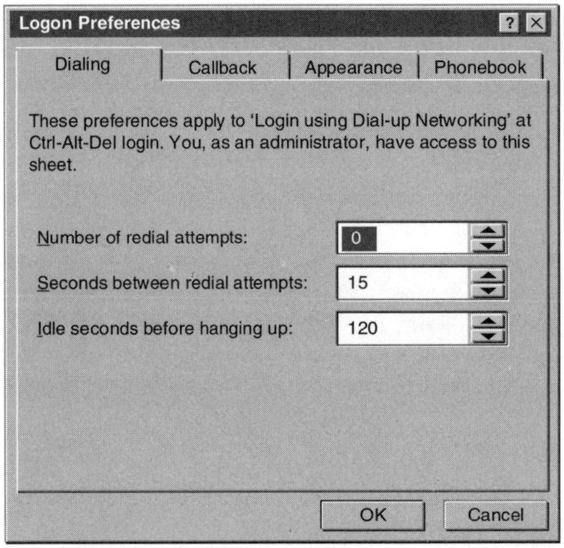

The following table describes the logon options that can be configured using the **Logon Preferences** dialog box.

Tab	Use this tab to
Dialing	Specify the number of and interval between redial attempts. It can also be used to set an idle connection timeout period.
Callback	Configure the server to disconnect and call the client back following authentication to reduce telephone charges and increase security.
Appearance	Configure the Dial-Up Networking interface that appears while logging on, including options to allow you to preview the number before dialing it, to show the location setting before dialing, to allow location edits during the logon process, to show connection progress while dialing, to close on dial, to allow phonebook edits during the logon process, and to use the wizard to create new phonebook entries.
Phonebook	Specify the system phonebook or an alternate phonebook to be used when logging on.

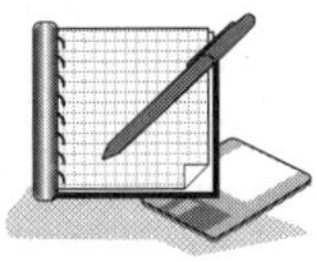

Practice

In this procedure, you configure logon preferences on your Dial-Up Networking client.

► To configure logon preferences

Note Complete this procedure on Workstation1, logged on as Administrator.

1. If you closed the **Dial-Up Networking** dialog box, double-click the Dial-Up Networking icon in My Computer.

   The **Dial-Up Networking** dialog box appears.
2. Under the **Phonebook entry to dial** box, click **More**.
3. On the **More** menu, click **Logon preferences**.

   The **Logon Preferences** dialog box appears.
4. On the **Dialing** tab, in the **Number of redial attempts** box, set the number to **3**.
5. Click **OK** to close the **Logon Preferences** dialog box.

User Profiles with Dial-Up Networking

The same logon process is used by Windows NT to log on to a LAN directly or through Dial-Up Networking. The reason this process is identical for direct and remote logon is that a copy of a user's profile is cached on the client each time the user logs off.

You may want to use the locally-cached user profile rather than the server-based profile when logging on through Dial-Up Networking. For example, if the server containing your server-based profile is unavailable, any customization of your desktop that is stored in that profile will not occur. However, if you have a locally-cached user profile, these customizations will occur. In order to configure Windows NT to use your locally-cached user profile, access the **User Profiles** tab through System on Control Panel.

AutoDial

Windows NT version 4.0 Dial-Up Networking supports a feature known as *AutoDial*. Windows 95 and Windows NT versions 3.51 and earlier do not support the AutoDial feature.

RAS AutoDial maps and maintains network addresses to phonebook entries, allowing them to be automatically dialed when referenced from an application or from the command line.

The database can include IP addresses (for example, "127.95.1.4"), Internet host names (for example, "www.microsoft.com"), or NetBIOS names (for example, "products1"). Associated with each address in the AutoDial database is a set of one or more entries. Each of these entries specifies a phonebook entry that RAS can dial to connect to the address from a particular TAPI dialing location.

AutoDial automatically creates entries in the AutoDial mapping database in two situations:

- When an attempt to connect to a network address fails.

  If there is no entry for the address in the mapping database, and the computer is not connected to a network (either directly or through RAS), AutoDial prompts the user to specify the information necessary to establish a dial-up connection. If the user provides the information and the dial-up connection operation is successful, AutoDial stores the information in the mapping database.

- When the computer is connected to a network through RAS.

  Whenever the user connects to a network address, AutoDial creates an entry in the database. The entry maps the network address to the phonebook entry that was used to establish the RAS connection.

AutoDial is enabled by default. A user can disable AutoDial in the **User Preferences** dialog box for a phonebook entry. To disable AutoDial, select an entry to dial from the phonebook list. Click **More**, and then click **User Preferences**. On the **Dialing** tab, clear each location listed in the **Enable auto-dial by location** list.

RAS AutoDial works only when the Remote Access AutoDial service is running. To determine if the Remote Access AutoDial service is running, use the Services program in Control Panel. If the Remote Access Autodial Manager is running, then the Remote Access AutoDial service is running. If the Remote Access Autodial Manager is not running, you can start it by selecting it, clicking **Startup**, setting the Startup Type to Automatic or Manual, and then clicking **Start**.

Note AutoDial does not support IPX connections. AutoDial only works with the TCP/IP and NetBEUI protocols. For more information on AutoDial, see Dial-Up Networking (RAS) Help.

The following illustration shows the User Preferences dialog box, with AutoDial enabled for Home and disabled for Hotel.

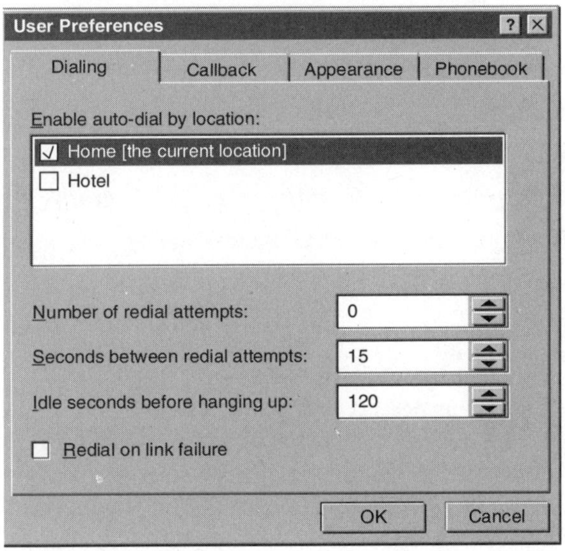

AutoDial also keeps track of all connections made over a Dial-Up Networking connection so that clients can be automatically reconnected.

AutoDial will attempt to make a connection in the following situations:

- When a user is disconnected from the network, AutoDial will attempt to establish a connection whenever an application references a network connection.
- When a user is connected to a network, AutoDial will attempt to create a network connection for addresses that it has previously learned.

Configuring AutoDial Preferences

Practice

In this procedure, you configure AutoDial preferences on your Dial-Up Networking client.

▸ **To configure AutoDial preferences**

Note Complete this procedure on Workstation1, logged on as Administrator.

---

1. If you closed the **Dial-Up Networking** dialog box, double-click the Dial-Up Networking icon in My Computer.

   The **Dial-Up Networking** dialog box appears.
2. Under the **Phonebook entry to dial** box, click **More**.
3. On the **More** menu, click **User preferences**.

   The **User Preferences** dialog box appears.
4. On the **Dialing** tab, in the **Number of redial attempts** box, set the number to **3**.
5. Click **OK** to close the **User Preferences** dialog box.
6. Click **Close** to close the **Dial-Up Networking** dialog box.

Testing the RAS Installation

To ensure that RAS has been properly installed and configured, you can perform a test procedure. There are two methods of testing your RAS installation: using a modem and telephone lines to dial in to a RAS server from your Dial-Up Networking client, or using a null modem cable to connect a Dial-Up Networking client and a RAS server.

Practice

In this procedure, you use the RAS simulation to practice the procedure you would normally use to test your RAS and Dial-Up Networking installations.

► **To run the RAS simulation**

Note Complete this procedure on Workstation1.

---

1. Click the **Start** button, point to **Programs**, and then point to **Technical Support Training**. Point to **Simulations**, and then click **RAS Simulation**.

   The simulation starts, and the **Logon Information** dialog box appears.
2. Click to select **Log on using Dial-Up Networking**.
3. Verify that the Domain is **Domain1**.
4. Log on as Administrator using *password* as the password, and then click **OK**.

   The **Dial-Up Networking** dialog box appears.
5. Verify the **Phonebook entry to dial** box contains **SERVER1**, and then click **Dial**.

   The **Connect to Server1** dialog box appears.
6. In the **Password** box, type **password** and then click **OK**.

   A **Connecting to Server1** dialog box appears, and the Remote Access Service connects to the RAS server.

   Note You are now looking at Server1. Whether you log on locally or remotely using RAS, your desktop is the same. Your desktop is controlled by your user profile and any System Policy settings that apply to your user account name or the computer to which you log on.

   ---

7. Double-click **Network Neighborhood**.
8. Double-click **Server1**.

   What shares are available on Server1?

   ___

9. In My Computer, double-click **Dial-Up Networking**.
10. Click **Hang-Up**.

    A **Dial-Up Networking** dialog box confirming that you want to disconnect from Server1 appears.
11. Click **Yes**, and then click **Close**.

    A **Windows NT RAS Simulation** dialog box appears.
12. Click **Continue** to close the simulation.

Note If you have a null modem cable, you can perform the actual test procedure on Server1 and Workstation1. First disconnect Workstation1 from the network by unplugging the network cable. Then connect Workstation1 to Server1 by plugging one end of the null modem cable into Workstation1's appropriate COM port (usually COM1) and the other end into Server1's appropriate COM port. You can then test your RAS installations by following the procedure listed in the practice.

Lesson 5: Troubleshooting RAS

This lesson describes some of the common errors that can occur when using RAS, along with guidelines and tools for solving these problems. Using the Event Viewer, which is accessed from the Administrative Tools (Common) group, and viewing the system log will be helpful as a first line of information in troubleshooting RAS.

After this lesson, you will be able to:

- Describe several of the tools that will enable you to diagnose and solve problems that may arise when using RAS.

Estimated lesson time: 15 minutes

Event Viewer

The Event Viewer is used to view the system log, which contains events for all Windows NT internal services and drivers. Event Viewer is useful in diagnosing RAS problems, because many RAS events are logged in the system log. For example, if the Windows NT Dial-Up Networking client fails to connect, or if the RAS server fails to start, you should check the system log.

Problems with PPP Connections

If the user is having problems being authenticated over PPP, a Ppp.log file can be created to provide debugging information to troubleshoot the problem. The Ppp.log file is stored in the *systemroot*\System32\Ras folder, and it is enabled by changing the following registry parameter to a value of 1:

\HKEY_LOCAL_MACHINE\SYSTEM\CurrentControlSet\Services\Rasman\PPP**Logging**

Authentication Problems

If a Dial-Up Networking client is having problems being authenticated over RAS, try to change the authentication settings for that client. Try the lowest authentication option on each side, and if successful, start increasing the authentication options to determine the highest level of authentication that can be used between the two systems.

Dial-Up Networking Monitor

The Dial-Up Networking Monitor, accessed through the Dial-Up Monitor program in Control Panel, shows the status of a session that is in progress. It shows the duration of the call, amount of data that is being transmitted and received, and the number of errors. In addition, it can show which lines are being used for Multilink sessions.

Multilink and Callback

If a client uses a Multilink-enabled phonebook entry to call a server and that server is configured to call the user back, when the callback is made it will be to one of the Multilink devices. The reason for this is that the RAS **Admin** utility allows only one number to be stored for callback purposes for each user account. Therefore, the RAS server calls only one of the devices and Multilink functionality is lost.

If the link between the Dial-Up Networking client and RAS server is made using ISDN with two channels that have the same telephone number, then Multilink will work with callback.

AutoDial Occurs During Logon

During the logon process, when Windows NT Explorer initializes, any persistent network connections or desktop shortcuts that reference network locations will cause AutoDial to attempt a connection. The only way to avoid this is to disable AutoDial or remove the persistent connections and shortcuts.

Note In order to set up your computer for the rest of the lessons in this book, perform the following procedure to remove RAS from Server1.

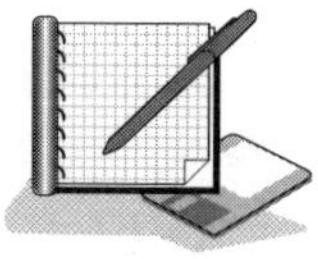

Practice

In this procedure, you remove RAS from Server1 to save resources.

Note Complete this procedure on Server1.

► **To remove RAS**

1. Double-click the Shortcut to Network icon.
2. Click the **Services** tab.
3. Click **Remote Access Service**, and then click **Remove**.

   A **Warning** dialog box appears, indicating that this action will permanently remove the component from your system, and asking if you still want to continue.
4. Click **Yes**, and then click **Close**.
5. When prompted to restart your computer, click **Yes**.

Note If you used a null-modem cable to test RAS using Server1 and Workstation1, remove the null-modem cable from the computers and plug the network cable into Workstation1.

Summary

The following information summarizes the key points in this chapter:

- RAS permits users who are not physically connected to the network to have network access through modems and telephone lines. The RAS server acts as a gateway between the remote client and the network. Any Microsoft Dial-Up Networking client can connect to any Microsoft RAS server.
- RAS can establish connections using standard telephone lines, X.25, and ISDN. RAS supports the SLIP and PPP protocols for WAN connections.
- An additional protocol, PPTP, enables you to remotely access your corporate network securely across the Internet. First you establish a connection to the Internet, and then establish a connection to the RAS server using PPTP.
- RAS provides several security features, including integrated domain security, encrypted logon, auditing, intermediary security hosts, and callback security.

Review

1. You would like to enable remote users to connect to your company's LAN through the Internet. However, your manager is concerned about potential unauthorized access from the Internet. How would you implement your plan while relieving your manager's concerns?

2. You are a frequent traveler, and you require dial-up access to your company's network through any of five remote access telephone numbers maintained by a RAS server. Changing all five access number properties to match your area code and dialing conditions is tedious; how can you simplify the process?

3. You use Dial-Up Networking frequently to access your company's network from home. You use a 28.8 Kbps modem to connect, and it takes a very long time to log on. Without buying another modem, how can you speed up the process?

4. Your network supports users who often work from home. These users only require remote access to their home directories, which are maintained on a RAS server. For security reasons, you do not want these users to be able to access the rest of your intranetwork from a remote location. What is the best way to implement this?

5. You receive a help desk call from a remote user who is having trouble connecting to the RAS server using PPP. How would you troubleshoot the problem?

Answer Key

Procedure Answers

Page 465

▸ **To run the RAS simulation**

8. Double-click **Server1**.

   What shares are available on Server1?

   PRINTERS and NETLOGON.

Review Answers

Page 470

1. You would like to enable remote users to connect to your company's LAN through the Internet. However, your manager is concerned about potential unauthorized access from the Internet. How would you implement your plan while relieving your manager's concerns?

   Implement PPTP, which uses the Internet as a connection medium but does not necessarily expose your network on the Internet. Only the RAS server needs to be on the Internet, and PPTP filtering can be enabled to prevent any packets other than PPTP packets from reaching the internal network.

2. You are a frequent traveler, and you require dial-up access to your company's network through any of five remote access telephone numbers maintained by a RAS server. Changing all five access number properties to match your area code and dialing conditions is tedious; how can you simplify the process?

   Configure a TAPI location with your local country and area code and any other necessary dialing properties. This location can be applied to all five of the Dial-Up Networking connections.

3. You use Dial-Up Networking frequently to access your company's network from home. You use a 28.8 Kbps modem to connect, and it takes a very long time to log on. Without buying another modem, how can you speed up the process?

   Configure your computer so that it does not download your server-based profile during logon across RAS.

4. Your network supports users who often work from home. These users only require remote access to their home directories, which are maintained on a RAS server. For security reasons, you do not want these users to be able to access the rest of your intranetwork from a remote location. What is the best way to implement this?

   Configure the RAS server so that it only allows access to itself and not to the entire network. If you apply permissions to other network servers and resources to restrict the remote users, these permissions would also apply when the users work at the office, restricting them unnecessarily.

5. You receive a help desk call from a remote user who is having trouble connecting to the RAS server using PPP. How would you troubleshoot the problem?

   Enable PPP logging for the RAS server and see how far the user is able to get in the connection process.

CHAPTER 13

Internetworking and Intranetworking

About This Chapter

Supporting Microsoft Windows NT requires a knowledge of how computers running Windows NT can both access resources and distribute them over the Internet or a private intranet. In this chapter, you will learn about the Windows NT tools to support publishing and accessing services on the Internet and intranets. These include Internet Information Server (IIS), Peer Web Services (PWS), and Microsoft Internet Explorer.

Before You Begin

To complete the lessons in this chapter, you must have:

- Two computers that meet the hardware and software requirements as specified in the Getting Started section of "About This Book."
- Completed all practices in Chapter 2, "Installing Windows NT."
- Server1 configured with the DNS service, as directed in Chapter 11, "Windows NT Networking Services."

Lesson 1: Internet and Intranet Overview

This lesson introduces you to the Internet and a private intranet and discusses their functions and characteristics. You will learn about the World Wide Web (WWW), a graphical interface that overlays the Internet to create a virtual network, or Web, of information. Finally, you will learn of the security issues that you should consider when connecting to the Internet as well as when integrating a local intranet with the Internet.

After this lesson, you will be able to:

- Describe the Internet and an intranet.
- Identify security considerations for integrating an intranet site with the Internet.

Estimated lesson time: 10 minutes

The *Internet* is a network of computers located around the world that are able to communicate with one another through telephone lines. An *intranet* exists at a local level, and consists of computers that are connected by means of LANs. The following illustration shows both Internet and intranet connectivity.

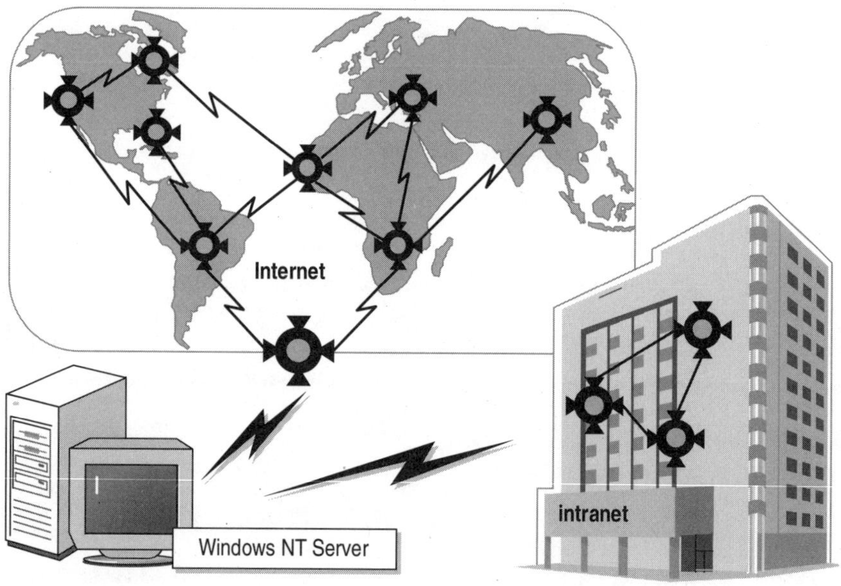

What Is the Internet?

The Internet is a global network of computers that communicate using common languages and protocols.

The Internet has been evolving since the early 1970s. Early servers on the Internet conformed to original Internet protocols, such as the File Transfer Protocol (FTP) or Virtual Terminal Protocol (VTP, now called Telnet). These protocols generally provide a way to copy files or issue commands or start programs through a character-based interface.

Internet technology has grown beyond the simple file transfers on character-based FTP or Telnet servers and incorporates graphical interfaces.

A key graphical network service on the Internet is the World Wide Web (WWW, or the Web). The user creates *Web pages* that are then linked together by means of the *Hypertext Transfer Protocol* (HTTP). Every Web page, including a Web site's *home page*, has a unique address called a *Uniform Resource Locator* (URL). The following shows a sample URL:

http://www.microsoft.com/ntserver/

Web pages are *hypertext* documents—files that have been formatted by using the *Hypertext Markup Language* (HTML)—that contain hyperlinks. *Hyperlinks* have Web addresses embedded in them and are represented as underlined or bordered words and graphics. When you click a hyperlink, you "jump" to the location on the Internet that was specified in the hyperlink.

Web servers automatically provide formatted text, graphics, sounds, and animation to Internet users. In order to connect to Web servers and view the information, you must use a Web *browser* such as *Microsoft Internet Explorer*. Microsoft Internet Explorer also supports the older standards, such as FTP, so you can use Microsoft Internet Explorer to access multiple servers and data types.

What Is an Intranet?

Intranets are networks, internal to a company or organization, that use Internet technology, such as the HTTP servers and Web browser services, to improve an organization's internal communications, information publishing, and application development process. In this chapter, intranet refers to any TCP/IP network using Internet technology that is not connected to the Internet.

Security Considerations When Connecting to the Internet

It is important to remember that the Internet, like other networks, provides two-way communication. When you are connected to the Internet, other computers can see your computer. By default, Windows NT security protects your computer from casual intrusion. However, while it is very unlikely that your computer will be attacked while you are browsing the Internet, it is still a good idea to configure your computer securely. Before you install and configure TCP/IP and Dial-Up Networking, you should review the security configuration of your computer.

Security Considerations for Integrating an Intranet Site with the Internet

It is possible to integrate a corporate intranet with the Internet. Both can be supported by the same network system. If your computer is also connected to an in-house network (an intranet), it is especially important to prevent access to your intranet from the Internet.

The following are security issues to keep in mind if you intend to integrate an intranet with the Internet:

- Usually, intranet sites are casual and informal, while Internet sites generally reflect the organization's public image.
- Separate the information that is downloaded to an intranet site from that distributed over the Internet. For example, proprietary documents are often distributed on intranets but would violate trade secrets if they were released to the Internet.
- It is usually not advisable to grant full intranet access to Internet users.

Lesson 2: IIS and PWS Networking Components

Windows NT is equipped with several components that support interoperability with the Internet and private intranets. You have learned about the Web browser, Microsoft Internet Explorer. Additional Internet and intranet components supported by Windows NT are the Internet Information Server (IIS) and Peer Web Services (PWS).

IIS and PWS provide computers running Windows NT with the ability to publish resources and services on the Internet and on private intranets. Use IIS and PWS for publishing hypertext Web pages and client/server applications, and for interactive Web applications. This lesson discusses IIS and PWS functions and features, and how they provide publishing services and resources to clients. In addition, you will learn how to install and configure both IIS and PWS.

After this lesson, you will be able to:

- Describe Internet Information Server (IIS) and Peer Web Services (PWS).
- Describe the procedures to install and configure IIS and PWS.

Estimated lesson time: 20 minutes

Functions of IIS and PWS

The following illustration shows the roles of IIS and PWS in Internet and intranet communications.

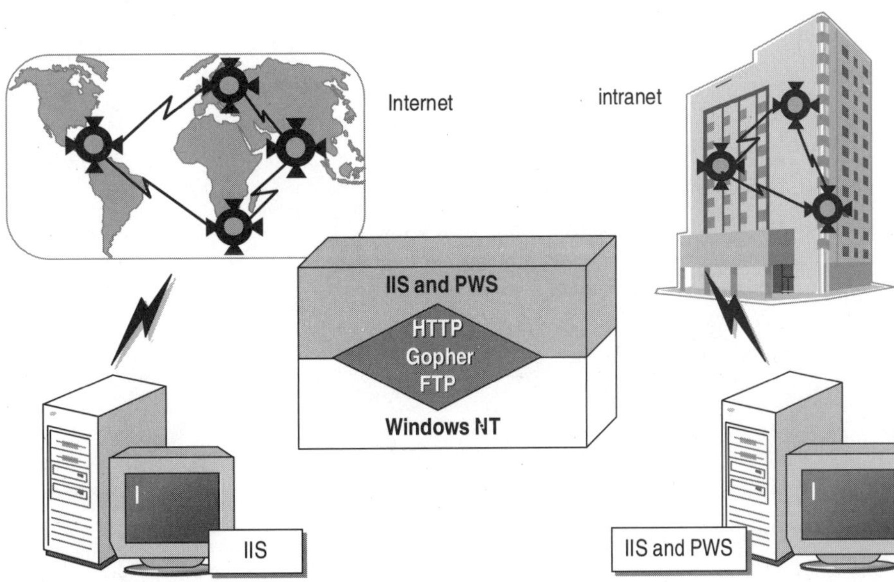

The IIS and PWS are network file and application servers that use HTTP, the Gopher service, and FTP to provide information over the Internet or an intranet.

- HTTP is used to link to and navigate Web hypertext documents and applications.
- The Gopher service is a hierarchical system used to create links to other computers or services, to put these links into custom menus, and to annotate files and directories.
- FTP is used to transfer files between two computers on a TCP/IP network.

Using IIS and PWS, it is possible to publish information or services such as Web pages, interactive applications, and catalogs for customers, and to post and track databases on the Web.

IIS and PWS support the Internet Server application programming interface (ISAPI). ISAPI is used to create interfaces that can be used for client/server applications. For example, ISAPI can be used to create applications that allow clients to access and enter information into a Web page.

IIS and PWS Comparison

Any computer running Windows NT Server can support IIS, and any computer running Windows NT Workstation can support PWS. IIS is designed to support the heavy usage that can occur on the Internet. PWS, on the other hand, is optimized for use as a small scale Web server suitable for exchanging information for a small department or individuals on an intranet.

Features of IIS and PWS

Among the features included with IIS and PWS are file publication, network management, and security. The following table provides an overview of some of the key features that IIS and PWS offer to a computer running Windows NT.

Feature	Use this feature to
File Publication	Publish existing files from Windows NT and other file servers.
Network Management	Monitor and record network activity and provide clients with access to valuable network resources such as HTML pages, shared files and printers, corporate databases, and legacy systems.
Security	Provide clients with secure access to Internet and intranet resources.
Support for common Internet standards	Enable development of Web applications, using such languages as CGI (Common Gateway Interface) and PERL (Practical Extraction and Report Language).
Microsoft Internet Explorer	Enable clients such as Microsoft Windows 3.11, Microsoft Windows for Workgroups, Windows NT, Microsoft Windows 95, and Macintosh to gain easy access to information on the Web.
Scalability	Enable Internet access to multiple platforms running on standard hardware packages, including single and multiprocessor servers using Intel 486, Pentium, Pentium Pro, Digital Alpha AXP, PowerPC, and MIPS processors.
Support for Microsoft BackOffice applications such as Microsoft SQL Server™ and Microsoft SNA Server	Provide businesses with the ability to deliver commercial solutions on the Web to customers.

Installing IIS

IIS can be installed when Windows NT Server is installed, or at a later time using either the Network program of Control Panel or the Install Internet Information Server icon located on the Windows NT Server desktop.

IIS Installation Requirements

Microsoft IIS has the following requirements for IIS installation:

- A computer running Windows NT Server 4.0 with TCP/IP.
- A CD-ROM drive for the *Windows NT Server* compact disc or a LAN connection to a server sharing the installation files.
- Adequate disk space for the published information content. It is recommended to use NTFS file and directory permissions to secure all of the disks used with IIS.

Changes can be made to a current installation of IIS through the Internet Information Server Setup icon located in the Microsoft Internet Server (Common) folder. Before adding or removing components, or reinstalling IIS, disable any previous versions of FTP, Gopher, or other Web service that may be installed on Windows NT Server.

Note See Windows NT Help for documentation on how to disable these services.

The following illustration shows the components available when installing IIS.

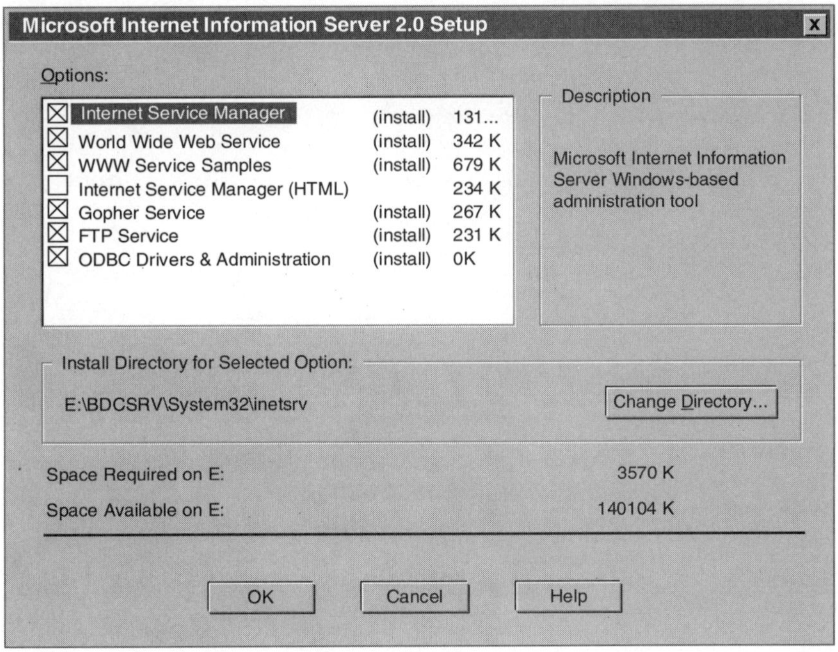

Installing PWS

Install Peer Web Services through the Network program in Control Panel.

PWS Installation Requirements

PWS requires the following components for installation:

- A computer running Windows NT Workstation 4.0 and TCP/IP.
- A CD-ROM drive for the *Windows NT Workstation* compact disc or a LAN connection to a server sharing the installation files.
- Adequate disk space for the published information content. It is recommended to use NTFS file and directory permissions to secure all drives used with PWS.

The following illustration shows the components that are available when installing PWS.

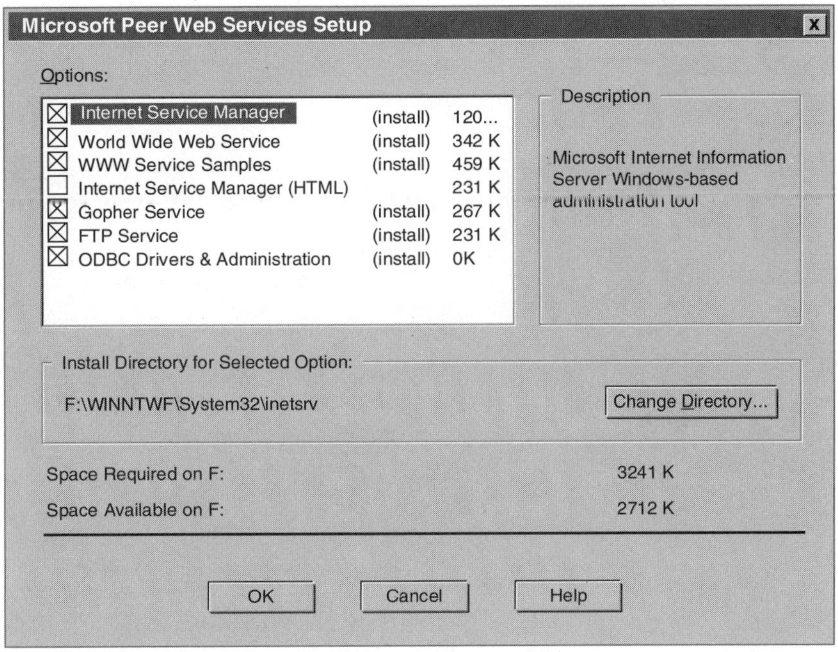

Changes can be made to a current installation of Peer Web Services through the Peer Web Services Setup icon located in the Microsoft Peer Web Services (Common) folder. Before adding or removing components, or reinstalling PWS, disable any previous versions of Gopher, FTP, or other Web services that may be installed on Windows NT Workstation.

The PWS default setup configurations are suitable for many publishing scenarios without any further modifications.

Configuring IIS and PWS

All of the Internet and intranet services can be configured and managed from one central point using a simple interface.

Use the Microsoft Internet Service Manager (ISM) to enhance IIS and PWS configuration and performance. ISM is located in the Microsoft Internet Server Tools (Common) folder on a computer running Windows NT Server, or in the Microsoft Peer Web Services Tools (Common) folder on a computer running Windows NT Workstation. ISM provides a mechanism to configure and monitor all of the Internet services running on any computer running Windows NT in the network.

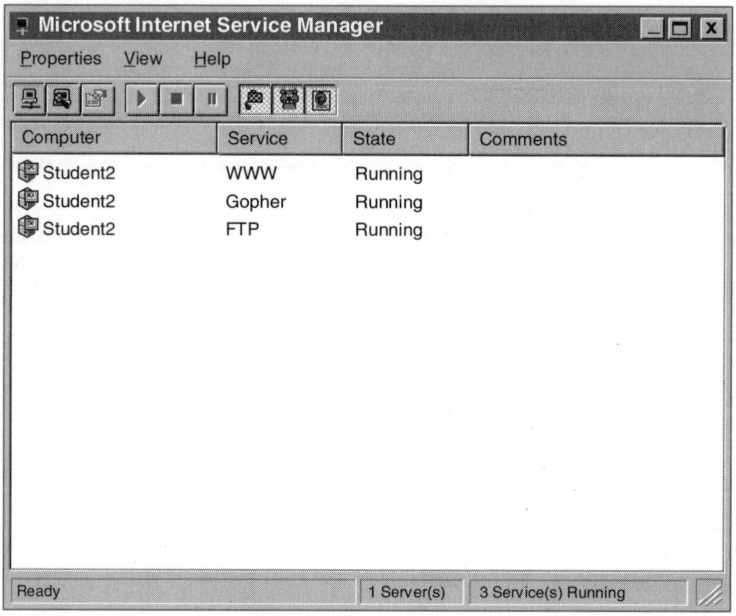

Internet Server Manager List Box

Using ISM, it is possible to manage multiple servers from one computer. ISM's default view is the Report view. Report view lists the computers on the network and the services installed on them. Report view also provides users with a mechanism to perform the following tasks:

- Connect to servers and view server properties.
- Start, stop, or pause a service.
- Select which services should be displayed.
- Configure properties of the services, if necessary.

Properties

In ISM, double-click a computer or service name to display its properties. The following illustration shows the WWW service properties displayed on the Service tab.

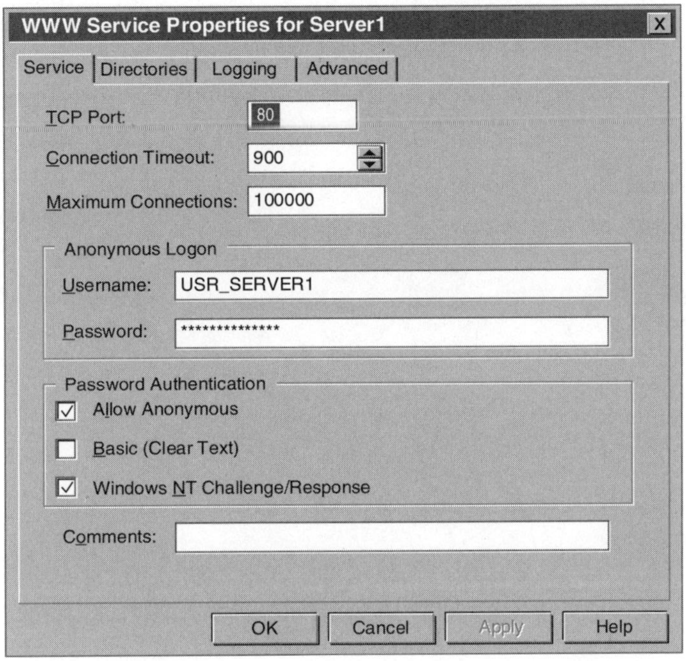

The different services (WWW, Gopher, FTP) have different properties. The properties that can be configured through the **Properties** dialog box include those listed below:

- **Service** tab. Connections, user logon, and authentication requirements.
- **Directories** tab. Directories used by each service, default document, and directory browsing.
- **Logging** tab. Server activity tracking and log file directory.
- **Advanced** tab. Secured access by IP address and bandwidth. The advanced tab is available only on IIS and not on PWS.

Configuring Services

ISM can also be used to configure the following:

- *WWW Service.* Set a default document so clients who are browsing can always receive the default document if they do not specify a particular file.
- *FTP Service.* Enable FTP clients to view files on NTFS partitions in the same format as a traditional UNIX FTP server.

For more information on	See
IIS	Product documentation available in the Microsoft Internet Server (Common) folder
PWS	Product documentation available in the Microsoft Peer Web Services (Common) folder

Lesson 3: Microsoft Internet Explorer

This lesson introduces you to Microsoft Internet Explorer. It describes the roles and functions of Microsoft Internet Explorer and the processes of accessing, navigating, and browsing the Internet or an intranet.

After this lesson, you will be able to:

- Describe the purpose and use of the Microsoft Internet Explorer.
- Use Microsoft Internet Explorer to access resources on the Internet.

Estimated lesson time: 5 minutes

Microsoft Internet Explorer is a Web browser that is used to navigate and access, or browse, information on the Web. After connecting to the Internet, use Microsoft Internet Explorer to view information on the Internet. Microsoft Internet Explorer can also be used to incorporate Internet information into a document or save the information as a file.

The Microsoft Internet Explorer toolbar provides a range of detailed functions and commands for managing Microsoft Internet Explorer.

The following methods can be used to begin exploring the Internet:

- Click a hyperlink in the Microsoft Internet Explorer main window.
- Enter a URL address directly into the white space on the address bar.
- Enter a URL in the **Run** dialog box available on the **Start** menu.

Windows NT 4.0 includes Microsoft Internet Explorer. In addition, versions of this browser are also available for Windows for Workgroups, Windows 3.1, Macintosh, and Windows 95.

Lesson 4: Securing Internet and Intranet Sites

This lesson describes the issues involved with securing your Internet and intranet sites. It provides guidelines for establishing an account policy to secure your sites from unwanted access and misuse.

After this lesson, you will be able to:

- Understand the major issues of Internet and intranet security.
- Explain how to secure Internet and intranet sites.
- Establish guidelines for creating an account policy.
- Install and configure IIS.

Estimated lesson time: 40 minutes

IIS and PWS are built on the Windows NT security model. Windows NT security helps protect Internet and intranet sites by requiring an assigned user account in order to access the site. When configuring these services, you specify whether to allow anonymous access to your site through the Internet Guest Account or another account designated by you, or to require a Windows NT user name and password. You can enable both anonymous connections and client authentication for the WWW and FTP services.

In addition, it is possible to control access to all computer resources by controlling the permissions assigned for each user or group to NTFS files and folders.

Allow Anonymous Access with the Internet Guest Account

On many Internet servers, access is anonymous; that is, the client request does not contain a user name and password. When you allow anonymous connections to your WWW, Gopher, and FTP services, Windows NT uses the user name and password configured for the service to make the anonymous connections.

The Internet Guest account, IUSR_*computername*, is created during the IIS or PWS installation. By default, this account is used when allowing anonymous connections.

Note The Internet Guest account is added to the Guests group. Changes to the Guests group user rights and resource permissions also apply to the Internet Guest account. Review the user rights and resource permissions for the Guests group to ensure that they are appropriate for the Internet Guest account.

If remote access is available only to the Internet Guest account, remote users do not provide a user name and password, and have only the permissions assigned to the Internet Guest account. This prevents unauthorized users from gaining access to sensitive information with fraudulent or illegally-obtained passwords.

Require a User Name and Password

The WWW and FTP services can be configured to require a valid user name and password to access your site's Internet resources. When this option is configured, the client request must contain a user name and password.

There are two types of authentication available when requiring a user name and password: Basic and Windows NT Challenge/Response.

- Basic authentication does not encrypt transmissions between the client and server, so names and passwords are sent in clear text over the networks. Intruders sniffing your transmissions could discover valid user names and passwords.
- Windows NT Challenge/Response authentication, supported by Microsoft Internet Explorer version 2.0 or later, protects the password, thereby providing for secure logon over the network. In this method, the user account obtained from the client is the one that the user is logged on with at the client computer.

Note The FTP service only supports basic authentication, so your FTP site is more secure if you only allow anonymous connections.

Guidelines for Securing an Internet and Intranet Site

The following are guidelines for creating an account policy for securing an Internet or intranet site:

- Do not allow blank passwords.
- Require a minimum password length.
- Require users to change their passwords frequently.
- Require users to use different passwords each time they are changed.
- Lock out accounts after multiple failed logon attempts.
- Require an administrator to unlock all locked accounts.
- Require users with restricted hours to be automatically disconnected.

Note For more information about securing your network, see Chapter 5, "Securing Your Site Against Intruders," in the *IIS Installation and Administration Guide*, or in the *PWS Installation and Administration Guide*. If you have IIS or PWS installed on your computer, click the **Start** button, point to **Programs**, point to **Microsoft Internet Server (Common)** or **Microsoft Peer Web Services (Common)**, and then click **Product Documentation**.

Practice

In these procedures, you examine the Windows NT Server environment before installing Microsoft Internet Information Server. You then install IIS, and again examine the Windows NT Server environment to determine changes made by IIS. You publish a document on your Web server, and access that document from Workstation1. Finally, you configure DNS to resolve IP addresses for IIS.

▸ To examine the Windows NT Server environment

In this procedure, you examine the Windows NT Server environment before installing Microsoft Internet Information Server.

Note Complete this procedure on Server1.

---

1. Log on as Administrator.
2. Click the **Start** button, point to **Settings**, and then click **Control Panel**.
3. Double-click the Services icon.

   The **Services** dialog box appears.
4. Scroll through the list of services available.

   Are there any publishing services listed? (Hint: Does the word *publishing* appear in the service name?)

5. Close the **Services** dialog box and minimize Control Panel.
6. Click the **Start** button, point to **Programs**, point to **Administrative Tools (Common)**, and then click **User Manager for Domains**.
7. In User Manager for Domains, examine the list of names.

   Is there an Internet Guest account listed?

8. Close User Manager for Domains.
9. In **Administrative Tools (Common)**, click **Performance Monitor**.
10. On the **Edit** menu in Performance Monitor, click **Add to Chart**.

    The **Add to Chart** dialog box appears.

11. In the **Object** box, scroll through the available objects.

    Are there any Internet-related items in the list?

    ____

12. Click **Cancel** to close the **Add to Chart** dialog box.
13. Close Performance Monitor.

► To install Internet Information Server

In this procedure, you install Internet Information Server.

Note Complete this procedure on Server1.

---

1. Double-click the Shortcut to Network icon.
2. Click the **Services** tab, and then click **Add**.
3. Click **Microsoft Internet Information Server 2.0**, and then click **OK**.

   The installation program prompts you for the path of the installation files.
4. In the **Installed from** box, type **\\Server1\Nts_source\I386** and then click **OK**.

   The **Microsoft Internet Information Server Setup** dialog box appears.
5. Read the information in the **Microsoft Internet Information 2.0 Server Setup** dialog box, and then click **OK**.

   The following installation options appear.

   - Internet Service Manager
   - World Wide Web Service
   - WWW Service Samples
   - Internet Service Manager (HTML)
   - Gopher Service
   - FTP Service
   - ODBC Drivers and Administration
6. Click **Internet Service Manager (HTML)**. Verify that all options are selected, and then click **OK**.

7. Click **Yes** to create the C:\WINNT\System32\Inetsrv directory.

   The **Publishing Directories** dialog box appears listing the following default directories.

Directory	Path
World Wide Web Publishing Directory	C:\InetPub\wwwroot
FTP Publishing Directory	C:\InetPub\ftproot
Gopher Publishing Directory	C:\InetPub\gophroot

8. Click **OK** to accept the default directories.
9. When prompted to create the default directories, click **Yes**.

   Setup installs the Internet Information Server software.

   Note If a dialog box appears prompting you to create an Internet domain name, click **OK**.

10. When prompted to install the Open Database Connectivity (ODBC) drivers, click **SQL Server**, and then click **OK**.
11. When Setup is complete, click **OK**.
12. Click **Close**.

▸ **To identify changes IIS made to the Windows NT Server environment**

In this procedure, you inspect the Windows NT Server environment after installing Microsoft Internet Information Server. If you do not remember how to determine the answers to the following questions, refer to the corresponding questions in the "To examine the Windows NT Server environment" procedure earlier in this lesson.

Note Complete this procedure on Server1.

1. What publishing services are now installed on your computer?

   ____

2. What Internet-related user account is on your computer?

   ____

3. What Internet-related objects are on your computer that Performance Monitor can monitor?

   ____

▸ To verify that your Microsoft Internet Information Server is working

In this procedure, you verify that IIS is working.

Note Complete this procedure on Workstation1.

---

1. Log on as Administrator.
2. Double-click **Internet Explorer**.
3. In Microsoft Internet Explorer, on the **File** menu, click **Open**, type **Server1** and then click **OK**.

   Does your Web server start?

   ____

4. In the **Address** box, type **ftp://Server1** and then press ENTER.

   Can you connect through FTP to your server?

   ____

5. Close Microsoft Internet Explorer.

▸ To publish from a new directory

In this procedure, you publish a document using a new directory that you create.

Note Complete this procedure on Server1.

---

1. Right-click **My Computer**, and then click **Explore**.
2. In the root of drive C, create a new folder called **NewWWW**.
3. Copy C:\Lab Files\IIS\Default.htm to C:\NewWWW.
4. Close Windows NT Explorer.
5. Click the **Start** button, point to **Programs**, point to **Microsoft Internet Server**, and then click **Internet Service Manager**.
6. Click **Server1** on the line where **Service** is **WWW**.
7. On the **Properties** menu, click **Service Properties**.

8. In the **WWW Service Properties** dialog box, click the **Directories** tab.

   What directories and aliases are listed?

Directory	**Alias**
______________________	______________
______________________	______________
______________________	______________

9. Click the **Add** button.

   The **Directory Properties** dialog box appears.
10. Click the **Browse** button.
11. Double-click **NewWWW** on drive C, and then click **OK**.

    The **Directory** box now contains **C:\NewWWW**.
12. Click **Virtual Directory**, and in the **Alias** box, type **Virtual**

    This will be the published name of the new directory.
13. Click **OK** to close the **Directory Properties** dialog box.

    What directory and alias were added?

    ____

14. Click **OK** to close the **WWW Service Properties** dialog box.
15. Exit Internet Service Manager.

► **To access the document**

In this procedure, you use Microsoft Internet Explorer to access the document you just published.

Note Complete this procedure on Workstation1.

---

1. On the desktop, double-click **Internet Explorer**.
2. On the **File** menu, click **Open**.
3. In the **Open** box, type **http://server1/virtual** and then click **OK**.

   Microsoft Internet Explorer displays the default page in the virtual share.
4. Close Microsoft Internet Explorer.

▸ **To set up DNS for the Internet Information Server**

In these procedures, you use DNS to resolve IP addresses for Internet Information Server.

Note Complete this procedure on Server1.

---

1. In **Administrative Tools (Common)**, click **DNS Manager**.
2. Double click **Server1**.
3. Double-click **corp1.com**.
4. Right-click **corp1.com**.
5. On the menu that appears, click **New Record**.
6. Click **CNAME**, and in the **Alias Name** box, type **WWW1**
7. In the **For Host DNS Name** box, type **Server1.corp1.com** and then click **OK**.
8. Verify that a resource record of type A exists for your computer. If not, create a new host resource record for your computer.
9. Close DNS Manager.

▸ **To test DNS name resolution for the Internet Information Server**

Note Complete this procedure on Server1.

---

1. At a command prompt, type **ping www1** and then press ENTER.

   What is the name of the host, and what is the IP address?

   ____

2. Start Microsoft Internet Explorer.
3. On the **File** menu, click **Open**.
4. In the **Open** box, type **WWW1** and then click **OK**.

   Does your Web server start?

   ____

5. Close Microsoft Internet Explorer.

Summary

The following information summarizes the key points in this chapter:

- The *Internet* is a network of computers located around the world that are able to communicate with one another through telephone lines; an *intranet* exists at a local level, and consists of computers that are connected by means of LANs.
- The Internet and intranets communicate using common languages and protocols.
- The World Wide Web (WWW) is a graphical interface that overlays the Internet to create a virtual network, or Web, of information. In order to connect to Web servers and view the information, you must use a Web *browser* such as *Microsoft Internet Explorer*.
- Additional Internet and intranet components supported by Windows NT are the Internet Information Server (IIS) and Peer Web Services (PWS). IIS and PWS provide computers running Windows NT with the ability to publish resources and services on the Internet and on private intranets. Use IIS and PWS for publishing hypertext Web pages and client/server applications, and for interactive Web applications.
- There are security issues that you need to be aware of when you connect an intranet to the Internet. The Internet, like other networks, provides two-way communication. When you are connected to the Internet, other computers can see your computer. By default, Windows NT security protects your computer from casual intrusion. However, while it is very unlikely that your computer will be attacked while you are browsing the Internet, it is still a good idea to configure your computer securely.

Review

1. Your company has an intranet for disseminating project information. Some of the executives have been hearing about potential security issues on the Internet and are concerned that external hackers could break in to the corporate network through this intranet. What difference between intranets and the Internet should ease their worries?

2. Your software company has many customers located throughout the world and must ensure that software updates are available to all customers worldwide. Should you install IIS or PWS? Which publishing service(s) would you use?

3. Your manager is concerned about allowing access to the corporate intranet from the Internet, because some internal Web pages contain confidential information. What would you tell your manager?

Answer Key

Procedure Answers

Page 492

▸ **To examine the Windows NT Server environment**

4. Scroll through the list of services available.

   Are there any publishing services listed? (Hint: Does the word *publishing* appear in the service name?)

   No.

7. In User Manager for Domains, examine the list of names.

   Is there an Internet Guest Account listed?

   No.

11. In the **Object** box, scroll through the available objects.

    Are there any Internet-related items in the list?

    No.

Page 494

▸ **To identify changes IIS made to the Windows NT Server environment**

1. What publishing services are now installed on your computer?

   Gopher Publishing Service, FTP Publishing Service, and World Wide Web Publishing Service.

2. What Internet-related user account is on your computer?

   IUSR_SERVER1

3. What Internet-related objects are on your computer that Performance Monitor can monitor?

   Gopher Service, FTP Server, HTTP Service, and Internet Information Services Global.

Page 495

▸ **To verify that your Microsoft Internet Information Server is working**

3. In Microsoft Internet Explorer, on the **File** menu, click **Open**, type **Server1** and then click **OK**.

   Does your Web server start?

   Yes.

4. In the **Address** box, type **ftp://Server1** and then press ENTER.

   Can you connect through FTP to your server?

   Yes.

Page 495

► **To publish from a new directory**

8. In the **WWW Service Properties** dialog box, click the **Directories** tab.

   What directories and aliases are listed?

Directory	Alias
C:\InetPub\wwwroot	**<Home>**
C:InetPub\scripts	**/Scripts**
C:\WINNT\System32\inetsrv\iisadmin	**/iisadmin**

13. Click **OK** to close the **Directory Properties** dialog box.

    What directory and alias were added?

    C:\NewWWW with an alias of /Virtual

Page 497

► **To test DNS name resolution for the Internet Information Server**

1. At a command prompt, type **ping www1** and then press ENTER.

   What is the name of the host, and what is the IP address?

   Server1.corp1.com is the name of the host, and the IP address is 131.107.2.200.

4. In the **Open** box, type **WWW1** and then click **OK**.

   Does your Web server start?

   Yes.

Review Answers

Page 499

1. Your company has an intranet for disseminating project information. Some of the executives have been hearing about potential security issues on the Internet and are concerned that external hackers could break in to the corporate network through this intranet. What difference between intranets and the Internet should ease their worries?

   Intranets, by definition, are internal to an organization. Adding WWW, Gopher, and FTP services does not change the security of the site.

2. Your software company has many customers located throughout the world and must ensure that software updates are available to all customers worldwide. Should you install IIS or PWS? Which publishing service(s) would you use?

   Use IIS, because it is optimized for heavy Internet traffic, and use the WWW and FTP publishing services.

3. Your manager is concerned about allowing access to the corporate intranet from the Internet, because some internal Web pages contain confidential information. What would you tell your manager?

   Windows NT security is fully integrated with IIS and PWS. Both IIS and PWS can be configured to require a valid user account and an encrypted authentication in order to access the site. Specific resources can be protected by granting permissions to appropriate users and groups.

CHAPTER 14

Interoperating with Novell NetWare

About This Chapter

Microsoft Windows NT Server and Microsoft Windows NT Workstation provide several features and services that enable computers running Windows NT to coexist and interoperate with Novell NetWare servers. Some of these services are included in Windows NT, while others are available as separate products, commonly called add-ons.

This chapter describes these NetWare connectivity tools and explains how they can be used to integrate Windows NT and NetWare environments.

Before You Begin

To complete the lessons in this chapter, you must have:

- Two computers that meet the hardware and software requirements as specified in the Getting Started section of "About This Book."
- Completed all practices in Chapter 2, "Installing Windows NT."

Lesson 1: Windows NT Connectivity with NetWare

In order for computers running Windows NT to access and share resources with computers running Novell NetWare, you must install some additional software on your computers running Windows NT. The type of connectivity you require determines the software that you must install. The software included with Windows NT is Client Service for NetWare (CSNW), Gateway Services for NetWare (GSNW), and Migration Tool for NetWare. In addition, there is a set of add-on utilities comprised of *File and Print Services for NetWare* (FPNW) and *Directory Service Manager for NetWare* (DSMN). FPNW enables a computer running Windows NT Server to function as a NetWare 3.12-compatible file and print server. DSMN extends Windows NT Server directory service features to NetWare servers.

This lesson explains how computers running Windows NT share file, print, and application services with NetWare-based computers.

After this lesson, you will be able to:

- List the features and services that allow computers running Windows NT to interoperate with computers running Novell NetWare.
- Explain the purpose of NWLink.
- Explain the function of Client Service for NetWare (CSNW).
- Explain the function Gateway Services for NetWare (GSNW).
- Explain the function of File and Print Services for NetWare (FPNW).
- Explain how Novell NetWare networks can be remotely administered by computers running Windows NT.
- Explain the function of Directory Service Manager for NetWare (DSMN).
- Describe the Migration Tool for NetWare.

Estimated lesson time: 30 minutes

NWLink

NetWare uses Internetwork Packet Exchange/Sequenced Packet Exchange (IPX/SPX) as its primary network protocol. Microsoft developed *NWLink IPX/SPX Compatible Transport* (NWLink) to provide computers running Windows NT with the ability to communicate with NetWare servers and clients. NWLink is a native 32-bit Windows NT implementation of IPX/SPX and supports application servers in a NetWare environment. NWLink is included with both Windows NT Server and Windows NT Workstation.

NWLink allows computers running Windows NT to communicate with other computers running Windows NT as well as with NetWare servers. Two networking application programming interfaces (APIs) are supported to allow these communications:

- *Windows Sockets.* This interface supports existing NetWare applications written to comply with the NetWare IPX/SPX Sockets interface.
- *NetBIOS.* This interface supports sending and receiving Novell NetBIOS packets between a computer running Novell NetWare and Novell NetBIOS, and a computer running Windows NT and NWLink NetBIOS.

By itself, NWLink does not provide access to NetWare file and print resources. To enable a computer running Windows NT to access services on NetWare networks, and to provide NetWare clients with the ability to use services on Windows NT servers, Microsoft has developed several tools for NetWare interoperability.

Client Service for NetWare

Client Service for NetWare (CSNW), included with Windows NT Workstation, enables computers running Windows NT Workstation to make direct connections to file and printer resources at NetWare servers running NetWare 2.*x* or later. CSNW supports NetWare 4.*x* servers running either NetWare Directory Services (NDS) or bindery emulation. Login script support is also included.

The following illustration shows two computers running Windows NT Workstation with CSNW and NWLink installed accessing file and print resources on NetWare Server.

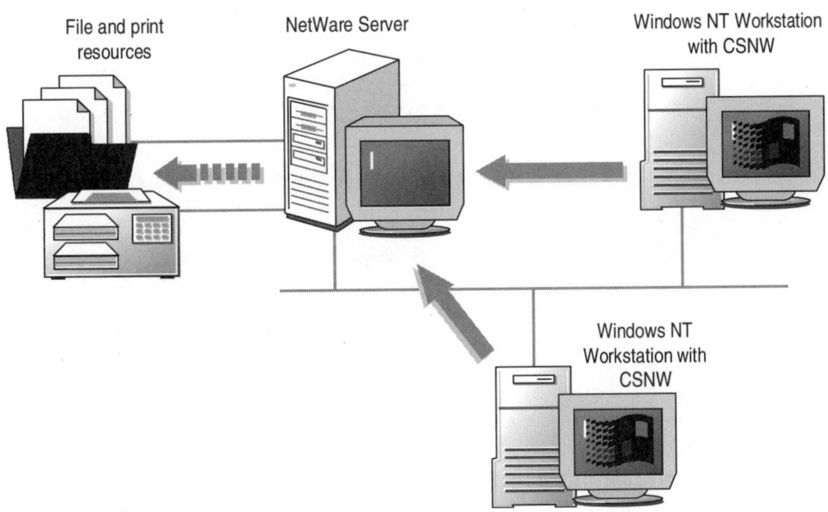

Computers running Windows NT that have CSNW and NWLink installed support the following:

- *NetWare Core Protocol* (NCP), which provides access to file and print services on a NetWare server. NCP provides similar functionality to the Microsoft *server message blocks* (SMBs) protocol, a file sharing protocol designed to allow systems to transparently access files that reside on remote systems.
- *Large Internet Protocol* (LIP), which determines and uses the largest allowable frame size when communicating with a server across a router.
- Long file names (LFNs), which can be used when the NetWare server is running OS/2 Name Space.

CSNW Support for NetWare Directory Services

Client Service for NetWare (CSNW) supports NetWare Directory Services (NDS). NDS organizes shared objects on participating NetWare Servers into a hierarchical tree. Thus, installing CSNW on Windows NT provides Windows NT clients with the ability to browse resources, use authentication, and use printing services on NDS hierarchies.

Note Although Windows NT Server and Windows NT Workstation versions 4.0 support connections to NetWare Directory Services (NDS), they do not support administration of NDS trees.

CSNW Support for Bindery Emulation

CSNW also supports the bindery-based version 3.*x* of Novell NetWare. User accounts and privileges are stored in the NetWare bindery, which is Novell's equivalent of the Windows NT directory database. Access to the network is validated based on user accounts and passwords in a Windows NT domain through the directory database, or on a Novell NetWare server through the bindery.

Gateway Services for NetWare

Gateway Services for NetWare (GSNW) enables computers running Windows NT Server and using NWLink as a transport protocol to access files and printers at NetWare servers. In addition, you can use GSNW to create gateways to NetWare resources. Creating a gateway enables computers running only Microsoft client software to access NetWare resources through the gateway. Any Microsoft network client, such as Windows NT Workstation, Microsoft Windows 95, or Microsoft Windows for Workgroups, that can access resources on the computer running Windows NT Server can access NetWare services through the Windows NT Server running GSNW.

In the following illustration, Windows clients, using SMBs, communicate with a NetWare Server, using NCPs, through a Windows NT server acting as a gateway.

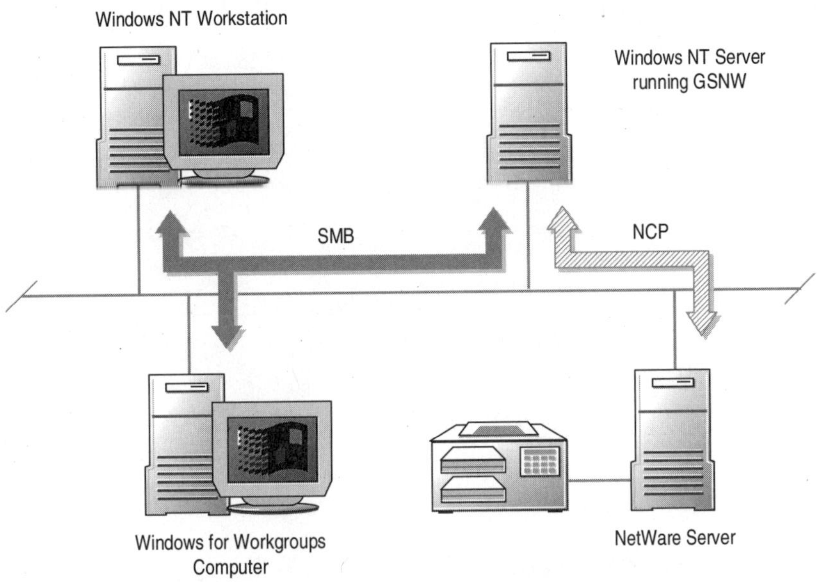

Using GSNW, a computer running Windows NT Server connects to a NetWare file server's directory and then shares it, just as if the directory were on the Windows NT server. Microsoft network clients can then access the directory on the NetWare server by connecting to the share created on the Windows NT server.

Note GSNW is available only on Windows NT Server. When GSNW is installed, CSNW is also installed automatically.

When to Use GSNW

GSNW is designed to provide Windows clients with occasional access to a NetWare network. GSNW is not designed to allow a computer running Windows NT Server to be a user-intensive, high-performance gateway.

GSNW can also serve as a migration path. For example, use GSNW to enable gradual migration from Novell NetWare to Windows NT.

Preparing to Install GSNW

For a computer running Windows NT Server to act as a gateway to resources on a NetWare server, the following steps must be taken on the Novell NetWare network:

1. A user account must be set up on the NetWare server, with the same name and password that the user will use to log on to the computer running Windows NT Server.
2. The user account set up on the NetWare server must have the necessary permissions assigned for the resources that are to be accessed.
3. A group account named NTGATEWAY must be created on the NetWare server.
4. The group NTGATEWAY on the NetWare server must include the user account that was set up in step 1.

Note Use one of the following NetWare utilities—System Console (Syscon), NWAdmin, or NetAdmin—to create the group and user accounts on the NetWare server.

Remote Client Access to NetWare Servers

RAS clients can use GSNW to access NetWare servers. Using GSNW, businesses can use Windows NT Server as a communications server and enable remote users to have reliable and secure remote access to a NetWare local area network (LAN).

Note Like Client Service for NetWare, GSNW supports NetWare Directory Services (NDS) as well as the bindery-based 3.*x* versions.

File and Print Services for NetWare

CSNW and GSNW provide computers running Windows NT with the ability to connect to NetWare servers for file, print, and application resources. To integrate NetWare clients into a Windows NT network and also allow them to access resources on computers running Windows NT Server, Microsoft provides File and Print Services for NetWare (FPNW).

The following illustration shows various connectivity methods between Windows NT networks and NetWare networks. The heavy black line shows the connectivity provided by installing FPNW on a Windows NT server.

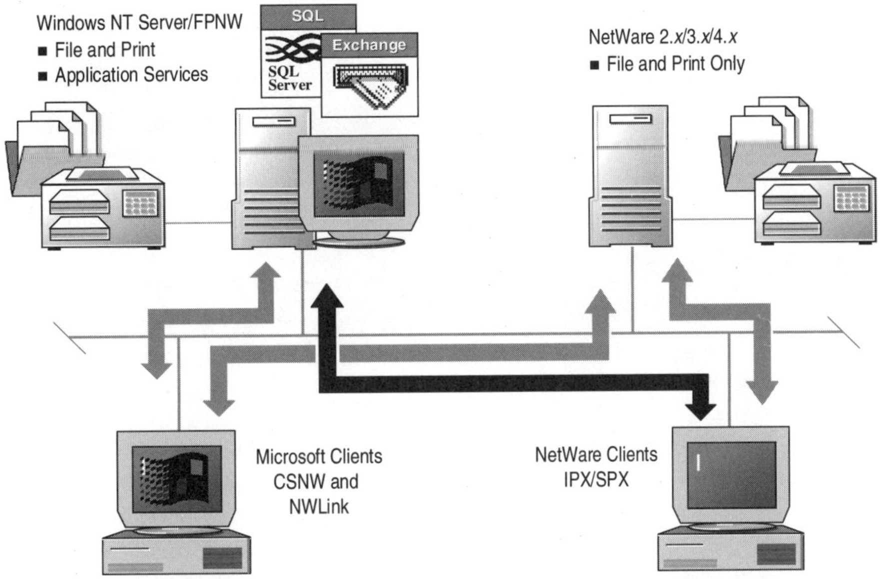

FPNW is not included with Windows NT. It is a Windows NT add-on utility that enables a computer running Windows NT Server to function as a NetWare 3.12-compatible file and print server. The server appears just like any other NetWare server to the NetWare clients, and the clients can access volumes, files, and printers at the server. No changes or additions to the NetWare client software are necessary, making integration with a Windows NT Server environment more cost-effective. You can add FPNW to an existing application server to maximize usage of hardware resources.

In summary, using FPNW, NetWare clients can transparently gain access to file, print, and application services on a Windows NT server. FPNW extends the interoperability of Windows NT Server and makes it easier for NetWare clients to make the transition to Windows NT Server.

Note For more information on FPNW, see the *Microsoft Services for NetWare Reviewer's Guide.*

Remote Administration of Novell Networks

Novell NetWare servers cannot be administered directly; instead, a NetWare client acts as the system console and controls the administration of the NetWare server.

A computer running Windows NT with GSNW or CSNW enabled can also act as a system console to administer the NetWare servers. Access to the NetWare administration utilities, Syscon, RConsole, and PConsole is accomplished on the Windows NT client as if the Windows NT client were a NetWare client.

- System Console (Syscon) is the primary administration tool and is used to set up user accounts, define policies, and grant user access permissions to the NetWare network.
- RConsole provides a remote view of the NetWare system console. The console functions can be performed on the remote console.
- PConsole provides the administrator with the tools necessary to manage print servers.

Multiple sessions of the administration tools can be run on a single Windows NT client. The information about each of the servers to which the client is connected is displayed in a separate window on the client. This ability to run multiple sessions of the administration tools on a single computer running Windows NT allows you to monitor all of the NetWare servers from one system console. This capability is not possible on computers running other operating systems such as Microsoft MS-DOS.

A major benefit of installing and configuring Windows NT Server services is the ability to administer *all* clients and servers on the network from a central point, regardless of the geographic location of the computer or which operating system is running.

Note For a NetWare client to access and administer a Windows NT server, FPNW must be installed on the computer running Windows NT Server. Once FPNW is installed and configured, a NetWare client can sign on to the computer running Windows NT Server and perform administration tasks.

Directory Service Manager for NetWare

Directory Service Manager for NetWare (DSMN) extends Windows NT Server directory service features to NetWare servers. With DSMN, you can centrally manage mixed Windows NT and NetWare 2.*x*, 3.*x*, and 4.*x* (in bindery emulation mode) environments with Windows NT Directory Services.

As can be seen in the following illustration, DSMN copies NetWare user and group account information, such as NWUSER1, NWUSER2, NWGRP1, and NWGRP2, to a primary domain controller (PDC) running Windows NT Server 4.0. DSMN also incrementally propagates any account changes, such as the user account NTUSER1 and group NTGRP1, which are created on the PDC back to NetWare servers.

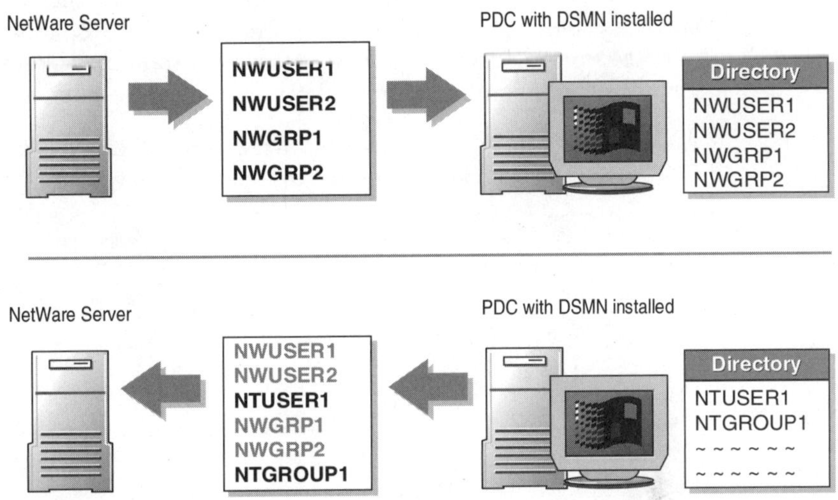

Sharing account information is accomplished without having to install additional software on NetWare servers.

DSMN is not included with Windows NT. It is a Windows NT add-on utility that allows a single network login for NetWare clients by synchronizing accounts across all NetWare servers. Clients need only remember one account name and password to gain access to file, print, and application resources on the network.

Use DSMN to accomplish the following tasks:

- Specify which NetWare user and group accounts to manage centrally from Windows NT Server. The specified accounts are copied to the domain's directory database on the PDC. These NetWare accounts become Windows NT Server accounts and must comply with the account policy of the Windows NT Server domain.
- Merge account names from multiple NetWare servers into one account name. If a client has accounts on two NetWare servers and these accounts have different user names, it is possible to merge the accounts' names when adding them to the domain. For example, DavidS and DavidSm could become DavidS.
- Specify which Windows NT Server domain accounts (user and group) to copy back to NetWare servers. This ensures that changes made to domain accounts are synchronized with the NetWare server.

Note For more information on DSMN, see the *Services for NetWare 4.0 Administrators Guide*.

Migration Tool for NetWare

The Windows NT Server Migration Tool for NetWare, included with Windows NT Server, enables you to easily transfer user and group accounts, volumes, folders, and files from a NetWare server to a computer running Windows NT Server. If the server you are migrating to runs FPNW, you can also migrate users' logon scripts.

The following illustration shows NetWare user and group accounts, folders, and files being transferred to a computer running Windows NT Server.

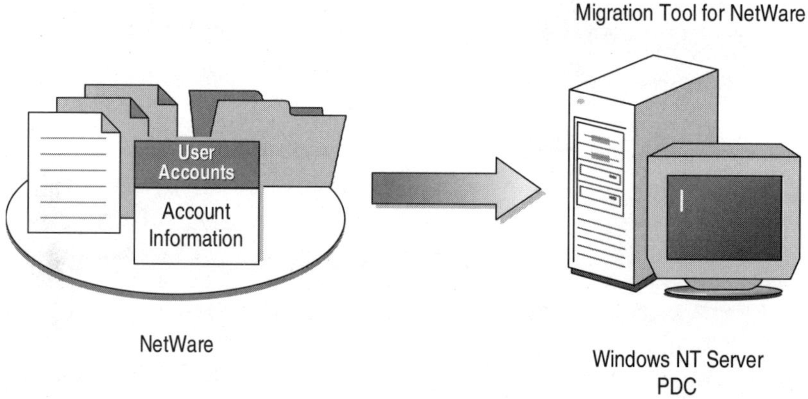

The Migration Tool for NetWare provides a computer running Windows NT with the capability to perform the following functions:

- Preserve appropriate user account information, including NetWare-specific information such as login and station restrictions.
- Preserve login scripts with the user account. Windows NT Server supports NetWare login script commands.
- Control how user and group names are transferred.
- Set passwords for transferred accounts.
- Control how account restrictions and administrative rights are transferred.
- Create a volume for NetWare users.
- Select the directories and files to transfer.
- Select a destination for transferred directories and files.
- Preserve effective rights on directories and files.

Note The executable file for launching the Migration Tool for NetWare is Nwconv.exe. For additional information on the Migration Tool for NetWare, see the *Networking Supplement* portion of Books Online or the Help file included with the source files. You can use the Expand.exe utility to decompress the **expand nwconv.hl_ expand.hlp** Help file.

Interoperability with Novell NetWare

Computers running Windows NT using NWLink can be integrated into Novell NetWare environments. Connections over NWLink can be made through a variety of communication mechanisms, such as Windows Sockets or NWLink NetBIOS.

The following illustration lists the interoperability options.

Platform	Running	Can Connect To
NetWare client	IPX with NetBIOS, Named Pipes, or Windows Sockets support	Windows NT–based computers, with NWLink, running IPX applications such as Microsoft SQL Server
Windows NT–based computer	NWLink	Client/server applications running on a NetWare server
Windows NT–based computer	NWLink and CSNW or NWLink and GSNW	Novell NetWare servers for file and print services
NetWare client	IPX	Windows NT Server, with NWLink and FPNW installed, for file and print services

Novell NetWare Integration

Recall that NWLink provides client/server application support for IPX-based applications, but by itself does not support access to file and print resources. If a Windows NT client requires connections to file and print resources on a NetWare server, CSNW must be installed on the Windows NT client.

If there are computers on the network that are not running NWLink or another IPX/SPX transport, you can create a gateway for these computers on a computer running Windows NT Server by installing and configuring GSNW.

If a Novell NetWare client requires file and print access to a computer running Windows NT, FPNW must be installed on that computer running Windows NT.

Lesson 2: Installing and Configuring CSNW and GSNW

Windows NT tools for NetWare enable file, print, and application sharing between Windows NT–based and NetWare-based computers. This lesson explains how to install and configure two of these tools, CSNW and GSNW.

After this lesson, you will be able to:

- Install and configure CSNW.
- Install and configure GSNW.
- Configure a GSNW gateway.

Estimated lesson time: 45 minutes

Installing and Configuring CSNW

CSNW is installed through the **Services** tab of the Network program in Control Panel.

Note Before installing CSNW, use the **Services** tab of the Network program in the Control Panel to remove any existing NetWare redirectors, such as *NetWare Services for Windows NT* from Novell, and then restart the computer.

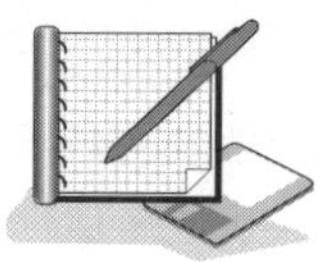

Practice

In this procedure, you install Client Service for NetWare.

Note Complete this procedure on Workstation1.

▸ **To install CSNW**

1. Double-click the Network icon in Control Panel.
2. Click the **Services** tab, and then click **Add**.

   The **Select Network Services** dialog box appears.
3. Click **Gateway (and Client) Services for NetWare**, and then click **OK**.
4. When prompted for the location of the CSNW installation files, type ***cd-rom_drive_letter*:\I386** and then click **Continue**.
5. Click **Close**.

   A series of **Bindings** dialog boxes appears while the binding's configuration, storing, and review occur.

6. Click **Yes** to restart the computer.
7. When Workstation1 restarts, log on to the domain as Administrator.
8. When the **Select NetWare Logon** dialog box appears, click **Cancel**.
9. When the **NetWare Network** dialog box appears indicating that you have not been authenticated by any server and asking if you would like to continue, click **Yes**.

Configuring CSNW

Configuration of CSNW is necessary for computers running Windows NT Workstation to be able to connect to a NetWare server. The CSNW installation creates a new icon, labeled CSNW, and adds it to Control Panel. You use this icon to configure CSNW.

To configure CSNW, double-click the CSNW icon in Control Panel. The **Client Service for NetWare** dialog box appears.

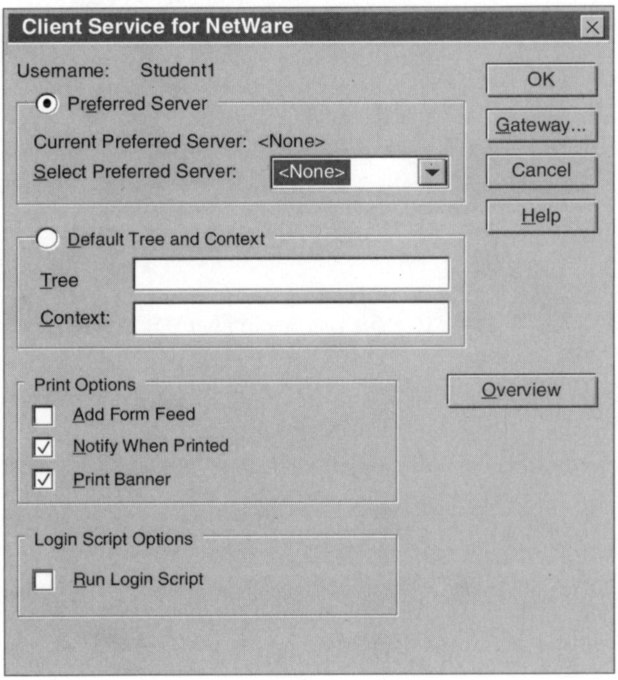

The **Client Service for NetWare** dialog box can be used to configure the options listed in the following table.

Option	Use this option to
Preferred Server	Choose a preferred server that the computer connects to by default during the login process. The preferred server is the one that is queried for information about resources available on the NetWare network. If you have not defined a default tree and context, the name of the NetWare server to which you connect by default when you log in appears in Current Preferred Server. If your network uses NDS, you should have a default tree and context instead of a preferred server.
Default Tree	Enter or change the default tree. In a NetWare Directory Services (NDS) environment, the default tree defines the NDS name of the user name that is used for login. All resources in the default tree can then be accessed without requiring further prompts. NDS is a global, distributed information database that maintains information about every resource on the network—including users, groups, printers, volumes, and other devices—in a hierarchical tree structure.
Default Context	Enter the default context, or position, of the user name used for login. The context can be in either a label or non-labeled format.
Print Options: Add Form Feed	Notify the printer to eject a page at the end of each document that is sent.
Print Options: Notify When Printed	Receive notification when documents have been printed.
Print Options: Print Banner	Notify the printer to print a banner page before each document that is printed.
Run Login Script	Run the user's login script whenever a user logs in to a NetWare server or NDS tree.

Next, you use the Novell NetWare simulation. The purpose of the simulation is to allow you to configure CSNW. The simulation presents two different CSNW configurations:

- *Bindery emulation.* Uses a preferred server. In the first configuration, you access a resource on a Novell NetWare server by specifying a preferred server.
- *NDS.* Uses a default tree and context. In the second configuration, you access a resource on a Novell NetWare server by specifying a default tree and context.

Practice

In these procedures, you use the Novell NetWare simulation to configure CSNW.

Note Complete this procedure on Workstation1.

► **To start the Novell NetWare simulation**

- Click the Start button, point to Programs, point to Technical Support Training, point to Simulations, and then click Novell NetWare Simulation.

  The simulation begins, simulating your desktop with Control Panel open.

► **To select a preferred server**

1. Double-click the CSNW icon in Control Panel.

   The **Client Service for NetWare** dialog box appears.
2. Click **Preferred Server**.
3. In the **Select Preferred Server** box, select **CANW312DPT01**.
4. Click **OK**.

   A message box appears, indicating your changes will take effect the next time you log in.
5. Click **OK**.

   A **Windows NT NetWare Simulation** dialog box appears stating that the simulation will proceed as if a shutdown occurs and you have logged on as Administrator.
6. Click **OK**.

   A dialog box appears prompting you to wait while the system writes unsaved data to the disk.

   The simulation continues with Control Panel open.

► **To use the Syscon resource on a NetWare server running bindery emulation**

1. Right-click My Computer, and then click **Map Network Drive**.
2. Double-click the CANW312DPT01 server.
3. Click the SYS folder, and then click **OK**.

   You are connected to the CANW312DPT01 NetWare server, with the SYS folder mapped to drive E. A window displaying the contents of the SYS folder is open on your desktop.
4. Double-click the Public folder.
5. Double-click **Syscon**.

   You are now running a utility that resides on the NetWare server. For this simulation, the menu options of Syscon have been disabled.
6. To exit Syscon, press ESC, use the arrow keys to select **Yes**, and then press ENTER.
7. Right-click My Computer, and then click **Disconnect Network Drive**.
8. Click **CANW312DPT01\SYS**, and then click **OK**.

► **To select a default tree and context**

1. Double-click the CSNW icon in Control Panel.

   The **Client Service for NetWare** dialog box appears.
2. Click **Default Tree and Context**.
3. In the **Tree** box, type **terra_flora**
4. In the **Context** box, type **terra_flora**
5. Click **OK**.

   A message box appears, indicating your changes will take effect the next time you log in.
6. Click **OK**.

   A **Windows NT NetWare Simulation** dialog box appears stating that the simulation will proceed as if a shutdown occurs and you have logged on as Administrator.
7. Click **OK**.

   A dialog box appears prompting you to wait while the system writes unsaved data to the disk.

   The simulation continues with Control Panel open.

▶ **To connect to a NetWare server running NDS**

1. Right-click My Computer, and then click **Map Network Drive**.
2. Double-click the Terra_flora tree.
3. Double-click the Terra_flora organization folder.
4. Click the CANW410DIV01_SYS folder, and then click **OK**.

   A window appears showing the connection to CANW410DIV01_SYS.terra_flora on the Terra_flora tree.
5. Double-click the Public folder.
6. Double-click **Pconsole**.

   You are now running a utility that resides on the NetWare server. In this simulation, the menu options of Pconsole have been disabled.
7. To exit Pconsole, press ESC, use the arrow keys to select **Yes**, and then press ENTER.
8. Right-click My Computer, and then click **Disconnect Network Drive**.
9. Click **TERRA_FLORA\CANW410DIV01_SYS.TERRA_FLORA**, and then click **OK**.

   A **Windows NetWare Simulation** dialog box appears.
10. Click **Exit** to end the Novell NetWare simulation.

Installing and Configuring GSNW

Like CSNW, GSNW is installed through the **Services** tab of the Network program in Control Panel.

Note Before installing GSNW, use the **Services** tab of the Network program in Control Panel to remove any existing NetWare redirectors, such as *NetWare Services for Windows NT* from Novell, and then restart the computer.

Practice

In this procedure, you install Gateway Services for NetWare.

Note Complete this procedure on Server1.

► To install GSNW

1. Double-click the Network icon in Control Panel.
2. Click the **Services** tab, and then click **Add**.

   The **Select Network Services** dialog box appears.
3. Click **Gateway (and Client) Services for NetWare**, and then click **OK**.
4. When prompted for the location to copy the necessary files, type **\\Server1\nts_source\I386** and then click **Continue**.

   A series of **Windows NT Setup** dialog boxes appear as files are installed on your system. When the installation is complete, the **Network** dialog box appears.
5. Click **Close**.
6. If you have multiple network adapters, you may be prompted to change the default internal network number (if it is 0) to a unique number, and asked if you would like to change that now. Click **No**.

   When the bindings review has completed, a **Network Settings Change** dialog box appears, prompting you to shut down and restart.
7. Click **Yes**.
8. When the computer restarts, log on as Administrator.

   When you log on, a **Select NetWare Logon** dialog box appears, and you are asked to specify a preferred server.
9. Click **Cancel**, and then click **Yes**.

   The GSNW installation creates a new icon, labeled GSNW, and adds it to Control Panel.

Configuring GSNW

Configuration of GSNW is necessary for computers running Windows NT Workstation to be able to connect to a NetWare server.

To configure GSNW, double-click the GSNW program in Control Panel.

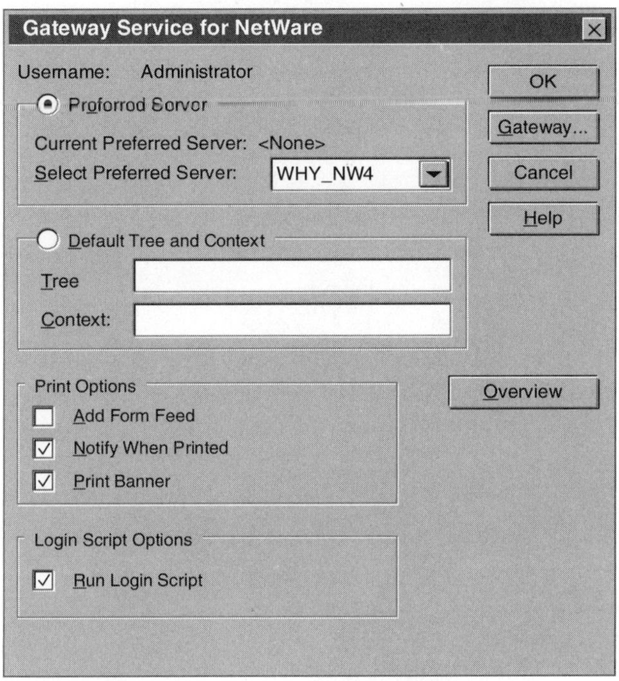

The **Gateway Service for NetWare** dialog box can be used to configure the options listed in the following table.

Option	Use this option to
Preferred Server	Choose a preferred server that the computer connects to by default during the login process. The preferred server is queried for information about resources available on the NetWare network.
Default Tree	Enter or change the default tree. In a NetWare Directory Services (NDS) environment, the default tree defines the NDS name of the user name that is used for login. All resources in the default tree can then be accessed without requiring further prompts.
Default Context	Enter the default context, or position, of the user name used for login. The context can be in either a label or non-labeled format.
Print Options: Add Form Feed	Notify the printer to eject a page at the end of each document that is sent.
Print Options: Notify When Printed	Receive notification when documents have been printed.
Print Options: Print Banner	Notify the printer to print a banner page before each document that is printed.
Run Login Script	Run login scripts.
Gateway	Display the **Configure Gateway** dialog box.
Overview	Display Help topics about Gateway Services for NetWare.

A Windows NT server needs to connect through a gateway to a NetWare server to enable Windows NT clients to transparently gain access to NetWare server file and print resources.

Specifying a Gateway

When you configure GSNW you need to specify a gateway and a gateway account that has supervisory privileges on the NetWare server. To specify a gateway and a gateway account, in the **Gateway Service for NetWare** dialog box, click **Gateway**. The **Configure Gateway** dialog box appears.

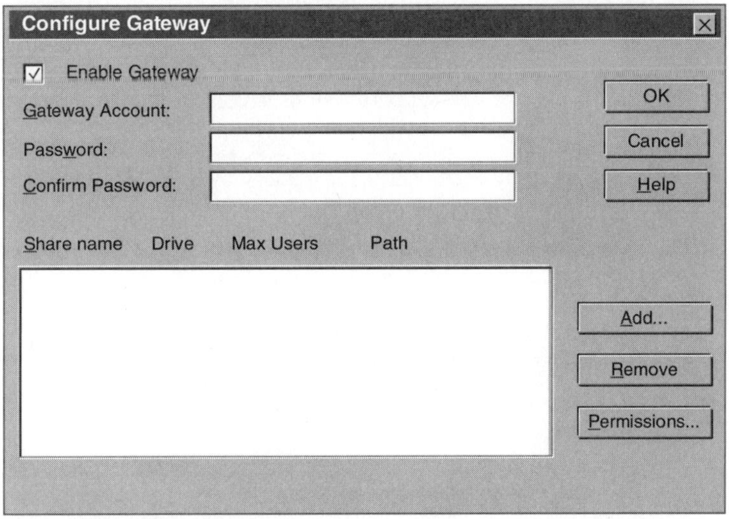

The **Configure Gateway** dialog box is used to enable the gateway to share NetWare file and print resources, to share NetWare volumes and directories, and to set permissions for the gateway. The options listed in the following table can be configured through this dialog box.

Option	Use this option to
Enable Gateway	Enable gateways on this server.
Gateway Account	Enter the user name for a gateway account. This account must exist and be a member of the NTGATEWAY group on all NetWare servers to which this server will have gateways.
Password	Enter the password for the gateway account.
Confirm Password	Retype the password for the gateway account.

(*continued*)

Option	Use this option to
Share name	List the existing gateways to NetWare resources created on this server.
Add	Create gateways to additional NetWare volumes or directories.
Remove	Disconnect clients and stop sharing selected NetWare file resources. You should warn clients before disconnecting them or stopping the sharing of a particular resource.
Permissions	Set permissions to control user access to a gateway.

Note The default permission for a gateway is **Full Control for Everyone**.

Once you have selected Enable Gateway and specified a gateway account and password, click **Add**. The **New Share** dialog box appears.

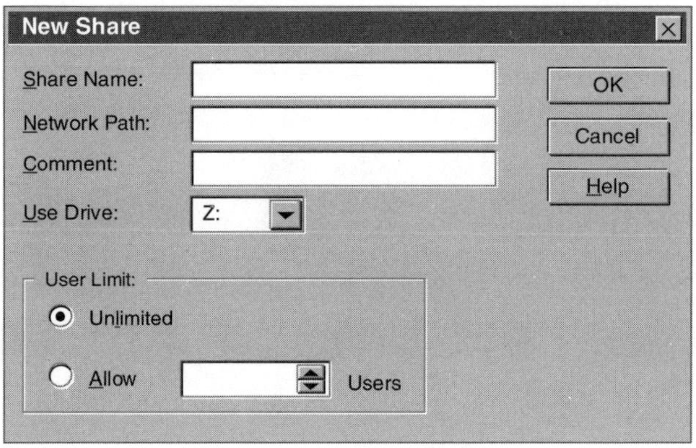

The options listed in the following table can be configured through the **New Share** dialog box.

Option	Use this option to
Share Name	Type the share name that the Microsoft client users will use to connect to the shared directory. In order for MS-DOS-based workstations to connect, the share name cannot exceed eight characters. Otherwise the share name can be as many as 12 characters.
Network Path	Type the path to a NetWare volume, including the name of the NetWare server and volume.

Practice

In this procedure, you view the options you can configure for GSNW. These options include selecting a preferred server, synchronizing your password with the Supervisor password on a Novell NetWare server, and sharing files on a Novell NetWare server.

Note Complete this exercise on Server1.

▸ **To configure GSNW**

1. Double-click the GSNW icon in Control Panel.

   The **Gateway Services for NetWare** dialog box appears.

2. In the **Gateway Services for NetWare** dialog box, click **Gateway**.

   The **Configure Gateway** dialog box appears.

3. Click **Enable Gateway**.
4. In the **Gateway Account** box, type **Administrator**
5. In the **Password** and **Confirm Password** boxes, type **password**
6. Click **Add**.

   The **New Share** dialog box appears.

7. In the **Share Name** text box, type **sysvol**
8. In the **Network Path** text box, type **\\netware1\sys**
9. In the **Use Drive** box, click **Z:**

   Note If you have a NetWare server on your network, you could use it to test this procedure.

   ---

10. Click **Cancel** to close the **New Share** dialog box.
11. Click **Cancel** to close the **Configure Gateway** dialog box.
12. Click **Cancel** to close the **Gateway Service for NetWare** dialog box.

    Note If you had entered a new share and clicked **OK** instead of **Cancel**, a dialog box would have appeared, stating that the changes will take effect the next time that you log on.

Summary

The following information summarizes the key points in this chapter:

- Microsoft provides several features and services that enable computers running Windows NT to interoperate with Novell networks and servers so that both computers running Windows NT and Novell-based computers can share resources. Some of these services are included in Windows NT, while others are available as separate products, commonly called add-ons.
- *NWLink protocol.* Microsoft developed NWLink to provide computers running Windows NT with the ability to communicate with NetWare servers and clients. NWLink is included with both Windows NT Server and Windows NT Workstation.
- *Client Service for NetWare* (CSNW). CSNW enables computers running Windows NT Workstation to make direct connections to file and printer resources at NetWare servers. Furthermore, CSNW supports NetWare Directory Services (NDS) which provides Windows NT clients with the ability to browse resources, use authentication, and use printing services on NDS hierarchies.
- *Gateway Services for NetWare* (GSNW). GSNW enables computers running Windows NT Server and NWLink to both directly access files and printers at NetWare servers, and create gateways to NetWare resources for Windows clients.
- *File and Print Services for NetWare* (FPNW). FPNW enables NetWare clients to access file, print, and application resources on computers running Windows NT Server. FPNW extends the interoperability of Windows NT Server and makes it easier for NetWare clients to make the transition to Windows NT Server.
- A computer running Windows NT with GSNW or CSNW enabled can also act as a system console to administer the NetWare servers. Multiple sessions of the NetWare administration tools can be run on a single Windows NT client. This ability to run multiple sessions of the administration tools on a single computer running Windows NT allows you to monitor all of the NetWare servers from one system console.
- *Directory Service Manager for NetWare* (DSMN). DSMN extends Windows NT Server directory service features to NetWare servers. DSMN copies NetWare user and group account information to Windows NT servers and then incrementally propagates any account changes back to NetWare servers.
- *Migration Tool for NetWare.* The Migration Tool for NetWare, included with Windows NT Server, enables the transfer of user and group accounts, volumes, folders, and files from a NetWare server to a computer running Windows NT Server.

Review

1. Your company is deploying Windows NT Workstation on its desktop computers. These computers need to access NetWare servers on the network. What components should be installed on the computers running Windows NT Workstation in order for them to gain access to the NetWare servers?

2. You have established a gateway on a computer running Windows NT Server to a NetWare volume. You have assigned full control permissions to your Domain Users group, and yet your users are complaining that they cannot save files to a directory through the gateway. What is the likely cause of the problem?

3. You want to integrate several NetWare clients into your Windows NT network. These clients need to be able to access printers located on Prntsrv, a computer running Windows NT Server. What software must be installed on the NetWare clients and what software must be installed on Prntsrv?

Answer Key

Review Answers

Page 527

1. Your company is deploying Windows NT Workstation on its desktop computers. These computers need to access NetWare servers on the network. What components should be installed on the computers running Windows NT Workstation in order for them to gain access to the NetWare servers?

   NWLink and CSNW.

2. You have established a gateway on a computer running Windows NT Server to a NetWare volume. You have assigned full control permissions to your Domain Users group, and yet your users are complaining that they cannot save files to a directory through the gateway. What is the likely cause of the problem?

   The NTGATEWAY group on the NetWare server has not been assigned the appropriate level of rights on the NetWare server. The gateway cannot grant greater permissions than the NetWare rights allow.

3. You want to integrate several NetWare clients into your Windows NT network. These clients need to be able to access printers located on Prntsrv, a computer running Windows NT Server. What software must be installed on the NetWare clients and what software must be installed on Prntsrv?

   No additional software needs to be installed on the NetWare clients; Prntsrv must be running NWLink and must have FPNW installed on it.

CHAPTER 15

Implementing Network Clients

About This Chapter

In order to connect to a computer running Microsoft Windows NT Server, the appropriate client software must be installed and configured on the client computer. In addition, the appropriate licensing for the servers and client computers must be obtained to ensure that network access complies with the Microsoft licensing legal requirements.

In Chapter 2, "Installing Windows NT," you learned that during installation of Windows NT Server you must select either the Per Server or Per Seat licensing mode. However, within a single organization you can choose the Per Server mode on some servers and the Per Seat mode on others. In this chapter, you learn about the Licensing program in Control Panel and License Manager in Administrative Tools (Common) to manage the client access licenses on your network. You learn which client operating systems can access a computer running Windows NT Server. You also learn how to install and configure client software, as well as Services for Macintosh.

Before You Begin

To complete the lessons in this chapter, you must have:

- Two computers that meet the hardware and software requirements as specified in the Getting Started section of "About This Book."
- Completed all practices in Chapter 2, "Installing Windows NT."

Lesson 1: Windows NT Server 4.0 Licensing

With the Microsoft BackOffice licensing model, Windows NT Servers and client computers are licensed separately. You purchase only the licenses required to accommodate your company's networking environment. A server license is required for each server and a Client Access License (CAL) is required for each client computer that accesses a server. Microsoft offers two licensing modes: Per Server licensing and Per Seat licensing. In this lesson, you learn how to determine which is the best licensing solution for a given network environment.

After this lesson, you will be able to:

- Describe a Client Access License.
- Describe Per Server and Per Seat licensing.
- Determine the preferred licensing configuration for a given network environment.
- Explain how to use the Licensing program in Control Panel to specify the licensing mode for a computer running Windows NT Server.
- Explain how to use the Licensing program in Control Panel to configure the license replication load.
- Explain how to use License Manager to manage Client Access Licenses across an organization.

Estimated lesson time: 50 minutes

What Is a Client Access License?

A *Client Access License* (CAL) provides the legal right for a computer to access a computer running Windows NT Server. Client Access Licenses are separate from the desktop operating system software you use to connect to Microsoft server products. Purchasing Microsoft Windows 95, Windows NT Workstation, or any other desktop operating system (such as an Apple Macintosh or any other non-Microsoft operating system) that connects to Microsoft server products does not constitute a legal license to connect to those Microsoft server products.

Example of Client Connections

Licensing is based upon the number of client connections to computers running Windows NT Server.

The following example illustrates how connections are defined for licensing purposes. A company has a computer running Windows NT Server named Products. It contains two shared folders, one named Word and the other named Excel.

- If User1 connects to the Word shared folder and the Excel shared folder from a *single* client computer, this is considered *one* connection to the server for licensing purposes.
- If User1 connects to the Word shared folder on Products from Workstation1 and concurrently logs on to Workstation2, as User1, and connects to the Excel shared folder on Products, that is considered *two* connections.
- Even if a user connects to the Word shared folder on Products from Workstation1 and concurrently logs on to Workstation2, as User1, and connects to the Word shared folder on Products, that is still considered *two* connections.

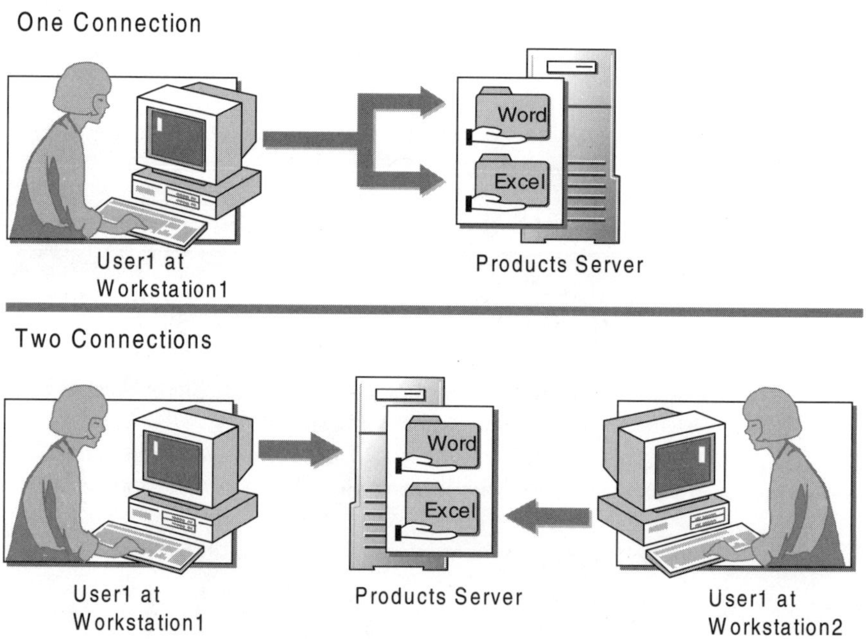

The Licensing Modes

Remember that Windows NT Server provides two licensing modes:

- *Per Server Licensing.* In Per Server licensing, *CALs are assigned to the server.* The number of CALs determines the number of simultaneous connections that can be made to *that* server.

  When you choose the Per Server licensing mode, you must enter the number of CALs purchased for that server. There must be at *least* as many CALs purchased for that server as the maximum number of client computers that connect simultaneously to that server. For example, if the maximum number of clients that will simultaneously connect to the server is 20, then you must have 20 CALs.

  The Per Server licensing mode can be the more economical choice when client computers:

  - Ordinarily connect to only one occasional-use or special-purpose server.
  - Do not all need to connect to the server at the same time.

  Important Under Per Server licensing, if the limit of concurrent connections to the server has been reached, and an additional client tries to connect to the server, Windows NT Server displays an error message on the client computer. This error is logged in the system log. No additional computers can connect to the server until an existing connection is closed or the server is configured for additional Client Access Licenses.

- *Per Seat Licensing.* In Per Seat licensing, *a CAL is purchased for each client computer.* With a Per Seat license, a client can access network resources such as file, print, and communications on *any* computer running Windows NT Server in the network, and can log on to multiple servers simultaneously.

  Thus, a user can legally connect to any server in the network from any client computer for which a CAL has been purchased. If the Per Seat licensing option is chosen, it will not prevent clients from connecting to a server if the number of simultaneous client connections exceeds the number of Per Seat licenses that have been purchased.

Licensing Considerations

The following examples will assist you in deciding whether to select either the Per Server or Per Seat licensing, or a combination of the two for the servers on your network.

If you have 200 clients that need simultaneous access to your server, then you must buy 200 CALs. If you select Per Server licensing, the 200 CALs would be placed on the server. If you purchase a second computer to run Windows NT Server, and continue to use Per Server licensing, you would need to purchase an additional 200 CALs for the second server in order for the clients to access resources on the second server. Thus, you would need a total of 400 CALs.

However, if you switched the first server to Per Seat mode, and you selected Per Seat mode during the Windows NT Server installation on the second server, you could assign the 200 CALs to the 200 clients. The clients would be able to access resources on either of the servers, or both of the servers simultaneously. You would only have to purchase a total of 200 CALs.

If all 200 clients occasionally need access to the two servers, but not all of the clients need access at the same time, you might find it more economical to use Per Server mode licensing. You could buy 100 CALs, with 50 CALs on each server. All 200 clients would have access to both servers, but a maximum of 50 clients at a time could be connected to each of the servers.

Topic Review

Your company is a small, newly created business that has one file and print server and 30 client computers. You configured the server using the Per Server licensing mode and obtained 30 Client Access Licenses, so that all 30 clients could access the server.

1. Your business is growing, so you purchase five new client computers and add them to the network. If 30 clients are currently connected to the server, will another client be able to connect to the server? Why or why not?

2. You decide to add a mail server that *all* clients will connect to. What would be the most economical licensing mode solution for the company?

Choosing Per Server vs. Per Seat Licensing

Use the following guidelines for selecting a licensing mode:

- If your network contains only one server, select the Per Server option and specify the maximum number of simultaneous connections that can be made to the server. The maximum number of simultaneous connections is the number of CALs you have purchased for that server. Any client computer in the network can log on to the server, as long as there are connections available. If you select the Per Seat mode, only those computers for which CALs were purchased would be able to connect to the server.

  If your needs change so that the Per Seat option is more economical, as is often the case when you purchase additional servers for your network, Windows NT Server allows you to perform a *one-time conversion* from a Per Server to a Per Seat configuration. If you chose Per Seat licensing at installation, and you later decide that you prefer the Per Server mode, you would need to reinstall Windows NT Server in order to use Per Server mode.
- If you have multiple servers and the total number of CALs across all servers to support the Per Server mode is equal to or greater than the number of computers or workstations, select or convert to the Per Seat option.

Use the following table to help you determine which licensing mode to use in your networking environment.

Licensing mode and computers	Result
Per Server option:	
Number of simultaneous connections needed to server1	
Number of simultaneous connections needed to server2	
Number of simultaneous connections needed to server*N*	
Total of simultaneous connections needed for all servers: A = server1 + server2 + ... + server*N*	A
Per Seat option:	
Number of seats (computers) that access *any* server is the number of CALs needed for Per Seat licensing	B

The following notes explain how to use the table:

- If A is less than B, then use Per Server licensing.
- If B is less than A, then use Per Seat licensing.

Note When you purchase Windows NT Server, a *server license* is included with the purchase. This server license entitles you to install Windows NT Server on one and only one computer. A server license should not be confused with Per Server licensing for CALs.

Topic Review

1. A company has one computer running Windows NT Server. There are 300 computers running Windows NT Workstation in the company, but only 250 of these will access the server simultaneously.

   What licensing mode would be the best solution for this company?

Licensing mode and computers	Result
Per Server option:	
Number of simultaneous connections needed to server1	
Number of simultaneous connections needed to server2	
Number of simultaneous connections needed to server*N*	
Total of simultaneous connections needed for all servers: A = server1 + server2 + ... + server*N*	A
Per Seat option:	
Number of seats (computers) that access *any* server is the number of CALs needed for Per Seat licensing	B

2. This company now adds an additional computer running Windows NT Server. Up to 200 of the workstations will also access the new server simultaneously.

   What licensing mode would now be the best solution for this company?

Licensing mode and computers	Result
Per Server option:	
Number of simultaneous connections needed to server1	
Number of simultaneous connections needed to server2	
Number of simultaneous connections needed to server*N*	
Total of simultaneous connections needed for all servers: A = server1 + server2 + ... + server*N*	A
Per Seat option:	
Number of seats (computers) that access *any* server is the number of CALs needed for Per Seat licensing	B

Licensing Administration

Tracking licenses manually on local computers within a small domain or across an entire organization with multiple domains can be time-consuming and expensive.

Windows NT Server 4.0 includes two administrative tools that help to reduce these costs and the administrative overhead of license tracking:

- Licensing program in Control Panel
- License Manager program on the Administrative Tools (Common) menu

These tools enable you to automatically replicate licensing data from all of the primary domain controllers (PDCs) in the organization to a centralized database on a specified master server, making it easier for you to comply with legal requirements.

The Licensing Program

The Licensing program is one of the tools that you can use to track licensing data and replicate the licensing data to a centralized database.

Start the Licensing program in Control Panel to access the **Choose Licensing Mode** dialog box shown in the following illustration.

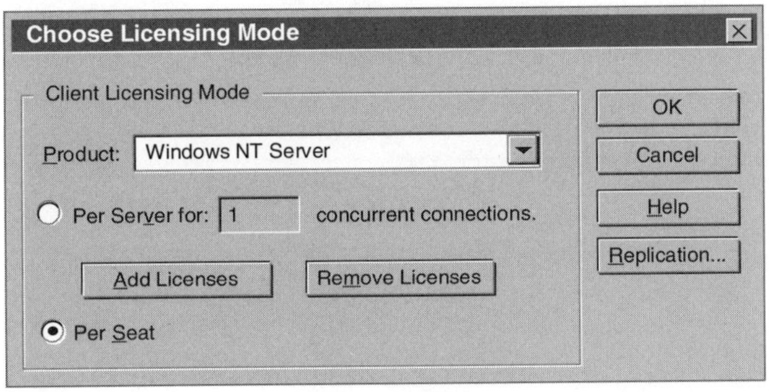

The **Choose Licensing Mode** dialog box allows you to view which licensing mode has been selected for each BackOffice product. The following table describes the tasks that you can perform using the Licensing program in Control Panel.

Option	Use this option to
Product	Specify the server product that requires CALs.
Per Server for *x* concurrent connections	View the number of concurrent client connections that are configured for a server if Per Server licensing mode has been selected.
Add licenses (Per Server licensing)	Add CALs to increase the number of concurrent client connections.
Remove licenses (Per Server licensing)	Remove CALs to decrease the number of concurrent client connections.
Replication	Display the **Replication Configuration** dialog box, which is used to specify how a computer replicates licensing information to a master server or enterprise server.
Per Seat	View whether the Per Seat licensing mode has been selected.

Note If the server uses the Per Seat licensing mode, use License Manager in the Administrative Tools (Common) group to enter CALs and configure Per Seat licensing options. You would also use License Manager if you want to perform the one-time conversion from a Per Server to a Per Seat configuration. License Manager is covered later in this chapter.

License Replication

You configure license replication on a server so that the server's licensing information is routed to a centralized database on a designated *master server* at specified intervals. The master server may be either the primary domain controller (PDC) for a single domain, or a specified *enterprise server* to which all of the PDCs in the organization replicate their licensing information.

The following illustration shows a PDC acting as a *master server* for license replication in a single domain. There are five stand-alone servers replicating licensing information to the PDC.

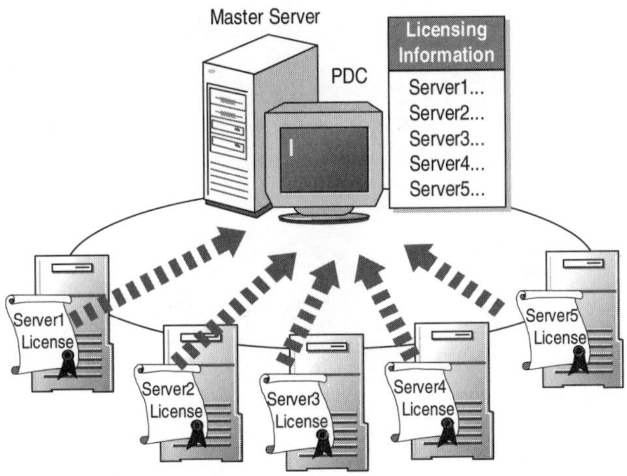

The following illustration shows an enterprise server acting as a *master server* for three domains. Each PDC acts as a master server for its domain. Then each of the three PDCs replicates the licensing information for its domain to the *master server* for the entire enterprise, where the servers' licensing information is stored in a centralized database.

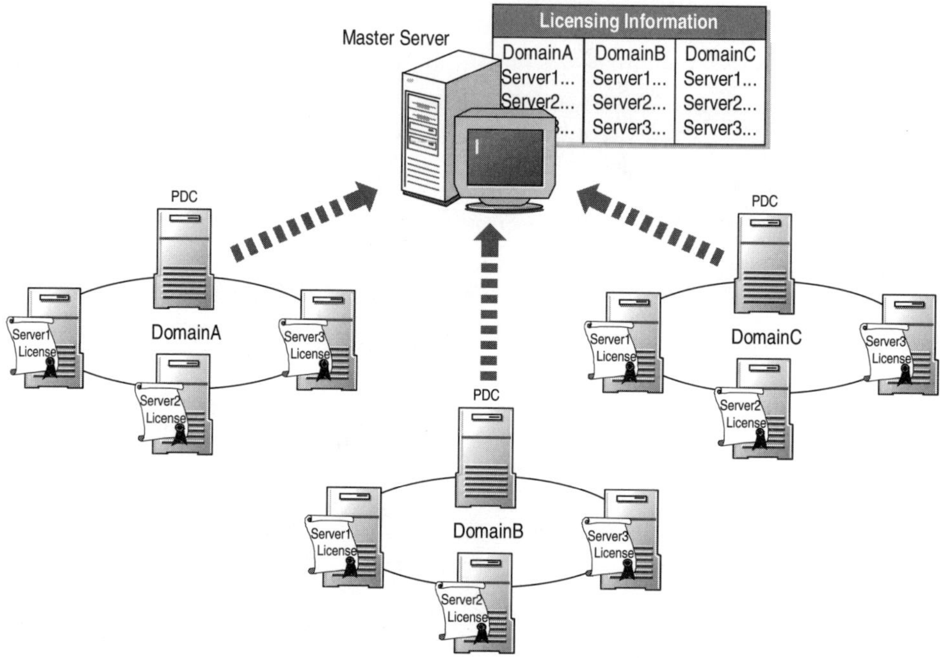

Configuring Licensing Replication

To configure licensing replication, start the Licensing program in Control Panel, and then click **Replication** in the **Choose Licensing Mode** dialog box. The **Replication Configuration** dialog box appears.

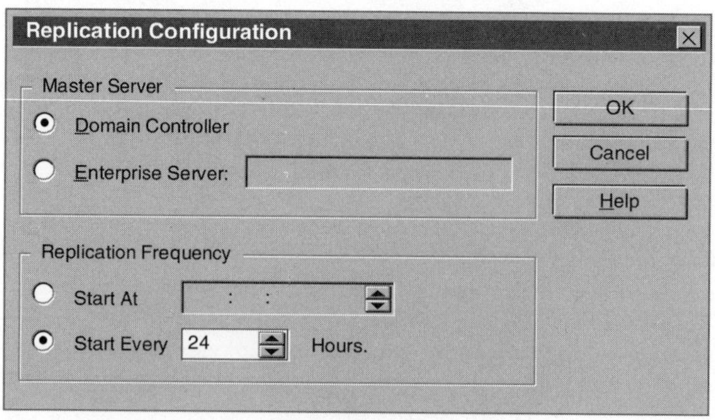

The following table describes the options in the **Replication Configuration** dialog box.

Option	Use this option to	Use this option when
Domain Controller (PDC)	Specify that the master server for this computer is the PDC.	This computer is a stand-alone server in a domain, or is a backup domain controller (BDC). This computer is a stand-alone server or a PDC, and you do not want to replicate further.
Enterprise Server	Specify that master server is an enterprise server and enter the name of the enterprise master server.	This computer is a stand-alone server, is part of an enterprise, and you want to replicate its licensing information directly to the enterprise master server. The computer is the PDC for its domain, and you want to replicate to an enterprise server.
Start At	Manually designate a time each day when licensing information is replicated to the master server.	You want to manually set a starting time for replication on this computer.
Start Every	Set the frequency for license replication.	The computer running Window NT Server will automatically stagger the replication of licensing data from each server. The default is every 24 hours, and the range from 1 to 72 hours.

Note Licensing replication is independent of Directory Replication. Directory Replication is discussed in Chapter 16 "Implementing File Synchronization and Directory Replication."

License Manager

License Manager is another tool that you can use to track licensing data and replicate the licensing data to a centralized database.

License Manager can be used to:

- View your organization's licensing.
- Administer license allocation and usage throughout an organization.
- Perform the one-time, one-way change from Per Server to Per Seat mode for qualifying BackOffice products.

Start **License Manager** from the **Administrative Tools (Common)** menu. The following illustration shows License Manager with the **Server Browser** tab selected.

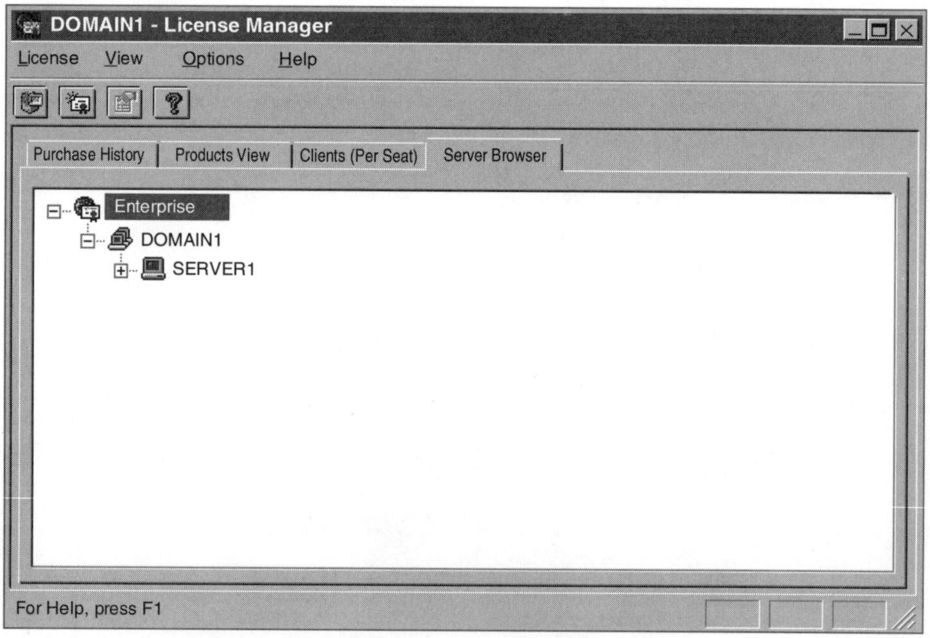

The following table describes the Per Server and Per Seat licensing functions that can be configured through the tabs in License Manager.

Tab	Use this tab to
Purchase History	View the product purchase date, product quantity, and identify the product administrator. This function can be used with either the Per Server or Per Seat licensing mode.
Products View	View the number of Per Server and Per Seat licenses by product in an organization.
Clients (Per Seat)	Survey licensed and unlicensed product usage. Click a user name to view the client's server usage history, to upgrade the user to a BackOffice license, or to revoke permission to access a server.
Server Browser	View servers in a domain or organization. Double-click to expand the domain to display servers in that domain. Double-click a server to display the **Choose Licensing Mode** dialog box.

Adding or Removing CALs for Per Server Licensing

Double-click a domain displayed by the **Server Browser** tab in License Manager to view the servers in that domain. Double-click a server to view the BackOffice products installed on that server. To add or remove CALs through the **Choose Licensing Mode** dialog box, double-click the appropriate BackOffice product.

The following illustration shows the **Choose Licensing Mode** dialog box for Windows NT Server.

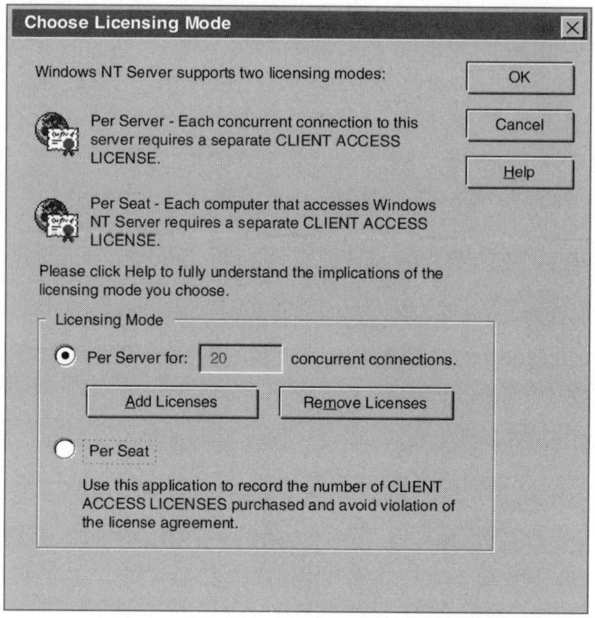

The following table describes the options in the **Choose Licensing Mode** dialog box.

Option	Use this option to
Per Server for *x* concurrent connections	View the number of concurrent client connections that are configured for a server, if the Per Server licensing mode has been chosen.
Add licenses (Per Server licensing)	Add CALs to increase the number of concurrent client connections.
Remove licenses (Per Server licensing)	Remove CALs to decrease the number of concurrent client connections.
Per Seat	View whether the Per Seat licensing mode has been selected.

Adding or Removing CALs for Per Seat Licensing

To add CALs for Per Seat licensing, in License Manager, click **New License** on the **License** menu. Select the appropriate product, enter the quantity of Client Access Licenses purchased, and then click **OK**.

To remove CALs for Per Seat licensing, in License Manager, click the **Products View** tab, and then click the appropriate BackOffice product. On the **License** menu, click **Delete**, and the **Select Certificate to Remove Licenses** dialog box appears. Select the appropriate Serial Number. In the **Number of Licenses to remove** box, enter the quantity of CALs to be removed, and then click **Remove**.

Creating License Groups

To obtain correct licensing information when working with Per Seat licenses, it may be necessary to group certain users and make them members of a *license group*.

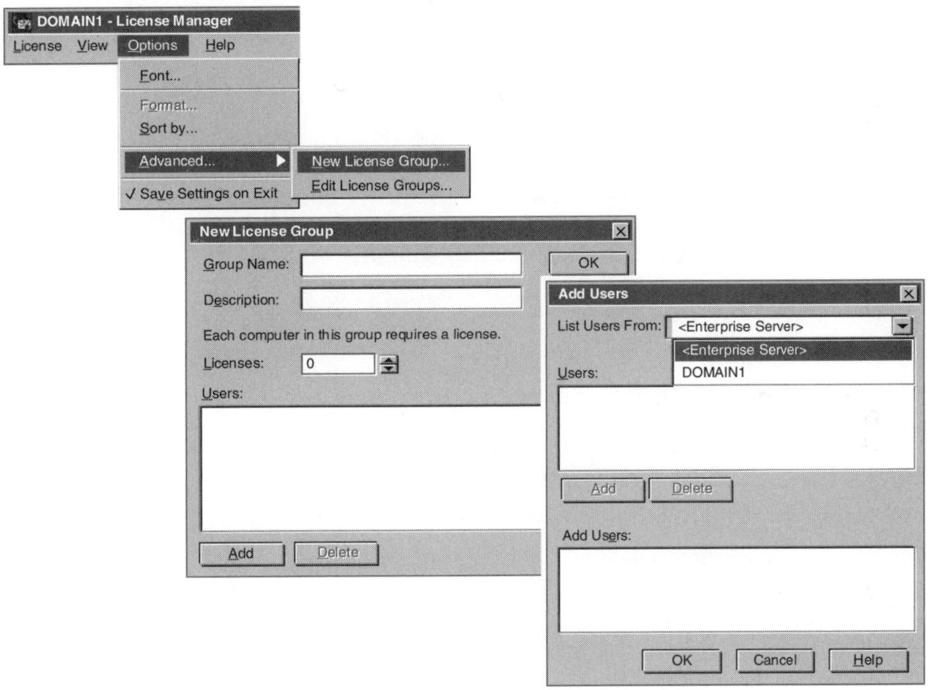

License groups show a relationship (also known as a mapping) between users and computers and should be used only when one of the following configurations is true:

- Multiple users use one computer, such as when people share jobs, or when multiple shifts of workers use the same computers.
- Multiple users use several computers, but there is an unequal number of users and computers, such as may occur in a university computer lab or in a retail store.
- One user uses multiple computers, such as often happens during software development when applications are developed on one computer and tested on several different platforms.

A license group is composed of the following components:

- A descriptive name for the group.
- A specified number of Per Seat licenses assigned to the group. The number of CALs required for a license group corresponds to the number of computers that are being used by the group, rather than the number of users in the group.
- A specific list of users who are members of the group.

Note For more information on licensing, see Chapter 12 of Microsoft Windows NT Server *Concepts and Planning*.

Lesson 2: Clients Included with Windows NT Server

For a computer to access a computer running Windows NT, you must install and configure client software on that computer. On computers running Windows NT Server, Windows NT Workstation, or Microsoft Windows 95, the client software is automatically installed during the installation of the operating system. If you need to set up computers that are running some other operating system, such as Microsoft MS-DOS, that does not include the networking components required to access a computer running Windows NT, Microsoft provides networking client software on the *Windows NT Server 4.0* compact disc. In this lesson, you learn what client software is included on the *Windows NT Server 4.0* compact disc and the protocols and redirectors that are supported by each client.

After this lesson, you will be able to:

- Describe the client software and the corresponding supported protocols for each client that are included with Windows NT Server.

Estimated lesson time: 15 minutes

Client Software Provided by Windows NT Server

The client software provided by Windows NT Server is located in the Clients folder on the *Windows NT Server 4.0* compact disc. The Clients folder contains subfolders that include the following software.

- *Microsoft Network Client 3.0 for MS-DOS and Windows.* Contained in the Msclient folder.
- *Microsoft LAN Manager 2.2c Client.* Contained in the Lanman folder.
- *Microsoft LAN Manager 2.2c Client for OS/2.* Contained in the Lanman.os2 folder.
- *Microsoft Windows 95 operating system.* Contained in the Win95 folder. Includes all operating system files required to install Windows 95.

Note Windows NT Server 4.0 also supports Windows for Workgroups as a client, but does not include the Windows for Workgroups software. Because the version of Transmission Control Protocol/Internet Protocol (TCP/IP) included with Windows for Workgroups does not support Dynamic Host Configuration Protocol (DHCP) and Windows Internet Name Service (WINS), Windows NT Server does include an add-on product, Microsoft TCP/IP-32 for Windows for Workgroups 3.11, which provides support for DHCP and WINS.

Microsoft Network Client 3.0 for MS-DOS and Windows

Microsoft Network Client 3.0 provides network connectivity for MS-DOS-based computers that need to access resources on computers running Windows NT.

The following illustration shows an MS-DOS based computer, with Microsoft Network Client 3.0 installed, accessing resources on a computer running Windows NT Server.

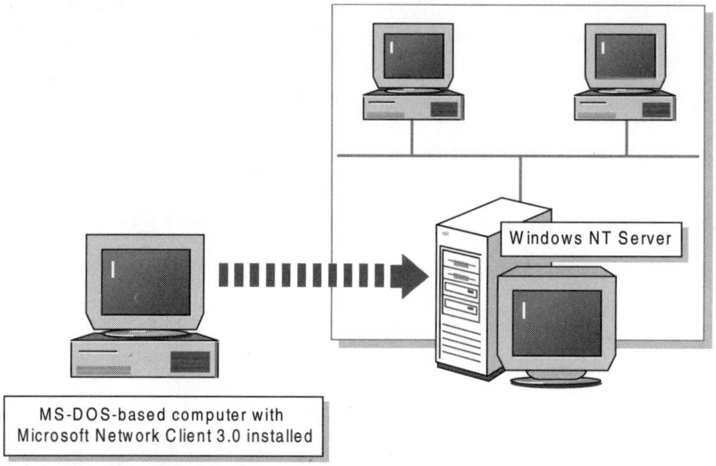

Supported Protocols

Microsoft Network Client 3.0 supports the following protocols:

- NetBEUI
- Internetwork Packet Exchange (IPX) Compatible Transport
- TCP/IP. The TCP/IP protocol included with this client software supports DHCP; it does not support either DNS or WINS name resolution.
- Data link control (DLC)

Full Redirector

By default, Microsoft Network Client 3.0 supports the full redirector, which enables clients to take advantage of the following network services:

- Domain logon capability and logon scripts
- Remote Access Service (RAS) version 1.1
- Messaging
- Interprocess communication mechanisms such as named pipes, remote procedure calls (RPC), and Windows Sockets (WinSock)

Note Neither Microsoft Network Client 3.0 nor MS-DOS have browsing capabilities. Therefore, to browse the network, there must be a Windows for Workgroups–based or a Windows NT–based computer running in the same workgroup.

LAN Manager 2.2c Clients

Windows NT Server includes software for the following two LAN Manager 2.2c clients: LAN Manager 2.2c for MS-DOS and LAN Manager 2.2c for OS/2.

LAN Manager 2.2c for MS-DOS

LAN Manager 2.2c for MS-DOS ships with NetBEUI, Microsoft DLC, and TCP/IP. The TCP/IP protocol stack that is included with LAN Manager 2.2c for MS-DOS supports the DHCP, which is the default setting, but it does not support DNS or WINS name resolution.

In addition, LAN Manager 2.2c for MS-DOS supports the Remoteboot service. MS-DOS and Microsoft Windows 3.*x*-based computers can be remotely started using the Remoteboot service.

LAN Manager 2.2c for OS/2

LAN Manager 2.2c for OS/2 supports OS/2 1.*x* and OS/2 2.*x*. This client ships with NetBEUI and TCP/IP; however, its version of TCP/IP does not support DHCP or WINS.

Microsoft Windows 95

Windows NT Server supports connectivity with Windows 95 clients.

Supported Protocols

Windows 95 supports the following protocols:

- NetBEUI
- Internetwork Packet Exchange/Sequenced Packet Exchange (IPX/SPX) Compatible Transport
- TCP/IP—the TCP/IP protocol supports DHCP, WINS, and DNS name resolution.

Support for 32-bit Networking

Windows 95 clients use a 32-bit protected mode redirector to log on to a network and access resources. The advantage of this redirector is that it supports the 32-bit WinNet32 programming interface and 32-bit protected mode drivers. The combination of the WinNet32 application programming interface (APIs) and 32-bit protected mode drivers provide faster, more robust network access than the corresponding 16-bit APIs and drivers.

Lesson 3: Network Client Administrator

In this lesson, you learn how to use the Network Client Administrator tool to install and configure the network client software and tools contained on the *Windows NT Server 4.0* compact disc.

After this lesson, you will be able to:

- Explain the methods provided by Network Client Administrator that enable you to install and update network client workstations.
- Describe the procedure to create and configure a network installation startup disk.
- Describe the procedure to create an installation disk set.

Estimated lesson time: 20 minutes

What Is Network Client Administrator?

The Network Client Administrator is used to:

- Install network client software by creating a network installation startup disk or an installation disk set.
- Share the installation files contained on the *Windows NT Server 4.0* compact disc.
- Copy the folders and files contained on the *Windows NT Server 4.0* compact disc to a network server and share them. Creating a network share is the recommended method for installing the client software.

The **Network Client Administrator** is located on the **Administrative Tools (Common)** menu on computers running Windows NT Server.

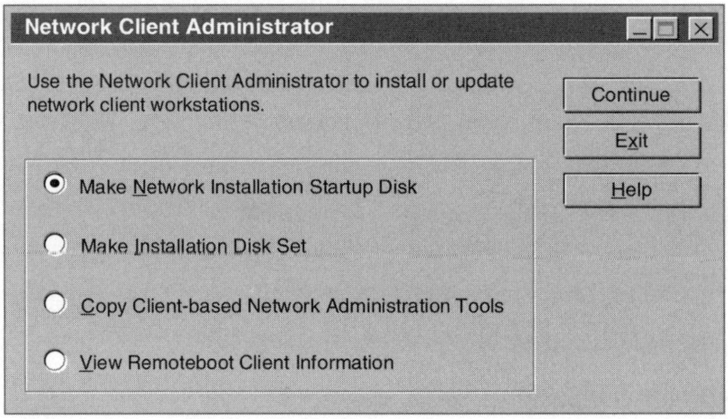

The following table describes each option in the **Network Client Administrator** dialog box.

Option	Use this option to
Make Network Installation Startup Disk	Create an MS-DOS network installation startup disk that can be used to automatically connect to a server and install Windows 95 or Microsoft Network Client 3.0 for MS-DOS and Windows.
Make Installation Disk Set	Create an installation disk set for Microsoft Network Client 3.0 for MS-DOS and Windows, LAN Manager 2.2c for MS-DOS, LAN Manager 2.2c for OS/2, Remote Access v1.1a for MS-DOS, or TCP/IP 32 for Windows for Workgroups 3.11.
Copy Client-based Network Administration Tools	Install client-based Windows NT administration tools on Windows NT Workstation or Microsoft Windows 95 clients to enable administration from those clients.
View Remoteboot Client Information	View Remoteboot client information. Remoteboot is a Windows NT service that can be used to start MS-DOS, Windows 3.*x*, and Microsoft Windows 95–based computers over the network. The Remoteboot service is installed through the Network program in Control Panel.

Network Installation Startup Disks

If client operating systems are to be installed from a computer running Windows NT Server, by means of either network share or a shared compact disc, then the clients must be able to connect to the Windows NT server. One method of providing access to the server would be to create a network installation startup disk and then start the client computer using that disk.

Creating a Network Installation Startup Disk

To create a network installation startup disk, select **Make Network Installation Startup Disk** in the **Network Client Administrator** dialog box, and then click **Continue**. The **Share Network Client Installation Files** dialog box appears.

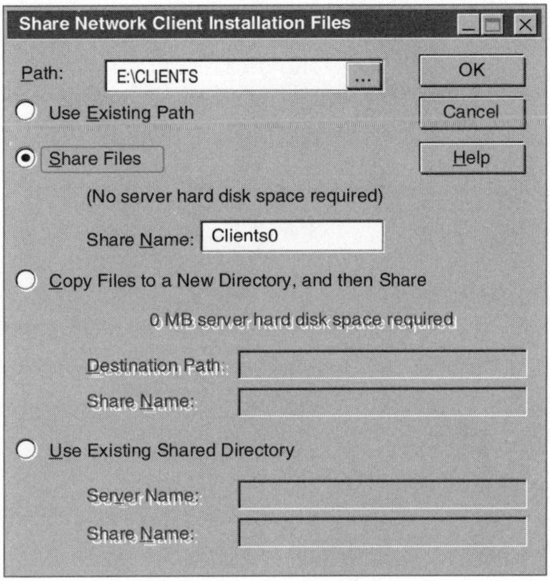

Use the **Share Network Client Installation Files** dialog box to specify how the share should be configured. The following table describes each option in this dialog box.

Option	Use this option to
Path	Indicate the location of the client files.
Use Existing Path	Specify an existing path.
Share Files	Share the client folders and files directly from the compact disc.
Copy Files to a New Directory, and then Share	Specify if files are copied to a new directory and then shared, or shared through an existing server directory.
Use Existing Shared Directory	Use files that have previously been copied and shared.

Note To save hard disk space, delete any folders that are copied from the Clients folder to the network share that are not required. For example, if you do not have any computers that require LAN Manager 2.2 for OS/2, then delete this folder from the network share.

Once the client software files have been shared, you can begin creating network installation startup disks or installation disk sets.

Specifying the Target Workstation Configuration

The next step in creating a network installation startup disk is to specify the configuration on the target workstations.

For example, to share the folders and files on the *Windows NT Server 4.0* compact disc, click **Share Files** in the **Share Network Client Installation Files** dialog box, and then Click **OK**. The **Target Workstation Configuration** dialog box appears.

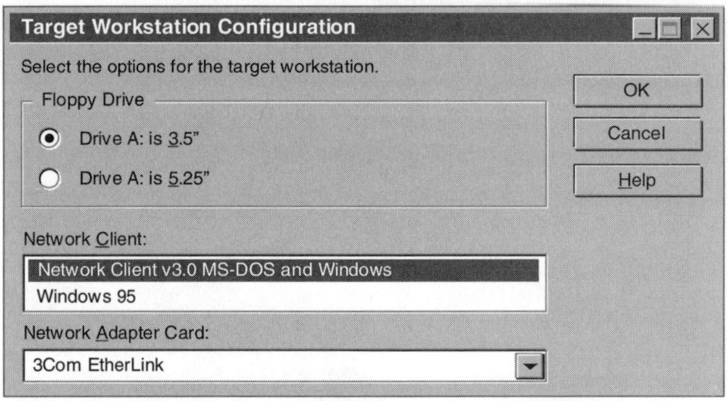

The following table describes the options in the **Target Workstation Configuration** dialog box.

Option	Use this option to
Floppy Drive	Select either 3.5" or 5.25", whichever is compatible with the drive on the target workstation.
Network Client	Identify the network client software that will be installed: Network Client v3.0 for MS-DOS and Windows or Windows 95
Network Adapter Card	Select the correct network adapter card for the client.

Configuring a Network Startup Disk

After you specify the configuration on the target workstation, you must configure the network startup disk.

For example, after specifying the appropriate floppy disk size, network client, and network adapter card, click **OK** in the **Target Workstation Configuration** dialog box. The **Network Startup Disk Configuration** dialog box appears.

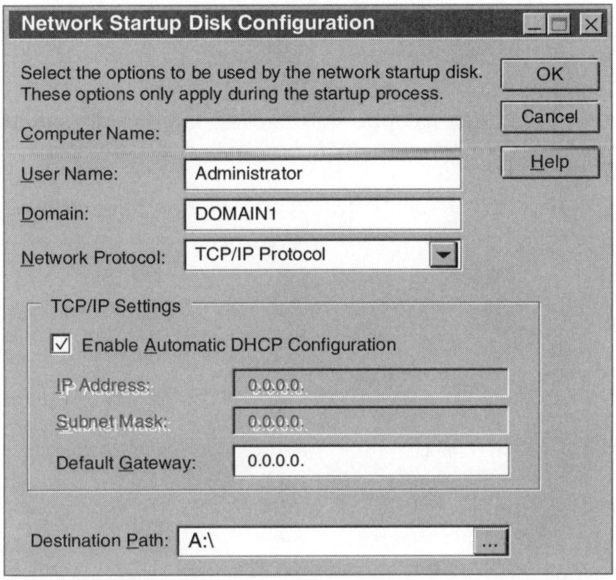

The **Network Startup Disk Configuration** dialog box is used to configure the network information described in the following table.

Option	Use this option to
Computer Name	Enter a unique name that identifies the computer on the network.
User Name	Enter a user name that identifies the user to the network.
Domain	Enter a domain name that identifies the domain to the network.
Network Protocol	Select which protocol to use when copying network client administration files.
Enable Automatic DHCP Configuration	Enable automatic DHCP configuration if the network has DHCP servers.
IP Address	Enter the IP address that identifies the computer to other computers on the network.
Subnet Mask	Enter the subnet mask.
Default Gateway	Enter the IP address of the default gateway.
Destination Path	Enter the destination path where files should be copied.

After supplying all information, you are prompted to insert a formatted, high-density system disk in the destination drive. The Network Client Administrator then copies files to the disk according to your specifications. You can then use the floppy disk to start a computer and automatically copy the client software to the computer.

Creating an Installation Disk Set

An installation disk set is used to *manually* install the following client software or service on a computer, as opposed to downloading it from a network server or installing it from the *Windows NT Server 4.0* compact disc:

- Microsoft Network Client 3.0 for MS-DOS and Windows.
- Remote Access v1.1a for MS-DOS.
- TCP/IP-32 for Windows for Workgroups 3.11.
- LAN Manager 2.2c for MS-DOS.
- LAN Manager 2.2c for OS/2.

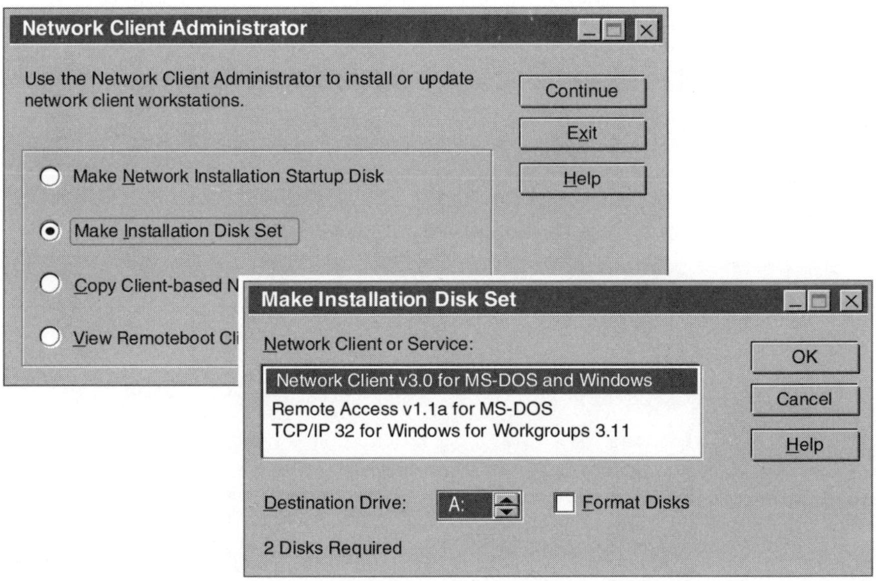

To create an installation disk set, start Network Client Administrator, select **Make Installation Disk Set**, and then click **Continue**. The **Make Installation Disk Set** dialog box appears. Select the appropriate options and then click **OK**. The **Share Network Client Installation Files** dialog box appears; configure the **Share Network Client Installation Files** dialog box and then click **OK**. The **Make Installation Disk Set** dialog box appears. The following table explains the options that can be configured in the **Make Installation Disk Set** dialog box.

Option	Use this option to
Network Client or Service	Specify the type of installation disks to create.
Destination Drive	Specify the destination drive for the disk.
Format Disks	Format disks to be used.

After you specify the appropriate information and click **OK**, the client software files are copied to floppy disks. The installation disk set you create can be used only for the specific client or service you selected. If you have multiple computers with different client(s) or service requirements, you must make separate installation disk sets for each network client or service.

Lesson 4: Client-based Network Administration Tools

The *Windows NT Server 4.0* compact disc includes client-based network administration tools that gives you the flexibility to manage computers running Windows NT and domains from either a computer running Windows NT Workstation or Windows 95. Though many of the administrative tools are the same for both operating systems, there are some differences among them. In this lesson, you learn how to install the client-based administration tools on computers running Windows NT Workstation or Windows 95 and learn which tools are installed for each operating system.

After this lesson, you will be able to:

- Explain the system requirements to install the administration tools on Windows NT Workstation and Windows 95 clients.
- Install the administration tools for Windows NT Workstation.
- Explain how to install the administration tools for Microsoft Windows 95.

Estimated lesson time: 25 minutes

Installing the Administration Tools on Windows NT Workstation

In order to use the Windows NT Server administration tools on a computer running Windows NT Workstation, you must first install them. The administration tools are installed in the *systemroot*\System32 folder on the computer's system partition.

System Requirements for Windows NT Workstation Clients

The minimum requirements needed to install the Windows NT Server administration tools for a computer running Windows NT Workstation are:

- A 486DX/33 CPU or higher.
- 12 MB of RAM.
- 2.5 MB of free disk space on the system partition.
- Workstation and Server services installed.

Practice

In this procedure, you install the Windows NT Server client-based administration tools from the *Windows NT Server 4.0* compact disc on Workstation1.

▸ To install the Windows NT Server client-based administrative tools

---

Note Complete this procedure on Workstation1, logged on as Administrator.

---

1. Insert the *Windows NT Server 4.0* compact disc in the CD-ROM drive on Workstation1.
2. From the *cd_rom_drive*:**\Clients\Srvtools\Winnt** folder, run Setup.

   A Command Prompt window is opened, and the administrative tools and their supporting files are copied to the *systemroot*\System32 folder.
3. Read the text in the Command Prompt window, and then press ENTER.
4. Remove the *Windows NT Server 4.0* compact disc from the CD-ROM drive.

The following table describes the administrative tools and their file names that are copied to computer running Windows NT Workstation.

Tool	File name	Use this tool to
DHCP Manager	Dhcpadmn.exe	Manage the DHCP service running on a computer running Windows NT Server. Use DHCP Manager to centrally configure global and scope-specific parameters.
Remote Access Administrator	Rasadmin.exe	Administer the Remote Access Service on a computer running Windows NT.
Remoteboot Manager	Rplmgr.exe	Configure the Remoteboot service on a computer running Windows NT Server.
Server Manager	Srvmgr.exe	Manage Windows NT–based domains and computers.
System Policy Editor	Poledit.exe	Control and change user and system configuration settings.
User Manager for Domains	Usrmgr.exe	Manage users, groups, and security policies for Windows NT–based domains and computers.
WINS Manager	Winsadmn.exe	Administer the Windows Internet Name Service (WINS) on a computer running Windows NT Server.
DNS Manager	N/A	Manage the Microsoft DNS Server service and database.

Note Once the administration tools have been copied to your Windows NT Workstation client computer, create shortcuts for the tools on your desktop.

Using the Administration Tools on Windows 95

System Requirements for Windows 95 Clients

To install the Windows NT Server tools on a computer running Windows 95, the computer must have:

- A 486DX/33 CPU or higher.
- 8 MB of RAM.
- 3 MB of free disk space on the system partition.

Installing the Administration Tools

To install the administration tools on a computer running Windows 95, use the following steps:

1. Insert the *Windows NT Server 4.0* compact disc in the CD-ROM drive on the computer running Windows 95.
2. Click the **Start** button, point to **Settings**, and then click **Control Panel**.
3. Double-click the Add/Remove Programs icon.
4. Click the **Windows Setup** tab, and then click **Have Disk**.
5. In **Copy manufacturer's files from**, type *cd-rom_drive_letter***Clients\Srvtools\Win95** and then click **OK**.
6. Click **Windows NT Server Tools**, and then click **Install**.

   The Windows NT Server client-based network administration tools are installed in a Srvtools folder on the computer's boot drive.
7. Edit the path in the Autoexec.bat file to include the appropriate folder, for example, add C:\Srvtools to the path.

Note You must restart the computer for the new path to take effect.

The following table describes the administrative tools and file names that are copied to the computer.

Tool	File name	Use this tool to
Event Viewer	Eventvwr.exe	View, access, manage, and archive event logs. Use Event Viewer to view and manage system, security, and application event logs.
File Security tab added to Windows NT Explorer and My Computer	N/A	Establish file and folder permissions. Use the server tools to view permissions over the network and change them, if required.
Print Security tab added to Windows NT Explorer and My Computer	N/A	Establish print permissions. Set print permissions through the **Properties** dialog box accessed through the **Printers** dialog box.
Server Manager	Srvmgr.exe	Manage shared folders and printers on computers running Windows NT. Use Server Manager to share folders, set permissions on shared folders, view who is using shared resources, and disconnect users from shared resources.
User Manager for Domains	Usrmgr.exe	Create and manage users, groups, and security policies for domains.
User Manager Extensions for Services for NetWare	N/A	Create a NetWare client user account, enable the account, configure account properties, create a NetWare home directory, and set restrictions. Although this tool is included on the *Windows NT Server 4.0* compact disc, it is only installed if File and Print Services for NetWare or Directory Services Manager for NetWare is installed.
File and Print Services for NetWare (FPNW)	N/A	Create and manage FPNW services, user accounts, volumes, printers and queues, and send messages. Although this tool is included on the *Windows NT Server 4.0* compact disc, it is installed only if FPNW is installed.

Note When using the administration tools on a Windows 95 client computer, the system requires the user to log on or enter a password several times for verification.

Lesson 5: Services for Macintosh

Windows NT Server includes Services for Macintosh; these services give you the ability to manage a Windows NT network environment that includes computers using an AppleTalk internetwork. Services for Macintosh also enables computers running Windows NT Server 4.0 to provide file and print services for computers using an AppleTalk internetwork. In addition, once Services for Macintosh are enabled, it is possible to connect networks with Macintosh clients to create an AppleTalk internetwork. In this lesson, you learn how to install and configure Services for Macintosh.

After this lesson, you will be able to:

- Describe the benefits provided by Services for Macintosh.
- Explain the requirements for running Services for Macintosh in a Windows NT Server environment.
- Install Services for Macintosh.

Estimated lesson time: 20 minutes

Services for Macintosh enables Microsoft clients and Apple Macintosh clients to share file, print, administrative, and other network resources. Using Services for Macintosh on a network provides the following benefits.

Function	Description
File sharing	Clients can work on the same documents, even if some clients work with the Macintosh version of an application and others work with the Windows or MS-DOS version.
Printer sharing	Clients can send print jobs to either a printer for personal computers or to a Macintosh-based printer.
Simplified administration	Mixed networks with both Windows-based or MS-DOS-based computers and Macintosh clients can be managed from a computer running Windows NT Server.
AppleTalk routing support	Apple Macintosh networks can be connected to create an AppleTalk internetwork.

Services for Macintosh Requirements

Setting up Services for Macintosh requires a computer running Windows NT Server, with 2 MB of disk space available, and a Windows NT File System (NTFS) partition, which is required for Macintosh-accessible volumes. The procedure for creating Macintosh-accessible volumes is described later in this lesson.

Requirements for Macintosh Clients

To use Services for Macintosh, a client computer must have the Macintosh operating system version 6.0.7 or later, and AppleShare (the Apple networking software for the Macintosh). This includes most Macintosh computers except for the Macintosh XL and Macintosh 128K models.

In addition, Services for Macintosh supports version 6.*x* or later of the LaserWriter printer driver, and the AppleTalk Filing Protocol versions 2.0 and 2.1.

Note Services for Macintosh supports LocalTalk, Ethernet, Token Ring, and fiber distributed data interface (FDDI). Ethernet and Token Ring are commonly used when integrating a Macintosh computer into a Windows- or MS-DOS-based network.

Installing Services for Macintosh

Services for Macintosh can be installed during the installation of Windows NT Server, or after installation, using the **Services** tab in the Network program located in Control Panel.

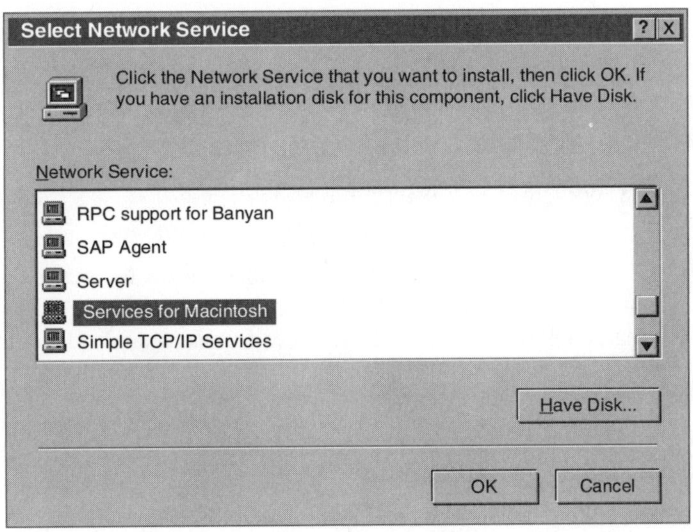

Creating a Macintosh-Accessible Volume

After Services for Macintosh is installed, a **MacFile** menu is added to Server Manager. You use the **MacFile** menu to create Macintosh-accessible volumes.

Note If you want documents that are stored on a Macintosh-accessible volume to also be available to your Windows- and MS-DOS-based network clients, you must share the folder from which the volume was created.

Macintosh computers have a maximum partition size of 2 GB. If Macintosh clients access a computer running Windows NT Server with an NTFS partition of more than 2 GB, the clients may get a message that there are 0 (zero) bytes available.

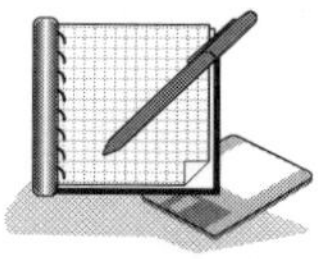

Practice

In this procedure, you install Services for Macintosh on Server2.

▸ **To install Services for Macintosh**

Note Complete this procedure on Server2, logged on as Administrator.

---

1. Start Server2, and then log on as Administrator.
2. Double-click the Network program in Control Panel.
3. Click the **Services** tab, and then click **Add**.
4. Click **Services for Macintosh**, and then click **OK**.

   A **Windows NT Setup** dialog box appears.
5. Type **\\Server1\Nts_source\I386** in the path, and then click **Continue**.
6. If you do not have an NTFS partition, a **Setup Message** dialog box appears stating that Services for Macintosh requires an NTFS partition, and that you can create one after you install Services for Macintosh. If this message appears, click **OK**.

   The **Network** dialog box reappears. Notice that Services for Macintosh is now included in the list of Network Services.
7. Click **Close**.

   A **Microsoft AppleTalk Protocol Properties** dialog box appears. This is where you would indicate the Zone.
8. Click **OK**.

   A **Network Settings Change** dialog box appears stating that you must shut down and restart your computer, and prompting you to restart your computer now.
9. Click **Yes**.

Features That Install Automatically with Services for Macintosh

When you install Services for Macintosh, the following features are also automatically installed:

- *The AppleTalk protocol.* Delivers data to its destination on the network. The AppleTalk protocol can be installed and configured through the **Protocols** tab in Control Panel.
- *File Service for Macintosh.* Manages Macintosh volumes, folders, and files.
- *Print Server for Macintosh.* Enables both Windows or MS-DOS clients and Macintosh clients to send print jobs to either AppleTalk (usually PostScript devices) or non-AppleTalk printing devices.

Removing Services for Macintosh

Services for Macintosh can be removed at any time by using the **Remove** button located on the **Services** tab in the Network program in Control Panel.

Summary

The following information summarizes the key points in this chapter:

- With the Microsoft BackOffice licensing model, Windows NT servers and client computers are licensed separately. A server license is required for each server, and a Client Access License (CAL) is required for each client computer that accesses a server.
- When you purchase Windows NT Server, a *server license* is included with the purchase. This server license entitles you to install Windows NT Server on one and only one computer.
- A Client Access License (CAL) provides the legal right for a computer to access a computer running Windows NT Server. CALs are separate from the desktop operating system software you use to connect to Microsoft server products.
- Microsoft offers two licensing modes: Per Server licensing and Per Seat licensing.
  - *Per Server Licensing.* In Per Server licensing, *CALs are assigned to the server.* The number of CALs determines the number of simultaneous connections that can be made to *that* server.
  - *Per Seat Licensing.* In Per Seat licensing, *a CAL is purchased for each client computer.* With a Per Seat license, a client can access network resources such as file, print, and communications on *any* computer running Windows NT Server in the network, and can log on to multiple servers simultaneously.
- Windows NT Server 4.0 includes two administrative tools that you can use to track licensing data and replicate the licensing data to a centralized database: the Licensing program in Control Panel and the License Manager program on the **Administrative Tools (Common)** menu.
- Windows NT Server 4.0 includes the Network Client Administrator, a tool that you can use to install client software.
- The *Windows NT Server 4.0* compact disc includes client-based network administration tools that gives you the flexibility to manage computers running Windows NT and domains from either a computer running Windows NT Workstation or Windows 95.
- Windows NT Server 4.0 includes Services for Macintosh, which enables Microsoft clients and Apple Macintosh clients to share file, print, administrative, and other network resources.

Review

1. You have recently added 50 new desktop computers to your network. Each of these computers requires access to the computers running Windows NT Server on the network. Your servers are licensed in the Per Seat mode. What utility must you use to add the new Client Access Licenses?

2. You are evaluating the clients included on the *Windows NT Server 4.0* compact disc. Your network uses both DHCP and WINS, and you require support for these protocols on your client computers. Which of the clients included with Windows NT Server would you deploy?

3. You must deploy 50 new desktop computers on your network. These computers will all run Windows NT Workstation, and the installation files are located in a shared folder on a computer running Windows NT Server. However, the new computers do not have a network client installed and therefore cannot connect to the server to download Windows NT Workstation. How would you enable the computers to connect to the server so that you can start the installation?

4. You are in charge of network operations for your company. You have many different administrators using various operating systems on their desktop computers. Which operating systems allow the administrators to work at their desktop computers and still be able to apply file and directory permissions to an NTFS partition on a computer running Windows NT Server?

5. Your computer running Windows NT Server provides file and print services to both Windows-based and Macintosh clients. You have installed Services for Macintosh and created a volume in which Macintosh users store their documents. You would like these documents to also be accessible from the Windows-based clients. What must you do?

____

____

Answer Key

Procedure Answers

Page 534

Licensing Considerations Review

Your company is a small, newly created business that has one file and print server and 30 client computers. You configured the server using the Per Server licensing mode and obtained 30 Client Access Licenses, so that all 30 clients could access the server.

1. Your business is growing, so you purchase five new client computers and add them to the network. If 30 clients are currently connected to the server, will another client be able to connect to the server? Why or why not?

   No. It will not be able to access the server, because the maximum number of server connections allowed is 30.

2. You decide to add a mail server that *all* clients will connect to. What would be the most economical licensing mode solution for the company?

   The most economical solution is to configure the mail server for the Per Seat licensing mode and then convert the file and print server to the Per Seat licensing mode. In this way, you could purchase 5 more Client Access Licenses and the 35 CALs will be assigned to the clients, allowing them to have access to either server.

Page 535

Choosing Per Server vs. Per Seat Licensing Review

1. A company has one computer running Windows NT Server. There are 300 computers running Windows NT Workstation in the company, but only 250 of these will access the server simultaneously.

   What licensing mode would be the best solution for this company?

Licensing mode and computers	Result
Per Server option:	
Number of simultaneous connections needed to server1	250
Total of simultaneous connections needed for all servers: A = server1 + server2 + ... + server*N*	A = 250
Per Seat option:	
Total number of seats (computers) that access *any* server This the number of CALs needed for Per Seat licensing	B = 300

A is less than B. Therefore the Per Server Licensing mode is the best licensing solution for this company.

2. This company now adds an additional computer running Windows NT Server. Up to 200 of the workstations will also access the new server simultaneously.

   What licensing mode would now be the best solution for this company?

Licensing mode and computers	Result
Per Server option:	
Number of simultaneous connections needed to server1	250
Number of simultaneous connections needed to server2	200
Total of simultaneous connections needed for all servers: A = server1 + server2 + ... + server*N*	A = 450
Per Seat option:	
Number of seats (computers) that access *any* server is the number of CALs needed for Per Seat licensing	B = 300

   A is now greater than B. Therefore the Per Seat Licensing mode is the best licensing solution for this company when it adds an additional server.

Review Answers

Page 567

1. You have recently added 50 new desktop computers to your network. Each of these computers requires access to the computers running Windows NT Server on the network. Your servers are licensed in the Per Seat mode. What utility must you use to add the new Client Access Licenses?

   You must use License Manager to enter the information for the new licenses.

2. You are evaluating the clients included on the *Windows NT Server 4.0* compact disc. Your network uses both DHCP and WINS, and you require support for these protocols on your client computers. Which of the clients included with Windows NT Server would you deploy?

   Windows 95 is the only included client that supports both DHCP and WINS. In addition, TCP/IP-32 for Windows for Workgroups (which is included with Windows NT Server) can be added to Windows for Workgroups computers to provide DHCP and WINS support.

   Windows NT Workstation, although not included on the *Windows NT Server 4.0* compact disc, also supports both DHCP and WINS.

3. You must deploy 50 new desktop computers on your network. These computers will all run Windows NT Workstation, and the installation files are located in a shared folder on a computer running Windows NT Server. However, the new computers do not have a network client installed and therefore cannot connect to the server to download Windows NT Workstation. How would you enable the computers to connect to the server so that you can start the installation?

   Use Network Client Administrator to create a network installation startup disk.

4. You are in charge of network operations for your company. You have many different administrators using various operating systems on their desktop computers. Which operating systems allow the administrators to work at their desktop computers and still be able to apply file and directory permissions to an NTFS partition on a computer running Windows NT Server?

   There are Windows NT administrative tools available that run on both Windows 95 and Windows NT.

5. Your computer running Windows NT Server provides file and print services to both Windows-based and Macintosh clients. You have installed Services for Macintosh and created a volume in which Macintosh users store their documents. You would like these documents to also be accessible from the Windows-based clients. What must you do?

   Share the folder from which the volume was created. Both types of clients will be able to access the files contained within the folder.

CHAPTER 16

Implementing File Synchronization and Directory Replication

About This Chapter

In Microsoft Windows NT, the Briefcase and the Directory Replicator service are used to minimize the administration involved in updating files over a network. The Briefcase supports mobile and distributed computing by transparently synchronizing updated files. The Directory Replicator service replicates information such as logon scripts, user profiles, and system policies from a designated export server to one or more import computers.

Before You Begin

To complete the lessons in this chapter, you must have:

- Two computers that meet the hardware and software requirements as specified in the Getting Started section of "About This Book."
- Completed all practices in Chapter 2, "Installing Windows NT."
- One blank, formatted 1.44 MB high-density disk.

Lesson 1: The Windows NT Briefcase

The Windows NT Briefcase, which appears as an icon on the desktop, allows users to copy files to their Briefcase, take their Briefcase with them, either on a disk or portable computer, modify the files in the Briefcase, and then on reconnecting to the network, synchronize the files with the original source.

After this lesson, you will be able to:

- Describe the function of the Windows NT Briefcase.
- Describe the mechanics involved in using the Briefcase.
- Use the Briefcase to synchronize remote file updates with centralized sources.

Estimated lesson time: 30 minutes

The following illustration summarizes the synchronization process that occurs when the Briefcase is used to work on files remotely.

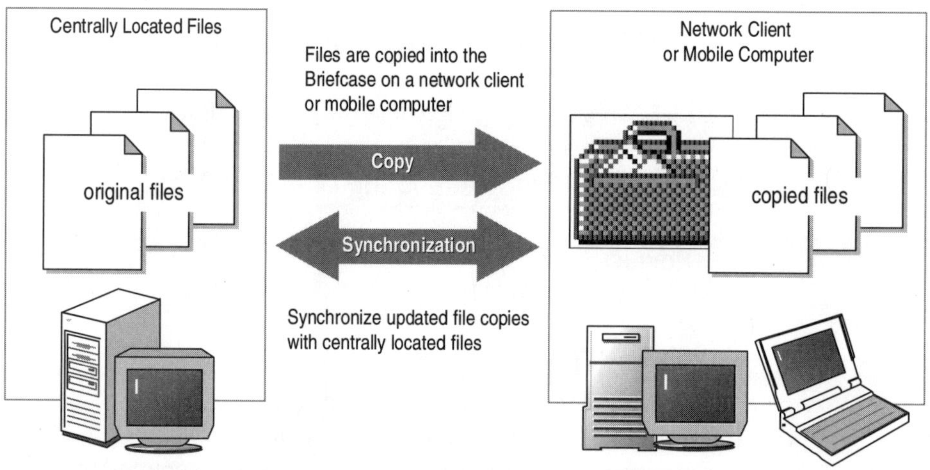

The Windows NT Briefcase can be deployed in any organization where employees spend a significant amount of time working on files off-site. The Briefcase can also be used to synchronize centrally located files with copies on local computers. In addition, it is possible to have a Briefcase synchronized with files on a network server.

For example, network or mobile users can connect to a file source, which could be on any computer that is visible to the user, drag files from it to their Briefcase and then work on these files. When the work on these files is complete, the user synchronizes files without having to move the updated file copies out of the Briefcase or manually replace the original files. The Briefcase notes whether either copy of the file has changed, and then updates the unchanged copy. If both copies of the file have changed, Briefcase notes this, but does not automatically update the copies. You can then choose which, if either, file to replace.

The Briefcase Database

The Briefcase Database stores the information required by Windows NT to synchronize files. If this database is deleted, it is impossible to synchronize updated files.

Note The Briefcase Database files are stored in the Briefcase. When the Briefcase is created, it is, by default, located in the following folder:

systemroot\Profiles*user_name*\Desktop\My Briefcase

These files may be accessed only from the command prompt. They are *not* displayed from Windows NT Explorer.

Using the Briefcase

Synchronizing files through the Briefcase involves copying files to the Briefcase, working on them, and synchronizing the updated files. When you open the Briefcase you see files and folders. These are the files and folders that will be synchronized.

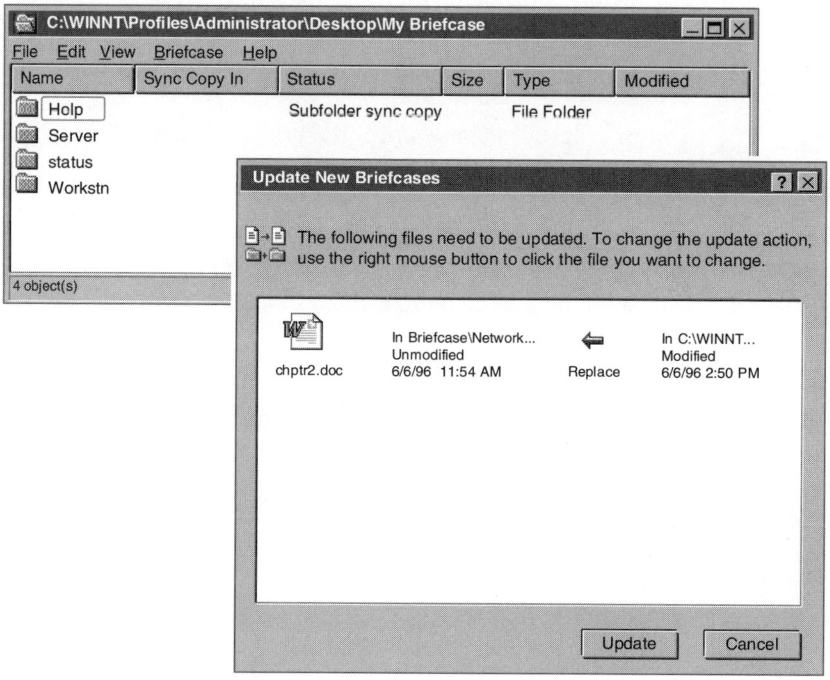

Copying Files to the Briefcase

Files can be copied to the Briefcase through the standard Windows NT methods: by performing a drag-and-drop operation, using the **Copy** and **Paste** commands, using the **Send To** menu command, and so on.

Important Files never get *moved* to the Briefcase; they are always *copied* to the Briefcase.

Working on Files in the Briefcase

To modify files in the Briefcase, open the Briefcase folder on the removable media, and then open the file and do your work. When you save your changes to the file, the changes are written to the file in the Briefcase folder.

Synchronizing Updated Files

If you put your Briefcase on a removable media, such as a floppy disk, drag your Briefcase folder back to your desktop.

You begin the file synchronization process by using the menus in Briefcase. When files are synchronized through the Briefcase **update** command, a dialog box appears requiring one of the following options to be chosen.

Option	This option appears when
Replace	The original file or the Briefcase copy has been updated, but not both.
Skip	Both the original file and the Briefcase copy have been updated.
Delete	The original file or the copy has been deleted.
Merge	Both the original file and the Briefcase copy have been updated, and the application that created the file supports the Briefcase merge feature. Microsoft Access version 7.0 is an example of an application that supports the Briefcase merge feature.

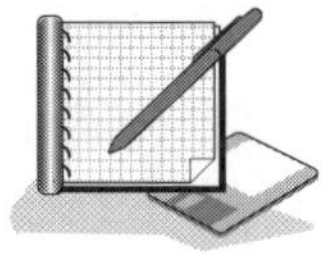

Practice

In these procedures, you use a Briefcase to synchronize files. You populate My Briefcase with four files from your hard disk; you then move My Briefcase to a floppy disk. After you modify some of the existing files in your Briefcase and some of the files on your hard disk, you synchronize the files on the disk with the original files still located on your computer's hard disk.

Note Complete these procedures on Workstation1.

▸ To enable My Briefcase

In this procedure, you start Briefcase.

1. Log on to the domain as Administrator.
2. On the desktop, double-click My Briefcase.
3. If this is the first time you have opened My Briefcase, read the directions in the **Welcome to the Windows Briefcase** dialog box, and then click **Finish**.

▸ To populate My Briefcase with files

In this procedure, you use My Computer to copy the C:\Lab Files\Briefcas folder to My Briefcase.

1. Open My Computer, locate the C:\Lab Files\Briefcas folder, and then open it to reveal the four files named W, X, Y, and Z (these are .rtf files).
2. For each of the four files, W, X, Y, and Z, right-click the file, and then click **Quick View** to see the data that is currently in the file.
3. Close Quick View when you are done.
4. Drag the entire Briefcas folder to My Briefcase and drop it there. This copies the Briefcas folder and all of the files in the Briefcas folder to My Briefcase.
5. Close My Briefcase.

▸ To move My Briefcase to another computer

In this procedure, you move My Briefcase to a floppy disk. This is the first procedure in moving My Briefcase to another computer.

1. Insert a blank disk in your disk drive.
2. Drag the My Briefcase icon to the disk.

   My Briefcase should now be located on the disk.

▸ To modify the contents of My Briefcase

The following change relationships are implemented in the following procedures.

	Original	Briefcase
File W	Not Modified	Modified
File X	Modified	Not Modified
File Y	Not Modified	Modified
File Z	Modified	Modified

▸ To modify the contents of W

1. In the Briefcas folder located in the Briefcase on your floppy disk, open W.
2. Modify W by inserting the following data at the beginning of the file:

   My name is *your name*. I have modified this file.
3. Exit WordPad, saving your changes.

   You have now modified W in your Briefcase. You do *not* modify the original W file.

▸ To modify the contents of X

1. In the C:\Lab Files\Briefcas folder, open X.
2. Select all of the text by pressing CTRL+A.
3. Copy the information to the Clipboard by pressing CTRL+C.
4. Position the cursor at the end of the file by pressing CTRL+END.
5. Paste the information from the Clipboard by pressing CTRL+V.
6. Exit WordPad, saving your changes.

   You have now modified your original X file. You do *not* modify the X file in your Briefcase.

▸ To modify the contents of Y

1. In the Briefcas folder located in the Briefcase on your floppy disk, open Y.
2. Select all of the text by pressing CTRL+A.
3. Copy the information to the Clipboard by pressing CTRL+C.
4. Position the cursor at the end of the file by pressing CTRL+END.
5. Paste the information from the Clipboard by pressing CTRL+V.
6. Exit WordPad, saving your changes.

   You have now modified the copy of Y in your Briefcase. You will *not* modify the original Y file.

▸ **To modify the contents of Z**

1. In the C:\Lab Files\Briefcas folder, open Z, and type today's date in the file.
2. Exit WordPad, saving your changes.
3. In the Briefcas folder located in the Briefcase on your floppy disk, open Z and type the name of your company in the file.
4. Exit WordPad, saving your changes.

   You have now modified your original Z file, and you have made a different modification to the copy of the Z file in your Briefcase.
5. Close My Briefcase.

▸ **To synchronize your files**

In this procedure, you synchronize the files in your Briefcase with those on your hard disk.

1. Drag My Briefcase from the floppy disk back to the desktop.

   My Briefcase moves to the desktop.
2. Open My Briefcase.
3. On the **Briefcase** menu, click **Update All**.
4. Click **Update**.

   The modified files are synchronized.
5. On the **Briefcase** menu, click **Update All**.

   Z should be the only file listed.

   Why was Z not updated?

   ____
6. Click **Cancel**.
7. Open each of the files (W, X, Y, and Z) to see the changes.
8. Close My Briefcase.
9. Remove the disk from drive A.

Lesson 2: Directory Replication Overview

One of the challenges in supporting multiple dedicated servers in a single-domain or multiple-domain environment is to keep shared resources current. For example, when managing a domain, make certain that all backup domain controllers maintain a copy of the logon scripts and system policy files for that domain. This enables each domain controller to provide a user with a requested logon script or system policy file. If these files are unavailable, then users may experience a problem when logging on to a computer.

Windows NT uses the *Directory Replicator* service to maintain identical folder hierarchies, which could include logon scripts, system policy files, and other commonly used files on multiple servers. This allows users to access multiple servers for their logon files and other information.

After this lesson, you will be able to:

- Describe the purpose of directory replication.
- Identify the directory replication components.
- Describe the directory replication process.

Estimated lesson time: 20 minutes

The Purpose of Directory Replication

Directory replication is a Microsoft Windows NT feature that is used to replicate logon scripts, system policy files, and commonly used information to computers in a domain or to multiple domains. Directory replication is used to set up identical directories on multiple computers running Microsoft Windows NT Server, but can also be set up on computers running Microsoft Windows NT Workstation. The *master directory* is maintained on a designated Windows NT Server. Updates made to the files in the master directory are replicated to the other designated computers.

The following illustration shows the propagation of logon scripts and system policy files to multiple servers by means of directory replication.

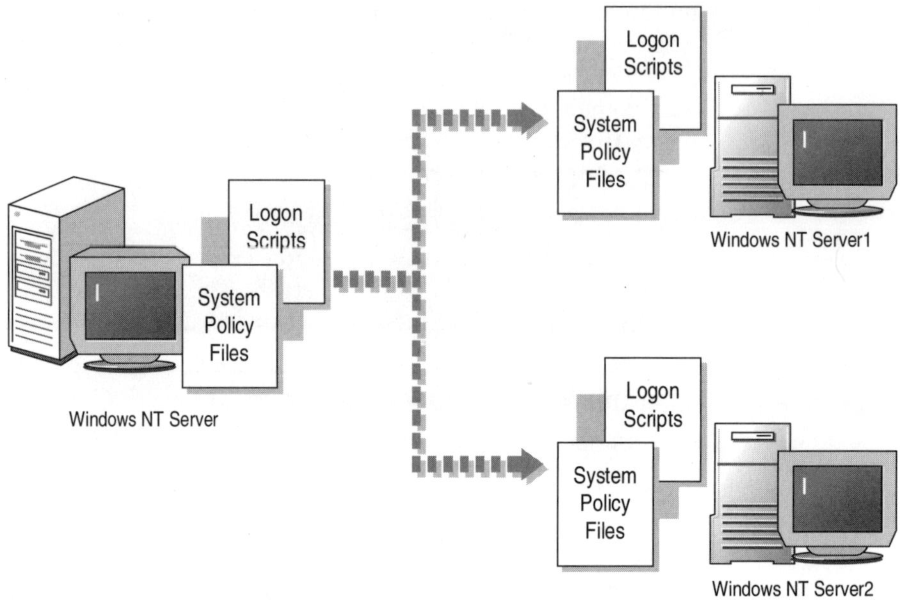

Directory replication makes the same files available at multiple servers. This is useful when a user logs on, because logon scripts must reside on the domain controller that validates the logon. In addition, directory replication helps to balance loads between multiple servers when several users need simultaneous access to a file, typically a read-only file, thereby avoiding overburdening any one server.

Types of Data Maintained by Directory Replication

Directory replication can be used to maintain any type of data. Some common examples of data that is replicated across servers using directory replication are logon scripts and system policy files.

Logon Scripts

Logon scripts are batch files, command files, or executable programs that can be assigned to user accounts. Logon scripts can be used to set up the user's environment without managing all aspects of it.

The logon script must reside on the domain controller that validates the user's logon request. When there is more than one Windows NT Server domain controller in a domain, it is recommended that logon scripts be replicated to all of them. This allows each domain controller to have a copy of all logon scripts. By using replication, only one copy of each script needs to be maintained.

Each time a user logs on, the assigned logon script is run. When a server processes a logon request, the system locates the logon script by combining a file name specified in User Manager for Domains with a path specified in Server Manager.

Note For information about how to manage logon scripts, see "Setting the Logon Script Path" in Server Manager Help.

System Policy Files

System policy files are used to control the user's work environment and implement uniform system configurations for all computers in an organization. Replicating system policy files ensures that proper system policy is downloaded regardless of the server that validates the logon request.

Note For more information on system policy files, see Chapter 4, "Managing System Policies."

Commonly Used Information

If many users need to access a file, such as an online telephone list, replicate the file to several computers. Replicating files to several servers allows you to set up *load balancing*, which can minimize bottlenecks by allowing different groups of users to access the file on different computers. These files are usually marked as read-only, because they typically contain information that is needed by many users, but should not be modified by those users. If any changes are made to the replicated copies of the file, they are overwritten the next time replication occurs.

Directory Replication Components

Replicating directory information in a Windows NT Server network requires an export server that replicates updated information and one or more import computers that receive a copy of these updated files.

The following illustration shows how an export server replicates files to the import servers.

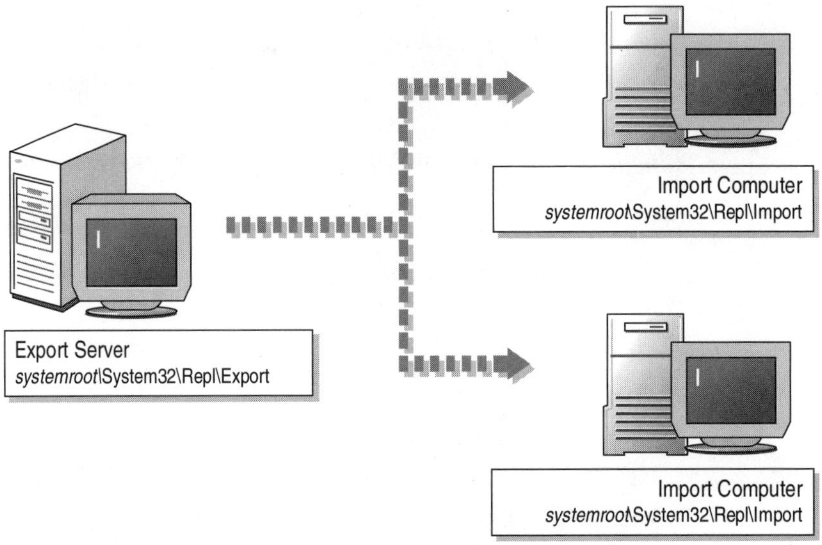

The Export Server

Export servers replicate updated files and directories from a designated master directory on an export server to a designated directory on an import computer. Only a computer running Windows NT Server can be an export server.

The Import Computer

Computers that receive updates, which are the replicated files and directories, from the export server are called *import computers*. Updates can be received from specified computers or domains. The following can be designated as import computers:

- Computers running Microsoft Windows NT Server.
- Computers running Microsoft Windows NT Workstation.
- Microsoft LAN Manager OS/2 servers.

Export and Import Directories

The export server keeps the directories to be replicated in a master export directory. By default, this directory is *systemroot*\System32\Repl\Export.

Note The directory *systemroot*\System32\Repl\Export is shared as **Repl$** when the Directory Replicator service is started.

Subdirectories under the *systemroot*\System32\Repl\Export directory must be created by the Administrator for each group of files that need to be replicated. These files are then placed in the appropriate subdirectories.

Caution In order for replication to occur, files must be placed in subdirectories in the *systemroot*\System32\Repl\Export directory. Any files placed directly in the *systemroot*\System32\Repl\Export directory are *not* replicated.

For example, to provide for replication of logon scripts, a computer running Windows NT Server exports logon scripts from the following directory:

systemroot\System32\Repl\Export\Scripts

Each import computer has an import directory that corresponds to the export server's export directory. By default, the import directory is *systemroot*\System32\Repl\Import.

The Directory Replicator service *automatically* creates subdirectories under this directory to match those on the export server.

For example, the logon scripts exported from the master export directory *systemroot*\System32\Repl\Export\Scripts on the export server would be imported to the *systemroot*\System32\Repl\Import\Scripts directory on import computers.

Note You use Server Manager to manage or change the default export or import directory paths.

The Directory Replication Process

After the files and directories have been set up for directory replication, the Directory Replicator service controls the replication process. This service operates on each export server and import computer that participates in replication. The service on each computer logs on using the same user account, for example the repl account, which you create for this purpose.

You configure export servers and import computers to send and receive updated files. An export directory on an export server contains all of the directories and subdirectories of files to be replicated, and when changes are saved to files in these directories, the files automatically replace the existing files on all of the import computers.

Periodically, the export server checks the export directory for changes. If any changes have occurred, the following process occurs, which replicates the updated information from export servers to import computers:

- The export server sends update notices to the import computers or domains.
- When an import computer receives an update notice, it calls the export server and reads the export directory structure.
- The import computer copies any new or changed files to its import directory structure, and deletes any of the import files that are no longer in the export directory structure.

The following illustration summarizes the directory replication process.

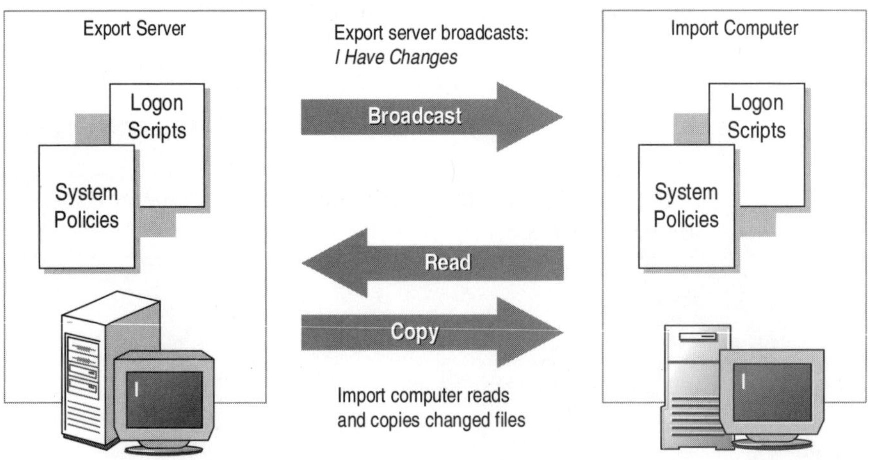

If nothing has changed in the export directories, the export server waits before sending a repeat update notice. The repeat notice allows import computers that missed the original update notice to receive the notice. The timing for checking replicated directories is set by the *Interval* parameter, which is discussed in the "Managing Replication from an Export Server" topic later in this chapter.

The parameters that control the Directory Replicator service are located in the following registry path:

HKEY_LOCAL_MACHINE\SYSTEM\CurrentControlSet\Services\
Replicator\Parameters.

Lesson 3: Preparing for Directory Replication

Directory replication begins with the configuration of both the export server and the import computer(s).

After this lesson, you will be able to:

- Prepare an export server to replicate directories to other computers and domains.
- Prepare an import computer to receive directories from an export server.

Estimated lesson time: 10 minutes

Preparing an Export Server

Any computer running Windows NT Server can be set up as an export server.

You would use the following steps to set up replication on an export server:

1. In User Manager for Domains, create a user account, such as repl, for the Directory Replicator service to use, according to the following specifications:
   - All logon hours are allowed.
   - The account is added to the domain's Backup Operators and Replicator groups.
   - The **User Must Change Password at Next Logon** check box is cleared.
   - The **Password Never Expires** option is selected.

2. From Server Manager, or the Services program in Control Panel configure the Directory Replicator service to start automatically and log on as the directory replicator user account.

   The following illustration shows the **Service** dialog boxes used to configure the Directory Replicator service to start automatically and to use the directory replicator user account.

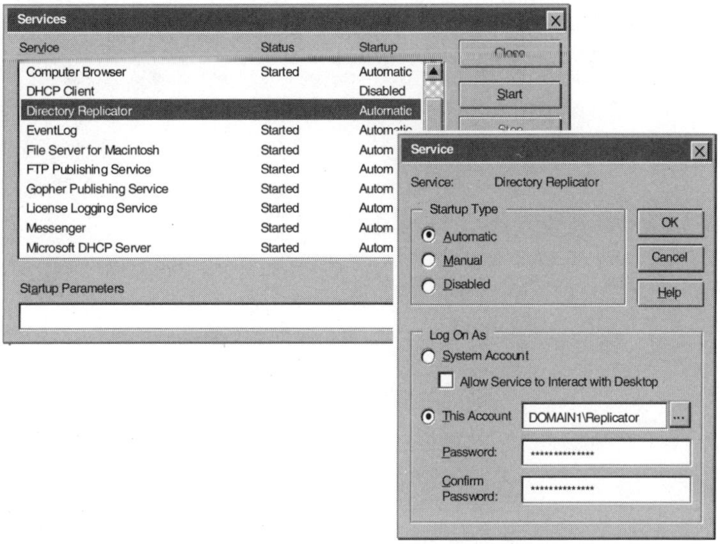

3. Place directories to be replicated in the following folder: *systemroot*\System32\Repl\Export
4. From Server Manager, configure the export server to export files to other computers or domains.

Note If the export directory is on an (NTFS) partition, the Replicator group on the export server should be granted Full Control to the export directory tree.

Preparing an Import Computer

Computers running Windows NT Server, computers running Windows NT Workstation, and Microsoft LAN Manager OS/2 servers can be set up as import computers. A computer running Windows NT Server that is configured as an export server can also be configured as an import computer.

The following describes the steps that are necessary for setting up replication on an import computer:

1. If the import computer is not part of the export server's domain or a trusting domain, create a replicator user account, using User Manager for Domains.
   - This account must have the same name and password as the account used to configure the export server because the account must have permission to access the export server's Repl$ share.
   - This account must be a member of the local Replicator group and the Backup Operators group.
2. From Server Manager, or the Services program in Control Panel, configure the Directory Replicator service to start automatically and to log on as the directory replicator user account.
3. Using Server Manager, configure the import computer to receive files from other servers or domains.

Lesson 4: Managing Directory Replication

You can manage directory replication between the export server and the import computer.

After this lesson, you will be able to:

- Use Server Manager to manage replication from the export server.
- Use Server Manager to manage replication to the import computer.
- Configure an export server to replicate directories and files.
- Configure an import computer to receive exported files.

Estimated lesson time: 45 minutes

Managing Replication from an Export Server

Server Manager is used to configure a server as an export server, to specify which computers to export to, and to manage the directories to be exported from the export server.

The following illustration shows the dialog boxes displayed in Server Manager that are used to set up an export server.

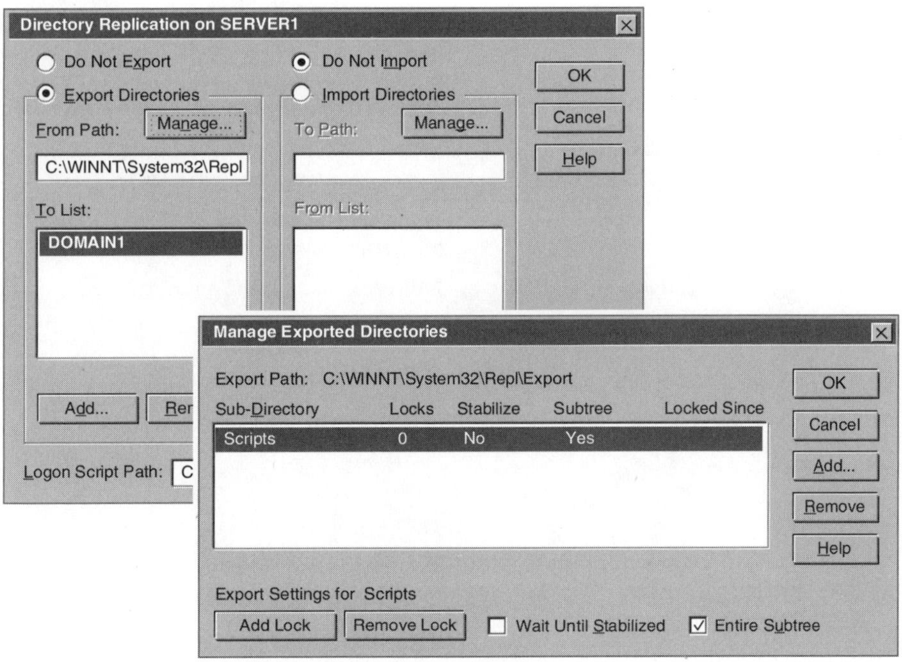

Note Ensure that an appropriate logon account is assigned to the Directory Replicator service before configuring the export options.

When managing directory replication from an export server, consider the following:

- Which computers are to receive the replicated directory. All computers on the network may not need to receive replicated information.
- Which directories are to be exported. Not all directories may need to be exported.
- Whether the entire tree or only top-level directories are to be replicated. In some instances, not all subdirectories need to be replicated.
- How long, if at all, the Directory Replicator service waits for the directory to stabilize before replicating. In many instances, it is not advisable to replicate a changing directory, as file integrity may not be preserved.
- Whether any directories need to be locked while modifications are being made to them. This provides control over when a directory can be replicated.

Use Server Manager to manage the replication options at the export server as shown in the following table.

Option	Description
From Path	Indicates the path from which directories are exported.
To List	Indicates the computers or the domains to which directories can be exported. If blank, replicate to any computer in the same domain configured as an import computer.
Locks	Prevents a directory from being exported. (Directories can be locked by more than one user.)
Stabilize	Indicates whether files in the export directory wait a specified time after changes before being exported.
Subtree	Indicates whether the entire subtree is exported.
Locked Since	Indicates the date and time a lock was placed on a directory.

The registry contains entries that control various aspects of replication. These are located in HKEY_LOCAL_MACHINE\SYSTEM\CurrentControlSet \Services\Replicator\Parameters.

There are two registry entries that are *not* configurable by Server Manager and that you may want to add to the registry in order to better manage replication are:

- *Interval*: **REG_DWORD** which sets how often an export server checks the replicated directories for changes. The range is from 1 through 60 minutes; the default is 5 minutes.
- *GuardTime*: **REG_DWORD** which sets the number of minutes an export directory must be stable (no changes to any files) before import servers can replicate its files. The range is from 0 through one-half of the Interval minutes; the default is 2 minutes.

Note For more information on registry parameters that control Directory Replication, see the Replicator entry in the Regentry.hlp file on the *Microsoft Windows NT Workstation Resource Kit CD-ROM*.

Managing Replication to an Import Computer

Server Manager allows you to manage replication to the import computer. When managing directory replication to an import computer consider the following:

- Which computers are going to be allowed to replicate to the import computer.
- Which directories are to be imported. Not all directories may be needed.
- Whether any directories need to be locked. This provides control over when a directory can be imported, because a locked directory can not be imported.

The following illustration shows the dialog boxes displayed in Server Manager that are used to set up an import computer.

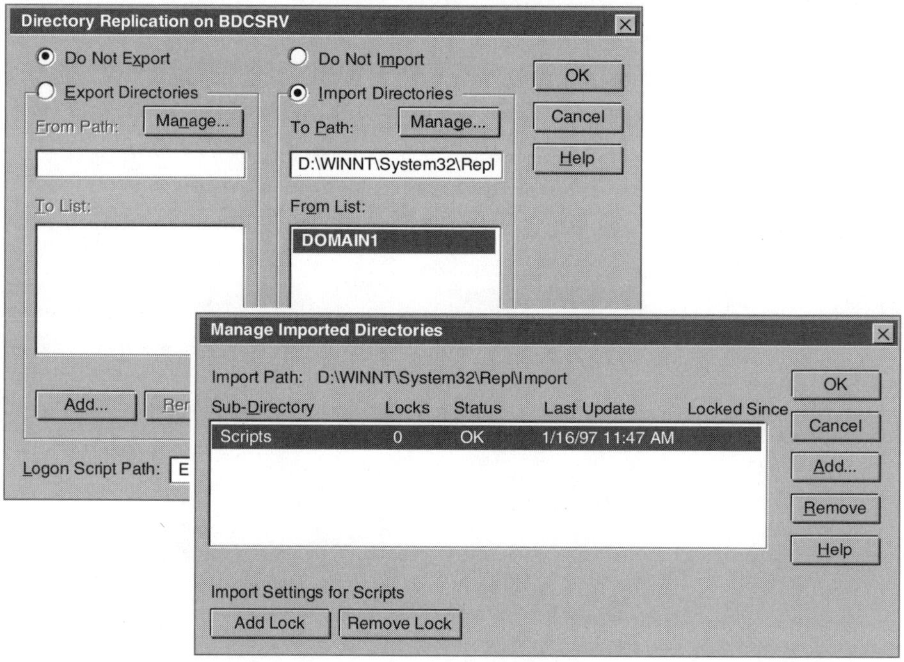

Use Server Manager to manage aspects of replication at the import computers as listed in the following table.

Option	Description
To Path	Indicates the path in which replicated directories are stored.
From List	Indicates the servers or domains which can export to this computer. If blank, receive replicated data from any export server in the same domain.
Locks	Prevents a directory from being imported.
Status	Indicates the status on receiving updates from the export server. Status options include the following: **OK**. Indicates that the directory is receiving regular updates from the export server and the imported data is identical to that exported. **No Master**. Indicates that the directory is not receiving updates from the export server. The export server may not be running or may have stopped exporting updates. **No Sync**. Indicates that the directory has received updates, but that the data is not up to date. This could be due to a communications failure, open files on the import computer or export server, the import computer not having access permissions to the export server, or an export server malfunction. **[blank]** Indicates that replication has never occurred for the directory. Replication may not be properly configured for this import computer, for the export server, or both.
Last Update	Provides the date and time that the last update was made to a file in the import directory.

Practice

In these procedures, you configure directory replication. Server1 is your export server, and Server2 is your import computer. In order to complete the procedures in this practice, you need to modify a registry setting on Server1.

► **To log on to Server2**

1. Shut down Workstation1, and restart the computer as Server2.
2. Log on at Server2 as Administrator.

▶ To modify an entry in the registry

Note Complete this procedure on Server1.

---

1. Verify that you are logged on to Server1 as Administrator.
2. Open Windows NT Registry Editor (Regedt32.exe).
3. On the **Options** menu, clear **Read Only Mode**.
4. Open the following key:

   HKEY_LOCAL_MACHINE\SYSTEM\CurrentControlSet\Control\SecurePipeServers\winreg\AllowedPaths
5. In the right pane, double-click **Machine: REG_MULTI_SZ**.

   The **Multi-String Editor** dialog box appears with four lines of data.
6. In the **Data** box add a fifth line by pressing the DOWN ARROW key to clear the highlight, and then press ENTER.
7. Type **System\CurrentControlSet\Services\Replicator**

Caution Verify that you have added a fifth line and typed the information correctly. If you made a mistake, correct it now or click **Cancel** and begin again.

---

8. Click **OK** to close the **Multi-String Editor** dialog box.
9. Close Registry Editor.
10. Shut down and restart your server.
11. Log on as Administrator.

▸ To create an account for the Directory Replicator service

In this procedure you create an account for the Directory Replicator service to use.

Note Complete this procedure on Server1.

---

1. Start User Manager for Domains.
2. Create a user account using the information in the following table.

Field	Response
Username	repl
Full Name	Replicator Service Account
Password	password
Confirm Password	password
User Must Change Password at Next Logon	Not selected
Password Never Expires	Selected
Groups	Add as a member of the Replicator group and the Backup Operators group

3. Close User Manager for Domains.

▸ To configure the Directory Replicator service on an export server

In this procedure, you configure the Directory Replicator service on your export server, Server1, to start automatically using the repl account.

Note Complete this procedure on Server1.

---

1. Click the **Start** button, point to **Programs**, point to **Administrative Tools (Common)**, and then click **Server Manager**.
2. Server Manager appears, click to select **Server1**.
3. On the **Computer** menu, click **Services**.
4. Click **Directory Replicator**, and then click **Startup**.

   A **Service** dialog box appears.
5. Under **Startup Type**, click **Automatic**.
6. Under **Log On As**, click **This Account**, and then click the ellipsis (…) button to the right of the **This Account** box.

   The **Add User** dialog box appears.
7. Click **repl**.

8. Click **Add**, and then click **OK**.

   The **Service** dialog box reappears, with **Domain1\repl** in the **This Account** box.

9. In the **Password** and **Confirm Password** fields, type **password**
10. Click **OK**.

    A **Services** dialog box appears, stating that the repl account has been granted the Log On As A Service right.

11. Click **OK**.
12. Click **Close** to close the **Services** dialog box.

► **To configure an export server**

In this procedure, you configure Server1 to be an export server for Domain1.

Note Complete this procedure on Server1.

---

1. In Server Manager, double-click **Server1**.
2. Click **Replication**.

   The **Directory Replication on Server1** dialog box appears.

3. Click **Export Directories**.
4. Click the **Add** button located under **Export Directories**.

   The **Select Domain** dialog box appears.

5. In the **Select Domain** list, double-click **Domain1**.

   The list of servers in Domain1 appears.

6. Click **Server2**, and then click **OK**.

   The **Directory Replication on Server1** dialog box reappears, with **Server2** listed in the **To List**.

7. Click **OK**.

   Service Control Manager starts the Directory Replicator service.

8. Click **OK** to close the **Properties for Server1** dialog box.
9. Close **Server Manager**.

▸ To create files for replication

In this procedure, you create files for the Directory Replicator service to replicate.

Note Complete this procedure on Server1, your export server.

---

1. In the C:\Winnt\System32\Repl\Export directory, create a new folder called Data.
2. Copy two or three files to the Data folder.
3. Close all windows that are open to the export folder or its subfolders.

▸ To configure the Directory Replicator service on an import computer

In this procedure, you configure the Directory Replicator service on your import computer, Server2, to start automatically using the repl account.

Note Complete this procedure on Server2.

---

1. Start Server Manager, and then click **Server2**.
2. On the **Computer** menu, click **Services**.
3. Click **Directory Replicator**, and then click **Startup**.

   A **Service** dialog box appears.
4. Under **Startup Type**, click **Automatic**.
5. Under **Log On As**, click **This Account** and then click the ellipsis (…) button to the right of the **This Account** box.

   The **Add User** dialog box appears.
6. Click **repl**.
7. Click **Add**, and then click **OK**.

   The **Service** dialog box reappears, with **Domain1\repl** in the **This Account** box.
8. In the **Password** and **Confirm Password** fields, type **password**
9. Click **OK**.
10. Click **Close** to close the Services dialog box.

▸ To configure an import computer

In this procedure, you configure Server2 to be an import computer for Domain1.

Note Complete this procedure on Server2.

---

1. In **Server Manager**, double-click **Server2**.
2. Click **Replication**.

   The **Directory Replication on Server2** dialog box appears.
3. Click **Import Directories**.
4. Click the **Add** button located under **Import Directories**.

   The **Select Domain** dialog box appears.
5. In the **Select Domain** list, double-click **Domain1**.

   The list of servers in **Domain1** appears.
6. Click **Server1** and then click **OK**.

   The **Directory Replication on Server2** dialog box reappears with **Server1** listed in the **From List**.
7. Click **OK**.

   Service Control Manager starts the Directory Replicator service.
8. Click **OK**.
9. Minimize **Server Manager**.

► **To verify file replication**

In this procedure, you verify that folders and files have been replicated to your import computer in D:\Server2\System32\Repl\Import directory on Server2.

Note Complete this procedure on Server2, your import computer.

---

1. Wait approximately six minutes.
2. In **Server Manager**, double-click **Server2**, and then click **Replication**.
3. Under **Import Directories**, click **Manage**.

   What is the status of the Data subdirectory?

   ____

4. If the status is not OK, wait a few more minutes. You may also want to check to see if the files are replicated on the import computer. It may take a while for the status in Server Manager to show that the files have been replicated, even after the files have successfully been copied to the import computer.
5. Close Server Manager.
6. Shut down Server2, and restart the computer as Workstation1.

Lesson 5: Troubleshooting Directory Replication

This lesson describes some of the problems that you may encounter when you use Directory Replication, and it identifies some troubleshooting measures.

After this lesson, you will be able to:

- Describe directory replication problems that can occur.
- Identify solutions to directory replication problems.

Estimated lesson time: 10 minutes

Replication Troubleshooting Overview

When the Directory Replicator service encounters an error, an event is written to the application log. You can use Event Viewer to view the error in the application log. The Event Viewer displays information about the **Status** column in the **Manage Import Directories** dialog box of Server Manager, and information about messages that appear while you are configuring directory replication servers.

The following illustration summarizes some of the common problems that can occur during directory replication, and the possible solutions to these problems.

Error	Possible Solution
Access denied	Use Server Manager to see if the Directory Replicator service is configured to log on using a specific account. Use User Manager for Domains to check logon properties.
Exporting to specific computers	Use Server Manager to make sure that the export servers that will export data, and the Import computers that should receive replicated information, are correctly set up.
Replication over a WAN link	In Server Manager, in the export **To List** and the import **From List**, specify the computer names in addition to the domain name.
Logon scripts are not working	Store logon scripts in a Scripts folder within the Import folder.

Replication Troubleshooting Procedures

Access Denied

If the application log in Event Viewer shows "access denied" errors for the Directory Replicator service, use Server Manager to check the following:

- Make sure that the Directory Replicator service is configured to log on using a specific account.
- Make sure that the account used by the import computer's Directory Replicator service has permission to read the files on the export server.

The default permissions for an export directory grant Full Control to the Replicator local group. If the Full Control permission is removed from the directory, exported files are copied to the import computers but receive the wrong permissions, and an access denied error is written to the event log. If necessary, use Windows NT Explorer and view the properties of the export directory. Then click **Permissions** on the export directory's **Sharing** tab and grant Full Control to the Replicator local group for the export directories.

Exporting to Specific Computers

Be sure to specify the correct export servers and import computers in the **From List** and **To List**, respectively, in the **Directory Replication** dialog box of Server Manager, or the Server program in Control Panel. If you do not specify the export server and import computers, exporting occurs to all import computers in the local domain, and importing occurs from all export servers in the local domain.

Replication to a Domain Name Over a WAN Link

Directory replication to a domain name does not always succeed when some or all replication import computers are located across a wide area network (WAN) bridge from an export server. When adding names to the export **To List** on an export server, and when adding names to the import **From List** on an import computer, specify the computer names (instead of—or in addition to—specifying the domain name) for those computers separated by a WAN bridge.

Logon Scripts Are Not Working

On non-domain controller computers running Windows NT Server or computers running Windows NT Workstation, store the logon scripts in the following local directory: *systemroot*\System32\Repl\Import\Scripts.

Summary

The following information summarizes the key points in this chapter:

- Both the Windows NT Briefcase and Directory Replicator service can provide considerable administrative benefits in managing distributed data.
  - The Briefcase supports mobile and distributed computing by transparently synchronizing updated files.
  - The Directory Replicator service replicates information such as logon scripts, user profiles, and system policies from a designated export server to one or more import computers.
- By copying files to the My Briefcase folder, users are able to work on files on a stand-alone computer, and then synchronize them with the original source upon reconnecting to the network.
- One of the challenges in supporting multiple dedicated servers in a single-domain or multiple-domain environment is to keep shared resources current. Windows NT uses the *Directory Replicator* service to maintain identical folder hierarchies, which could include logon scripts, system policy files, and other commonly used files on multiple servers. This allows users to access multiple servers for their logon files and other information.
- Windows NT Directory Replicator service uses export servers and import computers.
  - Only a computer running Windows NT Server can be an export server. Export servers replicate updated files and directories from a designated master directory on an export server to a designated directory on an import computer.
  - Import computers receive updates, which are the replicated files and directories, from the export server. Updates can be received from specified computers or domains. The following three types of computers can serve as import computers: computers running Microsoft Windows NT Server, computers running Microsoft Windows NT Workstation, and Microsoft LAN Manager OS/2 servers.
- Using the Directory Replicator service, identical directory trees are set up and maintained on the export servers and the corresponding import computers. Only one copy of each file needs to be maintained, yet every computer that participates has an available, identical copy of that file.

- Directory replication also helps alleviate potential bottlenecks through load balancing. If you have many users who need to periodically receive the same file, you can replicate the file to several computers to prevent any one server from becoming a bottleneck.
- When the Directory Replicator service encounters an error, an event is written to the application log. You can use Event Viewer to view the error in the application log. The Event Viewer displays information about the **Status** column in the **Manage Import Directories** dialog box of Server Manager, and information about messages that appear while you are configuring directory replication servers.

Review

1. You copy several files, including the file Qt_rpt01.doc, from a network server to the My Briefcase icon on your desktop computer. Then you copy My Briefcase to a floppy disk so that you can work at home on these files. The next day you copy My Briefcase back on to your desktop computer. When you open My Briefcase and use **Update All** to synchronize the files in My Briefcase with the copies of the files on the network server, all of the file except the Qt_rpt01.doc are updated on the server. What could be the problem?

2. You are one of several administrators on your network. Several of your users call reporting that the end of month reports that the third shift administrator had placed on the export server last night were not replicating correctly. You look in *systemroot*\System32\Repl\Export and find the file, Feb_eom.doc. Why is the file not being replicated?

Answer Key

Procedure Answers

Page 580

▸ **To synchronize your files**

5. On the **Briefcase** menu, click **Update All**.

   Z should be the only file listed.

   Why was Z not updated?

   Because the original and the Briefcase copy were both modified, Briefcase is unable to determine which direction to copy the file.

Page 601

▸ **To verify file replication**

3. Under **Import Directories**, click **Manage**.

   What is the status of the Data subdirectory?

   If the files replicated successfully, the status is OK.

Review Answers

Page 606

1. You copy several files, including the file Qt_rpt01.doc, from a network server to the My Briefcase icon on your desktop computer. Then you copy My Briefcase to a floppy disk so that you can work at home on these files. The next day you copy My Briefcase back on to your desktop computer. When you open My Briefcase and use **Update All** to synchronize the files in My Briefcase with the copies of the files on the network server, all of the file except the Qt_rpt01.doc are updated on the server. What could be the problem?

   The original and the Briefcase copy of Qt_rpt01.doc were both modified, and Briefcase was unable to determine which direction to copy the file.

2. You are one of several administrators on your network. Several of your users call reporting that the end of month reports that the third shift administrator had placed on the export server last night were not replicating correctly. You look in *systemroot*\System32\Repl\Export and find the file, Feb_eom.doc. Why is the file not being replicated?

   You must put the files to be replicated in a subdirectory under the *systemroot*\System32\Repl\Export directory. Files placed in the directory are not replicated.

CHAPTER 17

The Windows NT Boot Process

About This Chapter

Understanding the Microsoft Windows NT boot process facilitates restoring a system if a boot failure occurs. This chapter describes the boot process and introduces troubleshooting resources that help you solve Windows NT boot problems.

Before You Begin

To complete the lessons in this chapter, you must have:

- Two computers that meet the hardware and software requirements as specified in the Getting Started section of "About This Book."
- Completed all practices in Chapter 2, "Installing Windows NT."
- One blank, 1.44 MB high-density disk.

Lesson 1: Overview of the Windows NT Boot Process

The Windows NT boot process occurs in stages: the Power On Self Test (POST) process, the Initial Startup Process, the Boot loader process, the boot sequence, and the load phase. This lesson describes the boot process for the Intel x86 and RISC hardware platforms.

After this lesson, you will be able to:

- Identify the files necessary to boot Windows NT.
- Describe the boot sequence process on an Intel *x*86 platform.
- Describe the boot sequence process on a RISC platform.
- Identify the Windows NT load phases.

Estimated lesson time: 30 minutes

Files Required for Windows NT System Boot

The following illustration summarizes the files that are required for Windows NT system boot on Intel *x*86 platforms and those required by RISC-based systems. Note that some files are platform-specific while others are common to all platforms.

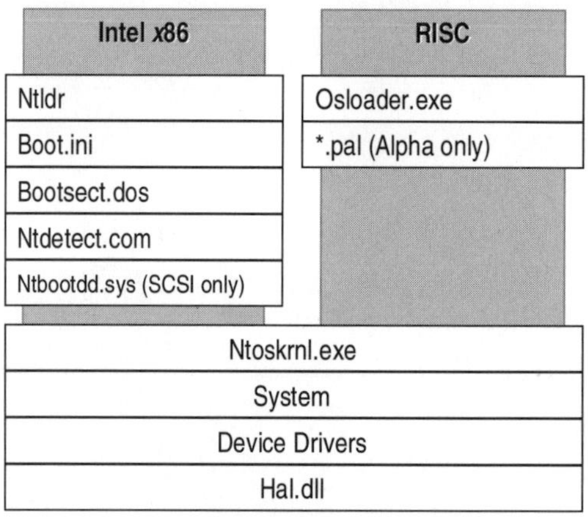

Intel *x*86 Boot Sequence Files

An Intel *x*86 computer requires all of the following files to be in the root folder of the system partition:

- *Ntldr.* This hidden, read-only system file loads the operating system.
- *Boot.ini.* This is a read-only system file, used to build the **Boot Loader Operating System Selection** menu on Intel *x*86-based computers.
- *Bootsect.dos.* This is a hidden system file loaded by Ntldr if another operating system, such as Microsoft MS-DOS, Microsoft Windows 95, or O/S 2 version 1.*x,* is selected instead of Windows NT. This file contains the boot sector that was on the hard disk before installing Windows NT.
- *Ntdetect.com.* This is a hidden, read-only system file used to examine the hardware available and to build a hardware list. This information is passed back to Ntldr to be added to the registry later in the boot process.
- *Ntbootdd.sys.* This hidden, read-only, system file is only on systems that boot from a SCSI hard disk and on which the BIOS on the SCSI adapter is disabled. This driver accesses devices attached to the SCSI adapter during the Windows NT boot sequence.

RISC Boot Sequence Files

RISC-based systems require the following two files:

- *Osloader.exe.* This is the operating system loader (equivalent to Ntldr on Intel *x*86-based computers).
- **.pal (Alpha only).* These files contain PAL code, software subroutines that provide an operating system with direct control of the processor.

Common Boot Sequence Files

The following files are common to both the Intel *x*86 and RISC platforms:

- *Ntoskrnl.exe.* This is the Windows NT kernel file, located in the *systemroot*\System32 folder.
- *System.* This file is a collection of system configuration settings. The file is in the *systemroot*\System32\Config folder. It controls which device drivers and services are loaded during the initialization process.
- *Device drivers.* These are files that support various device drivers, such as Ftdisk and Scsidisk.

The Windows NT Boot Sequence

In this section you now learn about the process of booting, and examine the steps that lead up to the Windows NT boot sequence, as well as the boot sequences for Intel *x*86 computers and those sequences for RISC-based computers.

The Intel *x*86 Boot Sequence

The following illustration presents a global look at the boot sequence for Intel systems.

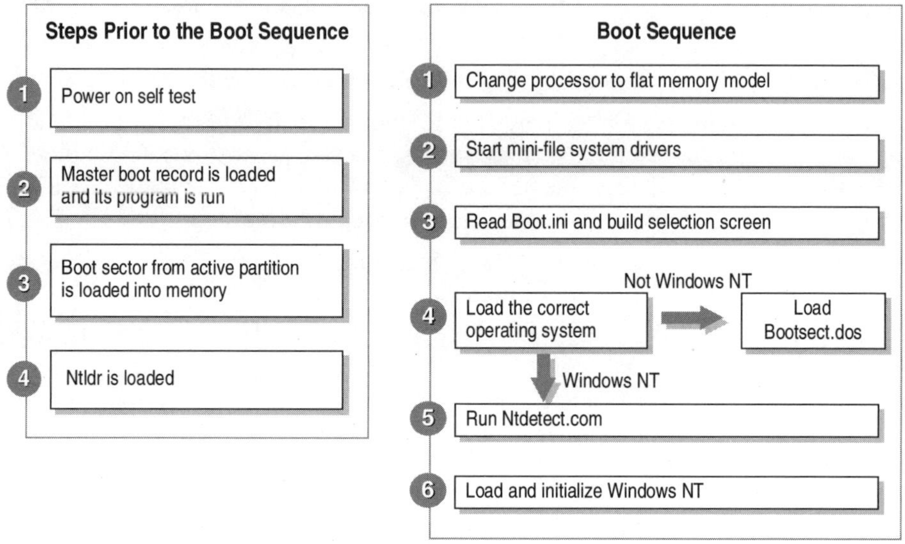

For Intel *x*86-based computers, several steps precede the actual boot sequence.

Steps Prior to the Boot Sequence

When you start a computer that has Windows NT installed on it, the computer initializes and locates the boot portion of the hard disk. The following steps are performed prior to the boot sequence:

1. Power On Self Test (POST) routines are run; for example, the memory check occurs.
2. The boot device is located, and the Master Boot Record (MBR) is loaded into memory. The program contained in the MBR is run.
3. The MBR program scans the Partition Boot Record (PBR) table to locate the active partition. The boot sector from the active partition is loaded into memory.
4. Ntldr is loaded and initialized from the boot sector.

Note When Windows NT is installed, it changes the boot sector so that Ntldr loads on system startup.

Boot Sequence

The boot sequence begins after Ntldr is loaded into memory. The boot sequence gathers information about hardware and drivers in preparation for the Windows NT load phases. The following files are used during the boot sequence: Ntldr, Boot.ini, Bootsect.dos, Ntdetect.com, and Ntoskrnl.exe. The boot sequence follows these steps:

1. Ntldr switches the processor from real mode into 32-bit flat memory mode. Ntldr, as is the case with any 32-bit code, requires this 32-bit flat memory mode before it can carry out any functions.
2. Ntldr starts the appropriate mini-file system drivers. Mini-file system drivers are built into Ntldr to find and load Windows NT from different file system formats (FAT or NTFS).
3. If there is a Boot.ini file, Ntldr reads it and displays the operating system selections contained within the Boot.ini file. This is called the **Boot Loader Operating System Selection** menu.
4. Ntldr loads the operating system. The operating system that is loaded is the one selected by the user or, if no selection is made, the default operating system.

Note If the user selects an operating system other than Windows NT, such as Microsoft Windows 95, Ntldr loads and runs Bootsect.dos and passes control to the selected operating system. The selected operating system then boots. At this point, the Windows NT boot process ends.

5. If Windows NT is selected, Ntldr runs Ntdetect.com. Ntdetect.com scans the hardware and then sends the list of detected hardware back to Ntldr for later inclusion in the registry under HKEY_LOCAL_MACHINE\HARDWARE.
6. Ntldr then loads Ntoskrnl.exe, Hal.dll, and the System hive.

   Ntldr scans the System hive and loads the device drivers configured to start at boot time.

   Finally, Ntldr starts Ntoskrnl.exe, at which point the boot process ends and the load phases begin.

Files Needed for Boot

The following table shows the files and their associated folders that are needed for the Windows NT boot sequence on Intel *x*86-based computers.

Intel *x*86-based file	Folder
Ntldr	system partition root
Boot.ini	system partition root
Bootsect.dos	system partition root
Ntdetect.com	system partition root
Ntbootdd.sys	system partition root
Ntoskrnl.exe	*systemroot*\System32
Hal.dll	*systemroot*\System32
System	*systemroot*\System32\Config
Device drivers	*systemroot*\System32\Drivers

The RISC Boot Sequence

The boot sequence for RISC-based computers is slightly different than Intel *x*86-based computers. The following illustration describes the Windows NT boot process for RISC-based computers.

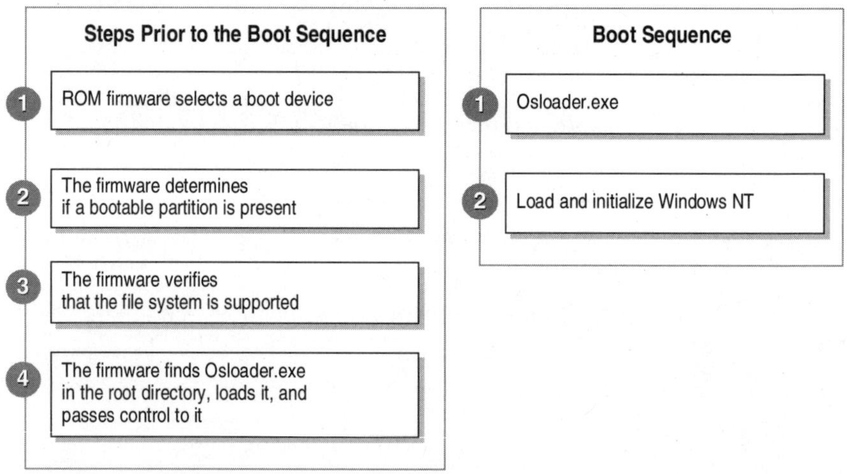

The Ntldr, Boot.ini, and Bootsect.dos files on Intel *x*86-based computers are not needed on RISC-based computers. On RISC-based computers, the Ntldr function is built into the firmware. The initial stages of loading the Windows NT operating system, that are controlled by Ntldr on Intel *x*86-based systems, are performed by Osloader.exe for RISC-based computers.

There is also no need for Ntdetect.com on RISC-based computers. The RISC POST routine collects the hardware information and passes it to Osloader.exe.

Steps Prior to the Boot Sequence

The following steps are performed before the boot sequence:

1. The ROM firmware selects a boot device by reading a boot precedence table from nonvolatile RAM. If the nonvolatile RAM is invalid or blank, the firmware either queries the user for the boot device, or defaults to a floppy or hard disk sequence.
2. For a hard disk boot, the firmware reads the Master Boot Record (MBR), and determines whether a system partition is present.
3. If a system partition exists, the firmware reads the first sector of the partition into memory. It then examines the BIOS Parameter Block (BPB) to determine whether the volume's file system is supported by the firmware.
4. If the file system is supported by the firmware, the firmware searches the root folder of the volume for Osloader.exe, loads the program, and passes control to it, along with a list of the available hardware on the system.

Boot Sequence

1. Osloader.exe loads Ntoskrnl.exe, Hal.dll, the *.pal files, and the System hive.
2. Osloader.exe scans the System hive and loads the device drivers configured to start at boot time.

Osloader.exe passes control to Ntoskrnl.exe, at which point the boot process ends and the load phases begin.

Files Needed for Boot

The following table shows the files and their associated folders that are needed for the boot sequence on RISC-based computers.

RISC file	Folder
Osloader.exe	os\nt40
Ntoskrnl.exe	*systemroot*\System32
Hal.dll	os\nt40
*.pal (Alpha only)	os\nt40
System	*systemroot*\System32\Config
Device drivers	*systemroot*\System32\Drivers

Windows NT Load Phases

The boot sequence for both the RISC and Intel *x*86-based platforms concludes when control is passed to Ntoskrnl.exe. At this point Windows NT begins to load and initializes in the following four phases: the kernel load phase, the kernel initialization phase, the services load phase, and the Win32 subsystem start phase.

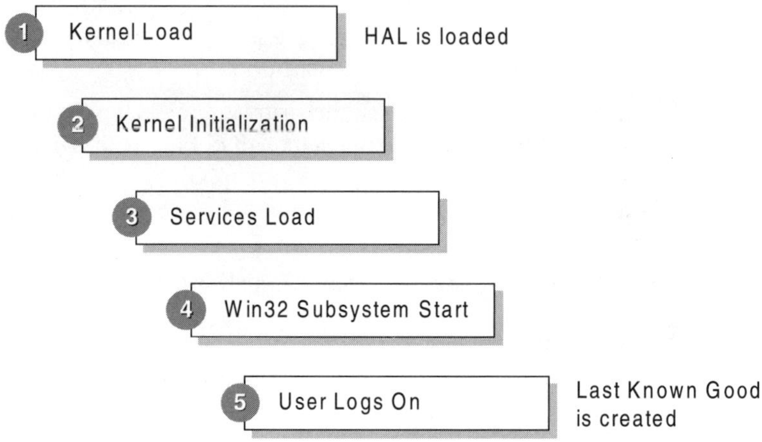

Kernel Load Phase

The kernel load phase begins as soon as Ntoskrnl.exe is loaded. The hardware abstraction layer (HAL), which hides platform-specific hardware issues from Windows NT, is loaded after the kernel.

Next, the System hive is loaded and scanned for drivers and services that should be loaded at this stage. These drivers and services are organized into groups. They are loaded into memory, but not initialized, in the order in which they appear beside "List" in the ServiceGroupOrder subkey. The ServiceGroupOrder subkey is found in the registry under:

HKEY_LOCAL_MACHINE\SYSTEM\CurrentControlSet\Control\
ServiceGroupOrder

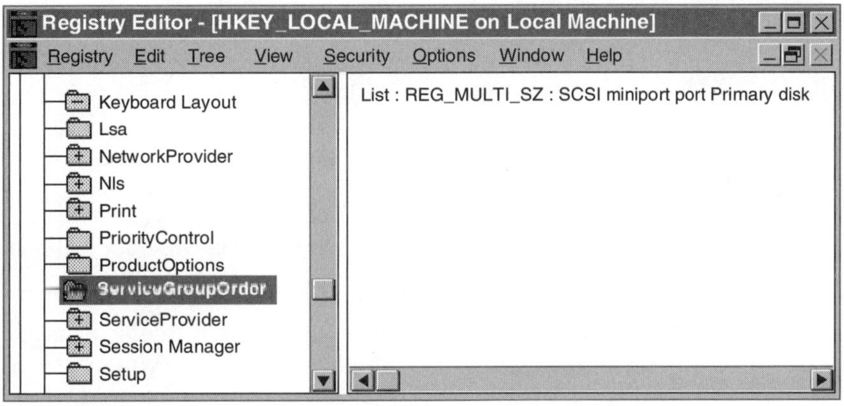

This portion of the boot sequence occurs when the screen clears after Ntdetect.com has run, and progress dots (...) are displayed across the top of the screen. It is possible to display the names of the drivers being loaded on this screen by adding an **/sos** switch to the appropriate operating system line in Boot.ini.

Kernel Initialization Phase

In this stage of the boot sequence the screen is painted blue. The kernel initialization phase initializes the kernel and the drivers that were loaded during the kernel load phase.

During this phase, the System hive is again scanned to determine which high-level drivers should be loaded. These drivers are initialized and loaded after the kernel has been initialized. The registry's CurrentControlSet is then saved, and the Clone control set is created and initialized, but not saved. The registry hardware list is then created, using the information from Ntdetect.com (for Intel-based computers) or Osloader.exe (for RISC-based computers).

Note A control set contains configuration data used to control the system, such as which device drivers and services to load and start. Control sets are stored in the registry as subkeys of HKEY_LOCAL_MACHINE\SYSTEM\Select.

For more information on the CurrentControlSet subkey, see Chapter 19, "What Happens When You Start Your Computer," in the *Workstation Resource Guide* of Books Online, or Chapter 23, "Overview of the Windows NT Registry," in the *Microsoft Windows NT Workstation Resource Kit.*

ErrorControl Values

If an error is encountered while loading and initializing the drivers for the system, action is taken based on the driver's **ErrorControl** value. There are four different **ErrorControl** levels:

- 0x0 – "Ignore"

  If an error occurs while loading a driver with this **ErrorControl** level, the boot sequence ignores the error and proceeds without displaying an error message.

- 0x1 – "Normal"

  If an error occurs while loading a driver with this **ErrorControl** level, an error message is displayed, but the boot sequence ignores the error and proceeds.

- 0x2 – "Severe"

  If an error occurs while loading a driver with this **ErrorControl** level, the boot sequence fails and then restarts using the LastKnownGood control set. If the boot sequence is currently using the LastKnownGood control set, the error is ignored and the boot sequence continues.

- 0x3 – "Critical"

  If an error occurs while loading a driver with this **ErrorControl** level, the boot sequence fails and then the boot sequence restarts using the LastKnownGood control set. However, if the LastKnownGood control set is being used and is causing the critical error, the boot sequence stops and an error message is displayed.

ErrorControl values are found in the registry under:

HKEY_LOCAL_MACHINE\SYSTEM\CurrentControlSet\Services\
*Name_of_service_or_driver***ErrorControl**

Services Load Phase

The services load phase starts the Session Manager (Smss.exe), which starts the higher-order subsystems and services for Windows NT. Session Manager carries out the instructions under the following four registry entries:

- BootExecute data item
- Memory Management key
- DOS Devices key
- Subsystems key

BootExecute Data Item

Session Manager immediately reads and carries out the list of programs in:
HKEY_LOCAL_MACHINE\SYSTEM\CurrentControlSet\Control\
Session Manager**BootExecute**

The default entry is: **autocheck autochk ***

Autocheck.exe is the boot-time version of Chkdsk. In this example, the wildcard (*) causes an automatic check of each partition. During system boot, Autocheck displays the check disk information about each partition. This display occurs on the blue screen portion of system boot and is your indication that the services load phase has started.

You can modify the entry for BootExecute. If this entry is changed to read **autocheck autochk /p ***, the **/p** forces the equivalent of a **Chkdsk /f** on each partition on every subsequent restart of the system.

The **BootExecute** value can also contain more than one command. Therefore, you could add a second command, such as the following:

autocheck autochk * autoconv \DosDevices\d: /FS:ntfs

In this example, the second command causes drive d to be converted to NTFS on the next system boot.

Memory Management Key

After all of the checks have been successfully performed on the system's hard disks, Session Manager sets up the paging files defined in:

HKEY_LOCAL_MACHINE\SYSTEM\CurrentControlSet\Control\
Session Manager\Memory Management**PagingFiles**

When the partitions are checked and the paging files are set up, the CurrentControlSet and the Clone control set are written to the registry.

DOS Devices Key

Next, the Session Manager creates symbolic links. These links direct certain classes of commands to the correct component in the file system. For example,

PRN : REG_SZ : \DosDevices\LPT1

This link redirects all output sent to PRN to LPT1.

Subsystems Key

The last step performed by Session Manager is to load the required subsystems, as defined in the registry in:

HKEY_LOCAL_MACHINE\SYSTEM\CurrentControlSet\Control\
Session Manager\SubSystems**Required**

By default, the only required subsystem is the Win32 subsystem, which appears as Windows in the **Required** data item.

Win32 Subsystem Start Phase

When the Win32 subsystem starts, it automatically starts Winlogon.exe, which starts the Local Security Authority (Lsass.exe) and displays the CTRL+ALT+DEL logon dialog box.

Next, the Service Controller (Screg.exe) is run, which makes a final pass through the registry looking for services that are marked to load automatically, such as the Workstation and Server services. The services that are loaded during this phase are loaded based on their dependencies, that is, their DependOnGroup or DependOnService entries.

User Logs On

The boot is not considered *good* until a user successfully logs on to the system.

Note After a successful logon, the Clone control set is copied to the LastKnownGood control set. The LastKnownGood control set is explained later in this chapter.

Lesson 2: Troubleshooting the Boot Process

Most problems related to booting Windows NT are caused by required files that are either missing or corrupted. Windows NT may also fail to boot if incorrect system configuration changes are made.

After this lesson, you will be able to:

- Identify common Windows NT boot process errors.
- Explain the function of the Boot.ini file.
- Identify troubleshooting strategies related to the Boot.ini file.
- Create a Windows NT boot disk.

Estimated lesson time: 45 minutes

Common Boot Process Errors

The errors presented in this section are the result of files that are missing. Some common boot error messages and symptoms are as follows:

- If the Ntldr file is missing, the following message appears before the **Boot Loader Operating System Selection** menu:

  ```
  BOOT: Couldn't find NTLDR
  Please insert another disk.
  ```

- If Ntdetect.com is missing, the following message appears after the **Boot Loader Operating System Selection** menu (on the same screen):

  ```
  NTDETECT V4.0 Checking Hardware...
  NTDETECT failed
  ```

- If Ntoskrnl.exe is missing, the following message appears after the Last Known Good prompt:

  ```
  Windows NT could not start because the following file is missing
  or corrupt:
  \winnt root\system32\ntoskrnl.exe
  Please re-install a copy of the above file.
  ```

- If Bootsect.dos is missing in a multiple-boot configuration, the following message appears after the **Boot Loader Operating System Selection** menu (on the same screen), when the user attempts to boot an MS-DOS-based system:

  ```
  I/O Error accessing boot sector file
  multi(0)disk(0)rdisk(0)partition(1):\bootss
  ```

In all of these cases, the Emergency Repair process, which is presented later in this chapter, can be used to recover the system and boot files, and to return the computer to a bootable state.

Note Bootsect.dos stores partition information specific to the computer. This file cannot be borrowed from another computer.

The Boot.ini File

If Windows NT does not start, the problem may be that the path for the *systemroot* folder, found in the Boot.ini file, is incorrect. If that is the case, you must edit the Boot.ini file.

However, when Windows NT is installed, it creates Boot.ini in the root of the active partition as a read-only, hidden, system text file. If you want to edit the Boot.ini file by using a text editor, you need to make the file visible, and you need to turn the Read-only option off to be able to make changes to it.

Changing the Attributes of Boot.ini

You can change the attributes of Boot.ini by using My Computer, Windows NT Explorer, or the command prompt.

Using My Computer or Windows NT Explorer to Change the Attributes of Boot.ini

1. Double-click drive C where Boot.ini is located.

   You can not see the Boot.ini file if its *hidden* attribute is set.
2. On the **View** menu, click **Options**.
3. In the **Options** dialog box, click the **View** tab.
4. Click **Show all files,** and then click **OK**.

   The "hidden" files now appear in the folder list.
5. Click **Boot.ini**.
6. On the **File** menu, click **Properties**.
7. In the **Attributes** box of the **General** tab, clear the **Read-only** check box, and then click **OK**.

Using Command Prompt to Change the Attributes of Boot.ini

- At the command prompt, type **attrib -s -h -r boot.ini**

Changing the Path to Windows NT System Files

If you have to change the path to the Windows NT system files, make sure you edit both the default path and the operating system path statements. If you change one but not both, a new choice is added to the **Boot Loader Operating System Selection** menu. The new choice has a DEFAULT designator next to it, indicating that this choice attempts to load the default operating system from the path designated on the default= line of the [boot loader] section of Boot.ini.

Components of the Boot.ini File

Boot.ini is a system file that has two sections: [boot loader] and [operating systems].

The following is an example of a Boot.ini file.

```
[boot loader]
timeout=30
default=multi(0)disk(0)rdisk(0)partition(1)\WINNT
[operating systems]
multi(0)disk(0)rdisk(0)partition(1)\WINNT="Windows NT
Workstation Version 4.0"
multi(0)disk(0)rdisk(0)partition(1)\WINNT="Windows NT
Workstation Version 4.0 [VGA mode]" /basevideo
C:\="Microsoft Windows"
```

[boot loader]

The [boot loader] section specifies the default operating system to start and a timeout value specifying how long to wait before starting automatically. The boot loader section has two parameters, as shown in the following table.

Parameter	Description
timeout	The number of seconds during which the user can select an operating system after the **Boot Loader Operating System Selection** menu appears. If the user does not select an operating system during this time, the default operating system starts. If timeout= is set to 0, the **Boot Loader Operating System Selection** menu may appear briefly or not at all, depending on processor speed, and the default operating system boots.
Default	The path to the default operating system that loads when the timeout reaches 0 (zero).

[operating systems]

The [operating systems] section of Boot.ini is a list of operating systems that are displayed in the **Boot Loader Operating System Selection** menu. Each entry includes the path to the operating system, the name displayed in the **Boot Loader Operating System Selection** menu (the text between the quotes), and optional parameters.

For example, if you installed Windows NT 4.0 Workstation, there will be two listings for Windows NT Workstation 4.0. The second listing provides an optional parameter of /BASEVIDEO to allow the user to boot Windows NT Workstation with a standard VGA driver. There will also be an entry of C:\="MS-DOS" on Microsoft MS-DOS-based dual-boot systems.

Troubleshooting Boot.ini Problems

You can use Control Panel to change some of the information in the Boot.ini file, such as the default operating system and the length of time allowed for you to choose which operating system to boot. You can also manually edit the Boot.ini file. However, manual editing errors may prevent Windows NT from booting properly.

The following sections discuss problems that can occur with Boot.ini.

The Boot.ini File Is Missing

If the Boot.ini file is missing, Ntldr automatically tries to boot Windows NT. If Windows NT is installed in the default folder of multi(0)disk(0)rdisk(0)partition(1)\Winnt or scsi(0)disk(0)rdisk(0)partition(1)\Winnt, Windows NT boots successfully. If Windows NT is installed in a folder other than the default, such as Windows, the following message appears after the Last Known Good prompt:

```
Windows NT could not start because the following file is missing
or corrupt:
<winnt root>\system32\ntoskrnl.exe
Please reinstall a copy of the above file.
```

A New Operating System Appears on the Boot Loader Operating System Selection Menu

If the path name for the *default* parameter in the [boot loader] section of Boot.ini does not match any of the path names in the [operating system] section of Boot.ini, the menu selection "NT (default)" appears. This selection is highlighted and loads unless the user selects another operating system.

Invalid Windows NT Path Name

If part of the path name to Windows NT is incorrect in the Boot.ini file, the following message appears:

```
Windows NT could not start because the following file is missing
or corrupt:
<winnt root>\system32\ntoskrnl.exe
Please reinstall a copy of the above file.
```

Invalid Device in Windows NT Path

If there is an invalid device in the path to Windows NT in the Boot.ini file, the following message appears:

```
OS Loader V4.0

Windows NT could not start because of a computer disk hardware
configuration problem.
Could not read from the selected boot disk. Check boot path
and disk hardware.
Please check the Windows NT (TM) documentation about hardware
disk configuration and your hardware reference manuals for
additional information.
```

In all of these cases, Boot.ini can be edited to fix the problem, or an Emergency Repair can restore the Boot.ini file.

Creating a Windows NT Boot Disk

If Windows NT fails to boot because a file is missing or corrupt in the system partition, a boot disk can be used to boot the system and restore the corrupt or missing file or files to the hard disk.

Required Boot Files

The files required on the boot disk depend on the processor in the computer. The following table shows the boot files required for Intel *x*86-based and RISC-based computers.

Platform	Required Windows NT boot files
Intel *x*86-based computers	Ntldr, Ntdetect.com, Boot.ini, Ntbootdd.sys (for computers with a BIOS-disabled SCSI adapter)
RISC-based computers	Osloader.exe, Hal.dll, *.pal (Alpha only)

Precautions

Observe the following precautions when creating a Windows NT boot disk:

- A Windows NT boot disk must be formatted on a computer running Windows NT, so that the boot sector on the disk can find and run Ntldr.
- If the computer is Intel *x*86-based, the Boot.ini file on the boot disk may need to be modified to reflect the ARC path to the system partition on the failed computer. This path includes the disk controller, disk drive, and partition to the Windows NT system files.

Note For additional information on ARC paths, see Chapter 7, "Managing Fault Tolerance."

- After the disk is created, insert it in the disk drive and use it to start Windows NT. It is important to note that only certain files are loaded from a floppy disk. All other files are accessed from the hard disk of the computer running Windows NT. If the Windows NT kernel (Ntoskrnl.exe) or other files are corrupt or missing, the boot disk is of no use. If this is the case, use the Emergency Repair process, as discussed later in this chapter, to restore the missing or corrupt files.

Practice

In these procedures, you create and test a Windows NT boot disk for Workstation1.

Note Complete these procedures on Workstation1.

▸ **To change attributes for Windows NT boot files**

1. Log on to the domain as Administrator.
2. In Windows NT Explorer, click drive C.
3. On the **View** menu, click **Options**.
4. Click **Show all files**.
5. Clear the **Hide file extensions for known file types** check box, and then click **OK**.
6. Select the following files: boot.ini, bootsect.dos, Ntdetect.com, ntldr, and Ntbootdd.sys (only if it exists).
7. On the **File** menu, click **Properties**.
8. Clear the **Hidden** and **Read-only** check boxes, and then click **OK**.

▸ **To create a Windows NT boot disk**

1. Format a floppy disk using Windows NT Explorer, or go to a command prompt and use the **Format.exe** command.
2. Copy the following files from the root of drive C to the root of drive A.

   Ntldr

   Ntdetect.com

   Boot.ini

   Bootsect.dos (only if it exists)

   Ntbootdd.sys (only if it exists)
3. Do not remove the disk from the drive.

▸ **To test the Windows NT boot disk**

1. Shut down and then restart your computer using the Windows NT boot disk you just created.

   Did Windows NT start successfully?

   ____

   ____

   ____
2. Remove the floppy from the disk drive, and then restart Workstation1.

Practice

In these procedures, you rename system files to produce booting problems. You then restart your computer to observe error messages for specific problems.

Note Complete these procedures on Workstation1.

▸ **To simulate missing files during system boot**

In this procedure, you rename four files that are used to start Windows NT. This enables you to simulate the effects of missing files, as presented in the next procedure.

1. Log on to the domain as Administrator.
2. In Windows NT Explorer, click drive C.

3. Rename each of the following files by adding a .lab extension, for example, Boot.ini.lab. Be sure to write down the new name.

   Boot.ini

   Bootsect.dos

   Ntdetect.com

   Ntldr

▸ To observe the effect of missing system files

In this procedure, you observe files in the boot sequence fail. You see an error message that gives appropriate information about the file that failed to load. In the following table, record the error message and the file that you think has failed.

1. Shut down and then restart the computer.

   What error message do you see? Record your answer in the following table.

   What file is missing? Record your answer in the following table.
2. Reboot the computer using the Windows NT Boot Disk that you created earlier, log on as Administrator, and then correct the problem by renaming the file back to its original name.
3. Remove the Windows NT Boot disk from drive A.

   If your solution is successful, the next boot process stops at the next missing file in the boot sequence.
4. Repeat steps 1–3 in this procedure, until you have a successful system boot.

Note The last missing file requires you to select another operating system, such as MS-DOS, from the **OS Loader Operating System Selection** menu.

Error message	Missing file
____________________	____________________
____________________	____________________
____________________	____________________
____________________	____________________

Lesson 3: Last Known Good Configuration

After a user has successfully logged on to Windows NT, current configuration information from the registry key HKEY_LOCAL_MACHINE is copied to a control set called *Last Known Good*. Last Known Good is a copy of the most recent control set used to successfully boot Windows NT.

If you change the Windows NT configuration and then have problems rebooting, the Last Known Good configuration stored in the registry can be used to boot Windows NT.

After this lesson, you will be able to:

- Describe the Last Known Good configuration and its function.
- Identify the situations in which you would use the Last Known Good configuration.
- Start Windows NT using the Last Known Good configuration.

Estimated lesson time: 25 minutes

The Function of Last Known Good Configuration

Windows NT provides two configurations in which you can start your computer:

- *Default.* The configuration that was saved when you *shut down* the computer.
- *Last Known Good.* The configuration that was saved when you last successfully *logged on* to your computer.

The configurations are stored as control sets in the registry key HKEY_LOCAL_MACHINE\SYSTEM. If you log on and then make changes to your configuration, such as adding drivers, changing services, or changing hardware, the two control sets will contain different information. However, as soon as you shut down, restart Windows NT, and log on again, the information in these control sets will be the same.

Therefore, if you are having problems with startup, and think the problems might be related to the changes that you made to your configuration, *do not log on*. Instead, shut down the computer and restart it. Then, select Last Known Good from the **Hardware Profile/Last Known Good** menu.

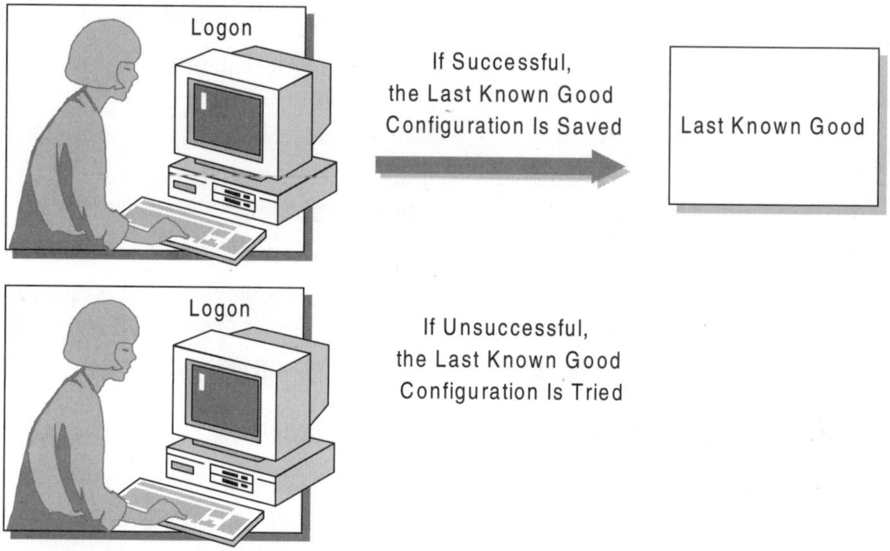

When to Use the Last Known Good Configuration

When Windows NT is selected from the **Boot Loader Operating System Selection** menu, the system loads the default control set. There are only two conditions that cause the system to load the Last Known Good configuration:

- When the system is recovering from a severe or critical device driver loading error.
- When the Last Known Good configuration is selected during the boot process.

Use the Last Known Good control set to recover from the following types of problems:

- You install a new device driver, restart Windows NT, and the system stops responding. The Last Known Good control set enables you to start Windows NT because it does not contain any reference to the new, faulty driver.
- You install a new video driver and are able to restart the system. However, you cannot see anything, because the new video resolution is incompatible with your video adapter. Do not try to log on. If you have the option to shut down the computer without logging on, do so. If that option is not available, you need to restart your computer by turning it off or using the reset button. Wait for all disk activity to stop before you initiate the restart, especially if the computer has FAT volumes.
- You accidentally disable a critical device driver (such as the SCSIport driver). Windows NT is not able to start and automatically reverts to the Last Known Good control set.

Using the Last Known Good control set does *not* help in the following situations:

- Any problem that is unrelated to changes in control set information, such as problems arising from incorrectly configured user profiles or incorrect file permissions.
- After you logged on after making changes. Here, the Last Known Good control set has already been updated to include the changes.
- Switching between different hardware profiles, such as docked and undocked laptops. The Last Known Good control set is only a method to switch between configuration information in the registry.
- Startup failures caused by hardware failures or missing or corrupted files.

In summary, booting from the Last Known Good configuration provides a way to recover from problems such as a newly added driver that may be incorrect for your hardware. It does not solve problems caused by corrupted or missing drivers or files. The Last Known Good option is used only in cases of incorrect configurations.

Important If the Last Known Good configuration is used, all configuration changes you made the last time you were logged on to Windows NT are lost.

How to Use the Last Known Good Configuration

When you have selected the version of Windows NT to start, and the boot loader has collected hardware information, you see the following screen:

OS Loader V4.00

Once you see the OS Loader V4.00 prompt, you have only a few seconds to press the SPACEBAR to invoke the **Hardware Profile/Configuration Recovery** menu.

After you press the SPACEBAR, the **Hardware Profile/Configuration Recovery** menu appears, from which you can do the following:

- Select a hardware profile to be used when Windows NT is started.
- Switch to the Last Known Good configuration.
- Restart the computer.

To switch to the Last Known Good Configuration, press L.

To exit this menu and restart your computer, press F3.

The boot loader uses the registry information that it saved at the completion of the last successful startup to configure this startup. All configuration changes that were made since your system was last successfully started are lost.

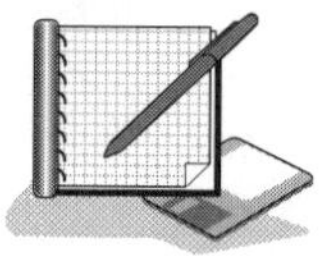

Practice

In these procedures, you disable the keyboard driver and use the Last Known Good configuration to successfully reboot your computer.

Note Complete these procedures on Workstation1.

► **To disable the keyboard driver**

1. Log on to the domain as Administrator.
2. Start the Devices program in Control Panel.
3. Click **i8042 Keyboard and PS/2 Mouse Port**. If this device is not listed, find your correct keyboard and mouse driver device in the list, and then click it.
4. Click **Startup**.
5. In the **Device** dialog box, click **Disabled**, and then click **OK**.

   A dialog box appears, warning you that changing the startup type for this device may leave the system in an unusable state.
6. Click **Yes**.
7. Click **Close**.
8. Shut down the computer.

▸ **To test the faulty configuration**

1. Restart Windows NT Workstation.
2. When the Begin Logon window appears, attempt to log on.

   Were you successful?

   ___

   Why?

   ___

3. Use the power switch to shut off your computer.

▸ **To restore the Last Known Good configuration**

1. Restart Windows NT Workstation, and when the Press spacebar now to invoke Hardware Profile/Last Known Good prompt appears, press the SPACEBAR.
2. When the **Hardware Profile/Configuration Recovery** menu appears, press L to use the Last Known Good configuration.
3. Press ENTER to select the original configuration.
4. When the Begin Logon window appears, attempt to log on as Administrator.

   Were you successful?

   ___

   Why?

   ___

Lesson 4: Emergency Repair

If Windows NT fails to boot or function correctly, and using the Last Known Good configuration does not solve the problem, you can use the Emergency Repair process in Windows NT Setup to restore Windows NT.

After this lesson, you will be able to:

- Create an Emergency Repair Disk.
- Complete the emergency repair process to restore Windows NT.

Estimated lesson time: 40 minutes

Creating and Updating an Emergency Repair Disk

If you ever have a serious system problem, your best recourse is the Emergency Repair folder or disk.

The Emergency Repair folder and disk are used to return a computer running Windows NT to the state of the last Emergency Repair update. The disk can repair missing or corrupt Windows NT files and restore the registry. Restored registry files include the Security Accounts Manager (SAM) database, security information, disk configuration information, software registry entries, and other system information. The Emergency Repair folder and disk also include a Setup.log file to verify files on the system.

The Repair Disk utility (Rdisk.exe) is used to either update repair information or create a new Emergency Repair Disk. Rdisk.exe is located in the *systemroot*\System32 folder, and has two options:

- Update Repair Info
- Create Repair Disk

Note In order to run Rdisk.exe, the user must be a member of the Administrators or Power Users group or have the appropriate privileges. For non-Administrators or non-Power Users, Rdisk.exe *appears* to work, but as it is saving files, the user gets an error message indicating that the utility could not save all configuration files.

The Update Repair Info Option

The Update Repair Info process overwrites the files in the *systemroot*\Repair folder. During the update process, a $$hive$$.tmp file is created. This file temporarily stores the registry information before it is copied to the appropriate file.

Note Because the Update Repair Info option deletes and creates files under *systemroot*\Repair, if Windows NT is installed on an NTFS partition, the user performing the update must have the appropriate permissions to the folder.

After the contents of the *systemroot*\Repair folder are updated, the repair process prompts the user to create an Emergency Repair Disk. This option formats a floppy disk and creates an Emergency Repair Disk. This has the same result as selecting the Create Repair Disk option.

When the contents of the *systemroot*\Repair folder are updated, copies of Autoexec.nt and Config.nt are also placed in the folder.

Note The Emergency Repair Disk utility (**rdisk**) does not back up the Default, SAM, and Security files, which contain the user accounts and file security, unless you specify the **/s** parameter with the **rdisk** command at the command prompt.

The Create Repair Disk Option

The Create Repair Disk option requests that a disk that can be formatted be inserted in drive A. If the current repair disk is used, the Create Repair Disk option does *not* update the disk; it reformats it and creates a new repair disk.

Setup.log

The Setup.log file is located in the Emergency Repair folder and on the Emergency Repair Disk. Setup.log is used to check the validity of the Windows NT files on the system.

Files Included on the Emergency Repair Disk

The Emergency Repair Disk contains the files listed in the following table.

File	Description
Setup.log	An information file used for verifying the files installed on the system. This file is a read-only, hidden system file. By default, this file does not appear in Windows NT Explorer.
System._	A copy of the System hive from the registry.
Sam._	A copy of the Security Accounts Manager (SAM) from the registry.
Security._	A copy of the Security hive from the registry.
Software._	A copy of the Software hive from the registry.
Default._	A copy of the Default hive from the registry.
Config.nt	The Windows NT version of the Config.sys file used when initializing an NTVDM.
Autoexec.nt	The Windows NT version of the Autoexec.bat file used when initializing an NTVDM.
Ntuser.da_	A compressed version of *systemroot*\Profiles\Default user\Ntuser.dat.

Note The files with an underscore extension (`._` or `.da_`) are compressed versions of the actual files. They can be uncompressed in the same manner as the Windows NT files on the source disks, by using the **expand** utility.

The Emergency Repair Process

This section discusses using the emergency repair process to restore a failed system.

To perform the emergency repair process, you need the following:

- The original installation compact disc, in case any files are detected as missing or corrupt.
- If the Security Account Manager (SAM) database is replaced, the Administrator password stored on the Emergency Repair Disk.

Using the Emergency Repair Process

To repair a Windows NT installation, Windows NT Setup needs either the configuration information that is saved in the *systemroot*\Repair folder or on the Emergency Repair Disk created when you installed Windows NT (or created later using the **rdisk** utility).

If your system becomes corrupt and you cannot repair it using the Emergency Repair Disk or using the information in the Repair folder, you must reinstall Windows NT from the original installation source.

Note For more information about restoring your system, see Chapter 20, "Preparing for and Performing Recovery," in the *Microsoft Windows NT Workstation Resource Kit.*

Restoring Windows NT Server on an Intel *x*86-based Computer

To restore Windows NT on an Intel *x*86-based computer using the repair process in Windows NT Setup, do the following:

1. If you installed Windows NT using the original Setup disks or compact disc, or using Winnt.exe, start Setup just as you did originally. That is, insert the Setup Boot disk in drive A and start the computer.

   If these disks cannot be located, create new disks from the Windows NT compact disc by running either Winnt.exe or Winnt32.exe and use the **/ox** switch. The **/ox** switch creates the Windows NT Setup disks without performing the entire installation.
2. In the text-based Setup screen that asks whether you want to install Windows NT or repair files, type **r** to indicate that you want to repair your Windows NT files.
3. Windows NT Setup prompts you for the Emergency Repair Disk. If you do not have one, Setup presents a list of the Windows NT installations that it found on your computer and lets you select the one you want to repair.
4. Follow the instructions on the screen, inserting the Emergency Repair Disk (if you have one) in drive A and providing any other Windows NT Setup disks as requested.
5. When the final message appears, remove the Emergency Repair Disk from drive A, and then press CTRL+ALT+DEL to restart your computer.

Restoring Windows NT on a RISC-based Computer

To restore Windows NT on a RISC-based computer with an Emergency Repair Disk, do the following:

1. Start the Windows NT Setup program as instructed in your manufacturer-supplied documentation. (How you start Windows NT Setup depends on the type of RISC-based computer you have.)
2. In the text-based Setup screen that asks whether you want to install Windows NT or repair files, type **r** to indicate that you want to repair your Windows NT files.

3. Follow the instructions on the screen, inserting the Emergency Repair Disk (if you have one) in drive A if Setup prompts you for it.
4. When the final message appears, remove the Emergency Repair Disk, and then press ENTER to restart your computer.

Caution Be sure to update the system repair information in the Repair folder on your hard disk and to create and maintain an up-to-date Emergency Repair Disk. This way, your system repair information includes new configuration information such as drive letter assignments, stripe sets, volume sets, mirror sets, and so on. Otherwise, drives can be inaccessible in the event of a system failure.

The repair process in Windows NT Setup enables you to choose what you want to repair. Four options during setup determine which emergency repair tasks are performed:

- *Inspect registry files.* Setup replaces one or more registry files with the files that were created when Windows NT was first installed, or when the Emergency Repair folder or disk was last updated. All changes made to the system since installation or the last update to the repair files are lost.
- *Inspect startup environment.* Select this option if Windows NT is installed but does not appear in the list of bootable systems. For this option, the Emergency Repair Disk is needed.
- *Verify Windows NT system files.* Select this option to verify that each file in the installation is good and matches the file that was installed from the distribution files. The repair process also verifies that files needed to start, such as Ntldr and Ntoskrnl.exe, are present and valid. When the repair process determines that the file on the disk does not match what was installed, it displays a message that identifies the file and asks whether you want to replace it.
- *Inspect boot sector.* Select this option if no system that is installed on the computer boots. Setup copies a new boot sector to the hard disk.

Note For more information about **rdisk** see the Windows NT Server *Start Here* book.

Practice

In these procedures, you use the **rdisk** utility to update your Emergency Repair Disk. Then, you perform an Emergency Repair to inspect your boot sector.

Note These procedures require you to have a CD-ROM drive in your computer, and that you have a *Windows NT Workstation 4.0* compact disc.

Note Complete these procedures on Workstation1.

▸ **To update the Emergency Repair Disk**

1. Log on to the domain as Administrator.
2. On the **Start** menu, click **Run**.
3. Type **rdisk** and then click **OK**.
4. Click **Update Repair Info**.

   A **Repair Disk Utility** dialog box appears, stating that the repair information that was saved when you installed the system or when you last ran this utility will be deleted. This message indicates that the information in the Repair folder will be updated to match the current system configuration.
5. Click **Yes** to continue this operation.

   After the configuration is saved, a **Repair Disk Utility** dialog box appears, stating that you can create an Emergency Repair Disk that contains a copy of the repair information in your system.
6. Click **Yes** to create an Emergency Repair Disk.
7. When prompted, insert the Emergency Repair Disk that was created during installation, and then click **OK**.

   The disk is formatted and the updated repair information is copied.
8. When updating is complete, click **Exit**.
9. Remove the Emergency Repair Disk from drive A.

► **To use the Emergency Repair process**

1. Restart your computer using the Windows NT Workstation Setup Boot disk.
2. When prompted, insert the Windows NT Workstation Setup Disk #2.
3. At the Welcome to Setup screen, type **r** to perform the Emergency Repair.

   The following options appear:

   ```
   [X] Inspect registry files
   [X] Inspect startup environment
   [X] Verify Windows NT system files
   [X] Inspect boot sector
       Continue (perform selected tasks)
   ```

4. Select **Inspect boot sector** and clear the other choices.
5. Choose **Continue (perform selected tasks)**, and then press ENTER.
6. Press ENTER to have Setup detect your mass storage devices.
7. When prompted, insert the Windows NT Workstation Setup Disk #3, and then press ENTER.
8. When prompted, press ENTER to confirm the detected mass storage devices.
9. When prompted, press ENTER to confirm that you have an Emergency Repair Disk.
10. When prompted, insert the Emergency Repair Disk, and then press ENTER.

    Setup completes the repair.
11. Remove the Emergency Repair Disk from drive A.
12. Press ENTER to restart your computer and boot Windows NT Workstation.

Summary

The following information summarizes the key points in this chapter:

- The Windows NT boot sequence requires the presence of a number of system files. For example, *Ntldr* is the main component for loading Windows NT on Intel-based computers, and *Osloader* is the main boot component for RISC-based computers.
- Windows NT is loaded and initialized in four phases: the kernel load phase, the kernel initialization phase, the services load phase, and the Win32 subsystem start phase.
- If Windows NT fails to boot, there are several troubleshooting techniques you can try to correct the problem, such as editing the Boot.ini file, using the Last Known Good configuration, and trying an Emergency Repair.
    - The problem may be that the path for the *systemroot* folder, found in the Boot.ini file, is incorrect. If that is the case, you must edit the Boot.ini file.
    - Booting from the Last Known Good configuration provides a way to recover from problems such as a newly added driver that may be incorrect for your system. It does not solve problems caused by corrupted or missing drivers or files. The Last Known Good option is used only in cases of incorrect configurations.
    - The Emergency Repair folder and disk are used to return a computer running Windows NT to the state of the last Emergency Repair update. The Emergency Repair folder and disk also include a Setup.log file to verify files on the system.

Review

1. One of the computers that you support can no longer boot to MS-DOS, even though it appears on the boot menu. You have identified the problem as a corrupted MS-DOS boot sector. Which file, containing the old MS-DOS boot sector, should you suspect has been corrupted?

2. You created a Windows NT boot disk that contains the following files:
   - Ntldr
   - Ntdetect.com
   - Boot.ini
   - Ntbootdd.sys

   When you try to boot Windows NT with the disk, you receive the following error message:

   ```
   Non-System disk or disk error
   Replace and press any key when ready
   ```

   What did you do wrong?

3. You change the settings for your network adapter card. When you reboot, you receive the following message: "One or more services failed to start." When you attempt to log on you receive a message stating that a domain controller could not be found, but you were logged on using cached credentials. After logging on, you discover that you cannot connect to network resources. You shut down your computer and restart using the Last Known Good configuration, but the same behavior results. What went wrong?

4. You need to perform an emergency repair on your computer that is running Windows NT Workstation. You have a CD-ROM drive in your computer, however, you originally installed Windows NT over the network and you do not have the original setup disks. You still have the original Windows NT Workstation compact disc, however, and can access it on other computers. How can you perform the emergency repair?

5. You receive a call from someone who tells you that he forgot the administrator password. He used the Emergency Repair Disk to restore the original administrator password, and now no one else can log on to the system. What happened and how can he correct the problem?

6. You have restarted a computer running Windows NT Workstation, and the following message appears:

```
BOOT: Couldn't find NTLDR
Please insert another disk
```

You suspect that Ntldr is missing or corrupt. How can you replace the file?

Answer Key

Procedure Answers

Page 627

▸ To test the Windows NT boot disk

1. Shut down and then restart your computer using the Windows NT boot disk you just created.

   Did Windows NT start successfully?

   Yes. The boot disk was created properly.

   No. Verify that you formatted the floppy disk using Windows NT, and then compare the files on your boot disk with those listed in the preceding procedure.

Page 628

▸ To observe the effect of missing system files

1. Shut down and then restart the computer.

   What error message do you see? Record your answer in the following table.

   What file is missing? Record your answer in the following table.

Error message	Missing file
BOOT: Couldn't find NTLDR Please insert another disk	**Ntldr**
NTDETECT failed	**Ntdetect.com**
No error message, but the Operating System Select menu failed to appear	**Boot.ini**
I/O Error accessing boot sector file multi(0)disk(0)rdisk(0)partition(1)\BOOTSS	**Bootsect.dos**

Page 633

▸ To test the faulty configuration

2. When the Begin Logon window appears, attempt to log on.

   Were you successful?

   No.

   Why?

   The keyboard device driver is not running.

Page 633

▶ **To restore the Last Known Good configuration**

4. When the Begin Logon window appears, attempt to log on as Administrator.

   Were you successful?

   Yes.

   Why?

   Because the Last Known Good configuration contained the correct startup setting for the keyboard device driver.

Review Answers

Page 642

1. One of the computers that you support can no longer boot to MS-DOS, even though it appears on the boot menu. You have identified the problem as a corrupted MS-DOS boot sector. Which file, containing the old MS-DOS boot sector, should you suspect has been corrupted?

   Bootsect.dos

2. You created a Windows NT boot disk that contains the following files:
   - Ntldr
   - Ntdetect.com
   - Boot.ini
   - Ntbootdd.sys

   When you try to boot Windows NT with the disk, you receive the following error message:

   ```
   Non-System disk or disk error
   Replace and press any key when ready
   ```

   What did you do wrong?

   The disk that you used was not formatted while running Windows NT.

3. You change the settings for your network adapter card. When you reboot, you receive the following message: "One or more services failed to start." When you attempt to log on you receive a message stating that a domain controller could not be found, but you were logged on using cached credentials. After logging on, you discover that you cannot connect to network resources. You shut down your computer and restart using the Last Known Good configuration, but the same behavior results. What went wrong?

   Last Known Good is updated with the current control set following the first successful logon after a reboot. When you notice something wrong following a restart, do not log on.

4. You need to perform an emergency repair on your computer that is running Windows NT Workstation. You have a CD-ROM drive in your computer, however, you originally installed Windows NT over the network and you do not have the original setup disks. You still have the original *Windows NT Workstation* compact disc, however, and can access it on other computers. How can you perform the emergency repair?

   Using another computer, run the Winnt.exe or Winnt32.exe program from the original *Windows NT Workstation* compact disc using the /ox switch. This makes the three setup disks that can be used to start the repair process.

5. You receive a call from someone who tells you that he forgot the administrator password. He used the Emergency Repair Disk to restore the original administrator password, and now no one else can log on to the system. What happened and how can he correct the problem?

   The Emergency Repair process replaces the entire directory database with the original directory database that was created during installation, or with the last updated version from using Rdisk.exe. If he had never updated the directory database stored on the Emergency Repair Disk, the only accounts present after the repair would be the Administrator and the Guest account (and possibly an initial user account) created during installation.

   To correct the situation, he could use the original administrator password to log on, and then restore the directory database from a tape backup.

6. You have restarted a computer running Windows NT Workstation, and the following message appears:

   ```
   BOOT: Couldn't find NTLDR
   Please insert another disk
   ```

   You suspect that Ntldr is missing or corrupt. How can you replace the file?

   Use a Windows NT Boot disk or the Emergency Repair process.

CHAPTER 18

Windows NT Troubleshooting Tools

About This Chapter

This chapter identifies many of the troubleshooting tools that are available in Microsoft Windows NT. In addition to learning about these resources, you will learn how to use them to diagnose and resolve problems that can occur in administering a Windows NT system or network.

Before You Begin

To complete the lessons in this chapter, you must have:

- Two computers that meet the hardware and software requirements as specified in the Getting Started section of "About This Book."
- Completed all practices in Chapter 2, "Installing Windows NT."
- Completed the practice in Chapter 3, "Configuring the Windows NT Environment," in which you used Add/Remove Programs in Control Panel to install the Windows NT games and wallpaper.

Lesson 1: Diagnostic Tools

This lesson describes some of the diagnostic tools included with Windows NT and how to use them to troubleshoot system problems.

After this lesson, you will be able to:

- Identify and use the diagnostic utilities available with Windows NT.
- Describe the contents and options of Event Viewer.
- Analyze system information through the log files.
- View event details to find system information.
- View system information through Windows NT Diagnostics.
- Describe the use of Performance Monitor to troubleshoot performance-related problems.
- Describe the use of Network Monitor to troubleshoot network-related problems.
- Describe the System Recovery utility used to capture information generated by STOP errors.

Estimated lesson time: 60 minutes

To help you troubleshoot system problems, Windows NT provides the following administration tools:

- Event Viewer
- Windows NT Diagnostics
- Performance Monitor
- Network Monitor
- System Recovery

These tools provide information concerning the type of problem and where it occurred.

Event Viewer

Event Viewer provides information about *events* such as errors, warnings, and the success or failure of tasks.

An event is any potentially significant occurrence in the system (or in an application). For example, there are events that can affect system security or network performance. Some critical events, such as a full disk drive or an interrupted power supply, are noted in on-screen messages, as well as in an *event log*. Non-critical events are merely logged. Event logging starts automatically each time you start Windows NT. With an event log and the Event Viewer, you can troubleshoot various hardware and software problems and monitor Windows NT security events.

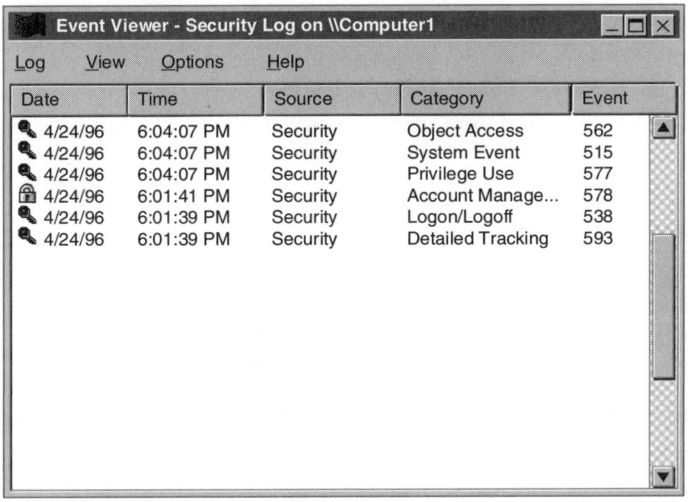

To start the Event Viewer, click **Start**, point to **Programs**, point to **Administrative Tools (Common)**, and then click **Event Viewer**.

Event Log Files

Windows NT records events in three kinds of logs: the *system log*, the *security log* and the *application log*. The system and application logs are automatically enabled; the security log must be manually enabled.

- The system log (*systemroot*\System32\Config\Sysevent.evt) contains events logged by the Windows NT system components and device drivers. For example, the failure of a driver or other system component to load during startup is recorded in the system log. The event types logged by system components are determined by Windows NT, and those logged by third party drivers are determined by the driver vendor.
- The security log (*systemroot*\System32\Config\Secevent.evt) can contain valid and invalid logon attempts, as well as events related to resource use, such as creating, opening, or deleting files or other objects. For example, if you use User Manager for Domains to enable Logon and Logoff auditing, attempts to log on to and log off of, the system are recorded in the security log.
- The application log (*systemroot*\System32\Config\Appevent.evt) contains events logged by applications. For example, a database program might record a file error in the application log. Application developers decide which events to monitor.

Note System and application logs can be viewed by all users; security logs are accessible only to administrators.

Enabling Security Logging

By default, security logging is turned off. To enable security logging, run User Manager for Domains to enable auditing and to determine what event to audit. You can also set auditing in the registry that causes the system to halt when the security log is full. To do this, use Registry Editor to create the following registry key value:

HKEY_LOCAL_MACHINE\SYSTEM\CurrentControlSet\Control\Lsa
\CrashOnAuditFail

The value type is REG_DWORD and it can have the following data values:

1 - Stop if the audit log is full.

2 - This data value will be set by the operating system just before the system crashes due to a full audit log. While the data value is 2, only the administrator can log on to the computer.

The *CrashOnAuditFail* registry entry directs the operating system to shut down abnormally and display a blue screen when the audit log is full. This assures that no auditable activities, including security violations, occur while the system is unable to log them.

Types of Events

The following table shows Event Viewer icons, event types, and descriptions.

Icon	Event type	Description
	**Error**	Significant problems, such as loss of data or loss of functionality. For example, an Error event will be logged if a service fails to load during Windows NT startup.
	**Warning**	Events that are not necessarily significant, but that indicate possible future problems. For example, a Warning event will be logged when disk space is low.
	**Information**	Infrequent but significant events that describe successful operations of drivers or services. For example, when a network driver loads successfully, it will log an Information event.
	**Success Audit**	Audited security access attempts that are successful. For example, a user's successful attempt to log on to the system will be logged as a Success Audit event.
	**Failure Audit**	Audited security access attempts that fail. For example, if a user tries to access a network drive and fails, the attempt will be logged as a Failure Audit event.

Interpreting an Event

Each event stored in the log files can be viewed in greater detail by clicking **Detail** on the **View** menu in Event Viewer. The **Event Detail** dialog box shows the following information:

- Date and time of the event
- Event identification
- Text description of the selected event

In some cases, the **Event Detail** dialog box displays hexadecimal data for the selected event. This information is generated by the component that was the source of the event record. If interpretation of the hexadecimal data is required to resolve a problem, a person who is familiar with the source component should be contacted. Not all events generate such hexadecimal data.

Note For more information about Windows NT Server events, see the Messages Database Help file on the *Windows NT Server Resource Kit 4.0* compact disc.

There are several methods to control the event display and to find specific events in Event Viewer. These methods include filtering, arranging, and searching.

Filtering

When Event Viewer starts, *all* events recorded in the selected log are displayed automatically. To view events with specific characteristics, click **Filter Events** on the **View** menu. Events can be filtered by the following properties:

- View From/View Through: From a specified date and time, or during a time frame
- Type: Error, Warning, Information, Success Audit, Failure Audit
- Source: Alerter, Browser, DLC error, floppy disk, and so on
- User
- Computer
- Event ID

Note Filtering has no effect on the contents of the event log; all events are logged whether the filter is active or not. The filter affects only what will be displayed.

Arranging

Events displayed in Event Viewer are listed in sequence, from the most recent to the oldest. On the **View** menu, the sequence can be changed to display the oldest events first.

Searching

To search for events in large logs, use the **Find** dialog box, which is accessible through the **View** menu. Search for an event by any one or more of the following: Type, Source, Category, Event ID, User, or Computer.

Options in the **Find** dialog box are in effect only during the current session. The settings in the **Find** dialog box can be saved by clicking **Save Settings On Exit** on the Event Viewer **Options** menu.

Archiving Log Files

When you archive an event log, you save it in one of three file formats:

- *Log file format.* This format enables you to view the archived log again in Event Viewer.
- *Text file format.* This format enables you to present the information in a text-oriented application, such as a word processor.
- *Comma-delimited text file format.* This format enables you to manage the information with an application, such as a spreadsheet or database.

Archived event logs can serve a variety of purposes, such as tracking and documenting system performance over time, or providing feedback to system and application developers.

Note For more information on using Event Viewer, see Chapter 9, "Monitoring Events," in Microsoft Windows NT Server *Concepts and Planning*.

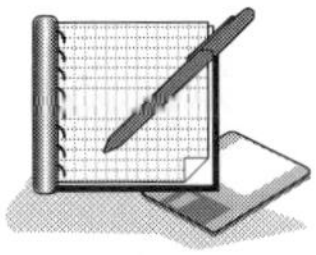

Practice

In these procedures, you use Event Viewer to view events in the system, security, and application event logs, and to control the size of the log files. You then use Event Viewer to filter events and search for specific events to locate existing and potential problems.

Note Complete these procedures on Server1.

▸ **To view events**

1. Log on as Administrator.
2. Click the **Start** button, point to **Programs**, point to **Administrative Tools (Common)**, and then click **Event Viewer**.

   Event Viewer appears.
3. On the **Log** menu, click **System**.

   Different symbols precede different types of events.
4. Double-click one of each of the symbols (Stop sign, exclamation point, and information symbol), one at a time to determine the type of event it represents and to see a description of the event.

   What types of events appear in your system log?

   ____

   ____

5. On the **Log** menu, click **Application**.

   What types of events appear in your application log?

   ____

   ____

▸ **To control the size and contents of a log file**

1. On the Event Viewer **Log** menu, click **Log Settings**.

   By default, what is the maximum log size for the system, security, and application log files?

   ____

2. In the **Change Settings for** box, select **System**.
3. Click **Overwrite Events As Needed**.

   How will this setting affect the system log?

   ____

4. Click **OK**.

▸ **To filter events**

1. On the **Log** menu, click **Open**.
2. In the C:\Lab Files\Events folder, open **Sample1.evt**.
3. Under **Open File of Type** window, click **System**, and then click **OK**.
4. On the **View** menu, click **Filter Events**.
5. In the **Source** box, click **Service Control Manager** from the list, and then click **OK**.
6. Double-click the oldest entry.

   What is the description of the problem?

   ____

   ____

   What could be the problem?

   ____

7. Click **Close** to close the event and return to the log.

▶ **To search for specific messages**

1. On the **Log** menu, click **Open**.
2. In the C:\Lab Files\Events folder, open **Sample2.evt** as a system log.
3. On the **View** menu, click **Filter Events**.
4. In the **Types** box, make sure that only the **Warning** box is checked, and then click **OK**.
5. Double-click the first entry.

   What is the description of the problem?

   ___

   What action is necessary?

   ___

6. Click **Close**.
7. On the **View** menu, click **Filter Events**.
8. In the **Types** box, select the **Error** check box, clear the **Warning** check box, and then click **OK**.
9. Double-click each entry and view its description one at a time until you determine what the problem is.

   What is the problem?

   ___

   What action is necessary?

   ___

10. Close Event Viewer.

Windows NT Diagnostics

Windows NT Diagnostics (Winmsd.exe) is a tool that shows computer hardware and operating system data stored in the Windows NT registry.

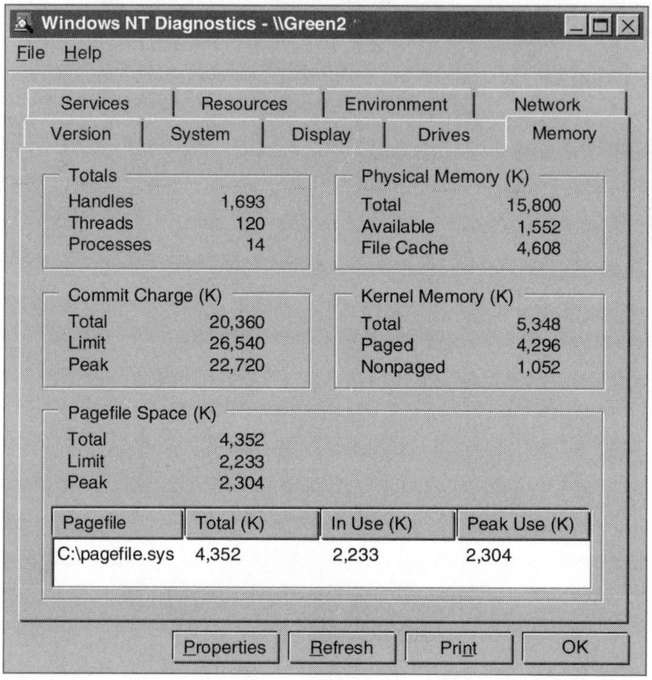

Note Configuration data cannot be modified using Windows NT Diagnostics.

Winmsd.exe is located in the *systemroot*\System32 directory. To start Windows NT Diagnostics, click the **Start** button, point to **Programs**, point to **Administrative Tools (Common)**, and then click **Windows NT Diagnostics**.

The following table describes the types of information displayed by Windows NT Diagnostics.

Tab	Description
Services	Lists services and devices in the CurrentControlSet, along with a state, or status, of running or stopped.
Resources	Displays system resources in use, including IRQs, I/O ports, DMA channels, memory allocation, and device drivers loaded.
Environment	Displays environment variables.
Network	Lists network-related configuration information, including current network statistics.
Version	Contains operating system information with version numbers, such as the build and Service Pack information, and the registered owner.
System	Displays BIOS, HAL, and CPU information.
Display	Contains information about the video adapter, driver, and display settings.
Drives	Lists all available drives and their types, including floppy and other removable drives, local disk drives, CD-ROM drives, and network-connected drives, as well as additional information, such as volume label, serial number, file system, and disk usage, for each drive.
Memory	Contains information about physical and virtual memory, such as the pagefile location, total memory, and available memory are displayed.

Practice

In these procedures, you use Windows NT Diagnostics (Winmsd) to view configuration information for Server1 and for a remote computer (Workstation1). You then save a report for the remote computer, and view the report.

Note Complete these procedures on Server1.

- **To view software configuration information**

In this procedure, you view your computer's configuration information.

1. Click the **Start** button, point to **Programs**, point to **Administrative Tools (Common)**, and then click **Windows NT Diagnostics**.
2. Locate the following information by reviewing the tabs in the Windows NT Diagnostics window. In the following table, record the name of the tab you chose and the value of the requested information.

Requested information	Tab	Value
Registered owner		
Registered organization		
Version number		
Build number		
systemroot (windir)		
Domain name		
CPU type		

3. Locate the following information.

Requested information	Your configuration
Total physical memory	
Available physical memory	
Total pagefile space	
Available pagefile space	
Paging files (location and size)	

4. List the service dependencies for the following services. (Hint: Click the **Services** tab, click the name of the service, and then click **Properties**.)

Service	Dependencies
ClipBook Server	
Network DDE	
Network DDE DSDM	
Server	
Messenger	

- **To view configuration information for Workstation1**

1. On the **File** menu, click **Select Computer**.

   The **Select Computer** dialog box appears.

2. In the **Computer** box, type **Workstation1** and then click **OK**.

   What tabs are available for remote computers?

   ____

   ____

3. Locate the following information about Workstation1.

Requested information	Workstation1 configuration
CPU type	
Network adapter IRQ	
Video driver in use	
Domain name	

- **To create a Windows NT Diagnostics report for Workstation1**

1. On the **File** menu, click **Save Report**.

   The **Create Report for Workstation1** dialog box appears.

2. Under **Scope**, click **All tabs**.
3. Under **Detail Level**, click **Complete**.
4. Under **Destination**, click **File**.

5. Click **OK**.

   The **Save WinMSD Report** dialog box appears.

6. Save the file as **C:\Msdrpt.txt**.

   The **Generating WinMSD Report** dialog box appears, which contains a status bar indicating the current progress.

7. Click **OK** to exit Windows NT Diagnostics.

▸ **To read a Windows NT Diagnostics report**

1. Start Windows NT Explorer and click drive C.

2. Double-click **Msdrpt.txt** to view your report.

   Notepad starts and displays the file Msdrpt.txt.

3. Use **Find** on the **Search** menu to locate the following information in Msdrpt.txt.

   For example, the results of a Find on PROCESSOR_ARCHITECTURE could be PROCESSOR_ARCHITECTURE=x86.

Requested information	Workstation1 configuration
PROCESSOR_ARCHITECTURE	
PROCESSOR_LEVEL	
PROCESSOR_IDENTIFIER	
PROCESSOR_REVISION	

4. Close Notepad when you have finished viewing your report.

Performance Monitor

Performance Monitor enables you to look at resource use for specific components and application processes through a dynamic display. These dynamic charts can be saved as logs or reports. With Performance Monitor, you can gauge your computer's efficiency, identify and troubleshoot possible problems (such as unbalanced resource use, insufficient hardware, or poor program design), and plan for additional hardware needs. You can also use alerts to notify you when resource use reaches a specified value.

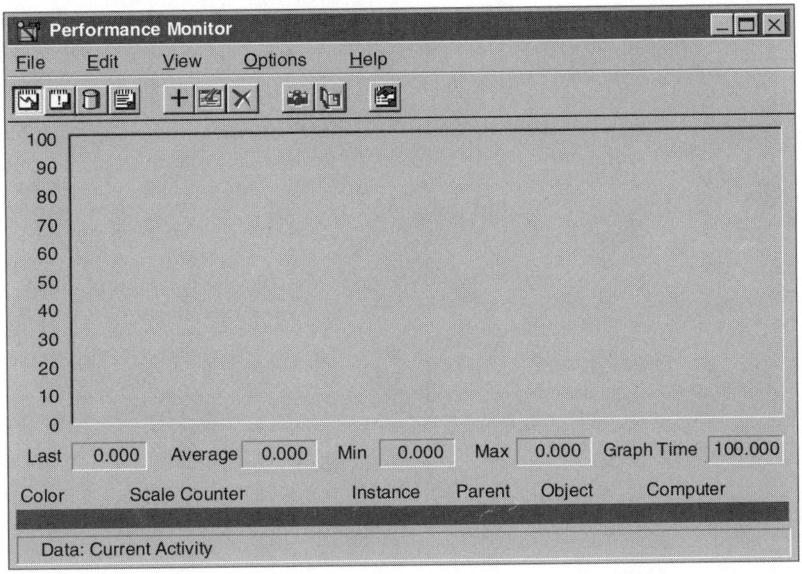

Performance Monitor treats system components as objects in order to track component and application performance. Start Performance Monitor through the Administrative Tools (Common) folder.

Use Performance Monitor by selecting specific features, or *counters*, of these objects for tracking. Counters can be monitored to identify performance problems. Three counters for the Processor and System objects are particularly useful for identifying problems: % Processor Time, Interrupts/Sec, and Processor Queue Length.

Processor: % Processor Time

The % Processor Time counter shows processor activity. During some operations this may reach 100 percent. If the processor returns to a level of use between 0 (zero) and 80 percent, with only occasional increases while loading applications, then the processor is probably not slowing down the performance of your system or network.

Processor: Interrupts/Sec

The Interrupts/Sec counter measures the rate of service requests from I/O devices. A dramatic increase in this value, without a corresponding increase in system activity, shows a hardware problem.

System: Processor Queue Length

The number of threads shown by the processor queue length is an indicator of system performance because each thread requires a certain number of processor cycles. If demand exceeds supply, long processor queues develop and system response slows. Therefore, a consistent processor queue length greater than two may mean that the processor is causing a problem.

Note For more information on Performance Monitor, see Chapter 8, "Monitoring Performance," in Microsoft Windows NT Server *Concepts and Planning*.

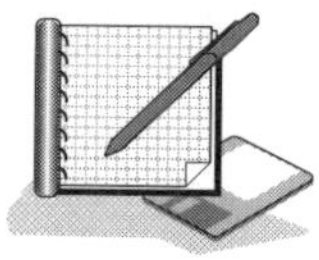

Practice

In these procedures, you create a chart in Performance Monitor to display performance data in real time. Real-time charts provide a quick overview of the current performance of your system.

Note Complete these procedures on Server1.

▸ **To configure the chart**

1. Click the **Start** button, point to **Programs**, point to **Administrative Tools (Common)**, and then click **Performance Monitor**.
2. On the **View** menu, click **Chart**.
3. On the **Edit** menu, click **Add To Chart**.

   Notice that Processor is the default object in the **Object** box.
4. In the **Counter** box, click **%DPC Time**, and then click **Explain**.

   Notice that the **Counter Definition** appears at the bottom of the window.
5. Click each of the counters for the **Processor** object, and read the **Counter Definition** for each.
6. In the **Counter** box, select all the counters available for **Processor**, and then click **Add**. (Hint: To select all counters, select the first counter, hold down the SHIFT key, and then select the last counter in the list.)
7. Click **Done**.

   A graph appears displaying the processor's real-time activities.

▶ **To generate data and view it on the chart**

1. Click the **Start** button, point to **Programs**, point to **Accessories**, point to **Games**, and then click **Pinball**.
2. Play one ball (and *only* one ball) of Pinball.
3. Close Pinball, and switch to Performance Monitor.
4. From the list of counters displayed in the lower part of your screen, click the **% Processor Time**, and notice the changing **Average** value.

Tip While looking at the activity of several counters on the Performance Monitor display, it may be difficult to distinguish a given counter's activity. In order to highlight the activity of a particular counter on the Performance Monitor display, select the counter name, and then press CTRL+H. Once you have turned on highlighting, you can click a different counter name to have its activity highlighted.

---

5. Minimize Performance Monitor.
6. Start and minimize both Server Manager and Disk Administrator.
7. Restore Performance Monitor.

   Notice the activity, such as spikes, on the chart.

You have created a chart displaying real-time processor utilization. This is useful to determine how your CPU is being used at the current time. In the next procedures, you will collect and save data for future reference, which can then be turned into a graph to compare with real time data to analyze performance.

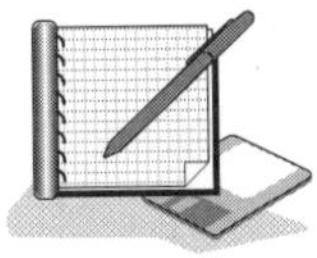

Practice

In these procedures, you use Performance Monitor to create and view a log of processor activity. Logs gather and record data to a file over a period of time. Logs are useful in predicting long-term trends or in troubleshooting short-term problems. You then view portions of the logged data in the chart to isolate specific information. You also use reports to view data in a non-graphical format.

Note Complete these procedures on Server1.

▶ **To create a log**

1. On the **View** menu, click **Log**.
2. On the **Edit** menu, click **Add To Log**.

3. In the **Objects** box, click **Processor**, and then click **Add**.

Note When you select an object for a log, all counters for that object will be recorded in the log automatically.

---

4. Click **Done**.
5. On the **Options** menu, click **Log**.
6. In the **File Name** box, type **pmlog1.log**
7. In the **Update Time** section, set the **Periodic Update Interval** to 1 second.
8. Click **Start Log**.

   The log window appears with real-time processor activity being collected in the log.
9. Create processor activity by starting applications or moving the mouse.
10. Check the **File Size** box in the Performance Monitor window periodically to determine the size of your data file.
11. Wait until the file has reached 100 KB, and then proceed with the next step.
12. On the **Options** menu, click **Log**, and then click **Stop Log**.

▸ **To view log data in a chart**

1. On the **View** menu, click **Chart**.
2. On the **File** menu, click **New Chart**.
3. On the **Options** menu, click **Data From**.
4. Click **Log File**, and then click the ellipsis (…) button.
5. Click the log file that you just created, and then click **Open**.
6. Click **OK** to return to the Performance Monitor window.

   An empty chart window appears.
7. On the **Edit** menu, click **Add To Chart**.
8. Select all counters available for **Processor**, and then click **Add**.
9. Click **Done**.

   The chart displays the processor counters collected in your log during the log collection period. You will notice data displayed on the chart as well as the status bar. The last, average, minimum, and maximum values are displayed with the total graph time from your log of data.

▸ **To view isolated segments of log data in a chart**

1. In the list of counters, select **% Processor Time**.
2. Using information from the status bar, record the average of % Processor Time.

 ____

3. On the **Edit** menu, click **Time Window**.

 The **Input Log File Timeframe** dialog box appears. This dialog box contains a slider that is used to adjust the portion of the chart shown in the Performance Monitor window. By default, the entire chart is shown.

 Note You may need to move the Input Log File Timeframe window to see the entire chart.

 ---

4. Click the left section of the slider and drag this section to the middle of the bar.
5. Click **OK**.

 The right half of the original chart is now displayed in the Performance Monitor window.

6. Record the average of % Processor Time again.

 ____

7. Repeat steps 3–5, this time adjusting the slider so that the last one-quarter of the chart is displayed.
8. Record the average of % Processor Time again.

 ____

9. Repeat steps 3–5, adjusting the left and right sections of the sliding bar as necessary, until the average % Processor Time for the portion of the chart displayed in the Performance Monitor window is greater than 40 percent.

 How accurate is this representation of the processor's use?

 ____

10. Edit the time window to view the entire graph.

▸ **To create a report showing the % Processor Time for the entire graph period**

1. On the **View** menu, click **Report**.

   A blank report window appears.

2. On the **Edit** menu, click **Add To Report**.
3. With **Processor** as the default object, select all counters in the **Counter** box, and then click **Add**.
4. Click **Done**.

   A report with the chosen counters is displayed, showing the averages.

   What was the average % Processor Time for the entire graph period?

   ---

5. Close Performance Monitor.

Network Monitor

Network Monitor monitors the network data stream, which consists of all information transferred over a network at any given time. Prior to transmission, this information is divided by the network software into smaller pieces, called frames or packets. Each frame contains the following information:

- The source address of the computer that sent the message.
- The destination address of the computer that received the frame.
- Headers from each protocol used to send the frame.
- The data or a portion of the information being sent.

For security reasons, Windows NT Network Monitor captures only those frames, including broadcast frames and multicast frames, that are sent to or from the local computer.

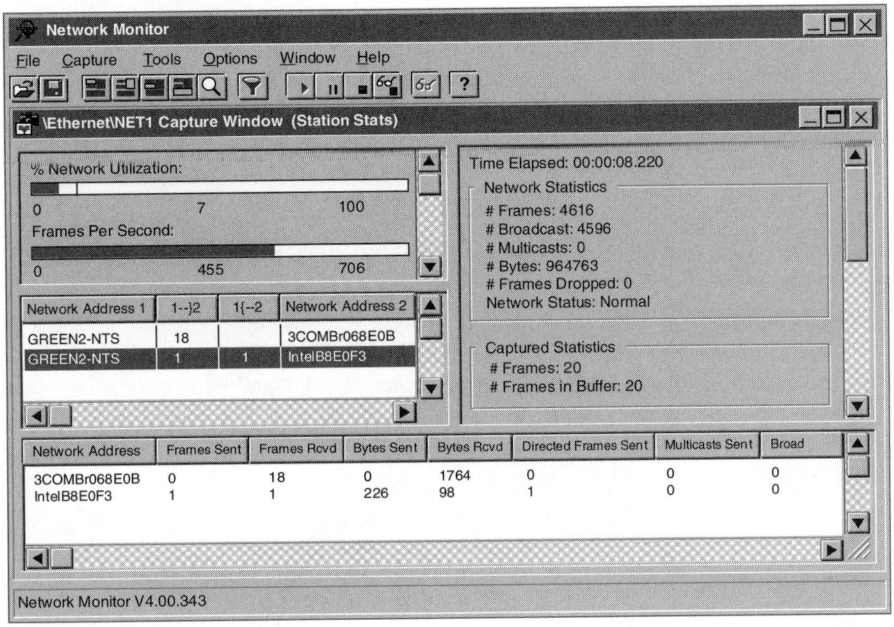

Installing Network Monitor

Network Monitor is installed as a service through the Network program in Control Panel. When Network Monitor is installed, it appears on the **Administrative Tools (Common)** menu.

The Network Monitor Capture Window

The Capture window in Network Monitor displays captured data. Four major *panes*, or sections, of the window display data. The following table describes the four panes.

Pane	Displays
Graph	The current activity as bar charts, showing the following: the percentage of network utilization, frames per second, bytes per second, broadcasts per second, and multicasts per second.
Session Statistics	A summary of the conversations between two hosts, and which host is initiating broadcasts and multicasts.
Total Statistics	Statistics for the traffic detected on the network as a whole, statistics for the frames captured, per second utilization statistics, and network adapter card statistics.
Station Statistics	A summary of the total number of frames initiated by a host, the number of frames and bytes sent and received, and the number of broadcast and multicast frames initiated.

Note For more information on Network Monitor, see Chapter 10, "Monitoring Your Network," in Microsoft Windows NT Server *Concepts and Planning*.

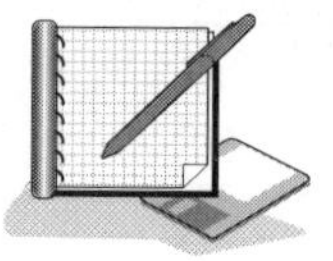

Practice

In these procedures, you install the Network Monitor Tools and Agent. You then use Network Monitor to capture and display network traffic.

Note Complete these procedures on Server1. Workstation1 should be online.

▸ **To install Network Monitor Tools and Agent**

1. Double-click the Shortcut to Network icon.
2. Click the **Services** tab.
3. Click **Add**.
4. In the **Network Service** box, click **Network Monitor Tools and Agent**, and then click **OK**.
5. In the **Windows NT Setup** dialog box, type **\\Server1\Nts_source\I386** and then click **Continue**.

   Windows NT Setup copies the required files.
6. After the files have been copied, click the **Close** button.
7. When prompted, click **Yes** to shut down and then restart your computer.
8. Restart Server1.

▸ **To set a trigger**

1. Log on as Administrator.
2. Click the **Start** button, point to **Programs**, point to **Administrative Tools (Common)**, and then click **Network Monitor**.

   The Network Monitor **Capture** window appears.
3. On the **Capture** menu, click **Trigger**.

   The **Capture Trigger** dialog box appears.
4. In the **Trigger on** box, click **Buffer Space**.
5. In the **Buffer Space** box, click **50%**.
6. In the **Trigger Action** box, click **Stop Capture**, and then click **OK**.

▸ **To capture network data and generate network traffic**

1. On the **Capture** menu, click **Start**.
2. On your desktop, click the **Start** button, and then click **Run**.
3. Type **\\Workstation1** and then click **OK**.

   A list of resources on \\Workstation1 appears.
4. Close the Workstation1 window.

▸ **To view captured network data**

1. On the **Capture** menu, click **Stop**.
2. On the **Capture** menu, click **Display Captured Data**.
3. Scroll through the list of captured frames. You should see your own computer name (**Server1**) and **Workstation1**.
4. Close Network Monitor. Do not save the capture.

System Recovery

When a severe error (called *STOP error*, or fatal system error or blue screen) occurs, Windows NT allows you to configure the way your system responds. This configuration is done through the **Recovery** options found on the **Startup/Shutdown** tab of the System program in Control Panel.

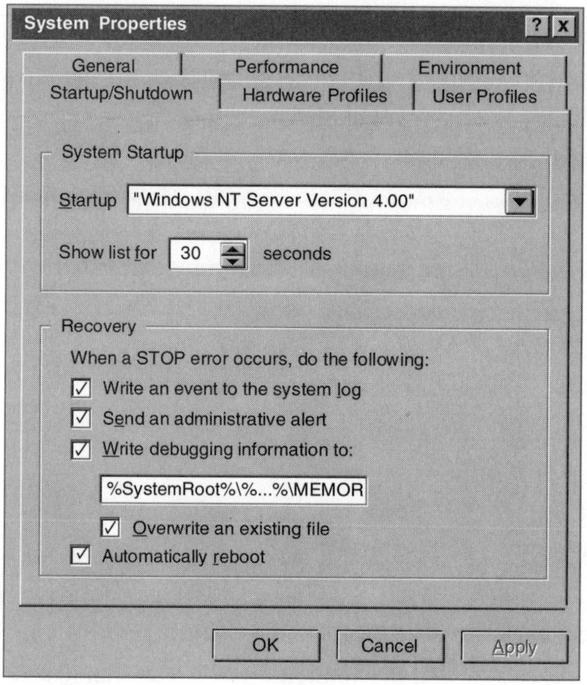

Configuring the Recovery Utility

The **Recovery** box on the **Startup/Shutdown** tab has the following options:

- Write an event to the system log.
- Send an administrative alert to the users and computers specified in the **Alerts** dialog box accessible through the **Server** dialog box in Control Panel.
- Write a debug file to a specified file name. This debug file contains a dump of system memory.
- Restart the system automatically. This allows the server to return to operation after a system crash, instead of requiring a manual reboot.

Recovery Operation

The **Write debugging information to** option is important for troubleshooting. If a STOP error occurs while this option is selected, a program named *Savedump.exe* writes (dumps) the entire contents of memory to the pagefile. For this reason, the pagefile must be at least as large as the amount of physical memory installed in the system. The pagefile must also reside on the partition that contains the *systemroot* folder.

Savedump.exe marks the part of the pagefile that contains the memory dump. When the system restarts, Windows NT automatically copies this part of the pagefile to the specified file name; by default, the file name is *Memory.dmp*. To preserve log files, you should copy them to a new file name after the computer restarts. A support engineer can then use the *Dumpexam.exe* program in the Support folder on the *Microsoft Windows NT Server* compact disc to debug the system.

Lesson 2: Resources for Troubleshooting

Whether you are a technical support engineer or network administrator, you should be aware of the Microsoft resources that are available to help you plan, configure, and troubleshoot Windows NT–based computers and domains. This lesson describes some of the key resources provided by Microsoft to help you maintain your Windows NT network.

After this lesson, you will be able to:

- Describe the purpose of TechNet.
- Name and access Microsoft online technical support resources.

Estimated lesson time: 10 minutes

The *Microsoft TechNet* compact disc is an important technical support tool. It is designed for professionals who perform any of the following tasks:

- Support or train users.
- Administer databases or networks.
- Integrate products and platforms.
- Evaluate and specify new products and solutions.

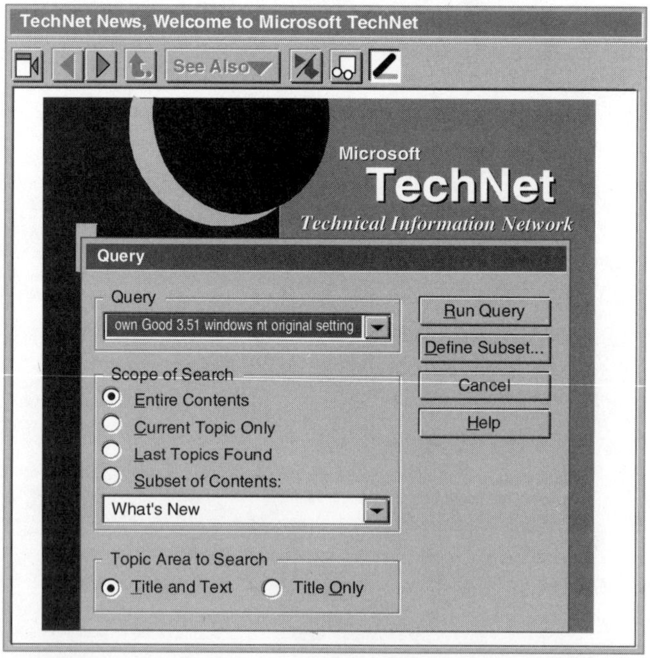

The *Microsoft TechNet* compact disc includes the following components:

- A complete set of online technical references to help install and support *all* Microsoft products. For example, the *Microsoft Windows NT Workstation Resource Kit* documentation describes how to install, configure, and optimize Windows NT Workstation.
- The entire Microsoft Knowledge Base, which is the same library of technical support articles developed and used by Microsoft's own support engineers to support customers.
- *TechNet Supplemental (Drivers & Patches)* compact disc, which contains the Microsoft Software Library. This compact disc includes drivers for the entire line of Microsoft software products, as well as patches and minor software updates for many Microsoft products, including Windows NT. This compact disc also includes code samples, utilities, and templates.

You can subscribe to TechNet by contacting:

Microsoft Corporation
PO Box 10296
Des Moines, IA 50336-0296
(800) 344-2121

Microsoft Internet and Online Services

To get up-to-date information on Microsoft Windows NT, Microsoft maintains online services to provide product and technical support information, such as the Microsoft Web site, the Microsoft Download Service (MSDL), and The Microsoft Network online service, MSN™.

- *Microsoft Web site (www.microsoft.com).* For example, to access articles on Windows NT, use Microsoft Internet Explorer to reach Microsoft support at the following address: http://www.microsoft.com/support
- *The Microsoft Download Service (MSDL).* This Microsoft electronic bulletin board provides support information and products. Access the MSDL by dialing (206) 936-6735. (Note that the modem settings for MSDL are 8 data bits, 1 stop bit, no parity, and no flow control.)

Note The course Web page that you installed from the *Course Materials* compact disc contains links to different Microsoft resources. See the Web Sites page to view this information.

Note The Microsoft Network (MSN) contains answers to the most common technical questions, as well as detailed articles about Microsoft products. In addition, subscribers can join online chat groups to both give and receive advice regarding technical issues from fellow members. Although much of the content of MSN can be accessed using Windows NT and Microsoft Internet Explorer, the full content of MSN can only be accessed from computers running Microsoft Windows 95.

Summary

The following information summarizes the key points in this chapter:

- In order to help you troubleshoot your system and your network, Windows NT provides the following tools: Event Viewer, Windows NT Diagnostics, Performance Monitor, Network Monitor, and System Recovery.
- Event Viewer provides information about events such as errors, warnings, and the success or failure of tasks that are maintained in an event log. An event is any potentially significant occurrence in the system (or in an application). With an event log and the Event Viewer, you can troubleshoot various hardware and software problems and monitor Windows NT security events.
- Windows NT records three kinds of logs: system, security, and application logs. System logs record information about the failure of a driver, or other system component. Security logs record information about valid and invalid logon attempts and events related to resource use such as creating, opening, and deleting files. Application logs record information about applications.
- Windows NT Diagnostics (Winmsd.exe) is a tool that shows computer hardware and operating system data stored in the Windows NT registry.
- Performance Monitor enables you to look at resource use for specific components and application processes through a dynamic display. These dynamic charts can be saved as logs or reports. With Performance Monitor, you can gauge your computer's efficiency, identify and troubleshoot possible problems, and plan for additional hardware needs. You can also use alerts to notify you when resource use reaches a specified value.
- Network Monitor is used to capture and display frames (also called packets) to detect and troubleshoot problems on LANs. For security reasons, Network Monitor captures only those frames, including broadcast frames and multicast frames, that are sent to or from the local computer.
- System Recovery allows you to configure the way your system responds when a STOP error occurs. You can configure the following System Recovery options: write an event to the system log, send an administrative alert, write a debug file that contains a dump of system memory when a STOP error occurs, and restart the system automatically, instead of requiring a manual reboot.
- Microsoft provides various resources, such as TechNet and MSDL, which you can use to get troubleshooting information about Microsoft products. You can also use the Internet to access one of the Microsoft Web sites, such as *www.microsoft.com,* to access the most recent information, as well as to download software, including drivers and Service Packs.

Review

1. A network user calls you and complains that her computer, which is running Windows NT Workstation, is unusually slow. Without going to her computer, what steps can you take to diagnose the problem?

2. Your manager wants you to track all unsuccessful logon attempts. You search the system log, but you cannot find any unsuccessful logon attempts recorded. What is the problem?

3. You are having a problem configuring a device to work with Windows NT. Where can you look for any reported problems?

Answer Key

Procedure Answers

Page 653

▸ **To view events**

4. Double-click one of each of the symbols (Stop sign, exclamation point, and information symbol), one at a time to determine the type of event it represents and to see a description of the event.

   What types of events appear in your system log?

   You may see messages with the following types: Information, Warning, and Errors.

5. On the **Log** menu, click **Application**.

   What types of events appear in your application log?

   You may see messages with the following types: Information, Warning, and Errors.

Page 654

▸ **To control the size and contents of a log file**

1. On the Event Viewer **Log** menu, click **Log Settings**.

   By default, what is the maximum log size for the system, security, and application log files?

   The default maximum log size for each log file is 512 KB.

3. Click **Overwrite Events As Needed**.

   How will this setting affect the system log?

   Older events will now be overwritten by new events.

Page 654

▸ **To filter events**

6. Double-click the oldest entry.

   What is the description of the problem?

   The 3Com EtherLink II Adapter Driver service failed to start due to the following error: A device attached to the system is not functioning.

   What could be the problem?

   The network adapter card is missing, configured incorrectly, or malfunctioning.

Page 655

▸ **To search for specific messages**

5. Double-click the first entry.

   What is the description of the problem?

   The drive D is at or near capacity.

   What action is necessary?

   You need to delete some files. The files can be backed up and then deleted from drive D.

9. Double-click each entry and view its description one at a time until you determine what the problem is.

   What is the problem?

   A duplicate computer name exists on the network.

   What action is necessary?

   Rename the computer and then restart Windows NT Server.

Page 658

▸ **To view software configuration information**

2. Locate the following information by reviewing the tabs in the Windows NT Diagnostics window. In the following table, record the name of the tab you chose and the value of the requested information.

   Answers recorded in the table will vary.

Requested information	Tab	Value
Registered owner	**Version**	**Answers will vary.**
Registered organization	**Version**	**Answers will vary.**
Version number	**Version**	**4.0**
Build number	**Version**	**1381**
systemroot (windir)	**Environment**	**C:\Winnt**
Domain name	**Network**	**Domain1**
CPU type	**System or Environment**	**Answers will vary. Example: *x*86 Family 5 Model 2 Stepping 1**

3. Locate the following information.

   Answers recorded in the table will vary.

Requested information	Your configuration
Total physical memory	**Answers will vary.**
Available physical memory	**Answers will vary.**
Total pagefile space	**Answers will vary.**
Available pagefile space	**(Pagefile Space: Total) - (Pagefile Space: Total in Use)**
Paging files (location and size)	**Answers will vary.**

4. List the service dependencies for the following services. (Hint: Click the **Services** tab, click the name of the service, and then click **Properties**.)

Service	Dependencies
ClipBook Server	**NetDDE**
Network DDE	**Network DDEDSDM**
Network DDE DSDM	**None**
Server	**TDI**
Messenger	**LANMAN Workstation, NetBIOS**

Page 659

▸ **To view configuration information for Workstation1**

2. In the **Computer** box, type **Workstation1** and then click **OK**.

   What tabs are available for remote computers?

   Version, System, Display, Services, Resources, Environment, and Network.

3. Locate the following information about Workstation1:

   Answers recorded in the table will vary.

Requested information	Workstation1 configuration
CPU type	**Example: *x*86 Family 5 Model 2 Stepping 1**
Network adapter IRQ	**Example: IRQ 5**
Video driver in use	**Example: Ati.sys**
Domain name	**Domain1**

Page 660

▸ **To read a Windows NT Diagnostics report**

3. Use **Find** on the **Search** menu to locate the following information in Msdrpt.txt.

   For example, the results of a Find on PROCESSOR_ARCHITECTURE could be PROCESSOR_ARCHITECTURE=x86.

Requested information	Workstation1 configuration
PROCESSOR_ARCHITECTURE	Answers will vary.
PROCESSOR_LEVEL	Answers will vary.
PROCESSOR_IDENTIFIER	Answers will vary.
PROCESSOR_REVISION	Answers will vary.

Page 665

▸ **To view isolated segments of log data in a chart**

2. Using information from the status bar, record the average of % Processor Time.

   Answers will vary.

6. Record the average of % Processor Time again.

   Answers will vary.

8. Record the average of % Processor Time again.

   Answers will vary.

9. Repeat steps 3–5, adjusting the left and right sections of the sliding bar as necessary, until the average % Processor Time for the portion of the chart displayed in the Performance Monitor window is greater than 40 percent.

   How accurate is this representation of the processor's use?

   It is accurate for this time slice, but will not reflect overall processor activity.

Page 666

▸ **To create a report showing the % Processor Time for the entire graph period**

4. Click **Done**.

   A report with the chosen counters is displayed, showing the averages.

   What was the average % Processor Time for the entire graph period?

   Answers will vary.

Review Answers

Page 676

1. A network user calls you and complains that her computer, which is running Windows NT Workstation, is unusually slow. Without going to her computer, what steps can you take to diagnose the problem?

   Use Event Viewer to examine the remote computer's event log to see if any errors have been reported. Then use Performance Monitor to see if any devices report a bottleneck. Finally, you can use Windows NT Diagnostics to document the computer's configuration.

2. Your manager wants you to track all unsuccessful logon attempts. You search the system log, but you cannot find any unsuccessful logon attempts recorded. What is the problem?

   Unsuccessful logon attempts are recorded in the security log, not in the system log. By default, security logging is turned off. To enable security logging, run User Manager for Domains and set the Audit policy.

3. You are having a problem configuring a device to work with Windows NT. Where can you look for any reported problems?

   Look in the Microsoft Knowledge Base available on TechNet, or www.microsoft.com.

Glossary

A

access control entry (ACE) An entry in an access control list (ACL). Each access control entry defines the protection or auditing to be applied to a file or other object for a specific user or group of users. *See also* access control list (ACL).

access control list (ACL) The part of a security descriptor that enumerates both the protections to accessing and the auditing of that accessing that are applied to an object. The owner of an object has discretionary access control of the object and can change the object's ACL to allow or disallow others access to the object. Access control lists are ordered lists of access control entries (ACEs). There are two types of ACLs: discretionary (DACL) and system (SACL). *See also* access control entry (ACE); discretionary access control list (DACL); system access control list (SACL).

access permission A rule associated with an object (usually a directory, file, or printer) to regulate which users can have access to the object and in what manner. *See also* user rights.

access privileges Permissions set by Macintosh users that allow them to view and make changes to folders on a server. By setting access privileges (called *permissions* when set on the computer running Windows NT Server), you control which Macintosh can use folders in a volume. Services for Macintosh (SFM) translates access privileges set by Macintosh users to the equivalent Windows NT permissions.

access token (or security token) An object that uniquely identifies a user who has logged on. An access token is attached to all of the user's processes and contains the user's security ID (SID), the SIDs of any groups to which the user belongs, any permissions that the user owns, the default owner of any objects that the user's processes create, and the default access control list (ACL) to be applied to any objects that the user's processes create. *See also* permissions.

access violation An attempt to carry out a memory operation that is not allowed by Windows NT memory management. This can include an invalid operation (such as writing to a read-only buffer); accessing memory beyond the limit of the current program's address space (a "length violation"); accessing a page to which the system forbids access; or accessing a page that is currently resident but dedicated to the use of an Executive component.

account *See* group account; user account.

account lockout A Windows NT Server security feature that locks a user account if a number of failed logon attempts occur within a specified amount of time, based on account policy lockout settings. (Locked accounts cannot log on.)

account policy Controls the way passwords must be used by all user accounts of a domain or of an individual computer. Specifics include minimum password length, how often a user must change his or her password, and how often users can reuse old passwords. Account policy can be set for all user accounts in a domain when administering a domain, and for all user accounts of a single workstation or member server when administering a computer.

ACK Short for acknowledgment. The Transmission Control Protocol (TCP) requires that the recipient of data packets acknowledge successful receipt of data. Such acknowledgments (ACKs) generate additional network traffic, diminishing the rate at which data passes in favor of reliability. To reduce the impact on performance, most hosts send an acknowledgment for every other segment or when a specified time interval has passed.

acknowledgment *See* ACK.

active Refers to the window or icon that you are currently using or that is currently selected. Windows NT always applies the next keystroke or command you choose to the active window. If a window is active, its title bar changes color to differentiate it from other windows. If an icon is active, its label changes color. Windows or icons on the desktop that are not selected are inactive.

ActiveX An umbrella term for Microsoft technologies that enable developers to create interactive content for the World Wide Web.

adapter card *See* network adapter.

address Within Network Monitor, an address refers to a hexadecimal number that identifies a computer uniquely on the network.

address classes Predefined groupings of Internet addresses, with each class defining networks of a certain size. The range of numbers that can be assigned for the first octet in the IP address is based on the address class. Class A networks (values 1–126) are the largest, with over 16 million hosts per network. Class B networks (128–191) have up to 65,534 hosts per network, and Class C networks (192–223) can have up to 254 hosts per network. *See also* octet.

address pairs Refers to the two specific computers between which you want to monitor traffic by using Network Monitor. Up to four specific address pairs can be monitored simultaneously to capture frames from particular computers on your network. *See also* frame.

Address Resolution Protocol (ARP) A network-maintenance protocol in the TCP/IP suite that provides IP address-to-MAC address resolution for IP packets. Not directly related to data transport. *See also* IP address; media access control (MAC); packet; Transmission Control Protocol/Internet Protocol (TCP/IP).

administrative account An account that is a member of the Administrators local group of a computer or domain.

administrative alerts Administrative alerts relate to server and resource use and warn about problems in areas such as security and access, user sessions, server shutdown due to power loss (when UPS is available), directory replication, and printing. When a computer generates an administrative alert, a message is sent to a predefined list of users and computers. *See also* Alerter service; uninterruptible power supply (UPS).

administrator A person responsible for setting up and managing domain controllers or local computers and their user and group accounts, assigning passwords and permissions, and helping users with networking issues. To use administrative tools such as User Manager or User Manager for Domains, an administrator must be logged on as a member of the Administrators local group of the computer or domain, respectively.

Administrator privilege One of three privilege levels you can assign to a Windows NT user account. Every user account has one of the three privilege levels (Administrator, Guest, and User). *See also* administrator; Guest privilege; User privilege.

Advanced RISC Computing (ARC) ARC names are a generic method of identifying devices within the ARC environment. *See also* reduced instruction set computing (RISC).

agent In SNMP, agent information consists of comments about the user, the physical location of the computer, and the types of service to report based on the computer's configuration. *See also* Simple Network Management Protocol (SNMP).

Alerter service Notifies selected users and computers of administrative alerts that occur on a computer. Used by the Server service and other services. Requires the Messenger service. *See also* administrative alerts; Messenger service.

anonymous-level security token The type of security token used when a server impersonates a client. If, when the client calls the server, the client specifies an anonymous impersonation mode, the server cannot access any of the client's identification information, such as its security identifier (SID) or privileges. The server will have to use an anonymous-level security token when representing the client in successive operations. *See also* access token.

Anonymous user A connection for which the request either did not contain a user name and password or whose user name and password were ignored because authentication is not permitted on the server.

API *See* application programming interface.

AppleShare Client software that is shipped with each Macintosh and with Apple Computer server software. With Services for Macintosh, a Macintosh uses its native AppleShare client software to connect to computers running Windows NT Server that have Services for Macintosh.

AppleTalk Apple Computer network architecture and network protocols. A network that has Macintosh clients and a computer running Windows NT Server with Services for Macintosh functions as an AppleTalk network.

AppleTalk Filing Protocol The presentation layer protocol that manages access of remote files in an AppleTalk network.

AppleTalk Phase 2 The extended AppleTalk Internet model designed by Apple Computer. It supports multiple zones within a network and extended addressing capacity.

AppleTalk Protocol The set of network protocols on which AppleTalk network architecture is based. Setting up Services for Macintosh installs its AppleTalk Protocol stack on a computer running Windows NT Server so that Macintosh clients can connect to it.

AppleTalk Transport The layer of AppleTalk Phase 2 protocols that deliver data to its destination on the network.

application A computer program used for a particular kind of work, such as word processing. This term is often used interchangeably with "program."

application log The application log contains specific events logged by applications. Applications developers decide which events to monitor (for example, a database program might record a file error in the application log). Use Event Viewer to view the application log.

application programming interface (API) A set of routines that an application program uses to request and carry out lower-level services performed by another component, such as the computer's operating system or a service running on a network computer. These maintenance chores are performed by the computer's operating system, and an API provides the program with a means of communicating with the system, telling it which system-level task to perform and when.

application window The main window for an application, which contains the application's menu bar and work area. An application window may contain multiple document windows.

ARC *See* Advanced RISC Computing.

archive bit Backup programs use the archive bit to mark the files after backing them up, if a normal or incremental backup is performed. *See also* backup types.

ARP *See* Address Resolution Protocol.

ARP reply packet All ARP-enabled systems on the local IP network detect ARP request packets, and the system that owns the IP address in question replies by sending its physical address to the requester in an ARP reply packet. The physical/IP address is then stored in the ARP cache of the requesting system for subsequent use. *See also* Address Resolution Protocol (ARP); ARP request packet; Internet Protocol (IP); MAC address.

ARP request packet If two systems are to communicate across a TCP/IP network, the system sending the packet must map the IP address of the final destination to the physical address of the final destination. This physical address is also referred to as a MAC address, a unique 48-bit number assigned to the network interface card by the manufacturer. IP acquires this physical address by broadcasting a special inquiry packet (an ARP request packet) containing the IP address of the destination system. *See also* Address Resolution Protocol (ARP); Internet Protocol (IP); MAC address; media access control (MAC).

AS/400 A type of IBM minicomputer.

ASCII file Also called a text file, a text-only file, or an ASCII text file, refers to a file in the universally recognized text format called ASCII (American Standard Code for Information Interchange). An ASCII file contains characters, spaces, punctuation, carriage returns, and sometimes tabs and an end-of-file marker, but it contains no formatting information. This generic format is useful for transferring files between programs that could not otherwise understand each other's documents. *See also* text file.

associate To identify a file name extension as "belonging" to a certain application so that when you open any file with that extension, the application starts automatically.

attributes Information that indicates whether a file is a read-only, hidden, system, or compressed file, and whether the file has been changed since a backup copy of it was made.

A-type resource record A line (record) in a computer's Domain Name System database that maps a computer's domain name (host name) to an IP address in a DNS zone.

auditing Tracking activities of users by recording selected types of events in the security log of a server or a workstation.

audit policy For the servers of a domain or for an individual computer, defines the type of security events that will be logged.

authentication Validation of a user's logon information. When a user logs on to an account on a computer running Windows NT Workstation, the authentication is performed by that workstation. When a user logs on to an account on a Windows NT Server domain, authentication may be performed by any server of that domain. *See also* Basic (clear-text) authentication; challenge/response authentication; server; trust relationship.

B

backup domain controller (BDC) In a Windows NT Server domain, a computer running Windows NT Server that receives a copy of the domain's directory database, which contains all account and security policy information for the domain. The copy is synchronized periodically and automatically with the master copy on the primary domain controller (PDC). BDCs also authenticate user logons and can be promoted to function as PDCs as needed. Multiple BDCs can exist on a domain. *See also* member server; primary domain controller (PDC).

backup set A collection of files from one drive that is backed up during a single backup operation.

backup set catalog At the end of each backup set, Windows NT Backup stores a summary of file or directory information in a backup set catalog. Catalog information includes the number of tapes in a set of tapes as well as the date they were created, and the dates of each file in the catalog. Catalogs are created for each backup set and are stored on the last tape in the set. *See also* backup set.

backup set map At the end of each tape used for backup, a backup set map maintains the exact tape location of the backup set's data and catalog.

backup types:

copy backup Copies all selected files, but does not mark each file as having been backed up. Copying is useful if you want to back up files between normal and incremental backups, because copying will not invalidate these other backup operations.

daily backup Copies all selected files that have been modified the day the daily backup is performed.

differential backup Copies those files created or changed since the last normal (or incremental) backup. It does not mark files as having been backed up.

incremental backup Backs up only those files created or changed since the last normal (or incremental) backup. It marks files as having been backed up.

normal backup Copies all selected files and marks each as having been backed up. Normal backups give you the ability to restore files quickly because files on the last tape are the most current.

bandwidth In communications, the difference between the highest and lowest frequencies in a given range. For example, a telephone line accommodates a bandwidth of 3000 Hz, the difference between the lowest (300 Hz) and highest (3300 Hz) frequencies it can carry. In computer networks, greater bandwidth indicates faster data-transfer capability and is expressed in bits per second (bps). Also known as "throughput."

Basic (clear-text) authentication A method of authentication that encodes user name and password data transmissions. Basic authentication is called "clear text" because the base-64 encoding can be decoded by anyone with a freely available decoding utility. Note that encoding is not the same as encryption. *See also* challenge/response authentication; encryption.

batch program An ASCII file (unformatted text file) that contains one or more Windows NT commands. A batch program's file name has a .cmd or .bat extension. When you type the file name at the command prompt, the commands are processed sequentially.

batch queue facility A program that effects a logon without user input, used for delayed logons.

BDC *See* backup domain controller.

binary A base-2 number system, in which values are expressed as combinations of two digits, 0 and 1.

binary-file transfer A method of transferring binary files from Windows NT HyperTerminal to a remote computer. Binary files consist of ASCII characters plus the extended ASCII character set. These files are not converted or translated during the transfer process. *See also* ASCII file.

binding A process that establishes the communication channel between a protocol driver (such as TCP/IP) and a network adapter. *See also* network adapter; Transmission Control Protocol/Internet Protocol (TCP/IP).

bits per second (bps) A measure of the speed at which a device, such as a modem, can transfer data.

blue screen The screen displayed when Windows NT encounters a serious error.

bookmarks A Windows NT feature that enables you to highlight major points of interest at various points in a Performance Monitor log file and then return to them easily when you work with that log file later on during performance monitoring. Bookmarks are also used in other applications, such as Microsoft Word.

boot loader Defines the information needed for system startup, such as the location for the operating system's files. Windows NT automatically creates the correct configuration and checks this information whenever you start your system.

boot partition The volume, formatted for either an NTFS or FAT file system, that contains the Windows NT operating system and its support files. The boot partition can be (but does not have to be) the same as the system partition. *See also* file allocation table (FAT); partition; Windows NT File System (NTFS).

Bootstrap protocol (BOOTP) A TCP/IP network protocol, defined by RFC 951 and RFC 1542, used to configure systems. DHCP is an extension of BOOTP. *See also* Dynamic Host Configuration Protocol (DHCP).

bps *See* bits per second.

branch A segment of the directory tree, representing a directory (or folder) and any subdirectories (or folders within folders) it contains.

bridge Connects multiple networks, subnets, or rings into one large logical network. A bridge maintains a table of node addresses and, based on this, forwards packets to a specific subnet, reducing traffic on other subnets. In a bridged network, there can be only one path to any destination (otherwise packets would circle the network, causing network storms). A bridge is more sophisticated than a repeater, but not as sophisticated as a router. *See also* packet; repeaters; router; subnet.

broadcast datagram An IP datagram sent to all hosts on the subnet. *See also* datagram; Internet Protocol (IP); subnet.

broadcast message A network message sent from a single computer that is distributed to all other devices on the same segment of the network as the sending computer.

broadcast name resolution A mechanism defined in RFC 1001/1002 that uses broadcasts to resolve names to IP addresses through a process of registration, resolution, and name release. *See also* broadcast datagram; IP address.

brouter Combines elements of the bridge and the router. Usually, a brouter acts as a router for one transport protocol (such as TCP/IP), sending packets of that format along detailed routes to their destinations. The brouter also acts as a bridge for all other types of packets (such as IPX), just passing them on, as long as they are not local to the LAN segment from which they originated. *See also* bridge; packet; router.

browse To view available network resources by looking through lists of folders, files, user accounts, groups, domains, or computers. Browsing allows users on a Windows NT network to see what domains and computers are accessible from their local computer. *See also* Windows NT browser system.

browse list A list kept by the master browser of all of the servers and domains on the network. This list is available to any workstation on the network requesting it. *See also* browse.

browse master *See* master browser; Windows NT browser system.

buffer A reserved portion of memory in which data is temporarily held pending an opportunity to complete its transfer to or from a storage device or another location in memory. Some devices, such as printers or the adapters supporting them, commonly have their own buffers. *See also* memory.

built-in groups Default groups, provided with Windows NT Server and Windows NT Workstation, that have been granted useful collections of rights and built-in abilities. In most cases, a built-in group provides all of the capabilities needed by a particular user. For example, if a domain user account belongs to the built-in Administrators group, logging on with that account gives a user administrative capabilities over the domain and the servers of the domain. To provide a needed set of capabilities to a user account, assign it to the appropriate built-in group. *See also* group; User Manager; User Manager for Domains.

bulk data encryption The encryption of all data sent over a network.

C

cache A special memory subsystem that stores the contents of frequently accessed RAM locations and the addresses where these data items are stored. In Windows NT, for example, user profiles have a locally cached copy of part of the registry.

caching In DNS name resolution, caching refers to a local cache where information about the DNS domain name space is kept. Whenever a resolver request arrives, the local name server checks both its static information and the cache for the name to IP address mapping. *See also* Domain Name System (DNS); IP address; mapping.

Callback Control Protocol (CBCP) A protocol that negotiates callback information with a remote client.

capture The process by which Network Monitor copies frames. (A *frame* is information that has been divided into smaller pieces by the network software prior to transmission.) *See also* frame.

capture buffer A reserved, resizable storage area in memory where Network Monitor copies all frames it detects from the network. When the capture buffer overflows, each new frame replaces the oldest frame in the buffer.

capture filter Functions like a database query to single out a subset of frames to be monitored in Network Monitor. You can filter on the basis of source and destination addresses, protocols, protocol properties, or by specifying a pattern offset. *See also* capture; frame.

capture password Required to be able to capture statistics from the network and to display captured data using Network Monitor.

capture trigger Performs a specified action (such as starting an executable file) when Network Monitor detects a particular set of conditions on the network.

catalog *See* backup set catalog.

CBCP *See* Callback Control Protocol.

CCP *See* Compression Control Protocol.

centralized network administration A centralized view of the entire network from any workstation on the network that provides the ability to track and manage information on users, groups, and resources in a distributed network.

CGI *See* Common Gateway Interface.

Challenge Handshake Authentication Protocol (CHAP) A protocol used by Microsoft RAS to negotiate the most secure form of encrypted authentication supported by both server and client. *See also* encryption.

challenge/response authentication A method of authentication in which a server uses challenge/response algorithms and Windows NT security to control access to resources. *See also* Basic (clear-text) authentication; encryption.

change log An inventory of the most recent changes made to the directory database such as new or changed passwords, new or changed user and group accounts, and any changes to associated group memberships and user rights. Change logs provide fault tolerance, so if your system crashes before a write completes, Windows NT can complete the write the next time you boot. This log holds only a certain number of changes, however, so when a new change is added, the oldest change is deleted. *See also* directory database; fault tolerance.

CHAP *See* Challenge Handshake Authentication Protocol.

check box A small box in a dialog box or property page that can be selected or cleared. Check boxes represent an option that you can turn on or off. When a check box is selected, an X or a check mark appears in the box.

checksum The mathematical computation used to verify the accuracy of data in TCP/IP packets. *See also* packet; Transmission Control Protocol/Internet Protocol (TCP/IP).

choose To pick an item that begins an action in Windows NT. You often click a command on a menu to perform a task, and you click an icon to start an application.

circular dependency A dependency in which an action that appears later in a chain is contingent upon an earlier action. For example, three services (A, B, and C) are linked. A is dependent upon B to start. B is dependent upon C to start. A circular dependency results when C is dependent upon A to start. *See also* dependency.

clear To turn off an option by removing the X or check mark from a check box. To clear a check box, you can click it, or you can select it and then press the SPACEBAR.

clear-text authentication *See* Basic (clear-text) authentication.

clear-text passwords Passwords that are not scrambled, thus making them more susceptible to network sniffers. *See also* network sniffer.

click To press and release a mouse button quickly.

client A computer that accesses shared network resources provided by another computer, called a server. *See also* server; workstation.

client application A Windows NT application that can display and store linked or embedded objects. For distributed applications, the application that imitates a request to a server application. *See also* DCOM Configuration tool; Distributed Component Object Module (DCOM); server application.

Client Service for NetWare Included with Windows NT Workstation, enabling workstations to make direct connections to file and printer resources at NetWare servers running NetWare 2.*x* or later.

Clipboard A temporary storage area in memory, used to transfer information. You can cut or copy information onto the Clipboard and then paste it into another document or application.

close Remove a window or dialog box, or quit an application. To close a window, you can click **Close** on the **Control** menu, or you can click the close button icon in the upper right corner of the dialog box. When you close an application window, you quit the application.

collapse To hide additional directory levels below a selected directory in the directory tree.

color scheme A combination of complementary colors for screen elements.

command A word or phrase, usually found on a menu, that you click to carry out an action. You click a command on a menu or type a command at the Windows NT command prompt. You can also type a command in the **Run** dialog box, which you open by clicking **Run** on the **Start** menu.

command button A button in a dialog box that carries out or cancels the selected action. Two common command buttons are **OK** and **Cancel**. If you click a command button that contains an ellipsis (for example, **Browse...**), another dialog box appears.

Common Gateway Interface (CGI) A standard interface for HTTP server application development. The standard was developed by the National Center for Supercomputing Applications.

common group Common groups appear in the program list on the **Start** menu for all users who log on to the computer. Only Administrators can create or change common groups.

communications settings Settings that specify how information is transferred from your computer to a device (usually a printer or modem).

community names A group of hosts to which a server belongs that is running the SNMP service. The community name is placed in the SNMP packet when the trap is sent. Typically, all hosts belong to Public, which is the standard name for the common community of all hosts. *See also* packet; Simple Network Management Protocol (SNMP); trap.

compact A command-line utility used to compress files on NTFS volumes. To see command line options, type **compact /?** at the command prompt. To access this utility, you can also right-click any file or directory on an NTFS volume in Windows NT Explorer, then click **Properties** to compress or decompress the files.

compound device A device that plays specific media files. For example, to run a compound device such as a MIDI sequencer, you must specify a MIDI file.

Compression Control Protocol (CCP) A protocol that negotiates compression with a remote client.

computer account Each computer running Windows NT Workstation and Windows NT Server that participates in a domain has its own account in the directory database. A computer account is created when the computer is first identified to the domain during network setup at installation time.

Computer Browser service Maintains an up-to-date list of computers, and provides the list to applications when requested. Provides the computer lists displayed in the **Network Neighborhood**, **Select Computer**, and **Select Domain** dialog boxes; and (for Windows NT Server only) in the Server Manager window.

computer name A unique name of up to 15 uppercase characters that identifies a computer to the network. The name cannot be the same as any other computer or domain name in the network.

configure To change the initial setup of a client, a Macintosh-accessible volume, a server, or a network.

connect To assign a drive letter, port, or computer name to a shared resource so that you can use it with Windows NT.

connected user A user accessing a computer or a resource across the network.

connection A software link between a client and a shared resource such as a printer or a shared directory on a server. Connections require a network adapter or modem.

connection-oriented protocol A network protocol with four important characteristics: the path for data packets is established in advance; the resources required for a connection are reserved in advance; a connection's resource reservation is enforced throughout the life of that connection; and when a connection's data transfer is completed, the connection is terminated and the allocated resources are freed.

control codes Codes that specify terminal commands or formatting instructions (such as linefeeds or carriage returns) in a text file. Control codes are usually preceded by a caret (^).

controller *See* backup domain controller (BDC); primary domain controller (PDC).

Control menu *See* window menu.

control set All Windows NT startup-related data that is not computed during startup is saved in a registry key. This startup data is organized into control sets, each of which contains a complete set of parameters for starting up devices and services. The registry always contains at least two control sets, each of which contains information about all of the configurable options for the computer: the current control set and the LastKnownGood control set. *See also* current control set; LastKnownGood (LKG) control set.

conventional memory Up to the first 640 KB of memory in your computer. MS-DOS uses this memory to run applications.

CRC *See* cyclic redundancy check.

current control set The control set that was used most recently to start the computer and that contains any changes made to the startup information during the current session. *See also* LastKnownGood (LKG) control set.

current directory The directory that you are currently working in. Also called "current folder."

cyclic redundancy check (CRC) A procedure used on disk drives to ensure that the data written to a sector is read correctly later. This procedure is also used in checking for errors in data transmission.

The procedure is known as a redundancy check because each data transmission includes not only data but extra (redundant) error-checking values. The sending device generates a number based on the data to be transmitted and sends its result along with the data to the receiving device. The receiving device repeats the same calculation after transmission. If both devices obtain the same result, it is assumed that the transmission is error-free.

D

DACL *See* discretionary access control list; *see also* system access control list (SACL).

daemon A networking program that runs in the background.

database query The process of extracting data from a database and presenting it for use.

data carrier In communications, either a specified frequency that can be modulated to convey information or a company that provides telephone and other communications services to consumers.

Data Carrier Detect (DCD) Tracks the presence of a data carrier. *See also* data carrier.

data communications equipment (DCE) An elaborate worldwide network of packet-forwarding nodes that participate in delivering an X.25 packet to its designated address, for example, a modem. *See also* node; packet; X.25.

Data Encryption Standard (DES) A type of encryption (the U.S. government standard) designed to protect against password discovery and playback. Microsoft RAS uses DES encryption when both the client and the server are using RAS.

data fork The part of a Macintosh file that holds most of the file's information. The data fork is the part of the file shared between Macintosh and PC clients.

datagram A packet of data and other delivery information that is routed through a packet-switched network or transmitted on a local area network. *See also* packet.

Data Source Name (DSN) The logical name used by ODBC to refer to the drive and other information required to access data. The name is use by Internet Information Server for a connection to an ODBC data source, such as a SQL Server database. To set this name, use ODBC in the Control Panel.

data stream Windows NT Network Monitor monitors the network data stream, which consists of all information transferred over a network at any given time.

Data Terminal Equipment (DTE) For example, a RAS server or client. *See also* Remote Access Service (RAS).

dbWeb Administrator The graphical user tool for Microsoft dbWeb that allows an administrator to create definition templates referred to as schemas. Schemas control how and what information from a private database is available to visitors who use the Internet to access the public Microsoft dbWeb gateway to the private database. *See also* schemas.

DCD *See* Data Carrier Detect.

DCE *See* data communications equipment.

DCOM *See* Distributed Component Object Model.

DCOM Configuration tool A Windows NT Server utility that can be used to configure 32-bit applications for DCOM communication over the network. *See also* Distributed Component Object Model (DCOM).

DDE *See* dynamic data exchange.

deadlock condition A run-time error condition that occurs when two threads of execution are blocked, each waiting to acquire a resource that the other holds, and both unable to continue running.

decision tree A geographical representation of a filter's logic used by Windows NT Network Monitor. When you include or exclude information from your capture specifications, the decision tree reflects these specifications.

default button In some dialog boxes, the command button that is selected or highlighted when the dialog box is initially displayed. The default button has a bold border, indicating that it will be chosen automatically if you press ENTER. To override a default button, you can click **Cancel** or another command button.

default gateway In TCP/IP, the intermediate network device on the local network that has knowledge of the network IDs of the other networks in the Internet, so it can forward the packets to other gateways until the packet is eventually delivered to a gateway connected to the specified destination. *See also* gateway; network ID; packet.

default network In the Macintosh environment, this refers to the physical network on which a server's processes reside as nodes and on which the server appears to users. A server's default network must be one to which that server is attached. Only servers on AppleTalk Phase 2 internets have default networks.

default owner The person assigned ownership of a folder on the server when the account of the folder or volume's previous owner expires or is deleted. Each server has one default owner; you can specify the owner.

default printer The printer that is used if you choose the **Print** command without first specifying which printer you want to use with an application. You can have only one default printer; it should be the printer you use most often.

default profile *See* system default profile; user default profile.

default user Every user profile begins as a copy of default user, a default user profile stored on each computer running Windows NT Workstation or Windows NT Server.

default zone The zone to which all Macintosh clients on the network are assigned by default.

dependency A situation in which one action must take place before another can happen. For example, if action A does not occur, then action D cannot occur. Some Windows NT drivers have dependencies on other drivers or groups of drivers. For example, driver A will not load unless some driver from the G group loads first. *See also* circular dependency.

dependent service A service that requires support of another service. For example, the Alerter service is dependent on the Messenger service. *See also* Alerter service; Messenger service.

DES *See* Data Encryption Standard.

descendent key All of the subkeys that appear when a key in the registry is expanded. A descendent key is the same thing as a subkey. *See also* key; registry; subkey.

desired zone The zone in which Services for Macintosh appears on the network. *See also* default zone.

desktop The background of your screen, on which windows, icons, and dialog boxes appear.

desktop pattern A design that appears across your desktop. You can create your own pattern or select a pattern provided by Windows NT.

destination directory The directory to which you intend to copy or move one or more files.

destination document The document into which a package or a linked or embedded object is being inserted. For an embedded object, this is sometimes also called the container document. *See also* embedded object; linked object; package.

device Any piece of equipment that can be attached to a network—for example, a computer, a printer, or any other peripheral equipment.

device contention The way Windows NT allocates access to peripheral devices, such as modems or printers, when more than one application is trying to use the same device.

device driver A program that enables a specific piece of hardware (device) to communicate with Windows NT. Although a device may be installed on your system, Windows NT cannot recognize the device until you have installed and configured the appropriate driver. If a device is listed in the Hardware Compatibility List, a driver is usually included with Windows NT. Drivers are installed when you run the Setup program (for a manufacturer's supplied driver) or by using Devices in Control Panel. *See also* Hardware Compatibility List (HCL).

DHCP *See* Dynamic Host Configuration Protocol.

DHCP Relay Agent The component responsible for relaying DHCP and BOOTP broadcast messages between a DHCP server and a client across an IP router. *See also* Bootstrap protocol (BOOTP); Dynamic Host Configuration Protocol (DHCP).

dialog box A window that is displayed to request or supply information. Many dialog boxes have options you must select before Windows NT can carry out a command.

dial-up line A standard dial-up connection such as telephone and ISDN lines.

dial-up networking The client version of Windows NT Remote Access Service (RAS), enabling users to connect to remote networks.

directory Part of a structure for organizing your files on a disk, a directory (also called a folder) is represented by the folder icon in Windows NT, Windows 95, and on Macintosh computers. A directory can contain files and other directories, called subdirectories or folders within folders.

With Services for Macintosh, directories on the computer running Windows NT Server appear to Macintosh users as volumes and folders if they are designated as Macintosh accessible.

See also directory tree; folder.

directory database A database of security information such as user account names and passwords, and the security policy settings. For Windows NT Workstation, the directory database is managed by using User Manager. For a Windows NT Server domain, it is managed by using User Manager for Domains. (Other Windows NT documents may refer to the directory database as the "Security Accounts Manager (SAM) database.") *See also* Windows NT Server Directory Services.

directory replication The copying of a master set of directories from a server (called an export server) to specified servers or workstations (called import computers) in the same or other domains. Replication simplifies the task of maintaining identical sets of directories and files on multiple computers, because only a single master copy of the data must be maintained. Files are replicated when they are added to an exported directory and every time a change is saved to the file. *See also* Directory Replicator service.

Directory Replicator service Replicates directories, and the files in those directories, between computers. *See also* directory replication.

Directory Service Manager for NetWare (DSMN) A component of Windows NT Server. Enables network administrators to add NetWare servers to Windows NT Server domains and to manage a single set of user and group accounts that are valid at multiple servers running either Windows NT Server or NetWare.

directory services *See* Windows NT Server Directory Services.

directory tree A graphical display of a disk's directory hierarchy. The directories and folders on the disk are shown as a branching structure. The top-level directory is the root directory.

disabled user account A user account that does not permit logons. The account appears in the user account list of the User Manager or User Manager for Domains window and can be re-enabled at any time. *See also* user account.

discovery A process by which the Windows NT Net Logon service attempts to locate a domain controller running Windows NT Server in the trusted domain. Once a domain controller has been discovered, it is used for subsequent user account authentication.

discretionary access control Allows the network administrator to allow some users to connect to a resource or perform an action while preventing other users from doing so. *See also* discretionary access control list; system access control list (SACL).

discretionary access control list (DACL) The discretionary ACL is controlled by the owner of an object and specifies the access particular users or groups can have to that object. *See also* system access control list (SACL).

disjoint networks Networks that are not connected to each other.

disk configuration information The Windows NT registry includes the following information on the configuration of your disk(s): assigned drive letters, stripe sets, mirror sets, volume sets, and stripe sets with parity. Disk configuration can be changed by using Disk Administrator. If you choose to create an Emergency Repair Disk, disk configuration information will be stored there, as well as in the registry.

display filter Functions like a database query, allowing you to single out specific types of information. Because a display filter operates on data that has already been captured, it does not affect the contents of the Network Monitor capture buffer. *See also* capture buffer.

display password Required to be able to open previously saved capture (.cap) files in Network Monitor.

Distributed Component Object Model (DCOM) Use the DCOM Configuration tool to integrate client/server applications across multiple computers. DCOM can also be used to integrate robust Web browser applications. *See also* DCOM Configuration tool.

distributed server system In Windows NT, a system in which individual departments or workgroups set up and maintain their own remote access domains.

DLL *See* dynamic-link library.

DNS *See* Domain Name System.

DNS name servers In the DNS client/server model, the servers containing information about a portion of the DNS database, which makes computer names available to client resolvers querying for name resolution across the Internet. *See also* Domain Name System (DNS).

DNS service The service that provides domain name resolution. *See also* DNS name servers.

document A self-contained file created with an application and, if saved on disk, given a unique file name by which it can be retrieved. A document can be a text file, a spreadsheet, or an image file, for example.

document file A file that is associated with an application. When you open a document file, the application starts and loads the file. *See also* associate.

Document file icon Represents a file that is associated with an application. When you double-click a document file icon, the application starts and loads the file. *See also* associate.

document icon Located at the left of a document window title bar, the document icon represents the open document. Clicking the document icon opens the window menu. Also known as the control menu box.

domain In Windows NT, a collection of computers, defined by the administrator of a Windows NT Server network, that share a common directory database. A domain provides access to the centralized user accounts and group accounts maintained by the domain administrator. Each domain has a unique name. *See also* directory database; user account; workgroup.

domain controller In a Windows NT Server domain, refers to the computer running Windows NT Server that manages all aspects of user-domain interactions, and uses information in the directory database to authenticate users logging on to domain accounts. One shared directory database is used to store security and user account information for the entire domain. A domain has one primary domain controller (PDC) and one or more backup domain controllers (BDCs). *See also* backup domain controller (BDC); directory database; member server; primary domain controller (PDC).

domain database *See* directory database.

domain model A grouping of one or more domains with administration and communication links between them that are arranged for the purpose of user and resource management.

domain name Part of the Domain Name System (DNS) naming structure, a domain name is the name by which a domain is known to the network. Domain names consist of a sequence of labels separated by periods. *See also* Domain Name System (DNS); fully qualified domain name (FQDN).

domain name space The database structure used by the Domain Name System (DNS). *See also* Domain Name System (DNS).

Domain Name System (DNS) Sometimes referred to as the BIND service in BSD UNIX, DNS offers a static, hierarchical name service for TCP/IP hosts. The network administrator configures the DNS with a list of host names and IP addresses, allowing users of workstations configured to query the DNS to specify remote systems by host names rather than IP addresses. For example, a workstation configured to use DNS name resolution could use the command **ping remotehost** rather than **ping 172.16.16.235** if the mapping for the system named **remotehost** was contained in the DNS database. DNS domains should not be confused with Windows NT networking domains. *See also* IP address; ping.

domain synchronization *See* synchronize.

dots per inch (DPI) The standard used to measure print device resolution. The greater the DPI, the better the resolution.

double-click To rapidly press and release a mouse button twice without moving the mouse. Double-clicking carries out an action, such as starting an application.

down level A term that refers to earlier operating systems, such as Windows for Workgroups or LAN Manager, that can still interoperate with Windows NT Workstation or Windows NT Server.

downloaded fonts Fonts that you send to your printer either before or during the printing of your documents. When you send a font to your printer, it is stored in printer memory until it is needed for printing. *See also* font; font types.

DPI *See* dots per inch.

drag To move an item on the screen by selecting the item and then pressing and holding down the mouse button while moving the mouse. For example, you can move a window to another location on the screen by dragging its title bar.

drive icon An icon in the All Folders column in Windows NT Explorer or the Names Column in My Computer that represents a disk drive on your system. Different icons depict floppy disk drives, hard disk drives, network drives, RAM drives, and CD-ROM drives.

driver *See* device driver.

drop folder In the Macintosh environment this refers to a folder for which you have the Make Changes permission but not the See Files or See Folders permission. You can copy files into a drop folder, but you cannot see what files and subfolders the drop folder contains.

DSDM Acronym for DDE share database manager. *See also* dynamic data exchange (DDE); Network DDE DSDM service.

DSMN *See* Directory Service Manager for NetWare.

DSN *See* Data Source Name.

DSR Acronym for Data Set Ready signal, used in serial communications. A DSR is sent by a modem to the computer to which it is attached to indicate that it is ready to operate. DSRs are hardware signals sent over line 6 in RS-232-C connections.

DTE *See* Data Terminal Equipment.

dual boot A computer that can boot two different operating systems. *See also* multiple boot.

DWORD A data type composed of hexadecimal data with a maximum allotted space of 4 bytes.

dynamic assignment The automatic assignment of TCP/IP properties in a changing network.

dynamic data exchange (DDE) A form of interprocess communication (IPC) implemented in the Microsoft Windows family of operating systems. Two or more programs that support dynamic data exchange (DDE) can exchange information and commands. *See also* interprocess communication (IPC).

Dynamic Host Configuration Protocol (DHCP) A protocol that offers dynamic configuration of IP addresses and related information. DHCP provides safe, reliable, and simple TCP/IP network configuration, prevents address conflicts, and helps conserve the use of IP addresses through centralized management of address allocation. *See also* IP address.

dynamic-link library (DLL) An operating system feature that allows executable routines (generally serving a specific function or set of functions) to be stored separately as files with .dll extensions and to be loaded only when needed by the program that calls them.

dynamic routing Dynamic routing automatically updates the routing tables, reducing administrative overhead (but increasing traffic in large networks). *See also* routing table.

dynamic Web pages Web pages that are derived or assembled only when the client requests them. Dynamic pages are used to deliver very current information, to deliver responses to forms and queries, and to provide a customized page. They are often associated with databases, such as SQL databases. *See also* static Web pages.

E

EISA *See* Extended Industry Standard Architecture.

embedded object Presents information, created in another application, which has been pasted inside your document. Information in the embedded object does not exist in another file outside your document.

EMS *See* Expanded Memory Specification.

encapsulated PostScript (EPS) file A file that prints at the highest possible resolution for your printer. An EPS file may print faster than other graphical representations. Some Windows NT and non-Windows NT graphical applications can import EPS files. *See also* font types; PostScript printer; print processor.

encryption The process of making information indecipherable to protect it from unauthorized viewing or use, especially during transmission or when it is stored on a transportable magnetic medium.

enterprise server Refers to the server to which multiple primary domain controllers (PDCs) in a large organization will replicate. *See also* primary domain controller (PDC).

environment variable A string consisting of environment information, such as a drive, path, or file name, associated with a symbolic name that can be used by Windows NT. To define environment variables, use System in Control Panel or use the **Set** command from the Windows NT command prompt.

EPS *See* encapsulated PostScript file.

error logging The process by which errors that cannot readily be corrected by the majority of end users are written to a file instead of being displayed on the screen. System administrators, support technicians, and users can use this log file to monitor the condition of the hardware in a computer running Windows NT to tune the configuration of the computer for better performance, and to debug problems as they occur.

event Any significant occurrence in the system or an application that requires users to be notified, or an entry to be added to a log.

Event Log service Records events in the system, security, and application logs. The Event Log service is located in Event Viewer.

exception A synchronous error condition resulting from the execution of a particular computer instruction. Exceptions can be either hardware-detected errors, such as division by zero, or software-detected errors, such as a guard-page violation.

Executive The Executive is the part of the Windows NT operating system that runs in kernel mode. *Kernel mode* is a privileged processor mode in which a thread has access to system memory and to hardware. (In contrast, *user mode* is a nonprivileged processor mode in which a thread can only access system resources by calling system services.) The Windows NT Executive provides process structure, thread scheduling, interprocess communication, memory management, object management, object security, interrupt processing, I/O capabilities, and networking. *See also* Hardware Abstraction Layer (HAL); Kernel.

Executive messages Two types of character-mode messages occur when the Windows NT Kernel detects an inconsistent condition from which it cannot recover: STOP messages and hardware-malfunction messages.

Character-mode STOP messages are always displayed on a full character-mode screen rather than in a Windows-mode message box. They are also uniquely identified by a hexadecimal number and a symbolic string.

Character-mode hardware-malfunction messages are caused by a hardware condition detected by the processor.

(continued)

Executive messages The Executive displays a Windows-mode STATUS message box when it detects conditions within a process (generally, an application) that you should know about.

expand To show hidden directory levels in the directory tree. With My Computer or Windows NT Explorer, directories that can expand have plus-sign icons which you click to expand.

expanded memory A type of memory, up to 8 megabytes, that can be added to an 8086 or 8088 computer, or to an 80286, 80386, 80486, or Pentium computer. The use of expanded memory is defined by the Expanded Memory Specification (EMS). Note: Windows NT requires an 80486 or higher computer.

Expanded Memory Specification (EMS) Describes a technique for adding memory to IBM PC systems. EMS bypasses the limits on the maximum amount of usable memory in a computer system by supporting memory boards containing a number of 16K banks of RAM that can be enabled or disabled by software. *See also* memory.

Explorer *See* Windows NT Explorer.

export path In directory replication, a path from which subdirectories, and the files in those subdirectories, are automatically exported from an export server. *See also* directory replication.

export server In directory replication, a server from which a master set of directories is exported to specified servers or workstations (called import computers) in the same or other domains. *See also* directory replication.

Extended Industry Standard Architecture (EISA) A 32-bit bus standard introduced in 1988 by a consortium of nine computer industry companies. EISA maintains compatibility with the earlier Industry Standard Architecture (ISA) but provides for additional features.

extended memory Memory beyond one megabyte in 80286, 80386, 80486, and Pentium computers. Note: Windows NT requires an 80486 or higher computer.

extended partition Created from free space on a hard disk, an extended partition can be subpartitioned into zero or more logical drives. Only one of the four partitions allowed per physical disk can be an extended partition, and no primary partition needs to be present to create an extended partition. *See also* free space; logical drive; primary partition.

extensible counters Performance Monitor counters that are not installed with Windows NT. Extensible counters typically are installed independently. Extensible counters should be monitored to make certain that they are working properly.

extension A file name extension usually indicates the type of file or directory, or the type of application associated with a file. In MS-DOS, this includes a period and up to three characters at the end of a file name. Windows NT supports long file names, up to the file name limit of 255 characters.

extension-type association The association of an MS-DOS file name extension with a Macintosh file type and file creator. Extension-type associations allow users of the PC and Macintosh versions of the same application to share the same data files on the server. Services for Macintosh has many predefined extension-type associations. *See also* name mapping.

external command A command that is stored in its own file and loaded from disk when you use the command.

F

family set A collection of related tapes containing several backup sets. *See also* backup set.

FAT *See* file allocation table.

fault tolerance Ensures data integrity when hardware failures occur. In Windows NT, fault tolerance is provided by the Ftdisk.sys driver. In Disk Administrator, fault tolerance is provided using mirror sets, stripe sets with parity, and volume sets. *See also* mirror set; stripe sets with parity; volume set.

FCB *See* file control block.

Fiber Distributed Data Interface (FDDI) A type of network media designed to be used with fiber-optic cabling. *See also* LocalTalk; Token Ring.

file A collection of information that has been given a name and is stored on a disk. This information can be a document or an application.

file allocation table (FAT) A table or list maintained by some operating systems to keep track of the status of various segments of disk space used for file storage. Also referred to as the FAT file system.

File and Print Services for NetWare (FPNW) A Windows NT Server component that enables a computer running Windows NT Server to provide file and print services directly to NetWare-compatible client computers.

file control block (FCB) A small block of memory temporarily assigned by a computer's operating system to hold information about a file that has been opened for use. An FCB typically contains such information as the file's identification, its location on disk, and a pointer that marks the user's current (or last) position in the file.

file creator A four-character sequence that tells the Macintosh Finder the name of the application that created a file. With Services for Macintosh, you can create extension-type associations that map PC file name extensions with Macintosh file creators and file types. These associations allow both PC and Macintosh users to share the same data files on the server. *See also* extension-type association.

file fork One of two subfiles of a Macintosh file. When Macintosh files are stored on a computer running Windows NT Server, each fork is stored as a separate file. Each fork can be independently opened by a Macintosh user.

file name The name of a file. MS-DOS supports the 8.3 naming convention of up to eight characters followed by a period and a three-character extension. Windows NT supports the FAT and NTFS file systems with file names up to 255 characters. Because MS-DOS cannot recognize long file names, Windows NT Server automatically translates long names of files and folders to 8.3 names for MS-DOS users. *See also* long name; name mapping; short name.

file name extension The characters that follow the period in a file name, following the FAT naming conventions. Filename extensions can have as many as three characters and are often used to identify the type of file and the application used to create the file (for example, spreadsheet files created by Microsoft Excel have the extension .xls). With Services for Macintosh, you can create extension-type associations that map PC file name extensions with Macintosh file creators and types.

File Replication service A Windows NT service that allows specified file(s) to be replicated to remote systems, ensuring that copies on each system are kept in synchronization. The system that maintains the master copy is called the exporter, and the systems that receive updates are known as importers.

File Server for Macintosh service A Services for Macintosh service that enables Macintosh clients and PC clients to share files. Also called MacFile.

file sharing The ability for a computer running Windows NT to share parts (or all) of its local file system(s) with remote computers. An administrator creates share points by using the file sharing command in My Computer or Windows NT Explorer or by using the **net share** command from the command prompt.

file system In an operating system, the overall structure in which files are named, stored, and organized. NTFS and FAT are types of file systems.

File Transfer Protocol (FTP) A service supporting file transfers between local and remote systems that support this protocol. FTP supports several commands that allow bidirectional transfer of binary and ASCII files between systems. The FTP Server service is part of the Internet Information Server. The FTP client is installed with TCP/IP connectivity utilities.

file type In the Macintosh environment, this refers to a four-character sequence that identifies the type of a Macintosh file. The file type and file creator are used by the Macintosh Finder to determine the appropriate desktop icon for that file.

find tab Displays the words you can use to search for related topics. Use this tab to look for topics related to a particular word. It is located in the Help button bar near the top of the Help window.

firewall A system or combination of systems that enforces a boundary between two or more networks and keeps intruders out of private networks. Firewalls serve as virtual barriers to passing packets from one network to another.

flat name space A naming system in which computer names are created from a short sequence of characters without any additional structure superimposed.

floppy disk A disk that can be inserted in and removed from a disk drive. Floppies are most commonly available in a 3.5- or 5.25-inch format.

flow control An exchange of signals, over specific wires, in which each device signals its readiness to send or receive data.

folder A grouping of files or other folders, graphically represented by a folder icon, in both the Windows NT and Macintosh environments. A folder is analogous to a PC's file system directory, and many folders are, in fact, directories. A folder may contain other folders as well as file objects. *See also* directory.

font A graphic design applied to a collection of numbers, symbols, and characters. A font describes a certain typeface along with other qualities such as size, spacing, and pitch. *See also* font set; font types.

font set A collection of font sizes for one font, customized for a particular display and printer. Font sets determine what text looks like on the screen and when printed. *See also* font.

font types:

device fonts Reside in the hardware of your print device. They can be built into the print device itself or can be provided by a font cartridge or font card.

downloadable soft fonts Fonts that are stored on disk and downloaded as needed to the print device.

plotter fonts A font created by a series of dots connected by lines. Plotter fonts can be scaled to any size and are most often printed on plotters. Some dot-matrix printers also support plotter fonts.

PostScript fonts Fonts that are defined in terms of the PostScript page-description language rules from Adobe Systems. When a document displayed in a screen font is sent to a PostScript printer, the printer uses the PostScript version if the font exists. If the font doesn't exist but a version is installed on the computer, that font is downloaded. If there is no PostScript font installed in either the printer or the computer, the bitmapped font is translated into PostScript and the printer prints text using the bitmapped font.

raster fonts Fonts that are stored as bitmaps. If a print device does not support raster fonts, it will not print them. Raster fonts cannot be scaled or rotated.

screen fonts Windows NT fonts that can be translated for output to the print device. Most screen fonts (including TrueType fonts) can be printed as well.

TrueType fonts Device-independent fonts that can be reproduced on all print devices. TrueType fonts are stored as outlines and can be scaled and rotated.

vector fonts Fonts that are useful on devices such as pen plotters that cannot reproduce bitmaps. They can be scaled to any size or aspect ratio. (*See also* plotter fonts, earlier in this entry.)

fork *See* data fork; file fork; resource fork.

FPNW *See* File and Print Services for NetWare.

FQDN *See* fully qualified domain name.

frame In synchronous communication, a package of information transmitted as a single unit from one device to another. *See also* capture.

Frame Relay A synchronous High-level Data Link Control (HDLC) protocol–based network that sends data in HDLC packets. *See also* High-level Data Link Control (HDLC).

framing rules Are established between a remote computer and the server, allowing continued communication (frame transfer) to occur. *See also* frame.

free space Free space is an unused and unformatted portion of a hard disk that can be partitioned or subpartitioned. Free space within an extended partition is available for the creation of logical drives. Free space that is not within an extended partition is available for the creation of a partition, with a maximum of four partitions allowed per disk. *See also* extended partition; logical drive; primary partition.

FTP *See* File Transfer Protocol.

full name A user's complete name, usually consisting of the last name, first name, and middle initial. The full name is information that can be maintained by User Manager and User Manager for Domains as part of the information identifying and defining a user account. *See also* user account.

full-screen application A non–Windows NT application that is displayed in the entire screen, rather than a window, when running in the Windows NT environment.

full synchronization Occurs when a copy of the entire database directory is sent to a backup domain controller (BDC). Full synchronization is performed automatically when changes have been deleted from the change log before replication takes place, and when a new BDC is added to a domain. *See also* backup domain controller (BDC); directory database.

fully qualified domain name (FQDN) Part of the TCP/IP naming convention known as the Domain Name System, DNS computer names consist of two parts: host names with their domain names appended to them. For example, a host with host name **corp001** and DNS domain name **trey-research.com** has an FQDN of **corp001.trey-research.com**. (DNS domains should not be confused with Windows NT networking domains.) *See also* Domain Name System (DNS).

G

gateway Describes a system connected to multiple physical TCP/IP networks, capable of routing or delivering IP packets between them. A gateway translates between different transport protocols or data formats (for example IPX and IP) and is generally added to a network primarily for its translation ability. Also referred to as an IP router. *See also* IP address; IP router.

Gateway Service for NetWare Included with Windows NT Server, enables a computer running Windows NT Server to connect to NetWare servers. Creating a gateway enables computers running only Microsoft client software to access NetWare resources through the gateway. *See also* gateway.

General MIDI A MIDI specification controlled by the MIDI Manufacturers Association (MMA). The specification provides guidelines that authors of MIDI files can use to create files that sound the same across a variety of different synthesizers.

global account For Windows NT Server, a normal user account in a user's domain. Most user accounts are global accounts. If there are multiple domains in the network, it is best if each user in the network has only one user account in only one domain, and each user's access to other domains is accomplished through the establishment of domain trust relationships. *See also* local account; trust relationship.

global group For Windows NT Server, a group that can be used in its own domain, member servers and workstations of the domain, and trusting domains. In all those places it can be granted rights and permissions and can become a member of local groups. However, it can only contain user accounts from its own domain. Global groups provide a way to create handy sets of users from inside the domain, available for use both in and out of the domain.

Global groups cannot be created or maintained on computers running Windows NT Workstation. However, for Windows NT Workstation computers that participate in a domain, domain global groups can be granted rights and permissions at those workstations, and can become members of local groups at those workstations. *See also* domain; group; local group; trust relationship.

globally unique identifier (GUID) *See* universally unique identifier (UUID).

Gopher A hierarchical system for finding and retrieving information from the Internet or an intranet. Similar to FTP, Gopher uses a menu system and enables links to other servers.

group In User Manager or User Manager for Domains, an account containing other accounts that are called members. The permissions and rights granted to a group are also provided to its members, making groups a convenient way to grant common capabilities to collections of user accounts. For Windows NT Workstation, groups are managed with User Manager. For Windows NT Server, groups are managed with User Manager for Domains. *See also* built-in groups; global group; local group; user account.

group account A collection of user accounts. Giving a user account membership in a group gives that user all of the rights and permissions granted to the group. *See also* local account; user account.

group category One of three categories of users to which you can assign Macintosh permissions for a folder. The permissions assigned to the group category are available to the group associated with the folder.

group memberships The groups to which a user account belongs. Permissions and rights granted to a group are also provided to its members. In most cases, the actions a user can perform in Windows NT are determined by the group memberships of the user account the user is logged on to. *See also* group.

group name A unique name identifying a local group or a global group to Windows NT. A group's name cannot be identical to any other group name or user name of its own domain or computer. *See also* global group; local group.

guest Users of Services for Macintosh who do not have a user account or who do not provide a password are logged on as a guest, using a user account with guest privileges. When a Macintosh user assigns permissions to everyone, those permissions are given to the group's guests and users.

guest account On computers running Windows NT Workstation or Windows NT Server, a built-in account used for logons by people who do not have a user account on the computer or domain or in any of the domains trusted by the computer's domain.

Guest privilege One of three privilege levels that you can assign to a Windows NT user account. The guest account used for Macintosh guest logons must have the Guest privilege. *See also* Administrator privilege; user account; User privilege.

GUID Acronym for globally unique identifier. *See* universally unique identifier (UUID).

H

HAL *See* Hardware Abstraction Layer.

handle A handle is a value used to uniquely identify a resource so that a program can access it.

In the registry, each of the first-level key names begins with HKEY_ to indicate to software developers that this is a handle that can be read by a program.

handshaking Refers to flow control in serial communication, which defines a method for the print device to tell Windows NT that its buffer is full. *See also* buffer.

Hardware Abstraction Layer (HAL) A thin layer of software provided by the hardware manufacturer that hides, or abstracts, hardware differences from higher layers of the operating system.

Through the filter provided by the HAL, different types of hardware all look alike to the rest of the operating system. This allows Windows NT to be portable from one hardware platform to another. The HAL also provides routines that allow a single device driver to support the same device on all platforms.

The HAL works closely with the Kernel.

See also Executive; Kernel.

Hardware Compatibility List (HCL) The Windows NT Hardware Compatibility List lists the devices supported by Windows NT. The latest version of the HCL can be downloaded from the Microsoft Web page (microsoft.com) on the Internet.

HCL *See* Hardware Compatibility List.

HDLC *See* High-level Data Link Control.

heterogeneous environment An internetwork with servers and workstations running different operating systems, such as Windows NT, Macintosh, or Novell NetWare, using a mix of different transport protocols.

hexadecimal A base-16 number system that consists of the digits 0 through 9 and the uppercase and lowercase letters A (equivalent to decimal 10) through F (equivalent to decimal 15).

High-level Data Link Control (HDLC) A protocol that governs information transfer. Under the HDLC protocol, messages are transmitted in units called frames, each of which can contain a variable amount of data but which must be organized in a particular way.

high memory area (HMA) The first 64 KB of extended memory (often referred to as HMA). *See also* memory.

High-Performance File System (HPFS) The file system designed for the OS/2 version 1.2 operating system.

hive A section of the registry that appears as a file on your hard disk. The registry subtree is divided into hives (named for their resemblance to the cellular structure of a beehive). A hive is a discrete body of keys, subkeys, and values that is rooted at the top of the registry hierarchy. A hive is backed by a single file and a .log file, which are in the *systemroot*\System32\Config or the *systemroot*\Profiles*user_name* folder. By default, most hive files (Default, SAM, Security, and System) are stored in the *systemroot*\System32\Config folder.

The *systemroot*\Profiles folder contains the user profile for each user of the computer. Because a hive is a file, it can be moved from one system to another but can only be edited by using a Registry Editor.

HMA *See* high memory area.

h-node A NetBIOS implementation that uses the p-node protocol first, then the b-node protocol if the name service is unavailable. For registration, it uses the b-node protocol, then the p-node protocol. *See also* NetBIOS; p-node; registration.

home directory A directory that is accessible to the user and contains files and programs for that user. A home directory can be assigned to an individual user or can be shared by many users.

home page The initial page of information for a collection of pages. The starting point for a Web site or section of a Web site is often referred to as the home page. Individuals also post pages that are called home pages.

hop Refers to the next router. In IP routing, packets are always forwarded one router at a time. Packets often hop from router to router before reaching their destination. *See also* IP address; packet; router.

host Any device that is attached to the network and uses TCP/IP. *See also* Transmission Control Protocol/Internet Protocol (TCP/IP).

host group A set of zero or more hosts identified by a single IP destination address. *See also* host; IP address.

host ID The portion of the IP address that identifies a computer within a particular network ID. *See also* IP address; network ID.

host name The name of a device on a network. For a device on a Windows or Windows NT network, this can be the same as the computer name, but it may not be. The host name must be in the host table or be known by a DNS server for that host to be found by another computer attempting to communicate with it. *See also* Domain Name System (DNS); host table.

HOSTS file A local text file in the same format as the 4.3 Berkeley Software Distribution (BSD) UNIX \etc\hosts file. This file maps host names to IP addresses. In Windows NT, this file is stored in the *systemroot*\System32\Drivers\Etc directory. *See also* IP address.

host table The HOSTS and LMHOSTS files, which contain mappings of known IP addresses mapped to host names.

HPFS *See* High-Performance File System.

HTML *See* Hypertext Markup Language.

HTTP *See* Hypertext Transport Protocol.

HTTP keep-alives An optimizing feature of the HTTP service. HTTP keep-alives maintain a connection even after the initial connection request is completed. This keeps the connection active and available for subsequent requests. HTTP keep-alives were implemented to avoid the substantial cost of establishing and terminating connections. Both the client and the server must support keep-alives. Keep-alives are supported by Internet Information Server version 1.0 and later and by Microsoft Internet Explorer version 2.0 and later. *See also* TCP/IP keep-alives.

hue The position of a color along the color spectrum. For example, green is between yellow and blue. To set this attribute, use Desktop in Control Panel.

hyperlink A way of jumping to another place on the Internet. Hyperlinks usually appear in a different format from regular text. You initiate the jump by clicking the link.

Hypertext Markup Language (HTML) A simple markup language used to create hypertext documents that are portable from one platform to another. HTML files are simple ASCII text files with codes embedded (indicated by markup tags) to indicate formatting and hypertext links. HTML is used for formatting documents on the World Wide Web.

Hypertext Transport Protocol (HTTP) The underlying protocol by which WWW clients and servers communicate. HTTP is an application-level protocol for distributed, collaborative, hypermedia information systems. It is a generic, stateless, object-oriented protocol. A feature of HTTP is the typing and negotiation of data representation, allowing systems to be built independently of the data being transferred.

I

ICMP *See* Internet Control Message Protocol.

icon A graphical representation of an element in Windows NT, such as a disk drive, directory, group, application, or document. Click the icon to enlarge an application icon to a window when you want to use the application. Within applications, there are also toolbar icons for commands such as cut, copy, and paste.

IDC *See* Internet Database Connector.

IDE *See* integrated device electronics.

IETF *See* Internet Engineering Task Force.

IGMP *See* Internet Group Management Protocol.

IIS *See* Internet Information Server.

IIS object cache An area of virtual memory that the IIS process uses to store frequently used objects, such as open file handles and directory listings. The IIS object cache is part of the working set of the IIS process, Inetinfo.exe, and it can be paged to disk.

IMC *See* Internet Mail Connector.

impersonation Impersonation occurs when Windows NT Server allows one process to take on the security attributes of another.

import To create a package by inserting an existing file into Object Packager. When you import a file, the icon of the application you used to create the file appears in the Appearance window, and the name of the file appears in the Contents window. *See also* package.

import computers In directory replication, the servers or workstations that receive copies of the master set of directories from an export server. *See also* directory replication; export server.

import path In directory replication, the path to which imported subdirectories, and the files in those subdirectories, will be stored on an import computer. *See also* directory replication; import computers.

Inetinfo A process containing the FTP, Gopher, and HTTP services. This process is about 400 KB in size. In addition to the FTP, Gopher, and HTTP services, this process contains the shared thread pool, cache, logging, and SNMP services of Internet Information Server.

input/output activity (I/O) Read or write actions that your computer performs. Your computer performs a "read" when you type information on your keyboard or you select and choose items by using your mouse. Also, when you open a file, your computer reads the disk on which the file is located to find and open it.

Your computer performs a "write" whenever it stores, sends, prints, or displays information. For example, your computer performs a write when it stores information on a disk, displays information on your screen, or sends information through a modem or to a printer. *See also* I/O addresses.

input/output control (IOCTL) An IOCTL command enables a program to communicate directly with a device driver. This is done, for example, by sending a string of control information recognized by the driver. None of the information passed from the program to the device driver is sent to the device itself (in other words, the control string sent to a printer driver is not displayed on the printer).

insertion point The place where text will be inserted when you type. The insertion point usually appears as a flashing vertical bar in an application's window or in a dialog box.

integrated device electronics (IDE)
A type of disk-drive interface in which the controller electronics reside on the drive itself, eliminating the need for a separate adapter card.

Integrated Services Digital Network (ISDN) A type of telephone line used to enhance WAN speeds, ISDN lines can transmit at speeds of 64 or 128 kilobits per second, as opposed to standard telephone lines, which typically transmit at only 9600 bits per second (bps). An ISDN line must be installed by the telephone company at both the server site and the remote site. *See also* bits per second (bps).

interactive logon A network logon from a computer keyboard, when the user types information in the **Logon Information** dialog box displayed by the computer's operating system. *See also* remote logon.

intermediary devices Microsoft RAS supports various kinds of intermediary devices (security hosts and switches) between the remote access client and the remote access server. These devices include a modem-pool switch or security host. *See also* Remote Access Service (RAS).

internal command Commands that are stored in the file Cmd.exe and that reside in memory at all times.

internet In Windows NT, a collection of two or more private networks, or private inter-enterprise TCP/IP networks.

In Macintosh terminology, refers to two or more physical networks connected by routers, which maintain a map of the physical networks on the internet and forward data received from one physical network to other physical networks. Network users in an internet can share information and network devices. You can use an internet with Services for Macintosh by connecting two or more AppleTalk networks to a computer running Windows NT Server.

Internet The global network of networks. *See also* World Wide Web (WWW).

Internet Assigned Numbers Authority (IANA) The central coordinator for the assignment of unique parameter values for Internet protocols. IANA is chartered by the Internet Society (ISOC) and the Federal Network Council (FNC) to act as the clearinghouse to assign and coordinate the use of numerous Internet protocol parameters. Contact IANA at http://www.iana.org/iana/.

Internet Assistant Several Internet Assistant add-on software components are available for Microsoft Office products. Each Internet Assistant adds functionality that is relevant to creating content for the Internet. For example, Internet Assistant for Microsoft Word enables Word to create HTML documents from within Microsoft Word.

Internet Control Message Protocol (ICMP) A maintenance protocol in the TCP/IP suite, required in every TCP/IP implementation, that allows two nodes on an IP network to share IP status and error information. ICMP is used by the ping utility to determine the readability of a remote system. *See also* ping; Transmission Control Protocol/Internet Protocol (TCP/IP).

Internet Database Connector (IDC) Provides access to databases for Internet Information Server by using ODBC. The Internet Database Connector is contained in Httpodbc.dll, which is an Internet Server API DLL.

Internet Engineering Task Force (IETF) A consortium that introduces procedures for new technology on the Internet. IETF specifications are released in documents called Requests for Comments (RFCs). *See also* Requests for Comments (RFCs).

Internet Group Management Protocol (IGMP) A protocol used by workgroup software products and supported by Microsoft TCP/IP.

Internet group name A name known by a DNS server that includes a list of the specific addresses of systems that have registered the name. *See also* Domain Name System (DNS).

Internet Information Server (IIS) A network file and application server that supports multiple protocols. Primarily, Internet Information Server transmits information in Hypertext Markup Language (HTML) pages by using the Hypertext Transport Protocol (HTTP).

Internet Mail Connector (IMC) The Internet Mail Connector is a component of Microsoft Exchange Server that runs as a Windows NT Server service. You can use the Internet Mail Connector to exchange information with other systems that use the Simple Mail Transfer Protocol (SMTP).

Internet Network Information Center (InterNIC) The coordinator for DNS registration. To register domain names and obtain IP addresses, contact InterNIC at http://internic.net.

Internet Protocol (IP) The messenger protocol of TCP/IP, responsible for addressing and sending TCP packets over the network. IP provides a best-effort, connectionless delivery system that does not guarantee that packets arrive at their destination or that they are received in the sequence in which they were sent. *See also* packet; Transmission Control Protocol (TCP); Transmission Control Protocol/Internet Protocol (TCP/IP).

Internet Protocol Control Protocol (IPCP) Specified by RFC 1332. Responsible for configuring, enabling, and disabling the IP protocol modules on both ends of the point-to-point (PPP) link. *See also* Point-to-Point Protocol (PPP); Requests for Comments (RFCs).

Internet Relay Chat (IRC) A protocol that enables two or more people, each in remote locations, who are connected to an IRC server to hold real-time conversations. IRC is defined in RFC 1459.

Internet router A device that connects networks and directs network information to other networks, usually choosing the most efficient route through other routers. *See also* router.

Internet Server Application Programming Interface (ISAPI) An API for developing extensions to the Microsoft Internet Information Server and other HTTP servers that support ISAPI. *See also* application programming interface (API).

Internet service provider (ISP) A company or educational institution that enables remote users to access the Internet by providing dial-up connections or installing leased lines.

internetworks Networks that connect local area networks (LANs) together.

interprocess communication (IPC) The ability, provided by a multitasking operating system, of one task or process to exchange data with another. Common IPC methods include pipes, semaphores, shared memory, queues, signals, and mailboxes. *See also* named pipe; queue.

interrupt An asynchronous operating system condition that disrupts normal execution and transfers control to an interrupt handler. Interrupts can be issued by both software and hardware devices requiring service from the processor. When software issues an interrupt, it calls an interrupt service routine (ISR). When hardware issues an interrupt, it signals an interrupt request (IRQ) line.

interrupt moderation A Windows NT performance optimizing feature that diverts interrupts from the network adapters when the rate of interrupts is very high. The system accumulates the interrupts in a buffer for later processing. Standard interrupt processing is resumed when the interrupt rate returns to normal.

interrupt request line (IRQ) A hardware line over which devices can send signals to get the attention of the processor when the device is ready to accept or send information. Typically, each device connected to the computer uses a separate IRQ.

intranet A TCP/IP network that uses Internet technology. May be connected to the Internet. *See also* Internet; Transmission Control Protocol/Internet Protocol (TCP/IP).

I/O addresses Locations within the input/output address space of your computer, used by a device such as a printer or modem. *See* also input/output activity (I/O).

IOCTL *See* input/output control.

IP *See* Internet Protocol.

IP address Used to identify a node on a network and to specify routing information. Each node on the network must be assigned a unique IP address, which is made up of the *network ID*, plus a unique *host ID* assigned by the network administrator. This address is typically represented in dotted-decimal notation, with the decimal value of each octet separated by a period (for example, 138.57.7.27).

In Windows NT, the IP address can be configured statically on the client or configured dynamically through DHCP. *See also* Dynamic Host Configuration Protocol (DHCP); node; octet.

IPC *See* interprocess communication.

IPCP *See* Internet Protocol Control Protocol.

IP datagrams The basic Internet Protocol (IP) information unit. *See also* datagram; Internet Protocol (IP).

IP router A system connected to multiple physical TCP/IP networks that can route or deliver IP packets between the networks. *See also* packet; routing; Transmission Control Protocol/Internet Protocol (TCP/IP).

IPX *See* IPX/SPX.

IPX/SPX Acronym for Internetwork Packet Exchange/Sequenced Packet Exchange, which is a set of transport protocols used in Novell NetWare networks. Windows NT implements IPX through NWLink.

IRC *See* Internet Relay Chat.

IRQ *See* interrupt request line.

ISAPI *See* Internet Server Application Programming Interface.

ISDN *See* Integrated Services Digital Network.

ISDN interface card Similar in function to a modem, an ISDN card is hardware that enables a computer to connect to other computers and networks on an Integrated Services Digital Network.

ISO Abbreviation for the International Standards Organization, an international association of member countries, each of which is represented by its leading standard-setting organization—for example ANSI (American National Standards Institute) for the United States. The ISO works to establish global standards for communications and information exchange.

ISP *See* Internet service provider.

iteration One of the three key concepts in DNS name resolution. A local name server keeps the burden of processing on itself and passes only iterative resolution requests to other name servers. An iterative resolution request tells the name server that the requester expects the best answer the name server can provide without help from others. If the name server has the requested data, it returns it, otherwise it returns pointers to name servers that are more likely to have the answer. *See also* Domain Name System (DNS).

In programming, iteration is the art of executing one or more statements or instructions repeatedly.

J

jump Text, graphics, or parts of graphics that provide links to other Help topics or to more information about the current topic. The pointer changes shape whenever it is over a jump. If you click a jump that is linked to another topic, that topic appears in the Help window. If you click a jump that is linked to more information, the information appears in a pop-up window on top of the main Help window.

K

keep-alives *See* HTTP keep-alives; TCP/IP keep-alives.

Kermit Protocol for transferring binary files that is somewhat slower than XModem/CRC. However, Kermit allows you to transmit and receive either seven or eight data bits per character. *See also* XModem/CRC.

Kernel The Windows NT Kernel is the part of the Windows NT Executive that manages the processor. It performs thread scheduling and dispatching, interrupt and exception handling, and multiprocessor synchronization. The Kernel synchronizes activities among Executive-level subcomponents, such as I/O Manager and Process Manager. It also provides primitive objects to the Windows NT Executive, which uses them to create User-mode objects. The Kernel works closely with the Hardware Abstraction Layer (HAL). *See also* Executive; Hardware Abstraction Layer (HAL).

Kernel debugger The Windows NT Kernel debugger (KD) is a 32-bit application that is used to debug the Kernel and device drivers, and to log the events leading up to a Windows NT Executive STOP, STATUS, or hardware-malfunction message.

The Kernel debugger runs on another Windows NT host computer that is connected to your Windows NT target computer. The two computers send debugging (troubleshooting) information back and forth through a communications port that must be running at the same baud rate on each computer.

Kernel driver A driver that accesses hardware. *See also* device driver.

key A folder that appears in the left pane of a Registry Editor window. A key can contain subkeys and value entries. For example: Environment is a key of HKEY_CURRENT_USER. *See also* subkey.

keyboard buffer A temporary storage area in memory that keeps track of keys you typed, even if the computer did not immediately respond to the keys when you typed them.

key map A mapping assignment that translates key values on synthesizers that do not conform to General MIDI standards. Key maps ensure that the appropriate percussion instrument is played or the appropriate octave for a melodic instrument is played when a MIDI file is played. *See also* Musical Instrument Digital Interface (MIDI).

kiosk A computer, connected to the Internet, made available to users in a commonly accessible location.

L

LAN *See* local area network.

LastKnownGood (LKG) control set The most recent control set that correctly started the system and resulted in a successful startup. The control set is saved as the LKG control set when you have a successful logon. *See also* current control set.

lease In Windows NT, the network administrator controls how long IP addresses are assigned by specifying lease durations that specify how long a computer can use an assigned IP address before having to renew the lease with the DHCP server. *See also* Dynamic Host Configuration Protocol (DHCP); IP address.

leased line A high-capacity line (most often a telephone line) dedicated to network connections.

license group License groups show a relationship (also known as a mapping) between users and computers. A license group comprises a single descriptive name for the group, a specified number of Per-Seat licenses assigned to the group, and a specific list of users who are members of the group.

line printer daemon (LPD) A line printer daemon (LPD) service on the print server receives documents from line printer remote (LPR) utilities running on client systems.

linked object A representation or placeholder for an object that is inserted into a destination document. The object still exists in the source file and, when it is changed, the linked object is updated to reflect these changes.

list box In a dialog box, a type of box that lists available choices—for example, a list of all files in a directory. If all of the choices do not fit in the list box, there is a scroll bar.

LMHOSTS file A local text file that maps IP addresses to the computer names of Windows NT networking computers outside the local subnet. In Windows NT, this file is stored in the *systemroot* \System32\Drivers\Etc directory. *See also* IP address; subnet.

local account For Windows NT Server, a user account provided in a domain for a user whose global account is not in a trusted domain. Not required where trust relationships exist between domains. *See also* global account; trust relationship; user account.

local area network (LAN) A group of computers and other devices dispersed over a relatively limited area and connected by a communications link that enables any device to interact with any other on the network.

local group For Windows NT Workstation, a group that can be granted permissions and rights only for its own workstation. However, it can contain user accounts from its own computer and (if the workstation participates in a domain) user accounts and global groups both from its own domain and from trusted domains.

For Windows NT Server, a group that can be granted permissions and rights only for the domain controllers of its own domain. However, it can contain user accounts and global groups both from its own domain and from trusted domains.

(continued)

local group Local groups provide a way to create handy sets of users from both inside and outside the domain, to be used only at domain controllers of the domain. *See also* global group; group; trust relationship.

local guest logon Takes effect when a user logs on interactively at a computer running Window NT Workstation or at a member server running Windows NT Server, and specifies Guest as the user name in the **Logon Information** dialog box. *See also* interactive logon.

Local Mail Delivery Agent The component of the SMTP server that processes messages that have been received by the SMTP server and downloads the messages to the user's local computer.

local printer A printer that is directly connected to one of the ports on your computer. *See also* port.

LocalTalk The name given by Apple Computer to the Apple networking hardware built into every Macintosh. LocalTalk includes the cables and connector boxes that connect components and network devices that are part of the AppleTalk network system. LocalTalk was formerly known as the AppleTalk Personal Network.

local user profiles User profiles that are created automatically on the computer at logon the first time a user logs on to a computer running Windows NT Workstation or Windows NT Server.

lock A method used to manage certain features of subdirectory replication by the export server. You can lock a subdirectory to prevent it from being exported to any import computers, or use locks to prevent imports to subdirectories on an import computer. *See also* directory replication; export server; import computers; subtree.

log books Kept by the system administrator to record the backup methods, dates, and contents of each tape in a backup set. *See also* backup set; backup types.

log files Created by Windows NT Backup and contain a record of the date the tapes were created and the names of files and directories successfully backed up and restored. Performance Monitor also creates log files.

logical drive A subpartition of an extended partition on a hard disk. *See also* extended partition.

Logical Unit (LU) A preset unit containing all of the configuration information needed for a user or a program to establish a session with a host or peer computer. *See also* host; peer.

log off To stop using the network and remove your user name from active use until you log on again.

log on To provide a user name and password that identifies you to the network.

logon hours For Windows NT Server, a definition of the days and hours during which a user account can connect to a server. When a user is connected to a server and the logon hours are exceeded, the user will either be disconnected from all server connections or allowed to remain connected but denied any new connections.

logon script A file that can be assigned to user accounts. Typically a batch program, a logon script runs automatically every time the user logs on. It can be used to configure a user's working environment at every logon, and it allows an administrator to affect a user's environment without managing all aspects of it. A logon script can be assigned to one or more user accounts. *See also* batch program.

logon script path When a user logs on, the computer authenticating the logon locates the specified logon script (if one has been assigned to that user account) by following that computer's local logon script path (usually C:\Winnt\System32\Repl\Imports\Scripts). *See also* authentication; logon script.

logon workstations In Windows NT Server, the computers from which a user is allowed to log on.

long name A folder name or file name longer than the 8.3 file name standard (up to eight characters followed by a period and a three-character extension) of the FAT file system. Windows NT Server automatically translates long names of files and folders to 8.3 names for MS-DOS users.

Macintosh users can assign long names to files and folders on the server, and by using Services for Macintosh, you can assign long names to Macintosh-accessible volumes when you create them. *See also* file allocation table (FAT); file name; name mapping; short name.

loopback address The IP address 127.0.0.1, which has been specified by the Internet Engineering Task Force as the IP address to use in conjunction with a loopback driver to route outgoing packets back to the source computer. *See also* loopback driver.

loopback driver A network driver that allows the packets to bypass the network adapter completely and be returned directly to the computer that is performing the test. *See also* loopback address.

LPD *See* line printer daemon.

LPR Acronym for line printer remote. *See also* line printer daemon.

LU *See* Logical Unit.

luminosity The brightness of a color on a scale from black to white on your monitor.

M

MAC *See* media access control.

MAC address A unique 48-bit number assigned to the network adapter by the manufacturer. MAC addresses (which are physical addresses) are used for mapping in TCP/IP network communication. *See also* Address Resolution Protocol (ARP); ARP request packet; media access control (MAC).

MacFile *See* File Server for Macintosh service.

MacFile menu The menu that appears in Windows NT Server when Services for Macintosh is set up. You can create Macintosh-accessible volumes, and set permissions and other options by using commands on this menu.

Macintosh-accessible volume Storage space on the server used for folders and files of Macintosh users. A Macintosh-accessible volume is equivalent to a shared directory for PC users. Each Macintosh-accessible volume on a computer running Windows NT Server will correspond to a directory. Both PC users and Macintosh users can be given access to files located in a directory that is designated as both a shared directory and a Macintosh-accessible volume.

Macintosh-style permissions Directory and volume permissions that are similar to the access privileges used on a Macintosh.

MacPrint *See* Print Server for Macintosh.

Mac volume *See* Macintosh-accessible volume.

Mail Server (MailSrv) The MailSrv utility no longer ships with the *Windows NT Server Resource Kit*.

Make Changes The Macintosh-style permission that gives users the right to make changes to a folder's contents; for example, modifying, renaming, moving, creating, and deleting files. When Services for Macintosh translates access privileges into Windows NT Server permissions, a user who has the Make Changes privilege is given Write and Delete permissions.

Management Information Base (MIB) A set of objects that represent various types of information about a device, used by SNMP to manage devices. Because different network-management services are used for different types of devices or protocols, each service has its own set of objects. The entire set of objects that any service or protocol uses is referred to as its MIB. *See also* Simple Network Management Protocol (SNMP).

mandatory user profile A profile that is downloaded to the user's desktop each time he or she logs on. A mandatory user profile is created by an administrator and assigned to one or more users to create consistent or job-specific user profiles. They cannot be changed by the user and remain the same from one logon session to the next. *See also* roaming user profile; user profile.

mapping In TCP/IP, refers to the relationship between a host or computer name and an IP address, used by DNS and NetBIOS servers on TCP/IP networks.

In Windows NT Explorer, refers to mapping a driver letter to a network drive.

In Windows NT License Manager, refers to the relationship between users and computers in license groups. *See also* Domain Name System (DNS); IP address; license group.

mapping file A file defining exactly which users and groups are to be migrated from NetWare to Windows NT Server, and what new user names and passwords are to be assigned to the migrated users.

Master Boot Record The most important area on a hard disk, the data structure that starts the process of booting the computer.

The Master Boot Record contains the partition table for the disk and a small amount of executable code. On *x*86-based computers, the executable code examines the partition table and identifies the system (or bootable) partition, finds the system partition's starting location on the disk, and loads an image of its Partition Boot Sector into memory. The Master Boot Record then transfers execution to the Partition Boot Sector. *See also* Partition Table.

master browser A kind of network name server which keeps a browse list of all of the servers and domains on the network. Also referred to as browse master. *See also* browse; Windows NT browser system.

master domain In the master domain model, the domain that is trusted by all other domains on the network and acts as the central administrative unit for user and group accounts.

maximize To enlarge a window to its maximum size by using the **Maximize** button (at the right of the title bar) or the **Maximize** command on the window menu.

Maximize button The small button containing a window icon at the right of the title bar. Mouse users can click the **Maximize** button to enlarge a window to its maximum size. Keyboard users can use the **Maximize** command on the window menu.

maximum password age The period of time a password can be used before the system requires the user to change it. *See also* account policy.

MCI *See* Media Control Interface.

media access control (MAC) A layer in the network architecture that deals with network access and collision detection.

media access control (MAC) driver *See* network card driver.

Media Control Interface (MCI) A standard control interface for multimedia devices and files. Using MCI, a multimedia application can control a variety of multimedia devices and files.

member server A computer that runs Windows NT Server but is not a primary domain controller (PDC) or backup domain controller (BDC) of a Windows NT domain. Member servers do not receive copies of the directory database. Also called a stand-alone server. *See also* backup domain controller (BDC); directory database; primary domain controller (PDC).

memory A temporary storage area for information and applications. *See also* expanded memory; extended memory.

menu A list of available commands in an application window. Menu names appear in the menu bar near the top of the window. The window menu, represented by the program icon at the left end of the title bar, is common to all applications for Windows NT. To open a menu, click the menu name.

menu bar The horizontal bar containing the names of all of the application's menus. It appears below the title bar.

Messenger service Sends and receives messages sent by administrators or by the Alerter service. *See also* Alerter service.

MIB *See* Management Information Base.

Microsoft dbWeb A database publishing gateway provided in the *Windows NT Server Resource Kit*. dbWeb can run under Internet Information Server to provide public access to private enterprise ODBC sources as specified by an administrator of the private enterprise.

MIDI *See* Musical Instrument Digital Interface.

MIDI setup Specifies the type of MIDI device you are using, the channel and patch settings needed to play MIDI files, and the port your device is using. *See also* Musical Instrument Digital Interface (MIDI).

Migration Tool for NetWare Included with Windows NT, it enables you to easily transfer user and group accounts, volumes, folders, and files from a NetWare server to a computer running Windows NT Server.

MIME *See* Multipurpose Internet Mail Extensions.

minimize To reduce a window to a button on the taskbar by using the **Minimize** button (at the right of the title bar) or the **Minimize** command on the **Control** menu. *See also* maximize.

Minimize button The small button containing a short line at the right of the title bar. Mouse users can click the **Minimize** button to reduce a window to a button on the taskbar. Keyboard users can use the **Minimize** command on the **Control** menu.

minimum password age The period of time a password must be used before the user can change it. *See also* account policy.

minimum password length The fewest characters a password can contain. *See also* account policy.

mirror set A fully redundant or shadow copy of data. Mirror sets provide an identical twin for a selected disk; all data written to the primary disk is also written to the shadow or mirror disk. This enables you to have instant access to another disk with a redundant copy of the information on a failed disk. Mirror sets provide fault tolerance. *See also* fault tolerance.

m-node A NetBIOS implementation that uses the b-node protocol first, then the p-node protocol if the broadcast fails to resolve a name to an IP address. *See also* IP address; network basic input/output system (NetBIOS); p-node.

modem Short for modulator/demodulator, a communications device that enables a computer to transmit information over a standard telephone line.

MPR *See* MultiProtocol Routing.

MS-DOS-based application An application that is designed to run with MS-DOS, and therefore may not be able to take full advantage of all Windows NT features.

multicast datagram IP multicasting is the transmission of an IP datagram to a host group (a set of zero or more hosts identified by a single IP destination address). An IP datagram sent to one host is called a unicast datagram. An IP datagram sent to all hosts is called a broadcast datagram. *See also* broadcast datagram; host; IP address.

multihomed computer A system that has multiple network adapters, or that has been configured with multiple IP addresses for a single network adapter. *See also* IP address; network adapter.

multihomed system A system with multiple network adapters attached to separate physical networks.

multilink dialing Multilink combines multiple physical links into a logical "bundle." This aggregate link increases your bandwidth. *See also* bandwidth.

multiple boot A computer that runs two or more operating systems. For example, Windows 95, MS-DOS, and Windows NT operating systems can be installed on the same computer. When the computer is started, any one of the operating systems can be selected. Also known as dual boot.

multiport serial adapter A communications device that enables a computer to simultaneously transmit information over standard telephone lines to multiple computers. Similar to multiple modems contained in one device. *See also* modem.

MultiProtocol Routing (MPR) Enables routing over IP and IPX networks by connecting LANs or by connecting LANs to WANs. *See also* IPX/SPX; local area network (LAN); wide area network (WAN).

Multipurpose Internet Mail Extensions (MIME) A standard mechanism for specifying and describing the format of Internet message bodies. MIME enables the exchanging of objects, different character sets, and multimedia in electronic mail on different computer systems. Defined in RFC 1521.

Musical Instrument Digital Interface (MIDI) An interface that enables several devices, instruments, or computers to send and receive messages for the purpose of creating music, sound, or lighting.

N

named pipe An interprocess communication mechanism that allows one process to communicate with another local or remote process.

name mapping Is provided by Windows NT Server and Windows NT Workstation to ensure access by MS-DOS users to NTFS and FAT volumes (which can have share names of up to 255 characters, as opposed to MS-DOS, which is restricted to eight characters followed by a period and a three-character extension). With name mapping, each file or directory with a name that does not conform to the MS-DOS 8.3 standard is automatically given a second name that does. MS-DOS users connecting the file or directory over the network see the name in the 8.3 format; Windows NT Workstation and Windows NT Server users see the long name. *See also* Domain Name System (DNS); long name; Windows Internet Name Service (WINS).

name resolution service TCP/IP internetworks require a name resolution service to convert computer names to IP addresses and IP addresses to computer names. (People use "friendly" names to connect to computers; programs use IP addresses.) *See also* IP address; Transmission Control Protocol/Internet Protocol (TCP/IP).

NDIS *See* network device interface specification.

NDS *See* NetWare Directory Services.

NetBEUI A network protocol usually used in small, department-size local area networks of 1 through 200 clients. It can use Token Ring source routing as its only method of routing. *See also* router; Token Ring.

NetBIOS *See* network basic input/output system.

NetBT Short for NetBIOS over TCP/IP. The session-layer network service that performs name-to-IP address mapping for name resolution. *See also* IP address; name resolution service; network basic input/output system (NetBIOS); Transmission Control Protocol/Internet Protocol (TCP/IP).

Net Logon service For Windows NT Server, performs authentication of domain logons, and keeps the domain's directory database synchronized between the primary domain controller (PDC) and the other backup domain controllers (BDCs) of the domain. *See also* backup domain controller (BDC); directory database; primary domain controller (PDC).

NetWare Directory Services (NDS) A NetWare service that runs on NetWare servers. The service enables the location of resources on the network.

network adapter An expansion card or other device used to connect a computer to a local area network (LAN). Also called a network card; network adapter card; adapter card; network interface card (NIC).

network adapter card *See* network adapter.

network administrator A person responsible for planning, configuring, and managing the day-to-day operation of the network. This person may also be referred to as a system administrator.

network basic input/output system (NetBIOS) An application programming interface (API) that can be used by applications on a local area network. NetBIOS provides applications with a uniform set of commands for requesting the lower-level services required to conduct sessions between nodes on a network and to transmit information back and forth. *See also* application programming interface (API).

network card *See* network adapter.

network card driver A network device driver that works directly with the network card, acting as an intermediary between the card and the protocol driver. With Services for Macintosh, the AppleTalk Protocol stack on the server is implemented as a protocol driver and is bound to one or more network drivers.

Network DDE DSDM service The Network DDE DSDM (DDE share database manager) service manages shared DDE conversations. It is used by the Network DDE service. *See also* dynamic data exchange (DDE).

Network DDE service The Network DDE (dynamic data exchange) service provides a network transport and security for DDE conversations. *See also* dynamic data exchange (DDE).

network device driver Software that coordinates communication between the network adapter and the computer's hardware and other software, controlling the physical function of the network adapters.

network device interface specification (NDIS) In Windows networking, the Microsoft/3Com specification for the interface of network device drivers. All transport drivers call the NDIS interface to access network cards. With Services for Macintosh, the AppleTalk Protocol stack on the server is implemented as an NDIS-compliant protocol and is bound to an NDIS network driver. All network drivers and protocol drivers shipped with Windows NT Workstation and Windows NT Server conform to NDIS.

network directory *See* shared directory.

network driver *See* network device driver.

network driver interface specification *See* network device interface specification (NDIS).

Network File System (NFS) A service for distributed computing systems that provides a distributed file system, eliminating the need for keeping multiple copies of files on separate computers.

network ID The portion of the IP address that identifies a group of computers and devices located on the same logical network.

Network Information Service (NIS) A service for distributed computing systems that provides a distributed database system for common configuration files.

network interface card (NIC) *See* network adapter.

Network News Transfer Protocol (NNTP) The protocol used to distribute network news messages to NNTP servers and to NNTP clients (news readers) on the Internet. NNTP provides for the distribution, inquiry, retrieval, and posting of news articles by using a reliable stream-based transmission of news on the Internet. NNTP is designed so that news articles are stored on a server in a central database, thus enabling a user to select specific items to read. Indexing, cross-referencing, and expiration of aged messages are also provided. Defined in RFC 977.

network number In the Macintosh environment, the network number (also referred to as the network range) is the address or range of addresses assigned to the network, which is used by AppleTalk routers to route information to the appropriate network. Each physical network can have a range of network numbers.

network protocol Software that enables computers to communicate over a network. TCP/IP is a network protocol, used on the Internet. *See also* Transmission Control Protocol/Internet Protocol (TCP/IP).

network range In the Macintosh environment, a range of network numbers (routing addresses) associated with a physical network in Phase 2. Apple manuals sometimes refer to a network range as a cable range. *See also* network number; routing.

network sniffer A hardware and software diagnostic tool that can also be used to decipher passwords, which may result in unauthorized access to network accounts. Clear-text passwords are susceptible to network sniffers.

NFS *See* Network File System.

NIC Acronym for network interface card. *See* network adapter.

NIS *See* Network Information Service.

NNTP *See* Network News Transfer Protocol.

node In the PC environment, a node is any device that is attached to the internetwork and uses TCP/IP. (A node can also be referred to as a host.) In the Macintosh environment, a node is an addressable entity on a network. Each Macintosh client is a node.

nonpaged memory Memory that cannot be paged to disk. *See also* memory; paging file.

non–Windows NT application Refers to an application that is designed to run with Windows 3.*x*, MS-DOS, OS/2, or POSIX, but not specifically with Windows NT, and that may not be able to take full advantage of all Windows NT features (such as memory management). *See also* POSIX.

NT *See* Windows NT Server; Windows NT Workstation.

NT File System *See* Windows NT File System.

NTFS *See* Windows NT File System.

NWLink IPX\SPX Compatible Transport A standard network protocol that supports routing, and can support NetWare client/server applications, where NetWare-aware Sockets-based applications communicate with IPX\SPX Sockets-based applications. *See also* IPX/SPX; Sockets.

O

object Any piece of information, created by using a Windows-based application, that can be linked or embedded into another document. *See also* embedded object; linked object.

object-cache scavenger A component of the IIS process that periodically flushes from the cache objects that have changed or that have not been referenced in its last timed interval. The default time interval for the object-cache scavenger is 30 seconds.

octet In programming, an octet refers to eight bits or one byte. IP addresses, for example, are typically represented in dotted-decimal notation, that is, with the decimal value of each octet of the address separated by a period. *See also* IP address.

ODBC *See* Open Database Connectivity.

offset When specifying a filter in Windows NT Network Monitor based on a pattern match (which limits the capture to only those frames containing a specific pattern of ASCII or hexadecimal data), you must specify where the pattern occurs in the frame. This number of bytes (from the beginning or end of the frame) is known as an offset. *See also* frame; hexadecimal.

OLE A way to transfer and share information between applications. *See also* ActiveX; embedded object; linked object.

one-way trust relationship One domain (the trusting domain) "trusts" the domain controllers in the other domain (the trusted domain) to authenticate user accounts from the trusted domain to use resources in the trusting domain. *See also* trust relationship; user account.

opcode Operation code; a code, usually a number, that specifies an operation to be performed. An opcode is often the first component in a contiguous block of data; it indicates how other data in the block should be interpreted.

open To display the contents of a directory, a document, or a data file in a window.

Open Database Connectivity (ODBC) ODBC is an application programming interface that enables applications to access data from a variety of existing data sources.

Open Systems Interconnection (OSI) model TCP/IP protocols map to a four-layered conceptual model consisting of Application, Transport, Internet, and Network Interface. Each layer in this TCP/IP model corresponds to one or more layers of the International Standards Organization (ISO) seven-layer OSI model consisting of Application, Presentation, Session, Transport, Network, Data-link, and Physical. *See also* ISO.

orphan A member of a mirror set or a stripe set with parity that has failed in a severe manner, such as in a loss of power or a complete head crash. When this happens, the fault-tolerance driver determines that it can no longer use the orphaned member and directs all new reads and writes to the remaining members of the fault-tolerance volume. *See also* fault tolerance; mirror set; stripe sets with parity.

orphaned member *See* orphan.

OSI *See* Open Systems Interconnection model.

owner In Windows NT, every file and directory on an NTFS volume has an owner, who controls how permissions are set on the file or directory and who can grant permissions to others.

P

package An icon that represents an embedded or linked object. When you choose the package, the application used to create the object either plays the object (for example, a sound file) or opens and displays the object. *See also* embedded object; linked object.

packet A transmission unit of fixed maximum size that consists of binary information representing both data and a header containing an ID number, source and destination addresses, and error-control data.

packet assembler/disassembler (PAD) A connection used in X.25 networks. X.25 PAD boards can be used in place of modems when provided with a compatible COM driver. *See also* X.25.

packet header The part of a packet that contains an identification number, source and destination addresses, and—sometimes—error-control data. *See also* packet.

PAD *See* packet assembler/disassembler.

page fault In the processor, a page fault occurs when a process refers to a virtual memory page that is not in its working set in main memory.

A *hard page fault* occurs when data that a program needs is not found in its working set (the physical memory visible to the program) or elsewhere in physical memory, and must be retrieved from disk.

A page fault will not cause the page to be fetched from disk if that page is on the standby list, and hence already in main memory, or if it is in use by another process with which the page is shared. In this case, a *soft page fault* occurs.

paging file A special file on a PC hard disk. With virtual memory under Windows NT, some of the program code and other information is kept in RAM while other information is temporarily swapped into virtual memory. When that information is required again, Windows NT pulls it back into RAM and, if necessary, swaps other information to virtual memory. Also called a swap file.

PAP *See* Password Authentication Protocol.

parity Redundant information that is associated with a block of information. In Windows NT Server, stripe sets with parity means that there is one additional parity stripe per row. Therefore, you must use at least three, rather than two, disks to allow for this extra parity information. Parity stripes contain the XOR (the Boolean operation called exclusive OR) of the data in that stripe. Windows NT Server, when regenerating a failed disk, uses the parity information in those stripes in conjunction with the data on the good disks to recreate the data on the failed disk. *See also* fault tolerance; stripe set; stripe sets with parity.

partial synchronization The automatic, timed delivery to all domain BDCs (backup domain controllers) of only those directory database changes that have occurred since the last synchronization. *See also* backup domain controller (BDC); synchronize.

partition A partition is a portion of a physical disk that functions as though it were a physically separate unit. *See also* extended partition; system partition.

Partition Table An area of the Master Boot Record that the computer uses to determine how to access the disk. The Partition Table can contain up to four partitions for each physical disk. *See also* Master Boot Record.

pass-through authentication When the user account must be authenticated, but the computer being used for the logon is not a domain controller in the domain where the user account is defined, nor is it the computer where the user account is defined, the computer passes the logon information through to a domain controller (directly or indirectly) where the user account is defined. *See also* domain controller; user account.

password A security measure used to restrict logons to user accounts and access to computer systems and resources. A password is a unique string of characters that must be provided before a logon or an access is authorized. For Windows NT, a password for a user account can be up to 14 characters, and is case-sensitive. There are four user-defined parameters to be entered in the **Account Policy** dialog box in User Manager or User Manager for Domains: maximum password age, minimum password age, minimum password length, and password uniqueness.

With Services for Macintosh, each Macintosh user must type a user password when accessing the Windows NT Server. You can also assign each Macintosh-accessible volume a volume password if you want, which all users must type to access the volume. *See also* account policy.

Password Authentication Protocol (PAP) A type of authentication that uses clear-text passwords and is the least sophisticated authentication protocol.

password uniqueness The number of new passwords that must be used by a user account before an old password can be reused. *See also* account policy; password.

patch map The part of a channel-map entry that translates instrument sounds, volume settings, and (optionally) key values for a channel.

path A sequence of directory (or folder) names that specifies the location of a directory, file, or folder within the directory tree. Each directory name and file name within the path (except the first) must be preceded by a backslash (\). For example, to specify the path of a file named Readme.wri located in the Windows directory on drive C, you type c:\windows\readme.wri.

PC Any personal computer (such as an IBM PC or compatible) using the MS-DOS, OS/2, Windows, Windows for Workgroups, Windows 95, Windows NT Server, or Windows NT Workstation operating systems.

PCMCIA *See* Personal Computer Memory Card International Association.

peer Any of the devices on a layered communications network that operate on the same protocol level.

Peer Web Services A collection of services that enable the user of a computer running Windows NT Workstation to publish a personal Web site from the desktop. The services include the WWW service, the FTP service, and the Gopher service.

pel Also known as a pixel, which is short for picture element, the smallest graphic unit that can be displayed on the screen.

Perl Practical Extraction and Report Language. A scripting (programming) language that is frequently used for CGI scripts.

permissions Windows NT Server settings you set on a shared resource that determine which users can use the resource and how they can use it. *See also* access permission.

Services for Macintosh automatically translates between permissions and Macintosh access privileges, so that permissions set on a directory (volume) are enforced for Macintosh users, and access privileges set by Macintosh users are enforced for PC users connected to the computer running Windows NT Server.

Personal Computer Memory Card International Association (PCMCIA) A standard for removable peripheral devices (called PC cards) about the size of a credit card, which plug into a special 68-pin connector found most commonly in portable computers. Currently available PCMCIA cards include memory, hard disk, modem, fax, network, and wireless communication devices.

personal group In the **Start** menu on the **Programs** list, a program group you have created that contains program items. Personal groups are stored with your logon information and each time you log on, your personal groups appear. *See also* group.

Physical Unit (PU) A network-addressable unit that provides the services needed to use and manage a particular device, such as a communications link device. A PU is implemented with a combination of hardware, software, and microcode.

PIF *See* program information file.

ping A command used to verify connections to one or more remote hosts. The **ping** utility uses the ICMP echo request and echo reply packets to determine whether a particular IP system on a network is functional. The ping utility is useful for diagnosing IP network or router failures. *See also* Internet Control Message Protocol (ICMP); router.

pipe An interprocess communication mechanism. Writing to and reading from a pipe is much like writing to and reading from a file, except that the two processes are actually using a shared memory segment to communicate data. *See also* named pipe.

pixel *See* pel.

plotter font *See* font types.

p-node A NetBIOS implementation that uses point-to-point communications with a name server to resolve names as IP addresses. *See also* h-node; IP address; network basic input/output system (NetBIOS).

pointer The arrow-shaped cursor on the screen that follows the movement of a mouse (or other pointing device) and indicates which area of the screen will be affected when you press the mouse button. The pointer changes shape during certain tasks.

Point-to-Point Protocol (PPP) A set of industry-standard framing and authentication protocols that is part of Windows NT RAS to ensure interoperability with third-party remote access software. PPP negotiates configuration parameters for multiple layers of the OSI model. *See also* Open Systems Interconnection model (OSI).

Point-to-Point Tunneling Protocol (PPTP) PPTP is a new networking technology that supports multiprotocol virtual private networks (VPNs), enabling remote users to access corporate networks securely across the Internet by dialing into an Internet service provider (ISP) or by connecting directly to the Internet. *See also* virtual private network (VPN).

POP *See* Post Office Protocol.

pop-up menu *See* window menu.

port A location used to pass data in and out of a computing device. This term can refer to an adapter card connecting a server to a network, a serial 232 port, a TCP/IP port, or a printer port.

port ID The method TCP and UDP use to specify which application running on the system is sending or receiving the data. *See also* Transmission Control Protocol (TCP); User Datagram Protocol (UDP).

POSIX Acronym for Portable Operating System Interface, an IEEE (Institute of Electrical and Electronics Engineers, Inc.) standard that defines a set of operating-system services. Programs that adhere to the POSIX standard can be easily ported from one system to another.

Post Office Protocol (POP) The Post Office Protocol version 3 (POP3) is a protocol that permits a workstation to dynamically access a mail drop on a server in a useful fashion. Usually, this means that a POP3 server is used to allow a workstation to retrieve mail that an SMTP server is holding for it. POP3 is specified in RFC 1725.

PostScript printer A printer that uses the PostScript page description language to create text and graphics on the output medium, such as paper or overhead transparency. Examples of PostScript printers include the Apple LaserWriter, the NEC LC-890, and the QMS PS-810. *See also* font types.

POTS Acronym for plain-old telephone service. Also an acronym for point of termination station, which refers to where a telephone call terminates.

power conditioning A feature of an uninterruptible power supply (UPS) that removes spikes, surges, sags, and noise from the power supply. *See also* uninterruptible power supply (UPS).

PPP *See* Point-to-Point Protocol.

PPTP *See* Point-to-Point Tunneling Protocol.

predefined key The key represented by a registry window, the name of which appears in the window's title bar. *See also* key; registry.

primary domain controller (PDC) In a Windows NT Server domain, the computer running Windows NT Server that authenticates domain logons and maintains the directory database for a domain. The PDC tracks changes made to accounts of all computers on a domain. It is the only computer to receive these changes directly. A domain has only one PDC. *See also* directory database.

primary partition A partition is a portion of a physical disk that can be marked for use by an operating system. There can be up to four primary partitions (or up to three, if there is an extended partition) per physical disk. A primary partition cannot be subpartitioned. *See also* extended partition; partition.

print device Refers to the actual hardware device that produces printed output.

printer Refers to the software interface between the operating system and the print device. The printer defines where the document will go before it reaches the print device (to a local port, to a file, or to a remote print share), when it will go, and various other aspects of the printing process.

printer driver A program that converts graphics commands into a specific printer language, such as PostScript or PCL. *See also* font types.

printer fonts Fonts that are built into your printer. These fonts are usually located in the printer's read-only memory (ROM). *See also* font; font types.

printer permissions Specify the type of access a user or group has to use the printer. The printer permissions are No Access, Print, Manage Documents, and Full Control.

printer window Shows information for one of the printers that you have installed or to which you are connected. For each printer, you can see what documents are waiting to be printed, who owns them, how large they are, and other information.

printing pool Consists of two or more identical print devices associated with one printer.

print processor A PostScript program that understands the format of a document's image file and how to print the file to a specific printer or class of printers. *See also* encapsulated PostScript (EPS) file.

print server Refers to the computer that receives documents from clients.

Print Server for Macintosh A Services for Macintosh service that enables Macintosh clients to send documents to printers attached to a computer running Windows NT; enables PC clients to send documents to printers anywhere on the AppleTalk network; and enables Macintosh users to spool their documents to the computer running Windows NT Server, thus freeing their clients to do other tasks. Also called MacPrint.

print sharing The ability for a computer running Windows NT Workstation or Windows NT Server to share a printer on the network. This is done by using the **Printers** folder or the **net share** command.

print spooler A collection of dynamic-link libraries (DLLs) that receive, process, schedule, and distribute documents.

privilege level One of three settings (User, Administrator, or Guest) assigned to each user account. The privilege level a user account has determines the actions that the user can perform on the network. *See also* Administrator privilege; Guest privilege; user account; User privilege.

process When a program runs, a Windows NT process is created. A process is an object type which consists of an executable program, a set of virtual memory addresses, and one or more threads.

processor affinity mask A Windows NT bit mask that associates processors with network adapters. All deferred procedure calls (DPCs) originating from the network adapter are handled by its associated processor.

program file A file that starts an application or program. A program file has an .exe, .pif, .com, or .bat file name extension.

program group On the **Start** menu, a collection of applications. Grouping your applications makes them easier to find when you want to start them. *See also* common group; personal group.

program icon Located at the left of the window title bar, the program icon represents the program being run. Clicking the program icon opens the window menu.

program information file (PIF) A PIF provides information to Windows NT about how best to run MS-DOS-based applications. When you start an MS-DOS-based application, Windows NT looks for a PIF to use with the application. PIFs contain such items as the name of the file, a start-up directory, and multitasking options.

program item An application, accessory, or document represented as an icon in the **Start** menu or on the desktop.

promiscuous mode A state of a network card in which it passes on to the networking software all of the frames that it detects on the network, regardless of the frames' destination address. *See also* frame; network adapter.

propagate Copy. For example, NetWare user accounts are propagated to the Windows NT primary domain controller when using Directory Service Manager for NetWare (DSMN).

property In Windows NT Network Monitor, a property refers to a field within a protocol header. A protocol's properties, collectively, indicate the purpose of the protocol.

protocol A set of rules and conventions for sending information over a network. These rules govern the content, format, timing, sequencing, and error control of messages exchanged among network devices.

protocol driver A network device driver that implements a protocol, communicating between Windows NT Server and one or more network adapter card drivers. With Services for Macintosh, the AppleTalk Protocol stack is implemented as an NDIS-protocol driver, and is bound to one or more network adapter card drivers.

protocol parser A dynamic-link library (DLL) that identifies the protocols used to send a frame onto the network. *See also* dynamic-link library (DLL); frame.

protocol properties Refers to the elements of information that define a protocol's purpose. Because the purposes of protocols vary, properties differ from one protocol to another.

protocol stack The implementation of a specific protocol family in a computer or other node on the network.

proxy A computer that listens to name query broadcasts and responds for those names not on the local subnet. The proxy communicates with the name server to resolve names and then caches them for a time period. *See also* caching; Domain Name System (DNS); subnet.

PSTN Acronym for public switched telephone network.

PU *See* Physical Unit.

public key cryptography A method of encrypting data transmissions to and from a server.

pull partner A WINS server that pulls in replicas from its push partner by requesting it and then accepting the pushed replicas. *See also* Windows Internet Name Service (WINS).

push partner A WINS server that sends replicas to its pull partner upon receiving a request from it. *See also* Windows Internet Name Service (WINS).

Q

queue In Windows NT terminology, a queue refers to a group of documents waiting to be printed. (In NetWare and OS/2 environments, queues are the primary software interface between the application and print device; users submit documents to a queue. However, with Windows NT, the printer is that interface—the document is sent to a printer, not a queue.)

quick format Deletes the file allocation table (FAT) and root directory of a disk but does not scan the disk for bad areas. This function is available in Disk Administrator or when checking disks for errors. *See also* file allocation table (FAT); root directory.

R

RAID Acronym for Redundant Array of Inexpensive Disks. A method used to standardize and categorize fault-tolerant disk systems. Six levels gauge various mixes of performance, reliability, and cost. Windows NT includes three of the RAID levels: Level 0, Level 1, and Level 5.

RAM An acronym for random-access memory. RAM can be read from or written to by the computer or other devices. Information stored in RAM is lost when you turn off the computer. *See also* memory.

RAS *See* Remote Access Service.

recursion One of the three key concepts in DNS name resolution. A resolver typically passes a recursive resolution request to its local name server, which tells the name server that the resolver expects a complete answer to the query, not just a pointer to another name server. Recursive resolution effectively puts the workload onto the name server and allows the resolver to be small and simple. *See also* Domain Name System (DNS); iteration.

reduce To minimize a window to an icon by using the **Minimize** button or the **Minimize** command. A minimized application continues running, and you can click the icon on the toolbar to make it the active application.

reduced instruction set computing (RISC) A type of microprocessor design that focuses on rapid and efficient processing of a relatively small set of instructions. RISC architecture limits the number of instructions that are built into the microprocessor, but optimizes each so that it can be carried out very rapidly—usually within a single clock cycle.

refresh To update displayed information with current data.

registration In Windows NT NetBT name resolution, registration is the process used to register a unique name for each computer (node) on the network. A computer typically registers itself when it starts.

registry The Windows NT registry is a hierarchical database that provides a repository for information about a computer's configuration on Windows NT Workstation and about hardware and user accounts on Windows NT Server. It is organized in subtrees and their keys, hives, and value entries. *See also* hive; key; subtree; user account.

registry size limit (RSL) The total amount of space that can be consumed by registry data is restricted by the registry size limit, which is a kind of universal maximum for registry space that prevents an application from filling the paged pool with registry data. *See also* hive; paging file.

Remote Access Service (RAS) A service that provides remote networking for telecommuters, mobile workers, and system administrators who monitor and manage servers at multiple branch offices. Users with RAS on a Windows NT–based computer can dial in to remotely access their networks for services such as file and printer sharing, electronic mail, scheduling, and SQL database access.

remote administration Administration of one computer by an administrator located at another computer and connected to the first computer across the network.

remote logon Occurs when a user is already logged on to a user account and makes a network connection to another computer. *See also* user account.

remote procedure call (RPC) A message-passing facility that allows a distributed application to call services available on various machines in a network. Used during remote administration of computers. *See also* remote administration.

Remote Procedure Call service *See* RPC service.

renew Client computers are periodically required to renew their NetBIOS name registrations with the WINS server. When a client computer first registers with a WINS server, the WINS server returns a message that indicates when the client will need to renew its registration. *See also* network basic input/output system (NetBIOS); Windows Internet Name Service (WINS).

repeaters The most basic LAN connection device, repeaters strengthen the physical transmission signal. A repeater simply takes the electrical signals that reach it and then regenerates them to full strength before passing them on. Repeaters generally extend a single network (rather than link two networks).

replication *See* directory replication.

replicators One of the Windows NT built-in local groups for workstations and member servers, used for directory replication functions. *See also* directory replication.

Requests for Comments (RFCs) The official documents of the IETF (Internet Engineering Task Force) that specify the details for protocols included in the TCP/IP family. *See also* Internet Engineering Task Force (IETF); Transmission Control Protocol/Internet Protocol (TCP/IP).

resolution In Windows NetBT name resolution, resolution is the process used to determine the specific address for a computer name.

resolvers DNS clients that query DNS servers for name resolution on networks. *See also* Domain Name System (DNS).

resource Any part of a computer system or a network, such as a disk drive, printer, or memory, that can be allotted to a program or a process while it is running, or shared over a local area network.

resource domain A trusting domain that establishes a one-way trust relationship with the master (account) domain, enabling users with accounts in the master domain to use resources in all of the other domains. *See also* domain; trust relationship.

resource fork One of two forks that make up each Macintosh file. The resource fork holds Macintosh operating system resources, such as code, menu, font, and icon definitions. Resource forks have no relevance to PCs, so the resource forks of files on the server are never accessed by PC clients. *See also* data fork; file fork.

response In Windows NT RAS, responses are strings expected from the device, which can contain macros.

RFC *See* Requests for Comments.

right *See* permissions; user rights.

RIP *See* routing information protocol.

RISC *See* reduced instruction set computing.

roaming user profile User profile that is enabled when an administrator enters a user profile path into the user account. The first time the user logs off, the local user profile is copied to that location. Thereafter, the server copy of the user profile is downloaded each time the user logs on (if it is more current than the local copy) and is updated each time the user logs off. *See also* user profile.

root directory The top-level directory on a computer, a partition, or Macintosh-accessible volume. *See also* directory tree.

router In the Windows NT environment, a router helps LANs and WANs achieve interoperability and connectivity and can link LANs that have different network topologies (such as Ethernet and Token Ring). Routers match packet headers to a LAN segment and choose the best path for the packet, optimizing network performance.

In the Macintosh environment, routers are necessary for computers on different physical networks to communicate with each other. Routers maintain a map of the physical networks on a Macintosh internet (network) and forward data received from one physical network to other physical networks. Computers running Windows NT Server with Services for Macintosh can act as routers, and you can also use third-party routing hardware on a network with Services for Macintosh. *See also* local area network (LAN); packet; wide area network (WAN).

routing The process of forwarding packets to other routers until the packet is eventually delivered to a router connected to the specified destination. *See also* packet; router.

routing information protocol (RIP)
Enables a router to exchange routing information with a neighboring router. *See also* routing.

routing table Controls the routing decisions made by computers running TCP/IP. Routing tables are built automatically by Windows NT based on the IP configuration of your computer. *See also* dynamic routing; routing; static routing; Transmission Control Protocol/Internet Protocol (TCP/IP).

RPC *See* remote procedure call.

RPC Locator service The Remote Procedure Call Locator service allows distributed applications to use the RPC Name service. The RPC Locator service manages the RPC Name service database.

The server side of a distributed application registers its availability with the RPC Locator service. The client side of a distributed application queries the RPC Locator service to find available compatible server applications. *See also* remote procedure call (RPC).

RPC service The Remote Procedure Call service is the RPC subsystem for Microsoft Windows NT. The RPC subsystem includes the endpoint mapper and other miscellaneous RPC services. *See also* remote procedure call (RPC).

RSL *See* registry size limit.

S

SACL *See* system access control list.

SAM Acronym for Security Accounts Manager. *See* directory database; Windows NT Server Directory Services.

SAP In the Windows environment, SAP is an acronym for Service Advertising Protocol, a service that broadcasts shared files, directories, and printers categorized first by domain or workgroup and then by server name.

In the context of routing and IPX, SAP is also an acronym for Service Advertising Protocol, used by servers to advertise their services and addresses on a network. Clients use SAP to determine what network resources are available.

In NetBEUI, SAP is an acronym for Service Access Point, in which each link-layer program identifies itself by registering a unique service access point.

Not to be confused with SAP financial database application software for the mainframe computer.

saturation The purity of a color's hue, moving from gray to the pure color.

scavenging Cleaning up the WINS database. *See also* Windows Internet Name Service (WINS).

Schedule service Supports and is required for use of the **at** command. The **at** command can schedule commands and programs to run on a computer at a specified time and date.

schemas Schemas control how and what information from a private database is available to visitors who use the Internet to access the public Microsoft dbWeb gateway to the private database. *See also* dbWeb Administrator.

Schema Wizard Interactive tool in dbWeb Administrator that leads a user through creation of HTML pages or through implementing an ISAPI application.

screen buffer The size reserved in memory for the command prompt display.

screen dump *See* snapshot.

screen elements The parts that make up a window or dialog box, such as the title bar, the **Minimize** and **Maximize** buttons, the window borders, and the scroll bars.

screen fonts Fonts displayed on your screen. Soft-font manufacturers often provide screen fonts that closely match the soft fonts for your printer. This ensures that your documents look the same on the screen as they do when printed. *See also* font; font types.

screen saver A moving picture or pattern that appears on your screen when you have not used the mouse or the keyboard for a specified period of time. To select a screen saver, either use Display in Control Panel or right-click on the desktop for properties.

scroll To move through text or graphics (up, down, left, or right) in order to see parts of the file that cannot fit on the screen.

scroll arrow An arrow on either end of a scroll bar that you use to scroll through the contents of the window or list box. Click the scroll arrow to scroll one screen at a time, or continue pressing the mouse button while pointing at the scroll arrow to scroll continuously.

scroll bar A bar that appears at the right or bottom edge of a window or list box whose contents are not completely visible. Each scroll bar contains two scroll arrows and a scroll box, which enable you to scroll through the contents of the window or list box.

scroll box In a scroll bar, a small box that shows the position of information currently visible in the window or list box relative to the contents of the entire window.

scroll buffer The area in memory that holds information that does not fit on the screen. You can use the scroll bars to scroll through the information.

SCSI *See* small computer system interface.

Search button *See* find tab.

section header In Windows NT RAS, a section header is a string, comprising up to 32 characters between square brackets, that identifies the specific device to which the section applies.

secure attention sequence A series of keystrokes (CTRL+ALT+DEL) that will always display the Windows NT operating system logon screen.

secure communications channel Created when computers at each end of a connection are satisfied that the computer on the other end has identified itself correctly by using its computer account. *See also* computer account.

Secure Sockets Layer (SSL) A protocol that supplies secure data communication through data encryption and decryption. SSL enables communications privacy over networks by using a combination of public key cryptography and bulk data encryption.

security A means of ensuring that shared files can be accessed only by authorized users.

Security Accounts Manager (SAM) *See* directory database; Windows NT Server Directory Services.

security database *See* directory database.

security host A third-party authentication device that verifies whether a caller from a remote client is authorized to connect to the Remote Access server. This verification supplements security already authorized to connect to the Remote-Access server.

security ID (SID) A unique name that identifies a logged-on user to the security system. Security IDs (SIDs) can identify one user or a group of users.

security identifier *See* security ID (SID).

security log Records security events. This helps track changes to the security system and identify any possible breaches of security. For example, depending on the Audit settings in User Manager or User Manager for Domains, attempts to log on to the local computer might be recorded in the security log. The security log contains both valid and invalid logon attempts as well as events related to resource use (such as creating, opening, or deleting files). *See also* event.

security policies For Windows NT Workstation, the security policies consist of the Account, User Rights, and Audit policies, and are managed by using User Manager.

For a Windows NT Server domain, the security policies consist of the Account, User Rights, Audit, and Trust Relationships policies, and are managed by using User Manager for Domains.

security token *See* access token.

seed router In the Macintosh environment, a seed router initializes and broadcasts routing information about one or more physical networks. This information tells routers where to send each packet of data. A seed router on an AppleTalk network initially defines the network number(s) and zone(s) for a network. Services for Macintosh servers can function as seed routers, and you can also use third-party hardware routers as seed routers. *See also* packet; router.

See Files The Macintosh-style permission that give users the right to open a folder and see the files in the folder. For example, a folder that has See Files and See Folders Macintosh-style permissions is given the Windows NT-style R (Read) permission. *See also* permissions.

See Folders The Macintosh-style permission that gives users the right to open a folder and see the files contained in that folder. *See also* permissions.

select To mark an item so that a subsequent action can be carried out on that item. You usually select an item by clicking it with a mouse or pressing a key. After selecting an item, you choose the action that you want to affect the item.

selection cursor The marking device that shows where you are in a window, menu, or dialog box and what you have selected. The selection cursor can appear as a highlight or as a dotted rectangle around text.

semaphore Generally, semaphores are signaling devices or mechanisms. However, in Windows NT, system semaphores are objects used to synchronize activities on an interprocess level. For example, when two or more processes share a common resource such as a printer, video screen, or memory segment, semaphores are used to control access to those resources so that only one process can alter them at any particular time.

sequence number The identifier with which TCP marks packets before sending them. The sequence numbers allow the receiving system to properly order the packets on the receiving system. *See also* packet; Transmission Control Protocol (TCP).

Serial Line Internet Protocol (SLIP) An older industry standard that is part of Windows NT RAS to ensure interoperability with third-party remote access software.

server In general, refers to a computer that provides shared resources to network users. *See also* member server.

server application A Windows NT application that can create objects for linking or embedding into other documents. For distributed applications, the application that responds to a client application. *See also* client application; DCOM Configuration tool; Distributed Component Object Model (DCOM); embedded object; linked object.

Server Manager In Windows NT Server, an application used to view and administer domains, workgroups, and computers.

server message block (SMB) A file-sharing protocol designed to allow systems to transparently access files that reside on remote systems.

Server service Provides RPC (remote procedure call) support, and file, print, and named pipe sharing. *See also* named pipe; remote procedure call (RPC).

server zone The AppleTalk zone on which a server appears. On a Phase 2 network, a server appears in the default zone of the server's default network. *See also* default network; default zone; desired zone; zone.

service A process that performs a specific system function and often provides an application programming interface (API) for other processes to call. Windows NT services are RPC-enabled, meaning that their API routines can be called from remote computers. *See also* application programming interface (API); remote procedure call (RPC).

Service Access Point (SAP) *See* SAP.

Service Advertising Protocol (SAP) *See* SAP.

Services for Macintosh *See* Windows NT Server Services for Macintosh.

session A link between two network devices, such as a client and a server. A session between a client and server consists of one or more connections from the client to the server.

SFM Acronym for Windows NT Services for Macintosh.

share To make resources, such as directories and printers, available to others.

shared directory A directory that network users can connect to.

shared network directory *See* shared directory.

shared resource Any device, data, or program that is used by more than one other device or program. For Windows NT, shared resources refer to any resource that is made available to network users, such as directories, files, printers, and named pipes. Also refers to a resource on a server that is available to network users. *See also* named pipe.

share name A name that refers to a shared resource on a server. Each shared directory on a server has a share name, used by PC users to refer to the directory. Users of Macintosh use the name of the Macintosh-accessible volume that corresponds to a directory, which may be the same as the share name. *See also* Macintosh-accessible volume.

share permissions Are used to restrict a shared resource's availability over the network to only certain users.

Shiva Password Authentication Protocol (SPAP) A two-way (reversible) encryption mechanism employed by Shiva. Windows NT Workstation, when connecting to a Shiva LAN Rover, uses SPAP, as does a Shiva client connecting to a Windows NT Server. *See also* encryption.

shortcut key A key or key combination, available for some commands, that you can press to carry out a command without first selecting a menu. Shortcut keys are listed to the right of commands on a menu.

short name A valid 8.3 (up to eight characters followed by a period and a three-character extension) MS-DOS or OS/2 file name that the computer running Windows NT Server creates for every Macintosh folder name or file name on the server. PC users refer to files on the server by their short names; Macintosh users refer to them by their long names. *See also* long name; name mapping.

SID *See* security ID.

silent mode During IP routing in silent mode, the computer listens to RIP broadcasts and updates its route table but does not advertise its own routes. *See also* routing; routing information protocol (RIP); routing table.

simple device A device that you use without specifying a related media file. An audio compact-disc player is a simple device.

Simple Mail Transfer Protocol (SMTP) A member of the TCP/IP suite of protocols that governs the exchange of electronic mail between message transfer agents.

Simple Network Management Protocol (SNMP) A protocol used by SNMP consoles and agents to communicate. In Windows NT, the SNMP service is used to get and set status information about a host on a TCP/IP network. *See also* Transmission Control Protocol/Internet Protocol (TCP/IP).

single user logon Windows NT network users can connect to multiple servers, domains, and applications with a single network logon.

SLIP *See* Serial Line Internet Protocol.

small computer system interface (SCSI) A standard high-speed parallel interface defined by the American National Standards Institute (ANSI). A SCSI interface is used for connecting microcomputers to peripheral devices such as hard disks and printers, and to other computers and local area networks.

SMB *See* server message block.

SMS *See* Systems Management Server.

SMTP *See* Simple Mail Transfer Protocol.

SNA *See* System Network Architecture.

snapshot A copy of main memory or video memory at a given instant, sent to a printer or hard disk. A graphical image of the video screen can be saved by taking a snapshot of video memory, more commonly called a screen dump.

sniffer *See* network sniffer.

Sniffer files Files saved from Network General Sniffer, a third-party protocol analyzer. *See also* network sniffer.

SNMP *See* Simple Network Management Protocol.

socket A bidirectional pipe for incoming and outgoing data between networked computers. The Windows Sockets API is a networking API used by programmers creating TCP/IP-based sockets applications. *See also* application programming interface (API); named pipe.

Sockets Windows Sockets is a Windows implementation of the widely used UC Berkeley sockets API. Microsoft TCP/IP, NWLink, and AppleTalk protocols use this interface. Sockets interfaces between programs and the transport protocol and works as a bidirectional pipe for incoming and outgoing data. *See also* application programming interface (API); named pipe; socket.

source directory The directory that contains the file or files you intend to copy or move.

source document The document where a linked or embedded object was originally created. *See also* embedded object; linked object.

SPAP *See* Shiva Password Authentication Protocol.

special access permission On NTFS volumes, a custom set of permissions. You can customize permissions on files and directories by selecting the individual components of the standard sets of permissions. *See also* access permission.

split bar Divides Windows NT Explorer into two parts: The directory tree is displayed on the left, and the contents of the current directory are on the right. *See also* directory tree.

spoofing Refers to a case where an Internet user mimics ("spoofs") the source IP address for an Internet server, proxy server, or firewall of a system to which it is trying to gain access.

spooler Software that accepts documents sent by a user to be printed, and then stores those documents and sends them, one by one, to available printer(s). *See also* spooling.

spooling A process on a server in which print documents are stored on a disk until a printing device is ready to process them. A spooler accepts each document from each client, stores it, then sends it to a printing device when it is ready.

SQL Acronym for structured query language, a database programming language used for accessing, querying, and otherwise managing information in a relational database system.

SSL *See* Secure Sockets Layer.

stabilize During subdirectory replication, when a subdirectory is stabilized, the export server waits two minutes after changes before exporting the subdirectory. The waiting period allows time for subsequent changes to take place so that all intended changes are recorded before being replicated. *See also* directory replication; export server; subtree.

stand-alone server *See* member server.

static mapping A method provided on a WINS server to assign a static (unchanging) IP address to a client.

static object Information that has been pasted into a document. Unlike embedded or linked objects, static objects cannot be changed from within the document. The only way you can change a static object is to delete it from the document, change it in the application used to create it, and paste it into the document again. *See also* embedded object; linked object.

static routing Static routing limits you to fixed routing tables, as opposed to dynamically updating the routing tables. *See also* dynamic routing; routing table.

static Web pages Standard Web pages that are created in advance and stored for later delivery to clients. *See also* dynamic Web pages.

status bar A line of information related to the application in the window. Usually located at the bottom of a window. Not all windows have a status bar.

STATUS message A message displayed by the Executive in a Windows-mode message box when the Executive detects a condition within a process that you should know about.

STATUS messages can be divided into three types:

System-information messages. Just read the information in the message box and click **OK**. The Kernel continues running the process or thread.

Warning messages. Some advise you to take an action that will enable the Kernel to keep running the process or thread. Others warn you that, although the process or thread will continue running, the results might be incorrect.

Application-termination messages. These warn you that the Kernel is about to terminate either a process or a thread.

See also Executive messages; STOP message.

STOP message A character-mode message that occurs when the Kernel detects an inconsistent condition from which it cannot recover. Always displayed on a full character-mode screen, uniquely identified by a hexadecimal number and a symbolic string. The content of the symbolic string can suggest, to a trained technician, the part of the Kernel that detected the condition from which there was no recourse but to stop. However, the cause may actually be in another part of the system. *See also* Executive messages; STATUS message.

string A data structure composed of a sequence of characters, usually representing human-readable text.

stripe set Refers to the saving of data across identical partitions on different drives. A stripe set does not provide fault tolerance; however stripe sets with parity do. *See also* fault tolerance; partition; stripe sets with parity.

stripe sets with parity A method of data protection in which data is striped in large blocks across all of the disks in an array. Data redundancy is provided by the parity information. This method provides fault tolerance. *See also* fault tolerance; stripe set.

subdirectory A directory within a directory. Also called a folder within a folder.

subkey A key within a key. Subkeys are analogous to subdirectories in the registry hierarchy. Keys and subkeys are similar to the section heading in .ini files; however subkeys can carry out functions. *See also* key; registry.

subnet A portion of a network, which may be a physically independent network segment, that shares a network address with other portions of the network and is distinguished by a subnet number. A subnet is to a network what a network is to an internet.

subnet mask A 32-bit value that allows the recipient of IP packets to distinguish the network ID portion of the IP address from the host ID. *See also* IP address; packet.

substitution macros Placeholders that are replaced in command strings.

subtree During directory replication, this refers to the export subdirectory and all of its subdirectories. *See also* directory replication.

swap file *See* paging file.

switched circuit *See* dial-up line.

SYN attack SYN (synchronizing character) messages maliciously generated by an intruder in an attempt to block legitimate access to a server by proliferating half-open TCP port connections. Also called SYN flooding.

synchronize To replicate the domain database from the primary domain controller (PDC) to one backup domain controller (BDC) of the domain, or to all of the BDCs of a domain. This is usually performed automatically by the system, but can also be invoked manually by an administrator. *See also* backup domain controller (BDC); domain; primary domain controller (PDC).

syntax The order in which you must type a command and the elements that follow the command. Windows NT commands have up to four elements: command name, parameters, switches, and values.

system access control list (SACL) The system ACL is controlled by the system administrator, and allows system-level security to be associated with an object. SACL APIs can be used only by a process with System Administrator privileges. *See also* discretionary access control list (DACL).

system default profile In Windows NT Server, the user profile that is loaded when Windows NT is running and no user is logged on. When the **Begin Logon** dialog box is visible, the system default profile is loaded. *See also* user default profile, user profile.

system disk A disk that contains the MS-DOS system files necessary to start MS-DOS.

system log The system log contains events logged by the Windows NT components. For example, the failure of a driver or other system component to load during startup is recorded in the system log. Use Event Viewer to view the system log.

System Network Architecture (SNA)
System Network Architecture is a communications framework developed by IBM. Microsoft System Network Architecture (SNA) is an optional solution that provides a gateway connection between personal computer LANs or WANs and IBM mainframe and AS/400 hosts. *See also* AS/400; gateway.

system partition The volume that has the hardware-specific files needed to load Windows NT. *See also* partition.

system policy A policy, created by using the System Policy Editor, to control user work environments and actions, and to enforce system configuration for Windows 95. System policy can be implemented for specific users, groups, computers, or for all users. System policy for users overwrites settings in the current user area of the registry, and system policy for computers overwrites the current local machine area of the registry. *See also* registry.

systemroot The name of the directory that contains Windows NT files. The name of this directory is specified when Windows NT is installed.

Systems Management Server Part of the Windows NT BackOffice suite. Systems Management Server includes desktop management and software distribution that significantly automates the task of upgrading software on client computers.

T

T1 or T3 connection Standard measurement of network bandwidth.

tag file A configuration file that contains information about a corresponding file on a Gopher server or links to other servers. This information is sent to clients in response to a Gopher request.

tape set A tape set (sometimes referred to as a tape family) in Windows NT Backup is a sequence of tapes in which each tape is a continuation of the backup on the previous tape. *See also* backup set; backup types.

TAPI *See* Telephony API.

Task list A window that shows all running applications and their status. View the Task list in the **Applications** tab in Task Manager.

Task Manager Task Manager enables you to start, end, or run applications, end processes (an application, application component, or system process), and view CPU and memory use data. Task Manager gives you a simple, quick view of how each process (application or service) is using CPU and memory resources. (Note: In previous versions of Windows NT, Task List handled some of these functions.)

To run Task Manager, right-click the toolbar and then click Task Manager.

TCP *See* Transmission Control Protocol.

TCP/IP *See* Transmission Control Protocol/Internet Protocol.

TCP/IP keep-alives An optimizing feature of the TCP/IP service. TCP/IP periodically broadcasts messages to determine whether an idle connection is still active. *See also* HTTP keep-alives.

TDI *See* transport driver interface.

Telephony API (TAPI) An API used by programs to make data/fax/voice calls, including HyperTerminal, Dial-up Networking, Phone Dialer, and other Win32 communications applications written for Windows NT.

Telnet (VTP) A terminal emulation protocol for logging on to remote computers. Once referred to as Virtual Terminal Protocol (VTP). Defined in RFC 854, among others.

template accounts Accounts that are not actually used by real users but serve as a basis for the real accounts (for administrative purposes).

terminate-and-stay-resident program (TSR) A program running under MS-DOS that remains loaded in memory even when it is not running so that it can be quickly invoked for a specific task performed while any other application is operating.

text box In a dialog box, a box in which you type information needed to carry out a command. The text box may be blank or may contain text when the dialog box opens.

text file A file containing text characters (letters, numbers, and symbols) but no formatting information. A text file can be a "plain" ASCII file that most computers can read. Text file can also refer to a word-processing file. *See also* ASCII file.

text-file transfer A method for transferring files from HyperTerminal to a remote computer. With this method, files are transferred as ASCII files with minimal formatting characters, such as linefeeds and carriage returns. All font-formatting information is removed. *See also* ASCII file.

text-only An ASCII file that contains no formatting. *See also* ASCII file.

TFTP *See* Trivial File Transfer Protocol.

thread Threads are objects within processes that run program instructions. They allow concurrent operations within a process and enable one process to run different parts of its program on different processors simultaneously.

throughput *See* bandwidth.

time-out If a device is not performing a task, the amount of time the computer should wait before detecting it as an error.

time slice The amount of processor time allocated to an application, usually measured in milliseconds.

title bar The horizontal bar (at the top of a window) that contains the title of the window or dialog box. On many windows, the title bar also contains the program icon and the **Maximize**, **Minimize**, and **Close** buttons.

Token Ring A type of network media that connects clients in a closed ring and uses token passing to enable clients to use the network. *See also* Fiber Distributed Data Interface (FDDI); LocalTalk.

toolbar A series of icons or shortcut buttons providing quick access to commands. Usually located directly below the menu bar. Not all windows have a toolbar.

topic Information in the Help window. A Help topic usually begins with a title and contains information about a particular task, command, or dialog box.

transforms Rules the administrator creates to add, remove, and modify domain names appended to inbound and outbound messages.

Transmission Control Protocol (TCP) A connection-based Internet protocol responsible for breaking data into packets, which the IP protocol sends over the network. This protocol provides a reliable, sequenced communication stream for network communication. *See also* Internet Protocol (IP); packet.

Transmission Control Protocol/Internet Protocol (TCP/IP) A set of networking protocols that provide communications across interconnected networks made up of computers with diverse hardware architectures and various operating systems. TCP/IP includes standards for how computers communicate and conventions for connecting networks and routing traffic.

transport driver interface (TDI) In Windows networking, the common interface for network components that communicate at the Session layer.

trap In SNMP, a discrete block of data that indicates that the request failed authentication. The SNMP service can send a trap when it receives a request for information that does not contain the correct community name and that does not match an accepted host name for the service. Trap destinations are the names or IP addresses of hosts to which the SNMP service is to send traps with community names. *See also* IP address; Simple Network Management Protocol (SNMP).

trigger A set of conditions that, when met, initiate an action. For example, before using Network Monitor to capture data from the network, you can set a trigger to stop the capture or to execute a program or command file.

Trivial File Transfer Protocol (TFTP) A file transfer protocol that transfers files to and from a remote computer running the TFTP service. TFTP was designed with less functions than FTP. Defined in RFC 1350, among others. *See also* File Transfer Protocol (FTP).

Trojan horse A program that masquerades as another common program in an attempt to receive information. An example of a Trojan horse is a program that masquerades as a system logon to retrieve user names and password information, which the writers of the Trojan horse can use later to break into the system.

TrueType fonts Fonts that are scalable and sometimes generated as bitmaps or soft fonts, depending on the capabilities of your printer. TrueType fonts can be sized to any height, and they print exactly as they appear on the screen.

trust *See* trust relationship.

trust relationship A link between domains that enables pass-through authentication, in which a trusting domain honors the logon authentications of a trusted domain. With trust relationships, a user who has only one user account in one domain can potentially access the entire network. User accounts and global groups defined in a trusted domain can be given rights and resource permissions in a trusting domain, even though those accounts do not exist in the trusting domain's directory database. *See also* directory database; global group; pass-through authentication; user account.

trust relationships policy A security policy that determines which domains are trusted and which domains are trusting domains. *See also* trust relationship.

TSR *See* terminate-and-stay-resident program.

two-way trust relationship Each domain trusts user accounts in the other domain to use its resources. Users can log on from computers in either domain to the domain that contains their account. *See also* trust relationship.

type *See* file type.

Type 1 fonts Scalable fonts designed to work with PostScript devices. *See also* font; font types; PostScript printer.

U

UAM *See* user authentication module.

UDP *See* User Datagram Protocol.

unavailable An unavailable button or command is displayed in light gray instead of black, and it cannot be clicked.

UNC name *See* universal naming convention name.

unicast datagram An IP datagram sent to one host. *See also* broadcast datagram; Internet Protocol (IP); multicast datagram.

Unicode A fixed-width, 16-bit character-encoding standard capable of representing the letters and characters of virtually all of the world's languages. Unicode was developed by a consortium of U.S. computer companies.

Uniform Resource Locator (URL) A naming convention that uniquely identifies the location of a computer, directory, or file on the Internet. The URL also specifies the appropriate Internet protocol, such as HTTP, FTP, IRC, or Gopher.

uninterruptible power supply (UPS) A battery-operated power supply connected to a computer to keep the system running during a power failure.

universally unique identifier (UUID) A unique identification string associated with the remote procedure call interface. Also known as a globally unique identifier (GUID).

universal naming convention (UNC) name A full Windows NT name of a resource on a network. It conforms to the *server_name**share_name* syntax, where *server_name* is the server's name and *share_name* is the name of the shared resource. UNC names of directories or files can also include the directory path under the share name, with the following syntax: *server_name**share_name**directory**file_name*.

UPS *See* uninterruptible power supply.

UPS service Manages an uninterruptible power supply connected to a computer. *See also* uninterruptible power supply (UPS).

URL *See* Uniform Resource Locator.

user account Consists of all of the information that defines a user to Windows NT. This includes such things as the user name and password required for the user to log on, the groups in which the user account has membership, and the rights and permissions the user has for using the system and accessing its resources. For Windows NT Workstation, user accounts are managed with User Manager. For Windows NT Server, user accounts are managed with User Manager for Domains. *See also* group.

user account database *See* directory database.

user authentication module Software component that prompts clients for their user names and passwords. *See also* clear-text passwords.

User Datagram Protocol (UDP) A TCP complement that offers a connectionless datagram service that guarantees neither delivery nor correct sequencing of delivered packets (much like IP). *See also* datagram; Internet Protocol (IP); packet.

user default profile In Windows NT Server, the user profile that is loaded by a server when a user's assigned profile cannot be accessed for any reason; when a user without an assigned profile logs on to the computer for the first time; or when a user logs on to the Guest account. *See also* system default profile; user profile.

User Manager A Windows NT Workstation tool used to manage the security for a workstation. User Manager administers user accounts, groups, and security policies.

User Manager for Domains A Windows NT Server tool used to manage security for a domain or an individual computer. User Manager for Domains administers user accounts, groups, and security policies.

user name A unique name identifying a user account to Windows NT. An account's user name cannot be identical to any other group name or user name of its own domain or workgroup. *See also* user account.

user password The password stored in each user's account. Each user generally has a unique user password and must type that password when logging on or accessing a server. *See also* password; volume password.

User privilege One of three privilege levels you can assign to a Windows NT user account. Every user account has one of the three privilege levels (Administrator, Guest, and User). Accounts with User privilege are regular users of the network; most accounts on your network probably have User privilege. *See also* Administrator privilege; Guest privilege; user account.

user profile Configuration information that can be retained on a user-by-user basis, and is saved in user profiles. This information includes all of the per-user settings of the Windows NT environment, such as the desktop arrangement, personal program groups and the program items in those groups, screen colors, screen savers, network connections, printer connections, mouse settings, window size and position. When a user logs on, the user's profile is loaded and the user's Windows NT environment is configured according to that profile. *See also* personal group; program item.

user rights Define a user's access to a computer or domain and the actions that a user can perform on the computer or domain. User rights permit actions such as logging onto a computer or network, adding or deleting users in a workstation or domain, and so forth.

user rights policy Manages the assignment of rights to groups and user accounts. *See also* user account; user rights.

users In the Macintosh environment, a special group that contains all users who have user permissions on the server. When a Macintosh user assigns permissions to everyone, those permissions are given to the groups users and guests. *See also* guest.

UUENCODE (UNIX-to-UNIX Encode) A utility that converts a binary file (such as a word-processing file or a program) to text so that it can be transmitted over a network. UUDECODE (UNIX-to-UNIX Decode) is the utility used to convert the file back to its original state.

UUID *See* universally unique identifier.

V

value entry The string of data that appears in the right pane of a Registry Editor window and that defines the value of the currently selected key. A value entry has three parts: name, data type, and the value itself. *See also* key; subkey.

Van Jacobsen header compression
A TCP/IP network layer compression technique, VJ compression reduces the size of IP and TCP headers. *See also* Internet Protocol (IP); Transmission Control Protocol (TCP); Transmission Control Protocol/ Internet Protocol (TCP/IP).

variables In programming, a variable is a named storage location capable of containing a certain type of data that can be modified during program execution. System environment variables are defined by Windows NT Server and are the same no matter who is logged on at the computer. (Administrator group members can add new variables or change the values, however.) User environment variables can be different for each user of a particular computer. They include any environment variables you want to define or variables defined by your applications, such as the path where application files are located.

VDD *See* virtual device driver.

VDM *See* virtual DOS machine.

verify operation Occurs after all files are backed up or restored, if specified. A verify operation compares files on disk to files that have been written to tape. *See also* backup types.

virtual device driver (VDD) A driver that enables MS-DOS-based and 16-bit Windows-based applications to run on Windows NT.

virtual directory An Internet Information Server directory outside the home directory. A virtual directory appears to browsers as a subdirectory of the home directory.

virtual DOS machine (VDM) Simulates an MS-DOS environment so that MS-DOS-based and Windows-based applications can run on Windows NT.

virtual memory The space on your hard disk that Windows NT uses as if it were actually memory. Windows NT does this through the use of paging files. The benefit of using virtual memory is that you can run more applications at one time than your system's physical memory would otherwise allow. The drawbacks are the disk space required for the virtual-memory paging file and the decreased execution speed when paging is required. *See also* paging file.

virtual printer memory In a PostScript printer, a part of memory that stores font information. The memory in PostScript printers is divided into two areas: banded memory and virtual memory. The banded memory contains graphics and page-layout information needed to print your documents. The virtual memory contains any font information that is sent to your printer either when you print a document or when you download fonts. *See also* font types; PostScript printer.

virtual private network (VPN) A remote LAN that can be accessed through the Internet by using the new PPTP. *See also* Point-to-Point Tunneling Protocol (PPTP).

virtual server A computer with several IP addresses assigned to the network adapter card. This configuration makes the computer look like several servers to a browser.

virus A program that attempts to spread from computer to computer and either cause damage (by erasing or corrupting data) or annoy users (by printing messages or altering what is displayed on the screen).

volume A partition or collection of partitions that have been formatted for use by a file system. *See also* Macintosh-accessible volume; partition.

volume password An optional, case-sensitive password you can assign to a Macintosh-accessible volume when you configure the volume. To access the volume, a user must type the volume password. *See also* Macintosh-accessible volume; user password.

volume set A combination of partitions on a physical disk that appear as one logical drive. *See also* logical drive; partition.

VPN *See* virtual private network.

VTP Acronym for Virtual Terminal Protocol. *See* Telnet.

W

WAIS *See* wide area information server.

wallpaper A picture or drawing stored as a bitmap file (a file that has a .bmp extension).

WAN *See* wide area network.

warning beep The sound that your computer makes when you encounter an error or try to perform a task that Windows NT does not recognize.

Web browser A software program, such as Microsoft Internet Explorer, that retrieves a document from a Web server, interprets the HTML codes, and displays the document to the user with as much graphical content as the software can supply.

WebCat Microsoft Web Capacity Analysis Tool. A script-driven utility that tests your client/server configuration by using a variety of predetermined, invariant workloads. WebCat can test how your server responds to different workloads or test the same workload on varying configurations of the server. WebCat is included on the *Windows NT Resource Kit Supplement 1* compact disc.

Web server A computer equipped with the server software to respond to HTTP requests, such as requests from a Web browser. A Web server uses the HTTP protocol to communicate with clients on a TCP/IP network.

Well Known Port Number The standard port numbers used by the Internet community for well known (commonly used) services. Ports are used in TCP to name the ends of logical connections that carry long-term conversations. Well known services are defined by RFC 1060. The relationship between the well known services and the well known ports is described in RFC 1340.

wide area information server (WAIS) A network publishing system designed to help users find information over a computer network. WAIS software has four main components: the client, the server, the database, and the protocol. Discussed in RFC 1625.

wide area network (WAN) A communications network that connects geographically separated areas.

wildcard A character that represents one or more characters. The question mark (?) wildcard can be used to represent any single character, and the asterisk (*) wildcard can be used to represent any character or group of characters that might match that position in other file names.

window A rectangular area on your screen in which you view an application or document. You can open, close, and move windows, and change the size of most windows. You can open several windows at a time, and you can often reduce a window to an icon or enlarge it to fill the entire desktop.

window menu A menu that contains commands you can use to manipulate a window. You click the program icon or document icon at the left of the title bar to open the window menu.

Windows Internet Name Service (WINS) A name resolution service that resolves Windows networking computer names to IP addresses in a routed environment. A WINS server handles name registrations, queries, and releases. *See also* IP address; routing.

Windows NT–based application Used as a shorthand term to refer to an application that is designed to run with Windows NT and does not run without Windows NT. All Windows NT–based applications follow similar conventions for arrangement of menus, style of dialog boxes, and keyboard and mouse use.

Windows NT browser system Consists of a master browser, backup browser, and client systems. The master browser maintains the browse list—of all of the available domains and servers—and periodically sends copies to the backup browsers. *See also* browse; master browser.

Windows NT Explorer A program that enables you to view and manage the files and folders on your computer and make network connections to other shared resources, such as a hard disk on a server. Windows NT Explorer replaces Program Manager and File Manager, which were programs available in earlier versions of Windows NT. Program Manager and File Manager are still available, and can be started in the same way you start other Windows-based programs.

Windows NT File System (NTFS) An advanced file system designed for use specifically within the Windows NT operating system. It supports file system recovery, extremely large storage media, long file names, and various features for the POSIX subsystem. It also supports object-oriented applications by treating all files as objects with user-defined and system-defined attributes. *See also* POSIX.

Windows NT Server A superset of Windows NT Workstation, Windows NT Server provides centralized management and security, fault tolerance, and additional connectivity. *See also* fault tolerance; Windows NT Workstation.

Windows NT Server Directory Services A Windows NT protected subsystem that maintains the directory database and provides an application programming interface (API) for accessing the database. *See also* application programming interface (API); directory database.

Windows NT Server Services for Macintosh A software component of Windows NT Server that allows Macintosh users access to the computer running Windows NT Server. The services provided with this component allow PC and Macintosh users to share files and resources, such as printers on the AppleTalk network or those attached to the Windows NT Server. *See also* File Server for Macintosh service; Print Server for Macintosh.

Windows NT Workstation The portable, secure, 32-bit, preemptive multitasking member of the Microsoft Windows operating system family.

Windows Open Services Architecture (WOSA) An open set of APIs for integrating Windows-based computers with back-end services on a broad range of vendor's systems. WOSA consists of an extensible set of APIs that enable Windows-based desktop applications to access available information without having to know anything about the type of network in use, the types of computers in the enterprise, or types of back-end services available. As a result, if the network computers or services change, the desktop applications built by using WOSA will not require rewriting. *See also* application programming interface (API).

Windows Sockets *See* Sockets.

WINS *See* Windows Internet Name Service.

workgroup For Windows NT, a workgroup is a collection of computers that are grouped for viewing purposes. Each workgroup is identified by a unique name. *See also* domain.

working set Every program running can use a portion of physical memory, its working set, which is the current number of physical memory bytes used by or allocated by a process.

workstation Any networked Macintosh or PC using server resources. *See also* backup domain controller (BDC); member server; primary domain controller (PDC).

Workstation service Provides network connections and communications.

World Wide Web (WWW) The software, protocols, conventions, and information that enable hypertext and multimedia publishing of resources on different computers around the world. *See also* Hypertext Markup Language (HTML); Internet.

WOSA *See* Windows Open Services Architecture.

WOW Acronym for Win16 on Win32. The translation of Windows 3.1-based application calls to standard mode for RISC-based computers and 386 enhanced mode for *x*86-based computers.

wrap To continue to the next line rather than stopping when the cursor reaches the end of the current line.

X

X.25 A recommendation published by the Comite Consultatif International de Telegraphique et Telephonique (CCITT) international communications standards organization that defines the connection between a terminal and a packet-switching network. An X.25 network is a type of packet-switching network that routes units of information (packets) as specified by X.25 and is used in public data communications networks. *See also* packet.

X.25 smart card A hardware card with a PAD (packet assembler/disassembler) embedded in it. *See also* packet assembler/disassembler (PAD); X.25.

X.400 system A messaging system that is compliant with the X.400 standards developed under the CCITT and the International Standards Organization (ISO).

XModem/CRC Protocol for transmitting binary files that uses a cyclic redundancy check (CRC) to detect any transmission errors. Both computers must be set to transmit and receive eight data bits per character.

XOR Short for exclusive OR. A Boolean operation in which the Windows NT Server stripe-sets-with-parity form of fault tolerance maintains an XOR of the total data to provide data redundancy. This enables the reconstruction of missing data (on a failed disk or sector) from the remaining disks in the stripe set with parity. *See also* fault tolerance; stripe sets with parity.

Z

zone In the Macintosh environment, a zone is a logical grouping that simplifies browsing the network for resources, such as servers and printers. It is similar to a domain in Windows NT Server networking.

In a DNS (Domain Name System) database, a zone is a subtree of the DNS database that is administered as a single separate entity, a DNS name server. This administrative unit can consist of a single domain or a domain with subdomains. A DNS zone administrator sets up one or more name servers for the zone. *See also* domain; Domain Name System (DNS).

zone data file A Domain Name System database for a zone in the DNS name space.

zone list In the Macintosh environment, a zone list includes all of the zones associated with a particular network. Not to be confused with Windows NT DNS zones.

Index

C

D

E

F

I

J

K

L

M

N

O

P

R

S

U

V

W

X

Z